Vauxhall/Opel Insignia
Owners Workshop Manual

Mark Storey & John S. Mead

Models covered

(5563 - 432 - 6BA2)

Hatchback, Saloon & Estate (Sports Tourer)
Petrol: 1.8 litre (1796cc)
Turbo-diesel: 1.6 litre (1598cc) & 2.0 litre (1956cc)

Does NOT cover VXR / OPC performance models or all-wheel-drive models
Does NOT cover 1.4 litre, 1.6 litre, 2.0 litre or 2.8 litre petrol engines or 2.0 litre twin-turbo ('BiTurbo') diesel engines
Does NOT cover new Insignia range introduced June 2017

© J H Haynes & Co Ltd 2020

ABCDE
FGHIJ
K

A book in the **Haynes Owners Workshop Manual Series**

ISBN **978 1 78521 440 0**

British Library Cataloguing in Publication Data
A catalogue record for this book is available from the British Library.

Printed in Malaysia

J H Haynes & Co Ltd
Sparkford, Yeovil, Somerset BA22 7JJ, England

Haynes North America, Inc
859 Lawrence Drive, Newbury Park, California 91320, USA

Printed using NORBRITE BOOK 48.8gsm (CODE: 40N6533) from NORPAC; procurement system certified under Sustainable Forestry Initiative standard. Paper produced is certified to the SFI Certified Fiber Sourcing Standard (CERT - 0094271)

Contents

LIVING WITH YOUR VAUXHALL/OPEL INSIGNIA

Contents

REPAIRS AND OVERHAUL

Engine and Associated Systems

Transmission

Brakes and suspension

Body equipment

REFERENCE

Index

The Vauxhall/Opel Insignia was introduced in the UK in the autumn of 2008 as a replacement for the Vectra. June 2013 saw a minor face lift and the introduction of a 1.6 diesel engine and an alternative 2.0 litre (LFS) diesel. Production ended in 2017 with the introduction of the second generation Insignia from June 2017 onwards. The Insignia is available in four-door Saloon, five-door Hatchback and five-door Estate configurations.

An extensive range of petrol and diesel engines are available in the Insignia range. This manual covers the most popular variants – the 1.8 litre petrol engine, the 1.6 litre diesel engine and the 2.0 litre diesel engines. 1.4, 1.6, 2.0 and 2.8 litre petrol engines are also available, but are not covered in this manual.

The 1.8 litre petrol engine is of 16-valve DOHC (double overhead camshaft) four-cylinder, in-line configuration. The engine is controlled by a sophisticated engine management system, which combines multipoint sequential fuel injection and distributorless ignition systems with evaporative emissions control, variable intake geometry and a three-way regulated catalytic converter to ensure compliance with increasingly stringent emissions control standards, while providing the expected levels of performance and fuel economy.

The diesel engines are all 16-valve DOHC four-cylinder, in-line turbo diesel unit. The engine incorporates the latest design of direct injection common rail fuel system, with a variable geometry turbocharger, intercooler, catalytic converter and exhaust particulate filter.

The transversely-mounted engines drive the front roadwheels through a six-speed manual transmission with a hydraulically-operated clutch. Diesel engines are also available with a six-speed, electronically controlled automatic transmission.

The fully-independent suspension is by MacPherson struts and transverse lower arms at the front, with multilink independent suspension at the rear; anti-roll bars are fitted at the front and rear.

The braking system has discs all round, with ABS, Electronic Stability Program (ESP) Emergency Brake Assist (EBA) and Electronic Brakeforce Distribution (EBD) for extra safety when braking in emergency situations.

Hydraulic power-assisted steering is standard on all models. Later models have electric power steering fitted. Air conditioning is available, and all models have an ergonomically-designed passenger cabin with high levels of safety and comfort for all passengers. A wide range of standard and optional equipment is available within the Insignia range to suit most tastes.

Provided that regular servicing is carried out in accordance with the manufacturer's recommendations, the Insignia should prove a reliable and economical car. The engine compartment is well-designed, and most of the items needing frequent attention are easily accessible.

Vauxhall/Opel Insignia manual

The aim of this manual is to help you get the best value from your vehicle. It can do so in several ways. It can help you decide what work must be done (even should you choose to get it done by a garage), provide information on routine maintenance and servicing, and give a logical course of action and diagnosis when random faults occur. However, it is hoped that you will use the manual by tackling the work yourself. On simpler jobs, it may even be quicker than booking the car into a garage and going there twice, to leave and collect it. Perhaps most important, a lot of money can be saved by avoiding the costs a garage must charge to cover its labour and overheads.

The manual has drawings and descriptions to show the function of the various components, so that their layout can be understood. Then the tasks are described and photo-graphed in a clear step-by-step sequence.

References to the 'left' or 'right' are in the sense of a person in the driver's seat, facing forward.

Acknowledgements

Thanks are due to Draper Tools Limited and AST tools, who provided some of the workshop tools, and to all those people at Sparkford who helped in the production of this manual.

We take great pride in the accuracy of information given in this manual, but vehicle manufacturers make alterations and design changes during the production run of a particular vehicle of which they do not inform us. No liability can be accepted by the authors or publishers for loss, damage or injury caused by any errors in, or omissions from, the information given.

Working on your car can be dangerous. This page shows just some of the potential risks and hazards, with the aim of creating a safety-conscious attitude.

General hazards

Scalding

• Don't remove the radiator or expansion tank cap while the engine is hot.
• Engine oil, transmission fluid or power steering fluid may also be dangerously hot if the engine has recently been running.

Burning

• Beware of burns from the exhaust system and from any part of the engine. Brake discs and drums can also be extremely hot immediately after use.

Crushing

• When working under or near a raised vehicle, always supplement the jack with axle stands, or use drive-on ramps.
Never venture under a car which is only supported by a jack.
• Take care if loosening or tightening high-torque nuts when the vehicle is on stands. Initial loosening and final tightening should be done with the wheels on the ground.

Fire

• Fuel is highly flammable; fuel vapour is explosive.
• Don't let fuel spill onto a hot engine.
• Do not smoke or allow naked lights (including pilot lights) anywhere near a vehicle being worked on. Also beware of creating sparks (electrically or by use of tools).
• Fuel vapour is heavier than air, so don't work on the fuel system with the vehicle over an inspection pit.
• Another cause of fire is an electrical overload or short-circuit. Take care when repairing or modifying the vehicle wiring.
• Keep a fire extinguisher handy, of a type suitable for use on fuel and electrical fires.

Electric shock

• Ignition HT and Xenon headlight voltages can be dangerous, especially to people with heart problems or a pacemaker. Don't work on or near these systems with the engine running or the ignition switched on.

• Mains voltage is also dangerous. Make sure that any mains-operated equipment is correctly earthed. Mains power points should be protected by a residual current device (RCD) circuit breaker.

Fume or gas intoxication

• Exhaust fumes are poisonous; they can contain carbon monoxide, which is rapidly fatal if inhaled. Never run the engine in a confined space such as a garage with the doors shut.
• Fuel vapour is also poisonous, as are the vapours from some cleaning solvents and paint thinners.

Poisonous or irritant substances

• Avoid skin contact with battery acid and with any fuel, fluid or lubricant, especially antifreeze, brake hydraulic fluid and Diesel fuel. Don't syphon them by mouth. If such a substance is swallowed or gets into the eyes, seek medical advice.
• Prolonged contact with used engine oil can cause skin cancer. Wear gloves or use a barrier cream if necessary. Change out of oil-soaked clothes and do not keep oily rags in your pocket.
• Air conditioning refrigerant forms a poisonous gas if exposed to a naked flame (including a cigarette). It can also cause skin burns on contact.

Asbestos

• Asbestos dust can cause cancer if inhaled or swallowed. Asbestos may be found in gaskets and in brake and clutch linings. When dealing with such components it is safest to assume that they contain asbestos.

Special hazards

Hydrofluoric acid

• This extremely corrosive acid is formed when certain types of synthetic rubber, found in some O-rings, oil seals, fuel hoses etc, are exposed to temperatures above 4000C. The rubber changes into a charred or sticky substance containing the acid. *Once formed, the acid remains dangerous for years. If it gets onto the skin, it may be necessary to amputate the limb concerned.*
• When dealing with a vehicle which has suffered a fire, or with components salvaged from such a vehicle, wear protective gloves and discard them after use.

The battery

• Batteries contain sulphuric acid, which attacks clothing, eyes and skin. Take care when topping-up or carrying the battery.
• The hydrogen gas given off by the battery is highly explosive. Never cause a spark or allow a naked light nearby. Be careful when connecting and disconnecting battery chargers or jump leads.

Air bags

• Air bags can cause injury if they go off accidentally. Take care when removing the steering wheel and trim panels. Special storage instructions may apply.

Diesel injection equipment

• Diesel injection pumps supply fuel at very high pressure. Take care when working on the fuel injectors and fuel pipes.

⚠ *Warning: Never expose the hands, face or any other part of the body to injector spray; the fuel can penetrate the skin with potentially fatal results.*

Remember...

DO

• Do use eye protection when using power tools, and when working under the vehicle.

• Do wear gloves or use barrier cream to protect your hands when necessary.

• Do get someone to check periodically that all is well when working alone on the vehicle.

• Do keep loose clothing and long hair well out of the way of moving mechanical parts.

• Do remove rings, wristwatch etc, before working on the vehicle – especially the electrical system.

• Do ensure that any lifting or jacking equipment has a safe working load rating adequate for the job.

DON'T

• Don't attempt to lift a heavy component which may be beyond your capability – get assistance.

• Don't rush to finish a job, or take unverified short cuts.

• Don't use ill-fitting tools which may slip and cause injury.

• Don't leave tools or parts lying around where someone can trip over them. Mop up oil and fuel spills at once.

• Don't allow children or pets to play in or near a vehicle being worked on.

The following pages are intended to help in dealing with common roadside emergencies and breakdowns. You will find more detailed fault finding information at the back of the manual, and repair information in the main chapters.

If your car won't start and the starter motor doesn't turn

- ☐ If it's a model with manual transmission, make sure that the clutch and brake pedals are fully depressed. On models with automatic transmission, make sure the selector is in P or N and the brake pedal is fully depressed.
- ☐ Open the bonnet and make sure that the battery terminals are clean and tight.
- ☐ Switch on the headlights and try to start the engine. If the headlights go very dim when you'r e trying to start, the battery is probably flat. Get out of trouble by jump starting using a friend's car.

If your car won't start even though the starter motor turns as normal

- ☐ Is there fuel in the tank?
- ☐ Is there moisture on electrical components under the bonnet? Switch off the ignition, then wipe off any obvious dampness with a dry cloth. Spray a water-repellent aerosol product (WD-40 or equivalent) on ignition and fuel system electrical connectors like those shown in the photos.

1 On petrol engines, check that the wiring to the ignition module is connected firmly.

2 Check that the airflow meter wiring is connected securely.

3 Check the security and condition of the battery connections.

Check that electrical connections are secure (with the ignition switched off) and spray with water dispersant if you suspect a problem due to damp.

4 Check all multi-plugs and wiring connectors for security.

5 Check that all fuses are still in good condition and none have blown.

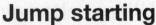

Jump starting

When jump-starting a car using a booster battery, observe the following precautions:

✔ Before connecting the booster battery, make sure that the ignition is switched off.

Caution: Remove the key in case the central locking engages when the jump leads are connected

✔ Ensure that all electrical equipment (lights, heater, wipers, etc) is switched off.

✔ Take note of any special precautions printed on the battery case.

✔ Make sure that the booster battery is the same voltage as the discharged one in the vehicle.

✔ If the battery is being jump-started from the battery in another vehicle, the two vehicles MUST NOT TOUCH each other.

✔ Make sure that the transmission is in neutral (or PARK, in the case of automatic transmission).

1 Connect one end of the red jump lead to the positive (+) terminal of the flat battery

2 Connect the other end of the red lead to the positive (+) terminal of the booster battery.

3 Connect one end of the black jump lead to the negative (-) terminal of the booster battery

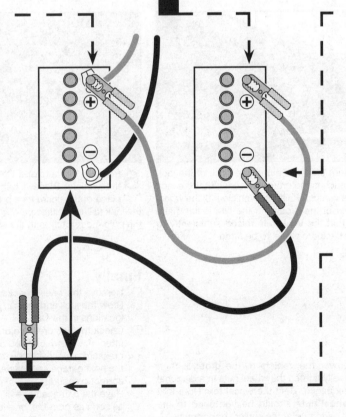

4 Connect the other end of the black jump lead to a bolt or bracket on the engine block, well away from the battery, on the vehicle to be started.

5 Make sure that the jump leads will not come into contact with the fan, drive-belts or other moving parts of the engine.

6 Start the engine using the booster battery and run it at idle speed. Switch on the lights, rear window demister and heater blower motor, then disconnect the jump leads in the reverse order of connection. Turn off the lights etc.

Wheel changing

Note: *Most Insignia models are equipped with a puncture repair kit and do not have a spare wheel and jack. If your car has a puncture repair kit, refer to the information contained in the next Section.*

 Warning: Do not change a wheel in a situation where you risk being hit by other traffic. On busy roads, try to stop in a lay-by or a gateway. Be wary of passing traffic while changing the wheel – it is easy to become distracted by the job in hand.

Preparation

☐ When a puncture occurs, stop as soon as it is safe to do so.
☐ Park on firm level ground, if possible, and well out of the way of other traffic.
☐ Use hazard warning lights if necessary.

☐ If you have one, use a warning triangle to alert other drivers of your presence.
☐ Apply the handbrake and engage first or reverse gear (or Park on models with automatic transmission).

☐ Chock the wheel diagonally opposite the one being removed – a couple of large stones will do for this.
☐ If the ground is soft, use a flat piece of wood to spread the load under the jack.

Changing the wheel

1 Lift the floor covering and unscrew the spare wheel clamp nut. Lift out the spare wheel.

2 Remove the tools from the carrier stored beneath the spare wheel.

3 On models with steel wheels, use the special tool to pull the wheel trim from the wheel. On models with alloywheels, use the screwdriver provided inserted at the wheel nut holes to prise off the trim.

4 Slacken each wheel nut by half a turn Locate the jack head below the jacking point nearest the wheel to be changed;the jacking point is indicated by an arrow in the sill.

5 Turn the handle until the base of the jack touches the ground ensuring that the jack is vertical. Raise the vehicleuntil the wheel is clear of the ground. If the tyre is flat make sure that the vehicle is raised sufficiently to allow thespare wheel to be fitted.

6 Remove the nuts and lift the wheel from the vehicle. Place it beneath the sill in place of the spare as a precautionagainst the jack failing. Fit the spare wheel and tighten the nuts moderately with the wheelbrace.

7 Lower the vehicle to the ground, then finally tighten the wheel nuts in a diagonal sequence. Refit the wheel trim.Note that the wheel nuts should be tightened to the specified torque at the earliest opportunity.

Finally . . .

☐ Remove the wheel chocks.
☐ Stow the jack and tools in the correct locations in the car.
☐ Check the tyre pressure on the wheel just fitted. If it is low, or if you don't have a pressure gauge with you, drive slowly to the next garage and inflate the tyre to the correct pressure.
☐ Have the damaged tyre or wheel repaired as soon as possible, or another puncture will leave you stranded.

Using the puncture repair kit

⚠️ *Warning: Do not change a wheel in a situation where you risk being hit by other traffic. On busy roads, try to stop in a lay-by or a gateway. Be wary of passing traffic while changing the wheel – it is easy to become distracted by the job in hand.*

⚠️ *Warning: Repair of a tyre using the puncture repair kit must be regarded as a 'get you home' emergency repair only. A new tyre must be fitted as soon as possible.*

Preparation

☐ When a puncture occurs, stop as soon as it is safe to do so.

☐ Park on firm level ground, if possible, and well out of the way of other traffic.

☐ Use hazard warning lights if necessary.

☐ If you have one, use a warning triangle to alert other drivers of your presence.

☐ Apply the handbrake and engage first or reverse gear (or Park on models with automatic transmission).

Repairing the puncture

1 Lift the luggage compartment floor covering and take out the sealant bottle and compressor from the stowage box.

2 Remove the air hose and electrical cable from the underside of the compressor.

3 Screw the air hose onto the sealant bottle connection.

4 Fit the sealant bottle in the retainer on the compressor, then position the compressor near the punctured tyre.

5 Unscrew the dust cap from the punctured tyre, and screw the sealant bottle air hose onto the tyre valve.

6 Ensure that the switch on the compressor is set to 'O', then plug the compressor electrical cable into the accessorysocket or cigarette lighter socket.

7 Switch on the ignition, then set the compressor switch to 'I' to start the compressor. To avoid discharging thebattery when the compressor is running, it is advisable to start the engine. The pump will initially pump the sealant into thetyre which will take approximately 30 seconds, and then start to inflate the tyre. During the initial 30 second period, thepressure gauge on the pump will indicate up to 6 bar (87 psi) and then drop. The correct tyre pressure should be obtainedwithin 10 minutes. The compressor can then be switched off by returning the switch to the 'O' position.

8 If it is necessary to release the pressure in the tyre, press the button above the pressure gauge on thecompressor.

Finally...

☐ Stow the puncture repair kit in the luggage compartment and refit the floor covering.

☐ Do not exceed 50 mph until until an undamaged wheel and tyre have been fitted.

☐ Obtain a new sealant bottle as soon as possible, or another puncture will leave you stranded.

Important notes

☐ If the correct tyre pressure is not obtained within 10 minutes, it is likely that the tyre is too badly damaged to be repaired.

☐ On completion, disconnect the tyre repair kit and connect the end of the air hose to the free connection on the sealant bottle. This will prevent any remaining sealant from leaking out.

☐ Continue driving immediately so that the sealant is evenly distributed around the inside of the tyre.

☐ After driving approximately 6 miles (but no more than 10 minutes) stop and check the tyre pressure by connecting the air hose to the tyre valve. As long as the pressure indicated on the gauge is more than 1.3 bar (19 psi) it may be adjusted to the prescribed value using the electric pump. If the pressure has fallen below 1.3 bar (19 psi) the repair has not been successful and the car should not be driven. It will therefore be necessary to seek roadside assistance.

Identifying leaks

Puddles on the garage floor or drive, or obvious wetness under the bonnet or underneath the car, suggest a leak that needs investigating. It can sometimes be difficult to decide where the leak is coming from, especially if an engine undershield is fitted. Leaking oil or fluid can also be blown rearwards by the passage of air under the car, giving a false impression of where the problem lies.

 Warning: Most automotive oils and fluids are poisonous. Wash them off skin, and change out of contaminated clothing, without delay.

 The smell of a fluid leaking from the car may provide a clue to what's leaking. Some fluids are distinctively coloured. It may help to remove the engine undershield, clean the car carefully and to park it over some clean paper overnight as an aid to locating the source of the leak. Remember that some leaks may only occur while the engine is running.

Sump oil

Engine oil may leak from the drain plug...

Oil from filter

...or from the base of the oil filter.

Gearbox oil

Gearbox oil can leak from the seals at the inboard ends of the driveshafts.

Antifreeze

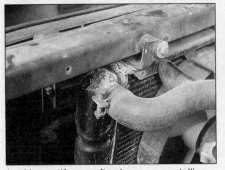

Leaking antifreeze often leaves a crystalline deposit like this.

Brake fluid

A leak occurring at a wheel is almost certainly brake fluid.

Power steering fluid

Power steering fluid may leak from the pipe connectors on the steering rack.

Towing

When all else fails, you may find yourself having to get a tow home – or of course you may be helping somebody else. Long-distance recovery should only be done by a garage or breakdown service. For shorter distances, DIY towing using another car is easy enough, but observe the following points:

☐ Use a proper tow-rope – they are not expensive. The vehicle being towed must display an ON TOW sign in its rear window.

☐ Always turn the ignition key to the 'On' position when the vehicle is being towed, so that the steering lock is released, and the direction indicator and brake lights work.

☐ Only attach the tow-rope to the towing eye provided with the tool kit in the luggage compartment.

☐ To fit the towing eye, remove the circular cover from the front or rear bumper, as required, then screw in the towing eye anti-clockwise as far as it will go using the handle of the wheel brace to turn the eye. **Note that the towing eye has a left-hand thread**.

☐ Before being towed, release the handbrake and select neutral on the transmission. On models with automatic transmission, special precautions apply. If in doubt, do not tow, or transmission damage may result.

☐ Note that greater-than-usual pedal pressure will be required to operate the brakes, since the vacuum servo unit is only operational with the engine running.

☐ Greater-than-usual steering effort will also be required.

☐ The driver of the car being towed must keep the tow-rope taut at all times to avoid snatching.

☐ Make sure that both drivers know the route before setting off.

☐ Only drive at moderate speeds and keep the distance towed to a minimum. Drive smoothly and allow plenty of time for slowing down at junctions.

Introduction

There are some very simple checks which need only take a few minutes to carry out, but which could save you a lot of inconvenience and expense.

These checks require no great skill or special tools, and the small amount of time they take to perform could prove to be very well spent, for example:

☐ Keeping an eye on tyre condition and pressures, will not only help to stop them wearing out prematurely, but could also save your life.

☐ Many breakdowns are caused by electrical problems. Battery-related faults are particularly common, and a quick check on a regular basis will often prevent the majority of these.

☐ If your car develops a brake fluid leak, the first time you might know about it is when your brakes don't work properly. Checking the level regularly will give advance warning of this kind of problem.

☐ If the oil or coolant levels run low, the cost of repairing any engine damage will be far greater than fixing the leak, for example.

Underbonnet check points

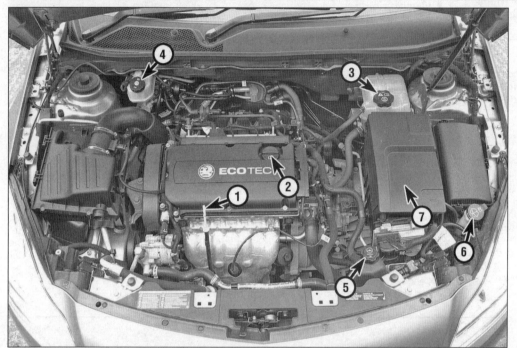

◄ Petrol engine models

1 *Engine oil level dipstick*

2 *Engine oil filler cap*

3 *Coolant reservoir (expansion tank)*

4 *Brake and clutch fluid reservoir*

5 *Power steering fluid reservoir*

6 *Washer fluid reservoir*

7 *Battery*

◄ Diesel engine models

1 *Engine oil level dipstick*

2 *Engine oil filler cap*

3 *Coolant reservoir (expansion tank)*

4 *Brake and clutch fluid reservoir*

5 *Power steering fluid reservoir*

6 *Washer fluid reservoir*

7 *Battery*

Engine oil level

Before you start
✔ Make sure that the car is on level ground.
✔ The oil level must be checked with the engine at normal operating temperature, however, wait at least 5 minutes after the engine has been switched off.

HAYNES HiNT *If the oil is checked immediately after driving the vehicle, some of the oil will remain in the upper engine components, resulting in an inaccurate reading on the dipstick.*

The correct oil
Modern engines place great demands on their oil. It is very important that the correct oil for your car is used (see *Lubricants and fluids*).

Car care
● If you have to add oil frequently, you should check whether you have any oil leaks. Place some clean paper under the car overnight, and check for stains in the morning. If there are no leaks, then the engine may be burning oil, or the oil may only be leaking when the engine is running
● Always maintain the level between the upper and lower dipstick marks (see photo 3). If the level is too low, severe engine damage may occur. Oil seal failure may result if the engine is overfilled by adding too much oil.

1 The dipstick is brightly coloured for easy identification (see *Underbonnet check points* for exact location). Withdraw the dipstick.

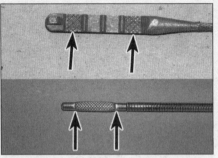

3 The level on the dipstick should be between the upper (MAX) mark and lower (MIN) mark. About 1.0 litre of oil willraise the level from the lower to the upper mark. On petrol engines (top), the MAX and MIN marks are indicated by the hatchedareas. On diesel engines (bottom) the MAX and MIN marks are above and below the hatched area on the dipstick.

2 Using a clean rag or paper towel remove all oil from the dipstick. Insert the clean dipstick into the tube as far asit will go, then withdraw it again.

4 Oil is added through the filler cap. Unscrew the cap and top-up the level. A funnel may help to reduce spillage. Addthe oil slowly, checking the level on the dipstick frequently. Avoid overfilling (see *Car care*).

Coolant level

⚠ Warning: Do not attempt to remove the expansion tank pressure cap when the engine is hot, as there is a very great risk of scalding. Do not leave open containers of coolant about, as it is poisonous.

Car care
● Adding coolant should not be necessary on a regular basis. If frequent topping-up is required, it is likely there is a leak. Check the radiator, all hoses and joint faces for signs of staining or wetness, and rectify as necessary.

● It is important that antifreeze is used in the cooling system all year round, not just during the winter months. Don't top up with water alone, as the antifreeze will become diluted.

1 The coolant level varies with the temperature of the engine. When the engine is cold, the coolant level should beslightly above the minimum level mark on the side of the tank (arrowed). When the engine is hot, the level will rise.

2 If topping-up is necessary, **wait until the engine is cold**. Slowly unscrew the expansion tank cap, to release anypressure present in the cooling system, and remove it.

3 Add a mixture of water and antifreeze to the expansion tank until the coolant is up to the minimum level mark. Refitthe cap and tighten it securely.

Brake and clutch fluid level

⚠️ **Warning:**
Hydraulic fluid can harm your eyes and damage painted surfaces, so use extreme caution when handling and pouring it.
Warning: Do not use fluid that has been standing open for some time, as it absorbs moisture from the air, which can cause a dangerous loss of braking effectiveness.

Before you start

✔ Make sure that the car is on level ground.
✔ Cleanliness is of great importance when dealing with the braking system, so take care to clean around the reservoir cap before topping-up. Use only clean brake fluid.

Safety first!

● If the reservoir requires repeated topping-up this is an indication of a fluid leak somewhere in the system, which should be investigated immediately.
● If a leak is suspected, the car should not be driven until the braking system has been checked. Never take any risks where brakes are concerned.

 HAYNES HINT *The fluid level in the reservoir will drop slightly as the brake pads wear down, but the fluid level must never be allowed to drop below the MIN mark.*

1 The MAX and MIN marks are indicated on the reservoir. The fluid level must be kept between the marks at alltimes.

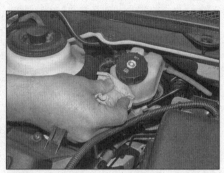

2 If topping-up is necessary, first wipe clean the area around the filler cap to prevent dirt entering the hydraulicsystem. Unscrew the reservoir cap.

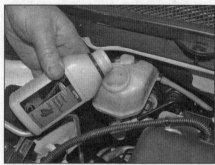

3 Carefully add fluid, taking care not to spill it onto the surrounding components. Use only the specified fluid;mixing different types can cause damage to the system. After topping-up to the correct level, securely refit the cap and wipeoff any spilt fluid.

Power steering fluid level (where fitted)

✔ Park the car on level ground.
✔ Set the steering wheel straight-ahead.
✔ The engine should be turned off.

✔ For the check to be accurate, the steering must not be turned once the engine has been stopped.

Safety first!

● The need for frequent topping-up indicates a leak, which should be investigated immediately.

1 The power steering fluid reservoir is located at the front, left-hand side of the engine compartment. With theengine stopped, wipe clean the area around the reservoir filler neck, and unscrew the filler cap from the reservoir.

2 Wipe all fluid from the cap dipstick with a clean rag. Refit the filler cap, then remove it again and note the fluidlevel on the dipstick. When the engine is cold, the fluid level should be between the lower (MIN) mark and the upper (MAX) markon the dipstick.

3 If the fluid level is on or below the lower (MIN) mark, top-up the fluid level to the upper (MAX) mark, using thespecified type of fluid (do not overfill). When the level is correct, securely refit the filler cap.

Tyre condition and pressure

It is very important that tyres are in good condition, and at the correct pressure - having a tyre failure at any speed is highly dangerous. Tyre wear is influenced by driving style - harsh braking and acceleration, or fast cornering, will all produce more rapid tyre wear. As a general rule, the front tyres wear out faster than the rears. Interchanging the tyres from front to rear ("rotating" the tyres) may result in more even wear. However, if this is completely effective, you may have the expense of replacing all four tyres at once! Remove any nails or stones embedded in the tread before they penetrate the tyre to cause deflation. If removal of a nail does reveal that the tyre has been punctured, refit the nail so that its point of penetration is marked. Then immediately change the wheel, and have the tyre repaired by a tyre dealer.

Regularly check the tyres for damage in the form of cuts or bulges, especially in the sidewalls. Periodically remove the wheels, and clean any dirt or mud from the inside and outside surfaces. Examine the wheel rims for signs of rusting, corrosion or other damage. Light alloy wheels are easily damaged by "kerbing" whilst parking; steel wheels may also become dented or buckled. A new wheel is very often the only way to overcome severe damage.

New tyres should be balanced when they are fitted, but it may become necessary to re-balance them as they wear, or if the balance weights fitted to the wheel rim should fall off. Unbalanced tyres will wear more quickly, as will the steering and suspension components. Wheel imbalance is normally signified by vibration, particularly at a certain speed (typically around 50 mph). If this vibration is felt only through the steering, then it is likely that just the front wheels need balancing. If, however, the vibration is felt through the whole car, the rear wheels could be out of balance. Wheel balancing should be carried out by a tyre dealer or garage.

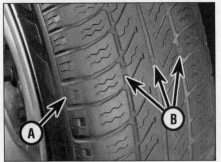

1 Tread Depth - visual check
The original tyres have tread wear safety bands (B), which will appear when the tread depth reaches approximately 1.6 mm. The band positions are indicated by a triangular mark on the tyre sidewall (A).

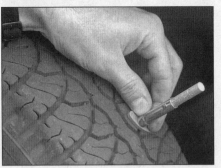

2 Tread Depth - manual check
Alternatively, tread wear can be monitored with a simple, inexpensive device known as a tread depth indicator gauge.

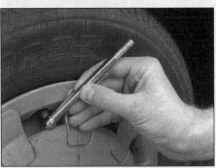

3 Tyre Pressure Check
Check the tyre pressures regularly with the tyres cold. Do not adjust the tyre pressures immediately after the vehicle has been used, or an inaccurate setting will result.

Tyre tread wear patterns

Shoulder Wear

Underinflation (wear on both sides)
Under-inflation will cause overheating of the tyre, because the tyre will flex too much, and the tread will not sit correctly on the road surface. This will cause a loss of grip and excessive wear, not to mention the danger of sudden tyre failure due to heat build-up.
Check and adjust pressures
Incorrect wheel camber (wear on one side)
Repair or renew suspension parts
Hard cornering
Reduce speed!

Centre Wear

Overinflation
Over-inflation will cause rapid wear of the centre part of the tyre tread, coupled with reduced grip, harsher ride, and the danger of shock damage occurring in the tyre casing.
Check and adjust pressures

If you sometimes have to inflate your car's tyres to the higher pressures specified for maximum load or sustained high speed, don't forget to reduce the pressures to normal afterwards.

Uneven Wear

Front tyres may wear unevenly as a result of wheel misalignment. Most tyre dealers and garages can check and adjust the wheel alignment (or "tracking") for a modest charge.
Incorrect camber or castor
Repair or renew suspension parts
Malfunctioning suspension
Repair or renew suspension parts
Unbalanced wheel
Balance tyres
Incorrect toe setting
Adjust front wheel alignment
Note: *The feathered edge of the tread which typifies toe wear is best checked by feel.*

Screen washer fluid level

● Screenwash additives not only keep the windscreen clean during bad weather, they also prevent the washer system freezing in cold weather – which is when you are likely to need it most. Don't top-up using plain water, as the screenwash will become diluted, and will freeze in cold weather.

 Warning: On no account use engine coolant antifreeze in the screen washer system – this may damage the paintwork.

1 The reservoir for the windscreen, rear window and headlight (where applicable) washer systems is located on the front left-hand side of the engine compartment. If topping-up is necessary, open the filler cap.

2 When topping-up the reservoir a screen-wash additive should be added in the quantities recommended on the bottle.

Wiper blades

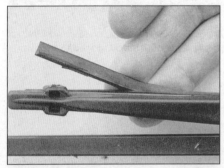

1 Check the condition of the wiper blades; if they are cracked or show any signs of deterioration, or if the glass swept area is smeared, renew them. Wiper blades should be renewed annually.

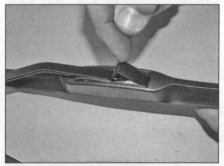

2 To remove a windscreen wiper blade, pull the arm fully away from the screen until it locks. Lift the locking tab with your finger ...

3 ... and slide the blade out of the arm's hooked end.

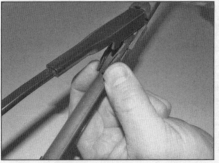

4 Don't forget to check the tailgate wiper blade as well. To remove the blade, depress the retaining tabs and pivot the blade away from the arm.

5 Disengage the blade from the tab on the arm and remove.

Battery

Caution: Before carrying out any work on the vehicle battery, read the precautions given in 'Safety first!' at the start of this manual. If the battery is to be disconnected, refer to 'Disconnecting the battery' in Chapter 5A, Section 4, before proceeding.
✔ Make sure that the battery tray is in good condition, and that the clamp is tight. Corrosion on the tray, retaining clamp and the battery itself can be removed with a solution of water and baking soda. Thoroughly rinse all cleaned areas with water. Any metal parts damaged by corrosion should be covered with a zinc-based primer, then painted.
✔ Periodically (approximately every three months), check the charge condition of the battery, as described in Chapter 5A, Section 3.
✔ If the battery is flat, and you need to jump start your vehicle, see *Roadside repairs*.

Battery corrosion can be kept to a minimum by applying a layer of petroleum jelly to the clamps and terminals after they are reconnected.

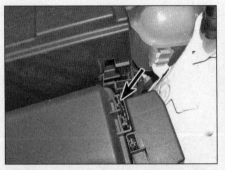

1 The battery is located at the front, left-hand side of the engine compartment, housed in a protective plastic box. Open the battery box for access to the terminals by depressing the tab at the rear left-hand side ...

2 ... and rear right-hand side ...

3 ... then pivot the lid upward to remove.

4 Lift up the plastic insulator cover over the battery positive terminal, then check the tightness of the battery clamps to ensure good electrical connections. You should not be able to move them. Also check each cable for cracks and frayed conductors.

5 If corrosion (white, fluffy deposits) is evident, remove the cables from the battery terminals, clean them with a small wire brush, then refit them. Automotive stores sell a tool for cleaning the battery post ...

6 ... as well as the battery cable clamps.

Electrical systems

✔ Check all external lights and the horn. Refer to the appropriate Sections of Chapter 12 for details if any of the circuits are found to be inoperative.

✔ Visually check all accessible wiring connectors, harnesses and retaining clips for security, and for signs of chafing or damage.

HAYNES HINT *If you need to check your brake lights and indicators unaided, back up to a wall or garage door and operate the lights. The reflected light should show if they are working properly.*

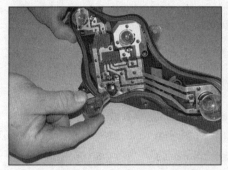

1 If a single indicator light, brake light or headlight has failed, it is likely that a bulb has blown and will need to be renewed. Refer to Chapter 12, Section 5 for details. If both brake lights have failed, it is possible that the switch has failed (see Chapter 9, Section 17).

2 If more than one indicator light or headlight has failed, it is likely that either a fuse has blown or that there is a fault in the circuit (see Chapter 12, Section 2). The main fuses are located in the fuse/relay box on the left-hand side of the engine compartment. Depress the three tabs and lift off the cover for access.

3 Additional fuses and relays are located behind a cover in the glovebox ...

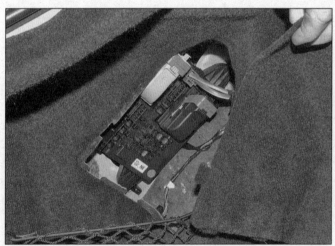

4 ... and (on some models) behind a cover in the left-hand side of the luggage compartment. Refer to the wiring diagrams at the end of Chapter 12 for details of the fuse locations and circuits protected.

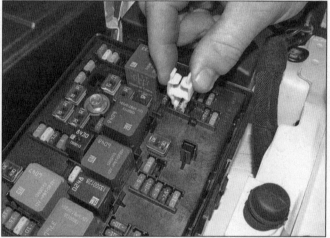

5 To renew a blown fuse, remove it, where applicable, using the plastic tool provided. Fit a new fuse of the same rating, available from car accessory shops. It is important that you find the reason that the fuse blew (see *Electrical fault finding* in Chapter 12, Section 2).

Lubricants and fluids

Engine

Recommended specification (all engines) . . . .   Multigrade engine oil, viscosity SAE 5W/30 to General Motors Dexos2™ specification

Alternative specification (if Dexos2 is unavailable)

   Petrol . . . .   Multigrade engine oil, viscosity SAE 5W/30 or 5W/40 to General Motors specification GM-LL-A-025

   Diesel . . . .   Multigrade engine oil, viscosity SAE 5W/30 or 5W/40 to General Motors specification GM-LL-B-025

Manual transmission . . . .   Vauxhall/Opel gear oil (93 165 290)

Automatic transmission. . . . .   Vauxhall/Opel automatic transmission fluid (93 165 147)

Power steering reservoir . . . .   Vauxhall/Opel power steering fluid (93 165 414)

Cooling system. . . . .   Vauxhall/Opel silicate-free coolant (93 170 402)

Brake/clutch fluid reservoir. . . . .   Hydraulic fluid to DOT 4

Tyre pressures

Details of the tyre pressures applicable to your vehicle are given on a sticker attached to the front door pillar on the left-hand side..

Chapter 1 Part A
Routine maintenance and servicing – petrol models

Contents

Degrees of difficulty

Easy, suitable for novice with little experience | **Fairly easy,** suitable for beginner with some experience | **Fairly difficult,** suitable for competent DIY mechanic | **Difficult,** suitable for experienced DIY mechanic | **Very difficult,** suitable for expert DIY or professional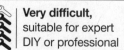

Specifications

Lubricants and fluids. . . . . Refer to Lubricants, fluids and tyre pressures

Capacities

Engine oil
Capacity including oil filter . . . . 4.5 litres
Difference between MIN and MAX dipstick marks. . . . . 1.0 litre

Cooling system
All models. . . . . 5.6 litres

Transmission
All models. . . . . 2.2 litres

Fuel tank
All models. . . . . 70 litres

Cooling system

Antifreeze mixture:
  50% antifreeze . . . . Protection down to -40°C

Ignition system

Spark plugs:
  Type   . . . . Bosch FQR 8 LEU2
  Electrode gap . . . . 0.75 to 0.9 mm

Brakes

Friction material minimum thickness . . . . 2.0 mm

Torque wrench settings

	Nm	lbf ft
Oil filter housing cap to filter housing.	25	18
Roadwheel nuts	150	111
Spark plugs	25	18
Sump drain plug.	14	10

1   Maintenance schedule – petrol models

1 The maintenance intervals in this manual are provided with the assumption that you, not the dealer, will be carrying out the work. These are the minimum maintenance intervals based on the standard service schedule recommended by the manufacturer for vehicles driven daily. If you wish to keep your vehicle in peak condition at all times, you may wish to perform some of these procedures more often. We encourage frequent maintenance, because it enhances the efficiency, performance and resale value of your vehicle.

2 If the vehicle is driven in dusty areas, used to tow a trailer, or driven frequently at slow speeds (idling in traffic) or on short journeys, more frequent maintenance intervals are recommended.

3 When the vehicle is new, it should be serviced by a dealer service department (or other workshop recognised by the vehicle manufacturer as providing the same standard of service) in order to preserve the warranty. The vehicle manufacturer may reject warranty claims if you are unable to prove that servicing has been carried out as and when specified, using only original equipment parts or parts certified to be of equivalent quality.

Every 250 miles or weekly
☐ Refer to *Weekly checks*.

Every 10 000 miles or 6 months – whichever comes first
☐ Renew the engine oil and filter (Section 5)*

*Note: *Vauxhall/Opel recommend that the engine oil and filter are changed every 20 000 miles or 12 months if the vehicle is being operated under the standard service schedule. However, oil and filter changes are good for the engine and we recommend that the oil and filter are renewed more frequently, especially if the vehicle is used on a lot of short journeys.*

Every 20 000 miles or 12 months – whichever comes first
☐ Check all underbonnet and underbody components, pipes and hoses for leaks (Section 6)
☐ Check the condition of the brake pads (renew if necessary), the calipers and discs (Section 7)
☐ Check the condition of all brake fluid pipes and hoses (Section 8)
☐ Check the condition of the front suspension and steering components, particularly the rubber gaiters and seals (Section 9)
☐ Check the condition of the driveshaft joint gaiters, and the driveshaft joints (Section 10)
☐ Check the condition of the exhaust system components (Section 11)
☐ Check the condition of the rear suspension components (Section 12)
☐ Check the bodywork and underbody for damage and corrosion, and check the condition of the underbody corrosion protection (Section 13)
☐ Check the tightness of the roadwheel nuts (Section 14)
☐ Lubricate all door, bonnet, boot lid and tailgate hinges and locks (Section 15)
☐ Check the operation of the horn, all lights, and the wipers and washers (Section 16)
☐ Carry out a road test (Section 17)
☐ Reset the service interval indicator (Section 18)

Every 40 000 miles or 2 years – whichever comes first
☐ Renew the pollen filter (Section 19)
☐ Check the auxiliary drivebelts and tensioner (Section 20)
☐ Check the headlight beam alignment (Section 21)

Every 2 years, regardless of mileage
☐ Renew the battery for the remote control handset (Section 22)
☐ Renew the brake and clutch fluid (Section 23)
☐ Renew the coolant (Section 24)*

*Note: *Vehicles using Vauxhall/Opel silicate-free coolant do not need the coolant renewed on a regular basis.*

Every 40 000 miles or 4 years – whichever comes first
☐ Renew the air cleaner filter element (Section 25)
☐ Renew the spark plugs (Section 26)
☐ Renew the timing belt, tensioner and idler pulleys (Section 27)*

*Note: *The manufacturer's specified timing belt renewal interval is 100 000 miles or 6 years. However, it is strongly recommended that the interval used is 40 000 miles on vehicles which are subjected to intensive use, ie, mainly short journeys or a lot of stop-start driving. The actual belt renewal interval is therefore very much up to the individual owner, but bear in mind that severe engine damage will result if the belt breaks.*

Every 80 000 miles or 6 years – whichever comes first
☐ Renew the auxiliary drivebelts and tensioner (Section 20)

Every 100 000 miles or 10 years – whichever comes first
☐ Check, and if necessary adjust, the valve clearances (Section 28)

2 Component location – petrol models

Front underbody view

1 Exhaust front pipe
2 Steering track rods
3 Front suspension lower arms
4 Front brake calipers
5 Engine mounting front torque link
6 Engine mounting rear torque link
7 Right-hand driveshaft
8 Manual transmission
9 Engine oil drain plug
10 Air conditioning compressor
11 Front subframe

Rear underbody view

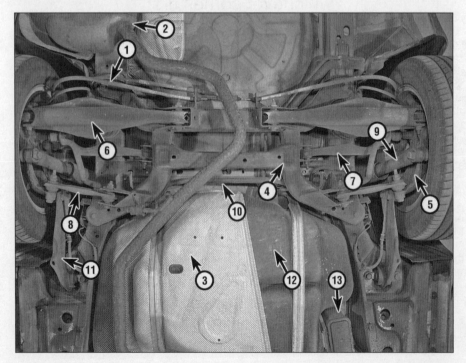

1 Handbrake cable
2 Exhaust rear silencer
3 Exhaust heat shield
4 Rear subframe
5 Rear hub carrier
6 Lower control arm
7 Upper control arm
8 Auxiliary control arm
9 Shock absorber
10 Rear anti-roll bar
11 Rear suspension trailing arm
12 Fuel tank
13 Charcoal canister

Underbonnet view

1 Engine oil level dipstick
2 Engine oil filler cap
3 Air cleaner assembly
4 Front suspension strut upper
 mounting

5 Screen washer fluid reservoir
6 Airflow meter
7 Brake (and clutch) fluid reservoir
8 Engine management ECU
9 Coolant expansion tank

10 Battery
11 Fuse/relay box
12 Power steering fluid reservoir
13 Oil filter

3   General Information

1 This Chapter is designed to help the home mechanic maintain his/her vehicle for safety, economy, long life and peak performance.
2 The Chapter contains a master maintenance schedule, followed by Sections dealing specifically with each task in the schedule. Visual checks, adjustments, component renewal and other helpful items are included. Refer to the accompanying illustrations of the engine compartment and the underside of the vehicle for the locations of the various components.
3 Servicing your vehicle in accordance with the mileage/time maintenance schedule and the following Sections will provide a planned maintenance programme, which should result in a long and reliable service life. This is a comprehensive plan, so maintaining some items but not others at the specified service intervals, will not produce the same results.

4 As you service your vehicle, you will discover that many of the procedures can – and should – be grouped together, because of the particular procedure being performed, or because of the proximity of two otherwise-unrelated components to one another. For example, if the vehicle is raised for any reason, the exhaust can be inspected at the same time as the suspension and steering components.
5 The first step in this maintenance programme is to prepare yourself before the actual work begins. Read through all the Sections relevant to the work to be carried out, then make a list and gather all the parts and tools required. If a problem is encountered, seek advice from a parts specialist, or a dealer service department.

4   Regular maintenance

1 If, from the time the vehicle is new, the routine maintenance schedule is followed

closely, and frequent checks are made of fluid levels and high-wear items, as suggested throughout this manual, the engine will be kept in relatively good running condition, and the need for additional work will be minimised.
2 It is possible that there will be times when the engine is running poorly due to the lack of regular maintenance. This is even more likely if a used vehicle, which has not received regular and frequent maintenance checks, is purchased. In such cases, additional work may need to be carried out, outside of the regular maintenance intervals.
3 If engine wear is suspected, a compression test (refer to Chapter 2A, Section 2 2) will provide valuable information regarding the overall performance of the main internal components. Such a test can be used as a basis to decide on the extent of the work to be carried out. If, for example, a compression test indicates serious internal engine wear, conventional maintenance as described in this Chapter will not greatly improve the performance of the engine, and may prove a waste of time and money, unless extensive overhaul work is carried out first.

4 The following series of operations are those most often required to improve the performance of a generally poor-running engine:

Primary operations

- Clean, inspect and test the battery (refer to *Weekly checks*).
- Check all the engine-related fluids (refer to *Weekly checks*).
- Check the condition and tension of the auxiliary drivebelts (Section 20).
- Renew the spark plugs (Section 26).
- Check the condition of the air filter element, and renew if necessary (Section 25).
- Check the condition of all hoses, and check for fluid leaks (Section 6).

5 If the above operations do not prove fully effective, carry out the following secondary operations:

Secondary operations

6 All items listed under *Primary operations*, plus the following:
- Check the charging system (refer to Chapter 5A, Section 3).
- Check the ignition system (refer to Chapter 5B, Section 2).
- Check the fuel, exhaust and emission control systems (refer to Chapter 4A and Chapter 4C).

5 Engine oil and filter renewal – petrol models

HAYNES HiNT *Frequent oil and filter changes are the most important prevent-ative maintenance procedures which can be undertaken by the DIY owner. As engine oil ages, it becomes diluted and contaminated, which leads to premature engine wear.*

1 Before starting this procedure, gather together all the necessary tools and materials. Also make sure that you have plenty of clean rags and newspapers handy, to mop up any spills. Ideally, the engine oil should be warm, as it will drain more easily, and more built-up sludge will be removed with it. Take care not to touch the exhaust or any other hot parts of the engine when working under the vehicle. To avoid any possibility of scalding, and to protect yourself from possible skin irritants and other harmful contaminants in used engine oils, it is advisable to wear gloves when carrying out this work.

2 Access to the underside of the vehicle will be greatly improved if it can be raised on a lift, driven onto ramps, or jacked up and supported on axle stands (see *Jacking and vehicle support*). Whichever method is chosen, make sure that the vehicle remains level, or if it is at an angle, that the drain plug is at the lowest point. The drain plug is located at the rear of the sump.

3 Remove the oil filler cap from the camshaft cover (twist it through a quarter-turn anti-clockwise and withdraw it).

4 Using a spanner, or preferably a suitable socket and bar, slacken the drain plug about half a turn. Position the draining container under the drain plug, then remove the plug completely **(see Haynes Hint)**.

5 Allow some time for the oil to drain, noting that it may be necessary to reposition the container as the oil flow slows to a trickle.

6 Position another container under the oil filter, located at the front left-hand side of the cylinder block.

7 Unscrew the oil filter housing cap and withdraw it, together with the element, then separate the element, and remove the O-ring seal from the cap **(see illustrations)**.

8 Use a clean rag to remove all oil, dirt and sludge from the oil filter housing.

9 Locate a new O-ring seal in the groove on the filter housing cap, then locate the new element in the cap. Lubricate the threads of the filter housing cap with clean engine oil, then insert the filter and cap into the housing. Screw on the cap and tighten it to the specified torque.

10 After all the oil has drained, wipe the drain plug and the sealing O-ring with a clean rag. Examine the condition of the O-ring, and renew it if it shows signs of damage which may prevent an oil-tight seal. Clean the area around the drain plug opening, and refit the

HAYNES HiNT *As the drain plug releases from the threads, move it away quickly so that the stream of oil running out of the sump goes into the drain pan and not up your sleeve.*

plug complete with the O-ring. Tighten the plug to the specified torque.

11 Remove the old oil and all tools from under the vehicle then lower the vehicle to the ground.

12 Fill the engine through the filler hole in the camshaft cover, using the correct grade and type of oil (refer to *Weekly checks* for details of topping-up). Pour in half the specified quantity of oil first, then wait a few minutes for the oil to drain into the sump. Continue to add oil, a small quantity at a time, until the level is up to the lower mark on the dipstick. Adding approximately a further 1.0 litre will bring the level up to the upper mark on the dipstick.

13 Start the engine and run it until it reaches normal operating temperature. While the engine is warming up, check for leaks around the oil filter and the sump drain plug.

14 Stop the engine, and wait at least five minutes for the oil to settle in the sump once more. With the new oil circulated and the filter now completely full, recheck the level on the dipstick, and add more oil as necessary.

15 Reset the service interval (oil life) display as described in Section 18.

16 Dispose of the used engine oil and filter safely, with reference to *General repair procedures*. Do not discard the old filter with domestic household waste. The facility for waste oil disposal provided by many local council refuse tips and/or recycling centres generally has a filter receptacle alongside.

6 Hose and fluid leak check

1 Visually inspect the engine joint faces, gaskets and seals for any signs of water or oil leaks. Pay particular attention to the areas around the camshaft cover, cylinder head, oil filter and sump joint faces. Similarly, check the transmission and the air conditioning compressor for oil leakage. Bear in mind that, over a period of time, some very slight

5.7a Separate the oil filter element from the cap ...

5.7b ... then remove the O-ring seal

A leak in the cooling system will usually show up as white- or antifreeze coloured deposits on the area adjoining the leak.

seepage from these areas is to be expected; what you are really looking for is any indication of a serious leak. Should a leak be found, renew the offending gasket or oil seal by referring to the appropriate Chapters in this manual.

2 Also check the security and condition of all the engine-related pipes and hoses. Ensure that all cable ties or securing clips are in place, and in good condition. Clips which are broken or missing can lead to chafing of the hoses pipes or wiring, which could cause more serious problems in the future.

3 Carefully check the radiator hoses and heater hoses along their entire length. Renew any hose which is cracked, swollen or deteriorated. Cracks will show up better if the hose is squeezed. Pay close attention to the hose clips that secure the hoses to the cooling system components. Hose clips can pinch and puncture hoses, resulting in cooling system leaks. If wire-type hose clips are used, it may be a good idea to replace them with screw-type clips.

4 Inspect all the cooling system components (hoses, joint faces, etc) for leaks. Where any problems of this nature are found on system components, renew the component or gasket with reference to Chapter 3 **(see Haynes Hint above)**.

For a quick check, the thickness of friction material remaining on the inner brake pad can be measured through the aperture in the caliper body.

5 With the vehicle raised, inspect the petrol tank and filler neck for punctures, cracks and other damage. The connection between the filler neck and tank is especially critical. Sometimes, a rubber filler neck or connecting hose will leak due to loose retaining clamps or deteriorated rubber.

6 Carefully check all rubber hoses and metal fuel lines leading away from the petrol tank. Check for loose connections, deteriorated hoses, crimped lines and other damage. Pay particular attention to the vent pipes and hoses, which often loop up around the filler neck and can become blocked or crimped. Follow the lines to the front of the vehicle, carefully inspecting them all the way. Renew damaged sections as necessary. Similarly, whilst the vehicle is raised, take the opportunity to inspect all underbody brake fluid pipes and hoses.

7 From within the engine compartment, check the security of all fuel hose attachments and pipe unions, and inspect the fuel hoses and vacuum hoses for kinks, chafing and deterioration.

7   Brake pad and disc check

1 Firmly apply the handbrake, then jack up the front and rear of the vehicle and support it securely on axle stands (see *Jacking and vehicle support*). Remove the roadwheels.

2 For a quick check, the pad thickness can be carried out via the inspection hole on the caliper **(see Haynes Hint below)**. Using a steel rule, measure the thickness of the pad lining including the backing plate. This must not be less than that indicated in the Specifications.

3 The view through the caliper inspection hole gives a rough indication of the state of the brake pads. For a comprehensive check, the brake pads should be removed and cleaned. The operation of the caliper can then also be checked, and the condition of the brake disc itself can be fully examined on both sides. Chapter 9, Section 6 contains a detailed description of how the brake disc should be checked for wear and/or damage.

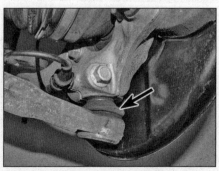

9.2a Inspect the balljoint dust covers ...

4 If any pad's friction material is worn to the specified thickness or less, *all four pads must be renewed as a set*. Refer to Chapter 9, Section 4 or Chapter 9 Section 5 for details.

5 On completion, refit the roadwheels and lower the vehicle to the ground.

8   Brake fluid pipe and hose check

1 The brake hydraulic system includes a number of metal pipes, which run from the master cylinder to the hydraulic modulator of the anti-lock braking system (ABS) and then to the front and rear brake assemblies. Flexible hoses are fitted between the pipes and the front and rear brake assemblies, to allow for steering and suspension movement.

2 When checking the system, first look for signs of leakage at the pipe or hose unions, then examine the flexible hoses for signs of cracking, chafing or deterioration of the rubber. Bend the hoses sharply between the fingers (but do not actually bend them double, or the casing may be damaged) and check that this does not reveal previously-hidden cracks, cuts or splits. Check that the pipes and hoses are securely fastened in their clips.

3 Carefully working along the length of the metal pipes, look for dents, kinks, damage of any sort, or corrosion. Light corrosion can be polished off, but if the depth of pitting is significant, the pipe must be renewed.

9   Front suspension and steering check

1 Apply the handbrake, then raise the front of the vehicle and securely support it on axle stands (see *Jacking and vehicle support*).

2 Inspect the balljoint dust covers and the steering gear gaiters for splits, chafing or deterioration **(see illustrations)**.

3 Any wear of these components will cause loss of lubricant, and may allow water to enter the components, resulting in rapid deterioration of the balljoints or steering gear.

4 Grasp each roadwheel at the 12 o'clock

9.2b ... and the steering gear gaiters for splits, chafing or deterioration

9.4 Check for wear in the hub bearings by grasping the wheel and trying to rock it

9.5 Check for wear in the track rod end ball joints

9.7 Check for signs of fluid leakage around the suspension struts, or from the rubber gaiters around the piston rods

and 6 o'clock positions, and try to rock it **(see illustration)**. Very slight free play may be felt, but if the movement is appreciable, further investigation is necessary to determine the source. Continue rocking the wheel while an assistant depresses the footbrake. If the movement is now eliminated or significantly reduced, it is likely that the hub bearings are at fault. If the free play is still evident with the footbrake depressed, then there is wear in the suspension joints or mountings.

5 Now grasp each wheel at the 9 o'clock and 3 o'clock positions, and try to rock it as before **(see illustration)**. Any movement felt now may again be caused by wear in the hub bearings or the steering track rod end balljoints. If the track rod end balljoint is worn, the visual movement will be obvious.

6 Using a large screwdriver or flat bar, check for wear in the suspension mounting bushes by levering between the relevant suspension component and its attachment point. Some movement is to be expected, as the mountings are made of rubber, but excessive wear should be obvious. Also check the condition of any visible rubber bushes, looking for splits, cracks or contamination of the rubber.

7 Check for any signs of fluid leakage around the suspension struts, or from the rubber gaiters around the piston rods **(see illustration)**. Should any fluid be noticed, the suspension strut is defective internally, and should be renewed. **Note:** *Suspension struts should always be renewed in pairs on the same axle.*

8 With the vehicle standing on its wheels,

have an assistant turn the steering wheel back-and-forth about an eighth of a turn each way. There should be very little, if any, lost movement between the steering wheel and roadwheels. If this is not the case, closely observe the joints and mountings previously described. In addition, check the steering column universal joints for wear, and also check the rack-and-pinion steering gear itself.

9 The efficiency of each suspension strut may be checked by bouncing the vehicle at each front corner. Generally speaking, the body will return to its normal position and stop after being depressed. If it rises and returns on a rebound, the suspension strut is probably suspect. Also examine the suspension strut upper mountings for any signs of wear.

10 Driveshaft check

1 Firmly apply the handbrake, then jack up the front of the car and support it securely on axle stands (see *Jacking and vehicle support*).

2 Turn the steering onto full lock then slowly rotate the roadwheel. Inspect the condition of the outer constant velocity (CV) joint rubber gaiters while squeezing the gaiters to open out the folds **(see illustration)**. Check for signs of cracking, splits or deterioration of the rubber which may allow the grease to escape and lead to water and grit entry into the joint. Also check the security and condition of the retaining clips. Repeat these checks on the

inner CV joints. If any damage or deterioration is found, the gaiters should be renewed as described in Chapter 8, Section 5.

3 At the same time, check the general condition of the CV joints themselves by first holding the driveshaft and attempting to rotate the wheel. Repeat this check by holding the inner joint and attempting to rotate the driveshaft. Any appreciable movement indicates wear in the joints, wear in the driveshaft splines or loose driveshaft retaining nut.

11 Exhaust system check

1 With the engine cold (at least an hour after the vehicle has been driven), check the complete exhaust system from the engine to the end of the tailpipe. The exhaust system is most easily checked with the vehicle raised on a hoist, or suitably-supported on axle stands, so that the exhaust components are readily visible and accessible (see *Jacking and vehicle support*).

2 Check the exhaust pipes and connections for evidence of leaks, severe corrosion and damage. Make sure that all brackets and mountings are in good condition, and that all relevant nuts and bolts are tight. Leakage at any of the joints or in other parts of the system will usually show up as a black sooty stain in the vicinity of the leak.

3 Rattles and other noises can often be traced to the exhaust system, especially the brackets and mountings **(see illustration)**. Try to move the pipes and silencers. If the components are able to come into contact with the body or suspension parts, secure the system with new mountings. Otherwise separate the joints (if possible) and twist the pipes as necessary to provide additional clearance.

12 Rear suspension check

1 Chock the front wheels, then jack up the rear of the vehicle and support securely on axle stands (see *Jacking and vehicle support*).

10.2 Check the condition of the driveshaft gaiters

11.3 Exhaust mountings

2 Inspect the rear suspension components for any signs of obvious wear or damage. Pay particular attention to the rubber mounting bushes, and renew if necessary (see Chapter 10, Section 18).

3 Grasp each roadwheel at the 12 o'clock and 6 o'clock positions **(see illustration 7.4)**, and try to rock it. Any excess movement indicates wear in the hub bearings. Wear may also be accompanied by a rumbling sound when the wheel is spun, or a noticeable roughness if the wheel is turned slowly. The hub bearing can be renewed as described in Chapter 10, Section 9.

4 Check for any signs of fluid leakage around the shock absorber bodies. Should any fluid be noticed, the shock absorber is defective internally, and should be renewed. **Note:** *Shock absorbers should always be renewed in pairs on the same axle.*

5 With the vehicle standing on its wheels, the efficiency of each shock absorber may be checked by bouncing the vehicle at each rear corner. Generally speaking, the body will return to its normal position and stop after being depressed. If it rises and returns on a rebound, the shock absorber is probably suspect.

13 Bodywork and underbody condition check

Note: *This work should be carried out by a Vauxhall/Opel dealer in order to validate the vehicle warranty. The work includes a thorough inspection of the vehicle paintwork and underbody for damage and corrosion.*

Bodywork damage/ corrosion check

1 Once the car has been washed, and all tar spots and other surface blemishes have been cleaned off, carefully check all paintwork, looking closely for chips or scratches. Pay particular attention to vulnerable areas such as the front body panels, and around the wheel arches. Any damage to the paintwork must be rectified as soon as possible, to comply with the terms of the manufacturer's anti-corrosion warranties; check with a Vauxhall/Opel dealer for details.

2 If a chip or light scratch is found which is recent and still free from rust, it can be touched-up using the appropriate touch-up stick which can be obtained from Vauxhall/Opel dealers. Any more serious damage, or rusted stone chips, can be repaired as described in Chapter 11, Section 4, but if damage or corrosion is so severe that a panel must be renewed, seek professional advice as soon as possible.

3 Always check that the door and ventilation opening drain holes and pipes are completely clear, so that water can drain out.

Corrosion protection check

4 The wax-based underbody protective coating should be inspected annually, preferably just prior to Winter, when the underbody should be washed down as thoroughly as possible without disturbing the protective coating. Any damage to the coating should be repaired using a suitable wax-based sealer. If any of the body panels are disturbed for repair or renewal, do not forget to re-apply the coating. Wax should be injected into door cavities, sills and box sections, to maintain the level of protection provided by the vehicle manufacturer – seek the advice of a Vauxhall/Opel dealer.

14 Roadwheel nut tightness check

1 Where applicable, remove the wheel trims from the wheels.

2 Using a torque wrench on each wheel nut in turn, ensure that the nuts are tightened to the specified torque.

3 Where applicable, refit the wheel trims on completion, making sure they are fitted correctly.

15 Hinge and lock lubrication

1 Work around the vehicle and lubricate the hinges of the bonnet, doors, boot lid and tailgate with a light machine oil.

2 Lightly lubricate the bonnet release mechanism and exposed section of inner cable with a smear of grease.

3 Check the security and operation of all hinges, latches and locks, adjusting them where required. Check the operation of the central locking system.

4 Check the condition and operation of the bonnet, boot lid or tailgate struts, renewing them both if either is leaking or no longer able to support the bonnet, boot lid/tailgate securely when raised.

16 Electrical systems check

1 Check the operation of all the electrical equipment, ie, lights, direction indicators, horn, etc. Refer to the appropriate sections of Chapter 12 for details if any of the circuits are found to be inoperative.

2 Note that the brake light switch is described in Chapter 9, Section 17.

3 Check all accessible wiring connectors, harnesses and retaining clips for security, and for signs of chafing or damage. Rectify any faults found.

17 Road test

Instruments/ electrical equipment

1 Check the operation of all instruments, warning lights and electrical equipment.

2 Make sure that all instruments read correctly, and switch on all electrical equipment in turn, to check that it functions properly.

Steering and suspension

3 Check for any abnormalities in the steering, suspension, handling or road 'feel'.

4 Drive the vehicle, and check that there are no unusual vibrations or noises.

5 Check that the steering feels positive, with no excessive 'sloppiness', or roughness, and check for any suspension noises when cornering and driving over bumps.

Drivetrain

6 Check the performance of the engine, clutch, transmission and driveshafts.

7 Listen for any unusual noises from the engine, clutch and transmission.

8 Make sure that the engine runs smoothly when idling, and that there is no hesitation when accelerating.

9 Check that the clutch action is smooth and progressive, that the drive is taken up smoothly, and that the pedal travel is not excessive. Also listen for any noises when the clutch pedal is depressed.

10 Check that all gears can be engaged smoothly without noise, and that the gear lever action is smooth and not abnormally vague or 'notchy'.

11 Listen for a metallic clicking sound from the front of the vehicle, as the vehicle is driven slowly in a circle with the steering on full-lock. Carry out this check in both directions. If a clicking noise is heard, this indicates wear in a driveshaft joint (see Chapter 8, Section 6).

Braking system

12 Make sure that the vehicle does not pull to one side when braking, and that the wheels do not lock when braking hard.

13 Check that there is no vibration through the steering when braking.

14 Check that the handbrake operates correctly, without excessive movement of the lever (manually operated handbrake), and that it holds the vehicle stationary on a slope.

15 Test the operation of the brake servo unit as follows. Depress the footbrake four or five times to exhaust the vacuum, then start the engine. As the engine starts, there should be a noticeable 'give' in the brake pedal as vacuum builds-up. Allow the engine to run for at least two minutes, and then switch it off. If the brake pedal is now depressed again, it should be possible to detect a hiss from the servo as the pedal is depressed. After about four or five applications, no further

19.2a Release the retaining catch and open the pollen filter housing cover ...

19.2b ... then remove the filter from the housing

hissing should be heard, and the pedal should feel considerably harder.

18 Service interval indicator reset

1 The procedure varies depending on the year of production and trim level.

Resetting the interval on early models

2 Switch on the ignition, but don't start the engine.
3 Press the 'Menu' button on the direction indicator stalk until 'Vehicle Information Menu' is displayed in the driver information centre.
4 Turn the adjuster wheel on the direction indicator stalk to select 'Remaining Oil Life'.
5 Depress the brake pedal, then press the 'SET/ CLR' button on the stalk to reset the system.
6 Release the brake pedal and switch off the ignition.

Resetting the interval on late models

7 Scroll through the menu on the information display until the 'oil life reset' message is displayed.
8 Press and hold the enter button for at least one second until the message 'acknowledged' is displayed.
9 Turn the ignition off.
10 The oil life system is now reset. Note that several attempts may be required to reset the system.

19 Pollen filter renewal

1 Remove the glovebox as described in Chapter 11, Section 30.
2 Release the retaining catch, open the pollen filter housing cover, then remove the filter from the housing (see illustrations).
3 Fit the new filter using a reversal of the removal procedure; make sure that the filter is fitted the correct way up as indicated on the edge of the filter.

20 Auxiliary drivebelt check and renewal

Checking

1 Two auxiliary drivebelts are fitted at the right-hand end of the engine. The main drivebelt drives the alternator, air conditioning compressor and coolant pump from the crankshaft pulley. The secondary drivebelt drives the power steering pump from the coolant pump pulley. The main drivebelt is tensioned by an automatic tensioner, whereas the secondary drivebelt is of the 'stretchy' type and is self-tensioning.
2 Due to their function and material make-up, drivebelts are prone to failure after a long period of time and should therefore be inspected regularly.

3 Apply the handbrake, then jack up the front of the vehicle and support it on axle stands (see *Jacking and vehicle support*). Remove the right-hand front roadwheel and the wheel arch liner lower cover for access to the right-hand side of the engine.
4 With the engine stopped, inspect the full length of both drivebelts for cracks and separation of the belt plies. It will be necessary to turn the engine (using a spanner or socket and bar on the crankshaft pulley bolt) so that the belts can be inspected thoroughly. Twist the belts between the pulleys so that both sides can be viewed. Also check for fraying, and glazing which gives the belts a shiny appearance. Check the pulleys for nicks, cracks, distortion and corrosion. If the belts show signs of wear or damage, they should be renewed as a precaution against breakage in service.

Renewal

Secondary drivebelt

Note: *No tensioner is used with the secondary drivebelt, so the only way to remove an old belt is to cut it off. Even if the old belt could be prised off without damaging it or the pulleys, a belt which has already been fitted has stretched, and may slip if re-used.*
Note: *Vauxhall/Opel special tool EN-50098 (or a suitable alternative) will be required to fit the new drivebelt.*
5 If not already done, apply the handbrake, then jack up the front of the vehicle and support it on axle stands (see *Jacking and vehicle support*). Remove the right-hand front roadwheel and the wheel arch liner lower cover for access to the crankshaft pulley.
6 Cut off the old drivebelt using a sharp knife or side cutters – take care that no damage is caused to surrounding components as this is done (see illustration).
7 Due to the fitting method required for this unusual type of belt, it is essential that the belt pulleys are as clean as possible before installing the new belt. Wipe the pulleys over with a suitable solvent, to ensure any traces of oil are removed. It's important that the new belt doesn't slip round the pulleys as it is stretched into place.
8 The fitting procedure for the 'stretchy' drivebelt involves the use of a special tool. Vauxhall/Opel tool EN-50098 is available for this purpose, however alternatives are readily available from automotive accessory outlets.
9 Fit the new drivebelt around the coolant pump pulley making sure the belt is seated properly in the pulley grooves.
10 Place the fitting tool on the top of the power steering pump pulley, then guide the drivebelt over the tool (see illustration).
11 Using a socket on the crankshaft pulley retaining bolt, turn the engine slowly in the normal direction of rotation (clockwise, as seen from the pulley itself). As the engine is turned, guide the belt onto the power steering pump pulley, with the help of the tool (see

20.6 Cut off the secondary drivebelt using a sharp knife or side cutters

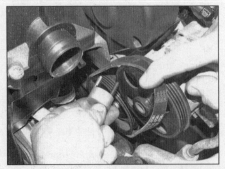

20.10 Guide the new drivebelt over the fitting tool

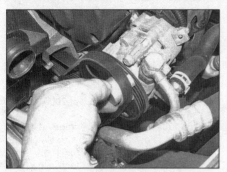

20.11 Slowly turn the engine and guide the belt onto the power steering pump pulley, with the help of the tool

20.18 Auxiliary drivebelt tensioner

1 Raised projection on tensioner arm
2 Locking pin/bolt hole

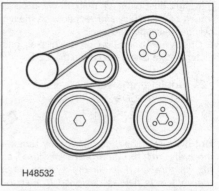

H48532

20.20 Main auxiliary drivebelt routing

illustration). Make sure that the belt goes in to its grooves properly.

12 Remove the fitting tool, then turn the engine through a full 360°, and check that the belt is sitting correctly in the pulley grooves.

13 Refit the wheel arch liner lower cover, then refit the roadwheel and lower the car to the ground.

Main drivebelt

Note: *The manufacturers recommend that the tensioner pulley is checked and if necessary renewed at the same time as the drivebelt.*

14 If not already done, apply the handbrake, then jack up the front of the vehicle and support it on axle stands (see *Jacking and vehicle support*). Remove the right-hand front roadwheel and the wheel arch liner lower cover for access to the right-hand side of the engine.

15 For additional working clearance, remove the air cleaner assembly as described in Chapter 4A, Section 2.

16 If the drivebelt is to be re-used, mark it to indicate its normal running direction.

17 Remove the secondary drivebelt as described previously in this Section.

18 Note the routing of the drivebelt, then, using a spanner on the raised projection on the tensioner arm, turn the tensioner anti-clockwise against the spring tension. Hold the tensioner in this position by inserting a suitable locking pin/bolt through the special hole provided **(see illustration)**.

19 Slip the drivebelt off the pulleys and remove it from the engine.

20 Locate the drivebelt onto the pulleys in

the correct routing **(see illustration)**. If the drivebelt is being re-used, make sure it is fitted the correct way around.

21 Turn back the tensioner and remove the locking pin/bolt then release it, making sure that the drivebelt ribs locate correctly on each of the pulley grooves.

22 Refit the air cleaner housing (if removed), then refit the wheel arch liner lower cover and roadwheel, and lower the vehicle to the ground.

23 Fit a new secondary drivebelt as described previously in this Section.

21 Headlight beam alignment check

1 Accurate adjustment of the headlight beam is only possible using optical beam-setting equipment, and this work should therefore be carried out by a Vauxhall/Opel dealer or service station with the necessary facilities. Refer to Chapter 12, Section 8 for further information.

22 Remote control battery renewal

1 Using a screwdriver, prise the battery cover from the ignition key fob **(see illustration)**.

2 Note how the circular battery is fitted, then carefully remove it from the contacts **(see illustration)**.

22.1 Remove the cover

22.2 Remove the battery. Note that the positive (+) side is up

3 Fit the new battery (type CR 2032) and refit the cover making sure that it clips fully onto the base.

4 After changing the battery, lock and unlock the driver's door with the key in the lock. The remote control unit will be synchronised when the ignition is switched on.

23 Hydraulic fluid renewal

⚠️ **Warning: Hydraulic fluid can harm your eyes and damage painted surfaces, so use extreme caution when handling and pouring it. Do not use fluid that has been standing open for some time, as it absorbs moisture from the air. Excess moisture can cause a dangerous loss of braking effectiveness.**

1 The procedure is similar to that for the bleeding of the hydraulic system as described in Chapter 9 (brake) and if applicable Chapter 6 (clutch).

2 Working as described in Chapter 9, Section 2, open the first bleed screw in the sequence, and pump the brake pedal gently until nearly all the old fluid has been emptied from the master cylinder reservoir. Top-up to the MAX level with new fluid, and continue pumping until only the new fluid remains in the reservoir, and new fluid can be seen emerging from the bleed screw. Tighten the screw, and top the reservoir level up to the MAX level line.

HAYNES HiNT *Old hydraulic fluid is invariably much darker in colour than the new, making it easy to distinguish the two.*

3 Work through all the remaining bleed screws in the sequence until new fluid can be seen at all of them. Be careful to keep the master cylinder reservoir topped-up to above the MIN level at all times, or air may enter the system and greatly increase the length of the task.

4 Bleed the fluid from the clutch hydraulic system as described in Chapter 6, Section 2.

5 When the operation is complete, check that all bleed screws are securely tightened, and that their dust caps are refitted. Wash off all traces of spilt fluid, and recheck the master cylinder reservoir fluid level.

6 Check the operation of the brakes and clutch before taking the car on the road.

24 Coolant renewal – petrol models

Note: *Vauxhall/Opel do not specify renewal intervals for the antifreeze mixture, as the mixture used to fill the system when the vehicle is new is designed to last the lifetime of the vehicle. However, it is strongly recommended that the coolant is renewed at the intervals specified in the 'Maintenance schedule', as a precaution against possible engine corrosion problems. This is particularly advisable if the coolant has been renewed using an antifreeze other than that specified by Vauxhall/Opel. With many antifreeze types, the corrosion inhibitors become progressively less effective with age. It is up to the individual owner whether or not to follow this advice.*

Cooling system draining

Warning: Wait until the engine is cold before starting this procedure. Do not allow antifreeze to come in contact with your skin, or with the painted surfaces of the vehicle. Rinse off spills immediately with plenty of water. Never leave antifreeze lying around in an open container, or in a puddle in the driveway or on the garage floor. Children and pets are attracted by its sweet smell, but antifreeze can be fatal if ingested.

1 To drain the cooling system, first cover the expansion tank cap with a wad of rag, and slowly turn the cap anti-clockwise to relieve the pressure in the cooling system (a hissing sound will normally be heard). Wait until any pressure remaining in the system is released, then continue to turn the cap until it can be removed.

2 The coolant drain plug is located at the bottom of the radiator right-hand end tank. Position a container beneath the radiator then unscrew the drain plug and allow the coolant to drain.

3 When the flow of coolant stops, refit and tighten the drain plug.

4 As no cylinder block drain plug is fitted, it is not possible to drain all of the coolant. Due consideration must be made for this when refilling the system, in order to maintain the correct concentration of antifreeze.

5 If the coolant has been drained for a reason other than renewal, then provided it is clean and less than two years old, it can be re-used.

Cooling system flushing

6 If coolant renewal has been neglected, or if the antifreeze mixture has become diluted, then in time, the cooling system may gradually lose efficiency, as the coolant passages become restricted due to rust, scale deposits, and other sediment. The cooling system efficiency can

be restored by flushing the system clean.

7 The radiator should be flushed independently of the engine, to avoid unnecessary contamination.

Radiator flushing

8 Disconnect the top and bottom hoses and any other relevant hoses from the radiator, with reference to Chapter 3, Section 2.

9 Insert a garden hose into the radiator top inlet. Direct a flow of clean water through the radiator, and continue flushing until clean water emerges from the radiator bottom outlet.

10 If after a reasonable period, the water still does not run clear, the radiator can be flushed with a good proprietary cleaning agent. It is important that the manufacturer's instructions are followed carefully. If the contamination is particularly bad, remove the radiator, insert the hose in the radiator bottom outlet, and reverse-flush the radiator.

Engine flushing

11 To flush the engine, the thermostat must be removed, because it will be shut, and would otherwise prevent the flow of water around the engine. The thermostat can be removed as described in Chapter 3, Section 4. Take care not to introduce dirt or debris into the system if this approach is used.

12 With the bottom hose disconnected from the radiator, insert a garden hose into the thermostat opening. Direct a clean flow of water through the engine, and continue flushing until clean water emerges from the radiator bottom hose.

13 On completion of flushing, refit the thermostat with reference to Chapter 3, Section 4, and reconnect the hoses.

Cooling system filling

14 Before attempting to fill the cooling system, make sure that all hoses and clips are in good condition, and that the clips are tight. Note that an antifreeze mixture must be used all year round, to prevent corrosion of the engine components.

15 Remove the expansion tank filler cap.

16 Open the bleed screw at the upper right-hand side of the radiator **(see illustration)**.

17 Fill the system by slowly pouring the coolant into the expansion tank until it is up to the filler neck.

24.16 Radiator bleed screw location

18 As soon as coolant begins to run from the radiator bleed screw, close the screw.

19 Top up the expansion tank until the coolant level is up to the KALT/COLD mark on the side of the tank.

20 Refit and tighten the expansion tank filler cap.

21 Start the engine and run it at 2000 to 2500 rpm for two minutes.

22 Continue running the engine at idling speed and allow it to warm-up. When the cooling fan cuts-in, briefly run the engine again at 2000 to 2500 rpm, then allow it to return to idle. Repeat this three times.

23 Stop the engine, and allow it to cool, then re-check the coolant level with reference to *Weekly checks*. Top-up the level if necessary and refit the expansion tank filler cap.

Antifreeze mixture

24 Always use a Vauxhall/Opel approved anti-freeze which is suitable for use in mixed-metal cooling systems. **Note:** *Vauxhall/Opel recommend the use of silicate-free 'red' coolant (93 170 402). The quantity of antifreeze and level of protection is given in the Specifications.*

25 Before adding antifreeze, the cooling system should be completely drained, preferably flushed, and all hoses checked for condition and security.

26 After filling with antifreeze, a label should be attached to the expansion tank, stating the type and concentration of antifreeze used, and the date installed. Any subsequent topping-up should be made with the same type and concentration of antifreeze.

27 Do not use engine antifreeze in the windscreen/tailgate washer system, as it will cause damage to the vehicle paintwork. A screenwash additive should be added to the washer system in the quantities stated on the bottle.

25 Air filter element renewal – petrol models

1 The air cleaner is located in the front right-hand corner of the engine compartment.

2 Disconnect the wiring connector from the airflow meter **(see illustration)**.

25.2 Disconnect the wiring connector from the airflow meter

25.3 Slacken the retaining clip and disconnect the air intake duct from the airflow meter

25.4 Disconnect the wiring harness from the side of the air cleaner cover

25.5 Undo the screws securing the air cleaner cover to the air cleaner housing

3 Slacken the retaining clip and disconnect the air intake duct from the airflow meter (**see illustration**).

4 Disconnect the wiring harness from the side of the air cleaner cover (**see illustration**).

5 Undo the screws securing the air cleaner cover to the air cleaner housing (**see illustration**).

6 Disengage the air cleaner cover retaining tabs, lift off the cover, then lift out the filter element (**see illustrations**).

7 Wipe out the casing and the cover.

8 Fit the new filter element, noting that the rubber locating flange should be uppermost, and secure the cover with the screws.

9 Reconnect the airflow meter wiring connector and the air intake duct, then reconnect the wiring harness.

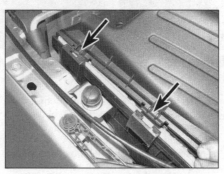

25.6a Disengage the air cleaner cover retaining tabs ...

25.6b ... then lift off the cover and lift out the filter element

26 Spark plug renewal

1 The correct functioning of the spark plugs is vital for the correct running and efficiency of the engine. It is essential that the plugs fitted are appropriate for the engine; a suitable type is specified at the beginning of this Chapter. If the correct type is used and the

engine is in good condition, the spark plugs should not need attention between scheduled replacement intervals. Spark plug cleaning is rarely necessary, and should not be attempted unless specialised equipment is available, as damage can easily be caused to the firing ends.

2 Remove the ignition module from the spark plugs with reference to Chapter 5B, Section 3.

3 It is advisable to remove the dirt from the spark plug recesses using a clean brush, vacuum cleaner or compressed air before removing the plugs, to prevent dirt dropping into the cylinders.

4 Unscrew the spark plugs from the cylinder

head using a spark plug spanner, suitable box spanner or a deep socket and extension bar (**see illustrations**). Keep the socket aligned with the spark plug – if it is forcibly moved to one side, the ceramic insulator may be broken off.

5 Examination of the spark plugs will give a good indication of the condition of the engine. As each plug is removed, examine it as follows. If the insulator nose of the spark plug is clean and white, with no deposits, this is indicative of a weak mixture or too hot a plug (a hot plug transfers heat away from the electrode slowly, a cold plug transfers heat away quickly).

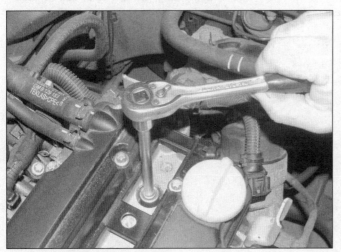

26.4a Unscrew the spark plugs ...

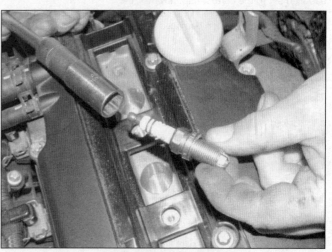

26.4b ... and remove them

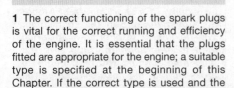
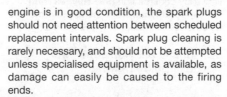

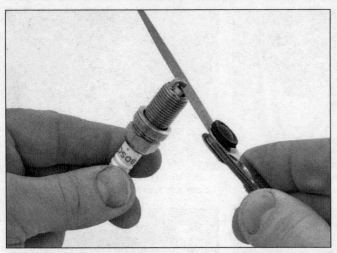

26.9a Check the electrode gap using a feeler gauge …

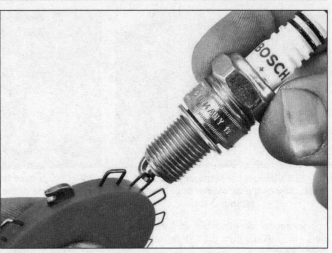

26.9b … or a wire gauge

6 If the tip and insulator nose are covered with hard black-looking deposits, then this is indicative that the mixture is too rich. Should the plug be black and oily, then it is likely that the engine is fairly worn, as well as the mixture being too rich.

7 If the insulator nose is covered with light tan to greyish-brown deposits, then the mixture is correct and it is likely that the engine is in good condition.

8 The spark plug electrode gap is of considerable importance. If the gap is too large or too small, the size of the spark and its efficiency will be seriously impaired and it will not perform correctly under all engine speed and load conditions. For the best results, the spark plug gap should checked against the Specifications at the beginning of this Chapter.

9 To check the gap, measure it with a feeler blade or spark plug gap gauge **(see illustrations)**. Do not attempt to reset the spark plug gap. If the gap is outside the specifications then the spark plugs must be replaced. Replacement spark plugs are supplied set to the correct gap, however they should be checked before installation in case the spark plugs have been damaged in transit.

10 Before fitting the spark plugs, check that the connector sleeves on the top of the plug are tight, and that the plug exterior surfaces and threads are clean.

11 Screw in the spark plugs by hand where possible, then tighten them to the specified torque. Take extra care to enter the plug threads correctly, as the cylinder head is of light alloy construction **(see Haynes Hint)**.

12 On completion, refit the ignition module as described in Chapter 5B, Section 3.

27 Timing belt, tensioner and idler pulley renewal

1 Refer to the procedures contained in Chapter 2A, Section 8.

28 Valve clearance check and adjustment

1 Refer to the procedures contained in Chapter 2A, Section 11.

HAYNES HiNT

It is very often difficult to insert spark plugs into their holes without crossthreading them. To avoid this possibility, fit a short length of rubber hose over the end of the spark plug. The flexible hose acts as a universal joint to help align the plug with the plug hole. Should the plug begin to cross-thread, the hose will slip on the spark plug, preventing thread damage to the aluminium cylinder head.

Chapter 1 Part B
Routine maintenance and servicing – diesel models

Contents

Degrees of difficulty

Easy, suitable for novice with little experience	**Fairly easy,** suitable for beginner with some experience	**Fairly difficult,** suitable for competent DIY mechanic	**Difficult,** suitable for experienced DIY mechanic	**Very difficult,** suitable for expert DIY or professional

Specifications

Lubricants and fluids . . . . Refer to Lubricants, fluids and tyre pressures

Capacities

Engine oil

Capacity including oil filter:
1.6 litre engine	5.0 litres
2.0 litre engine (A20)	4.5 litres
2.0 litre engine (B20)	4.9 litres
Difference between MIN and MAX dipstick marks (approximately)	1.0 litre

Cooling system
1.6 litre engine	8.3 litres
2.0 litre engine	9.0 litres

Transmission

Manual transmission:
M32	2.3 litres
F40	1.8 litres
Automatic transmission (at fluid change)	3.0 litres (approximately)

Fuel tank
All models	70 litres

Cooling system

Antifreeze mixture:
50% antifreeze	Protection down to -40°C

Brakes

Friction material minimum thickness	2.0 mm

Torque wrench settings

	Nm	lbf ft
Engine oil filter housing cap	25	18
Fuel filter base	25	18
Roadwheel nuts	150	111
Sump drain plug	25	18
Sump drain plug B20 engine	20	15

1 Maintenance schedule – diesel models

1 The maintenance intervals in this manual are provided with the assumption that you, not the dealer, will be carrying out the work. These are the minimum maintenance intervals based on the standard service schedule recommended by the manufacturer for vehicles driven daily. If you wish to keep your vehicle in peak condition at all times, you may wish to perform some of these procedures more often. We encourage frequent maintenance, because it enhances the efficiency, performance and resale value of your vehicle.

2 If the vehicle is driven in dusty areas, used to tow a trailer, or driven frequently at slow speeds (idling in traffic) or on short journeys, more frequent maintenance intervals are recommended.

3 When the vehicle is new, it should be serviced by a dealer service department (or other workshop recognised by the vehicle manufacturer as providing the same standard of service) in order to preserve the warranty. The vehicle manufacturer may reject warranty claims if you are unable to prove that servicing has been carried out as and when specified, using only original equipment parts or parts certified to be of equivalent quality.

Every 250 miles or weekly
☐ Refer to *Weekly checks*

Every 10 000 miles or 6 months – whichever comes first
☐ Renew the engine oil and filter (Section 5)*

*Note: *Vauxhall/Opel recommend that the engine oil and filter are changed every 20 000 miles or 12 months if the vehicle is being operated under the standard service schedule. However, oil and filter changes are good for the engine and we recommend that the oil and filter are renewed more frequently, especially if the vehicle is used on a lot of short journeys.*

Every 20 000 miles or 12 months – whichever comes first
☐ Check all underbonnet and underbody components, pipes and hoses for leaks (Section 6)
☐ Drain the water from the fuel filter (Section 7)
☐ Check the condition of the brake pads (renew if necessary), the calipers and discs (Section 8)
☐ Check the condition of all brake fluid pipes and hoses (Section 9)
☐ Check the condition of the front suspension and steering components, particularly the rubber gaiters and seals (Section 10)
☐ Check the condition of the driveshaft joint gaiters, and the driveshaft joints (Section 11)
☐ Check the condition of the exhaust system components (Section 12)
☐ Check the condition of the rear suspension components (Section 13)
☐ Check the bodywork and underbody for damage and corrosion, and check the condition of the underbody corrosion protection (Section 14)
☐ Check the tightness of the roadwheel nuts (Section 15)
☐ Lubricate all door, bonnet, boot lid and tailgate hinges and locks (Section 16)
☐ Check the operation of the horn, all lights, and the wipers and washers (Section 17)
☐ Carry out a road test (Section 18)
☐ Reset the service interval indicator (Section 19)

Every 40 000 miles or 2 years – whichever comes first
☐ Renew the pollen filter (Section 20)
☐ Renew the fuel filter (Section 21)
☐ Check the auxiliary drivebelt and tensioner (Section 22)
☐ Check the headlight beam alignment (Section 23)

Every 2 years, regardless of mileage
☐ Renew the battery for the remote control handset (Section 24)
☐ Renew the brake and clutch fluid (Section 25)
☐ Renew the coolant (Section 26)

*Note: *Vehicles using Vauxhall/Opel silicate-free coolant do not need the coolant renewed on a regular basis.*

Every 40 000 miles or 4 years – whichever comes first
☐ Renew the air cleaner filter element (Section 27)
☐ Renew the timing belt, tensioner and idler pulleys (Section 28)*

*Note: *The manufacturer's specified timing belt renewal interval is 100 000 miles or 6 years for the A20 engine. The manufacturer's interval for the B20 engine is 80,000 miles or 6 years up to VIN number G1030020 and 100,000 miles or 6 years for later engines. However, it is strongly recommended that the interval used is 40 000 miles on vehicles which are subjected to intensive use, ie, mainly short journeys or a lot of stop-start driving. The actual belt renewal interval is therefore very much up to the individual owner, but bear in mind that severe engine damage will result if the belt breaks.*

Every 80 000 miles or 6 years – whichever comes first
☐ Renew the auxiliary drivebelt and tensioner (Section 22)

2 Component location –
diesel models

Underbonnet view (1.6 litre diesel engine)

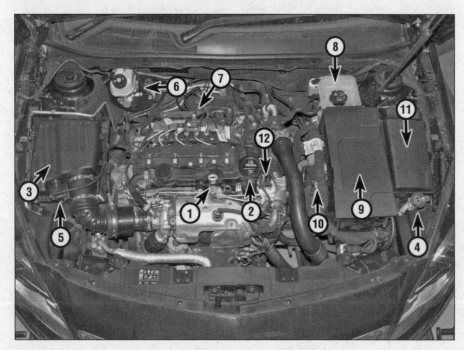

1 Engine oil level dipstick
2 Engine oil filler cap
3 Air filter assembly
4 Screen washer fluid reservoir
5 Mass airflow meter
6 Brake (and clutch) fluid reservoir
7 Boost pressure sensor
8 Coolant expansion tank
9 Battery (under cover)
10 Engine management ECU
11 Fuse/relay box
12 Brake vacuum pump

Underbonnet view (2.0 litre, A20 engine)

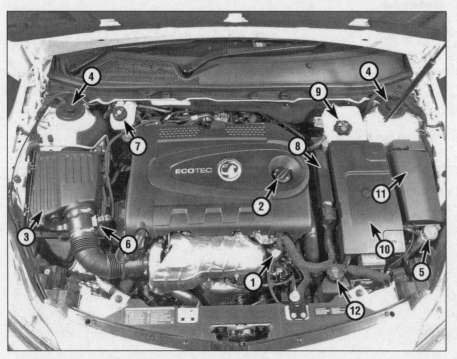

1 Engine oil level dipstick
2 Engine oil filler cap
3 Air cleaner assembly
4 Front suspension strut upper mounting
5 Screen washer fluid reservoir
6 Airflow meter
7 Brake (and clutch) fluid reservoir
8 Engine management ECU
9 Coolant expansion tank
10 Battery
11 Fuse/relay box
12 Power steering fluid reservoir

Underbonnet view (2.0 litre, B20 engine)

1 Engine oil level dipstick
2 Engine oil filler cap
3 Air cleaner assembly
4 Screen washer fluid reservoir
5 Mass airflow meter
6 Brake (and clutch) fluid reservoir
7 Engine management ECU
8 Coolant expansion tank
9 Battery (under cover)
10 Fuse/relay box

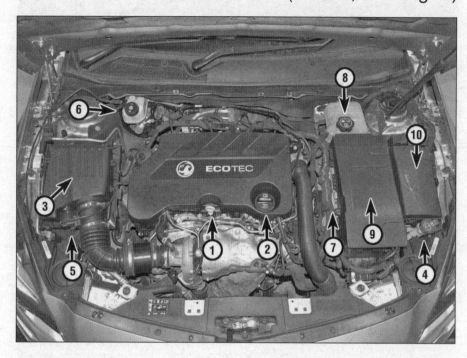

Front underbody view (2.0 litre A20 engine shown, but all similar)

1 Exhaust front pipe
2 Steering track rods
3 Front suspension lower arms
4 Front brake calipers
5 Engine mounting front torque link
6 Engine mounting rear torque link
7 Right-hand driveshaft
8 Manual transmission
9 Engine oil drain plug
10 Front subframe

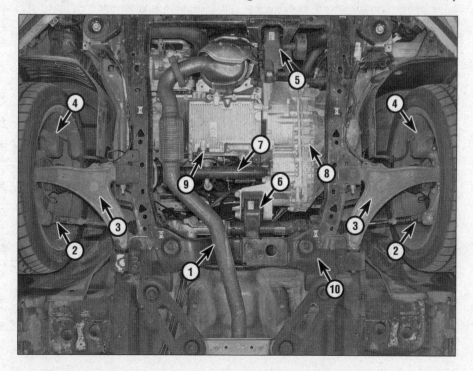

Rear underbody view (2.0 litre B20 shown, but all similar)

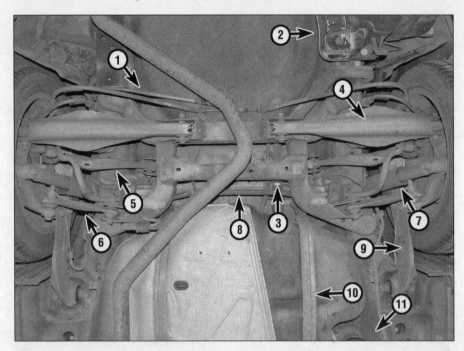

1 Handbrake cable
2 Diesel exhaust fluid (Adblue) tank
3 Rear subframe
4 Lower control arm
5 Upper control arm
6 Auxiliary control arm
7 Shock absorber
8 Rear anti-roll bar
9 Rear suspension trailing arm
10 Fuel tank
11 Fuel filter

3 General Information

1 This Chapter is designed to help the home mechanic maintain his/her vehicle for safety, economy, long life and peak performance.
2 The Chapter contains a master maintenance schedule, followed by Sections dealing specifically with each task in the schedule. Visual checks, adjustments, component renewal and other helpful items are included. Refer to the accompanying illustrations of the engine compartment and the underside of the vehicle for the locations of the various components.
3 Servicing your vehicle in accordance with the mileage/time maintenance schedule and the following Sections will provide a planned maintenance programme, which should result in a long and reliable service life. This is a comprehensive plan, so maintaining some items but not others at the specified service intervals, will not produce the same results.
4 As you service your vehicle, you will discover that many of the procedures can – and should – be grouped together, because of the particular procedure being performed, or because of the proximity of two otherwise-unrelated components to one another. For example, if the vehicle is raised for any reason, the exhaust can be inspected at the same time as the suspension and steering components.
5 The first step in this maintenance

programme is to prepare yourself before the actual work begins. Read through all the Sections relevant to the work to be carried out, then make a list and gather all the parts and tools required. If a problem is encountered, seek advice from a parts specialist, or a dealer service department.

4 Regular maintenance

1 If, from the time the vehicle is new, the routine maintenance schedule is followed closely, and frequent checks are made of fluid levels and high-wear items, as suggested throughout this manual, the engine will be kept in relatively good running condition, and the need for additional work will be minimised.
2 It is possible that there will be times when the engine is running poorly due to the lack of regular maintenance. This is even more likely if a used vehicle, which has not received regular and frequent maintenance checks, is purchased. In such cases, additional work may need to be carried out, outside of the regular maintenance intervals.
3 If engine wear is suspected, a compression test (refer to Chapter 2B Section 2, Chapter 2C, Section 2, or Chapter 2D Section 2) will provide valuable information regarding the overall performance of the main internal components. Such a test can be used as a basis to decide on the extent of the work to be carried out. If, for example, a compression

test indicates serious internal engine wear, conventional maintenance as described in this Chapter will not greatly improve the performance of the engine, and may prove a waste of time and money, unless extensive overhaul work is carried out first.
4 The following series of operations are those most often required to improve the performance of a generally poor-running engine:

Primary operations

● Clean, inspect and test the battery (refer to Weekly checks).
● Check all the engine-related fluids (refer to Weekly checks).
● Check the condition and tension of the auxiliary drivebelt (Section 22).
● Check the condition of the air filter, and renew if necessary (Section 27).
● Renew the fuel filter (Section 21).
● Check the condition of all hoses, and check for fluid leaks (Section 6).
5 If the above operations do not prove fully effective, carry out the following secondary operations:

Secondary operations

6 All items listed under Primary operations, plus the following:
● Check the charging system (refer to Chapter 5A, Section 3).
● Check the pre/post-heating system (refer to Chapter 5A, Section 16).
● Check the fuel, exhaust and emission control systems (refer to Chapter 4B and Chapter 4C).

5.4a Slacken the drain plug using a spanner or socket and bar ...

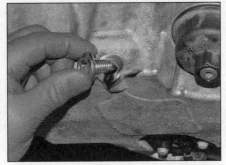

5.4b ... then remove the plug completely

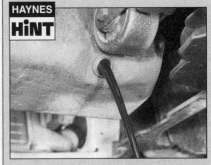

As the drain plug releases from the threads, move it away quickly so that the stream of oil running out of the sump goes into the drain pan and not up your sleeve.

5   Engine oil and filter renewal – diesel models

HAYNES HiNT *Frequent oil and filter changes are the most important preventative maintenance procedures which can be undertaken by the DIY owner. As engine oil ages, it becomes diluted and contaminated, which leads to premature engine wear.*

1 Before starting this procedure, gather together all the necessary tools and materials. Also make sure that you have plenty of clean rags and newspapers handy, to mop up any spills. Ideally, the engine oil should be warm, as it will drain more easily, and more built-up sludge will be removed with it. Take care not to touch the exhaust or any other hot parts of the engine when working under the vehicle. To avoid any possibility of scalding, and to protect yourself from possible skin irritants and other harmful contaminants in used engine oils, it is advisable to wear gloves when carrying out this work.
2 Access to the underside of the vehicle will be greatly improved if it can be raised on a lift, driven onto ramps, or jacked up and supported on axle stands (see *Jacking and vehicle support*). Whichever method is

chosen, make sure that the vehicle remains level, or if it is at an angle, that the drain plug is at the lowest point.

1.6 litre engines

3 Lift up and remove the engine cover and then remove the oil filler cap from the camshaft cover. Remove the engine undershield, then position a draining container under the sump drain plug.
4 Using a spanner, or preferably a suitable socket and bar, slacken the drain plug about half a turn, then remove the plug completely **(see illustrations and Haynes Hint)**.
5 Allow some time for the oil to drain, noting that it may be necessary to reposition the container as the oil flow slows to a trickle.
6 After all the oil has drained, clean the area around the drain plug opening. Fit a new seal to the drain plug **(see illustration)**. Fit

5.6 Fit a new seal to the drain plug

the drain plug and tighten it to the specified torque, using a torque wrench.
7 Reposition the container under the oil filter which is located in the sump.
8 Using a suitable Torx bit, slacken the filter drain plug located in the centre of the oil filter cap, then unscrew the plug completely **(see illustrations)**. Allow the oil in the filter housing to drain.
9 Using a large socket, unscrew and remove the oil filter housing cap, withdraw the filter element, and remove the O-ring seal from the cap **(see illustrations)**.
10 Use a clean rag to remove all oil, dirt and sludge from the oil filter housing and cap.

5.8a Slacken the drain plug in the oil filter cap ...

5.8b ... then remove the drain plug and allow the oil in the filter housing to drain

5.9a Unscrew the oil filter housing cap ...

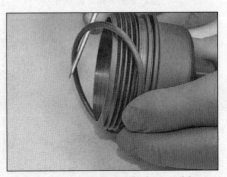

5.9b ... and remove the O-ring seal from the cap

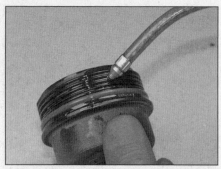

5.11 Lubricate the new O-ring seal and filter housing cap threads with clean engine oil

5.12a Fit the new filter to the housing ...

5.12b ... then screw on the cap and tighten it to the specified torque

5.13 Renew the oil filter cap drain plug O-ring

2.0 litre A20 engines

14 Remove the right-hand front roadwheel and engine cover.

15 Remove the engine undertray and the right-hand front wheel arch liner as described in Chapter 11, Section 24.

16 Remove the oil filler cap from the oil filler housing (twist it through a quarter-turn anti-clockwise and withdraw it).

17 Using a spanner, or preferably a suitable socket and bar, slacken the drain plug about half a turn. Position the draining container under the drain plug, then remove the plug completely **(see illustrations)**.

18 Allow some time for the oil to drain, noting that it may be necessary to reposition the container as the oil flow slows to a trickle.

19 The oil filter on the 2.0 litre A20 series of engines is located in a slightly awkward location at the rear of the engine and is only accessible from under the car. It will be necessary to make up a guiding channel to allow the filter to drain and be removed from under the wheel arch on the right-hand side. We used a suitable length of cardboard, bent in the centre and positioned under the filter housing and extending out to a convenient point under the wheel arch **(see illustration)**. If a length of household guttering, cut to a suitable length can be obtained, this would be an ideal substitute. Position another container under the end of the guiding channel.

20 Unscrew the oil filter housing cap a few turns and allow the oil in the filter housing to drain from the drain orifice on the underside of the filter housing **(see illustrations)**.

11 Locate a new O-ring seal in the groove on the filter housing cap, then lubricate the seal and the cap threads with clean engine oil **(see illustration)**.

12 Fit the new filter to the housing, then screw on the cap and tighten it to the specified torque **(see illustrations)**.

13 Renew the O-ring seal on the oil filter cap drain plug, then refit the drain plug and tighten it securely **(see illustration)**.

5.17a Using a spanner, or preferably a suitable socket and bar, slacken the drain plug about half a turn

5.17b Position the draining container under the drain plug ...

5.17c ... then remove the plug completely

5.19 Position a folded length of cardboard or similar under the filter housing and extending out to a container under the wheel arch

5.20a Unscrew the oil filter housing cap a few turns ...

5.20b ... and allow the oil in the filter housing to drain from the drain orifice on the underside of the housing

21 Once the filter housing has drained, fully unscrew the filter housing cap and withdraw it, together with the element, then separate the element, and remove the O-ring seal from the cap **(see illustration)**.
22 Use a clean rag to remove all oil, dirt and sludge from the oil filter housing and cap.
23 Locate a new O-ring seal in the groove on the filter housing cap, then lubricate the O-ring seal and the filter housing cap threads with clean engine oil **(see illustrations)**.
24 Fit the new filter to the oil filter housing, then screw on the cap and tighten it to the specified torque **(see illustration)**.
25 After all the oil has drained, wipe the drain plug and the sealing washer/O-ring with a clean rag. Examine the condition of the sealing washer/O-ring, and renew it if it shows signs of damage which may prevent an oil-tight seal. Clean the area around the drain plug opening, and refit the plug complete with the washer/O-ring. Tighten the plug to the specified torque, using a torque wrench.

2.0 litre B20 engines

26 Remove the engine cover by pulling it up.
27 The oil filter is positioned at the top of the engine on the rear right-hand side.
28 Unscrew the cap from the oil filter, pull up the oil filter from the housing **(see illustrations)** and allow the oil to drain into the housing and down into the sump. Not that the cap may become detached from the filter, if this is the case pull up the filter to allow the oil to drain.
29 Remove the oil filler cap from the camshaft cover, then position a container under the sump drain plug.
30 Using a spanner, or preferably a suitable socket and bar, slacken the drain plug about half a turn, then remove the plug completely **(see illustration and Haynes Hint)**.
31 Allow some time for the oil to drain, noting that it may be necessary to reposition the container as the oil flow slows to a trickle.
32 After all the oil has drained, clean the area around the drain plug opening. Fit a new seal to the drain plug **(see illustration 5.6)**. Fit the drain plug and tighten it to the specified torque, using a torque wrench.
33 Use a clean rag to remove all oil, dirt and sludge from the oil filter housing and cap.

5.21 Once the filter housing has drained, fully unscrew the filter housing cap and withdraw it, together with the element

5.23b ... then lubricate the O-ring seal and the filter housing cap threads with clean engine oil

34 Locate a new O-ring seal in the groove on the filter housing cap, then lubricate the O-ring seal and the filter housing cap threads with clean engine oil **(see illustrations)**.

5.28a Unscrew the filter cap

5.30 The 2.0 litre (B20) engine drain plug

5.23a Locate a new O-ring seal in the groove on the filter housing cap ...

5.24 Fit the new filter to the oil filter housing, then screw on the cap

35 Check that the oil seals fitted to the filter are correctly positioned. Filters maybe supplied with the lower seals separately – there should be two seals on the filter itself.

5.28b Allow the oil to drain into the sump

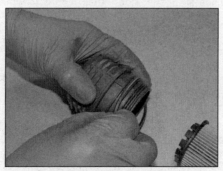

5.34a Fit the new seal to the cap

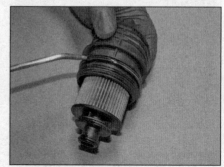

5.34b Lubricate the main seal and ...

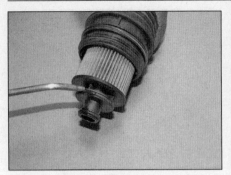

5.34c ... the filter seals

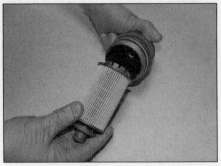

5.34d Fit the filter to the cap. It should snap into place and stay there

5.36 Tighten the cap to the specified torque

36 Fit the element to the cap and install it in the engine. Tighten the filter cap to the specified torque **(see illustration)**.

All engines

37 Remove the old oil and all tools from under the vehicle. Where removed, refit the wheel arch liner and wheel. Lower the vehicle to the ground. If the wheel was removed (A20 engines only) tighten the wheel nuts to the specified torque.

38 Fill the engine through the oil filler cap, using the correct grade and type of oil (refer to *Weekly checks* for details of topping-up). Pour in half the specified quantity of oil first, then wait a few minutes for the oil to drain into the sump. Continue to add oil, a small quantity at a time, until the level is up to the lower mark on the dipstick. Adding approximately a further 1.0 litre will bring the level up to the upper mark on the dipstick.

39 Start the engine and run it until it reaches normal operating temperature. While the engine is warming up, check for leaks around the oil filter and the sump drain plug.

40 Stop the engine, and wait at least five minutes for the oil to settle in the sump once more. With the new oil circulated and the filter now completely full, recheck the level on the dipstick, and add more oil as necessary.

41 On models fitted with an engine undershield raise the vehicle and support it on axle stands (see *Jacking and vehicle support*). Refit the engine undershield.

A leak in the cooling system will usually show up as white- or antifreeze coloured deposits on the area adjoining the leak.

42 Reset the service interval (oil life) display as described in Section 19.

43 Dispose of the used engine oil and filter safely, with reference to *General repair procedures*. Do not discard the old filter with domestic household waste. The facility for waste oil disposal provided by many local council refuse tips and/or recycling centres generally has a filter receptacle alongside.

6 Hose and fluid leak check

1 Visually inspect the engine joint faces, gaskets and seals for any signs of water or oil leaks. Pay particular attention to the areas around the camshaft cover, cylinder head, oil filter and sump joint faces. Similarly, check the transmission and the air conditioning compressor for oil leakage. Bear in mind that, over a period of time, some very slight seepage from these areas is to be expected; what you are really looking for is any indication of a serious leak. Should a leak be found, renew the offending gasket or oil seal by referring to the appropriate Chapters in this manual.

2 Also check the security and condition of all the engine-related pipes and hoses. Ensure that all cable ties or securing clips are in place, and in good condition. Clips which are broken or missing can lead to chafing of the hoses pipes or wiring, which could cause more serious problems in the future.

3 Carefully check the radiator hoses and heater hoses along their entire length. Renew any hose which is cracked, swollen or deteriorated. Cracks will show up better if the hose is squeezed. Pay close attention to the hose clips that secure the hoses to the cooling system components. Hose clips can pinch and puncture hoses, resulting in cooling system leaks. If wire-type hose clips are used, it may be a good idea to replace them with screw-type clips.

4 Inspect all the cooling system components (hoses, joint faces, etc) for leaks. Where any problems of this nature are found on system components, renew the component or gasket with reference to Chapter 3, Section 2 **(see Haynes Hint)**.

5 Where applicable, inspect the automatic transmission fluid cooler hoses for leaks or deterioration.

6 With the vehicle raised, inspect the fuel tank and filler neck for punctures, cracks and other damage. The connection between the filler neck and tank is especially critical. Sometimes, a rubber filler neck or connecting hose will leak due to loose retaining clamps or deteriorated rubber.

7 Carefully check all rubber hoses and metal fuel lines leading away from the fuel tank. Check for loose connections, deteriorated hoses, crimped lines and other damage. Pay particular attention to the vent pipes and hoses, which often loop up around the filler neck and can become blocked or crimped. Follow the lines to the front of the vehicle, carefully inspecting them all the way. Renew damaged sections as necessary. Similarly, whilst the vehicle is raised, take the opportunity to inspect all underbody brake fluid pipes and hoses.

8 From within the engine compartment, check the security of all fuel hose attachments and pipe unions, and inspect the fuel hoses and vacuum hoses for kinks, chafing and deterioration.

7 Fuel filter water draining – diesel models

Caution: Before starting any work on the fuel filter, wipe clean the filter assembly and the area around it; it is essential that no dirt or other foreign matter is allowed into the system. Obtain a suitable container into which the filter can be drained and place rags or similar material under the filter assembly to catch any spillages.

1 The fuel filter is located under the car, attached to the right-hand side of the fuel tank.

2 Chock the front wheels, then jack up the rear of the vehicle, and support it securely on axle stands (see *Jacking and vehicle support*).

3 Using a screwdriver, unscrew and remove the filter drain screw at the base of the filter housing and allow the filter to drain until

7.3a Unscrew and remove the fuel filter drain screw at the base of the filter housing ...

7.3b ... and allow the filter to drain until clean fuel, free of dirt or water, emerges

For a quick check, the thickness of friction material remaining on the inner brake pad can be measured through the aperture in the caliper body.

clean fuel, free of dirt or water, emerges **(see illustrations)**.

4 Refit the drain screw, and tighten the screw securely. Lower the vehicle to the ground.

5 On completion, dispose of the drained fuel safely. Check all disturbed components to ensure that there are no leaks (of air or fuel) when the engine is restarted.

8 Brake pad and disc check

1 Firmly apply the handbrake, then jack up the front and rear of the vehicle and support it securely on axle stands (see *Jacking and vehicle support*). Remove the roadwheels.

2 For a quick check, the pad thickness can be carried out via the inspection hole on the caliper **(see Haynes Hint)**. Using a steel rule, measure the thickness of the pad lining including the backing plate. This must not be less than that indicated in the Specifications.

3 The view through the caliper inspection hole gives a rough indication of the state of the brake pads. For a comprehensive check, the brake pads should be removed and cleaned. The operation of the caliper can then also be checked, and the condition of the brake disc itself can be fully examined on both sides. Chapter 9, Section 6 contains a detailed description of how the brake disc should be checked for wear and/or damage.

4 If any pad's friction material is worn to the specified thickness or less, *all four pads must be renewed as a set.* Refer to Chapter 9 Section 4 or Chapter 9 Section 5 for details.

5 On completion, refit the roadwheels and lower the vehicle to the ground.

9 Brake fluid pipe and hose check

1 The brake hydraulic system includes a number of metal pipes, which run from the master cylinder to the hydraulic modulator of the anti-lock braking system (ABS) and then to the front and rear brake assemblies. Flexible hoses are fitted between the pipes and the front and rear brake assemblies, to allow for steering and suspension movement.

2 When checking the system, first look for signs of leakage at the pipe or hose unions, then examine the flexible hoses for signs of cracking, chafing or deterioration of the rubber. Bend the hoses sharply between the fingers (but do not actually bend them double, or the casing may be damaged) and check that this does not reveal previously-hidden cracks, cuts or splits. Check that the pipes and hoses are securely fastened in their clips.

3 Carefully working along the length of metal pipes, look for dents, kinks, damage of any sort, or corrosion. Light corrosion can

be polished off, but if the depth of pitting is significant, the pipe must be renewed.

10 Front suspension and steering check

1 Apply the handbrake, then raise the front of the vehicle and securely support it on axle stands (see *Jacking and vehicle support*).

2 Inspect the balljoint dust covers and the steering gear gaiters for splits, chafing or deterioration **(see illustrations)**.

3 Any wear of these components will cause loss of lubricant, and may allow water to enter the components, resulting in rapid deterioration of the balljoints or steering gear.

4 Grasp each roadwheel at the 12 o'clock and 6 o'clock positions, and try to rock it **(see illustration)**. Very slight free play may be felt, but if the movement is appreciable, further investigation is necessary to determine the source. Continue rocking the wheel while an assistant depresses the footbrake. If the movement is now eliminated or significantly reduced, it is likely that the hub bearings are at fault. If the free play is still evident with the footbrake depressed, then there is wear in the suspension joints or mountings.

5 Now grasp each wheel at the 9 o'clock

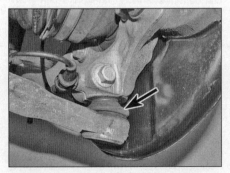

10.2a Inspect the balljoint dust covers ...

10.2b ... and the steering gear gaiters for splits, chafing or deterioration

10.4 Check for wear in the hub bearings by grasping the wheel and trying to rock it

10.5 Check for wear in the track rod end ball joints

10.7 Check for signs of fluid leakage around the suspension struts, or from the rubber gaiters around the piston rods

and 3 o'clock positions, and try to rock it as before **(see illustration)**. Any movement felt now may again be caused by wear in the hub bearings or the steering track rod end balljoints. If the track rod end balljoint is worn, the visual movement will be obvious.

6 Using a large screwdriver or flat bar, check for wear in the suspension mounting bushes by levering between the relevant suspension component and its attachment point. Some movement is to be expected, as the mountings are made of rubber, but excessive wear should be obvious. Also check the condition of any visible rubber bushes, looking for splits, cracks or contamination of the rubber.

7 Check for any signs of fluid leakage around the suspension struts, or from the rubber gaiters around the piston rods **(see illustration)**. Should any fluid be noticed, the suspension strut is defective internally, and should be renewed. **Note:** *Suspension struts should always be renewed in pairs on the same axle.*

8 With the vehicle standing on its wheels, have an assistant turn the steering wheel back-and-forth about an eighth of a turn each way. There should be very little, if any, lost movement between the steering wheel and roadwheels. If this is not the case, closely observe the joints and mountings previously described. In addition, check the steering column universal joints for wear, and also check the rack-and-pinion steering gear itself.

9 The efficiency of each suspension strut may be checked by bouncing the vehicle at each front corner. Generally speaking, the body will

return to its normal position and stop after being depressed. If it rises and returns on a rebound, the suspension strut is probably suspect. Also examine the suspension strut upper mountings for any signs of wear.

11 Driveshaft check

1 Firmly apply the handbrake, then jack up the front of the car and support it securely on axle stands (see *Jacking and vehicle support*).

2 Turn the steering onto full lock then slowly rotate the roadwheel. Inspect the condition of the outer constant velocity (CV) joint rubber gaiters while squeezing the gaiters to open out the folds **(see illustration)**. Check for signs of cracking, splits or deterioration of the rubber which may allow the grease to escape and lead to water and grit entry into the joint. Also check the security and condition of the retaining clips. Repeat these checks on the inner CV joints. If any damage or deterioration is found, the gaiters should be renewed as described in Chapter 8, Section 5.

3 At the same time, check the general condition of the CV joints themselves by first holding the driveshaft and attempting to rotate the wheel. Repeat this check by holding the inner joint and attempting to rotate the driveshaft. Any appreciable movement indicates wear in the joints, wear in the drive-shaft splines or loose driveshaft retaining nut.

11.2 Check the condition of the driveshaft gaiters

12.3 Exhaust mountings

12 Exhaust system check

1 With the engine cold (at least an hour after the vehicle has been driven), check the complete exhaust system from the engine to the end of the tailpipe. The exhaust system is most easily checked with the vehicle raised on a hoist, or suitably-supported on axle stands, so that the exhaust components are readily visible and accessible (see *Jacking and vehicle support*).

2 Check the exhaust pipes and connections for evidence of leaks, severe corrosion and damage. Make sure that all brackets and mountings are in good condition, and that all relevant nuts and bolts are tight. Leakage at any of the joints or in other parts of the system will usually show up as a black sooty stain in the vicinity of the leak.

3 Rattles and other noises can often be traced to the exhaust system, especially the brackets and mountings **(see illustration)**. Try to move the pipes and silencers. If the components are able to come into contact with the body or suspension parts, secure the system with new mountings. Otherwise separate the joints (if possible) and twist the pipes as necessary to provide additional clearance.

13 Rear suspension check

1 Chock the front wheels, then jack up the rear of the vehicle and support securely on axle stands (see *Jacking and vehicle support*).

2 Inspect the rear suspension components for any signs of obvious wear or damage. Pay particular attention to the rubber mounting bushes, and renew if necessary (see Chapter 10, Section 18).

3 Grasp each roadwheel at the 12 o'clock and 6 o'clock positions **(see illustration 8.4)**, and try to rock it. Any excess movement indicates wear in the hub bearings. Wear may also be accompanied by a rumbling sound when the wheel is spun, or a noticeable roughness if the wheel is turned slowly. The hub bearing can be renewed as described in Chapter 10, Section 9.

4 Check for any signs of fluid leakage around the shock absorber bodies. Should any fluid be noticed, the shock absorber is defective internally, and should be renewed. **Note:** *Shock absorbers should always be renewed in pairs on the same axle.*

5 With the vehicle standing on its wheels, the efficiency of each shock absorber may be checked by bouncing the vehicle at each rear corner. Generally speaking, the body will return to its normal position and stop after being depressed. If it rises and returns on a rebound, the shock absorber is probably suspect.

14 Bodywork and underbody condition check

Note: *This work should be carried out by a Vauxhall/Opel dealer in order to validate the vehicle warranty. The work includes a thorough inspection of the vehicle paintwork and underbody for damage and corrosion.*

Bodywork damage/ corrosion check

1 Once the car has been washed, and all tar spots and other surface blemishes have been cleaned off, carefully check all paintwork, looking closely for chips or scratches. Pay particular attention to vulnerable areas such as the front body panels, and around the wheel arches. Any damage to the paintwork must be rectified as soon as possible, to comply with the terms of the manufacturer's anti-corrosion warranties; check with a Vauxhall/Opel dealer for details.

2 If a chip or light scratch is found which is recent and still free from rust, it can be touched-up using the appropriate touch-up stick which can be obtained from Vauxhall/Opel dealers. Any more serious damage, or rusted stone chips, can be repaired as described in Chapter 11, Section 4, but if damage or corrosion is so severe that a panel must be renewed, seek professional advice as soon as possible.

3 Always check that the door and ventilation opening drain holes and pipes are completely clear, so that water can drain out.

Corrosion protection check

4 The wax-based underbody protective coating should be inspected annually, preferably just prior to Winter, when the underbody should be washed down as thoroughly as possible without disturbing the protective coating. Any damage to the coating should be repaired using a suitable wax-based sealer. If any of the body panels are disturbed for repair or renewal, do not forget to re-apply the coating. Wax should be injected into door cavities, sills and box sections, to maintain the level of protection provided by the vehicle manufacturer – seek the advice of a Vauxhall/Opel dealer.

15 Roadwheel nut tightness check

1 Where applicable, remove the wheel trims from the wheels.

2 Using a torque wrench on each wheel nut in turn, ensure that the nuts are tightened to the specified torque.

3 Where applicable, refit the wheel trims on completion, making sure they are fitted correctly.

16 Hinge and lock lubrication

1 Work around the vehicle and lubricate the hinges of the bonnet, doors, boot lid and tailgate with a light machine oil.

2 Lightly lubricate the bonnet release mechanism and exposed section of inner cable with a smear of grease.

3 Check the security and operation of all hinges, latches and locks, adjusting them where required. Check the operation of the central locking system.

4 Check the condition and operation of the bonnet, boot lid or tailgate struts, renewing them both if either is leaking or no longer able to support the bonnet, boot lid/tailgate securely when raised.

17 Electrical systems check

1 Check the operation of all the electrical equipment, ie, lights, direction indicators, horn, etc. Refer to the appropriate sections of Chapter 12 for details if any of the circuits are found to be inoperative.

2 Note that the brake light switch is described in Chapter 9, Section 17.

3 Check all accessible wiring connectors, harnesses and retaining clips for security, and for signs of chafing or damage. Rectify any faults found.

18 Road test

Instruments/electrical equipment

1 Check the operation of all instruments, warning lights and electrical equipment.

2 Make sure that all instruments read correctly, and switch on all electrical equipment in turn, to check that it functions properly.

Steering and suspension

3 Check for any abnormalities in the steering, suspension, handling or road 'feel'.

4 Drive the vehicle, and check that there are no unusual vibrations or noises.

5 Check that the steering feels positive, with no excessive 'sloppiness', or roughness, and check for any suspension noises when cornering and driving over bumps.

Drivetrain

6 Check the performance of the engine, clutch, transmission and driveshafts.

7 Listen for any unusual noises from the engine, clutch and transmission.

8 Make sure that the engine runs smoothly when idling, and that there is no hesitation when accelerating.

9 Check that, where applicable, the clutch action is smooth and progressive, that the drive is taken up smoothly, and that the pedal travel is not excessive. Also listen for any noises when the clutch pedal is depressed.

10 Check that all gears can be engaged smoothly without noise, and that the gear lever action is smooth and not abnormally vague or 'notchy'.

11 On automatic transmission models, make sure that all gearchanges occur smoothly, without snatching, and without an increase in engine speed between changes. Check that all of the gear positions can be selected with the vehicle at rest. If any problems are found, they should be referred to a Vauxhall/Opel dealer.

12 Listen for a metallic clicking sound from the front of the vehicle, as the vehicle is driven slowly in a circle with the steering on full-lock. Carry out this check in both directions. If a clicking noise is heard, this indicates wear in a driveshaft joint (see Chapter 8, Section 6).

Braking system

13 Make sure that the vehicle does not pull to one side when braking, and that the wheels do not lock when braking hard.

14 Check that there is no vibration through the steering when braking.

15 Check that the handbrake operates correctly, without excessive movement of the lever (manually operated handbrake), and that it holds the vehicle stationary on a slope.

16 Test the operation of the brake servo unit as follows. Depress the footbrake four or five times to exhaust the vacuum, then start the engine. As the engine starts, there should be a noticeable 'give' in the brake pedal as vacuum builds-up. Allow the engine to run for at least two minutes, and then switch it off. If the brake pedal is now depressed again, it should be possible to detect a hiss from the servo as the pedal is depressed. After about four or five applications, no further hissing should be heard, and the pedal should feel considerably harder.

19 Service interval indicator reset

1 The procedure varies depending on the year of production and trim level.

Resetting the interval on early models

2 Switch on the ignition, but don't start the engine.

3 Press the 'Menu' button on the direction indicator stalk until 'Vehicle Information

20.2a Release the retaining catch and open the pollen filter housing cover ...

20.2b ... then remove the filter from the housing

Menu' is displayed in the driver information centre.

4 Turn the adjuster wheel on the direction indicator stalk to select 'Remaining Oil Life'.

5 Depress the brake pedal, then press the 'SET/CLR' button on the stalk to reset the system.

6 Release the brake pedal and switch off the ignition.

Resetting the interval on late models

7 Scroll through the menu on the information display until the 'oil life reset' message is displayed.

8 Press and hold the enter button for at least one second until the message 'acknowledged' is displayed.

9 Turn the ignition off.

10 The oil life system is now reset. Note that several attempts may be required to reset the system.

20 Pollen filter renewal

1 Remove the glovebox as described in Chapter 11, Section 30.

2 Release the retaining catch, open the pollen filter housing cover, then remove the filter from the housing **(see illustrations)**.

3 Fit the new filter using a reversal of the removal procedure; make sure that the filter is fitted the correct way up as indicated on the edge of the filter.

21 Fuel filter renewal – diesel models

Caution: Before starting any work on the fuel filter, wipe clean the filter assembly and the area around it; it is essential that no dirt or other foreign matter is allowed into the system. Obtain a suitable container into which the filter can be drained and place rags or similar material under the filter assembly to catch any spillages.

1 The fuel filter is located under the car, attached to the right-hand side of the fuel tank.

2 Chock the front wheels, then jack up the rear of the car, and support it securely on axle stands (see *Jacking and vehicle support*).

3 Drain the water from the filter housing as described in Section 7.

4 When the filter has completely drained, unscrew and remove the filter base **(see illustrations)**.

5 Remove the sealing ring from the filter housing **(see illustration)**.

6 Using pliers, pull the old filter from the housing **(see illustration)**.

7 Thoroughly clean the filter base and filter housing.

8 Locate the new filter in the housing and push it up until it engages with the retainers **(see illustration)**.

9 Fit a new sealing ring to the filter housing **(see illustration)**.

21.4a Unscrew the fuel filter base ...

21.4b ... and remove it from the housing

21.5 Remove the sealing ring from the filter housing

21.6 Using pliers, pull the old filter from the housing

21.8 Locate the new filter in the housing and push it up until it engages with the retainers

21.9 Fit a new sealing ring to the filter housing

21.10a Refit the filter base ...

21.10b ... and tighten it to the specified torque

22.8a Release the tension ...

10 Refit the filter base and tighten it to the specified torque **(see illustrations)**. Tighten the drain screw on the filter base securely.

11 Lower the car to the ground, then prime and bleed the fuel system as described in Chapter 4B, Section 5.

22 Auxiliary drivebelt check and renewal

Checking

1 Due to their function and material make-up, drivebelts are prone to failure after a long period of time and should therefore be inspected regularly.

2 Apply the handbrake, then jack up the front of the vehicle and support it on axle stands (see *Jacking and vehicle support*). Remove the right-hand front roadwheel.

3 Remove the engine undertray and the right-hand front wheel arch liner as described in Chapter 11, Section 24.

4 With the engine stopped, inspect the full length of the drivebelt for cracks and separation of the belt plies. It will be necessary to turn the engine (using a spanner or socket and bar on the crankshaft pulley bolt) so that the belt can be inspected thoroughly. Twist the belt between the pulleys so that both sides can be viewed. Also check for fraying, and glazing which gives the belt a shiny appearance. Check the pulleys for nicks, cracks, distortion and corrosion. If the belt shows signs of wear or damage, it should be renewed as a precaution against breakage in service.

Renewal

5 If not already done, apply the handbrake, then jack up the front of the vehicle and support it on axle stands (see *Jacking and vehicle support*). Remove the right-hand front roadwheel, then remove the engine undertray and the right-hand front wheel arch liner as described in Chapter 11, Section 24.

6 On some versions, for additional working clearance, remove the air filter housing as described in Chapter 4B, Section 3.

7 If the drivebelt is to be re-used, mark it to indicate its normal running direction.

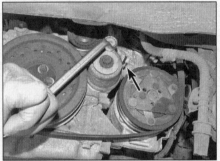

22.8b ... fit a locking pin (we used and old drill bit) to hold the tensioner ...

8 Using a socket or spanner on the pulley centre bolt, turn the tensioner anti-clockwise against the spring tension. Hold the tensioner in this position and slip the drivebelt from the pulleys. Some models have the provision for a locking pin to be fitted to the tensioner **(see illustrations)**.

9 Hold the tensioner in the released position and locate the new drivebelt on the pulleys

22.8c ... and remove the belt

in the correct routing **(see illustration)**. If the drivebelt is being re-used, make sure it is fitted the correct way around.

10 Release the tensioner, making sure that the drivebelt ribs locate correctly on each of the pulley grooves.

11 Refit the air cleaner housing (if removed), then refit the wheel arch liner lower cover and roadwheel, and lower the vehicle to the ground.

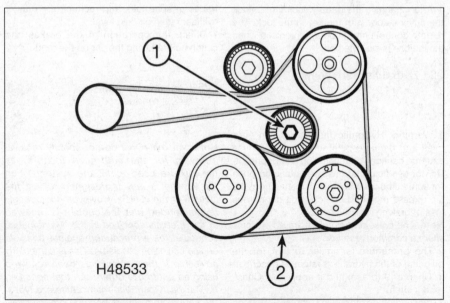

H48533

22.9 Auxiliary drivebelt routing (2.0 litre A20 engine shown, but all models are similar)

1 Tensioner pulley centre bolt   2 Auxiliary drivebelt

24.1 Remove the cover

24.2 Lift out the battery. Note the battery is fitted positive (+) side up

26.2 The coolant drain plug (shown with bumper cover removed)

23 Headlight beam alignment check

1 Accurate adjustment of the headlight beam is only possible using optical beam-setting equipment, and this work should therefore be carried out by a Vauxhall/Opel dealer or service station with the necessary facilities. Refer to Chapter 12, Section 8 for further information.

24 Remote control battery renewal

1 Using a screwdriver, prise the battery cover from the ignition key fob **(see illustration)**.
2 Note how the circular battery is fitted, then carefully remove it from the contacts **(see illustration)**.
3 Fit the new battery (type CR 20 32) and refit the cover making sure that it clips fully onto the base.
4 After changing the battery, lock and unlock the driver's door with the key in the lock. The remote control unit will be synchronised when the ignition is switched on.

25 Hydraulic fluid renewal

1 Warning: Hydraulic fluid can harm your eyes and damage painted surfaces, so use extreme caution when handling and pouring it. Do not use fluid that has been standing open for some time, as it absorbs moisture from the air. Excess moisture can cause a dangerous loss of braking effectiveness.
Note: The brake and clutch hydraulic systems share a common reservoir.
2 The procedure is similar to that for the bleeding of the hydraulic system as described in Chapter 9 (brake) and if applicable Chapter 6 (clutch).
3 Working as described in Chapter 9, Section 2, open the first bleed screw in the sequence, and pump the brake pedal gently until nearly

all the old fluid has been emptied from the master cylinder reservoir. Top-up to the MAX level with new fluid, and continue pumping until only the new fluid remains in the reservoir, and new fluid can be seen emerging from the bleed screw. Tighten the screw, and top the reservoir level up to the MAX level line.

 Old hydraulic fluid is invariably much darker in colour than the new, making it easy to distinguish the two.

4 Work through all the remaining bleed screws in the sequence until new fluid can be seen at all of them. Be careful to keep the master cylinder reservoir topped-up to above the MIN level at all times, or air may enter the system and greatly increase the length of the task.
5 Bleed the fluid from the clutch hydraulic system as described in Chapter 6, Section 2.
6 When the operation is complete, check that all bleed screws are securely tightened, and that their dust caps are refitted. Wash off all traces of spilt fluid, and recheck the master cylinder reservoir fluid level.
7 Check the operation of the brakes and clutch before taking the car on the road.

26 Coolant renewal – diesel models

Note: *Vauxhall/Opel do not specify renewal intervals for the antifreeze mixture, as the mixture used to fill the system when the vehicle is new is designed to last the lifetime of the vehicle. However, it is strongly recommended that the coolant is renewed at the intervals specified in the 'Maintenance schedule', as a precaution against possible engine corrosion problems. This is particularly advisable if the coolant has been renewed using an antifreeze other than that specified by Vauxhall/Opel. With many antifreeze types, the corrosion inhibitors become progressively less effective with age. It is up to the individual owner whether or not to follow this advice.*

Cooling system draining

⚠️ *Warning: Wait until the engine is cold before starting this procedure. Do not allow antifreeze to come in contact with your skin, or with the painted surfaces of the vehicle. Rinse off spills immediately with plenty of water. Never leave antifreeze lying around in an open container, or in a puddle in the driveway or on the garage floor. Children and pets are attracted by its sweet smell, but antifreeze can be fatal if ingested.*

1 To drain the cooling system, first cover the expansion tank cap with a wad of rag, and slowly turn the cap anti-clockwise to relieve the pressure in the cooling system (a hissing sound will normally be heard). Wait until any pressure remaining in the system is released, then continue to turn the cap until it can be removed.
2 The coolant drain plug is located at the bottom of the radiator right-hand end tank **(see illustration)**. A short length of garden hose can be fitted to direct the coolant into a container. Position a container beneath the radiator then unscrew the drain plug and allow the coolant to drain.
3 When the flow of coolant stops, refit and tighten the drain plug.
4 As no cylinder block drain plug is fitted, it is not possible to drain all of the coolant. Due consideration must be made for this when refilling the system, in order to maintain the correct concentration of antifreeze.
5 If the coolant has been drained for a reason other than renewal, then provided it is clean and less than two years old, it can be re-used.

Cooling system flushing

6 If coolant renewal has been neglected, or if the antifreeze mixture has become diluted, then in time, the cooling system may gradually lose efficiency, as the coolant passages become restricted due to rust, scale deposits, and other sediment. The cooling system efficiency can be restored by flushing the system clean.
7 The radiator should be flushed independently of the engine, to avoid unnecessary contamination.

Radiator flushing

8 Disconnect the top and bottom hoses and

26.16a Open the bleed screw at the upper right-hand side of the radiator ...

26.16b ... and the bleed screw on the thermostat housing (A20 engines only)

any other relevant hoses from the radiator, with reference to Chapter 3, Section 2.

9 Insert a garden hose into the radiator top inlet. Direct a flow of clean water through the radiator, and continue flushing until clean water emerges from the radiator bottom outlet.

10 If after a reasonable period, the water still does not run clear, the radiator can be flushed with a good proprietary cleaning agent. It is important that the manufacturer's instructions are followed carefully. If the contamination is particularly bad, remove the radiator, insert the hose in the radiator bottom outlet, and reverse-flush the radiator.

Engine flushing

11 To flush the engine, the thermostat must be removed, because it will be shut, and would otherwise prevent the flow of water around the engine. The thermostat can be removed as described in Chapter 3, Section 4. Take care not to introduce dirt or debris into the system if this approach is used.

12 With the bottom hose disconnected from the radiator, insert a garden hose into the thermostat opening. Direct a clean flow of water through the engine, and continue flushing until clean water emerges from the radiator bottom hose.

13 On completion of flushing, refit the thermostat with reference to Chapter 3, Section 4, and reconnect the hoses.

Cooling system filling

14 Before attempting to fill the cooling system, make sure that all hoses and clips are in good condition, and that the clips are tight. Note that an antifreeze mixture must be used all year round, to prevent corrosion of the engine components.

15 Remove the expansion tank filler cap.

16 Open the bleed screw at the upper right-hand side of the radiator. 2.0 litre engines also have a bleed screw on the thermostat housing **(see illustrations)**.

17 Fill the system by slowly pouring the coolant into the expansion tank until it is up to the filler neck.

18 As soon as coolant begins to run from the bleed screw(s), close the screw(s).

19 Top up the expansion tank until the coolant level is up to the KALT/COLD mark on the side of the tank. On models fitted with a vent hose on the expansion tank, only fill up with coolant to just below the vent hose.

20 Start the engine and top up the coolant to the immediately to the KALT/COLD mark on the expansion tank.

21 Refit and tighten the expansion tank filler cap.

22 Start the engine and run it at 2000 to 2500 rpm for two minutes.

23 Continue running the engine at idling speed and allow it to warm-up. When the cooling fan cuts-in, briefly run the engine

again at 2000 to 2500 rpm, then allow it to return to idle. Repeat this three times.

24 Stop the engine, and allow it to cool, then re-check the coolant level with reference to *Weekly checks*. Top-up the level if necessary and refit the expansion tank filler cap.

Antifreeze mixture

25 Always use a Vauxhall/Opel approved anti-freeze which is suitable for use in mixed-metal cooling systems. **Note:** *Vauxhall/ Opel recommend the use of silicate-free 'red' coolant (93 170 402).* The quantity of antifreeze and level of protection is given in the Specifications.

26 Before adding antifreeze, the cooling system should be completely drained, preferably flushed, and all hoses checked for condition and security.

27 After filling with antifreeze, a label should be attached to the expansion tank, stating the type and concentration of antifreeze used, and the date installed. Any subsequent topping-up should be made with the same type and concentration of antifreeze.

28 Do not use engine antifreeze in the windscreen/tailgate washer system, as it will cause damage to the vehicle paintwork. A screenwash additive should be added to the washer system in the quantities stated on the bottle.

27 Air filter element renewal – diesel models

1 The air cleaner is located in the front right-hand corner of the engine compartment.

2 Slacken the retaining clip and disconnect the airflow meter from the air cleaner cover **(see illustration)**.

3 Release the wiring harness from the side of the air cleaner cover **(see illustration)**.

4 Undo the screws securing the air cleaner cover to the air cleaner housing **(see illustration)**.

5 Disengage the air cleaner cover retaining

27.2 Slacken the retaining clip and disconnect the airflow meter from the air cleaner cover

27.3 Release the wiring harness from the side of the air cleaner cover

27.4 Undo the screws securing the air cleaner cover to the air cleaner housing

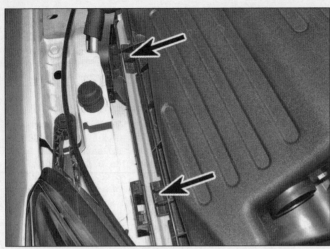

27.5a Disengage the retaining tabs and lift off the cover ...

27.5b ... then lift out the filter element

27.6 Vacuum out the housing if required

tabs, lift off the cover, then lift out the filter element **(see illustrations)**.

6 Remove any debris from the housing **(see illustration)** and wipe out the cover.

7 Fit the new filter element, noting that the rubber locating flange should be uppermost, and secure the cover with the screws.

8 Reconnect the airflow meter and the wiring harness.

28 Timing belt, tensioner and idler pulley renewal

1 Refer to the procedures contained in Chapter 2C Section 6 (2.0 litre A20 engine) or Chapter 2D Section 5 (2.0 litre B20 engine).

Chapter 2 Part A
1.8 litre petrol engine in-car repair procedures

Contents

Degrees of difficulty

Easy, suitable for novice with little experience	**Fairly easy,** suitable for beginner with some experience	**Fairly difficult,** suitable for competent DIY mechanic	**Difficult,** suitable for experienced DIY mechanic	**Very difficult,** suitable for expert DIY or professional

Specifications

General

Engine type.	Four-cylinder, in-line, water-cooled. Double overhead camshafts, belt-driven
Manufacturer's engine code*	2HO/A18XER
Bore	80.5 mm
Stroke	88.2 mm
Capacity	1796 cc
Compression ratio	10.5: 1
Firing order.	1-3-4-2 (No 1 cylinder at timing belt end)
Direction of crankshaft rotation	Clockwise (viewed from timing belt end of engine)

* For details of engine code location, see 'Vehicle identification' in the Reference Chapter.

Compression pressures

Standard	14 to 16 bar
Maximum difference between any two cylinders.	1 bar

Valve clearances

Engine cold:

Inlet	0.21 to 0.29 mm
Exhaust.	0.26 to 0.34 mm

Lubrication system

Minimum oil pressure at 80ºC	1.3 bar at idle speed
Oil pump type.	Rotor-type, driven directly from crankshaft
Rotor-to-housing clearance (endfloat)	0.02 to 0.058 mm

Torque wrench settings

	Nm	lbf ft
Auxiliary drivebelt tensioner bolt*	50	37
Camshaft bearing cap bolts	8	6
Camshaft bearing support bolts	8	6
Camshaft cover bolts	8	6
Camshaft sprocket closure bolt	30	22
Camshaft sprocket retaining bolt*:		
Stage 1	65	48
Stage 2	Angle-tighten a further 120°	
Stage 3	Angle-tighten a further 15°	
Connecting rod big-end bearing cap bolt*:		
Stage 1	35	26
Stage 2	Angle-tighten a further 45°	
Stage 3	Angle-tighten a further 15°	
Crankshaft pulley bolt*:		
Stage 1	95	70
Stage 2	Angle-tighten a further 45°	
Stage 3	Angle-tighten a further 15°	
Cylinder head bolts*:		
Stage 1	25	18
Stage 2	Angle-tighten a further 90°	
Stage 3	Angle-tighten a further 90°	
Stage 4	Angle-tighten a further 90°	
Stage 5	Angle-tighten a further 45°	
Engine mountings:		
Front mounting/torque link:		
Mounting-to-transmission	62	46
Mounting to subframe	100	74
Left-hand mounting:		
Mounting-to-body bolts/nut	22	16
Mounting bracket-to-transmission bracket	80	59
Transmission bracket-to-transmission	100	74
Rear mounting/torque link:		
Mounting bracket-to-transmission	62	46
Mounting-to-subframe	110	81
Mounting-to-transmission bracket	100	74
Right-hand mounting:		
Engine bracket-to-engine bolts	100	74
Mounting-to-body bolts	62	46
Mounting-to-engine bracket bolts	62	46
Engine-to-transmission bolts	60	44
Exhaust front pipe-to-catalytic converter nuts	22	16
Flywheel bolts*:		
Stage 1	35	26
Stage 2	Angle-tighten a further 30°	
Stage 3	Angle-tighten a further 15°	
Main bearing cap bolts*:		
Stage 1	50	37
Stage 2	Angle-tighten a further 45°	
Stage 3	Angle-tighten a further 15°	
Oil pump:		
Retaining bolts	20	15
Oil pressure relief valve cap	20	15
Roadwheel nuts	150	111
Sump bolts:		
Sump-to-cylinder block/oil pump bolts	10	7
Sump flange-to-transmission bolts	40	30
Timing belt cover bolts	6	4
Timing belt idler pulley bolt*	25	18
Timing belt tensioner bolt*	20	15
VVT oil control valve bolts	6	4

Use new nut/bolts

1 General Information

How to use this Chapter

1 This Chapter describes the repair procedures which can reasonably be carried out on the engine while it remains in the vehicle. If the engine has been removed from the vehicle and is being dismantled as described in Chapter 2E, any preliminary dismantling procedures can be ignored.

2 Note that, while it may be possible physically to overhaul items such as the piston/connecting rod assemblies while the engine is in the vehicle, such tasks are not usually carried out as separate operations, and usually require the execution of several additional procedures (not to mention the cleaning of components and of oil ways); for this reason, all such tasks are classed as major overhaul procedures, and are described in Chapter 2E.

3 Chapter 2E, Section 4 describes the removal of the engine/transmission unit from the vehicle, and the full overhaul procedures which can then be carried out.

Engine description

4 The engine is a double overhead camshaft, four-cylinder, in-line unit, mounted transversely at the front of the car, with the transmission attached to its left-hand end.

5 The crankshaft is supported within the cylinder block on five shell-type main bearings. Thrustwashers are fitted to number 3 main bearing, to control crankshaft endfloat.

6 The connecting rods are attached to the crankshaft by horizontally-split shell-type big-end bearings, and to the pistons by gudgeon pins which are retained by circlips. The aluminium alloy pistons are of the slipper type, and are fitted with three piston rings, comprising two compression rings and a scraper-type oil control ring.

7 The camshafts run directly in the cylinder head, and are driven by the crankshaft via a toothed composite rubber timing belt. One camshaft operates the inlet valves, and the other operates the exhaust valves. The camshafts operate each valve via a solid camshaft follower. The camshaft followers are available in various thicknesses to facilitate valve clearance adjustment.

8 A variable valve timing (VVT) system is employed. The VVT system allows the inlet and exhaust camshaft timing to be varied under the control of the engine management system, to boost both low-speed torque and top-end power, as well as reducing exhaust emissions. The VVT camshaft adjuster is integral with each camshaft timing belt sprocket, and is supplied with two pressurised oil feeds through passages in the camshaft itself. Two electro-magnetic oil control valves,

one for each camshaft and operated by the engine management system, are fitted to the cylinder head, and are used to supply the pressurised oil to each camshaft adjuster through the two oil feeds. Each adjuster contains two chambers – depending on which of the two oil feeds is enabled by the control valve, the oil pressure will turn the camshaft clockwise (advance) or anti-clockwise (retard) to adjust the valve timing as required. If pressure is removed from both feeds, this induces a timing 'hold' condition. Thus the valve timing is infinitely variable within a given range.

9 Lubrication is by pressure-feed from a rotor-type oil pump, which is mounted on the right-hand end of the crankshaft. The pump draws oil through a strainer located in the sump, and then forces it through an externally mounted full-flow oil filter. The oil flows into galleries in the cylinder block/crankcase, from where it is distributed to the crankshaft (main bearings) and camshafts. The big-end bearings are supplied with oil via internal drillings in the crankshaft, while the camshaft bearings also receive a pressurised supply. The camshaft lobes and valves are lubricated by splash, as are all other engine components.

10 A semi-closed crankcase ventilation system is employed; crankcase fumes are drawn from camshaft cover, and passed via a hose to the inlet manifold.

Repair operations possible with the engine in the car

11 The following operations can be carried out without having to remove the engine from the car.

a) *Removal and refitting of the camshaft cover.*
b) *Adjustment of the valve clearances.*
c) *Removal and refitting of the VVT oil control valves.*
d) *Removal and refitting of the cylinder head.*
e) *Removal and refitting of the timing belt, tensioner and sprockets.*
f) *Renewal of the camshaft oil seals.*
g) *Removal and refitting of the camshafts and followers.*
h) *Removal and refitting of the sump.*
i) *Removal and refitting of the connecting rods and pistons*.*
j) *Removal and refitting of the oil pump.*
k) *Renewal of the crankshaft oil seals.*
l) *Renewal of the engine mountings.*
m) *Removal and refitting of the flywheel.*

*Although the operation marked with an asterisk can be carried out with the engine in the car (after removal of the sump), it is preferable for the engine to be removed, in the interests of cleanliness and improved access. For this reason, the procedure is described in Chapter 2E.

2 Compression test – general information

1 When engine performance is down, or if misfiring occurs which cannot be attributed to the ignition or fuel systems, a compression test can provide diagnostic clues as to the engine's condition. If the test is performed regularly, it can give warning of trouble before any other symptoms become apparent.

2 The engine must be fully warmed-up to normal operating temperature, the battery must be fully-charged, and the spark plugs must be removed (see Chapter 1A, Section 26). The aid of an assistant will also be required.

3 Disable the fuel system by removing the fuel pump relay from the engine compartment fuse/relay box **(see illustration)**.

4 Remove the throttle housing as described in Chapter 4A, Section 8.

5 Fit a compression tester to the number 1 cylinder spark plug hole. The type of tester which screws into the plug thread is to be preferred.

6 Have the assistant crank the engine on the starter motor; after one or two revolutions, the compression pressure should build-up to a maximum figure, and then stabilise. Record the highest reading obtained.

7 Repeat the test on the remaining cylinders, recording the pressure in each.

8 All cylinders should produce very similar pressures; any difference greater than that specified indicates the existence of a fault. Note that the compression should build-up quickly in a healthy engine. Low compression on the first stroke, followed by gradually-increasing pressure on successive strokes, indicates worn piston rings. A low compression reading on the first stroke, which does not build-up during successive strokes, indicates leaking valves or a blown head gasket (a cracked head could also be the cause). Deposits on the undersides of the valve heads can also cause low compression.

9 If the pressure in any cylinder is the specified minimum or less, carry out the following test to isolate the cause. Introduce a teaspoonful of clean oil into that cylinder through its spark plug hole, and repeat the test.

2.3 Fuel pump relay location

3.5a Align the camshaft timing marks ...

3.5b ... and the notch on the crankshaft pulley rim with the mark on the timing belt lower cover

3.6 Crankshaft sprocket timing mark (A) aligned with mark (B) on timing belt rear cover (crankshaft pulley removed)

10 If the addition of oil temporarily improves the compression pressure, this indicates that bore or piston wear is responsible for the pressure loss. No improvement suggests that leaking or burnt valves, or a blown head gasket, may be to blame.

11 A low reading from two adjacent cylinders is almost certainly due to the head gasket having blown between them; the presence of coolant in the engine oil will confirm this.

12 If one cylinder is about 20 per cent lower than the others, and the engine has a slightly rough idle, a worn camshaft lobe could be the cause.

13 If the compression reading is unusually high, the combustion chambers are probably coated with carbon deposits. If this is the case, the cylinder head should be removed and decarbonised.

14 On completion of the test, refit the spark plugs (Chapter 1A, Section 26), throttle housing (Chapter 4A, Section 8) and fuel pump relay.

3 Top Dead Centre (TDC) for No 1 piston – locating

1 Top dead centre (TDC) is the highest point in the cylinder that a piston reaches as the crankshaft turns. Each piston reaches TDC at the end of the compression stroke, and again at the end of the exhaust stroke. For the purpose of timing the engine, TDC refers

to the position of No 1 piston at the end of its compression stroke. No 1 piston and cylinder are at the timing belt end of the engine.

2 Disconnect the battery negative terminal (refer to Chapter 5A, Section 4). If necessary, remove all the spark plugs as described in Chapter 1A, Section 26 to enable the engine to be easily turned over.

3 Remove the timing belt upper cover as described in Section 6.

4 Apply the handbrake, then jack up the front of the vehicle and support it on axle stands (see *Jacking and vehicle support*). Remove the right-hand front roadwheel, then remove the wheel arch liner lower cover for access to the crankshaft pulley.

5 Using a socket and extension bar on the crankshaft pulley bolt, rotate the crankshaft until the timing marks on the camshaft sprockets are facing towards each other, and an imaginary straight line can be drawn through the camshaft sprocket bolts and the timing marks. With the camshaft sprocket marks correctly positioned, align the notch on the crankshaft pulley rim with the mark on the timing belt lower cover **(see illustrations)**. The engine is now positioned with No 1 piston at TDC on its compression stroke.

6 If the crankshaft pulley and lower timing belt cover have been removed, the timing mark on the crankshaft sprocket can be used instead of the mark on the pulley. The mark on the crankshaft sprocket must align with the corresponding mark on the timing belt rear cover **(see illustration)**.

4 Camshaft cover – removal and refitting

Removal

1 Remove the ignition module from the spark plugs as described in Chapter 5B, Section 3.

2 Lift the wiring harness up and out of the support on the right-hand end of the camshaft cover **(see illustration)**.

3 Unclip the wiring harness trough from the rear of the camshaft cover **(see illustration)**.

4 Pull out the retaining wire clip and disconnect the breather hose from the camshaft cover **(see illustration)**.

5 Unscrew the eleven bolts securing the camshaft cover to the cylinder head.

6 Lift the camshaft cover away from the cylinder head and recover the rubber seal. Examine the seal for signs of wear or damage and renew if necessary.

Refitting

7 Ensure that the camshaft cover grove and rubber seal are clean and dry with all traces of oil removed. If necessary, de-grease the seal and cover groove with brake cleaner or a similar product.

8 Clean the mating surface of the cylinder head and the area around the camshaft bearing caps at the timing belt end, ensuring that all traces of oil are removed.

9 Locate the rubber seal into the grooves of

4.2 Lift the wiring harness out of the support on the camshaft cover

4.3 Unclip the wiring harness trough from the rear of the camshaft cover

4.4 Pull out the retaining wire clip and disconnect the breather hose from the camshaft cover

4.9 Locate the rubber seal into the grooves of the camshaft cover

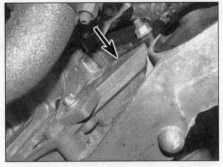

5.3 Engage a strip of metal with the flywheel ring gear teeth through the access slot

5.5 Align the pulley cut-out with the raised notch

the camshaft cover, ensuring that it is fully seated, with no chance of it falling out as the cover is fitted **(see illustration)**.

10 Carefully manoeuvre the camshaft cover into position, taking great care to ensure the seal remains correctly seated. Screw in all the cover retaining bolts and tighten them to the specified torque, working in a spiral pattern from the centre outwards.

11 Reconnect the engine breather hose, then clip the wiring harness trough back into position. Engage the wiring harness with the support on cover.

12 Refit the ignition module to the spark plugs as described in Chapter 5B, Section 3.

5 Crankshaft pulley – removal and refitting

Note: *A new pulley retaining bolt will be required on refitting.*

Removal

1 Firmly apply the handbrake, then jack up the front of the car and support it securely on axle stands (see *Jacking and vehicle support*). Remove the right-hand roadwheel, then remove the wheel arch liner lower cover for access to the crankshaft pulley.

2 Remove the auxiliary drivebelts as described in Chapter 1A, Section 20. Prior to removal of the main drivebelt, mark the direction of rotation on the belt to ensure the belt is refitted the same way around.

3 Slacken the crankshaft pulley retaining bolt. To prevent crankshaft rotation, have an assistant select top gear and apply the brakes firmly. Alternatively, engage a strip of metal with the flywheel ring gear teeth through the access slot located just above the front engine mounting/torque link **(see illustration)**.

4 Unscrew the retaining bolt and washer and remove the crankshaft pulley from the end of the crankshaft.

Refitting

5 Refit the crankshaft pulley, aligning the pulley cut-out with the raised notch on the timing belt sprocket, then fit the washer and new retaining bolt **(see illustration)**.

6 Lock the crankshaft by the method used on removal, and tighten the pulley retaining bolt to the specified Stage 1 torque setting, then angle-tighten the bolt through the specified Stage 2 angle, using a socket and extension bar, and finally through the specified Stage 3 angle. It is recommended that an angle-measuring gauge is used during the final stages of the tightening, to ensure accuracy. If a gauge is not available, use white paint to make alignment marks between the bolt head and pulley prior to tightening; the marks can then be used to check that the bolt has been rotated through the correct angle.

7 Refit the auxiliary drivebelts as described in Chapter 1A, Section 20 using the mark made prior to removal to ensure the main drivebelt is fitted the correct way around.

8 Refit the wheel arch liner lower cover and the roadwheel. Lower the car to the ground and tighten the wheel nuts to the specified torque.

6 Timing belt covers – removal and refitting

Upper cover

Removal

1 Remove the air cleaner assembly and intake ducts as described in Chapter 4A, Section 2.

2 Undo the two retaining bolts then withdraw

the upper cover from the rear cover and remove it from the engine compartment **(see illustration)**.

Refitting

3 Refitting is the reverse of removal, tightening the cover retaining bolts to the specified torque.

Lower cover

Removal

4 Remove the crankshaft pulley as described in Section 5.

5 Undo the retaining bolt and remove the auxiliary drivebelt tensioner **(see illustration)**.

6 Undo the four retaining bolts then manoeuvre the lower cover off the engine.

Refitting

7 Refitting is the reverse of removal, tightening the cover retaining bolts to the specified torque.

Centre cover

Removal

8 Remove the upper and lower covers as described previously.

9 Remove the right-hand engine mounting as described in Section 18, then undo the three retaining bolts and remove the mounting bracket bolted to the cylinder block.

10 Release the two clips securing the centre cover to the rear cover and manoeuvre the centre cover off the engine.

6.2 Undo the two retaining bolts and withdraw the upper cover from the rear cover

6.5 Undo the retaining bolt and remove the auxiliary drivebelt tensioner

Refitting

11 Refitting is the reverse of removal, tightening the engine mounting bracket retaining bolts to the specified torque.

Rear cover

Removal

12 Remove the timing belt as described in Section 7.
13 Remove the camshaft sprockets and timing belt tensioner as described in Section 8.
14 Unclip the wiring harness from the cover, then undo the four retaining bolts and manoeuvre the rear cover off the engine.

Refitting

15 Refitting is the reverse of removal, tightening the cover retaining bolts to the specified torque.

---

7 Timing belt –
removal and refitting

Note: *The timing belt must be removed and refitted with the engine cold.*

Removal

1 Position No 1 cylinder at TDC on its compression stroke as described in Section 3.
2 Remove the timing belt lower and centre covers as described in Section 6.
3 Check that the timing marks on the camshaft sprockets are still correctly aligned and facing towards each other, and the timing mark on the crankshaft sprocket is aligned with the corresponding mark on the oil pump housing (Section 3).
4 Using an Allen key inserted in the slot on the face of the timing belt tensioner, rotate the tensioner clockwise to relieve the tension in the timing belt. Insert a small drill bit or similar into the slot on the inner edge of the tensioner body to lock the tensioner in the released position.
5 Slide the timing belt from its sprockets and remove it from the engine. If the belt is to be re-used, use white paint or similar to mark the direction of rotation on the belt. **Do not** rotate the crankshaft or camshafts until the timing belt has been refitted.

8.3 Insert the special tool into the slots on the end of the camshafts to lock the camshafts in the TDC position

6 Check the timing belt carefully for any signs of uneven wear, splitting or oil contamination, and renew it if there is the slightest doubt about its condition. If the engine is undergoing an overhaul and is approaching the manufacturer's specified interval for belt renewal (see Chapter 1A) renew the belt as a matter of course, regardless of its apparent condition. If signs of oil contamination are found, trace the source of the oil leak and rectify it, then wash down the engine timing belt area and all related components to remove all traces of oil.

Refitting

7 On reassembly, thoroughly clean the timing belt sprockets and tensioner/idler pulleys.
8 Check that the camshaft and crankshaft sprocket timing marks are still correctly aligned as described in Section 3.
9 Fit the timing belt over the crankshaft and camshaft sprockets and around the idler pulley, ensuring that the belt front run is taut (ie, all slack is on the tensioner side of the belt), then fit the belt over the tensioner pulley. Do not twist the belt sharply while refitting it. Ensure that the belt teeth are correctly seated centrally in the sprockets, and that the timing marks remain in alignment. If a used belt is being refitted, ensure that the arrow mark made on removal points in the normal direction of rotation, as before.
10 Using the Allen key, turn the tensioner clockwise slightly and remove the drill bit or similar tool used to lock the tensioner. Slowly release the tensioner and allow it to turn anti-clockwise and automatically tension the timing belt.
11 Check the sprocket timing marks are still correctly aligned. If adjustment is necessary, release the tensioner again then disengage the belt from the sprockets and make any necessary adjustments.
12 Using a socket on the temporarily refitted crankshaft pulley bolt, rotate the crankshaft smoothly through two complete turns (720°) in the normal direction of rotation to settle the timing belt in position.

A camshaft locking tool can be made from a steel strip approximately 4.5 mm thick, with two grooves filed in the strip to clear the camshaft sensor trigger lugs

13 Set the crankshaft back in the timing position and check that all the sprocket timing marks are still correctly aligned. If this is not the case, repeat the timing belt refitting procedure.
14 If everything is satisfactory, refit the timing belt covers as described in Section 6.

---

8 Timing belt sprockets, tensioner and idler pulley –
removal and refitting

Camshaft sprockets

Note: *Vauxhall/Opel special tools KM-6340 and KM-6628 or suitable alternatives will be required for this procedure.*
Note: *New sprocket retaining bolt(s) and a new sprocket closure bolt seal will be required for refitting.*

Removal

1 Remove the camshaft cover as described in Section 4.
2 Remove the timing belt as described in Section 7.
3 Insert Vauxhall/Opel special tool KM-6628 into the slots on the end of the camshafts to lock the camshafts in the TDC position. In the absence of the special tool, a suitable alternative can be fabricated from a steel strip **(see Tool Tip and illustration)**. It may be necessary to turn the camshafts slightly using an open-ended spanner on the flats provided, to allow the tool to fully engage with the slots.
4 Unscrew the closure bolt from the relevant camshaft sprocket **(see illustration)**. Note that a new closure bolt seal will be required for refitting.
5 Hold the camshaft using an open-ended spanner on the flats provided, and unscrew the camshaft sprocket retaining bolt. Withdraw the sprocket from the end of the camshaft.
6 If necessary, remove the remaining sprocket using the same method.

Refitting

7 Prior to refitting check the oil seal(s) for signs of damage or leakage. If necessary, renew as described in Section 10.

8.4 Camshaft sprocket closure bolts

8 Refit the sprocket to the camshaft end and fit the new retaining bolt. Tighten the bolt finger tight only at this stage. If both sprockets have been removed, ensure each sprocket is fitted to the correct shaft; the exhaust camshaft sprocket has the timing belt guide flange on its inner face and the inlet sprocket has the guide flange on its outer face.

9 Turn the camshaft sprocket(s) until the timing marks are facing towards each other and aligned. It will now be necessary to retain the sprockets in the timing position while the sprocket retaining bolt is tightened. Engage Vauxhall/Opel special tool KM-6340 or a suitable alternative with the teeth on both sprockets, to lock the sprockets together.

10 With the camshafts and sprockets locked in the timing position with the special tools, hold the camshaft using an open-ended spanner on the flats provided and tighten the sprocket retaining bolt to the specified Stage 1 torque setting. Now angle-tighten the bolt through the specified Stage 2 angle, using a socket and extension bar, and finally through the specified Stage 3 angle. It is recommended that an angle-measuring gauge is used during the final stages of the tightening, to ensure accuracy. If a gauge is not available, use white paint to make alignment marks between the bolt head and sprocket prior to tightening; the marks can then be used to check that the bolt has been rotated through the correct angle.

11 Fit a new seal to the camshaft sprocket closure bolt, then refit the closure bolt and tighten to the specified torque.

12 Remove the special tools, then refit the timing belt as described in Section 7, and the camshaft cover as described in Section 4.

Crankshaft sprocket

Removal

13 Remove the timing belt as described in Section 7.

14 Slide the sprocket off from the end of the crankshaft, noting which way around it is fitted.

Refitting

15 Align the sprocket locating key with the crankshaft groove then slide the sprocket into position, making sure its timing mark is facing outwards.

16 Refit the timing belt as described in Section 7.

Tensioner assembly

Note: *A new tensioner retaining bolt will be required for refitting.*

Removal

17 Remove the timing belt as described in Section 7.

18 Slacken and remove the retaining bolt and remove the tensioner assembly from the engine.

Refitting

19 Clean the tensioner retaining bolt threads in the oil pump housing, ensuring that all traces of sealant, oil or grease are removed.

20 Fit the tensioner to the engine, making sure that the lug on the backplate is correctly located in the oil pump housing hole. On later models, also ensure that the projecting end of the tensioner spring engages with the slot on the oil pump housing. Ensure the tensioner is correctly seated then refit the new retaining bolt and tighten it to the specified torque.

21 Refit the timing belt as described in Section 7.

Idler pulley

Removal

Note: *A new idler pulley retaining bolt will be required for refitting.*

22 Remove the timing belt as described in Section 7.

23 Slacken and remove the retaining bolt and remove the idler pulley from the engine.

Refitting

24 Refit the idler pulley and tighten the new retaining bolt to the specified torque.

25 Refit the timing belt as described in Section 7.

9 VVT oil control valves – removal and refitting

Removal

1 The VVT oil control valves are fitted to the camshaft bearing support, adjacent to the camshaft sprockets. Two oil control valves are used, one for each camshaft.

2 Disconnect the wiring connector from the relevant oil control valve **(see illustration)**.

3 Undo the retaining bolt located below the valve, and withdraw the valve from the camshaft bearing support. Be prepared for oil spillage.

Refitting

4 Lubricate the valve sealing rings with clean engine oil and insert the valve into the camshaft bearing support.

5 Refit and tighten the retaining bolt and reconnect the wiring connector.

6 On completion, check and if necessary top-up the engine oil as described in *Weekly checks.*

10.2 Camshaft oil seal removal method

9.2 Disconnect the wiring connector from the VVT oil control valve

10 Camshaft oil seals – renewal

1 Remove the relevant camshaft sprocket as described in Section 8.

2 Carefully punch or drill two small holes opposite each other in the oil seal. Screw a self-tapping screw into each, and pull on the screws with pliers to extract the seal **(see illustration)**.

3 Clean the seal housing, and polish off any burrs or raised edges which may have caused the seal to fail in the first place.

4 Press the new seal into position using a suitable tubular drift (such as a socket) which bears only on the hard outer edge of the seal **(see illustration)**. Take care not to damage the seal lips during fitting; note that the seal lips should face inwards.

5 Refit the camshaft sprocket as described in Section 8.

11 Valve clearances – checking and adjustment

Checking

1 The importance of having the valve clearances correctly adjusted cannot be overstressed, as they vitally affect the performance of the engine. The engine must be cold for the check to be accurate. The clearances are checked as follows.

10.4 Using the old camshaft sprocket bolt and a socket to fit the new camshaft oil seal

11.7a Using feeler blades, measure the clearance between the base of both No 2 cylinder inlet cam lobes ...

11.7b ... and No 3 cylinder exhaust cam lobes and their followers

2 Firmly apply the handbrake, then jack up the front of the car and support it securely on axle stands (see *Jacking and vehicle support)*. Remove the right-hand front roadwheel then remove the wheel arch liner lower cover for access to the crankshaft pulley.

3 Remove the camshaft cover as described in Section 4.

4 Position No 1 cylinder at TDC on its compression stroke as described in Section 3.

5 With the engine at TDC on compression for No 1 cylinder, the inlet camshaft lobes for No 2 cylinder and the exhaust camshaft lobes for No 3 cylinder are pointing upwards and slightly towards the centre. This indicates that these valves are completely closed, and the clearances can be checked.

6 On a piece of paper, draw the outline of the engine with the cylinders numbered from the timing belt end. Show the position of each valve, together with the specified valve clearance.

7 With the cam lobes positioned as described in paragraph 5, using feeler blades, measure the clearance between the base of both No 2 cylinder inlet cam lobes and No 3 cylinder exhaust cam lobes and their followers. Record the clearances on the paper **(see illustrations)**.

8 Rotate the crankshaft pulley in the normal direction of rotation through a half a turn (180°) to position No 1 cylinder inlet camshaft lobes and No 4 cylinder exhaust camshaft lobes pointing upwards and slightly towards the centre. Measure the clearance between the base of the camshaft lobes and their followers and record the clearances on the paper.

9 Rotate the crankshaft pulley through a half a turn (180°) to position No 3 cylinder inlet camshaft lobes and No 2 cylinder exhaust camshaft lobes pointing upwards and slightly towards the centre. Measure the clearance between the base of the camshaft lobes and their followers and record the clearances on the paper.

10 Rotate the crankshaft pulley through a half a turn (180°) to position No 4 cylinder inlet camshaft lobes and No 1 cylinder exhaust camshaft lobes pointing upwards and slightly towards the centre. Measure the clearance between the base of the camshaft lobes and their followers and record the clearances on the paper.

11 If all the clearances are correct, refit the camshaft cover (see Section 4), then refit the wheel arch liner lower cover and the roadwheel. Lower the vehicle to the ground and tighten the wheel nuts to the specified torque. If any clearance measured is not correct, adjustment must be carried out as described in the following paragraphs.

Adjustment

12 If adjustment is necessary, remove the relevant camshaft(s) and camshaft followers as described in Section 12.

13 Clean the followers of the valves that require clearance adjustment and note the thickness marking on the follower. The thickness marking is stamped on the underside of each follower. For example, a 3.20 mm thick follower will have a 20 thickness marking, a 3.21 mm thick follower will have a 21 thickness marking etc.

14 Add the measured clearance of the valve to the thickness of the original follower then subtract the specified valve clearance from this figure. This will give you the thickness of the follower required. For example:

Clearance measured of inlet valve	*0.31 mm*
Plus thickness of the original follower	*3.20 mm*
Equals	*3.51 mm*
Minus clearance required	*0.25 mm*
Thickness of follower required	*3.26 mm*

15 Repeat this procedure on the remaining valves which require adjustment, then obtain the correct thickness of follower(s) required.

16 Refit the camshaft followers and the relevant camshaft(s) as described in Section 12. Rotate the crankshaft a few times to settle all the components, then recheck the valve clearances before refitting the camshaft cover (Section 4).

17 Refit the wheel arch liner lower cover and roadwheel then lower the vehicle to the ground and tighten the wheel nuts to the specified torque.

12 Camshafts and followers – removal, inspection and refitting

Note: *New timing belt end oil seals, and a tube of suitable sealant will be required when refitting.*

Removal

1 Remove the camshaft cover as described in Section 4.

2 Remove the timing belt as described in Section 7.

3 Remove the camshaft sprockets as described in Section 8.

4 Remove the timing belt rear cover as described in Section 6.

5 Remove the special tool used to lock the camshafts in the TDC position.

6 Remove the camshaft sensors as described in Chapter 4A, Section 11.

7 Disconnect the wiring connector at the inlet camshaft and exhaust camshaft VVT oil control valves **(see illustration 9.2)**.

8 Undo the four bolts securing the camshaft bearing support at the timing belt end of the engine **(see illustration)**. Undo the two outer bolts first, followed by the two inner bolts. Using a plastic mallet, gently tap the bearing support free and remove it from the cylinder head.

9 Starting on the inlet camshaft, working in a spiral pattern from the outside inwards, slacken the camshaft bearing cap retaining bolts by half a turn at a time, to relieve the pressure of the valve springs on the bearing caps gradually and evenly **(the reverse of illustration 12.21)**. Once the valve spring pressure has been relieved, the bolts can be fully unscrewed and removed along with the caps; the bearing caps are numbered inlet camshaft 2 to 5, exhaust camshaft 6 to 9 to

12.8 Camshaft bearing support retaining bolts

12.9 Camshaft bearing cap numbers (inlet camshaft shown)

ensure the caps are correctly positioned on refitting **(see illustration)**. Take care not to lose the locating dowels (where fitted).

Caution: If the bearing cap bolts are carelessly slackened, the bearing caps might break. If any bearing cap breaks then the complete cylinder head assembly must be renewed; the bearing caps are matched to the head and are not available separately.

10 Lift the camshaft out of the cylinder head and slide off the oil seal.

11 Repeat the operations described in paragraphs 4 and 5 and remove the exhaust camshaft.

12 Obtain sixteen small, clean plastic containers, and label them for identification. Alternatively, divide a larger container into compartments. Using a rubber sucker tool, lift the followers out from the top of the cylinder head and store each one in its respective fitted position **(see illustration)**.

Inspection

13 Examine the camshaft bearing surfaces and cam lobes for signs of wear ridges and scoring. Renew the camshaft if any of these conditions are apparent. Examine the condition of the bearing surfaces both on the camshaft journals and in the cylinder head. If the head bearing surfaces are worn excessively, the cylinder head will need to be renewed.

14 Examine the follower bearing surfaces which contact the camshaft lobes for wear ridges and scoring. Check the followers and their bores in the cylinder head for signs of wear or damage. If any follower is thought to be faulty or is visibly worn it should be renewed.

Refitting

15 Commence refitting by turning the crankshaft anti-clockwise by 60°. This will position Nos 1 and 4 pistons a third of the way down the bore, and prevent any chance of the valves touching the piston crowns as the camshafts are being fitted.

16 Thoroughly clean the mating surfaces of the camshaft bearing support and cylinder head, ensuring all traces of old sealant are removed.

17 Where removed, lubricate the followers with clean engine oil and carefully insert each one into its original location in the cylinder head.

18 Lubricate the camshaft followers with molybdenum disulphide paste (or clean engine oil) then lay the camshafts in position.

19 Ensure the mating surfaces of the bearing caps and cylinder head are clean and dry and lubricate the camshaft journals and lobes with clean engine oil.

20 Ensure the locating dowels (where fitted) are in position then refit camshaft bearing caps 2 to 9 and the retaining bolts in their original locations on the cylinder head.

21 Working on the inlet camshaft, tighten the bearing cap bolts by hand only then, working

12.12 Use a valve lapping tool to remove the cam followers

in a spiral pattern from the centre outwards, tighten the bolts by half a turn at a time to gradually impose the pressure of the valve springs on the bearing caps **(see illustration)**. Repeat this sequence until all bearing caps are in contact with the cylinder head then go around and tighten the camshaft bearing cap bolts to the specified torque.

Caution: If the bearing cap bolts are carelessly tightened, the bearing caps might break. If any bearing cap breaks then the complete cylinder head assembly must be renewed; the bearing caps are matched to the head and are not available separately.

22 Tighten the exhaust camshaft bearing cap bolts as described in paragraph 21.

23 Apply a smear of sealant to the mating surface of the camshaft bearing support, ensuring that the oil grooves remain free of sealant. Do not apply sealant to the area immediately adjacent to the bearing surface on the inside of the oil groove.

24 Place the camshaft bearing support in position and refit the four retaining bolts. Tighten the bolts to the specified torque, starting with the two inner bolts, then the two outer bolts.

25 If new components have been fitted, the valve clearances should now be checked and, if necessary adjusted, before proceeding with the refitting procedure. Temporarily refit the camshaft sprockets and secure with their retaining bolts, to allow the camshafts to be turned for the check. Refer to the procedure contained in Section 11, but as the timing belt is not fitted, check the clearances of each camshaft individually. Use the sprocket retaining bolt to turn the camshafts as necessary until the cam lobes for each pair of valves are pointing upward, away from the valves.

26 Once the valve clearances have been checked and if necessary adjusted, position the camshafts so that their timing slots are parallel with the cylinder head surface and refit the locking tool to the slots. Undo the retaining bolts and remove the camshaft sprockets.

27 Refit the camshaft sensors as described in Chapter 4A, Section 11.

28 Reconnect the wiring connector at the inlet camshaft and exhaust camshaft VVT oil control valves.

12.21 Camshaft bearing cap tightening sequence (inlet camshaft shown – exhaust identical)

29 Refit the timing belt rear cover as described in Section 6.

30 Fit new camshaft oil seals as described in Section 10.

31 Refit the camshaft sprockets as described in Section 8.

32 Align all the sprocket timing marks to bring the camshafts and crankshaft back to TDC then refit the timing belt as described in Section 7.

33 Refit the camshaft cover as described in Section 4.

13 Cylinder head – removal and refitting

Note: *The engine must be cold when removing the cylinder head. A new cylinder head gasket and new cylinder head bolts must be used on refitting.*

Removal

1 Depressurise the fuel system as described in Chapter 4A, Section 5.

2 Disconnect the battery negative terminal (refer to Chapter 5A, Section 1).

3 Apply the handbrake, then jack up the front of the vehicle and support it on axle stands (see *Jacking and vehicle support*). Remove the right-hand front roadwheel and the wheel arch liner lower cover for access to the right-hand side of the engine.

4 Drain the cooling system as described in Chapter 1A, Section 24.

5 Remove the spark plugs as described in Chapter 1A, Section 26.

6 Remove the camshaft cover as described in Section 4.

7 Remove the timing belt as described in Section 7.

8 Remove the camshaft sprockets, timing belt tensioner, and the timing belt idler pulleys, as described in Section 8.

9 Remove the rear timing belt cover with reference to Section 6.

10 Refer to Chapter 4A, Section 14 and unbolt the exhaust front pipe from the catalytic converter, taking care to support the flexible section. **Note:** *Angular movement in excess of 10° can cause permanent damage*

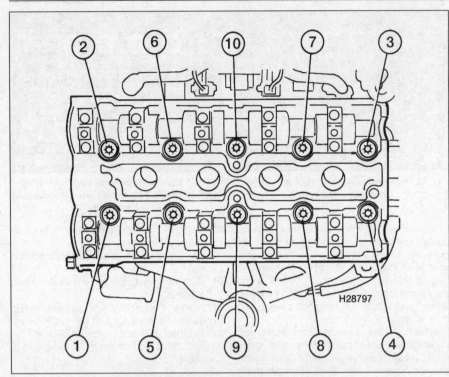

13.20 Cylinder head bolt loosening sequence

to the flexible section. Release the mounting rubbers and support the front of the exhaust pipe to one side.

11 Disconnect the engine management wiring loom from the following, noting its routing:
a) *Crankshaft speed/position sensor.*
b) *Oil pressure switch.*
c) *Oil level sensor.*

12 Release the cable ties and place the wiring loom to one side.

13 Remove the inlet and exhaust manifolds as described in Chapter 4A, Section 12 and 13.

14 Referring to Chapter 3, Section 2, unclip the coolant hoses from the heater matrix unions on the engine compartment bulkhead to drain the coolant from the cylinder block.

15 Once the flow of coolant has stopped, reconnect both hoses and mop up any spilt coolant.

13.29 Ensure the head gasket is fitted with its OBEN/TOP marking uppermost

16 Loosen the clips and remove the upper hose from the radiator and thermostat housing.

17 Loosen the clips and disconnect the heater hoses from the left-hand end of the cylinder head or thermostat housing.

18 Undo the bolt and free the oil dipstick guide tube from the cylinder head.

19 Make a final check to ensure that all relevant hoses, pipes and wires have been disconnected.

20 Working in the sequence shown, progressively loosen the cylinder head bolts **(see illustration)**. First loosen all the bolts by quarter of a turn, then loosen all the bolts by half a turn, then finally slacken all the bolts fully and withdraw them from the cylinder head. Recover the washers.

21 Lift the cylinder head from the cylinder block. If necessary, tap the cylinder head gently with a soft-faced mallet to free it from the block, but **do not** lever at the mating faces. Note that the cylinder head is located on dowels.

22 Recover the cylinder head gasket, and discard it.

Preparation for refitting

23 The mating faces of the cylinder head and block must be perfectly clean before refitting the head. Use a scraper to remove all traces of gasket and carbon, and also clean the tops of the pistons. Take particular care with the aluminium surfaces, as the soft metal is damaged easily. Also, make sure that debris is not allowed to enter the oil and water channels – this is particularly important for the

oil circuit, as carbon could block the oil supply to the camshaft or crankshaft bearings. Using adhesive tape and paper, seal the water, oil and bolt holes in the cylinder block. To prevent carbon entering the gap between the pistons and bores, smear a little grease in the gap. After cleaning the piston, rotate the crankshaft so that the piston moves down the bore, then wipe out the grease and carbon with a cloth rag. Clean the other piston crowns in the same way.

24 Check the block and head for nicks, deep scratches and other damage. If slight, they may be removed carefully with a file. More serious damage may be repaired by machining, but this is a specialist job.

25 If warpage of the cylinder head is suspected, use a straight-edge to check it for distortion. Refer to Chapter 2E, Section 7 if necessary.

26 Ensure that the cylinder head bolt holes in the crankcase are clean and free of oil. Syringe or soak up any oil left in the bolt holes. This is most important in order that the correct bolt tightening torque can be applied and to prevent the possibility of the block being cracked by hydraulic pressure when the bolts are tightened.

27 Renew the cylinder head bolts regardless of their apparent condition.

Refitting

28 Ensure that the two locating dowels are in position at each end of the cylinder block/crankcase surface.

29 Fit the new cylinder head gasket to the block, making sure it is fitted with the correct way up with its OBEN/TOP mark uppermost **(see illustration)**.

30 Carefully refit the cylinder head, locating it on the dowels.

31 Fit the washers to the new cylinder head bolts then carefully insert them into position **(do not drop)**, tightening them finger-tight only at this stage.

32 Working progressively and in the sequence shown, first tighten all the cylinder head bolts to the Stage 1 torque setting **(see illustrations)**.

33 Once all bolts have been tightened to the Stage 1 torque, again working in the sequence shown, tighten each bolt through its specified Stage 2 angle, using a socket and extension bar. It is recommended that an angle-measuring gauge is used during this stage of the tightening, to ensure accuracy **(see illustration)**.

34 Working in the specified sequence, go around again and tighten all bolts through the specified Stage 3 angle.

35 Working again in the specified sequence, go around and tighten all bolts through the specified Stage 4 angle.

36 Finally go around in the specified sequence again and tighten all bolts through the specified Stage 5 angle.

37 Refit the exhaust manifold as described in Chapter 4A, Section 13.

38 Reconnect the heater hoses to the

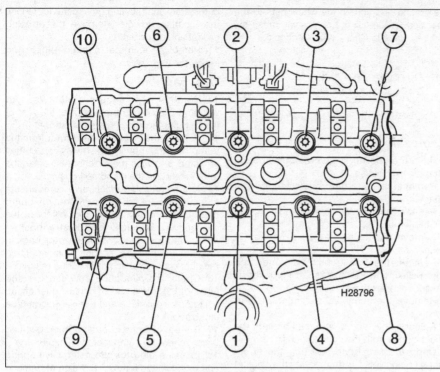

13.32a Cylinder head bolt tightening sequence

13.32b Tighten the cylinder head bolts to the specified Stage 1 torque setting ...

13.33 ... and then through the various specified angles as described in the text

left-hand end of the cylinder head or thermostat housing and tighten the clips.

39 Refit the upper hose to the radiator and thermostat housing and tighten the clips.

40 Refit the inlet manifold as described in Chapter 4A, Section 12.

41 Reconnect the wiring to the components listed in paragraph 11, then secure the wiring with cable ties.

42 Refer to Chapter 4A, Section 14 and refit the exhaust front pipe to the exhaust manifold. Refit the mounting rubbers.

43 Refit the rear timing belt cover with reference to Section 6.

44 Refit the camshaft sprockets, timing belt tensioner, and the timing belt idler pulleys, with reference to Section 8.

45 Refit the timing belt as described in Section 7.

46 Refit the spark plugs as described in Chapter 1A, Section 26.

47 Refit the camshaft cover as described in Section 4.

48 Refit the wheel arch liner inner cover and front roadwheel, then lower the vehicle to the ground.

49 Reconnect the battery negative terminal.

50 Check that all relevant hoses, pipes and wires, etc, have been reconnected. Check the security of the fuel hose connections.

51 Refill and bleed the cooling system with reference to Chapter 1A, Section 24.

52 When the engine is started, check for signs of oil or coolant leakage.

14 Sump – removal and refitting

Removal

1 Disconnect the battery negative terminal (refer to Chapter 5A, Section 4).

2 Apply the handbrake, then jack up the front of the vehicle and support it on axle stands (see *Jacking and vehicle support*). Remove the right-hand front roadwheel and the wheel arch liner lower cover for access to the right-hand side of the engine.

3 Drain the engine oil as described in Chapter 1A, Section 5, then fit a new sealing washer and refit the drain plug, tightening it to the specified torque.

4 Remove the exhaust system front pipe as described in Chapter 4A, Section 14.

5 Disconnect the wiring connector from the oil level sensor.

6 Undo the retaining bolt and remove the oil dipstick guide tube from the cylinder head.

7 Slacken and remove the bolts securing the sump flange to the transmission housing.

8 Progressively slacken and remove the bolts securing the sump to the base of the cylinder block/oil pump. Using a wide bladed scraper or similar tool inserted between the sump and cylinder block, carefully break the joint, then remove the sump from under the car.

9 While the sump is removed, take the opportunity to check the oil pump pick-up strainer for signs of clogging or splitting. Undo the bolts and remove the baffle plate from the sump. Withdraw the pick-up strainer from its location in the sump. The strainer can then be cleaned easily in solvent or renewed.

Refitting

10 Thoroughly clean the sump, baffle plate and pick-up strainer, then remove all traces of sealer and oil from the mating surfaces of the sump and cylinder block.

11 Where removed, refit the oil pick-up strainer and baffle plate to the sump.

12 Ensure the sump and cylinder block mating surfaces are clean and dry and remove all traces of locking compound from the sump bolts.

13 Apply a smear of suitable sealant (available from Vauxhall/Opel dealers) to the areas of the cylinder block mating surface around the areas of the of the oil pump housing and rear main bearing cap joints **(see illustration)**.

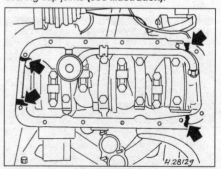

14.13 Apply sealant to the oil pump and rear main bearing cap joints before the sump is refitted

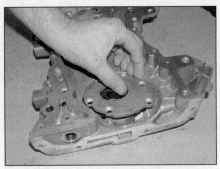

15.12 Remove the securing screws and withdraw the oil pump cover from the rear of the housing

14 Apply a bead of suitable sealant (available from Vauxhall/Opel dealers) approximately 2.5 mm thick to the sealing surface of the sump. Around the No 5 main bearing cap area, increase the thickness of the bead to 3.5 mm.
15 Offer up the sump, and loosely refit all the retaining bolts. Working out from the centre in a diagonal sequence, progressively tighten the bolts securing the sump to the cylinder block/oil pump to their specified torque setting.
16 Tighten the bolts securing the sump flange to the transmission housing to their specified torque settings.
17 Refit the exhaust system front pipe (see Chapter 4A, Section 14) and reconnect the oil level sensor wiring connector.
18 Refit the wheel arch liner lower cover and front roadwheel, then lower the vehicle to

the ground and tighten the wheel nuts to the specified torque. Fill the engine with fresh oil, with reference to Chapter 1A, Section 5.

15 Oil pump – removal, overhaul and refitting

Removal

1 Drain the cooling system as described in Chapter 1A, Section 24.
2 Remove the alternator as described in Chapter 5A, Section 8.
3 Remove the exhaust manifold as described in Chapter 4A, Section 13.
4 Remove the timing belt as described in Section 7.
5 Remove the timing belt tensioner and idler pulley, and the crankshaft sprocket as described in Section 8.
6 Remove the sump as described in Section 14.
7 Release the clamp and disconnect the coolant hose from the coolant pump.
8 Undo the two bolts securing the upper metal coolant pipe to the rear of the coolant pump.
9 Undo the support bracket bolt securing the lower metal coolant pipe to the oil filter housing.
10 Slacken and remove the eight retaining bolts (noting their different lengths) then slide the oil pump housing assembly off of the end

of the crankshaft, taking great care not to lose the locating dowels. Remove the housing gasket and discard it.
11 Remove the metal coolant pipes and renew the four seals.

Overhaul

12 Remove the securing screws and withdraw the oil pump cover from the rear of the oil pump housing **(see illustration)**.
13 Remove the inner and outer rotor from the pump housing, noting which way round they are fitted, and wipe them clean. Also clean the rotor location in the oil pump housing.
14 The oil pressure relief valve components can also be removed from the oil pump housing by unscrewing the cap. Withdraw the cap, spring and plunger **(see illustrations)**.
15 Locate the inner and outer rotor back in the oil pump housing, ensuring they are fitted the right way round as noted during removal.
16 Check the clearance between the end faces of the rotors and the housing (endfloat) using a straight-edge and a feeler gauge **(see illustration)**.
17 If the clearance is outside the specified limits, renew the components as necessary.
18 Examine the pressure relief valve spring and plunger, and renew if any sign of damage or wear is evident.
19 Ensure that the rotor location in the interior of the oil pump housing is scrupulously clean before commencing reassembly.
20 Thoroughly clean the pressure relief valve components, and lubricate them with clean engine oil before refitting. Insert the plunger and spring, then refit the cap and tighten to the specified torque.
21 Ensure that the rotors are clean, then lubricate them with clean engine oil, and refit them to the pump body ensuring they are fitted the right way round as noted during removal.
22 Wipe clean the mating faces of the rear cover and the pump housing, then refit the rear cover. Refit and tighten the securing screws securely. Prime the oil pump by filling it with clean engine oil whilst rotating the inner rotor

Refitting

23 Prior to refitting, carefully lever out the crankshaft oil seal using a flat-bladed screwdriver. Fit the new oil seal, ensuring its sealing lip is facing inwards, and press it squarely into the housing using a tubular drift which bears only on the hard outer edge of the seal. Press the seal into position so that it is flush with the housing.
24 Refit the two previously removed metal coolant pipes.
25 Ensure the mating surfaces of the oil pump housing and cylinder block are clean and dry and the locating dowels are in position.
26 Fit a new gasket to the cylinder block.
27 Carefully manoeuvre the oil pump into position and engage the inner rotor with the crankshaft end. Engage the coolant pipes,

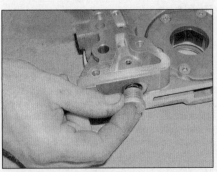

15.14a Unscrew the oil pressure relief valve cap ...

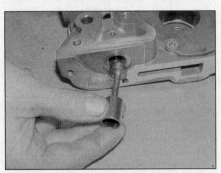

15.14c ... and the plunger

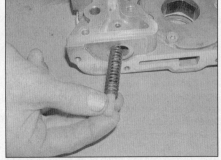

15.14b ... then withdraw the spring ...

15.16 Check the oil pump rotor endfloat using a straight-edge and feeler gauge

16.2 Prevent the flywheel from turning by locking the ring gear teeth with a suitable tool

16.8a Tighten the flywheel bolts to the specified torque using a torque wrench ...

16.8b ... then through the specified angle using an angle tightening gauge

then locate the pump on the dowels, taking great care not damage the oil seal lip.

28 Refit the pump housing retaining bolts in their original locations and tighten them to the specified torque.

29 Refit the metal coolant pipe retaining bolts and tighten securely.

30 Reconnect the coolant hose to the pump and secure with the retaining clip.

31 Refit the sump as described in Section 14.

32 Refit the timing belt tensioner and idler pulley and the crankshaft sprocket, then refit the timing belt as described in Sections 8 and 7.

33 Refit the exhaust manifold as described in Chapter 4A, Section 13.

34 Refit the alternator as described in Chapter 5A, Section 8.

35 On completion, refer to Chapter 1A, Section 5 and fit a new oil filter and fill the engine with clean oil, then refill the cooling system.

16 Flywheel – removal, inspection and refitting

Note: New flywheel retaining bolts will be required on refitting.

Removal

1 Remove the transmission as described in Chapter 7A, Section 8, then remove the clutch assembly as described in Chapter 6, Section 6.

2 Prevent the flywheel from turning by locking the ring gear teeth with a similar arrangement to that shown **(see illustration)**. Alternatively, bolt a strap between the flywheel and the cylinder block/crankcase. Make alignment marks between the flywheel and crankshaft using paint or a suitable marker pen.

3 Slacken and remove the retaining bolts and remove the flywheel. Do not drop it, as it is very heavy.

Inspection

4 Examine the flywheel for scoring of the clutch face. If the clutch face is scored, the flywheel may be surface-ground, but renewal

is preferable. Also check for wear or chipping of the ring gear teeth.

5 If there is any doubt about the condition of the flywheel, seek the advice of a Vauxhall/Opel dealer or engine reconditioning specialist. They will be able to advise if it is possible to recondition it or whether renewal is necessary.

Refitting

6 Clean the mating surfaces of the flywheel and crankshaft.

7 Offer up the flywheel and fit the new retaining bolts. If the original is being refitted align the marks made prior to removal.

8 Lock the flywheel by the method used on removal, and tighten the retaining bolts to the specified Stage 1 torque setting then angle-tighten the bolts through the specified Stage 2 angle, using a socket and extension bar, and finally through the specified Stage 3 angle. It is recommended that an angle-measuring gauge is used during the final stages of the tightening, to ensure accuracy **(see illustrations)**. If a gauge is not available, use white paint to make alignment marks between the bolt head and flywheel prior to tightening; the marks can then be used to check that the bolt has been rotated through the correct angle.

9 Refit the clutch as described in Chapter 6, Section 6, then remove the locking tool, and refit the transmission as described in Chapter 7A, Section 8.

17 Crankshaft oil seals – renewal

Right-hand (timing belt end)

1 Remove the crankshaft sprocket as described in Section 8.

2 Carefully punch or drill two small holes opposite each other in the oil seal. Screw a self-tapping screw into each and pull on the screws with pliers to extract the seal **(see illustration)**.

Caution: Great care must be taken to avoid damage to the oil pump

3 Clean the seal housing and polish off any burrs or raised edges which may have caused the seal to fail in the first place.

4 Ease the new seal into position on the end of the crankshaft. Press the seal squarely into position until it is flush with the housing. If necessary, a suitable tubular drift, such as a socket, which bears only on the hard outer edge of the seal can be used to tap the seal into position **(see illustration)**. Take great care not to damage the seal lips during fitting and ensure that the seal lips face inwards.

5 Wash off any traces of oil, then refit the crankshaft sprocket as described in Section 8.

Left-hand (flywheel end)

6 Remove the flywheel as described in Section 16.

17.2 Removing the crankshaft oil seal

17.4 Fitting a new crankshaft oil seal

17.8 Left-hand crankshaft oil seal – transmission and flywheel removed

7 Remove the crankshaft position sensor as described in Chapter 4A, Section 11.

8 Note the fitted depth of the oil seal, then carefully punch or drill two small holes opposite each other in the seal. Screw a self-tapping screw into each and pull on the screws with pliers to extract the seal **(see illustration)**.

9 Ease the new seal into position on the end of the crankshaft. Press the seal squarely into position until it is at the depth previously noted. If necessary, a suitable tubular drift, such as a socket, which bears only on the hard outer edge of the seal can be used to tap the seal into position. Take great care not to damage the seal lips during fitting. Ensure that the seal lips face inwards and that the new seal is fitted to the depth noted during removal.

10 Refit the flywheel as described in Section 16.

11 Refit the crankshaft position sensor as described in Chapter 4A, Section 11.

18.6 Front mounting/torque link through-bolt

18.15 Rear mounting/torque link bracket to subframe mounting bolt nuts

18 Engine/transmission mountings – inspection and renewal

Inspection

1 If improved access is required, firmly apply the handbrake, then jack up the front of the car and support it securely on axle stands (see *Jacking and vehicle support*).

2 Check the mounting rubber to see if it is cracked, hardened or separated from the metal at any point; renew the mounting if any such damage or deterioration is evident.

3 Check that all the mounting's fasteners are securely tightened; use a torque wrench to check if possible.

4 Using a large screwdriver or a pry bar, check for wear in the mounting by carefully levering against it to check for free play; where this is not possible, enlist the aid of an assistant to move the engine/transmission unit back-and-forth, or from side-to-side, while you watch the mounting. While some free play is to be expected even from new components, excessive wear should be obvious. If excessive free play is found, check first that the fasteners are correctly secured, then renew any worn components as described below.

Renewal

Note: *Before slackening any of the engine mounting bolts/nuts, the relative positions of the mountings to their various brackets should*

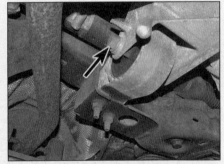

18.14 Rear mounting/torque link through-bolt

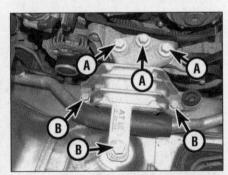

18.22 Right-hand mounting bracket-to-engine bracket bolts (A) and mounting-to-body bolts (B)

be marked to ensure correct alignment upon refitting.

Front mounting/torque link

5 Apply the handbrake, then jack up the front of the vehicle and support it on axle stands (see *Jacking and vehicle support*).

6 Slacken and remove the through-bolt securing the mounting to the subframe bracket **(see illustration)**.

7 Undo the bolts securing the mounting bracket to the transmission, then manoeuvre the mounting and bracket out of position.

8 Check all components for signs of wear or damage, and renew as necessary.

9 Locate the mounting in the subframe, refit the through bolt and tighten the bolt finger tight at this stage.

10 Refit the mounting bracket to the transmission and tighten its bolts to the specified torque.

11 Tighten the through bolt to the specified torque.

12 On completion, lower the vehicle to the ground.

Rear mounting/torque link

13 Apply the handbrake, then jack up the front of the vehicle and support it on axle stands (see *Jacking and vehicle support*).

14 Undo the three bolts securing the mounting bracket to the transmission and the through-bolt securing the mounting to the bracket **(see illustration)**.

15 Undo the nuts and remove the two bolts securing the mounting to the subframe **(see illustration)**. Manoeuvre the mounting and bracket out from under the car.

16 Refit the bracket to the transmission and tighten the bolts to the specified torque.

17 Locate the new mounting in position. Insert the bolts and tighten the bolt/nuts to the specified torque.

18 On completion, lower the vehicle to the ground.

Right-hand mounting

19 Apply the handbrake, then jack up the front of the vehicle and support it on axle stands (see *Jacking and vehicle support*).

20 Remove the air cleaner as described in Chapter 4A, Section 2.

21 Attach a suitable hoist and lifting tackle to the engine lifting brackets on the cylinder head, and support the weight of the engine.

22 Mark the position of the three bolts securing the mounting bracket to the engine bracket and undo the bolts. Undo the three bolts securing the mounting to the body and remove the mounting assembly **(see illustration)**. If necessary, undo the three bolts and remove the mounting bracket from the engine.

23 Place the mounting assembly in position and refit the bolts securing the mounting to the body. Tighten the bolts to the specified torque. Align the mounting in its original position, then tighten the three mounting bracket bolts to the specified torque.

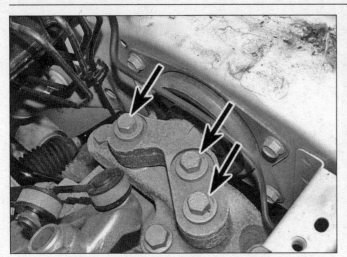

18.31 Left-hand mounting bracket-to-transmission bracket retaining bolts – diesel model shown, petrol similar

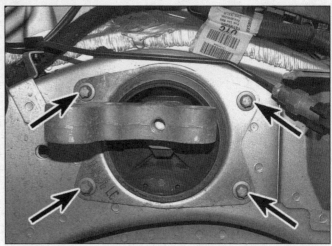

18.32 Left-hand mounting-to-body retaining bolts – shown with engine/transmission removed

24 Remove the hoist, then refit the air cleaner as described in Chapter 4A, Section 4.

25 On completion, lower the vehicle to the ground.

Left-hand mounting

26 Remove the battery and battery box as described in Chapter 5A, Section 4.

27 Apply the handbrake, then jack up the front of the vehicle and support it on axle stands (see *Jacking and vehicle support*).

28 Remove the left-hand front roadwheel, then remove the wheel arch liner from under the front wing.

29 Attach a suitable hoist and lifting tackle to the engine lifting brackets on the cylinder head, and support the weight of the engine. Alternatively, support the transmission on a jack with a block of wood between the transmission and jack head.

30 Working under the front wing, unscrew the nut securing the mounting to the body.

31 From within the engine compartment, unscrew the three bolts securing the mounting bracket to the transmission bracket **(see illustration)**.

32 Undo the four bolts securing the mounting to the body and the three bolts securing the transmission bracket to the transmission **(see illustration)**. Remove the mounting assembly from the car.

33 Locate the mounting brackets in position then refit the nut and bolts and tighten them to the specified torque.

34 Disconnect the hoist and lifting tackle, or remove the jack, as applicable.

35 Refit the wheel arch liner and roadwheel, then lower the vehicle to the ground and tighten the wheel nuts to the specified torque.

36 Refit the battery box and battery as described in Chapter 5A, Section 4.

Chapter 2 Part B
1.6 litre diesel engine in-car repair procedures

Contents

Degrees of difficulty

Easy, suitable for novice with little experience 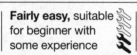	**Fairly easy,** suitable for beginner with some experience	**Fairly difficult,** suitable for competent DIY mechanic	**Difficult,** suitable for experienced DIY mechanic	**Very difficult,** suitable for expert DIY or professional

Specifications

General

Engine type	Four-cylinder, in-line, water-cooled. Chain-driven double overhead camshafts, 16 valves
Manufacturer's engine code*	B16DTH (LVL) or B16DTJ (LVL)
Bore	79.7 mm
Stroke	80.1 mm
Capacity	1598 cc
Firing order	1-3-4-2 (No 1 cylinder at right-hand end of engine)
Direction of crankshaft rotation	Clockwise (viewed from right-hand end of engine)
Compression ratio	16.0: 1

For details of engine code location, see 'Vehicle identification' in Chapter 13 Section 3

Compression pressures

Minimum	20.0 bar
Maximum difference between cylinders	25%

Lubrication system

Oil pump type	Variable displacement vane type with integral vacuum pump
Oil pressure at 80ºC (approximate)	1.0 bar at idle speed

Torque wrench settings

	Nm	lbf ft
Auxiliary drivebelt tensioner-to-cylinder block	55	41
Big-end bearing cap bolts*:		
Stage 1	25	18
Stage 2	Angle-tighten a further 110º	

Torque wrench settings (continued)

	Nm	lbf ft
Camshaft bearing cap bolts (except rear bearing cap)	10	7
Camshaft bearing cap bolts (rear bearing cap)	25	18
Camshaft cover bolts	10	7
Camshaft sprocket bolts	25	18
Crankshaft pulley bolts*:		
Stage 1	50	37
Stage 2	Angle-tighten a further 45°	
Cylinder block baseplate bolts (main bearings):		
M10 bolts (bolts 1 to 10)*:		
Stage 1	50	37
Stage 2	Angle-tighten a further 90°	
Stage 3	Angle-tighten a further 90°	
M8 bolts (bolts 11 to 21)	34	25
Cylinder head bolts (except two outer bolts)*:		
Stage 1	50	37
Stage 2	Angle-tighten a further 90°	
Stage 3	Angle-tighten a further 90°	
Stage 4	Angle-tighten a further 90°	
Cylinder head bolts (two outer bolts)*:		
Stage 1	20	15
Stage 2	Angle-tighten a further 45°	
Engine lifting bracket bolts	58	43
Engine mountings:		
Front mounting:		
Through bolt	100	74
Bracket to transmission	62	46
Left-hand mounting:		
Mounting-to-body bolts/nut	22	16
Mounting bracket-to-transmission bracket*:		
Stage 1	50	37
Stage 2	Angle-tighten a further 60°	
Bracket to transmission	100	74
Rear mounting/torque link:		
Through bolt	100	74
Bracket to transmission	100	74
Mounting-to-subframe	110	82
Right-hand mounting:		
Mounting bracket-to-engine	62	46
Mounting-to-body	62	46
Mounting-to-mounting bracket*:		
Stage 1	50	37
Stage 2	Angle-tighten a further 60°	
Engine-to-transmission bolts	58	43
Flywheel/driveplate bolts*:		
Stage 1	60	44
Stage 2	Angle-tighten a further 45°	
Fuel pump sprocket retaining nut*	64	47
Idler sprocket retaining bolts	25	18
Main vacuum pipe assembly retaining bolts	10	7
Oil cooler retaining bolts	25	18
Oil pump chain tensioner bolts:		
Lower bolt	10	7
Upper bolt	25	18
Oil pump retaining bolts	25	18
Oil pump sprocket bolt*:		
Stage 1	25	18
Stage 2	Angle-tighten a further 60°	
Roadwheel nuts	150	111
Sump-to-cylinder block baseplate and timing cover	25	18
Sump baffle plate	10	7
Sump-to-transmission	58	43
Timing chain guide rail bolts	10	7
Timing chain tensioner bolts	10	7
Timing chain tensioner rail pivot bolt	25	18
Timing cover retaining bolts	25	18
Timing cover sleeve bolt	25	18

*Use new fasteners

1 General Information

How to use this Chapter

1 This Part of Chapter 2 describes the repair procedures which can reasonably be carried out on the engine while it remains in the vehicle. If the engine has been removed from the vehicle and is being dismantled as described in Chapter 2E, any preliminary dismantling procedures can be ignored.

2 Note that, while it may be possible physically to overhaul items such as the piston/connecting rod assemblies while the engine is in the vehicle, such tasks are not usually carried out as separate operations, and usually require the execution of several additional procedures (not to mention the cleaning of components and of oil ways); for this reason, all such tasks are classed as major overhaul procedures, and are described in Chapter 2E.

3 Chapter 2E describes the removal of the engine/transmission unit from the vehicle, and the full overhaul procedures which can then be carried out.

Engine description

4 The 1.6 litre common-rail diesel engine is of sixteen-valve, in-line four-cylinder, double overhead camshaft (DOHC) type, mounted transversely at the front of the car with the transmission attached to its left-hand end.

5 The crankshaft runs in five main bearings. Thrustwashers are fitted to No 3 main bearing shell (upper half) to control crankshaft endfloat.

6 The cylinder block is made of aluminium incorporating cast iron dry liners. An aluminium baseplate is bolted to the cylinder block and forms the lower half of the crankcase.

7 The connecting rods rotate on horizontally-split bearing shells at their big-ends. The pistons are attached to the connecting rods by gudgeon pins, which are a sliding fit in the connecting rod small-end eyes and retained by circlips. The aluminium-alloy pistons are fitted with three piston rings – two compression rings and an oil control ring.

8 The camshafts run directly in the cylinder head. The inlet camshaft is driven by the crankshaft by a hydraulically tensioned timing chain and drives the exhaust camshaft via a spur gear. Each cylinder has four valves (two inlet and two exhaust), operated via rocker arms which are supported at their pivot ends by hydraulic self-adjusting valve lifters (tappets). One camshaft operates the inlet valves, and the other operates the exhaust valves. In what is an unusual configuration, the timing chain and timing gear components are situated at the left-hand (flywheel/driveplate) end of the engine

9 The inlet and exhaust valves are each closed by a single valve spring, and operate in guides pressed into the cylinder head.

10 A variable displacement vane-type oil pump is located below the cylinder block baseplate, and is driven by a chain from the left-hand end of the crankshaft. The brake servo vacuum pump is integral with the oil pump.

11 The coolant pump is located externally at the right-hand end of the engine, and is driven by the auxiliary drivebelt.

Operations with engine in place

12 The following operations can be carried out without having to remove the engine from the vehicle.
a) Removal and refitting of the cylinder head.
b) Removal and refitting of the timing covers.
c) Removal and refitting of the timing chain, tensioner, sprockets and guide rails.
d) Removal and refitting of the hydraulic tappets and rocker arms.
e) Removal and refitting of the camshafts.
f) Removal and refitting of the sump.
g) Removal and refitting of the big-end bearings, connecting rods, and pistons*.
h) Removal and refitting of the oil pump.
i) Removal and refitting of the oil cooler.
j) Renewal of the crankshaft oil seals.
k) Renewal of the engine mountings.
l) Removal and refitting of the flywheel/ driveplate.

*Although the operation marked with an asterisk can be carried out with the engine in the vehicle (after removal of the sump), it is preferable for the engine to be removed, in the interests of cleanliness and improved access. For this reason, the procedure is described in Chapter 2E Section 3.

2 Compression test – description and interpretation

Compression test

Note: *A compression tester specifically designed for diesel engines must be used for this test.*

1 When engine performance is down, or if misfiring occurs which cannot be attributed to the fuel system, a compression test can provide diagnostic clues as to the engine's condition. If the test is performed regularly, it can give warning of trouble before any other symptoms become apparent.

2 A compression tester specifically intended for diesel engines must be used, because of the higher pressures involved. The tester is connected to an adapter which screws into the glow plug or injector hole. On these models, an adapter suitable for use in the injector holes will be required. It is unlikely to be worthwhile buying such a tester for occasional use, but it may be possible to borrow or hire one – if not, have the test performed by a garage.

3 It should be noted that the factory diagnostic tool (Tech 2 or MDI) is capable of performing a non-invasive cylinder contribution test. Whilst this may not be as definitive as a traditional compression test it requires little or no preparatory work to conduct the test. An automotive oscilloscope can also be used (in conjunction with an inductive amps clamp) to asses each cylinders contribution as the engine is cranked over. Many properly equipped garages should have this equipment.

4 Unless specific instructions to the contrary are supplied with the tester, observe the following points:
a) *The battery must be in a good state of charge, the air filter must be clean, and the engine should be at normal operating temperature.*
b) *The fuel injectors (Chapter 4B Section 11) or the glow plugs (Chapter 5A Section 17) must be removed before starting the test.*
c) *Open the cover on the engine compartment fuse/relay box and remove the fuel pump relay. Refer to the wiring diagrams in Chapter 12 for information on fuse and relay locations.*

5 Screw the compression tester and adaptor into ether the fuel injector hole or the glow plug hole of No 1 cylinder.

6 With the help of an assistant, crank the engine on the starter motor; after one or two revolutions, the compression pressure should build-up to a maximum figure, and then stabilise. Record the highest reading obtained.

7 Repeat the test on the remaining cylinders, recording the pressure in each.

8 All cylinders should produce very similar pressures; any difference greater than that specified indicates the existence of a fault. Note that the compression should build-up quickly in a healthy engine; low compression on the first stroke, followed by gradually-increasing pressure on successive strokes, indicates worn piston rings. A low compression reading on the first stroke, which does not build-up during successive strokes, indicates leaking valves or a blown head gasket (a cracked head could also be the cause).

Note: *The cause of poor compression is less easy to establish on a diesel engine than on a petrol one. The effect of introducing oil into the cylinders ('wet' testing) is not conclusive, because there is a risk that the oil will sit in the recess on the piston crown instead of passing to the rings.*

9 On completion of the test, refit the fuel pump relay, then refit the fuel injectors as described in Chapter 4B Section 11 or the glow plugs as described in Chapter 5A Section 17.

Leakdown test

10 A leakdown test measures the rate at which compressed air fed into the cylinder is lost. It is an alternative to a compression test, and in many ways it is better, since the

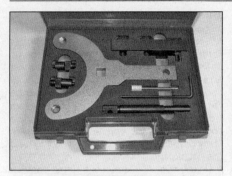

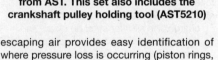

3.2 A comprehensive set of timing tools from AST. This set also includes the crankshaft pulley holding tool (AST5210)

3.6 Camshaft locking tool inserted through the bearing cap and into the exhaust camshaft timing gear

3.7 Crankshaft locking tool securing the crankshaft in the TDC position

escaping air provides easy identification of where pressure loss is occurring (piston rings, valves or head gasket).

11 The equipment needed for leakdown testing is unlikely to be available to the home mechanic. If poor compression is suspected, have the test performed by a Vauxhall/Opel dealer or suitably-equipped garage.

3 Engine assembly/valve timing tools – general information and usage

Note: *Do not attempt to rotate the engine whilst the camshafts and crankshaft are locked in position. If the engine is to be left in this state for a long period of time, it is a good idea to place suitable warning notices inside the car, and in the engine compartment. This will reduce the possibility of the engine being accidentally cranked on the starter motor, which is likely to cause damage with the locking tools in place.*

1 To accurately set the valve timing for all operations requiring removal and refitting of the timing chain, a hole is machined in the exhaust camshaft timing gear to allow a locking tool to be inserted. When the hole (and locking tool) are aligned with a corresponding hole in the camshaft bearing cap, No 1 piston will be at TDC on its compression stroke. An additional tool is used to lock the crankshaft in the TDC position. With the crankshaft pulley removed, the locking tool is bolted to the crankshaft using the pulley bolts, and a projection on the tool engages with a timing hole in the cylinder block. This arrangement ensures that the correct valve timing can be obtained. The design of the engine is such that there are no conventional timing marks on the crankshaft or camshafts to indicate the normal TDC position. Therefore, for any work on the timing chain, camshafts or cylinder head, the locking tools must be used.

2 The Vauxhall/Opel tools required are EN-51143 (camshaft locking) and EN-51140 (crankshaft locking). Similar tools are available in the aftermarket **(see illustration)**.

3 To position the engine at TDC for No 1

piston on compression, first remove the camshaft cover as described in Section 5.

4 Remove the crankshaft pulley as described in Section 4. Refit the crankshaft pulley retaining bolts and screw them in a few turns to allow the crankshaft to be turned.

5 Using a large screwdriver or pry bar engaged with the crankshaft pulley bolts, turn the crankshaft in the normal direction of rotation (clockwise as viewed from the right-hand side of the engine) until the hole in the exhaust camshaft timing gear is aligned with the corresponding hole in the camshaft bearing cap.

6 Insert the camshaft locking tool through the hole in the bearing cap and into the hole in the gear **(see illustration)**.

7 Remove the crankshaft pulley retaining bolts and place the crankshaft locking tool in position. Ensure that the projection on the tool engages with the timing hole in the cylinder block. Refit two of the crankshaft pulley retaining bolts to secure the tool in position and tighten them securely **(see illustration)**.

HAYNES HINT

To make a pulley/sprocket holding tool, obtain two lengths of steel strip about 6 mm thick by about 30 mm wide or similar, one 600 mm long, the other 200 mm long (all dimensions are approximate). Bolt the two strips together, leaving the bolt slack so that the shorter strip can pivot freely. At the other end of each 'prong' of the fork, drill a suitable hole and fit a nut and bolt to allow the tool to engage with the holes in the pulley.

4 Crankshaft pulley – removal and refitting

Removal

1 Firmly apply the handbrake, then jack up the front of the car and support it securely on axle stands (see Jacking and vehicle support 13 Section 5), Section. Remove the right-hand roadwheel, then remove the wheel arch liner as described in Chapter 11 Section 24.

2 Remove the auxiliary drivebelt as described in Chapter 1B Section 22.

3 It will now be necessary to hold the crankshaft pulley to enable the retaining bolts to be removed. Vauxhall/Opel special tools EN-49979 and EN-49979-100 are available for this purpose, however, a home-made tool can easily be fabricated **(see Tool-Tip)**.

4 Using the holding tool to prevent rotation of the crankshaft, slacken the four pulley retaining bolts. Remove the holding tool, unscrew the retaining bolts and remove the pulley **(see illustration)**. Note that new pulley retaining bolts will be required for refitting.

Refitting

5 Locate the pulley in position on the crankshaft.

6 Fit the new pulley retaining bolts and tighten them to the specified torque, then through the specified angle while preventing crankshaft rotation using the method employed on removal.

4.4 Undo the four retaining bolts and remove the crankshaft pulley

5.3 Lift the retaining catch and disconnect the fuel pressure sensor wiring connector

5.5a Undo the nut and four bolts ...

5.5b ... and lift off the turbocharger upper heat shield

7 Refit the auxiliary drivebelt as described in Chapter 1B Section 22.

8 Refit the wheel arch liner as described in Chapter 11 Section 24, then refit the roadwheel and lower the car to the ground. Tighten the wheel nuts to the specified torque.

5 Camshaft cover –
removal and refitting

Removal

1 Disconnect the battery negative lead as described in Chapter 5A Section 4.
2 Remove the fuel injectors as described in Chapter 4B Section 11.
3 Disconnect the wiring connector at the fuel pressure sensor on the fuel rail (see illustration).
4 Remove the oxygen sensor from the top of the diesel particulate filter as described in Chapter 4C Section 3.
5 Undo the nut and four bolts securing the upper heat shield to the turbocharger. Remove the washer from the particulate filter stud, then lift off the heat shield (see illustrations).
6 Undo the two bolts and remove the turbocharger inner heat shield (see illustration).
7 Release the two retaining clips and remove the crankcase ventilation hose from the camshaft cover and turbocharger (see illustration).

8 Undo the bolts securing the turbocharger wastegate actuator pipe and turbocharger coolant pipe support brackets to their

attachments. Disconnect the pipe hose ends from the vacuum pipe and wastegate actuator and remove the pipe (see illustrations).

5.6 Undo the two bolts and remove the inner heat shield

5.7 Release the clips and remove the crankcase ventilation hose

5.8a Undo the turbocharger coolant pipe bracket bolt ...

5.8b ... and wastegate actuator pipe bracket bolt at the left-hand end of the engine ...

5.8c ... at the centre of the engine ...

5.8d ... and at the right-hand end of the engine ...

5.8e ... then disconnect the hose ends and remove the wastegate actuator pipe

5.9 Unbolt and remove the left-hand engine lifting bracket

5.10 Undo the bolt securing the right-hand engine lifting bracket to the cylinder head

5.11 Undo the two bolts and move the wiring harness and engine lifting bracket to one side

5.16 Locate the new rubber seal into the grooves of the camshaft cover

9 Undo the retaining bolt and remove the left-hand engine lifting bracket **(see illustration)**.
10 Undo the bolt securing the right-hand engine lifting bracket to the cylinder head **(see illustration)**.
11 Undo the two bolts securing the wiring harness support bracket to the camshaft cover **(see illustration)**. Move the wiring harness and the engine lifting bracket to one side.
12 Remove the engine oil level dipstick.
13 Progressively unscrew the fifteen outer bolts followed by the five inner bolts securing the camshaft cover to the cylinder head.

Carefully lift up the cover and remove it from the engine.
14 Remove the camshaft cover rubber seal and the washer and rubber seal from each of the retaining bolts, noting the larger diameter of the washers and seals on the inner bolts. Check the condition of the retaining bolt seals and renew as necessary. It is recommended that the cover rubber seal is renewed as a matter of course.

Refitting

15 Ensure that the camshaft cover grove and rubber seal are clean and dry with all traces

of oil removed. If necessary, de-grease the seal and cover groove with brake cleaner or a similar product.
16 Locate the rubber seal into the grooves of the camshaft cover, ensuring that it is fully seated, with no chance of it falling out as the cover is fitted **(see illustration)**.
17 Insert the retaining bolts into the camshaft cover ensuring that the bushing and rubber seal are correctly seated **(see illustration)**.
18 Clean the mating surface of the cylinder head ensuring that all traces of oil are removed, then lower the camshaft cover into position. Initially tighten all the bolts lightly to draw the cover down into contact with the cylinder head, then tighten them in the sequence shown to the specified torque **(see illustration)**.
19 Refit the engine oil level dipstick.
20 Locate the wiring harness support bracket back in position on the camshaft cover, then refit and securely tighten the two retaining bolts.
21 Refit the bolt securing the right-hand engine lifting bracket to the cylinder head and tighten the bolt to the specified torque.
22 Refit the left-hand engine lifting bracket and tighten the retaining bolt to the specified torque.
23 Attach the wastegate actuator pipe ends to the vacuum pipe and actuator, then refit the support brackets and tighten the bolts securely.
24 Refit the crankcase ventilation hose to the camshaft cover and turbocharger.
25 Refit the turbocharger inner heat shield and upper heat shield, securely tightening the retaining bolts.
26 Refit the oxygen sensor to the diesel particulate filter as described in Chapter 4C Section 3.
27 Reconnect the wiring connector to the fuel pressure sensor on the fuel rail.
28 Refit the fuel injectors as described in Chapter 4B Section 11.
29 On completion, reconnect the battery negative terminal as described in Chapter 5A Section 4.

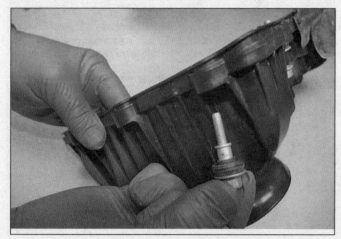

5.17 Insert the bolts into the camshaft cover ensuring the bushing and seal are correctly seated

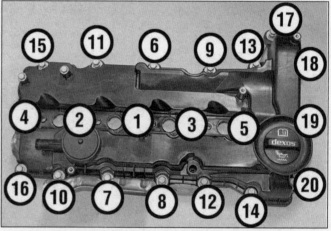

5.18 Camshaft cover bolt tightening sequence

6.7 Disconnect the wastegate actuator solenoid vacuum hose from the main vacuum pipe assembly

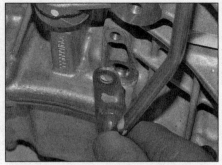

6.8a Undo the main vacuum pipe assembly retaining bolts at the lower flange …

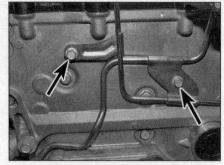

6.8b … at the upper timing cover …

6 Timing chain covers – removal and refitting

Removal

Upper cover

1 Disconnect the battery negative lead as described in Chapter 5A Section 4.
2 Lift off the cover from the top of the engine.
3 Remove the throttle body as described in Chapter 4B Section 8.
4 Remove the EGR valve cooler as described in Chapter 4C Section 3.
5 Disconnect the brake servo unit vacuum hose at the quick-release connector on the main vacuum pipe assembly.
6 Disconnect the turbocharger wastegate actuator pipe hose end from the main vacuum pipe assembly **(see illustration 5.8e)**.
7 Disconnect the turbocharger wastegate actuator solenoid vacuum hose from the main vacuum pipe assembly **(see illustration)**.
8 Undo the main vacuum pipe assembly retaining bolts at the lower flange, at the centre of the upper timing cover, and at the top, then remove the main vacuum pipe assembly **(see illustrations)**.
9 Remove the camshaft cover as described in Section 5.
10 Undo the seven bolts securing the upper timing cover to the cylinder head **(see illustration)**.

6.8c … and at the top …

11 Carefully work the upper cover free from the cylinder head and lower cover. Use a knife or spatula to cut through the sealant. Considerable patience will be required to avoid damaging the mating surfaces. Remove the upper timing cover.
12 Once the upper timing cover has been removed, fully unscrew the sleeve **(see illustration)**.
13 Thoroughly clean the timing cover and remove all traces of sealant from all the mating surfaces. Similarly clean the lower timing cover, cylinder block and cylinder head mating surfaces. Ensure that all traces of old sealant are removed, particularly from the joint areas between these components.

Lower cover

14 Remove the timing chain upper cover as described previously in this Section.

6.8d … then remove the main vacuum pipe assembly

15 Remove the transmission as described in Chapter 7A Section 8(manual transmission) or Chapter 7B Section 10(automatic transmission).
16 Remove the flywheel/driveplate as described in Section 17.
17 Remove the crankshaft speed/position sensor as described in Chapter 4B Section 8.
18 Carefully withdraw the crankshaft speed/position sensor reluctor ring from the left-hand end of the crankshaft **(see illustration)**.
19 Remove the sump as described in Section 12. Note that is possible to remove the lower cover with the sump in place, however reassembly will be difficult since the lower cover must slide over the sump. This action will remove the liquid gasket from the sump and more than likely led to an oil leak at the interface.

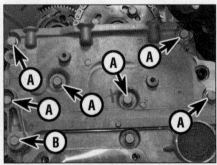

6.10 Upper timing cover retaining bolts (A) Note the special sleeve and bolt (B)

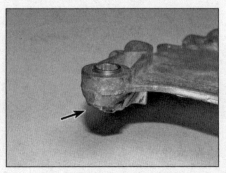

6.12 Fully unscrew the sleeve

6.18 Withdraw the crankshaft speed/position sensor reluctor ring

6.20 Lower timing cover retaining bolt locations

6.21 A prying point is provided

6.24 Fit two new seals to the timing cover recesses

20 Undo the bolts securing the lower timing cover to the cylinder block **(see illustration)**.
21 Use a knife or spatula to cut through the sealant, then carefully prise the cover free and remove it from the engine **(see illustration)**. Recover the two rubber seals from the rear of the cover.
22 Carefully prise out the old crankshaft oil seal with a screwdriver or similar hooked tool. Clean the oil seal seat with a wooden or plastic scraper.
23 Thoroughly clean the timing cover and cylinder block to remove all traces of sealant from all the mating surfaces.

Refitting

Lower cover

Note: *The lower cover must be fitted before the upper.*
24 Fit the two new rubber seals to the

recesses on the rear of the lower timing cover **(see illustration)**.
25 Apply a 2 to 3 mm bead of silicone sealant to the mating surfaces on each side of the lower timing cover. The sealant bead should be around the inside of the bolt holes on the sides of the cover **(see illustration)**.
26 Place the lower cover in position on the cylinder block and refit the eleven retaining bolts. Progressively tighten the retaining bolts to the specified torque in the sequence shown **(see illustrations)**.
27 Fit a new crankshaft left-hand oil seal to the lower timing cover as described in Section 15.
28 Refit the crankshaft speed/position sensor reluctor ring.
29 Refit the crankshaft speed/position sensor as described in Chapter 4B Section 8.
30 Refit the flywheel/driveplate as described in Section 17.
31 Refit the transmission as described in

Chapter 7A Section 8 (manual transmission) or Chapter 7B Section 10 (automatic transmission).
32 Refit the timing chain upper cover as described below.

Upper cover

33 Apply a 2 to 3 mm bead of silicone sealant to the mating surfaces of the upper timing cover. The sealant bead should be around the inside of the bolt holes on the sides of the cover and there should be two beads, one each side of the groove along the lower face of the cover. Ensure that a bead of sealant is also applied around the two central bolt holes **(see illustrations)**.
34 Place the upper timing cover in position on the engine and refit the six retaining bolts (don't fit the sleeve bolt at this stage). Tighten the bolts to the specified torque in the sequence shown **(see illustration)**.
35 Screw in the sleeve until it just makes

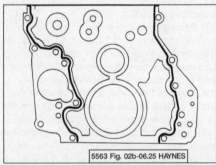

6.25 Apply a bead of sealant to each side of the lower timing cover

6.26a Refit the lower timing cover …

6.26b … and tighten the retaining bolts in the sequence shown

6.33a Apply a bead of sealant to the timing cover mating surfaces …

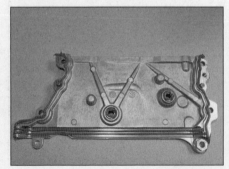

6.33b … in the areas shown. Note the double row of sealant at the lower edge

6.34 Upper timing cover retaining bolt tightening sequence

contact with the lower timing cover. Refit the sleeve bolt and tighten it to the specified torque **(see illustration)**.

36 Refit the camshaft cover as described in Section 5.

37 Place the main vacuum pipe assembly in position and refit the retaining bolts at the lower flange, at the centre of the upper timing cover, and at the top. Tighten the bolts to the specified torque.

38 Reconnect the turbocharger wastegate actuator pipe hose end and actuator solenoid hose to the main vacuum pipe assembly

39 Resconnect the brake servo unit vacuum hose to the quick-release connector on the main vacuum pipe assembly.

40 Refit the EGR valve cooler as described in Chapter 4C Section 3.

41 Refit the throttle housing as described in Chapter 4B Section 8.

42 Refit the plastic cover over the top of the engine, then reconnect the battery negative terminal.

6.35 Refit the sleeve bolt and tighten it to the specified torque

TDC for No. 1 piston. Insert the camshaft and crankshaft locking tools to retain the engine in the TDC position.

3 Push the timing chain tensioner plunger back into its bore and insert a suitable drill bit or similar tool to retain it in the released position **(see illustration)**.

4 Hold the camshaft using a spanner on the camshaft hexagon, then undo the three bolts and withdraw the sprocket and timing chain from the inlet camshaft **(see illustration)**. Disengage the sprocket from the chain and remove the sprocket.

5 Undo the two bolts and remove the timing chain upper guide rail **(see illustration)**.

6 Disengage the timing chain from the idler sprocket and fuel pump sprocket and remove the chain from the engine **(see illustration)**.

7 Inspect the timing chain, sprockets, tensioner rail and guide rails for any sign of wear or deformation, and renew any suspect components as necessary.

8 Push the timing chain tensioner plunger into the tensioner body and remove the locking drill bit. Check that the tensioner plunger is free to move in out of the tensioner body with no trace of binding. If any binding or sticking of the plunger is felt, renew the tensioner assembly. On completion of the check, or if a new tensioner is being fitted, compress the plunger and refit the locking drill bit.

Refitting

9 Remove all traces of thread locking compound from the timing chain upper guide rail retaining bolt holes by running a suitable tap through the bolt hole threads. Also, suitably clean the threads of the retaining bolts.

10 Hold the timing chain so that the two coloured links, separated by a plain link are uppermost. Half way down the right-hand side of the chain is another coloured link. Engage the chain with the fuel pump sprocket so that the coloured link is adjacent to the dot on the sprocket **(see illustration)**.

11 Feed the chain around the idler sprocket aligning the coloured link with the mark on the sprocket **(see illustration)**.

12 Apply thread locking compound to the two upper guide rail retaining bolts. Refit the timing chain upper guide rail and tighten the retaining bolts to the specified torque.

7 Timing chain – removal and refitting

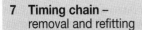

Removal

1 Remove the upper and lower timing covers as described in Section 6.

2 Refer to Section 3 and set the engine at

7.3 Push the timing chain tensioner plunger back into its bore and retain it using a suitable drill bit

7.4 Undo the three bolts and withdraw the sprocket and timing chain from the camshaft

7.5 Remove the timing chain upper guide rail

7.6 Disengage the chain from the sprockets and remove the chain

7.10 Engage the chain with the fuel pump sprocket so that the coloured link is adjacent to the dot

7.11 Feed the chain around the idler sprocket so that the coloured link is aligned with the sprocket mark

7.13a Locate the camshaft sprocket in the chain so that the plain link between the two coloured links is aligned with the dot on the sprocket …

7.13b … then fit the retaining bolts and tighten them to the specified torque

7.14 Withdraw the locking drill bit and release the tensioner plunger

13 Locate the camshaft sprocket in the chain so that the plain link between the two coloured links is aligned with the dot on the sprocket. Fit the sprocket to the inlet camshaft, insert the three bolts and tighten them to the specified torque **(see illustrations)**. Hold the camshaft using a spanner on the camshaft hexagon as the bolts are tightened.

14 Depress the timing chain tensioner plunger, withdraw the locking drill bit and release the plunger to apply tension to the chain **(see illustration)**.

15 Remove the tools used to lock the camshaft and crankshaft in the TDC position. Refit the crankshaft pulley retaining bolts and rotate the crankshaft through two complete revolutions.

16 Remove the crankshaft pulley retaining bolts, refit the tool used to lock the crankshaft in the TDC position and secure with the pulley retaining bolts. Check that it is possible to insert the camshaft sprocket locking tool. If the tool cannot be inserted, slacken the inlet camshaft sprocket retaining bolts. Using a spanner on the camshaft hexagon, rotate the camshaft slightly until the tool can be inserted. When all is correct, tighten the camshaft sprocket retaining bolts to the specified torque, then remove the locking tools.

17 Refit the crankshaft pulley with reference to Section 4.

18 Refit the timing covers as described in Section 6.

8 Timing chain sprockets, tensioner and guide rails – removal and refitting

Camshaft sprocket

1 Removal and refitting of the timing chain camshaft sprocket is part of the timing chain removal and refitting procedures contained in Section 7.

Fuel pump sprocket

Removal

2 Remove the timing chain as described in Section 7.

3 If the timing chain is to be replaced, then the old chain can be used to lock the pump sprocket. If the timing chain is to be reused, then the sprocket can be locked with a large adjustable spanner.

4 Lock the sprocket and slacken the nut **(see illustration)**.

5 A puller may be required to release the sprocket from the fuel pump **(see illustration)**.

6 Pull off the sprocket and recover the key.

Refitting

7 Clean the fuel pump shaft and the sprocket hub ensuring that all traces of oil or grease are removed.

8 Refit the woodruff key and refit the sprocket.

9 Fit a new nut to the pump shaft and tighten the nut to the specified torque **(see illustration)**.

10 Refit the timing chain as described in Section 7.

Idler sprocket

Removal

11 Remove the timing chain as described in Section 7.

12 The idler sprocket incorporates a backlash compensating gear. This must now be locked to the fixed gear by attaching either the Vauxhall/Opel special tool (EN-51141) to the gear teeth or by aligning the gear teeth with a screwdriver and fitting a locking pin – a drill bit or similar **(see illustration)**.

8.4 Lock the sprocket and remove the nut

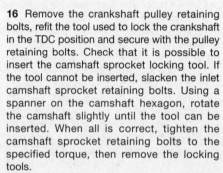

8.5 Use a puller to release the sprocket

8.9 The old chain used again to lock the sprocket and allow the nut to be tightened to the correct torque setting

8.12 When using the special tool engage the special tool with the teeth of the idler sprocket

8.13a Undo the three bolts ...

8.13b ... and remove the idler sprocket and special tool

8.14 The mark on the idler sprocket tooth must be between the two dots on the crankshaft sprocket teeth

This prevents the spring preload of the compensating gear being lost when the sprocket is removed. Note that if the sprocket is to be replaced, then the sprocket can be simply unbolted as replacement sprockets are supplied with a locking pin fitted.

13 Undo the three bolts and remove the sprocket and special tool from the cylinder block **(see illustrations)**. If used, do not remove the tool if the existing sprocket is to be refitted.

Refitting

14 Engage the idler sprocket gear teeth with the crankshaft sprocket gear teeth so that the timing mark on the idler sprocket tooth is between the two dots on the crankshaft sprocket teeth **(see illustration)**.

15 Refit the sprocket retaining bolts, remove the special tool, and tighten the bolts to the specified torque. If a new sprocket is fitted (or the old one was locked using a drill bit or similar) then remove the locking pin.

16 Refit the timing chain as described in Section 7.

Tensioner

Removal

17 Remove the upper timing cover as described in Section 6.

18 Refer to Section 3 and set the engine at TDC for No. 1 piston. Insert the camshaft and crankshaft locking tools to retain the engine in the TDC position.

19 Push the timing chain tensioner plunger back into its bore and insert a suitable drill bit or similar tool to retain it in the released position **(see illustration 7.3)**.

20 Undo the two retaining bolts and remove the tensioner from the cylinder head.

21 Push the timing chain tensioner plunger into the tensioner body and remove the locking drill bit. Check that the tensioner plunger is free to move in out of the tensioner body with no trace of binding. If any binding or sticking of the plunger is felt, renew the tensioner assembly. On completion of the check, or if a new tensioner is being fitted, compress the plunger and refit the locking drill bit.

Refitting

22 Refit the timing chain tensioner and tighten the two retaining bolts to the specified torque. Depress the tensioner plunger, withdraw the locking drill bit and release the plunger.

23 Remove the TDC locking tools, then refit the upper timing cover as described in Section 6.

Upper guide rail

Note: *The upper and lower guide rails can be removed with the timing chain partiality removed. Removing the camshaft sprocket and lowering it with the chain will allow enough slack in the chain to release the guides. However it is more than likely that the guides need replacement because the chain has worn, so chain removal will be required anyway.*

Removal

24 Remove the timing chain as described in Section 7.

25 Undo the two bolts and remove the timing chain upper guide rail **(see illustration)**.

Refitting

26 Remove all traces of thread locking compound from the upper guide rail retaining bolt holes by running a suitable tap through the bolt hole threads. Also, suitably clean the threads of the retaining bolts.

27 Apply thread locking compound to the two upper guide rail retaining bolts. Refit the upper guide rail and chain together. Fit the

guide rail bolts and tighten the retaining bolts to the specified torque.

28 Align the chain with the timing marks on the fuel pump, idler sprocket and camshaft sprocket. Tension the chain and proceed as described in Section 7.

Lower guide rail

Removal

29 Remove the timing chain as described in Section 7.

30 Undo the two retaining bolts and remove the lower guide rail from the cylinder block **(see illustration)**.

Refitting

31 Locate the lower guide rail in position, refit the two bolts and tighten them to the specified torque.

32 Refit the timing chain as described in Section 7.

Tensioner rail

Removal

33 Remove the timing chain covers as described in Section 6.

34 Refer to Section 3 and set the engine at TDC for No. 1 piston. Insert the camshaft and crankshaft locking tools to retain the engine in the TDC position.

35 Push the timing chain tensioner plunger back into its bore and insert a suitable drill bit or similar tool to retain it in the released position **(see illustration 7.3)**.

36 Undo the lower pivot bolt and remove

8.25 Undo the bolts and remove the upper guide rail

8.30 Lower guide rail retaining bolts

the tensioner rail from the cylinder block **(see illustration)**.

Refitting

37 Locate the tensioner rail in position, refit the pivot bolt and tighten it to the specified torque.

38 Depress the timing chain tensioner plunger, withdraw the locking drill bit and release the plunger to apply tension to the chain.

39 Remove the TDC locking tools, then refit the timing chain covers as described in Section 6.

9 Camshafts – removal, inspection and refitting

Removal

1 Remove camshaft cover as described in Section 5.

2 Lock the engine in the TDC (Top Dead Centre) position as described in Section 3.

3 Locate the lower (hidden) camshaft sprocket bolt. Remove the timing tools and refit the crankshaft pulley bolts. Using a screwdriver or similar between the bolts rotate the crankshaft (in the normal clockwise direction only) until the hidden bolt is accessible.

4 Mark the position of the bolt in the slot and then using a spanner on the camshaft flats, remove the now exposed bolt.

5 Install the special tool (EN-51188) or fabricate a similar tool from sections of angle iron. The tool is designed to hold and support the timing chain in position whilst the camshafts are removed. This is the only

8.36 Tensioner rail lower pivot bolt

9.6 Remove the bolts. Note the spanner on the camshaft flats

function of the tool. If you are removing the camshafts for access to the cylinder head bolts the tool is not required.

6 With the tool in position remove the upper camshaft sprocket bolts **(see illustration)**.

7 Slide the camshaft sprocket away from the camshaft gears and onto the tool **(see illustration)**.

8 Undo the four bolts and lift off the camshaft left-hand bearing cap **(see illustrations)**.

9 Mark the position of the camshafts gears, before proceeding further **(see illustration)**. Note that factory alignment marks are provided on the front of the gears, but these are not visible with the camshaft chain sprocket special tool fitted **(see illustration 9.26a)**.

10 The exhaust camshaft gear incorporates a backlash compensating gear. This must now be locked to the fixed exhaust camshaft gear by inserting a suitably-sized bolt/rod into the

hole on the inboard face of the fixed gear, and through into the backlash compensating gear. Alternatively a simply locking tool can be fabricated from a long nut and bolt and a couple of brackets **(see illustrations)**. This mimics the factory tool. The tool prevents the spring preload of the compensating gear being lost when either camshaft is removed.

11 Working in a spiral pattern from the outside in, slacken the remaining camshaft bearing cap retaining bolts by one turn at a time, to relieve the pressure of the valve springs on the bearing caps gradually and evenly. Once the valve spring pressure has been relieved, the bolts can be fully unscrewed and removed.

12 Remove the bearing caps, noting each caps correct fitted location. The exhaust camshaft bearing caps are numbered 1 to 4 starting at the crankshaft pulley end of the engine. The inlet camshaft bearing caps are

9.7 The sprocket positioned on the nose of the tool

9.8a Undo the four bolts …

9.8b … and lift off the camshaft left-hand bearing cap

9.9 Mark the meshing point of the gears

9.10a Use a nut and bolt to lock the backlash gear to the fixed gear …

9.10b … or fabricate a locking tool. The better method if the engine needs to remain at TDC

9.12 The camshaft bearing caps are numbered 1 to 4 (exhaust) and 5 to 8 (inlet) and the arrow points toward the outside of the engine

9.13 Lift the camshafts out of the cylinder head

9.14 Lift out the camshaft rear bearing base

9.20a Liberally oil the cylinder head tappet bores and tappets …

9.20b … then refit the tappets and rocker arms to their original locations

9.21 Refit the camshaft rear bearing base

numbered 5 to 8 starting at the flywheel/driveplate end of the engine. On all the bearing caps the arrow on each cap points towards the outside of the engine (see illustration).

13 Carefully lift the camshafts from their locations in the cylinder head (see illustration). If both camshafts are removed, identify them as exhaust and inlet.

14 With the camshafts removed, lift out the rear bearing base (see illustration).

15 If required, remove the rocker arms and hydraulic tappets from the cylinder head as described in Section 10.

Inspection

16 Examine the camshaft bearing surfaces and cam lobes for signs of wear ridges and scoring. Renew the camshaft if any of these conditions are apparent. Examine the condition of the bearing surfaces in the cylinder head. If the any wear or scoring is evident, the cylinder head will need to be renewed.

17 If either camshaft is being renewed, it will be necessary to renew all the rocker arms and tappets for that particular camshaft also (see Section 10).

18 Check the condition of the camshaft drive gears for chipped or damaged teeth, wear ridges and scoring. Renew any components as necessary.

Refitting

19 Before refitting, thoroughly clean all the components and the cylinder head and bearing cap journals.

20 Liberally oil the cylinder head hydraulic tappet bores and the tappets. Carefully refit

the tappets and rocker arms to the cylinder head, ensuring that each tappet is refitted to its original bore (see illustrations).

21 Refit the camshaft rear bearing base to the cylinder head, ensuring that it locates correctly over the positioning dowels (see illustration).

22 Liberally oil the exhaust camshaft bearings

in the cylinder head, then place the exhaust camshaft in position (see illustrations).

23 Liberally oil the exhaust camshaft bearing journals and the bearing caps, Refit the bearing caps to their respective locations ensuring they are fitted the correct way round as noted during removal (see illustrations).

9.22a Liberally oil the exhaust camshaft bearings in the cylinder head …

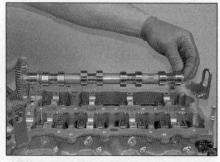

9.22b … then place the exhaust camshaft in position

9.23a Liberally oil the camshaft bearings and bearing caps …

9.23b … then refit the bearing caps to their respective locations

9.26a Refit the inlet camshaft so that the timing marks on the camshaft gears are aligned (shown from the front with the chain removed) ...

9.26b ... noting that it may be necessary to align the backlash compensating gear to allow the gear teeth to engage

9.27 Place the camshaft rear bearing cap in position

24 Refit the bearing cap bolts and initially tighten them, one at a time, by half a turn, working from the centre outward in a spiral pattern. When all the bolts have been initially tightened, repeat the procedure, tightening the bolts by a further half a turn. Continue until all the bearing caps are in contact with the cylinder head and the bolts are lightly tightened.

25 Again, working in the same sequence, tighten all the bolts to the specified torque.

26 Liberally oil the inlet camshaft bearings in the cylinder head. Place the inlet camshaft in position, ensuring that the timing marks on the camshaft gears are aligned. Note that it may be necessary to use a large screwdriver to align the teeth of the backlash compensating gear to allow the gear teeth to engage **(see illustrations)**.

27 Liberally oil the rear camshaft bearing journals and the camshaft rear bearing cap, then place the cap in position. Refit the four retaining bolts and tighten them to the specified torque starting with the two outer bolts, then the two inner bolts **(see illustration)**.

28 Refit the timing chain as described in Section 7.

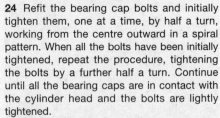

10 Hydraulic tappets and rocker arms – removal, inspection and refitting

Removal

1 Remove the camshafts as described in Section 9.

2 Obtain sixteen small, clean plastic containers, and number them inlet 1 to 8 and exhaust 1 to 8; alternatively, divide a larger container into sixteen compartments and number each compartment accordingly. The best practise is to use an oil tight container (or containers) and keep them fully submerged in clean engine oil.

3 Withdraw each rocker arm and hydraulic tappet in turn, unclip the rocker arm from the tappet, and place them in their respective container **(see illustrations)**. Do not interchange the rocker arms and tappets, or the rate of wear will be much increased.

Inspection

4 Examine the rocker arm and hydraulic tappet bearing surfaces for wear ridges and scoring. Renew any rocker arm or tappet on which these conditions are apparent.

Refitting

5 Liberally oil the cylinder head hydraulic tappet bores and the tappets. Working on one assembly at a time, clip the rocker arm back onto the tappet, then refit the tappet to the cylinder head, ensuring that it is refitted to its original bore. Lay the rocker arm over its respective valve.

6 Refit the remaining tappets and rocker arms in the same way.

7 With all the tappets and rocker arms in place, refit the camshafts as described in Section 9.

11 Cylinder head – removal and refitting

Removal

Note: *New cylinder head retaining bolts will be required for refitting.*

1 Remove the camshafts as described in Section 9, the hydraulic tappets and rocker arms as described in Section 10.

2 Remove the inlet manifold as described in Chapter 4B Section 12.

3 Remove the exhaust manifold as described in Chapter 4B Section 17.

4 Remove the fuel rail as described in Chapter 4B Section 10 and the glow plugs as described in Chapter 5A Section 17.

5 The engine must now be supported while the right-hand engine mounting is removed. To do this, use a hoist attached to the top of the engine, or make up a wooden frame to locate beneath the sump and use a trolley jack.

6 Remove the right-hand engine mounting as described in Section 18.

7 Undo the four bolts and remove the right-hand engine mounting bracket.

8 Undo and remove the two outer cylinder head retaining bolts at the timing chain end of the engine.

9 Working in the reverse of the tightening sequence **(see illustration 11.28)**, progressively slacken the cylinder head bolts by half a turn at a time, until all bolts can be unscrewed by hand. Remove the cylinder head bolts.

10 Engage the help of an assistant and lift the cylinder head from the cylinder block. Take care as it is a bulky and heavy assembly.

11 Remove the gasket and keep it for identification purposes (see paragraph 18).

12 If the cylinder head is to be dismantled for overhaul, then refer to Part E of this Chapter.

10.3a Withdraw each rocker arm and hydraulic tappet in turn ...

10.3b ... then unclip the rocker arm from the tappet

Preparation for refitting

13 The mating faces of the cylinder head and cylinder block/crankcase must be perfectly clean before refitting the head. Use a hard plastic or wood scraper to remove all traces of gasket and carbon; also clean the piston crowns. Take particular care, as the surfaces are damaged easily. Also, make sure that the carbon is not allowed to enter the oil and water passages – this is particularly important for the lubrication system, as carbon could block the oil supply to any of the engine's components. Using adhesive tape and paper, seal the water, oil and bolt holes in the cylinder block/crankcase. To prevent carbon entering the gap between the pistons and bores, smear a little grease in the gap. After cleaning each piston, use a small brush to remove all traces of grease and carbon from the gap, then wipe away the remainder with a clean rag. Clean all the pistons in the same way.

14 Check the mating surfaces of the cylinder block/crankcase and the cylinder head for nicks, deep scratches and other damage. If slight, they may be removed carefully with a fine grade of wet and dry paper, but if excessive, machining may be the only alternative to renewal.

15 Ensure that the cylinder head bolt holes in the crankcase are clean and free of oil. Syringe or soak up any oil left in the bolt holes. This is most important in order that the correct bolt tightening torque can be applied and to prevent the possibility of the block being cracked by hydraulic pressure when the bolts are tightened.

16 The cylinder head bolts must be discarded and renewed, regardless of their apparent condition.

17 If warpage of the cylinder head gasket surface is suspected, use a straight-edge to check it for distortion. Refer to Part E of this Chapter if necessary.

18 On this engine, the cylinder head-to-piston clearance is controlled by fitting different thickness head gaskets. The gasket thickness can be determined by looking at the tab located adjacent to No. 2 cylinder, on the inlet manifold side, and checking the position of the identification hole **(see illustration)**.

11.25 Genuine gaskets are clearly marked

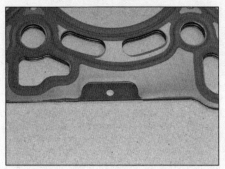

11.18 Head gasket with the punched hole in the centre (1.35 mm thick)

Identification hole position	Gasket thickness
Left-hand side of tab	1.25 mm
Centre of tab	1.35 mm
Right-hand side of tab	1.45 mm

19 The correct thickness of gasket required is selected by measuring the piston protrusions as follows:

20 Remove the crankshaft locking tool and temporarily refit the four crankshaft pulley retaining bolts to enable the crankshaft to be turned.

21 Mount a dial test indicator securely on the block so that its pointer can be easily pivoted between the piston crown and block mating surface. Turn the crankshaft to bring No 1 piston roughly to the TDC position. Move the dial test indicator probe over and in contact with No 1 piston. Turn the crankshaft back and forth slightly until the highest reading is shown on the gauge, indicating that the piston is at TDC.

22 Zero the dial test indicator on the gasket surface of the cylinder block then carefully move the indicator over No 1 piston. Measure its protrusion at the highest point between the valve cut-outs, and then again at its highest point between the valve cut-outs at 90° to the first measurement **(see illustration)**. Repeat this procedure with No 4 piston.

23 Rotate the crankshaft half a turn (180°) to bring No 2 and 3 pistons to TDC. Ensure the crankshaft is accurately positioned then measure the protrusions of No 2 and 3 pistons at the specified points. Once all pistons have been measured, rotate the crankshaft to

11.28 Cylinder head bolt tightening sequence

11.22 Using a dial test indicator to measure piston protrusion

return No 1 piston to the TDC position and refit the crankshaft locking tool.

24 Select the correct thickness of head gasket required by determining the largest amount of piston protrusion, and using the following table.

Piston protrusion measurement	Gasket thickness required
0.440 to 0.535 mm	1.25 mm (hole on left-hand side of tab)
0.535 to 0.630 mm	1.35 mm (hole in centre of tab)
0.630 to 0.725 mm	1.45 mm (hole on right-hand side of tab)

Refitting

25 Wipe clean the mating surfaces of the cylinder head and cylinder block/crankcase. Place the new gasket in position with the words ALTO/TOP uppermost **(see illustration)**.

26 With the aid of an assistant, carefully refit the cylinder head assembly to the block, aligning it with the locating dowels.

27 Carefully enter each new cylinder head bolt into its relevant hole (*do not drop them in*). Screw all bolts in, by hand only, until finger-tight.

28 Working progressively in the sequence shown, tighten the cylinder head bolts to their Stage 1 torque setting, using a torque wrench and suitable socket **(see illustration)**.

29 Once all bolts have been tightened to the Stage 1 torque, working again in the same sequence, go around and tighten all bolts through the specified Stage 2 angle, then through the specified Stage 3 and Stage 4 angles using an angle-measuring gauge.

30 Fit two new outer cylinder head retaining bolts at the timing chain end of the engine and tighten them to the specified torque.

31 Refit the right-hand engine mounting bracket and engine mounting as described in Section 18.

32 Refit the fuel rail as described in Chapter 4B Section 10, and the glow plugs as described in Chapter 5A Section 17.

33 Refit the exhaust manifold as described in Chapter 4B Section 17.

34 Refit the inlet manifold as described in Chapter 4B Section 12.

35 Refit the hydraulic tappets and rocker arms as described in Section 10, and the camshafts as described in Section 9.

12 Sump – removal and refitting

Removal

1 Disconnect the battery negative lead as described in Chapter 5A Section 4.
2 Apply the handbrake, then jack up the front of the vehicle and support it on axle stands (see *Jacking and vehicle support*).
3 Remove the engine undertray as described in Chapter 11 Section 24.
4 Drain the engine oil and remove the oil filter as described in Chapter 1B Section 5.
5 Remove the exhaust system front pipe as described in Chapter 4B Section 18.
6 Remove the engine oil dipstick.
7 Disconnect the wiring connector from the oil level sensor **(see illustration)**.
8 Undo the three bolts (manual transmission models) or two bolts (automatic transmission models) securing the sump flange to the transmission casing.
9 Undo the fifteen bolts securing the sump to the cylinder block baseplate and lower timing cover, noting the locations of the different length bolts. Using a wide bladed scraper or similar tool inserted between the sump and baseplate, carefully break the joint, then remove the sump from under the car. Recover

the oil filter housing seal from the sump upper face **(see illustrations)**. Obtain a new seal for refitting.
10 If required, the oil level sensor can be removed as described in Chapter 5A Section 15.

Refitting

11 Thoroughly clean the inside and outside of the sump ensuring that all traces of old sealant are removed from the mating face. Preferably, undo the six bolts and remove the baffle plate so the inside of the sump can be completely cleaned. Also clean the cylinder block baseplate mating face to remove all traces of old sealant. Refit the baffle plate on completion.
12 If removed, refit the oil level sensor as described in Chapter 5A Section 14.
13 Fit a new oil filter housing seal to the sump upper face, ensuring that it seats fully in the housing groove.
14 Apply a 3 to 4 mm bead of silicone sealant to the sump mating face, ensuring the sealant bead runs around the inside of the bolt holes **(see illustration)**. Position the sump on the cylinder block baseplate, then refit the retaining bolts. Progressively tighten the bolts to the specified torque.
15 Refit the three bolts (manual transmission models) or two bolts (automatic transmission models) securing the sump flange to the transmission casing, and tighten the bolts to the specified torque.
16 Reconnect the oil level sensor wiring connector.
17 Refit the engine oil dipstick.

18 Refit the exhaust system front pipe as described in Chapter 4B Section 18.
19 Fit a new oil filter, then fill the engine with oil as described in Chapter 1B Section 5.
20 Refit the engine undertray as described in Chapter 11 Section 24, then lower the vehicle to the ground.
21 Reconnect the battery negative terminal.

13 Oil pump – removal and refitting

Note: *The oil pump also incorporates the brake servo vacuum pump as an integral assembly.*

Removal

Note: *The following procedure assumes that the transmission and flywheel/driveplate have been removed. Although it is possible to remove the oil pump with the transmission and flywheel/driveplate installed, it is an awkward operation and clearance is extremely limited.*
1 Remove the sump as described in Section 12.
2 Screw one of the sump retaining bolts into the outer front bolt hole on the lower timing cover. Push the oil pump chain tensioner forward to remove the tension in the chain and retain it in the released position using a short length of stiff wire or similar, suitably bent to shape. Engage the wire with the tensioner arm, then wrap it around the sump bolt **(see illustrations)**.
3 Undo the oil pump sprocket retaining bolt, while preventing the sprocket from rotating

12.7 Disconnect the oil level sensor wiring connector

12.9a Undo the fifteen sump retaining bolts

12.9b A prying point is provided

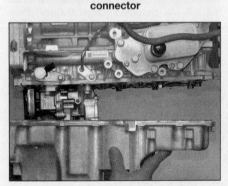

12.9c Remove the sump from the baseplate ...

12.9d ... and recover the oil filter housing seal

12.14 Apply a bead of sealant to the sump mating face, ensuring the bead runs around the inside of the bolt holes

with a suitable forked tool engaged with the sprocket holes **(see illustrations)**. Note that a new bolt will be required for refitting.

4 Using a suitable screwdriver, ease the sprocket off the pump shaft.

5 Undo the four bolts securing the oil pump to the cylinder block baseplate. Withdraw the pump from its location and recover the two rubber seals **(see illustrations)**. Note that new seals will be required for refitting.

6 The oil pump and integral vacuum pump is a sealed assembly. No internal components are available and no repair is possible.

Refitting

7 Thoroughly clean the pump and cylinder block baseplate contact areas, paying particular attention to the oil seal locations.

8 Fit a new rubber seal to each side of the pump, then refit the pump to the cylinder block baseplate **(see illustrations)**. Refit the four retaining bolts and tighten them to the specified torque.

9 Turn the oil pump shaft as necessary until the flat on the shaft aligns with the flat on the sprocket, then fit the sprocket to the pump shaft.

10 Fit a new sprocket retaining bolt and tighten it to the specified torque, then through the specified angle. Hold the sprocket stationary as the bolt is tightened using the method employed on removal.

11 Undo the sump retaining bolt used to retain the tensioner in the released position and allow the tensioner to contact and tension the chain.

12 Refit the sump as described in Section 12.

14 Oil pump sprocket, chain and tensioner – removal and refitting

Removal

1 Remove the lower timing cover as described in Section 6.

2 Undo the oil pump sprocket retaining bolt, while preventing the sprocket from rotating with a suitable forked tool engaged with the sprocket holes **(see illustrations 13.03a and 13.03b)**. Note that a new bolt will be required for refitting.

13.8a Fit a new rubber seal ...

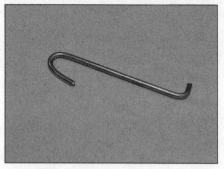

13.2a Make up a tool out of welding rod or stiff wire ...

13.3a Use a suitable forked tool to hold the sprocket ...

13.5a Undo the four oil pump retaining bolts ...

3 Using a suitable screwdriver, ease the sprocket off the pump shaft. Push the tensioner arm away from the oil pump chain and disengage the sprocket from the chain.

4 Disengage the chain from the crankshaft

13.8b ... to each side of the oil pump

13.2b ... to hold the chain tensioner arm in the released position

13.3b ... then undo and remove the sprocket retaining bolt

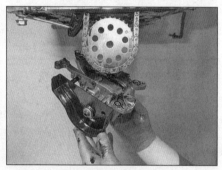

13.5b ... and withdraw the pump from the cylinder block baseplate

and remove the chain from the engine **(see illustration)**.

5 To remove the tensioner, undo the two retaining bolts and remove it from the cylinder block baseplate.

14.4 Disengage the chain from the crankshaft

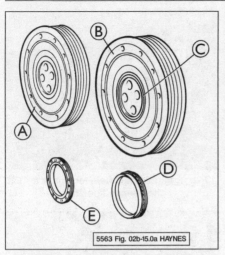

15.0a Crankshaft pulley details

A: *Crankshaft pulley with no groove – must be replaced.*
B: *Replacement pulley with groove (C).*
D: *Replacement seal with lip.*
E: *Flat faced seal – no longer available*

Refitting

6 Refitting is a reversal of removal, bearing in mind the following points:

a) *Tighten all retaining bolts to the specified torque and, where applicable, through the specified angle.*

b) *When refitting the oil pump sprocket, turn the oil pump shaft as necessary until the flat on the shaft aligns with the flat on the sprocket, then fit the sprocket to the pump shaft.*

c) *Refit the lower timing cover as described in Section 6.*

15 Crankshaft oil seals –
renewal
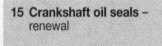

Front (crankshaft pulley end) oil seal

Caution: One of two versions of the oil seal maybe fitted. Replacement oil seals are only supplied with a lip. If a flat faced

15.7 Withdraw the crankshaft speed/ position sensor reluctor ring

oil seal is fitted then the crankshaft pulley must also be replaced if it has a flat face. Replacement crankshaft pulleys have a groove machine into them that matches the lip on the oil seal (see illustration).

1 Remove the crankshaft pulley as described in Section 4.

2 Carefully punch or drill a small hole in the seal. Screw in a self-tapping screw and pull on the screw with pliers to extract the seal.

3 Clean the oil seal seat with a wooden or plastic scraper.

4 Tap the new seal into position until it is flush with the outer face of the housing, using a wooden block or preferably, an oil seal installer tool.

5 Refit the crankshaft pulley as described in Section 4.

Rear (transmission end) oil seal

6 Remove the flywheel/driveplate as described in Section 17.

7 Carefully withdraw the crankshaft speed/ position sensor reluctor ring from the end of the crankshaft **(see illustration)**.

8 Carefully punch or drill a small hole in the seal. Screw in a self-tapping screw and pull on the screw with pliers to extract the seal **(see illustration)**.

9 Clean the oil seal seat with a wooden or plastic scraper.

10 Fit the new seal to the fitting tool supplied with the seal, so that the seal lip is spread open toward the crankshaft side **(see illustration)**.

15.8 Screw in a self-tapping screw and pull on the screw with pliers to extract the seal

11 Position the seal, together with the fitting tool over the end of the crankshaft. Remove the fitting tool then tap the seal into position using a suitable socket or tube, or a wooden block The seal will bottom out on the flange in the lower timing cover when correctly positioned **(see illustrations)**.

12 Refit the crankshaft speed/position sensor reluctor ring to the end of the crankshaft.

13 Refit the flywheel/driveplate as described in Section 17.

16 Oil cooler –
removal and refitting

Removal

1 Disconnect the battery negative lead as described in Chapter 5A Section 4.

2 Drain the cooling system as described in Chapter 1B Section 26.

3 Remove the driveshaft intermediate shaft and bracket as described in Chapter 8 Section 2.

4 Remove the exhaust system front pipe as described in Chapter 4B Section 18.

5 Release the retaining spring clip and disconnect the coolant hose from the oil cooler.

6 Undo the six retaining bolts **(see illustration)** and remove the oil cooler from the cylinder block. Recover the three rubber seals from the rear of the housing. Note that new seals will be required for refitting.

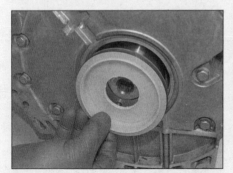

15.10 Fit the oil seal to the fitting tool, so that the seal lip is spread open toward the crankshaft side

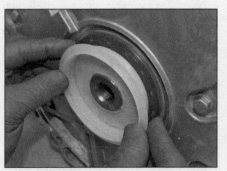

15.11a Position the seal, together with the fitting tool over the end of the crankshaft, then remove the tool

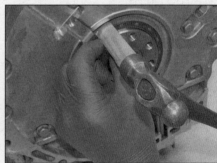

15.11b Tap the seal into position using a suitable wooden block or similar

16.6 Remove the bolts

17.4 Prevent the flywheel from turning by jamming the ring gear teeth using a suitable tool

Refitting

7 Fit the three new rubber seals to the rear of the oil cooler.

8 Position the oil cooler on the cylinder block and fit the six retaining bolts. Tighten the bolts to the specified torque.

9 Connect the coolant hose to the oil cooler and secure with the retaining spring clip.

10 Refit the exhaust system front pipe as described in Chapter 4B Section 18.

11 Refit the driveshaft intermediate shaft and bracket as described in Chapter 8 Section 2.

12 Lower the vehicle to the ground, then reconnect the battery negative terminal.

13 Refill the cooling system as described in Chapter 1B Section 26.

---

17 Flywheel/driveplate – removal, inspection and refitting

Removal

Note: *New flywheel/driveplate securing bolts must be used on refitting.*

Flywheel (manual transmission models)

1 Remove the transmission as described in Chapter 7A Section 8.

2 Remove the clutch assembly as described in Chapter 6 Section 6.

3 Although the flywheel bolt holes are offset so that the flywheel can only be fitted in one position, it will make refitting easier if alignment marks are made between the flywheel and the end of the crankshaft.

4 Prevent the flywheel from turning by jamming the ring gear teeth using a suitable tool **(see illustration)**.

5 Unscrew the eight retaining bolts, and remove the flywheel **(see illustrations)**.

Caution: Take care, as the flywheel is heavy.

Driveplate (automatic transmission models)

6 Remove the transmission as described in Chapter 7B Section 10, then remove the driveplate as described in paragraphs 4 and 5.

Inspection

Flywheel

7 A dual-mass flywheel is fitted and has the effect of reducing engine and transmission vibrations and harshness. The flywheel consists of a primary mass and a secondary mass constructed in such a way that the secondary mass is allowed to rotate slightly in relation to the primary mass. Springs within the assembly restrict this movement to set limits.

8 Dual-mass flywheels have earned an unenviable reputation for unreliability and have been known to fail at quite low mileages (sometimes as low as 20 000 miles).

9 Examine the flywheel for wear or chipping of the ring gear teeth. Renewal of the ring gear is not possible and if the wear or chipping is significant, a new flywheel will be required.

10 Examine the flywheel for scoring of the clutch face. If the clutch face is scored significantly, a new flywheel will be required.

11 Look through the bolt hole and inspection openings in the secondary mass and check

for any visible damage in the area of the centre bearing.

12 Place your thumbs on the clutch face of the secondary mass at the 3 o'clock and 9 o'clock positions and try to rock it. The maximum movement should not exceed 3 mm. Repeat this check with your thumbs at the 12 o'clock and 6 o'clock positions.

13 Rotate the secondary mass clockwise and anti-clockwise. It should move freely in both directions until spring resistance is felt, with no abnormal grating or rattling noises. The maximum rotational movement should not exceed a distance of eight teeth of the ring gear.

14 If there is any doubt about the condition of the flywheel, seek the advice of a Vauxhall/Opel dealer or engine reconditioning specialist. They will be able to advise if the flywheel is an acceptable condition, or whether renewal is necessary.

Driveplate

15 Closely examine the driveplate and ring gear teeth for signs of wear or damage and check the driveplate surface for any signs of cracks.

16 If there is any doubt about the condition of the driveplate, seek the advice of a Vauxhall/Opel dealer or engine reconditioning specialist.

17.5a Unscrew the retaining bolts ...

17.5b ... and remove the flywheel

Refitting

Flywheel

17 Offer the flywheel to the end of the crankshaft, and align the previously-made marks on the flywheel and crankshaft (if applicable).

18 Coat the threads of the new flywheel bolts with thread-locking compound (note that new bolts may be supplied ready-coated), then fit the bolts and tighten them to the specified torque, then through the specified angle whilst preventing the flywheel from turning as during removal **(see illustrations).**

19 Refit the clutch as described in Chapter 6 Section 6 then refit the transmission as described in Chapter 7A Section 8.

Driveplate

20 Clean the mating surfaces of the driveplate and crankshaft

21 Offer the driveplate and engage it on the crankshaft. Coat the threads of the new retaining bolts with thread-locking compound (note that new bolts may be supplied ready-coated), then fit the bolts and tighten them to the specified torque. Prevent the driveplate from turning as during removal.

22 Remove the locking tool and refit the transmission as described in Chapter 7B Section 10.

18 Engine/transmission mountings – inspection and renewal

Inspection

1 If improved access is required, firmly apply the handbrake, then jack up the front of the car and support it securely on axle stands (see *Jacking and vehicle support)*. Remove the engine undertray as described in Chapter 11 Section 24.

2 Check the mounting rubber to see if it is cracked, hardened or separated from the metal at any point; renew the mounting if any such damage or deterioration is evident.

3 Check that all the mounting's fasteners are securely tightened; use a torque wrench to check if possible.

17.18a Tighten the flywheel retaining bolts to the specified torque ...

4 Using a large screwdriver or a pry bar, check for wear in the mounting by carefully levering against it to check for free play; where this is not possible, enlist the aid of an assistant to move the engine/transmission unit back-and-forth, or from side-to-side, while you watch the mounting. While some free play is to be expected even from new components, excessive wear should be obvious. If excessive free play is found, check first that the fasteners are correctly secured, then renew any worn components as described below.

Renewal

Note: *Before slackening any of the engine mounting bolts/nuts, the relative positions of the mountings to their various brackets should be marked to ensure correct alignment upon refitting.*

Front mounting/torque link

5 Apply the handbrake, then jack up the front of the vehicle and support it on axle stands (see *Jacking and vehicle support)*.

6 Remove the engine undertray as described in Chapter 11 Section 24.

7 Slacken and remove the through-bolt securing the mounting and vibration damper to the subframe bracket **(see illustration).**

8 Undo the bolts securing the mounting bracket to the transmission, then manoeuvre the mounting and bracket out of position.

9 Check all components for signs of wear or damage, and renew as necessary.

10 Locate the mounting in the subframe, refit

17.18b ... then through the specified angle

the through bolt and tighten the bolt finger tight at this stage.

11 Refit the mounting bracket to the transmission and tighten its bolts to the specified torque.

12 Tighten the through bolt to the specified torque.

13 On completion, refit the engine undertray and lower the vehicle to the ground.

Rear mounting/torque link

14 Apply the handbrake, then jack up the front of the vehicle and support it on axle stands (see *Jacking and vehicle support)*.

15 Remove the engine undertray.

16 Undo the three bolts securing the mounting bracket to the transmission and the through-bolt securing the mounting to the bracket **(see illustration).**

17 Undo the nuts and remove the two bolts securing the mounting to the subframe **(see illustration).** Manoeuvre the mounting and bracket out from under the car.

18 Refit the bracket to the transmission and tighten the bolts to the specified torque.

19 Locate the new mounting in position. Insert the bolts and tighten the bolt/nuts to the specified torque.

20 On completion, refit the engine undertray and lower the vehicle to the ground.

Right-hand mounting

21 Apply the handbrake, then jack up the front of the vehicle and support it on axle stands (see *Jacking and vehicle support)*.

22 Remove the air cleaner assembly as described in Chapter 4B Section 3.

18.7 Front mounting/torque link through-bolt

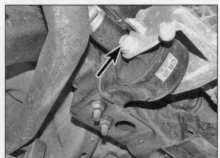

18.16 Rear mounting/torque link through-bolt

18.17 Rear mounting/torque link bracket-to-subframe mounting bolt nuts (arrowed)

23 Attach a suitable hoist and lifting tackle to the engine lifting brackets on the cylinder head, and support the weight of the engine.

24 Mark the position of the three bolts securing the mounting bracket to the engine bracket and undo the bolts. Undo the three bolts securing the mounting to the body and remove the mounting assembly **(see illustrations)**. If necessary, undo the three bolts and remove the mounting bracket from the engine.

25 Place the mounting assembly in position and refit the bolts securing the mounting to the body. Tighten the bolts to the specified torque. Align the mounting in its original position, then tighten the three mounting bracket bolts to the specified torque.

26 Remove the hoist, then refit the air cleaner as described in Chapter 4B Section 3.

27 On completion, lower the vehicle to the ground.

Left-hand mounting

28 Remove the battery and battery box as described in Chapter 5A Section 4.

29 Apply the handbrake, then jack up the front of the vehicle and support it on axle stands (see *Jacking and vehicle support*).

30 Remove the left-hand front roadwheel, then remove the wheel arch liner from under the front wing.

31 Attach a suitable hoist and lifting tackle to the engine lifting brackets on the cylinder head, and support the weight of the engine. Alternatively, support the transmission on a jack with a block of wood between the transmission and jack head.

32 Working under the front wing, unscrew the nut securing the mounting to the body.

33 From within the engine compartment,

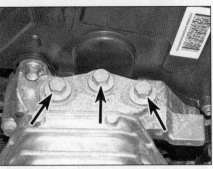

18.24a Right-hand mounting bracket-to-engine bracket bolts …

18.33 Left-hand mounting bracket-to-transmission bracket retaining bolts

18.24b … and mounting-to-body bolts

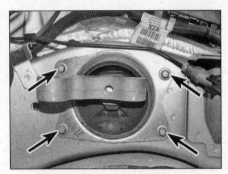

18.34 Left-hand mounting-to-body retaining bolts – shown with engine/transmission removed

unscrew the three bolts securing the mounting bracket to the transmission bracket **(see illustration)**.

34 Undo the four bolts securing the mounting to the body and the three bolts securing the transmission bracket to the transmission **(see illustration)**. Remove the mounting assembly from the car.

35 Locate the mounting brackets in position

then refit the nut and bolts and tighten them to the specified torque.

36 Disconnect the hoist and lifting tackle, or remove the jack, as applicable.

37 Refit the wheel arch liner and roadwheel, then lower the vehicle to the ground and tighten the wheel nuts to the specified torque.

38 Refit the battery box and battery as described in Chapter 5A Section 4.

Chapter 2 Part C
2.0 litre (A20) diesel engine in-car repair procedures

Contents

Degrees of difficulty

Easy, suitable for novice with little experience	**Fairly easy,** suitable for beginner with some experience	**Fairly difficult,** suitable for competent DIY mechanic	**Difficult,** suitable for experienced DIY mechanic	**Very difficult,** suitable for expert DIY or professional

Specifications

General

Engine type.	Four-cylinder, in-line, water-cooled. Double overhead camshaft, belt-driven
Manufacturer's engine code*	LBS/A20DTH, LBX/A20DTJ, LBR/A20DT and LHV/A20DTE
Bore	83.0 mm
Stroke	90.4 mm
Capacity	1956 cc
Compression ratio	16.5: 1
Firing order	1-3-4-2 (No 1 cylinder at timing belt end of engine)
Direction of crankshaft rotation	Clockwise (viewed from timing belt end of engine)

For details of engine code location, see 'Vehicle identification 13 Section 3 ' in the Reference Chapter.

Compression pressures

Minimum	26.0 bar
Maximum difference between any two cylinders.	2.6 bar

Lubrication system

Minimum oil pressure at 100°C	1.0 bar at idle speed
Oil pump type.	Rotor-type, driven by crankshaft pulley/vibration damper from crankshaft

Torque wrench settings

	Nm	lbf ft
Auxiliary drivebelt idler pulley bolt	22	16
Auxiliary drivebelt tensioner assembly bolts	22	16
Camshaft drive gear bolts*:		
Stage 1	30	22
Air conditioning compressor mounting bracket-to-cylinder block/sump . .	50	37
Stage 2	Angle-tighten a further 52°	
Camshaft housing closure bolts.	16	12
Camshaft housing-to-cylinder head.	25	18
Camshaft sprocket bolt	120	89
Connecting rod big-end bearing cap bolt*:		
Stage 1	25	18
Stage 2	Angle-tighten a further 60°	

Torque wrench settings (continued)

	Nm	lbf ft
Crankshaft pulley/vibration damper bolts	25	18
Crankshaft sprocket bolt*†	380	280
Crankshaft rear oil seal housing	9	7
Cylinder head bolts*:		
With M14 RIBE bolts:		
Stage 1	20	15
Stage 2	65	48
Stage 3	Angle-tighten a further 90°	
Stage 4	Angle-tighten a further 90°	
Stage 5	Angle-tighten a further 90°	
With Torx T60 bolts:		
Stage 1	20	15
Stage 2	65	48
Stage 3	Angle-tighten a further 90°	
Stage 4	Angle-tighten a further 90°	
Stage 5	Angle-tighten a further 90°	
Stage 6	Angle-tighten a further 90°	
Engine mountings:		
Front mounting/torque link:		
Mounting-to-transmission:		
M32 manual transmission	62	46
F40 manual transmission and AF40 automatic transmission . . .	100	74
Mounting to subframe	100	74
Left-hand mounting:		
Mounting-to-body bolts/nut	22	16
Mounting bracket-to-transmission bracket:		
M32 manual transmission	80	59
F40 manual transmission and AF40 automatic transmission*:		
Stage 1	50	37
Stage 2	Angle-tighten a further 60°	
Stage 3	Angle-tighten a further 15°	
Transmission bracket-to-transmission	100	74
Rear mounting/torque link:		
Mounting bracket-to-transmission:		
M32 manual transmissions	62	46
F40 manual transmissions and AF40 automatic transmission . .	100	74
Mounting-to-subframe	110	81
Mounting-to-transmission bracket	100	74
Right-hand mounting:		
Engine bracket-to-engine bolts:		
Long bolts	48	35
Short bolts	24	17
Mounting-to-body bolts:		
Long bolts	58	43
Short bolt	63	46
Mounting-to-engine bracket bolts	58	43
Engine-to-transmission unit bolts	60	44
Flywheel/driveplate bolts*	160	118
High-pressure fuel pump sprocket nut*	50	37
Intermediate shaft bearing housing support bracket bolts	55	41
Main bearing cap bolts*:		
Stage 1	25	18
Stage 2	Angle-tighten a further 100°	
Oil cooler to block	25	18
Oil filter housing-to-cylinder block	25	18
Oil pump housing-to-cylinder block	9	7
Roadwheel nuts	150	111
Sump bolts:		
M6 bolts	9	7
M8 bolts	25	18
M10 bolts	40	30
Timing belt idler pulley bolt	25	18
Timing belt tensioner bolt	25	18
Timing belt upper cover bolts	9	7

*Use new nuts/bolts

† Left-hand thread

1 General Information

How to use this Chapter

1 This Chapter describes the repair procedures which can reasonably be carried out on the engine while it remains in the vehicle. If the engine has been removed from the vehicle and is being dismantled as described in Chapter 2E, any preliminary dismantling procedures can be ignored.

2 Note that, while it may be possible physically to overhaul items such as the piston/connecting rod assemblies while the engine is in the vehicle, such tasks are not usually carried out as separate operations, and usually require the execution of several additional procedures (not to mention the cleaning of components and of oil ways); for this reason, all such tasks are classed as major overhaul procedures, and are described in Chapter 2E.

3 Chapter 2E, Section 4 describes the removal of the engine/transmission unit from the vehicle, and the full overhaul procedures which can then be carried out.

Engine description

4 The 2.0 litre DOHC diesel engine is of the sixteen-valve, in-line four-cylinder, double overhead camshaft type, mounted transversely at the front of the car, with the transmission on its left-hand end.

5 The crankshaft is supported within the cylinder block on five shell-type main bearings. Thrustwashers are fitted to number 3 main bearing, to control crankshaft endfloat.

6 The connecting rods rotate on horizontally-split bearing shells at their big-ends. The pistons are attached to the connecting rods by gudgeon pins, which are retained by circlips. The aluminium-alloy pistons are fitted with three piston rings – two compression rings and scraper-type oil control ring.

7 The camshafts are situated in a separate housing bolted to the top of the cylinder head. The exhaust camshaft is driven by the crankshaft via a toothed composite rubber timing belt (which also drives the high-pressure fuel pump and the coolant pump). The exhaust camshaft drives the inlet camshaft via a spur gear. Each cylinder has four valves (two inlet and two exhaust), operated via followers which are supported at their pivot ends by hydraulic self-adjusting tappets. One camshaft operates the inlet valves, and the other operates the exhaust valves.

8 The inlet and exhaust valves are each closed by a single valve spring, and operate in guides pressed into the cylinder head.

9 Lubrication is by pressure-feed from a rotor-type oil pump, which is mounted on the right-hand end of the crankshaft. The pump draws oil through a strainer located in the sump, and then forces it through an externally mounted full-flow cartridge-type filter. The oil flows into galleries in the cylinder block/crankcase, from where it is distributed to the crankshaft (main bearings) and camshafts. The big-end bearings are supplied with oil via internal drillings in the crankshaft, while the camshaft bearings also receive a pressurised supply. The camshaft lobes and valves are lubricated by splash, as are all other engine components.

10 A semi-closed crankcase ventilation system is employed; crankcase fumes are drawn from the oil separator attached to the cylinder block via a hose to the camshaft housing. The fumes are then passed via a hose to the inlet manifold.

Repair operations possible with the engine in the car

11 The following operations can be carried out without having to remove the engine from the car.

a) Removal and refitting of the cylinder head.
b) Removal and refitting of the timing belt, tensioner, idler pulleys and sprockets.
c) Renewal of the camshaft oil seal.
d) Removal and refitting of the camshaft housing.
e) Removal and refitting of the camshafts and followers.
f) Removal and refitting of the sump.
g) Removal and refitting of the connecting rods and pistons*.
h) Removal and refitting of the oil pump.
i) Removal and refitting of the oil filter housing.
j) Renewal of the crankshaft oil seals.
k) Renewal of the engine mountings.
l) Removal and refitting of the flywheel/driveplate.

*Although the operation marked with an asterisk can be carried out with the engine in the car (after removal of the sump), it is preferable for the engine to be removed, in the interests of cleanliness and improved access. For this reason, the procedure is described in Chapter 2E.

2 Compression and leakdown tests – description and interpretation

Compression test

Note: *A compression tester specifically designed for diesel engines must be used for this test.*

Note: *The battery must be in a good state of charge, the air filter must be clean, and the engine should be at normal operating temperature.*

1 When engine performance is down, or if misfiring occurs which cannot be attributed to the fuel system, a compression test can provide diagnostic clues as to the engine's condition. If the test is performed regularly, it can give warning of trouble before any other symptoms become apparent.

2 A compression tester specifically intended for diesel engines must be used, because of the higher pressures involved. The tester is connected to an adapter which screws into the glow plug holes. It is unlikely to be worthwhile buying such a tester for occasional use, but it may be possible to borrow or hire one – if not, have the test performed by a Vauxhall/Opel dealer, or suitably-equipped garage. If the necessary equipment is available, proceed as follows.

3 Remove the glow plugs as described in Chapter 5A Section 17, then disconnect the wiring connector from the crankshaft sensor (see Chapter 4B, Section 8).

4 Screw the compression tester adapter in to the glow plug hole of No 1 cylinder.

5 With the help of an assistant, crank the engine on the starter motor; after one or two revolutions, the compression pressure should build-up to a maximum figure, and then stabilise. Record the highest reading obtained.

6 Repeat the test on the remaining cylinders, recording the pressure in each.

7 All cylinders should produce very similar pressures; any difference greater than the maximum figure given in the Specifications indicates the existence of a fault. Note that the compression should build-up quickly in a healthy engine; low compression on the first stroke, followed by gradually-increasing pressure on successive strokes, indicates worn piston rings. A low compression reading on the first stroke, which does not build-up during successive strokes, indicates leaking valves or a blown head gasket (a cracked head could also be the cause). **Note:** *The cause of poor compression is less easy to establish on a diesel engine than on a petrol one. The effect of introducing oil into the cylinders ('wet' testing) is not conclusive, because there is a risk that the oil will sit in the recess on the piston crown instead of passing to the rings.*

8 On completion of the test refit the glow plugs as described in Chapter 5A, Section 17, and reconnect the wiring connector to the crankshaft sensor.

Leakdown test

9 A leakdown test measures the rate at which compressed air fed into the cylinder is lost. It is an alternative to a compression test, and in many ways it is better, since the escaping air provides easy identification of where pressure loss is occurring (piston rings, valves or head gasket).

10 The equipment needed for leakdown testing is unlikely to be available to the home mechanic. If poor compression is suspected, have the test performed by a Vauxhall/Opel dealer, or suitably-equipped garage.

3.0a Vauxhall/Opel special tool EN-46788 (or equivalent) is required to set the TDC position for No 1 piston. . .

3.0b. . .together with Vauxhall/Opel special tool EN-46789 (or equivalent) to set the camshaft position

3 Top Dead Centre (TDC) for No 1 piston – locating

Note: *To accurately determine the TDC position for No 1 piston, it will be necessary to use Vauxhall/Opel special tool EN-46788 (or suitable equivalent) to set the crankshaft at the TDC position, together with the camshaft positioning tool, Vauxhall/Opel special tool EN-46789 (or suitable equivalent)* **(see illustrations).**

1 In its travel up and down its cylinder bore, Top Dead Centre (TDC) is the highest point that each piston reaches as the crankshaft rotates. While each piston reaches TDC both at the top of the compression stroke and again at the top of the exhaust stroke, for the purpose of timing the engine, TDC refers to the piston position of No 1 cylinder at the top of its compression stroke.

2 Number 1 piston (and cylinder) is at the right-hand (timing belt) end of the engine, and its TDC position is located as follows. Note that the crankshaft rotates clockwise when viewed from the right-hand side of the car.

3 Disconnect the battery negative terminal (refer to Chapter 5A, Section 4), then lift off the plastic cover over the top of the engine.

4 Remove the crankshaft pulley/vibration damper as described in Section 5.

5 Remove the air cleaner assembly and turbocharger intake duct as described in Chapter 4B, Section 3.

6 Unscrew the closure bolt from the valve timing checking hole in the camshaft housing **(see illustration)**.

7 Screw the camshaft positioning tool (Vauxhall/Opel special tool EN-46789) into the valve timing checking hole **(see illustration)**.

8 Using a socket and extension bar on the crankshaft sprocket bolt, rotate the crankshaft in the normal direction of rotation until the spring-loaded plunger of the positioning tool slides into engagement with the slot in the camshaft. There will be an audible click from the tool when this happens.

9 Unscrew the bolt from the lower left-hand side of the oil pump housing and screw in the fastening stud of Vauxhall/Opel special tool EN-46788 **(see illustration)**.

10 Fit the positioning ring of tool EN-46788 over the fastening stud and engage it with the crankshaft sprocket. Ensure that the hole in the positioning ring engages with the lug on the sprocket. Secure the tool in position with the retaining bolt and nut **(see illustration)**.

11 With the crankshaft positioning ring in place and the camshaft positioning tool engaged with the slot in the camshaft, the engine is positioned with No 1 piston at TDC on compression.

4 Valve timing – checking and adjustment

Note: *To check and adjust the valve timing, it will be necessary to use Vauxhall/Opel special tool EN-46788 (or suitable equivalent) to set the crankshaft at the TDC position. Additionally, it will be necessary to use Vauxhall/Opel special tools EN-46789 and EN46789-100 (or suitable equivalents) to lock the camshafts in the TDC position.*

Checking

1 Disconnect the battery negative terminal (refer to Chapter 5A, Section 4), then lift off the plastic cover over the top of the engine.

2 Unscrew the closure bolt from the valve timing checking hole in the exhaust side of camshaft housing **(see illustration 3.6)**.

3 Screw the exhaust camshaft positioning tool (Vauxhall/Opel special tool EN-46789) into the valve timing checking hole **(see illustration 3.7)**.

4 Unscrew the closure bolt from the valve timing checking hole in the inlet side of the camshaft housing. The closure bolt is located below the fuel pressure sensor on the fuel rail **(see illustration)**.

5 Screw the inlet camshaft positioning tool (Vauxhall/Opel special tool EN-46789-100) into the valve timing checking hole.

3.6 Unscrew the closure bolt from the valve timing checking hole in the camshaft housing

3.7 Screw the camshaft positioning tool into the valve timing checking hole

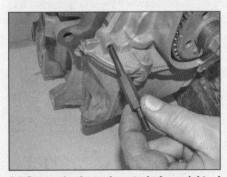

3.9 Screw the fastening stud of special tool EN-46788 into the oil pump housing

3.10 Positioning ring of tool EN-46788 attached to the fastening stud and crankshaft sprocket

4.4 Unscrew the closure bolt from the valve timing checking hole in the inlet side of the camshaft housing

6 Remove the crankshaft pulley/vibration damper as described in Section 5.

7 Using a socket and extension bar on the crankshaft sprocket bolt, rotate the crankshaft in the normal direction of rotation until the spring-loaded plungers of the positioning tools slide into engagement with the slots in the camshafts. There will be an audible click from the tools when this happens.

8 Unscrew the bolt from the lower left-hand side of the oil pump housing and screw in the fastening stud of Vauxhall/Opel special tool EN-46788 **(see illustration 3.9)**.

9 Fit the positioning ring of tool EN-46788 over the fastening stud and engage it with the crankshaft sprocket. Ensure that the hole in the positioning ring engages with the lug on the sprocket. Secure the tool in position with the retaining bolt and nut **(see illustration 3.10)**.

10 If it is not possible to fit the positioning ring of tool EN-46788 as described, or if the camshaft positioning tools did not engage with the camshaft slots, adjust the valve timing as follows.

Adjustment

11 Remove the timing belt as described in Section 6.

12 Using a socket and extension bar on the crankshaft sprocket bolt, rotate the crankshaft anti-clockwise by 90°. This will position all the pistons half way down their bores, and prevent any chance of the valves touching the piston crowns during the following procedure.

13 Remove the inlet and exhaust camshaft positioning tools from the valve timing checking holes.

14 Using a suitable tool engaged with the timing belt sprocket on the exhaust camshaft, rotate the sprocket approximately 90° clockwise. Vauxhall/Opel special tools EN-47634 and EN-956-1 are available for this purpose, however, a home-made tool can easily be fabricated **(see Tool Tip in Section 7)**. Take care not to damage the camshaft sensor with the tool as the sprocket is rotated.

15 Screw the inlet camshaft positioning tool (Vauxhall/Opel special tool EN-46789-100) into the valve timing checking hole.

16 Rotate the camshaft sprocket clockwise until the spring-loaded plunger of the positioning tool slides into engagement with the slot in the inlet camshaft. There will be an

audible click from the tool when this happens.

17 Remove the throttle housing intake duct as described in Chapter 4B, Section 3.

18 Undo the three retaining bolts and remove the oil filter housing.

19 Remove the braking system vacuum pump as described in Chapter 9, Section 22.

20 Working through the oil filler housing aperture, and using the holding tool to prevent rotation of the camshaft, slacken the inlet camshaft drive gear retaining bolt. Working through the vacuum pump aperture, slacken the exhaust camshaft drive gear retaining bolt in the same way.

21 Screw the exhaust camshaft positioning tool (Vauxhall/Opel special tool EN-46789) into the valve timing checking hole.

22 Rotate the camshaft sprocket clockwise until the spring-loaded plunger of the positioning tool slides into engagement with the slot in the exhaust camshaft. There will be an audible click from the tool when this happens.

23 Hold the camshaft sprocket with the tool and tighten both drive gear retaining bolts to the specified torque.

24 Remove the positioning tool from the inlet camshaft and refit the closure bolt. Tighten the bolt to the specified torque.

25 Refit the oil filter housing to the camshaft housing using a new gasket, refit the retaining bolts and tighten the bolts to the specified torque.

26 Refit the braking system vacuum pump as described in Chapter 9, Section 22.

27 Refit the throttle housing intake duct as described in Chapter 4B, Section 3.

28 Refit the timing belt as described in Section 6.

5 Crankshaft pulley/vibration damper – removal and refitting

Removal

1 Apply the handbrake, then jack up the front of the vehicle and support it on axle stands (see *Jacking and vehicle support*). Remove the right-hand front roadwheel.

2 Remove the engine undertray and the front wheel arch liner on the right-hand side as described in Chapter 11, Section 24.

3 Remove the auxiliary drivebelt as described

5.4 Crankshaft pulley/vibration damper retaining bolts

in Chapter 1B, Section 22. Prior to removal, mark the direction of rotation on the belt to ensure the belt is refitted the same way around.

4 Undo the four bolts securing the pulley to the crankshaft sprocket and remove the pulley from the sprocket **(see illustration)**.

Refitting

5 Locate the crankshaft pulley on the sprocket, ensuring that the hole on the rear face of the pulley engages with the lug on the sprocket.

6 Refit the four retaining bolts and tighten them progressively to the specified torque.

7 Refit the auxiliary drivebelt as described in Chapter 1B, Section 22 using the mark made prior to removal to ensure the belt is fitted the correct way around.

8 Refit the wheel arch liner, engine undertray and roadwheel, then lower the car to the ground and tighten the wheel nuts to the specified torque.

6 Timing belt – removal and refitting

Note: *The timing belt must be removed and refitted with the engine cold.*

Removal

1 Position No 1 cylinder at TDC on its compression stroke as described in Section 3.

2 Unclip the wiring harness from the side of the upper timing belt cover. Unscrew the seven retaining bolts and lift off the upper timing belt cover **(see illustrations)**.

3 Place a trolley jack beneath the right-hand

6.2a Unclip the wiring harness from the side of the upper timing belt cover. . .

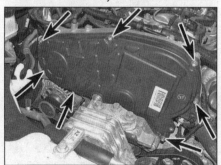

6.2b. . .unscrew the seven retaining bolts. . .

6.2c. . .and lift off the upper timing belt cover

6.5a Undo the two lower bolts. . .

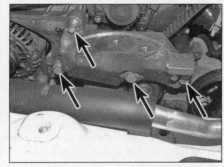

6.5b. . .and the four upper bolts. . .

6.5c. . .and remove the engine bracket from the engine

end of the engine with a block of wood on the jack head. Raise the jack until it is supporting the weight of the engine.

4 Remove the right-hand engine mounting as described in Section 18.

5 Undo the two lower bolts, and the four upper bolts, and remove the engine bracket from the engine **(see illustrations)**.

6 Undo the nut and bolt and remove the crankshaft positioning tool (EN-46788) from the crankshaft sprocket.

7 Slacken the timing belt tensioner retaining bolt and allow the tensioner to retract, relieving the tension on the timing belt.

8 Slide the timing belt from its sprockets and remove it from the engine. If the belt is to be re-used, use white paint or similar to mark the direction of rotation on the belt. **Do not** rotate the crankshaft or camshafts until the timing belt has been refitted.

9 Check the timing belt carefully for any signs of uneven wear, splitting or oil contamination, and renew it if there is the slightest doubt about its condition. If the engine is undergoing an overhaul and is approaching the manufacturer's specified interval for belt renewal (see Chapter 1B) renew the belt as a matter of course, regardless of its apparent condition. If signs of oil contamination are found, trace the source of the oil leak and rectify it, then wash down the engine timing belt area and all related components to remove all traces of oil.

Refitting

10 On reassembly, thoroughly clean the timing belt sprockets and tensioner/idler pulleys.

11 Using a suitable tool to hold the timing belt sprocket, slacken the sprocket retaining bolt until the sprocket is free to move on the

camshaft. Vauxhall/Opel special tools EN-47634 and EN-956-1 are available for this purpose, however, a home-made tool can easily be fabricated **(see Tool Tip in Section 7)**.

12 Place the timing belt in position over the crankshaft sprocket. If the original belt is being refitted, ensure that the arrow mark made on removal points in the normal direction of rotation, as before.

13 Check that the camshaft and crankshaft are still positioned with No 1 piston at TDC on compression as described in Section 3, and with the camshaft positioning tool still in place. Now refit the crankshaft positioning tool.

14 Check the timing belt tensioner bolt is still slackened.

15 As the timing belt is fitted, ensure that the marks on the edge of the belt align with the marks on the sprockets **(see illustrations)**. Start by fitting the belt over the crankshaft sprocket, then over the tensioner pulley, coolant pump sprocket, fuel pump sprocket, camshaft sprocket and finally over the idler pulley. Do not twist the belt sharply while refitting it. Ensure that the belt teeth are correctly seated centrally in the sprockets.

16 Screw in a suitable bolt, approximately 50 mm in length, into the threaded hole directly below the timing belt tensioner. Using a screwdriver resting on the bolt as a pivot, move the adjusting lever on the tensioner until the tensioner pointer is aligned with the mark on the backplate. Hold the tensioner in this position and tighten the tensioner retaining bolt **(see illustrations)**.

6.15a Ensure that the marks on the edge of the timing belt align with the marks on the crankshaft sprocket. . .

6.15b. . .fuel pump sprocket. . .

6.15c. . .and camshaft sprocket

6.16a Using a screwdriver resting on a pivot bolt, move the adjusting lever on the tensioner. . .

6.16b. . .until the tensioner pointer is aligned with the mark on the backplate

17 Retain the camshaft sprocket using the holding tool, and tighten the retaining bolt to the specified torque.

18 Remove the crankshaft and camshaft positioning tools.

19 Using a socket on the crankshaft sprocket bolt, rotate the crankshaft smoothly through two complete turns (720°) in the normal direction of rotation to settle the timing belt in position. Stop rotating the crankshaft just before completing the second turn.

20 Refit the camshaft positioning tool and continue turning the crankshaft until the camshaft positioning tool engages.

21 Check that it is possible to refit the positioning ring of tool EN-46788 over the fastening stud and engage it with the lug on the crankshaft sprocket. If it is not possible to refit the positioning ring, repeat the timing belt refitting procedure.

22 When all is correct, remove all the positioning tools and remove the tensioner position pivot bolt. Refit the bolt removed from the oil pump housing and tighten it to the specified torque. Refit the closure plug to the camshaft housing and tighten to the specified torque.

23 Place the engine bracket in position and refit the two lower bolts, and the four upper bolts. Tighten the bolts to the specified torque.

24 Refit the upper timing belt cover and tighten the retaining bolts to the specified torque. Clip the wiring harness back into position.

25 Refit the right-hand engine mounting as described in Section 18.

26 Refit the air cleaner assembly and intake duct as described in Chapter 4B, Section 3.

27 Refit the crankshaft pulley/vibration damper as described in Section 5, then refit the auxiliary drivebelt as described in Chapter 1B, Section 22.

28 Refit the plastic cover to the top of the engine.

29 Refit the wheel arch liner, engine undertray and roadwheel, then lower the car to the ground and tighten the wheel nuts to the specified torque.

---

7 Timing belt sprockets, tensioner and idler pulley – removal and refitting

Note: *Certain special tools will be required for the removal and refitting of the sprockets. Read through the entire procedure to familiarise yourself with the work involved, then either obtain the manufacturer's special tools, or use the alternatives described.*

Camshaft sprocket

Removal

1 Remove the timing belt as described in Section 6, then remove camshaft positioning tool from the valve timing checking hole.

2 It will now be necessary to hold the camshaft sprocket to enable the retaining bolt

to be removed. Vauxhall/Opel special tools EN-47634 and EN-956-1 are available for this purpose, however, a home-made tool can easily be fabricated **(see Tool Tip)**.

3 Engage the tool with the holes in the camshaft sprocket, taking care not to damage the camshaft sensor located behind the sprocket

4 Unscrew the retaining bolt and remove the sprocket from the end of the camshaft.

Refitting

5 Prior to refitting check the oil seal for signs of damage or leakage. If necessary, renew it as described in Section 8.

6 Refit the sprocket to the camshaft end, aligning its cut-out with the locating peg, and fit the retaining bolt finger tight only at this stage. Final tightening is carried out after the timing belt has been fitted and tensioned.

7 Refit the camshaft positioning tool to the valve timing checking hole. If necessary, rotate the camshaft slightly, by means of the sprocket, until the tool audibly engages.

8 Proceed with the timing belt refitting procedure as described in Section 6, paragraphs 10 to 29.

Crankshaft sprocket

Note: *The crankshaft sprocket retaining bolt is extremely tight. Ensure that the holding tool used to prevent rotation as the bolt is slackened is of sturdy construction and securely attached.*

Note: *A new sprocket retaining bolt will be required for refitting.*

Removal

9 Remove the timing belt as described in Section 6.

10 It will now be necessary to hold the crankshaft sprocket to enable the retaining bolt to be removed. Vauxhall special tools EN-47630 and EN-977 are available for this purpose, however, a home-made tool similar to that described in paragraph 2, can easily be fabricated.

11 Using the crankshaft pulley retaining bolts, securely attach the tool to the crankshaft sprocket. With the help of an assistant, hold the sprocket stationary and unscrew the retaining bolt. **Note:** *The sprocket retaining bolt has a **left-hand thread** and is unscrewed by turning it clockwise.*

To make a sprocket holding tool, obtain two lengths of steel strip about 6 mm thick by about 30 mm wide or similar, one 600 mm long, the other 200 mm long (all dimensions are approximate). Bolt the two strips together to form a forked end, leaving the bolt slack so that the shorter strip can pivot freely. At the other end of each 'prong' of the fork, drill a suitable hole and fit a nut and bolt to allow the tool to engage with the spokes in the sprocket.

12 Remove the bolt and washer and slide the sprocket off the end of the crankshaft **(see illustrations)**. Note that a new bolt will be required for refitting.

Refitting

13 Align the sprocket location key with the crankshaft groove and slide the sprocket into position. Fit the new retaining bolt and washer.

14 Hold the sprocket stationary using the holding tool and tighten the retaining bolt to the specified torque. Remove the holding tool.

15 Refit the timing belt as described in Section 6.

High-pressure fuel pump sprocket

Note: *A new sprocket retaining nut will be required for refitting.*

Removal

16 Remove the timing belt as described in Section 6.

17 It will now be necessary to hold the fuel pump sprocket to enable the retaining nut to be

7.12a Remove the bolt and washer. . .

7.12b . . .and slide the sprocket off the end of the crankshaft

7.18 Engage the holding tool with the holes in the fuel pump sprocket and undo the retaining nut

7.19 Use a suitable puller to release the fuel pump sprocket taper

19 Attach a suitable puller to the threaded holes in the fuel pump sprocket using bolts and washers similar to the arrangement shown **(see illustration)**.

20 Tighten the puller centre bolt to release the sprocket from the taper on the pump shaft. Once the taper releases, remove the puller and withdraw the sprocket. Collect the Woodruff key from the pump shaft **(see illustrations)**.

Refitting

21 Clean the fuel pump shaft and the sprocket hub ensuring that all traces of oil or grease are removed.

22 Refit the Woodruff key to the pump shaft, then locate the sprocket in position. Fit the new retaining nut.

23 Hold the sprocket stationary using the holding tool and tighten the retaining nut to the specified torque. Remove the holding tool.

24 Refit the timing belt as described in Section 6.

removed. Vauxhall special tools KM-6347 and KM-956-1 are available for this purpose, however, a home-made tool similar to that described in paragraph 2, can easily be fabricated.

18 Engage the tool with the holes in the fuel pump sprocket and undo the sprocket retaining nut **(see illustration)**. Note that a new nut will be required for refitting.

7.20a Once the taper releases, withdraw the sprocket. . .

7.20b. . .and collect the Woodruff key from the pump shaft

Tensioner assembly

Removal

25 Remove the timing belt as described in Section 6.

26 Slacken and remove the retaining bolt and remove the tensioner assembly from the engine **(see illustrations)**.

Refitting

27 Fit the tensioner to the engine, making sure that the slot on the tensioner backplate is correctly located over the peg on the engine bracket **(see illustration)**.

28 Clean the threads of the retaining bolt and apply thread locking compound to the bolt threads. Screw in the retaining bolt, set the tensioner in the retracted position and tighten the retaining bolt.

29 Refit the timing belt as described in Section 6.

7.26a Slacken and remove the retaining bolt. . .

7.26b. . .and remove the timing belt tensioner assembly

Idler pulley

Removal

30 Remove the timing belt as described in Section 6.

31 Slacken and remove the retaining bolt and remove the idler pulley from the engine **(see illustration)**.

Refitting

32 Refit the idler pulley and tighten the retaining bolt to the specified torque.

33 Refit the timing belt as described in Section 6.

7.27 The slot on the tensioner backplate must locate over the peg on the engine bracket

7.31 Slacken and remove the retaining bolt and remove the idler pulley from the engine

8 Camshaft oil seal – renewal

1 Remove the camshaft sprocket as described in Section 7.

2 Carefully punch or drill a small hole in the oil seal. Screw in a self-tapping screw, and pull on the screw with pliers to extract the seal.

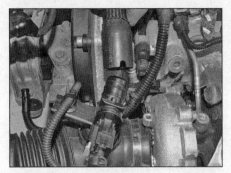

9.3 Disconnect the crankcase ventilation hose from the heating element

9.4a Unclip the wiring harness from the crankcase ventilation pipe. . .

9.4b. . .then undo the upper bolt. . .

3 Clean the seal housing, and polish off any burrs or raised edges which may have caused the seal to fail in the first place.

4 Press the new oil seal into position using a suitable tubular drift (such as a socket) which bears only on the hard outer edge of the seal. Take care not to damage the seal lips during fitting; note that the seal lips should face inwards.

5 Refit the camshaft sprocket as described in Section 7.

9.4c. . .and lower bolt at the rear. . .

9.4d. . .and move the crankcase ventilation pipe to one side

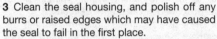

9 Camshaft housing – removal and refitting

Removal

1 Remove the timing belt as described in Section 6.

2 Remove the EGR valve cooler as described in Chapter 4C Section 3.

3 Disconnect the crankcase ventilation hose from the heating element **(see illustration)**.

4 Unclip the wiring harness from the crankcase ventilation pipe, then undo the two bolts and move the crankcase ventilation pipe to one side **(see illustrations)**.

5 Disconnect the fuel return hose quick-release fitting, then undo the bolts securing the engine lifting eye and hose/cable support bracket and move the bracket clear of the fuel pump **(see illustrations)**.

6 Disconnect the quick-release fitting and detach the vacuum servo unit vacuum hose from the vacuum pump. Disconnect the

9.5a Disconnect the fuel return hose quick-release fitting. . .

smaller vacuum hose from the outlet on the side of the pump.

7 Disconnect the wiring connectors from the four glow plugs **(see illustration)**.

8 Disconnect the wiring harness connector

9.5b. . .then undo the bolt and move the engine lifting eye and support bracket clear of the fuel pump

above the inlet manifold, then undo the retaining bolts and move the wiring harness support bracket and the harness to one side **(see illustrations)**.

9 Disconnect the coolant hose at the

9.7 Disconnect the wiring connectors from the four glow plugs

9.8a Disconnect the wiring harness connector above the inlet manifold. . .

9.8b. . .then undo the retaining bolts and move the wiring harness and support bracket to one side

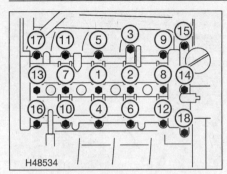

9.23 Camshaft housing retaining bolt tightening sequence

quick-release fitting at the rear of the manifold.

10 Release the clips and disconnect the crankcase breather hoses from the top and bottom of the oil separator.

11 Undo the retaining bolts and remove the oil separator from the inlet manifold.

12 Disconnect the wiring connector from the changeover flap actuator drive on the underside of the inlet manifold.

13 Remove the fuel rail and the fuel injectors as described in Chapter 4B, Section 10 and Chapter 4B Section 11.

14 Unscrew the turbocharger oil supply pipe banjo union from the top of the camshaft housing and collect the two copper washers.

15 Disconnect any remaining wiring connectors, fuel hoses or vacuum hoses likely to impede removal of the camshaft housing as necessary.

16 Working in the reverse of the tightening sequence **(see illustration 9.23)**, progressively slacken, then remove, the bolts, securing the camshaft housing to the cylinder head. Ensure that the housing releases evenly from the cylinder block.

17 Lift the camshaft housing off the cylinder head and recover the gasket.

18 Thoroughly clean the mating faces of the cylinder head, camshaft housing and vacuum pump and obtain a new gasket for refitting.

Refitting

19 Check that all the hydraulic tappets and rocker arms are correctly positioned in the cylinder head and none have been disturbed.

20 Commence refitting by turning the crankshaft anti-clockwise by 90°. This will position all the pistons half way down their bores, and prevent any chance of the valves touching the piston crowns as the camshaft housing is being fitted.

21 Place a new gasket on the cylinder head, then locate the camshaft housing in position aligning it with the locating dowels.

22 Refit the camshaft housing retaining bolts. Progressively screw in the bolts to gradually draw the housing down and into contact with the cylinder head.

23 Working progressively in the sequence shown, tighten the retaining bolts to the specified torque **(see illustration)**.

24 Using new copper washers, refit the turbocharger oil supply pipe banjo union to the top of the camshaft housing and tighten the banjo bolt securely.

25 Refit the fuel injectors and fuel rail as described in Chapter 4B, Section 10 and Chapter 4B Section 11.

26 Reconnect the wiring connector to the changeover flap actuator drive on the underside of the inlet manifold.

27 Refit the oil separator and the crankcase breather hoses, then reconnect the coolant hose to the rear of the inlet manifold.

28 Reconnect the wiring harness connector above the inlet manifold, then refit the wiring harness support bracket and secure with the two bolts.

29 Reconnect the wiring connectors to the glow plugs.

30 Reconnect the vacuum hoses to the vacuum pump.

31 Reconnect the fuel return hose quick-release fitting, then refit the bolts securing the engine lifting eye and hose/cable support bracket.

32 Refit the crankcase ventilation pipe and secure the wiring harness to the pipe with the retaining clips.

33 Refit the EGR cooler as described in Chapter 4C Section 3.

34 Turn the crankshaft clockwise by 90° to bring No 1 and 4 pistons to approximately the TDC position.

35 Refit the timing belt as described in Section 6.

36 On completion, refill the cooling system as described in Chapter 1B, Section 26.

10 Camshafts – removal, inspection and refitting

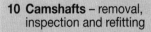

Note: *Vauxhall/Opel special tools EN-46789 and EN46789-100 (or suitable equivalents) will be required for this operation to lock the camshafts in the TDC position.*

Removal

1 Carry out the operations described in Section 9, paragraphs 1 to 15.

2 Undo the three retaining bolts and remove the oil filler housing.

3 Remove the braking system vacuum pump as described in Chapter 9, Section 22.

4 Undo the retaining bolt and remove the camshaft sensor from the right-hand end of the camshaft housing.

5 Before removing the camshaft housing completely, the retaining bolts for the camshaft drive gears and sprocket should be slackened as follows.

6 Remove the exhaust camshaft positioning tool from the valve timing checking hole.

7 It will be necessary to hold the camshaft sprocket to enable the drive gear and sprocket retaining bolts to be slackened. Vauxhall special tools EN-46787 and KM-956-1 are available for this purpose, however, a home-made tool can easily be fabricated **(see Tool tip in Section 7)**.

8 Working through the oil filler housing aperture, and using the holding tool to prevent rotation of the camshaft, slacken the inlet camshaft drive gear retaining bolt. Working through the vacuum pump aperture, slacken the exhaust camshaft drive gear retaining bolt in the same way.

9 Again, using the holding tool, slacken the camshaft sprocket retaining bolt.

10 Continue with the camshaft housing removal procedure as described in Section 9, paragraphs 16 to 18.

11 With the camshaft housing placed upside down on the bench, unscrew and remove the previously slackened retaining bolt, and remove the timing belt sprocket from the exhaust camshaft.

12 At the other end of the housing, unscrew and remove the two previously slackened

10.12a Unscrew and remove the two previously slackened retaining bolts. . .

10.12b. . .then lift out the exhaust camshaft drive gear. . .

10.12c. . .and the inlet camshaft drive gear

retaining bolts, and lift off the drive gears from the inlet and exhaust camshafts **(see illustrations)**.

13 Carefully prise out the exhaust camshaft oil seal with a screwdriver or similar hooked tool. Carefully withdraw the exhaust camshaft out from the timing belt end of the camshaft housing **(see illustration)**.

14 Using a wooden dowel or similar, carefully tap the end of the inlet camshaft toward the timing belt end of the housing, to release the blanking cap. Remove the cap, then carefully withdraw the inlet camshaft from the housing **(see illustration)**.

Inspection

15 Examine the camshaft bearing surfaces and cam lobes for signs of wear ridges and scoring. Renew the camshaft(s) if any of these conditions are apparent. Examine the condition of the bearing surfaces in the camshaft housing. If the any wear or scoring is evident, the camshaft housing will need to be renewed.

16 If either camshaft is being renewed, it will be necessary to renew all the camshaft followers and hydraulic tappets for that particular camshaft also (see Section 10).

17 Check the condition of the camshaft drive gears and sprocket for chipped or damaged teeth, wear ridges and scoring. Renew any components as necessary.

Refitting

18 Prior to refitting, thoroughly clean all components and dry with a lint-free cloth.

10.13 Withdraw the exhaust camshaft. . .

Ensure that all traces of oil and grease are removed from the contact faces of the drive gears, sprocket and camshafts.

19 Lubricate the camshaft bearing journals in the camshaft housing and carefully insert the inlet and exhaust camshafts.

20 Ensuring that the contact faces are clean and dry, refit the drive gear to each camshaft. Note that the gear with the vacuum pump drive dogs is fitted to the exhaust camshaft, and the plain gear is fitted to the inlet camshaft.

21 Screw in a new drive gear retaining bolt for each camshaft and tighten both bolts finger tight only at this stage.

22 Refit the camshaft positioning tool to the valve timing checking hole of the exhaust camshaft. If necessary, rotate the exhaust camshaft slightly, until the tool audibly engages **(see illustration)**.

10.14. . .and inlet camshaft from the camshaft housing

23 Unscrew and remove the closure bolt from the inlet camshaft side of the camshaft housing and fit a second camshaft positioning tool **(see illustrations)**. If necessary, rotate the camshaft slightly, until the tool audibly engages.

24 With both camshafts locked by means of the positioning tools, tighten both drive gear retaining bolts to the specified torque **(see illustration)**. It may be beneficial to have an assistant securely support the camshaft housing as the bolts are tightened.

25 Remove the positioning tool from the inlet camshaft and refit the closure bolt. Tighten the bolt to the specified torque.

26 Fit a new inlet camshaft blanking cap to the timing belt end of the camshaft housing and tap it into position until it is flush with the outer face of the housing, using a suitable socket or tube, or a wooden block **(see illustrations)**.

10.22 Refit the camshaft positioning tool to the valve timing checking hole of the exhaust camshaft

10.23a Unscrew the closure bolt from the inlet camshaft side of the camshaft housing. . .

10.23b. . .and fit a camshaft positioning tool for the inlet camshaft

10.24 With both camshafts locked, tighten both drive gear retaining bolts to the specified torque

10.26a Fit a new inlet camshaft blanking cap to the camshaft housing. . .

10.26b. . .and tap it into position until it is flush with the outer face of the housing

27 Similarly, fit a new exhaust camshaft oil seal to the timing belt end of the camshaft housing and tap it into position until it is flush with the outer face of the housing, using a suitable socket or tube, or a wooden block **(see illustration)**.

28 Refit the timing belt sprocket to the exhaust camshaft, aligning its cut-out with the locating peg, and fit the new retaining bolt finger tight only at this stage. Final tightening is carried out after the timing belt has been fitted and tensioned.

29 Refit the camshaft sensor to the camshaft housing and tighten the retaining bolt securely.

30 Refit the oil filler housing to the camshaft housing using a new gasket, refit the retaining bolts and tighten the bolts to the specified torque.

31 Refit the braking system vacuum pump as described in Chapter 9, Section 22.

32 Thoroughly clean the mating faces of the cylinder head and camshaft housing.

33 Refit the camshaft housing to the cylinder head as described in Section 9.

11 Camshaft followers and hydraulic tappets – removal, inspection and refitting

Removal

1 Remove the camshaft housing as described in Section 9.

2 Obtain sixteen small, oil tight clean plastic containers, and number them inlet 1 to 8 and

11.3a Withdraw each camshaft follower. . .

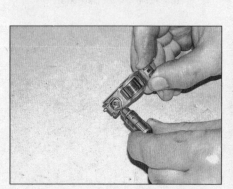

11.6a Clip the follower back onto the tappet. . .

10.27 Similarly, fit a new exhaust camshaft oil seal to the camshaft housing

exhaust 1 to 8; alternatively, divide a larger container into sixteen compartments and number each compartment accordingly.

3 Withdraw each camshaft follower and hydraulic tappet in turn, unclip the follower from the tappet, and place them in their respective container **(see illustrations)**. Do not interchange the followers and tappets, or the rate of wear will be much increased. Fill each container with clean engine oil and ensure that the tappet is submerged.

Inspection

4 Examine the followers and hydraulic tappet bearing surfaces for wear ridges and scoring. Renew any follower or tappet on which these conditions are apparent.

5 If any new hydraulic tappets are obtained, they should be immersed in a container of clean engine oil prior to refitting.

11.3b. . .and hydraulic tappet in turn, and place them in their respective container

11.6b. . .then refit the tappet to its original bore, and lay the follower over its respective valve

Refitting

6 Liberally oil the cylinder head hydraulic tappet bores and the tappets. Working on one assembly at a time, clip the follower back onto the tappet, then refit the tappet to the cylinder head, ensuring that it is refitted to its original bore. Lay the follower over its respective valve **(see illustrations)**.

7 Refit the remaining tappets and followers in the same way.

8 With all the tappets and followers in place, refit the camshaft housing as described in Section 9.

12 Cylinder head – removal and refitting

Note: *New cylinder head bolts will be required for refitting.*

Removal

1 Disconnect the battery negative terminal (refer to Chapter 5A, Section 1).

2 Drain the cooling system as described in Chapter 1B, Section 26.

3 Remove the camshaft housing as described in Section 9.

4 Remove the camshaft followers and hydraulic tappets as described in Section 11.

5 Remove the inlet and exhaust manifolds as described in Chapter 4B, Section 12 and Chapter 4B Section 17.

6 Undo the bolt securing the high-pressure fuel pump mounting bracket to the cylinder head **(see illustration)**.

7 Make a final check to ensure that all relevant hoses, pipes and wires have been disconnected.

8 Working in the reverse of the tightening sequence **(see illustration 12.21)**, progressively slacken the cylinder head bolts by half a turn at a time, until all bolts can be unscrewed by hand. Note that either an M14 RIBE socket bit, or a Torx T60 socket bit will be required to unscrew the bolts, depending on year of vehicle manufacture. Remove the cylinder head bolts and recover the washers.

9 Engage the help of an assistant, if

12.6 Undo the bolt securing the high-pressure fuel pump mounting bracket to the cylinder head

necessary, and lift the cylinder head from the cylinder block (see illustration).
Caution: Do not lay the head on its lower mating surface; support the head on wooden blocks, ensuring each block only contacts the head mating surface.
10 Remove the gasket and keep it for identification purposes (see paragraph 17).
11 If the cylinder head is to be dismantled for overhaul, then refer to Chapter 2E.

Preparation for refitting

12 The mating faces of the cylinder head and cylinder block/crankcase must be perfectly clean before refitting the head. Use a hard plastic or wood scraper to remove all traces of gasket and carbon; also clean the piston crowns. Take particular care, as the surfaces are damaged easily. Also, make sure that the carbon is not allowed to enter the oil and water passages – this is particularly important for the lubrication system, as carbon could block the oil supply to any of the engine's components. Using adhesive tape and paper, seal the water, oil and bolt holes in the cylinder block/crankcase. To prevent carbon entering the gap between the pistons and bores, smear a little grease in the gap. After cleaning each piston, use a small brush to remove all traces of grease and carbon from the gap, then wipe away the remainder with a clean rag. Clean all the pistons in the same way.
13 Check the mating surfaces of the cylinder block/crankcase and the cylinder head for nicks, deep scratches and other damage. If slight, they may be removed carefully with a file, but if excessive, machining may be the only alternative to renewal.
14 Ensure that the cylinder head bolt holes in the crankcase are clean and free of oil. Syringe or soak up any oil left in the bolt holes. This is most important in order that the correct bolt tightening torque can be applied and to prevent the possibility of the block being cracked by hydraulic pressure when the bolts are tightened.
15 The cylinder head bolts must be discarded and renewed, regardless of their apparent condition.
16 If warpage of the cylinder head gasket surface is suspected, use a straight-edge to check it for distortion. Refer Chapter 2E if necessary.

12.9 Lift the cylinder head from the cylinder block

17 On this engine, the cylinder head-to-piston clearance is controlled by fitting different thickness head gaskets. The gasket thickness can be determined by looking at the holes stamped on the edge of the gasket (see illustration). Obtain a new cylinder head gasket with the same number of holes as the original.

Number of holes	Gasket thickness
No holes	0.89 mm
One hole	1.05 mm
Two holes	1.15 mm

Refitting

18 Wipe clean the mating surfaces of the cylinder head and cylinder block/crankcase. Place the new gasket in position with the words ALTO/TOP uppermost (see illustration).
19 Carefully refit the cylinder head assembly to the block, aligning it with the locating dowels.
20 Apply a thin film of engine oil to the bolt threads and the underside of the bolt heads. Carefully enter each new cylinder head bolt into its relevant hole (*do not drop them in*). Screw all bolts in, by hand only, until finger-tight.
21 Working progressively in the sequence shown, tighten the cylinder head bolts to their Stage 1 torque setting, using a torque wrench and suitable socket (see illustration). Working again in the same sequence, go around and tighten all bolts through the specified Stage 2 torque setting.
22 Once all bolts have been tightened to the Stage 2 torque, working again in the same sequence, go around and tighten all bolts through the specified Stage 3 angle, then

through the specified Stage 4 angle, and then through the specified Stage 5 angle using an angle-measuring gauge. If Torx T60 cylinder head bolts are fitted, go around one more time and tighten all the bolts through the Stage 6 angle.
23 Refit the bolt securing the high-pressure fuel pump mounting bracket to the cylinder head and tighten the bolt securely.
24 Refit the inlet and exhaust manifolds as described in Chapter 4B, Section 12 and Chapter 4B Section 17.
25 Refit the camshaft followers and hydraulic tappets as described in Section 11.
26 Refit the camshaft housing as described in Section 9.
27 On completion, reconnect the battery negative terminal, then refill the cooling system as described in Chapter 1B, Section 26.

13 Sump – removal and refitting

Removal

1 Disconnect the battery negative terminal (refer to Chapter 5A, Section 4).
2 Apply the handbrake, then jack up the front of the vehicle and support it on axle stands (see *Jacking and vehicle support*). Remove the right-hand front roadwheel.
3 Remove the engine undertray as described in Chapter 11, Section 24.
4 Drain the engine oil as described in Chapter 1B, Section 5. When the oil has completely drained, refit the drain plug with new sealing washer, and tighten to the specified torque.
5 Remove the right-hand driveshaft and the intermediate shaft as described in Chapter 8, Section 2 and Chapter 8 Section 3.
6 Undo the three bolts securing the intermediate shaft bearing housing support bracket to the cylinder block and remove the support bracket.
7 Undo the two bolts securing the catalytic converter support bracket to the sump (see illustration).
8 Remove the exhaust system front pipe as described in Chapter 4B, Section 18.
9 Undo the retaining bolt and remove the oil separator pipe from the sump.

12.17 Cylinder head gasket thickness identification hole

12.18 Place the new gasket in position with the words ALTO/TOP uppermost

12.21 Cylinder head bolt tightening sequence

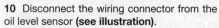

13.7 Undo the two bolts securing the catalytic converter support bracket to the sump

13.10 Disconnect the wiring connector from the oil level sensor

13.11 Undo the two bolts securing the sump flange to the transmission bellhousing

10 Disconnect the wiring connector from the oil level sensor **(see illustration)**.

11 Undo the two bolts securing the sump flange to the transmission bellhousing **(see illustration)**.

12 Using a socket and extension on the crankshaft pulley bolt, rotate the crankshaft in the normal direction of rotation (clockwise when viewed from the right-hand end of the engine) until the opening in the flywheel is positioned to allow access to one of the rear sump retaining bolts. Undo and remove the bolt, then rotate the crankshaft again until the flywheel allows access to the second rear retaining bolt. Undo and remove the bolt.

13 Progressively slacken and remove the remaining bolts securing the sump to the base of the cylinder block and oil pump housing. Note the bolt locations as they are of differing lengths. Using a wide-bladed scraper or similar tool inserted between the sump and cylinder block, carefully break the joint to release the sump, then manoeuvre the sump out from under the car.

14 Recover the oil pump pick-up/strainer sealing ring from the base of the oil pump. Renew the sealing ring prior to refitting

15 If required, undo the retaining bolts and remove the oil baffle plate from inside the sump.

16 While the sump is removed, take the opportunity to check the oil pump pick-up/strainer for signs of clogging or splitting. Unbolt the oil pump pick-up/strainer and remove it from the sump. The strainer can then be cleaned easily in solvent or renewed.

Refitting

17 Thoroughly clean the sump and remove all traces of silicone sealer and oil from the mating surfaces of the sump and cylinder block. If removed, refit the pick-up/strainer and oil baffle plate and tighten the retaining bolts securely.

18 Fit the new oil pump pick-up/strainer sealing ring to the installation cap provided with the new sealing ring. Push the sealing ring, by means of the installation cap, into position on the oil pump. Using a tube or socket of suitable diameter, in contact with the installation cap, tap the sealing ring fully home on the oil pump. Ensure that the sealing ring is fitted squarely, then remove the installation cap.

19 Apply a continuous bead of silicone sealing compound (available from your Vauxhall/Opel dealer) at approximately 1.0 mm from the inner edge of the sump. The bead of sealant should be between 2.0 and 2.5 mm in diameter.

20 Engage the sump with the cylinder block and loosely refit all the retaining bolts.

21 Working out from the centre in a diagonal sequence, progressively tighten the bolts securing the sump to the cylinder block and oil pump housing. Tighten all the bolts to their specified torque setting.

22 Tighten the two bolts securing the sump flange to the transmission bellhousing to their specified torque settings.

23 Reconnect the wiring connector to the oil level sensor.

24 Refit the oil separator pipe and tighten the retaining bolt securely.

25 Refit the exhaust system front pipe as described in Chapter 4B, Section 18.

26 Refit the two catalytic converter support bracket bolts and tighten them securely.

27 Position the intermediate shaft bearing housing support bracket on the cylinder block and secure with the three retaining bolts tightened to the specified torque.

28 Refit the intermediate shaft and right-hand driveshaft as described in Chapter 8, Section 2 and Chapter 8 Section 3.

29 Refit the roadwheel and engine undertray, then lower the car to the ground and tighten the wheel nuts to the specified torque.

30 Fill the engine with fresh engine oil as described in Chapter 1B, Section 5.

31 On completion, reconnect the battery negative terminal.

14 Oil pump – removal, overhaul and refitting

Removal

1 Remove the timing belt as described in Section 6.

2 Remove the crankshaft sprocket as described In Section 7.

3 Remove the sump and oil pump pick-up/strainer as described in Section 13.

4 Slacken and remove the seven retaining bolts then slide the oil pump housing assembly off of the end of the crankshaft **(see illustration)**. Remove the housing gasket and discard it.

Overhaul

5 Undo the retaining screws and lift off the pump cover from the rear of the housing **(see illustration)**.

6 Check the inner and outer rotors for identification dots indicating which way round they are fitted **(see illustration)**. If no marks are visible, use a suitable marker pen to mark the surface of both the pump inner and outer rotors.

7 Lift out the inner and outer rotors from the pump housing.

14.4 Oil pump housing retaining bolts

14.5 Undo the retaining screws and lift off the oil pump cover

8 Unscrew the oil pressure relief valve bolt from the base of the housing and withdraw the spring and plunger, noting which way around the plunger is fitted **(see illustrations)**. Remove the sealing washer from the valve bolt.
9 Clean the components, and carefully examine the rotors, pump body and relief valve plunger for any signs of scoring or wear. If any damage or wear is noticed, it will be necessary to renew the complete pump assembly.
10 If the pump is satisfactory, reassemble the components in the reverse order of removal, noting the following.
a) *Ensure both rotors are fitted the correct way around.*
b) *Fit a new sealing ring to the pressure relief valve bolt and securely tighten the bolt.*
c) *Apply a little locking compound to the threads, and securely tighten the pump cover screws.*
d) *On completion prime the oil pump by filling it with clean engine oil whilst rotating the inner rotor(see illustration).*

Refitting

11 Prior to refitting, carefully lever out the crankshaft oil seal using a flat-bladed screwdriver. Fit the new oil seal, ensuring its sealing lip is facing inwards, and press it squarely into the housing using a tubular drift which bears only on the hard outer edge of the seal. Press the seal into position so that it is flush with the housing and lubricate the oil seal lip with clean engine oil.
12 Ensure the mating surfaces of the oil pump and cylinder block are clean and dry.
13 Fit a new gasket to the oil pump housing and bend down the tabs on the edge of the gasket to retain it on the pump housing **(see illustration)**.
14 Locate the pump housing over the end of the crankshaft and into position on the cylinder block.
15 Refit the pump housing retaining bolts and tighten them to the specified torque.
16 Refit the oil pump pick-up/strainer and sump as described in Section 13.
17 Refit the crankshaft sprocket as described in Section 7.
18 Refit the timing belt as described in Section 6.
19 On completion, fit a new oil filter and fill the engine with clean oil as described in Chapter 1B, Section 5.

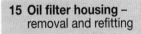

15 Oil filter housing – removal and refitting

Removal

1 The oil filter housing with integral oil cooler is located at the rear of the cylinder block, above the right-hand driveshaft.
2 Disconnect the battery negative terminal (refer to Chapter 5A, Section 4).
3 Apply the handbrake, then jack up the front of the vehicle and support it on axle stands

14.6 Oil pump inner and outer rotor identification dots

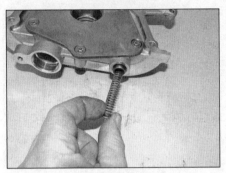

14.8b. . .and withdraw the spring. . .

(see *Jacking and vehicle support*). Remove the right-hand front roadwheel.
4 Remove the engine undertray as described in Chapter 11, Section 24.
5 Drain the engine oil and remove the oil filter element as described in Chapter 1B, Section 5. When the oil has completely drained, refit the drain plug with new sealing washer, and tighten to the specified torque.
6 Drain the cooling system as described in Chapter 1B, Section 26.
7 Disconnect the wiring connector from the oil pressure switch.
8 Release the retaining clips and disconnect the two coolant hoses from the oil cooler on the oil filter housing.
9 Undo the three retaining bolts and remove the oil filter housing from the cylinder block. Recover the two rubber seals from the rear of the housing. Note that new seals will be required for refitting.

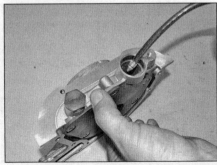

14.10a Prime the oil pump by filling it with clean engine oil whilst rotating the inner rotor

14.8a Unscrew the oil pressure relief valve bolt. . .

14.8c. . .and plunger

Refitting

10 Thoroughly clean the oil filter housing, then fit the two new sealing rings.
11 Position the oil filter housing on the cylinder block and refit the retaining bolts. Tighten the bolts to the specified torque.
12 Refit the two coolant hoses and secure with their retaining clips. Reconnect the oil pressure switch wiring connector.
13 Fit a new oil filter element as described in Chapter 1B, Section 5.
14 Refit the roadwheel and engine undertray, then lower the car to the ground and tighten the wheel nuts to the specified torque.
15 Refill the cooling system as described in Chapter 1B, Section 26.
16 Top-up the engine oil as described in *Weekly checks*.
17 On completion, reconnect the battery negative terminal.

14.13 Bend down the tabs on the edge of the gasket to retain it on the oil pump housing

16.2 Screw in a self-tapping screw and pull on the screw with pliers to extract the oil seal

16.4 Using a socket as a tubular drift to fit the new oil seal

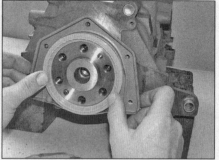

16.10 Fitting the new oil seal housing, with integral oil seal over the crankshaft

16.12 After fitting, remove the protector sleeve from the housing

16 Crankshaft oil seals – renewal

Right-hand (timing belt end)

1 Remove the crankshaft sprocket as described in Section 7.
2 Carefully punch or drill a small hole in the oil seal. Screw in a self-tapping screw and pull on the screw with pliers to extract the seal **(see illustration)**.
3 Clean the seal housing and polish off any burrs or raised edges which may have caused the seal to fail in the first place.
4 Ease the new oil seal into position on the end of the crankshaft. Press the seal squarely into position until it is flush with the housing. If necessary, a suitable tubular drift which bears only on the hard outer edge of the seal

17.2 Prevent the flywheel from turning by locking the ring gear teeth

can be used to tap the seal into position **(see illustration)**. Take great care not to damage the seal lips during fitting and ensure that the seal lips face inwards.
5 Wash off any traces of oil, then refit the crankshaft sprocket as described in Section 7.

Left-hand (flywheel/driveplate end)

6 Remove the flywheel/driveplate as described in Section 17.
7 Remove the sump as described in Section 13.
8 Undo the five bolts and remove the rear oil seal housing. Note that the oil seal and the housing are a single assembly.
9 Clean the crankshaft and polish off any burrs or raised edges which may have caused the seal to fail in the first place.
10 Position the new oil seal housing, complete with seal over the crankshaft and into position on the cylinder block **(see**

17.3 Flywheel retaining bolts

illustration). Note that the new oil seal housing is supplied with a protector sleeve over the oil seal. Leave the sleeve in position as the housing is fitted.
11 Refit the five retaining bolts and tighten to the specified torque.
12 Remove the protector sleeve from the housing **(see illustration)**.
13 Refit the sump as described in Section 13.
14 Refit the flywheel/driveplate as described in Section 17.

17 Flywheel/driveplate – removal, inspection and refitting

Note: *New flywheel/driveplate retaining bolts will be required on refitting.*

Removal
Manual transmission models

1 Remove the transmission as described in Chapter 7A, Section 8 then remove the clutch assembly as described in Chapter 6, Section 6.
2 Prevent the flywheel from turning by locking the ring gear teeth with a similar arrangement to that shown **(see illustration)**.
3 Slacken and remove the retaining bolts and remove the flywheel **(see illustration)**. Do not drop it, as it is very heavy.

Automatic transmission models

4 Remove the transmission as described in Chapter 7B, Section 10, then remove the driveplate as described in paragraphs 2 and 3.

Inspection

5 If there is any doubt about the condition of the flywheel/driveplate, seek the advice of a Vauxhall/Opel dealer or engine reconditioning specialist. They will be able to advise if it is possible to recondition it or whether renewal is necessary.

Refitting
Manual transmission models

6 Clean the mating surfaces of the flywheel and crankshaft.
7 Offer up the flywheel and engage it over the positioning dowel on the crankshaft. Apply a drop of locking compound to the threads of each new flywheel retaining bolt (unless they are already precoated) and install the new bolts.
8 Lock the flywheel by the method used on removal then, working in a diagonal sequence, evenly and progressively tighten the retaining bolts to the specified torque.
9 Refit the clutch as described in Chapter 6, Section 6 then remove the locking tool, and refit the transmission as described in Chapter 7A, Section 8.

Automatic transmission models

10 Refit the driveplate as described in paragraphs 6 to 8.
11 Remove the locking tool, and refit the transmission as described in Chapter 7B, Section 10.

18 Engine/transmission mountings – inspection and renewal

Inspection

1 If improved access is required, firmly apply the handbrake, then jack up the front of the car and support it securely on axle stands (see *Jacking and vehicle support*). Remove the engine undertray as described in Chapter 11, Section 24.

2 Check the mounting rubber to see if it is cracked, hardened or separated from the metal at any point; renew the mounting if any such damage or deterioration is evident.

3 Check that all the mounting's fasteners are securely tightened; use a torque wrench to check if possible.

4 Using a large screwdriver or a pry bar, check for wear in the mounting by carefully levering against it to check for free play; where this is not possible, enlist the aid of an assistant to move the engine/transmission unit back-and-forth, or from side-to-side, while you watch the mounting. While some free play is to be expected even from new components, excessive wear should be obvious. If excessive free play is found, check first that the fasteners are correctly secured, then renew any worn components as described below.

Renewal

Note: *Before slackening any of the engine mounting bolts/nuts, the relative positions of the mountings to their various brackets should be marked to ensure correct alignment upon refitting.*

Front mounting/torque link

5 Apply the handbrake, then jack up the front of the vehicle and support it on axle stands (see *Jacking and vehicle support*).

6 Remove the engine undertray as described in Chapter 11, Section 24.

7 Slacken and remove the through-bolt securing the mounting and vibration damper to the subframe bracket **(see illustration)**.

8 Undo the bolts securing the mounting bracket to the transmission, then manoeuvre the mounting and bracket out of position.

9 Check all components for signs of wear or damage, and renew as necessary.

10 Locate the mounting in the subframe, refit the through bolt and tighten the bolt finger tight at this stage.

11 Refit the mounting bracket to the transmission and tighten its bolts to the specified torque.

12 Tighten the through bolt to the specified torque.

13 On completion, refit the engine undertray and lower the vehicle to the ground.

Rear mounting/torque link

14 Apply the handbrake, then jack up the front of the vehicle and support it on axle stands (see *Jacking and vehicle support*).

15 Remove the engine undertray as described in Chapter 11, Section 24.

16 Undo the three bolts securing the mounting bracket to the transmission and the through-bolt securing the mounting to the bracket **(see illustration)**.

17 Undo the nuts and remove the two bolts securing the mounting to the subframe **(see illustration)**. Manoeuvre the mounting and bracket out from under the car.

18 Refit the bracket to the transmission and tighten the bolts to the specified torque.

19 Locate the new mounting in position. Insert the bolts and tighten the bolt/nuts to the specified torque.

20 On completion, refit the engine undertray and lower the vehicle to the ground.

Right-hand mounting

21 Apply the handbrake, then jack up the front of the vehicle and support it on axle stands (see *Jacking and vehicle support*).

22 Remove the air cleaner assembly as described in Chapter 4B, Section 3.

23 Attach a suitable hoist and lifting tackle to the engine lifting brackets on the cylinder head, and support the weight of the engine.

24 Mark the position of the three bolts securing the mounting bracket to the engine bracket and undo the bolts. Undo the three bolts securing the mounting to the body and remove the mounting assembly **(see illustrations)**. If necessary, undo the three bolts and remove the mounting bracket from the engine.

25 Place the mounting assembly in position and refit the bolts securing the mounting to the body. Tighten the bolts to the specified

18.7 Front mounting/torque link through-bolt

torque. Align the mounting in its original position, then tighten the three mounting bracket bolts to the specified torque.

26 Remove the hoist, then refit the air cleaner as described in Chapter 4B, Section 3.

27 On completion, lower the vehicle to the ground.

Left-hand mounting

28 Remove the battery, battery box and battery tray as described in Chapter 5A, Section 4.

29 Apply the handbrake, then jack up the front of the vehicle and support it on axle stands (see *Jacking and vehicle support*).

30 Remove the left-hand front roadwheel, then remove the wheel arch liner from under the front wing.

31 Attach a suitable hoist and lifting tackle to the engine lifting brackets on the cylinder head, and support the weight of the engine. Alternatively, support the transmission on

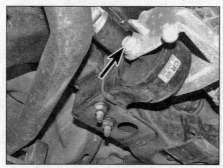

18.16 Rear mounting/torque link through-bolt

18.17 Rear mounting/torque link bracket-to-subframe mounting bolt nuts

18.24a Right-hand mounting bracket-to-engine bracket bolts. . .

18.24b. . .and mounting-to-body bolts

18.33 Left-hand mounting bracket-to-transmission bracket retaining bolts

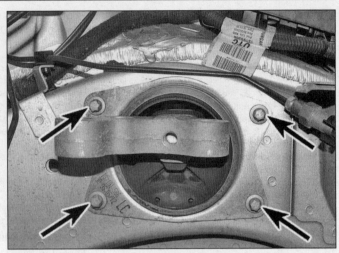

18.34 Left-hand mounting-to-body retaining bolts – shown with engine/transmission removed

a jack with a block of wood between the transmission and jack head.

32 Working under the front wing, unscrew the nut securing the mounting to the body.

33 From within the engine compartment, unscrew the three bolts securing the mounting bracket to the transmission bracket (see illustration).

34 Undo the four bolts securing the mounting to the body and the three bolts securing the transmission bracket to the transmission (see illustration). Remove the mounting assembly from the car.

35 Locate the mounting brackets in position then refit the nut and bolts and tighten them to the specified torque.

36 Disconnect the hoist and lifting tackle, or remove the jack, as applicable.

37 Refit the wheel arch liner and roadwheel, then lower the vehicle to the ground and tighten the wheel nuts to the specified torque.

38 Refit the battery tray, battery box and battery as described in Chapter 5A, Section 4.

Chapter 2 Part D
2.0 litre (B20) diesel engine in-car repair procedures

Contents

Degrees of difficulty

Easy, suitable for novice with little experience	**Fairly easy,** suitable for beginner with some experience	**Fairly difficult,** suitable for competent DIY mechanic	**Difficult,** suitable for experienced DIY mechanic	**Very difficult,** suitable for expert DIY or professional

Specifications

General

Engine type	Four-cylinder, in-line, water-cooled. Double overhead camshaft, belt-driven
Manufacturer's engine code*	B20DTH (LFS)
Bore	83.0 mm
Stroke	90.0 mm
Capacity	1956 cc
Compression ratio	16.5: 1
Firing order	1-3-4-2 (No 1 cylinder at timing belt end of engine)
Direction of crankshaft rotation	Clockwise (viewed from timing belt end of engine)

* For details of engine code location, see 'Vehicle identification' in the Reference Chapter.

Compression pressures

Minimum	Not less than 70% of the highest cylinder

Lubrication system

Minimum oil pressure at 100°C	2.5 bar at idle speed (solenoid inactive)
Oil pressure at 4000 rpm (hot):	
Solenoid active	1.9 to 2.3 bar
Solenoid inactive	4.5 to 5 bar
Oil pump type	Rotor-type, driven by crankshaft pulley/vibration damper from crankshaft

Torque wrench settings

	Nm	lbf ft
Auxiliary drivebelt tensioner assembly bolts	22	16
Auxiliary drivebelt idler bolt	58	43
Balancer shaft housing bolts*:		
Stage 1	20	15
Stage 2	Angle-tighten a further 90°	
Camshaft bearing cap bolts (double cap)	25	18
Camshaft bearing cap bolts (inner caps)	10	7
Camshaft bearing cap bolts (oil seal cap at exhaust)	25	18
Camshaft cover bolts.	10	7
Camshaft sprocket bolts (belt end)	25	18
Camshaft timing chain sprocket bolts*:		
Stage 1	40	30
Stage 2	Angle-tighten a further 55°	
Camshaft hub/timing plate bolt*:		
Stage 1	30	22
Stage 2	Angle-tighten a further 40°	
Camshaft hydraulic tensioner bolts	10	7
Connecting rod big-end bearing cap bolt*:		
Stage 1	25	18
Stage 2	Angle-tighten a further 60°	
Crankshaft pulley/vibration damper bolts*:		
Stage 1	20	15
Stage 2	Angle-tighten a further 90°	
Crankshaft sprocket bolt*†:		
Stage 1	90	55
Stage 2	Angle-tighten a further 75°	
Crankshaft rear oil seal housing.	10	7
Cylinder head bolts*:		
Stage 1	65	48
Stage 2	Angle-tighten a further 90°	
Stage 3	Angle-tighten a further 90°	
Stage 4	Angle-tighten a further 90°	
Stage 5	Angle-tighten a further 90°	
Engine-to-transmission bolts.	60	45
Engine end plate (at transmission).	10	7
Engine mountings:		
Front mounting/torque link:		
Mounting to transmission.	100	75
Mounting to subframe	100	75
Left-hand mounting:		
Mounting to body bolts/nut	22	16
Mounting to transmission*:		
Stage 1	50	37
Stage 2	Angle-tighten a further 90° to 105°	
Mounting bracket to transmission	100	75
Rear mounting/torque link:		
Mounting bracket to transmission:	100	75
Mounting to subframe (manual transmission)	110	81
Mounting to subframe (automatic transmission)	62	46
Mounting connector bolt	100	75
Right-hand mounting:		
Engine bracket to engine bolts.	58	43
Mounting to body bolts:	62	46
Mounting to engine bracket bolts*:		
Stage 1	50	37
Stage 2	Angle-tighten a further 75°	
Engine oil level sensor bolts.	10	7
Flywheel bolts (manual transmission)*:		
Stage 1	20	15
Stage 2	100	74
Stage 3	Angle-tighten a further 30°	
Flywheel/driveplate bolts (auto transmission)*.	160	118
High-pressure fuel pump sprocket nut.	80	59
Main bearing cap bolts*:		
Stage 1	25	18
Stage 2	Angle-tighten a further 100°	
Oil filter housing-to-cylinder block	10	7

Torque wrench settings (continued)

	Nm	lbf ft
Oil pump pick up pipe bolts*	10	7
Oil pump mounting bolts	10	7
Oil pump cover bolts	11	8
Oil cooler sleeve bolt (in cylinder head)	25	18
Oil pressure sensor	35	26
Oil seal housing bolts (transmission end)*	10	7
Roadwheel nuts	150	111
Sump baffle plate bolts	10	7
Sump bolts (lower sump)	10	7
Sump bolts (upper sump):		
M6 bolts	10	7
M8 bolts	25	18
Timing belt idler pulley bolt (upper idler)	58	43
Timing belt idler pulley bolt (lower idler)	28	18
Timing belt tensioner bolt*:		
Stage 1 (Initial setting)	15	11
Stage 2	25	18
Stage 3	Angle-tighten a further 60°	
Timing belt cover bolts	10	7
Turbocharger banjo bolt (at oil filter)	35	26

†*Left-hand thread*
**Use new nuts/bolts*

1 General Information

How to use this Chapter

1 This Chapter describes the repair procedures which can reasonably be carried out on the engine while it remains in the vehicle. If the engine has been removed from the vehicle and is being dismantled as described in Chapter 2E, any preliminary dismantling procedures can be ignored.

2 Note that, while it may be possible physically to overhaul items such as the piston/connecting rod assemblies while the engine is in the vehicle, such tasks are not usually carried out as separate operations, and usually require the execution of several additional procedures (not to mention the cleaning of components and of oil ways); for this reason, all such tasks are classed as major overhaul procedures, and are described in Chapter 2E.

3 Chapter 2E, Section 4 describes the removal of the engine/transmission unit from the vehicle, and the full overhaul procedures which can then be carried out.

Engine description

4 The 2.0 litre DOHC diesel engine is of the sixteen-valve, in-line four-cylinder, double overhead camshaft type, mounted transversely at the front of the car, with the transmission on its left-hand end.

5 The crankshaft is supported within the cylinder block on five shell-type main bearings. The third main bearing acts as the thrust bearing to control end float. A gear driven balancer shaft assembly is also fitted to control torsional vibration.

6 The connecting rods rotate on horizontally-split bearing shells at their big-ends. The pistons are attached to the connecting rods by gudgeon pins, which are retained by circlips. The aluminium-alloy pistons are fitted with three piston rings – two compression rings and scraper-type oil control ring.

7 The camshafts are fitted to the top of the cylinder head. The exhaust camshaft is driven by the crankshaft via a toothed composite rubber timing belt (which also drives the high-pressure fuel pump). The exhaust camshaft drives the inlet camshaft via a chain. Each cylinder has four valves (two inlet and two exhaust), operated via followers which are supported at their pivot ends by hydraulic self-adjusting tappets. One camshaft operates the inlet valves, and the other operates the exhaust valves.

8 The inlet and exhaust valves are each closed by a single valve spring, and operate in guides pressed into the cylinder head.

9 Lubrication is by pressure-feed from a rotor-type oil pump, which is mounted on the right-hand end of the crankshaft. The pump draws oil through a strainer located in the sump, and then forces it through an externally mounted full-flow cartridge-type filter. The oil flows into galleries in the cylinder block/crankcase, from where it is distributed to the crankshaft (main bearings) and camshafts. The big-end bearings are supplied with oil via internal drillings in the crankshaft, while the camshaft bearings also receive a pressurised supply. The camshaft lobes and valves are lubricated by splash, as are all other engine components. The output of the pump can be controlled by activating a solenoid that control the pressure output.

10 A semi-closed crankcase ventilation system is employed; crankcase fumes are drawn from the oil separator attached to the cylinder block via a hose to the camshaft housing. The fumes are then passed via a hose to the inlet manifold.

Repair operations possible with the engine in the car

11 The following operations can be carried out without having to remove the engine from the car.

a) Removal and refitting of the cylinder head.
b) Removal and refitting of the timing belt, tensioner, idler pulleys and sprockets.
c) Renewal of the camshaft oil seal.
d) Removal and refitting of the camshafts and followers.
e) Removal and refitting of the lower and upper sump.
f) Removal and refitting of the connecting rods and pistons*.
g) Removal and refitting of the balancer shaft assembly*.
h) Removal and refitting of the oil pump.
i) Removal and refitting of the oil filter housing.
j) Renewal of the crankshaft oil seals.
k) Renewal of the engine mountings.
l) Removal and refitting of the flywheel/driveplate.

*Although the operation marked with an asterisk can be carried out with the engine in the car (after removal of the sump), it is preferable for the engine to be removed, in the interests of cleanliness and improved access. For this reason, the procedure is described in Chapter 2E.

2 Compression and leakdown tests – description and interpretation

Compression test

Note: *A compression tester specifically designed for diesel engines must be used for this test.*

Note: *The battery must be in a good state of charge, the air filter must be clean, and*

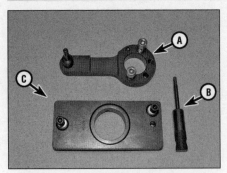

3.0a Vauxhall/Opel special timing tools

A: Sets the crankshaft at TDC position for No 1 piston (EN-51412)
B: Sets the camshaft position (EN-51414)
C: Sets the fuel pump position when changing the timing belt (EN-51413-2)

the engine should be at normal operating temperature.

1 When engine performance is down, or if misfiring occurs which cannot be attributed to the fuel system, a compression test can provide diagnostic clues as to the engine's condition. If the test is performed regularly, it can give warning of trouble before any other symptoms become apparent.

2 A compression tester specifically intended for diesel engines must be used, because of the higher pressures involved. The tester is connected to an adapter which screws into the glow plug holes. It is unlikely to be worthwhile buying such a tester for occasional use, but it may be possible to borrow or hire one – if not, have the test performed by a Vauxhall/Opel dealer, or suitably-equipped garage. If the necessary equipment is available, proceed as follows.

3 Remove the glow plugs as described in Chapter 5A, Section 18, then disconnect the wiring connector from the crankshaft sensor (see Chapter 4B, Section 8).

4 Screw the compression tester adapter in to the glow plug hole of No 1 cylinder.

5 With the help of an assistant, crank the engine on the starter motor; after one or two revolutions, the compression pressure should build-up to a maximum figure, and

then stabilise. Record the highest reading obtained.

6 Repeat the test on the remaining cylinders, recording the pressure in each.

7 All cylinders should produce very similar pressures; any difference greater than the minimum figure given in the Specifications indicates the existence of a fault. Note that the compression should build-up quickly in a healthy engine; low compression on the first stroke, followed by gradually-increasing pressure on successive strokes, indicates worn piston rings. A low compression reading on the first stroke, which does not build-up during successive strokes, indicates leaking valves or a blown head gasket (a cracked head could also be the cause). **Note:** *The cause of poor compression is less easy to establish on a diesel engine than on a petrol one. The effect of introducing oil into the cylinders ('wet' testing) is not conclusive, because there is a risk that the oil will sit in the recess on the piston crown instead of passing to the rings.*

8 On completion of the test refit the glow plugs as described in Chapter 5A, Section 17, and reconnect the wiring connector to the crankshaft sensor.

Leakdown test

9 A leakdown test measures the rate at which compressed air fed into the cylinder is lost. It is an alternative to a compression test, and in many ways it is better, since the escaping air provides easy identification of where pressure loss is occurring (piston rings, valves or head gasket).

10 The equipment needed for leakdown testing is unlikely to be available to the home mechanic. If poor compression is suspected, have the test performed by a Vauxhall/Opel dealer, or suitably-equipped garage.

3 Top Dead Centre (TDC) for No 1 piston – locating

Note: *To accurately determine the TDC position for No 1 piston, it will be necessary to use Vauxhall/Opel special tool EN-51412*

(or suitable equivalent) to set the crankshaft at the TDC position, together with the camshaft positioning tool, Vauxhall/Opel special tool EN-51414 (or suitable equivalent) **(see illustration).**

1 In its travel up and down its cylinder bore, Top Dead Centre (TDC) is the highest point that each piston reaches as the crankshaft rotates. While each piston reaches TDC both at the top of the compression stroke and again at the top of the exhaust stroke, for the purpose of timing the engine, TDC refers to the piston position of No 1 cylinder at the top of its compression stroke.

2 Number 1 piston (and cylinder) is at the right-hand (timing belt) end of the engine, and its TDC position is located as follows. Note that the crankshaft rotates clockwise when viewed from the right-hand side of the car.

3 Disconnect the battery negative terminal (refer to Chapter 5A, Section 4) and remove the engine cover.

4 Remove the air filter housing and associated pipe work as described in Chapter 4B Section 3.

5 Jack up and support the front of the vehicle (see Jacking and vehicle support 13 Section 5).

6 Remove the starter motor and lock the engine using either a large screw driver in the flywheel/driveplate ring gear or with the special tool (EN-50432 – manual transmission or EN-51411 – automatic transmission).

7 Remove the crankshaft pulley/vibration damper as described in Section 4.

8 Using a block of wood to spread the load, place a trolley jack under the sump and take the weight of the engine. Take extreme care when placing the jack under the sump as the pressed steel sump pan can easily be damaged.

9 Remove the right-hand engine mount as described in Section 18.

10 Remove the auxiliary drivebelt as described in Chapter 1B Section 22.

11 Remove the engine mounting bracket from the engine **(see illustration).**

12 Remove the drivebelt tensioner **(see illustration).**

13 Unbolt the auxiliary drivebelt idler pulley **(see illustration).**

3.11 Remove the bracket

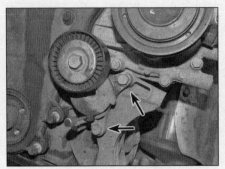

3.12 Unbolt and remove the tensioner

3.13 Remove the idler pulley

3.14 Remove the pump cover

3.15a The camshaft sprocket correctly positioned

3.15b The crankshaft correctly positioned, prior to fitting the locking tool

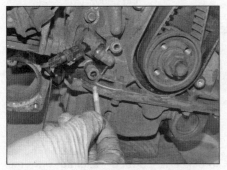

3.16a Remove the oil pump lower bolt ...

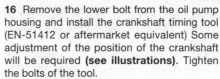

3.16b ... and fit the crankshaft locking tool

3.17 Fit the timing pin to the camshaft sprocket

14 Remove the timing belt high pressure pump cover **(see illustration)** and then working in reverse order to that shown remove the main timing belt cover **(see illustration 3.19)**.

15 If still fitted remove the crankshaft locking tool from the flywheel/driveplate and using a socket on the crankshaft pulley rotate the engine (clockwise) so that the pin in the crankshaft sprocket is at the 6 o'clock position. The hole for the camshaft locking tool will be in the 11 o'clock position **(see illustrations)**. If the hole for the camshaft locking tool is not in the 11 o'clock position, rotate the engine a further 360 degrees.

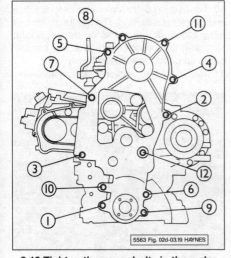

3.19 Tighten the cover bolts in the order shown

16 Remove the lower bolt from the oil pump housing and install the crankshaft timing tool (EN-51412 or aftermarket equivalent) Some adjustment of the position of the crankshaft will be required **(see illustrations)**. Tighten the bolts of the tool.

17 Fit the camshaft timing tool to the camshaft sprocket **(see illustration)**.

18 With the crankshaft locking tool in place and the camshaft positioning tool engaged with the slot in the camshaft, the engine is positioned with No 1 piston at TDC on compression.

19 Refitting is a reversal of removal. Tighten the main timing belt cover bolts to the specified torque in the order shown **(see illustration)**.

4   Crankshaft pulley/vibration damper – removal and refitting

Removal

1 Apply the handbrake, then jack up the front of the vehicle and support it on axle stands (see *Jacking and vehicle support*). Remove the right-hand front roadwheel.

2 Remove the engine undertray and the front wheel arch liner on the right-hand side as described in Chapter 11, Section 24.

3 Remove the auxiliary drivebelt as described in Chapter 1B, Section 22. Prior to removal, mark the direction of rotation on the belt to ensure the belt is refitted the same way around.

4 The crankshaft musts be locked in position to remove the pulley bolts. Remove the starter motor and lock the engine using either a

large screw driver in the flywheel/driveplate ring gear or with the special tool (EN-50432 – manual transmission or EN-51411 – automatic transmission). Alternatively a strap wrench can be used on the pulley itself.

5 Undo the bolts securing the pulley to the crankshaft sprocket and remove the pulley from the sprocket. Dispose of the bolts – new ones must be used.

Refitting

6 Locate the crankshaft pulley on the sprocket, ensuring that the hole on the rear face of the pulley engages with the lug on the sprocket.

7 Fit the new retaining bolts and tighten them in a diagonal sequence to the specified torque and angle.

8 Refit the auxiliary drivebelt as described in Chapter 1B, Section 22 using the mark made prior to removal to ensure the belt is fitted the correct way around.

9 Refit the wheel arch liner, engine undertray and roadwheel, then lower the car to the ground and tighten the wheel nuts to the specified torque.

5   Timing belt – removal and refitting

Note: *The timing belt must be removed and refitted with the engine cold.*

Removal

Caution: The timing belt, idler pulleys and belt tensioner have been modified by

5.0a The modified camshaft pulley …

5.0b … and the original without the belt retaining flange

5.0c A steel idler pulley is included in the updated kit. Note the extreme wear on the old pulley

Vauxhall. The replacement belt kit includes a new (modified) camshaft pulley with a belt retaining flange (see illustrations). If the vehicle does not already have the updated camshaft pulley, idlers and tensioner fitted then a updated timing belt kit must be fitted.

1 Position No 1 cylinder at TDC on its compression stroke as described in Section 3 with the timing tools installed.

2 If the belt is to be refitted, mark the direction of rotation and the position of the indicator on the belt tensioner. If the Vauxhall special high pressure pump alignment tool is not available mark the exact position of the high pressure pump before removing the belt **(see illustration)**.

3 Slacken the belt tensioner, remove the belt locking tools and ease the belt of the sprockets **(see illustration)**.

4 Check the timing belt carefully for any signs of uneven wear, splitting or oil contamination, and renew it if there is the slightest doubt about its condition. If the engine is undergoing an overhaul and is approaching the manufacturer's specified interval for belt renewal (see Chapter 1B Section 28) renew the belt as a matter of course, regardless of its apparent condition. If signs of oil contamination are found, trace the source of the oil leak and rectify it, then wash down the engine timing belt area and all related components to remove all traces of oil.

Refitting

Note: *If the old belt is to be refitted the belt tensioner bolt must be replaced. See also the caution note above.*

Note: *It is standard practise to replace the belt tensioner, idler pulleys and all bolts when the timing belt is replaced. Timing belt manufactures will often not guarantee the belt unless these component are replaced.*

5 On reassembly, thoroughly clean the timing belt, pump and crankshaft sprockets. Replace the tensioner and idler pulleys as described in Section 6.

6 Refit the camshaft timing tool and slacken the three camshaft sprocket bolts **(see illustration)**. DO NOT slacken the centre bolt.

7 Check that the high pressure pump sprocket is correctly aligned with the previously made mark. Where available, install the Vauxhall special tool (EN-51413 or aftermarket equivalent) and set the high pressure pump in position and lock it in place **(see illustration)**. Note that the tool is only used to position the fuel pump. Once correctly set, remove the tool.

8 Fit the belt to the crankshaft sprocket and fit the crankshaft timing tool. The engine must be at TDC (see Section 3).

9 Rotate the camshaft sprocket fully clockwise and then working anti-clockwise fit the timing belt around the idler pulleys and over the camshaft sprocket. Continue anti-clockwise under the idler, round the high pressure pump and finally over the belt tensioner.

10 New timing belts are marked for direction and correct positioning. The marks on the belt must align with the marks on the crankshaft sprocket, the camshaft sprocket and the fuel pump sprocket **(see illustrations)**.

11 Adjust the belt tensioner so that the belt is

5.2 Mark the position of the pump sprocket

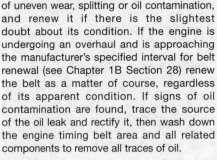

5.3 Remove the belt

5.6 Slacken the camshaft sprocket bolts

5.7 Lock the pump in position

5.10a The belt correctly installed on the camshaft sprocket …

5.10b ... the fuel pump sprocket and ...

5.10c the crankshaft sprocket

5.11 Tighten the belt tensioner just past the correct mark

slightly over tensioned **(see illustration)** and then tighten the belt tensioner to the specified torque. Note that the final adjustment is a torque and angle setting. The bolt must always be replaced.

12 Tighten the camshaft sprocket bolts to the correct torque **(see illustration)**.

13 Remove the locking tools and rotate the engine twice (720 degrees) in a clockwise direction. Note that the marks on the new timing belt will not align after rotating the engine.

14 Slacken the belt tensioner and adjust the tensioner to the correct position **(see illustration)**.

15 Tighten the new belt tensioner bolt to the specified torque and angle.

16 Refit the crankshaft timing tool and the camshaft timing tool. If the timing is correct the camshaft timing tool will fit easily. Note that if marks had been made to align the fuel pump then they maybe slightly out of alignment. This is normal.

17 Remove the timing tools and refit the oil pump bolt.

18 Refit the main timing belt cover and tighten the retaining bolts to the specified torque. Refit the high pressure pump cover.

19 Refit the engine bracket and tighten the bolts to the specified torque.

20 Refit the right-hand engine mounting as described in Section 18.

21 Refit the air cleaner assembly and intake duct as described in Chapter 4B, Section 3.

22 Refit the crankshaft pulley/vibration damper as described in Section 4, then refit

the auxiliary drivebelt as described in Chapter 1B, Section 22.

23 Refit the engine cover.

24 Refit the wheel arch liner, engine undertray and roadwheel, then lower the car to the ground and tighten the wheel nuts to the specified torque.

6 Timing belt sprockets, tensioner and idler pulley – removal and refitting

Note: *Certain special tools will be required for the removal and refitting of the sprockets. Read through the entire procedure to familiarise yourself with the work involved, then either obtain the manufacturer's special tools, or use the alternatives described.*

Camshaft sprocket and hub

Removal

1 Remove the timing belt as described in Section 5. Remove the camshaft positioning tool from the camshaft sprocket.

2 Fully remove the three sprocket adjustment bolts and lift off the sprocket.

3 The hub and timing plate are now accessible. Special tools are avialable (EN-51417 and EN-956-1) to hold the camshaft in position whilst the hub bolt is removed **(see illustration)**. A home made alternative can easily be fabricated.

4 Unscrew the retaining bolt and remove the

hub/timing plate from the end of the camshaft. Dispose of the bolt – a new one must be fitted.

Refitting

5 Prior to refitting check the oil seal for signs of damage or leakage. If necessary, renew it as described in Section 7.

6 Refit the hub to the camshaft and fit the retaining bolt. Hold the camshaft with the fabricated tool and tighten the new bolt to the specified torque and angle.

7 Refit the camshaft sprocket. Tighten the bolts so that the sprocket can rotate but is not loose on the shaft.

8 Proceed with the timing belt refitting procedure as described in Section 5.

Crankshaft sprocket

Caution: The bolt has a left-hand thread.
Note: *The crankshaft sprocket retaining bolt is extremely tight. Ensure that the holding tool used to prevent rotation as the bolt is slackened is of sturdy construction and securely attached.*
Note: *A new sprocket retaining bolt will be required for refitting.*

Removal

9 Remove the timing belt as described in Section 5.

10 It will now be necessary to hold the crankshaft sprocket to enable the retaining bolt to be removed. Vauxhall special tools EN-47630 and EN-956-1 are available for this purpose, however, a home-made tool can be fabricated. Alternatively, remove the starter motor as described in Chapter 5A Section 11 and use a flywheel locking tool to lock the

5.12 Tighten the camshaft sprocket bolts

5.14 Adjust the tensioner to the correct position

6.3 Hold the camshaft with the tool and slacken the bolt

6.10a A fabricated crankshaft locking tool

6.10b Alternatively lock the crankshaft at the flywheel

6.12a Remove the bolt and washer ...

crankshaft (see illustrations). If the sprocket is being removed to gain access to the oil pump locking the crankshaft with a block of wood between the crankshaft web and the engine block is another suitable method.

11 Using the crankshaft pulley retaining bolts, securely attach the tool to the crankshaft sprocket. With the help of an assistant, hold the sprocket stationary and unscrew the retaining bolt. **Note:** *The sprocket retaining bolt has a **left-hand thread** and is unscrewed by turning it clockwise.*

12 Remove the bolt and washer and slide the sprocket off the end of the crankshaft (see illustrations). Note that a new bolt will be required for refitting.

Refitting

13 Align the sprocket location key with the crankshaft groove and slide the sprocket into position. Fit the new retaining bolt and washer.

14 Hold the sprocket stationary using the holding tool and tighten the retaining bolt to the specified torque. Remove the holding tool.

15 Refit the timing belt as described in Section 5.

High-pressure fuel pump sprocket
Removal

Note: *Special tools (EN-51413, EN-51420 and EN-51585) are available to release the sprocket from the pump with the timing belt installed. These allow replacement of the high pressure fuel pump without disturbing the timing belt. If the sprocket is to be removed whilst the timing belt is replaced then only Vauxhall special tool EN-51413 (and a suitable puller) will be required. The use of the special tool is unavoidable, as any alternative method will damage the housing or the sprocket.*

16 Remove the timing belt as described in Section 5.

17 It will now be necessary to hold the fuel pump sprocket to enable the retaining nut to be removed. Vauxhall special tools EN-51413 (see illustration) and EN-51420 are available for this purpose.

18 Engage the tool with the holes in the fuel pump sprocket and undo the sprocket retaining nut (see illustrations).

19 Attach a suitable puller (or where available special tool EN-51420) and pull the sprocket off the pump shaft (see illustration).

6.12b ... and slide the sprocket off the end of the crankshaft

6.18a Fit the special tool so that the movable section (A) engages with the sprocket teeth

20 When the sprocket releases, remove the puller and withdraw the sprocket. Collect the Woodruff key from the pump shaft.

Refitting

21 Clean the fuel pump shaft and the sprocket hub ensuring that all traces of oil or grease are removed.

6.19 Use a suitable puller to release the fuel pump sprocket taper

6.17 The HP pump sprocket holding tool

6.18b Remove the nut

22 Refit the Woodruff key to the pump shaft, then locate the sprocket in position. Fit the retaining nut.

23 Hold the sprocket stationary using the holding tool and tighten the retaining nut to the specified torque (see illustration). Remove the holding tool.

6.23 Tighten the sprocket nut to the specified torque

6.27 The slot on the tensioner backplate must locate over the peg on the engine bracket

24 Refit the timing belt as described in Section 5.

Tensioner assembly

Removal

25 Remove the timing belt as described in Section 5.
26 Slacken and remove the retaining bolt and remove the tensioner assembly from the engine. Dispose of the bolt – a new one must be fitted.

Refitting

27 Fit the tensioner to the engine, making sure that the slot on the tensioner backplate is correctly located over the peg on the engine bracket **(see illustration)**.
28 Fit the new retaining bolt, set the tensioner in the retracted position and finger tighten the retaining bolt. Follow the timing belt fitting procedure to tighten the bolt, noting that the final angle setting is only carried out after confirming the correct timing (and tensioning) of the belt.
29 Refit the timing belt as described in Section 5.

Idler pulleys

Removal

30 Remove the timing belt as described in Section 5.
31 Slacken and remove the retaining bolt and remove the idler pulley(s) from the engine **(see illustration)**.

7.2 The seal before removal

6.31 Slacken and remove the retaining bolt and remove the idler pulley from the engine

Refitting

32 Refit the idler pulley and tighten the retaining bolt to the specified torque **(see illustration)**. Note the different torque settings for the upper and lower idler pulleys.
33 Refit the timing belt as described in Section 5.

---

7 Camshaft oil seal – renewal

1 Remove the camshaft sprocket and hub/timing plate as described in Section 6.
2 Note the position of the oil seal before removal. The edge of the seal should be in line with the bevelled edge of the camshaft bearing cap **(see illustration)**.
3 Carefully punch or drill a small hole in the oil seal. Screw in a self-tapping screw, and pull on the screw with pliers to extract the seal.
4 Clean the seal housing, and polish off any burrs or raised edges which may have caused the seal to fail in the first place.
5 Press the new oil seal into position using a suitable tubular drift (such as a socket) which bears only on the hard outer edge of the seal. Take care not to damage the seal lips during fitting; note that the seal lips should face inwards.
6 Refit the camshaft sprocket as described

8.5 Remove the camshaft position sensor

6.32 Fit the lower modified steel idler

in Section 6 and then refit the timing belt as described in Section 5.

8 Camshaft cover – removal and refitting

Removal

1 Remove the engine cover and oil dipstick.
2 Remove the fuel injectors as described in Chapter 4B Section 11.
3 Remove the turbocharger oil feed pipe.
4 Release the hose clips and remove the crankcase ventilation hose.
5 Unbolt the top fixing bolts from the timing belt cover (the bolts are captive in the cover) and then unbolt the camshaft position sensor **(see illustration)**.
6 Slacken the camshaft cover bolts and lift off the cover **(see illustration)**.
7 Remove the gasket from the cover (and dispose of it) and then remove the seals from the bolts. The bolt seals can be reused if in good condition. Note that given the amount of work involved removing the cover it would be a wise precaution to replace them anyway.

Refitting

8 Thoroughly clean the cover and inspect it for damage. Fit new seals and a gasket to the cover.
9 Clean the mounting surface on the cylinder head and then apply a small bead of sealant (Vauxhall 93165267 or equivalent) to the edge

8.6 Remove the cover

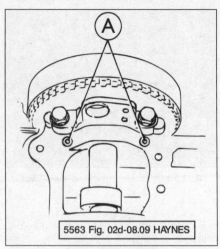

5563 Fig. 02d-08.09 HAYNES

8.9 Apply a 3 to 4 mm thick bead of sealant to the area shown (A)

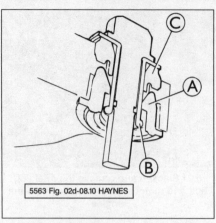

5563 Fig. 02d-08.10 HAYNES

8.10 The bolts must retain the gasket.
A = Valve cover gasket,
B = Bolt sleeve
C = Bolt insulator/gasket

8.11 Tighten the bolts in the order shown

of the exhaust camshaft bearing cap at the timing belt end **(see illustration)**.

10 Fit the bolts to the cover. They must be correctly located so that they are held in place. The bolt extends through the gasket **(see illustration)**.

11 Fit the cover to the cylinder head and tighten the bolts in the order shown **(see illustration)**, to the specified torque.

12 Refitting of the remaining components is a reversal of removal.

9 Camshafts – removal, inspection and refitting

Note: *Vauxhall/Opel special tools EN-51415 and EN-51418 (or suitable equivalents) will be required for this operation to lock the camshafts in the TDC position.*

Removal

1 Remove the timing belt as described in Section 5.

2 Remove the exhaust camshaft hub/timing plate as described in Section 6.

3 Remove the camshaft cover as described in Section 8.

4 Remove the braking system vacuum pump as described in Chapter 9, Section 22.

5 Install the camshaft locking tool (EN-51415) and lock the camshafts in the TDC position **(see illustrations)**. This tool is available in the aftermarket

6 At the base of the chain tensioner lift the tensioner with a trim tool (or thumb pressure) and install the locking pin (EN-51418). A simple pin can be fabricated from welding rod where the correct tool is not available **(see illustration)**.

7 Remove the tensioner bolt and then remove the sprocket bolts **(see illustrations)**. Dispose of all the bolts – they must be replaced. Note that the bolts (at the time of writing) are only supplied as part of a chain and tensioner kit.

8 The chain, tensioner assembly and sprockets are removed as a single item.

9 If required the chain tensioner can be dismantled and inspected.

10 Remove the camshaft locking tool and unbolt the double camshaft bearing cap at the chain end. Recover the guide dowels from the cylinder head if further work is required.

11 At the timing belt end of the engine unbolt the bearing cap from the exhaust camshaft **(see illustration)**.

12 Mark the position and direction of the bearing caps.

13 Slacken each bolt a turn at a time in reverse order to that shown **(see illustration 9.27)** Remove the exhaust camshaft bearing caps keeping them in the marked order.

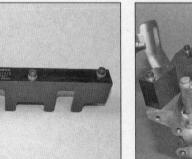

9.5a The camshaft locking tool

9.5b The tool installed on the camshafts

9.6 Lift up the tensioner and install the locking pin

9.7a Remove the tensioner bolts and the chain gear bolts

9.7b Spanners fitted to the flats on the camshaft help take the load of the camshaft tool when removing the sprocket bolts

9.11 Remove the exhaust camshaft bearing cap

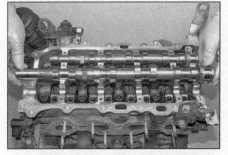

9.14 Remove the exhaust camshaft

9.15 The caps should be marked. The arrow points to the outside of the cylinder head

9.17 Remove the lower bearing support

14 Lift out the camshaft **(see illustration)**, slide off the oil seal and dispose of it. A new one will be required.

15 Mark the position and direction of the inlet camshaft bearing caps **(see illustration)**.

16 Remove the bearing caps in reverse order to that shown **(see illustration 9.25)** and lift out the camshaft.

17 If required lift out the lower bearing support saddle from the cylinder head **(see illustration)**.

Inspection

18 Examine the camshaft bearing surfaces and cam lobes for signs of wear ridges and scoring. Renew the camshaft(s) if any of these conditions are apparent. Examine the condition of the bearing surfaces in the cylinder head and bearing caps. If the any wear or scoring is evident, the cylinder head will need to be replaced.

19 If either camshaft is being renewed, it will be necessary to renew all the camshaft

followers and hydraulic tappets for that particular camshaft also (see Section 10).

20 Check the condition of the camshaft drive chain and sprocket for chipped or damaged teeth, wear ridges and scoring **(see illustration)**. Renew any components as necessary.

Refitting

21 Prior to refitting, thoroughly clean all components and dry with a lint-free cloth. Ensure that all traces of oil and grease are removed from the contact faces of the drive gears, sprocket and camshafts.

22 Refit the lower bearing support where applicable, then lubricate the camshaft bearing journals in the cylinder head and carefully insert the inlet camshaft.

23 If the engine is set at TDC, remove the crankshaft locking tool and rotate the crankshaft to lower the pistons in the bores. This will avoid any chance of the camshaft lobes opening a valve and making contact with

the piston crown. The height of the pistons can be checked through the injector holes.

24 Rotate the inlet camshaft so that the cam lobes on cylinder number 1 (at the timing belt end of the engine) point to the outside of the cylinder head.

25 Lubricate the camshaft bearing journals, lobes and bearing caps with engine oil and install the bearing caps. Tighten the bearing caps in the order shown to the specified torque **(see illustration)**.

26 Install the exhaust camshaft following the same procedure, but fit the camshaft so that the lobes on the camshaft (again on number 1 cylinder) point to the outside of the cylinder head. The groove for the camshaft hub/timing wheel will be in the 12 o'clock position.

27 Lubricate the camshaft bearing journals, lobes and bearing caps with engine oil and install the bearing caps. Tighten the bearing caps in the order shown to the specified torque **(see illustration)**.

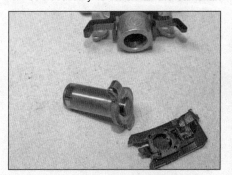

9.20 This tensioner was damaged by a stretched chain

9.25 Tighten the inlet camshaft cap bolts in the order shown

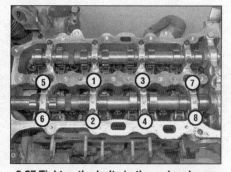

9.27 Tighten the bolts in the order shown

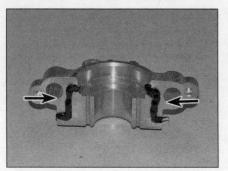

9.28 Apply sealant to the area shown

9.30 Fit the double bearing cap

28 Clean the mounting surface of engine oil and then apply gasket sealant to the front exhaust camshaft bearing cap in the area shown **(see illustration)**. The sealant should be no more that 3 millimetres thick and the cap must be fitted within 8 minutes of applying the sealant.

29 Tighten the bearing cap to the specified torque and then remove any sealant from the oil seal housing. Note that the specified torque is higher than the centre bearing caps.

30 Fit the rear (chain end) bearing cap and tighten the bolts from the centre outwards to the specified torque **(see illustration)**.

31 Fit a new oil seal to the exhaust camshaft as described in Section 7.

32 Fit the camshaft locking tool (EN-51415) to the camshafts.

33 Clean the camshaft bores and fit the complete chain, sprockets and tensioner assembly to the camshafts. Fit new bolts to the camshaft sprockets and tighten them so that they are just free to rotate. Fit the tensioner bolts and tighten them to the specified torque.

34 Remove the tensioner locking pin and allow the tensioner to take up the chain slack – the sprockets will rotate slightly. Tighten the camshaft chain sprocket bolts to the specified torque whist restring the camshafts with spanners on the flats of the camshaft **(see illustration 9.7b)**. This saves loading the camshaft locking tool and allows easy removal of the tool. Remove the camshaft locking tool.

35 Refit the remaining components in reverse order to removal.

10 Camshaft followers and hydraulic tappets – removal, inspection and refitting

Removal

1 Remove the camshaft cover and then remove the camshafts as described in Section 9.

2 Obtain sixteen small, oil tight clean plastic containers, and number them inlet 1 to 8 and exhaust 1 to 8; alternatively, divide a larger container into sixteen compartments and number each compartment accordingly.

3 Withdraw each camshaft follower and hydraulic tappet in turn, unclip the follower from the tappet, and place them in their respective container **(see illustrations)**. Do not interchange the followers and tappets, or the rate of wear will be much increased. Fill each container with clean engine oil and ensure that the tappet is submerged.

Inspection

4 Examine the followers and hydraulic tappet bearing surfaces for wear ridges and scoring. Renew any follower or tappet on which these conditions are apparent.

5 If any new hydraulic tappets are obtained, they should be immersed in a container of clean engine oil prior to refitting.

Refitting

6 Liberally oil the cylinder head hydraulic tappet bores and the tappets. Working on one assembly at a time, clip the follower back onto the tappet, then refit the tappet to the cylinder head, ensuring that it is refitted to its original bore. Lay the follower over its respective valve **(see illustration)**.

7 Refit the remaining tappets and followers in the same way.

8 With all the tappets and followers in place, refit the camshafts and camshaft cover as described in Section 9.

11 Cylinder head – removal and refitting

Note: *New cylinder head bolts will be required for refitting.*

Removal

1 Disconnect the battery negative terminal (refer to Chapter 5A Section 4).

2 Drain the cooling system as described in Chapter 1B, Section 26.

3 Remove the exhaust manifold as described in Chapter 4B Section 17.

4 Remove the EGR cooler as described in Chapter 4C Section 3.

5 Remove the inlet manifold as described in Chapter 4B, Section 12.

6 Remove the fuel rail (Chapter 4B Section 10) and fuel injectors as described in Chapter 4B Section 11.

7 Remove the brake servo vacuum pump as described in Chapter 9 Section 22.

8 Jack up and support the engine (see Jacking and vehicle support 13 Section 5) and then remove:

a) The right-hand engine mount.
b) The timing belt (Section 5).
c) The camshaft cover (Section 8).
d) The camshafts (Section 9).
e) The camshaft followers and hydraulic tappets (Section 10).

9 If not already done so, lift out the lower bearing saddle **(see illustration)**.

10 Remove the heater matrix coolant

10.3a Withdraw each camshaft follower and hydraulic tappet in turn

10.3b Place them in order in their respective container

10.6 Clip the follower back onto the tappet

11.9 Remove the bearing bracket

11.10 The cylinder head temperature sensor

11.12 Slacken the head bolts in the order shown

hose and then remove the cylinder head temperature sensor **(see illustration)**.

11 At the rear of the cylinder head (above the fuel pump), unbolt and remove the oil cooler upper bolt from the cylinder head.

12 Working in the order shown **(see illustration)** progressively slacken the cylinder head bolts by half a turn at a time, until all bolts can be unscrewed by hand. Remove the cylinder head bolts.

13 Engage the help of an assistant, if necessary, and lift the cylinder head from the cylinder block. Check that the guide sleeves in the engine block have not been disturbed. *Caution: Do not lay the head on its lower mating surface; support the head on wooden blocks, ensuring each block only contacts the head mating surface.*

14 Remove the gasket and keep it for identification purposes (see paragraph 22).

15 Dispose of the bolts – new ones must be used.

16 If the cylinder head is to be dismantled for overhaul, then refer to Chapter 2E Section 7.

Preparation for refitting

17 The mating faces of the cylinder head and cylinder block/crankcase must be perfectly clean before refitting the head. Use a hard plastic or wood scraper to remove all traces of gasket and carbon; also clean the piston crowns. Take particular care, as the surfaces are damaged easily. Also, make sure that the carbon is not allowed to enter the oil and water passages – this is particularly important for the lubrication system, as carbon could block the oil supply to any of the engine's components. Using adhesive tape and paper, seal the water, oil and bolt holes in the cylinder block/crankcase. To prevent carbon entering the gap between the pistons and bores, smear a little grease in the gap. After cleaning each piston, use a small brush to remove all traces of grease and carbon from the gap, then wipe away the remainder with a clean rag. Clean all the pistons in the same way.

18 Check the mating surfaces of the cylinder block/crankcase and the cylinder head for nicks, deep scratches and other damage. If slight, they may be removed carefully with a file, but if excessive, machining may be the only alternative to renewal.

19 Ensure that the cylinder head bolt holes in the crankcase are clean and free of oil. Syringe or soak up any oil left in the bolt holes. This is most important in order that the correct bolt tightening torque can be applied and to prevent the possibility of the block being cracked by hydraulic pressure when the bolts are tightened.

20 The cylinder head bolts must be discarded and renewed, regardless of their apparent condition.

21 If warpage of the cylinder head gasket surface is suspected, use a straight-edge to check it for distortion. Refer Chapter 2E Section 7 if necessary.

22 On this engine, the cylinder head-to-piston clearance is controlled by fitting different thickness head gaskets. The piston protrusion is represented by the position of holes in the gasket **(see illustration)**. Select the new gasket which has the same thickness/letter/number of notches as the original, unless new piston and connecting rod assemblies have been fitted or either gasket surface has been machined. In that case, the correct thickness of gasket required is selected by measuring the piston protrusions as follows:

23 Mount a dial test indicator securely on the block so that its pointer can be easily pivoted between the piston crown and the block mating surface.

24 Ensure the piston is at exactly TDC, then zero the dial test indicator on the gasket surface of the cylinder block. Carefully move the indicator over No. 1 piston. Measure

the piston protrusion on both the left- and right-hand sides **(see illustration)**. Repeat this procedure on No. 4 piston.

25 Remove the crankshaft locking tool and rotate the crankshaft 180° to bring Nos. 2 and 3 pistons to TDC. Measure the protrusions of Nos. 2 and 3 pistons, again taking two measurements for each piston. Once both pistons have been measured, rotate the crankshaft 180° to bring Nos. 1 and 4 pistons back to TDC and refit the crankshaft timing tool.

26 Take the average of each piston's measurements and record the highest average protrusion found. Use the table below to select the appropriate gasket. Note that this should only be required if the engine block has been machined or the pistons and connecting rods replaced.

Number of holes	Piston protrusion	Gasket thickness
No holes	0.266 to 0.393 mm	1.15 mm
One hole	0.393 to 0.463 mm	1.25 mm
Two holes	0.463 to 0.590 mm	1.35 mm

Refitting

27 Wipe clean the mating surfaces of the cylinder head and cylinder block/crankcase. Ensure the guide sleeves are in position and fit the new gasket.

28 Carefully refit the cylinder head assembly to the block, aligning it with the locating dowels.

29 Carefully enter each new cylinder head bolt into its relevant hole (*do not drop them in*). Screw all bolts in, by hand only, until finger-tight.

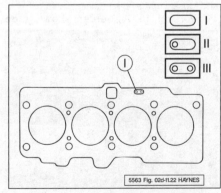

11.22 The holes denote the gasket thickness

11.24 Measure the piston protrusion

12.6 Remove the pick-up pipe

12.8 Fit a new gasket to the oil pump pick-up pipe

12.9 Apply a continuous bead of sealant as shown

30 Working progressively in the sequence shown, tighten the cylinder head bolts to their Stage 1 torque setting, using a torque wrench and suitable socket **(see illustration 11.12)**.

31 Once all bolts have been tightened to the Stage 1 torque, working again in the same sequence, go around and tighten all bolts through the specified Stage 2 angle, then through the specified Stage 3 angle, Stage 4 angle and then the specified Stage 5 angle using an angle-measuring gauge.

32 Fit the oil cooler upper bolt and sleeve.

33 Refitting of the remaining components is a reversal of removal.

34 On completion, reconnect the battery negative terminal, then refill the cooling system as described in Chapter 1B, Section 26.

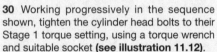

12 Sump – removal and refitting

Note: *The engine has a lower oil sump and and upper. The lower must be removed first.*

Lower sump

Removal

1 Disconnect the battery negative terminal (refer to Chapter 5A, Section 4).

2 Apply the handbrake, then jack up the front

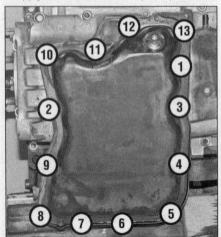

12.11 Tighten the bolts in the order shown

of the vehicle and support it on axle stands (see *Jacking and vehicle support*).

3 Remove the engine undertray as described in Chapter 11, Section 24.

4 Drain the engine oil as described in Chapter 1B, Section 5. When the oil has completely drained, refit the drain plug with a new drain plug and sealing washer. Tighten to the specified torque.

5 Remove the mounting bolts and carefully release the pressed steel sump away from the upper sump. Extreme care should be taken so as not to distort the sump.

6 While the sump is removed, take the opportunity to check the oil pump pick-up/strainer for signs of clogging or splitting. Unbolt the oil pump pick-up/strainer **(see illustration)** and remove it from the sump. The strainer can then be cleaned easily in solvent or renewed.

Refitting

7 Thoroughly clean the sump and remove all traces of silicone sealer and oil from the mating surfaces of the sump and cylinder block.

8 Fit the new oil pump pick-up/strainer gasket **(see illustration)** and refit the pick up pipe with new bolts.

9 Apply a continuous bead of silicone sealing compound (available from your Vauxhall/Opel dealer) at approximately 1.0 mm from the inner edge of the sump. The bead of sealant should be between 3.0 and 4.0 mm in thick **(see illustration)**.

10 Engage the sump with the cylinder block and loosely refit all the retaining bolts.

11 Working in the order shown **(see**

12.22 A prying point is provide below the crankshaft position sensor

illustration) progressively tighten the bolts to their specified torque setting.

12 Fill the engine with fresh engine oil as described in Chapter 1B, Section 5.

13 On completion, reconnect the battery negative terminal.

Upper sump

Removal

14 On model fitted with a manual transmission, remove the transmission as described in Chapter 7A Section 8.

15 On models fitted with an automatic transmission remove the exhaust front pipe as described in Chapter 4B Section 18.

16 On manual transmission models remove the flywheel as described in Section 17.

17 Remove the lower sump and oil pump pick-up pipe as as described above.

18 On models fitted with automatic transmission remove the two lower transmission to engine bolts and then remove the two hidden upper sump bolts.

19 Disconnect the wiring plug for the oil level sensor.

20 On manual transmission models remove the engine end plate.

21 Remove the upper sump bolts, noting the location of each bolt, as they are different lengths.

22 Carefully work around the upper sump and pry it free from the main engine block **(see illustration)**. Do not damage the mounting surfaces. Recover the seal and dispose of it – a new one must be fitted.

23 If required the baffle plate and oil level sensor can now be removed from the upper sump. Unbolt the baffle plate and level sensor. Remove the circlip and pull out the sensor wiring plug. Recover the seal and dispose of it – a new one must be fitted.

Refitting

24 Clean all the old sealant from the sump and engine block. Pay attention to the threaded holes in the block and run a tap down the threads to completely clean them if needed.

25 If removed refit the baffle plate and oil level sensor. A new seal must be fitted to the oil level sensor wiring plug.

26 Cut the head of two old bolts and cut

slots in the bolts so that they can be screwed into the engine block to act as guides to aid alignment of the upper sump. The bolts should protrude below the upper sump and the slot will enable them to be removed later.

27 Fit a new seal and then apply sealant to the upper sump as shown **(see illustrations)**. The sealant bead should be 3 to 4 mm thick and the sump must be installed within 10 minutes.

28 Install all the bolts and hand tighten them. On manual transmission models, place a straight edge across the front of the block and align the upper sump to the engine block. Both the front and rear edges at the transmission end must be flush.The aid of an assistant is recommended.

29 Evenly and in order fully tighten the upper sump bolts **(see illustration)**. Note the different torques for the different diameter bolts.

30 Refit the engine end plate and lower sump.

31 Refitting the remaining components in reverse order of removal. Do not fill the engine with oil for at least 3 hours.

12.27a Fit a new seal

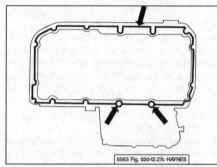

12.27c The bead must pass inside all the bolt holes. Note the additional sealant around the holes

12.27b Apply a bead of sealant to the upper sump

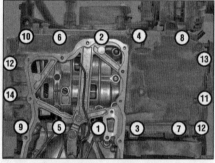

12.29 Tighten the bolts in the order shown

---

13 Oil pump – removal and refitting

Removal

1 Remove the timing belt as described in Section 5.

2 Remove the crankshaft sprocket as described In Section 6.

3 Remove the lower and upper sumps as described in Section 12.

4 Slacken and remove the retaining bolts then slide the oil pump housing assembly off of the end of the crankshaft **(see illustration)**. Remove the housing gasket and discard it.

5 It is possible to strip and inspect the oil pump, however Vauxhall provide no tolerance data, so if the pump is suspect it should be replaced. Details of the procedure are given in Chapter 2C Section 14. If removal of the pump was part of an engine overhaul it would

be foolish not to replace the pump regardless of the condition.

Refitting

6 If the pump has been replaced transfer the oil pressure control solenoid to the new pump.

7 Prior to refitting, carefully lever out the crankshaft oil seal using a flat-bladed screwdriver. Fit the new oil seal, ensuring its sealing lip is facing inwards, and press it squarely into the housing using a tubular drift which bears only on the hard outer edge of the seal. Press the seal into position so that it is flush with the housing and lubricate the oil seal lip with clean engine oil.

8 Ensure the mating surfaces of the oil pump and cylinder block are clean and dry.

9 Fit a new gasket to the oil pump housing and bend down the tabs on the edge of the gasket to retain it on the pump housing. Before fitting the oil pump push the bolts through the pump where the gasket has bolt retaining tabs incorporated **(see illustration)**.

10 Locate the pump housing over the end of the crankshaft and into position on the cylinder block.

11 Refit the pump housing retaining bolts and tighten them to the specified torque.

12 Refit the upper and lower sumps as described in Section 12.

13 Refit the crankshaft sprocket as described in Section 6.

14 Refit the timing belt as described in Section 5.

15 On completion, fit a new oil filter and fill the engine with clean oil as described in Chapter 1B, Section 5.

---

14 Balancer shaft assembly – removal and refitting

Removal

1 Remove the lower and upper sumps as described in Section 12.

2 Remove the crankshaft pulley as described in Section 4 and then set the engine to TDC (Top dead Centre) as described in Section 3.

3 Inspect the position of the balancer shafts

13.4 Remove the oil pump

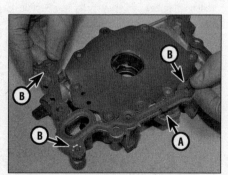

13.9 Bend down the tabs (A) on the edge of the gasket and install the bolts where retaining tabs are fitted (B).

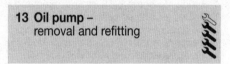

14.3 The shafts must be aligned before removal

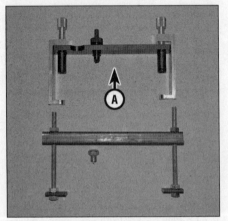

14.5a The factory tool (A) is easy to replicate

14.5b The locking pin on the tool. The pin locks the back lash compensator to the main gear

14.6a Remove the bolts. Note the mounting hole for the special tool (A)

14.4 The factory locking tool correctly aligned

in the housing. They must be aligned as shown **(see illustration)**.

4 A special tool (EN-51426-A) is available to lock the balancer shafts in position whilst the housing is removed. Where the tool is available, fit the tool ensuring that the locking pin is correctly aligned **(see illustration)**. The locking pin locks the backlash adjuster to the primary gear and locks the complete assembly together.

5 If the factory locking tool is not available then it can be easily replicated using threaded bar and a section of square bar **(see illustrations)**.

6 Remove the housing mounting bolts and lower the housing from the engine block **(see illustrations)**. Dispose of the bolts (new ones must be fitted) and recover the O-ring seal. Dispose of the seal a new one must be fitted.

Refitting

7 If the old housing is to be refitted, do not remove the tool. If a new balancer shaft assembly is to be fitted remove the tool. Replacement balancer shaft housings are supplied with a locking pin that is removed after installation.

8 Fit the housing with a new O-ring seal **(see illustration)** and then ft the housing to the engine block using new bolts. Tighten the bolts in a diagonal sequence to the specified torque.

9 Check that the shafts are aligned **(see illustration 14.3)** correctly with the engine still set at TDC.

10 Refit the upper and lower sumps as described in Section 12.

11 Remove the TDC timing tool and fit the crankshaft pulley using new bolts (see Section 4).

14.6b Leave the special tool attached

12 Fit the remaining components in reverse order of removal.

15 Oil filter housing – removal and refitting

Removal

1 The oil filter housing with integral oil cooler is located at the rear of the cylinder block, above the right-hand driveshaft.

2 Disconnect the battery negative terminal (refer to Chapter 5A, Section 4).

3 Remove the engine cover and then remove the air filter housing as described in Chapter 4B Section 3.

4 Apply the handbrake, then jack up the front of the vehicle and support it on axle stands (see *Jacking and vehicle support*).

5 Remove the engine undertray as described in Chapter 11, Section 24.

6 Drain the engine oil and remove the oil filter element as described in Chapter 1B, Section 5. When the oil has completely drained, fit a new drain plug and tighten to the specified torque.

7 Anticipate some oil loss and remove the turbocharger oil feed pipe banjo bolt. Dispose of the sealing washers – they must be replaced.

8 Disconnect the wiring connector from the oil pressure switch and remove the switch.

9 Undo the retaining bolts and remove the oil filter housing from the cylinder block. Recover the gasket. Note that a new gasket will be required for refitting.

Refitting

10 Thoroughly clean the oil filter housing, then fit the new gasket.

11 Position the oil filter housing on the cylinder block and refit the retaining bolts. Tighten the bolts to the specified torque.

12 Fit a new oil filter element and refill the engine with oil, as described in Chapter 1B, Section 5.

13 Refit the engine undertray, then lower the car to the ground.

14 Top-up the engine oil as described in *Weekly checks*.

15 On completion, reconnect the battery negative terminal.

14.8 Fit a new seal

16.2 Screw in a self-tapping screw and pull on the screw with pliers to extract the oil seal

16.4 Using a socket as a tubular drift to fit the new oil seal

16.11 Fitting the new oil seal housing, with integral oil seal over the crankshaft

16 Crankshaft oil seals – renewal

Right-hand (timing belt end)

1 Remove the crankshaft sprocket as described in Section 6.

2 Carefully punch or drill a small hole in the oil seal. Screw in a self-tapping screw and pull on the screw with pliers to extract the seal **(see illustration)**.

3 Clean the seal housing and polish off any burrs or raised edges which may have caused the seal to fail in the first place.

4 Ease the new oil seal into position on the end of the crankshaft. Press the seal squarely into position until it is flush with the housing. If necessary, a suitable tubular drift which bears only on the hard outer edge of the seal can be used to tap the seal into position **(see illustration)**. Note that Vauxhall list a special seal installer tool (EN-46793) and where this is available it should be used. Take great care not to damage the seal lips during fitting and ensure that the seal lips face inwards.

5 Wash off any traces of oil, then refit the crankshaft sprocket as described in Section 6.

Left-hand (flywheel/driveplate end)

6 Remove the flywheel/driveplate as described in Section 17.

7 Remove the lower and upper sumps as described in Section 12.

8 On manual transmission models remove the engine plate.

9 Undo the five bolts and remove the rear oil seal housing. Note that the oil seal and the housing are a single assembly.

10 Clean the crankshaft and polish off any burrs or raised edges which may have caused the seal to fail in the first place.

11 Position the new oil seal housing, complete with seal over the crankshaft and into position on the cylinder block **(see illustration)**. Note that the new oil seal housing maybe supplied with a protector sleeve over the oil seal. Where supplied, leave the sleeve in position as the housing is fitted.

12 Refit the five retaining bolts and tighten to the specified torque.

13 If fitted, remove the protector sleeve from the housing.

14 Refit the sump as described in Section 12.

15 Refit the flywheel/driveplate as described in Section 17.

17 Flywheel/driveplate – removal, inspection and refitting

Note: *New flywheel/driveplate retaining bolts will be required on refitting.*

Removal

Manual transmission models

1 Remove the transmission as described in Chapter 7A, Section 8 then remove the clutch assembly as described in Chapter 6, Section 6.

2 Prevent the flywheel from turning by locking the ring gear teeth with a similar arrangement to that shown **(see illustration)**.

3 Slacken and remove the retaining bolts and remove the flywheel **(see illustration)**. Do not drop it, as it is very heavy.

Automatic transmission models

4 Remove the transmission as described in Chapter 7B, Section 10, then remove the driveplate as described in paragraphs 2 and 3.

Inspection

5 Check the flywheel for wear and damage. Examine the starter ring gear for excessive wear to the teeth. If the driveplate or its ring gear is damaged, the complete driveplate must be renewed.

6 There should be no cracks in the drive surface of the flywheel. If cracks are evident, the flywheel must be replaced.

7 The following are *guidelines* only, but should indicate whether professional inspection is necessary. The dual-mass flywheel should be checked as follows:

Warpage

8 Place a straightedge across the face of the drive surface, and check by trying to insert a feeler gauge between the straightedge and the drive surface **(see illustration)**. The flywheel will normally warp like a bowl – i.e. higher on the outer edge. If the warpage is more than 0.40 mm, the flywheel may need renewing.

17.2 Prevent the flywheel from turning by locking the ring gear teeth

17.3 Flywheel retaining bolts

17.8 Flywheel warpage check – see text

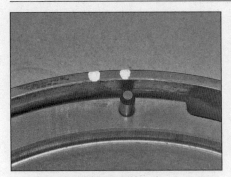

17.9 Flywheel free rotational movement check alignment marks – see text

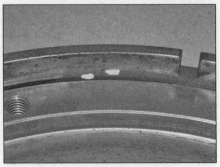

17.11 Flywheel lateral movement check marks – see text

Free rotational movement

9 This is the distance the drive surface of the flywheel can be turned independently of the flywheel primary element, using finger effort alone. Move the drive surface in one direction and make a mark where the locating pin aligns with the flywheel edge. Move the drive surface in the other direction (finger pressure only) and make another mark **(see illustration)**. The total of free movement should not exceed 20.0 mm. If it's more, the flywheel may need renewing.

Total rotational movement

10 This is the total distance the drive surface can be turned independently of the flywheel primary element. Insert two bolts into the clutch pressure plate/damper unit mounting holes, and with the crankshaft/flywheel held stationary, use a lever/pry bar between the bolts and use some effort to move the drive surface fully in one direction – make a mark where the locating pin aligns with the flywheel edge. Now force the drive surface fully in the opposite direction, and make another mark. The total rotational movement should not exceed 44.0 mm. If it does, have the flywheel professionally inspected.

Lateral movement

11 The lateral movement (up and down) of the drive surface in relation to the primary element of the flywheel should not exceed 2.0 mm. If it does, the flywheel may need renewing. This can be checked by pressing the drive surface down on one side into the flywheel (flywheel horizontal) and making an alignment mark between the drive surface and the inner edge of the primary element. Now press down on the opposite side of the drive surface, and make another mark above the original one. The difference between the two marks is the lateral movement **(see illustration)**.

Refitting

Manual transmission models

12 Clean the mating surfaces of the flywheel and crankshaft.
13 Offer up the flywheel and engage it over the positioning dowel on the crankshaft and install the new bolts.
14 Lock the flywheel by the method used on

removal then, working in a diagonal sequence, evenly and progressively tighten the retaining bolts to the specified torque.
15 Refit the clutch as described in Chapter 6, Section 6 then remove the locking tool, and refit the transmission as described in Chapter 7A, Section 8.

Automatic transmission models

16 Refit the driveplate as described in paragraphs 13 and 14.
17 Remove the locking tool, and refit the transmission as described in Chapter 7B, Section 10.

---

18 Engine/transmission mountings – inspection and renewal

Inspection

1 If improved access is required, firmly apply the handbrake, then jack up the front of the car and support it securely on axle stands (see *Jacking and vehicle support*). Remove the engine undertray as described in Chapter 11, Section 24.
2 Check the mounting rubber to see if it is cracked, hardened or separated from the metal at any point; renew the mounting if any such damage or deterioration is evident.
3 Check that all the mounting's fasteners are securely tightened; use a torque wrench to check if possible.
4 Using a large screwdriver or a pry bar, check for wear in the mounting by carefully levering

against it to check for free play; where this is not possible, enlist the aid of an assistant to move the engine/transmission unit back-and-forth, or from side-to-side, while you watch the mounting. While some free play is to be expected even from new components, excessive wear should be obvious. If excessive free play is found, check first that the fasteners are correctly secured, then renew any worn components as described below.

Renewal

Note: *Before slackening any of the engine mounting bolts/nuts, the relative positions of the mountings to their various brackets should be marked to ensure correct alignment upon refitting.*

Front mounting/torque link

5 Apply the handbrake, then jack up the front of the vehicle and support it on axle stands (see *Jacking and vehicle support*).
6 Remove the engine undertray as described in Chapter 11, Section 24.
7 Slacken and remove the through-bolt securing the mounting and vibration damper to the subframe bracket **(see illustration)**.
8 Undo the bolts securing the mounting bracket to the transmission, then manoeuvre the mounting and bracket out of position.
9 Check all components for signs of wear or damage, and renew as necessary.
10 Locate the mounting in the subframe, refit the through bolt and tighten the bolt finger tight at this stage.
11 Refit the mounting bracket to the transmission and tighten its bolts to the specified torque.
12 Tighten the through bolt to the specified torque.
13 On completion, refit the engine undertray and lower the vehicle to the ground.

Rear mounting/torque link

14 Apply the handbrake, then jack up the front of the vehicle and support it on axle stands (see *Jacking and vehicle support*).
15 Remove the engine undertray as described in Chapter 11, Section 24.
16 Undo the three bolts securing the mounting bracket to the transmission and the through-bolt securing the mounting to the bracket **(see illustration)**.

18.7 Front mounting/torque link through-bolt

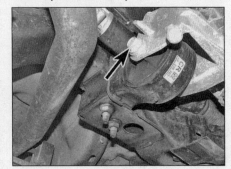

18.16 Rear mounting/torque link through-bolt

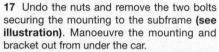

18.17 Rear mounting/torque link bracket-to-subframe mounting bolt nuts

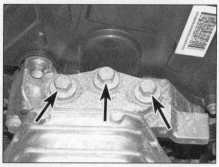

18.24a Right-hand mounting bracket-to-engine bracket bolts ...

18.24b ... and mounting-to-body bolts

17 Undo the nuts and remove the two bolts securing the mounting to the subframe (see illustration). Manoeuvre the mounting and bracket out from under the car.

18 Refit the bracket to the transmission and tighten the bolts to the specified torque.

19 Locate the new mounting in position. Insert the bolts and tighten the bolt/nuts to the specified torque.

20 On completion, refit the engine undertray and lower the vehicle to the ground.

Right-hand mounting

21 Apply the handbrake, then jack up the front of the vehicle and support it on axle stands (see Jacking and vehicle support).

22 Remove the air cleaner assembly as described in Chapter 4B, Section 3.

23 Attach a suitable hoist and lifting tackle to the engine lifting brackets on the cylinder head, and support the weight of the engine.

24 Mark the position of the three bolts securing the mounting bracket to the engine bracket and undo the bolts. Undo the three bolts securing the mounting to the body and remove the mounting assembly (see illustrations). If necessary, undo the three bolts and remove the mounting bracket from the engine.

25 Place the mounting assembly in position and refit the bolts securing the mounting to the body. Tighten the bolts to the specified torque. Align the mounting in its original position, then tighten the three mounting bracket bolts to the specified torque.

26 Remove the hoist, then refit the air cleaner as described in Chapter 4B, Section 3.

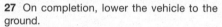

18.33 Left-hand mounting bracket-to-transmission bracket retaining bolts

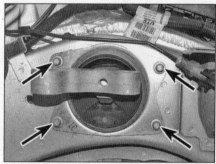

18.34 Left-hand mounting-to-body retaining bolts – shown with engine/transmission removed

27 On completion, lower the vehicle to the ground.

Left-hand mounting

28 Remove the battery, battery box and battery tray as described in Chapter 5A, Section 4.

29 Apply the handbrake, then jack up the front of the vehicle and support it on axle stands (see Jacking and vehicle support).

30 Remove the left-hand front roadwheel, then remove the wheel arch liner from under the front wing.

31 Attach a suitable hoist and lifting tackle to the engine lifting brackets on the cylinder head, and support the weight of the engine. Alternatively, support the transmission on a jack with a block of wood between the transmission and jack head.

32 Working under the front wing, unscrew the nut securing the mounting to the body.

33 From within the engine compartment, unscrew the three bolts securing the mounting bracket to the transmission bracket (see illustration).

34 Undo the four bolts securing the mounting to the body and the three bolts securing the transmission bracket to the transmission (see illustration). Remove the mounting assembly from the car.

35 Locate the mounting brackets in position then refit the nut and bolts and tighten them to the specified torque.

36 Disconnect the hoist and lifting tackle, or remove the jack, as applicable.

37 Refit the wheel arch liner and roadwheel, then lower the vehicle to the ground and tighten the wheel nuts to the specified torque.

38 Refit the battery tray, battery box and battery as described in Chapter 5A, Section 4.

Chapter 2 Part E
Engine removal and overhaul procedures

Contents

Degrees of difficulty

Easy, suitable for novice with little experience 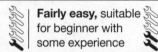	**Fairly easy,** suitable for beginner with some experience	**Fairly difficult,** suitable for competent DIY mechanic	**Difficult,** suitable for experienced DIY mechanic	**Very difficult,** suitable for expert DIY or professional

Specifications

Engine identification

1.8 litre (1796 cc) DOHC 16-valve petrol engine	2HO/A18XER
1.6 litre (1598 cc) DOHC 16-valve diesel engine	LVL/B16DTH/J
2.0 litre (1956 cc) DOHC 16-valve diesel engine	LBS/A20DTH, LBX/A20DTJ and LBR/A20DT
2.0 litre (1956 cc) DOHC 16-valve diesel engine	LFS/B20DTH

Petrol engines

Note: *Where specifications are given as N/A, no information was available at the time of writing. Refer to your Vauxhall/Opel dealer for the latest information available.*

Cylinder head

Maximum gasket face distortion	0.05 mm
Cylinder head height	N/A
Valve seat angle in cylinder head.	90° 30'
Valve seat width in cylinder head:	
Inlet	1.0 to 1.4 mm
Exhaust.	1.4 to 1.8 mm

Valves and guides

Stem diameter:	
Inlet valve:	
Standard size	4.965 to 4.980 mm
Exhaust valve:	
Standard size	4.950 to 4.965 mm
Valve head diameter:	
Inlet valve	31.10 to 31.30 mm
Exhaust valve	27.40 to 27.60 mm
Valve length:	
Inlet valve:	
Standard size	113.60 to 114.00 mm
Exhaust valve:	
Standard size	112.96 to 113.36 mm
Maximum permissible valve stem play in guide:	
Inlet	0.020 to 0.051 mm
Exhaust.	0.035 to 0.066 mm
Valve clearances (cold):	
Inlet valve	0.21 to 0.29 mm
Exhaust valve	0.26 to 0.34 mm

Petrol engines (continued)

Cylinder block
Maximum gasket face distortion	0.05 mm
Cylinder bore diameter	80.492 to 80.558 mm (nominal)
Maximum cylinder bore ovality and taper	0.013 mm

Crankshaft and bearings
Number of main bearings	5
Main bearing journal diameter:	
Standard size	54.980 to 54.997 mm
Big-end bearing journal diameter:	
Standard size	42.971 to 42.987 mm
Crankshaft endfloat	0.100 to 0.202 mm

Pistons
Piston diameter	80.455 to 80.515 mm (nominal)

Piston rings
Number of rings (per piston)	2 compression, 1 oil control
Ring end gap:	
Top compression	0.20 to 0.40 mm
Second compression	0.40 to 0.60 mm
Oil control	0.25 to 0.75 mm

Torque wrench settings
Refer to Chapter 2A.

Diesel engines

Note: *Where specifications are given as N/A, no information was available at the time of writing. Refer to your Vauxhall/Opel dealer for the latest information available.*

Cylinder head
Maximum gasket face distortion	0.10 mm
Cylinder head height:	
1.6 litre engine	127 mm ± 0.15 mm
2.0 litre (A20) engine	107 mm ± 0.05 mm
2.0 litre (B20) engine	130 mm ± 0.05 mm
Valve seat angle in cylinder head	
1.6 litre engine	45° ± 20'
2.0 litre (A20) engine	N/A
2.0 litre (B20) engine	45° ± 0.33°
Valve seat width in cylinder head	N/A

Valves and guides
Stem diameter:	
1.6 litre engine	
Inlet valve	4.969 to 4.985 mm
Exhaust valve	4.959 to 4.975 mm
2.0 litre (A20) engine	
Inlet valve	5.982 to 6.000 mm
Exhaust valve	5.972 to 5.990 mm
2.0 litre (B20) engine	
Inlet valve	4.90 to 4.94 mm
Exhaust valve	4.90 to 4.94 mm
Valve head diameter:	
1.6 litre engine	
Inlet valve	26.54 to 26.8 mm
Exhaust valve	24.24 to 24.5 mm
2.0 litre (A20) engine	N/A
2.0 litre (B20) engine	
Inlet valve	27.74 to 28.0 mm
Exhaust valve	24.24 to 24.5 mm
Valve length (inlet and exhaust):	
1.6 litre engine	N/A
2.0 litre (A20) engine	107.95 mm
2.0 litre (B20) engine	104.0 ± 2.5 mm
Maximum permissible valve stem play in guide	N/A
Valve clearances	Automatic adjustment by hydraulic cam followers

Diesel engines (continued)

Cylinder block

Maximum gasket face distortion	0.15 mm
Cylinder bore diameter	
1.6 litre engine	79.692 to 79.708 mm
2.0 litre (A20) engine	82.000 to 82.030 mm
2.0 litre (B20) engine	83.00 to 83.03 mm
Maximum cylinder bore ovality:	
1.6 litre engine	± 0.013 mm
2.0 litre (A20) engine	± 0.050 mm
2.0 litre (B20) engine	N/A
Maximum cylinder bore taper	0.005 mm

Crankshaft and bearings

Number of main bearings	5
Main bearing journal diameter:	
1.6 litre engine (standard size)	52.982 to 52.998 mm
2.0 litre (A20) engine (standard size)	59.855 to 60.000 mm
2.0 litre (B20) engine (standard size)	59.988 to 59.994 mm
Big-end bearing journal diameter:	
1.6 litre engine	N/A
2.0 litre (A20) engine	50.660 to 50.805 mm
2.0 litre (B20) engine	N/A
Crankshaft endfloat:	
1.6 litre engine	N/A
2.0 litre (A20) engine	0.049 to 0.211 mm
2.0 litre (B20) engine	0.027 to 0.197 mm

Pistons

Piston diameter:	
1.6 litre engine	79.655 ± 0.007 mm
2.0 litre (A20) engine	81.920 to 81.950 mm
2.0 litre (B20) engine	82.332 to 82.930 mm

Piston rings

Number of rings (per piston)	2 compression, 1 oil control
Ring end gap:	
1.6 litre engine	
Top compression	0.20 to 0.35 mm
Second compression	0.50 to 0.70 mm
Oil control ring	0.25 to 0.50 mm
2.0 litre (A20) engine	
Top compression	0.20 to 0.35 mm
Second compression	0.60 to 0.80 mm
Oil control	0.25 to 0.50 mm
2.0 litre (B20) engine	
Top compression	0.20 to 0.35 mm
Second compression	0.50 to 0.70 mm
Oil control	0.25 to 0.50 mm

Torque wrench settings

Refer to Chapter 2B (1.6 litre engine) Chapter 2C (2.0 litre A20 engine) or Chapter 2D (2.0 litre B20 engine).

1 General Information

1 Included in this Chapter are details of removing the engine/transmission from the car and general overhaul procedures for the cylinder head, cylinder block/crankcase and all other engine internal components.

2 The information given ranges from advice concerning preparation for an overhaul and the purchase of replacement parts, to detailed step-by-step procedures covering removal, inspection, renovation and refitting of engine internal components.

3 After Section 5, all instructions are based on the assumption that the engine has been removed from the car. For information concerning in-car engine repair, as well as the removal and refitting of those external components necessary for full overhaul, refer to Part A, B, C or D of this Chapter (as applicable) and to Section 5. Ignore any preliminary dismantling operations described in Part A, B, C or D that are no longer relevant once the engine has been removed from the car.

4 Apart from torque wrench settings, which are given at the beginning of Part A, B, C or D (as applicable), all specifications relating to engine overhaul are at the beginning of this Chapter.

2 Engine overhaul –
general information

1 It is not always easy to determine when, or if, an engine should be completely overhauled, as a number of factors must be considered.

2 High mileage is not necessarily an indication that an overhaul is needed, while low mileage does not preclude the need for an overhaul. Frequency of servicing is probably the most important consideration. An engine which has had regular and frequent oil and filter changes, as well as other required maintenance, should give many thousands of miles of reliable

service. Conversely, a neglected engine may require an overhaul very early in its life.

3 Excessive oil consumption is an indication that piston rings, valve seals and/or valve guides are in need of attention. Make sure that oil leaks are not responsible before deciding that the rings and/or guides are worn. Have a compression test performed, as described in Chapter 2A (petrol engines) Chapter 2B (1.6 litre diesel engine) Chapter 2C (2.0 litre A20 diesel engines) or Chapter 2D (2.0 litres B20 diesel engines) to determine the likely cause of the problem.

4 Check the oil pressure with a gauge fitted in place of the oil pressure switch, and compare it with that specified. If it is extremely low, the main and big-end bearings, and/or the oil pump, are probably worn out.

5 Loss of power, rough running, knocking or metallic engine noises, excessive valve gear noise, and high fuel consumption may also point to the need for an overhaul, especially if they are all present at the same time. If a complete service does not cure the situation, major mechanical work is the only solution.

6 A full engine overhaul involves restoring all internal parts to the specification of a new engine. During a complete overhaul, the pistons and the piston rings are renewed, and the cylinder bores are reconditioned. New main and big-end bearings are generally fitted; if necessary, the crankshaft may be reground, to compensate for wear in the journals. The valves are also serviced as well, since they are usually in less-than-perfect condition at this point. Always pay careful attention to the condition of the oil pump when overhauling the engine, and renew it if there is any doubt as to its serviceability. The end result should be an as-new engine that will give many trouble-free miles.

7 Critical cooling system components such as the hoses, thermostat and coolant pump should be renewed when an engine is overhauled. The radiator should also be checked carefully, to ensure that it is not clogged or leaking.

8 Before beginning the engine overhaul, read through the entire procedure, to familiarise yourself with the scope and requirements of the job. Check on the availability of parts and make sure that any necessary special tools and equipment are obtained in advance. Most work can be done with typical hand tools, although a number of precision measuring tools are required for inspecting parts to determine if they must be renewed.

9 The services provided by an engineering machine shop or engine reconditioning specialist will almost certainly be required, particularly if major repairs such as crankshaft regrinding or cylinder reboring are necessary. Apart from carrying out machining operations, these establishments will normally handle the inspection of parts, offer advice concerning reconditioning or renewal and supply new components such as pistons, piston rings and bearing shells. It is recommended that the establishment used is a member of the Federation of Engine Re-Manufacturers, or a similar society.

10 Always wait until the engine has been completely dismantled, and until all components (especially the cylinder block/ crankcase and the crankshaft) have been inspected, before deciding what service and repair operations must be performed by an engineering works. The condition of these components will be the major factor to consider when determining whether to overhaul the original engine, or to buy a reconditioned unit. Do not, therefore, purchase parts or have overhaul work done on other components until they have been thoroughly inspected. As a general rule, time is the primary cost of an overhaul, so it does not pay to fit worn or sub-standard parts.

11 As a final note, to ensure maximum life and minimum trouble from a reconditioned engine, everything must be assembled with care, in a spotlessly-clean environment.

3 Engine removal – methods and precautions

1 If you have decided that the engine must be removed for overhaul or major repair work, several preliminary steps should be taken.

2 Engine/transmission removal is extremely complicated and involved on these vehicles. It must be stated, that unless the vehicle can be positioned on a ramp, or raised and supported on axle stands over an inspection pit, it will be very difficult to carry out the work involved.

3 Cleaning the engine compartment and engine/transmission before beginning the removal procedure will help keep tools clean and organised.

4 An engine hoist will also be necessary. Make sure the equipment is rated in excess of the combined weight of the engine and transmission. Safety is of primary importance, considering the potential hazards involved in removing the engine/transmission from the car.

5 The help of an assistant is essential. Apart from the safety aspects involved, there are many instances when one person cannot simultaneously perform all of the operations required during engine/transmission removal.

6 Plan the operation ahead of time. Before starting work, arrange for the hire of or obtain all of the tools and equipment you will need. Some of the equipment necessary to perform engine/transmission removal and installation safely (in addition to an engine hoist) is as follows: a heavy duty trolley jack, complete sets of spanners and sockets as described in the rear of this manual, wooden blocks, and plenty of rags and cleaning solvent for mopping up spilled oil, coolant and fuel. If the hoist must be hired, make sure that you arrange for it in advance, and perform all of the operations possible without it beforehand. This will save you money and time.

7 Plan for the car to be out of use for quite a while. An engineering machine shop or engine reconditioning specialist will be required to perform some of the work which cannot be accomplished without special equipment. These places often have a busy schedule, so it would be a good idea to consult them before removing the engine, in order to accurately estimate the amount of time required to rebuild or repair components that may need work.

8 During the engine/transmission removal procedure, it is advisable to make notes of the locations of all brackets, cable ties, earthing points, etc, as well as how the wiring harnesses, hoses and electrical connections are attached and routed around the engine and engine compartment. An effective way of doing this is to take a series of photographs of the various components before they are disconnected or removed; the resulting photographs will prove invaluable when the engine/transmission is refitted.

9 Always be extremely careful when removing and refitting the engine/transmission. Serious injury can result from careless actions. Plan ahead and take your time, and a job of this nature, although major, can be accomplished successfully.

10 On all Insignia models, the engine must be removed complete with the transmission as an assembly. There is insufficient clearance in the engine compartment to remove the engine leaving the transmission in the vehicle.

4 Engine and transmission unit – removal, separation and refitting

Note: The engine can be removed from the car only as a complete unit with the transmission; the two are then separated for overhaul. The official factory method is to lower the engine out of position, and withdrawn from under the vehicle. If the factory procedure is used (and also bearing in mind the information contained in Section 3), ensure the vehicle is raised sufficiently so that there is enough clearance between the front of the vehicle and the floor to allow the engine/transmission unit to be slid out once it has been lowered out of position. However for the home mechanic it is possible to remove the engine and transmission up and out of the engine bay. For most of the engines covered in this manual this will require removal of the AC compressor and the crankshaft pulley.
Note: Such is the complexity of the power unit arrangement on these vehicles, and the variations that may be encountered according to model and optional equipment fitted, that the following should be regarded as a guide to the work involved, rather than a step-by-step procedure. Where differences are encountered, or additional component disconnection or removal is necessary, make notes of the work involved as an aid to refitting.

Removal

1 Have the air conditioning system fully discharged by an air conditioning specialist.

2 Position the vehicle as described in Section 3, paragraph 2 and remove both front roadwheels. On petrol engine models, remove the right-hand wheel arch liner lower cover. On diesel engine models, remove the engine undertray as described in Chapter 11, Section 24.

3 Remove the bonnet and the front bumper as described in Chapter 11, Section 6.

4 On diesel engine models, remove the cover from the top of the engine.

5 Remove the engine management ECU as described in Chapter 4A, Section 11 (petrol engine models) or Chapter 4B Section 8 (diesel engine models).

6 Remove the battery, battery box and battery tray as described in Chapter 5A, Section 4.

7 Carry out the following operations as described in Chapter 2A or Chapter 1B, as applicable:

a) *Drain the engine oil.*
b) *Drain the cooling system.*
c) *Remove the auxiliary drivebelt(s).*

8 Remove the air cleaner assembly and intake ducts as described in Chapter 4A, Section 2 (petrol engine models) or Chapter 4B, Section 3 (diesel engine models).

9 Lift off the cover from the engine compartment fuse/relay box, and unscrew the bolts securing the upper section of the fuse/relay box to the lower section. Lift the upper section off the lower section, while at the same time disconnecting the engine wiring harness block connectors.

10 Disconnect the reversing light switch wiring connector and release the wiring harness from the transmission **(see illustration)**.

11 Disconnect the wiring connector(s) from the radiator cooling fan housing. Release the wiring harness from the retaining clips so that it is free to be removed with the engine.

12 Remove the air conditioning system compressor as described in Chapter 3, Section 11.

Petrol engine models

13 Depressurise the fuel system with reference to Chapter 4A, Section 5, then disconnect the fuel supply pipe from the fuel rail and support bracket **(see illustration)**. Be prepared for fuel spillage, and take adequate precautions. Clamp or plug the open unions, to minimise further fuel loss.

14 Disconnect the brake vacuum servo hose, and fuel evaporation purge hose.

15 Disconnect the engine wiring harness connectors at the front left-hand side of the engine compartment **(see illustration)**.

16 Undo the retaining nuts and disconnect the earth leads at the front left-hand side of the engine compartment.

Diesel engine models

17 Disconnect the brake vacuum servo hose from the vacuum pump.

18 Disconnect the fuel return hose quick-release fitting, then release the retaining

4.10 Disconnect the reversing light switch wiring connector

clip and disconnect the fuel supply hose from the top of the fuel pump. Suitably plug or cover the open unions to prevent dirt entry.

19 Disconnect the wiring connector and vacuum hose, then undo the two bolts securing the turbocharger wastegate (charge pressure) solenoid valve to the upper body panel **(see illustration)**. Note not applicable to all engines.

20 Disconnect the wiring connector and vacuum hose from the vane position actuator on the underside of the turbocharger.

All models

21 Loosen the clips and remove the upper and lower radiator hoses.

22 Release the retaining clips and disconnect the coolant hoses at the cooling system expansion tank.

23 Using a small screwdriver, lift up the wire clips securing the two heater hoses to the

4.15 Disconnect the engine wiring harness connectors at the front left-hand side of the engine compartment

4.23 Lift up the wire clips and disconnect the heater hoses from the heater matrix pipe stubs

4.13 Disconnect the fuel supply pipe from the fuel rail

heater matrix pipe stubs, and disconnect the hoses from the stubs **(see illustration)**.

24 Wipe clean the area around the power steering pump reservoir filler neck, and unscrew the filler cap. Siphon as much of the power steering fluid from the reservoir as possible. **Note:** *Do not siphon the fluid by mouth, as it is poisonous; use a syringe or an old hydrometer.*

25 On models with hydraulic power steering, disconnect the high-pressure pipe and the reservoir supply hose from the power steering pump as described in Chapter 10, Section 23.

26 On automatic transmission models, disconnect the selector cable from the transmission as described in Chapter 7B Section 4. On manual transmission models, using a large screwdriver, prise the inner cable end fittings from the transmission selector lever ballpins **(see illustrations)**.

4.19 Undo the two bolts and remove the turbocharger wastegate (charge pressure) solenoid valve from the upper bodypanel

4.26 On manual transmission models, prise the selector cable end fittings from the transmission selector leverballpins

4.27 Push the retaining sleeves rearward and detach the outer cables from the transmission bracket

4.33a Prise out the clip securing the clutch hydraulic hose to the end fitting on the transmission bellhousing ...

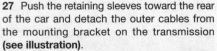

4.37 Right-hand engine mounting bracket-to-engine bracket retaining bolts

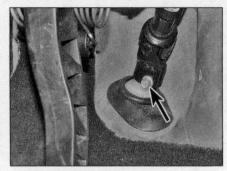

4.31 Unscrew the bolt securing the steering column intermediate shaft to the steering gear pinion

4.33b ... then detach the hose from the end fitting

4.38 Left-hand engine mounting-to-transmission bracket retaining bolts

27 Push the retaining sleeves toward the rear of the car and detach the outer cables from the mounting bracket on the transmission **(see illustration)**.

28 Drain the manual transmission oil or automatic transmission fluid as described in Chapter 7A, Section 2 (manual transmission) or Chapter 7B, Section 2 (automatic transmission).

29 Remove both driveshafts as described in Chapter 8, Section 2.

30 Position the steering with the front roadwheels straight-ahead, and lock the steering by removing the ignition key.

31 If the engine is to be lowered out of the engine bay, then working in the driver's footwell, unscrew the bolt securing the bottom of the steering column intermediate shaft to the steering gear pinion **(see illustration)**.

Use paint or a suitable marker pen to make alignment marks between the intermediate shaft and the steering gear pinion, then pull the shaft from the pinion and position to one side.

Caution: To prevent damage to the airbag wiring contact unit, the steering lock must remain locked until the intermediate shaft is re-attached to the pinion shaft.

32 On manual transmission models, remove the filler cap from the brake/clutch fluid reservoir on the bulkhead, then tighten it onto a piece of polythene. This will reduce the loss of fluid when the clutch hydraulic hose is disconnected. Alternatively, fit a hose clamp to the flexible hose next to the clutch hydraulic connection on the transmission housing.

33 Place some cloth rags beneath the hose,

then prise out the retaining clip securing the clutch hydraulic hose to the end fitting on top of the transmission bellhousing. Detach the hose from the end fitting **(see illustrations)**. Gently squeeze the two legs of the retaining clip together and re-insert the retaining clip back into position in the end fitting. Discard the sealing ring from the hose end; a new sealing ring must be used on refitting. Plug/cover both the end fitting and hose end to minimise fluid loss and prevent the entry of dirt into the hydraulic system. **Note:** *Whilst the hose is disconnected, do not depress the clutch pedal.*

34 On automatic transmission models, unscrew the central retaining bolt (or nut) and detach the fluid cooler pipes from the transmission. Suitably cover the pipe ends and plug the transmission orifices to prevent dirt entry.

35 Attach a suitable hoist and lifting tackle to the engine lifting brackets on the cylinder head, and support the weight of the engine/transmission.

36 If the factory method is used, then remove the front subframe as described in Chapter 10, Section 6.

37 Mark the position of the three bolts securing the right-hand engine mounting bracket to the engine bracket and undo the bolts. **(see illustration)**.

38 Mark the position of the three bolts securing the left-hand engine mounting to the transmission bracket **(see illustration)**.

39 Make a final check to ensure that all relevant pipes, hoses, wires, etc, have been disconnected, and that they are positioned clear of the engine and transmission.

40 If the engine is to be lifted out then remove the crankshaft pulley (B20 engine) and AC compressor.

41 If following the factory method (and with the help of an assistant), carefully lower the engine/transmission assembly to the ground. Make sure that the surrounding components in the engine compartment are not damaged. Ideally, the assembly should be lowered onto a trolley jack or low platform with castors, so that it can easily be withdrawn from under the car.

42 If lifting the engine out of the engine bay have an assistant operate the engine crane and carefully guide the engine out of the engine bay. Some rotation of the engine will be required as it is a very tight fit in the engine bay.

43 Ensure that the assembly is adequately supported, then disconnect the engine hoist and lifting tackle. If the engine was lowered out, withdraw the engine/transmission assembly from under the front of the vehicle.

44 Clean away any external dirt using paraffin or a water-soluble solvent and a stiff brush.

45 With reference to Chapter 7A, Section 8 or Chapter 7B, Section 10, unbolt the transmission from the engine. Carefully withdraw the transmission from the engine. On manual transmission models, ensure that

its weight is not allowed to hang on the input shaft while engaged with the clutch friction disc. On automatic transmission models, ensure that the torque converter is removed together with the transmission so that it remains engaged with the oil pump. Note that the transmission locates on dowels positioned in the rear of the cylinder block.

Refitting

46 With reference to Chapter 7A, Section 8 or Chapter 7B, Section 10, refit the transmission to the engine and tighten the bolts to the specified torque.

47 If using the factory method, raise the front of the vehicle and support it on axle stands. Move the engine/transmission assembly under the vehicle, ensuring that the assembly is adequately supported.

48 If using the alternative method connect the engine/transmission to the engine crane using the method used for removal.

49 If using the factory method, reconnect the hoist and lifting tackle to the engine lifting brackets, and carefully raise the engine/ transmission assembly up into the engine compartment with the help of an assistant.

50 If using the alternative method raise the engine/transmission on the engine crane and lower it into the engine bay.

51 Reconnect the right- and left-hand engine/transmission mountings and tighten the bolts to the specified torque given in the relevant Part of this Chapter. Ensure that the marks made on removal are correctly aligned when tightening the retaining bolts.

52 Where removed, refit the front subframe as described in Chapter 10, Section 6.

53 Disconnect the hoist and lifting tackle from the engine lifting brackets.

54 Refit the driveshafts as described in Chapter 8, Section 2.

55 The remainder of refitting is a reversal of removal, noting the following additional points:

a) Make sure that all mating faces are clean, and use new gaskets where necessary.

b) Tighten all nuts and bolts to the specified torque setting, where given.

c) Check and if necessary adjust the gearchange/selector cables as described in Chapter 7A, Section 3 or Chapter 7B, Section 3.

d) Refill the transmission with lubricant as described in Chapter 7A, Section 2 or Chapter 7B, Section 3.

e) Top-up and bleed the clutch hydraulic system as described in Chapter 6, Section 2.

f) Refill the engine with coolant and oil as described in the Chapter 1A or Chapter 1B.

g) Where fitted, fill and bleed the power steering hydraulic system as described in Chapter 10, Section 24.

h) Have the air conditioning system evacuated, charged and leak-tested by the specialist who discharged it.

5 Engine overhaul – dismantling sequence

1 It is much easier to dismantle and work on the engine if it is mounted on a portable engine stand. These stands can often be hired from a tool hire shop. Before the engine is mounted on a stand, the flywheel/driveplate should be removed, so that the stand bolts can be tightened into the end of the cylinder block/crankcase.

2 If a stand is not available, it is possible to dismantle the engine with it blocked up on a sturdy workbench, or on the floor. Be extra-careful not to tip or drop the engine when working without a stand.

3 If you are going to obtain a reconditioned engine, all the external components must be removed first, to be transferred to the replacement engine (just as they will if you are doing a complete engine overhaul yourself). These components include the following:

a) Engine wiring harness and supports.

b) Alternator, air conditioning compressor and power steering pump mounting brackets (as applicable).

c) Coolant pump (where applicable) and inlet/ outlet housings.

d) Dipstick tube.

e) Fuel system components.

f) All electrical switches and sensors.

g) Inlet and exhaust manifolds and, where fitted, the turbocharger.

h) Oil filter and oil cooler/heat exchanger.

i) Flywheel/driveplate.

Note: When removing the external components from the engine, pay close attention to details that may be helpful or important during refitting. Note the fitted position of gaskets, seals, spacers, pins, washers, bolts, and other small items.

4 If you are obtaining a 'short' engine (which consists of the engine cylinder block/crankcase, crankshaft, pistons and connecting rods all assembled), then the cylinder head, sump, oil pump, and timing belt will have to be removed also.

5 If you are planning a complete overhaul, the engine can be dismantled, and the internal components removed, in the order given below.

Petrol engines

a) Inlet and exhaust manifolds (see Chapter 4A, Section 12 and 13).

b) Timing belt, sprockets, tensioner and idler pulleys (see Chapter 2A, Section 8).

c) Coolant pump (see Chapter 3, Section 7).

d) Cylinder head (see Chapter 2A, Section 13).

e) Flywheel (see Chapter 2A, Section 16).

f) Sump (see Chapter 2A, Section 14).

g) Oil pump (see Chapter 2A, Section 15).

h) Pistons/connecting rod assemblies (see Section 9).

i) Crankshaft (see Section 10).

Diesel engines

a) Inlet and exhaust manifolds (see Chapter 4B, Section 12 and Chapter 4B Section 17).

b) Timing belt (or chain) sprockets, tensioner and idler pulleys (see Chapter – 1.6 litre engine, Chapter 2C – 2.0 litre A20 engine or Chapter 2D – 2.0 litre B20 engine).

c) Coolant pump (see Chapter 3, Section 7).

d) Cylinder head (see – 1.6 litre engine, Chapter 2C Section 12 – 2.0 litre A20 engine or Chapter 2D Section 11 – 2.0 litre B20 engine).

e) Flywheel/driveplate (see Chapter 2C, Section 17).

f) Sump (see – 1.6 litre engine, Chapter 2C Section 13 – 2.0 litre A20 engine or Chapter 2D Section 12 – 2.0 litre B20 engine).

g) Oil pump (see – 1.6 litre engine, Chapter 2C Section 14 – 2.0 litre A20 engine or Chapter 2D Section 13 – 2.0 litre B20 engine).

h) Piston/connecting rod assemblies (see Section 9).

i) Crankshaft (see Section 10).

6 Before beginning the dismantling and overhaul procedures, make sure that you have all of the correct tools necessary. See for further information.

6 Cylinder head – dismantling

Note: New and reconditioned cylinder heads are available from the manufacturer, and from engine overhaul specialists. Due to the fact that some specialist tools are required for the dismantling and inspection procedures, and new components may not be readily available, it may be more practical and economical for the home mechanic to purchase a reconditioned head rather than to dismantle, inspect and recondition the original head. A valve spring compressor tool will be required for this operation.

1 With the cylinder head removed as described in Chapter 2A, Section 13, Chapter 2B Section 11, Chapter 2C Section 12 or Chapter 2D Section 11 clean away all external dirt, and remove the following components as applicable, if not already done:

a) Manifolds (petrol engines – see Chapter 4A, Section 12 and Chapter 4A Section 13)

b) Manifolds (diesel engines – see Chapter 4B, Section 12 and Chapter 4B Section 17).

c) Spark plugs (petrol engines – see Chapter 1A, Section 26).

d) Glow plugs (diesel engines – see Chapter 5A, Section 17).

e) Camshafts and associated valve train components (see Chapter 2A Section 12, Chapter 2B Section 9, Chapter 2C Section 10 or Chapter 2D Section 9)

f) Fuel injectors (diesel engines – see Chapter 4B, Section 11).

g) Engine lifting brackets.

2 To remove a valve, fit a valve spring compressor tool. Ensure that the arms of the compressor tool are securely positioned on the head of the valve and the spring cap **(see**

illustration). The valves are deeply-recessed on petrol engines, and a suitable extension piece may be required for the spring compressor.

3 Compress the valve spring to relieve the pressure of the spring cap acting on the collets.

>
> **HAYNES HINT** *If the spring cap sticks to the valve stem, support the compressor tool, and give the end a light tap with a soft-faced mallet to help free the spring cap.*

4 Extract the two split collets by hooking them out using a small screwdriver, then slowly release the compressor tool **(see illustration)**.

5 Remove the valve spring cap and the spring, then withdraw the valve through the combustion chamber. Using pliers, remove the valve stem oil seal, which also incorporates the spring seat **(see illustrations)**.

6 Repeat the procedure for the remaining valves, keeping all components in strict order so that they can be refitted in their original positions, unless all the components are to be renewed. If the components are to be kept and used again, place each valve assembly in a labelled polythene bag or a similar small container **(see illustration)**. Note that as with cylinder numbering, the valves are numbered from the timing belt end of the engine. Make sure that the valve components are identified as inlet and exhaust, as well as numbered.

---

7 **Cylinder head and valves –** cleaning and inspection

---

1 Thorough cleaning of the cylinder head and valve components, followed by a detailed inspection, will enable you to decide how much valve service work must be carried out during the engine overhaul. **Note:** *If the engine has been severely overheated, it is best to assume that the cylinder head is warped – check carefully for signs of this.*

Cleaning

2 Scrape away all traces of old gasket material from the cylinder head.

6.6 Place each valve assembly in a labelled polythene bag or similar container

6.2 Using a valve spring compressor, compress the valve spring to relieve the pressure on the collets

6.5a Remove the valve spring cap ...

6.5c ... then withdraw the valve through the combustion chamber

3 Scrape away the carbon from the combustion chambers and ports, then wash the cylinder head thoroughly with paraffin or a suitable solvent.

4 Scrape off any heavy carbon deposits that may have formed on the valves, then

7.6 Using a straight-edge and feeler gauge to check cylinder head surface distortion

6.4 Extract the two split collets by hooking them out using a small screwdriver

6.5b ... and the spring ...

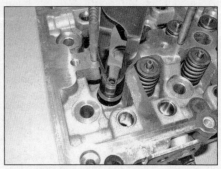

6.5d Using pliers, remove the valve stem oil seal, which also incorporates the spring seat

use a power-operated wire brush to remove deposits from the valve heads and stems.

Inspection

Note: *Be sure to perform all the following inspection procedures before concluding that the services of a machine shop or engine overhaul specialist are required. Make a list of all items that require attention.*

Cylinder head

5 Inspect the head very carefully for cracks, evidence of coolant leakage, and other damage. If cracks are found, a new cylinder head should be obtained.

6 Use a straight-edge and feeler gauge blade to check that the cylinder head surface is not distorted **(see illustration)**. If it is, it will be necessary to obtain a new or reconditioned cylinder head.

7 Examine the valve seats in each of the combustion chambers. If they are severely pitted, cracked or burned, then they will need

to be recut by an engine overhaul specialist. If they are only slightly pitted, this can be removed by grinding-in the valve heads and seats with fine valve-grinding compound, as described below.

8 If the valve guides are worn, indicated by a side-to-side motion of the valve, oversize valve guides are available, and valves with oversize stems can be fitted. This work is best carried out by an engine overhaul specialist. A dial gauge may be used to determine whether the amount of side play of a valve exceeds the specified maximum.

9 Check the tappet bores in the cylinder head for wear. If excessive wear is evident, the cylinder head must be renewed. Also check the tappet oil holes in the cylinder head for obstructions.

Valves

10 Examine the head of each valve for pitting, burning, cracks and general wear, and check the valve stem for scoring and wear ridges. Rotate the valve, and check for any obvious indication that it is bent. Look for pitting and excessive wear on the tip of each valve stem. Renew any valve that shows any such signs of wear or damage.

11 If the valve appears satisfactory at this stage, measure the valve stem diameter at several points using a micrometer **(see illustration)**. Any significant difference in the readings obtained indicates wear of the valve stem. Should any of these conditions be apparent, the valve(s) must be renewed.

12 If the valves are in satisfactory condition, they should be ground (lapped) into their respective seats, to ensure a smooth gas-tight

7.11 Using a micrometer to measure valve stem diameter

seal. If the seat is only lightly pitted, or if it has been recut, fine grinding compound **only** should be used to produce the required finish. Coarse valve-grinding compound should **not** be used unless a seat is badly burned or deeply pitted; if this is the case, the cylinder head and valves should be inspected by an expert to decide whether seat recutting, or even the renewal of the valve or seat insert, is required.

13 Valve grinding is carried out as follows. Place the cylinder head upside-down on a bench, with a block of wood at each end to give clearance for the valve stems.

14 Smear a trace of the appropriate grade of valve-grinding compound on the seat face, and press a suction grinding tool onto the valve head. With a semi-rotary action, grind the valve head to its seat, lifting the valve occasionally to redistribute the grinding compound **(see illustration)**. A light spring placed under the valve head will greatly ease this operation.

7.14 Grinding-in a valve

15 If coarse grinding compound is being used, work only until a dull, matt even surface is produced on both the valve seat and the valve, then wipe off the used compound and repeat the process with fine compound. When a smooth unbroken ring of light grey matt finish is produced on both the valve and seat, the grinding operation is complete. **Do not** grind in the valves any further than absolutely necessary, or the seat will be prematurely sunk into the cylinder head.

16 When all the valves have been ground-in, carefully wash off all traces of grinding compound using paraffin or a suitable solvent before reassembly of the cylinder head.

Valve components

17 Examine the valve springs for signs of damage and discoloration; if possible; also compare the existing spring free length with new components.

18 Stand each spring on a flat surface, and check it for squareness. If any of the springs are damaged, distorted or have lost their tension, obtain a complete new set of springs.

---

8 Cylinder head – reassembly

1 Lubricate the stems of the valves, and insert them into their original locations **(see illustration)**. If new valves are being fitted, insert them into the locations to which they have been ground.

2 Working on the first valve, dip the new valve stem seal in fresh engine oil, then carefully locate it over the valve and onto the guide. Take care not to damage the seal as it is passed over the valve stem. Use a suitable socket or metal tube to press the seal firmly onto the guide. **Note:** *If genuine seals are being fitted, use the oil seal protector which is supplied with the seals; the protector fits over the valve stem and prevents the oil seal lip being damaged on the valve (see illustrations)*

3 Locate the spring on the seat and fit the spring cap **(see illustration)**.

4 Compress the valve spring, and locate the split collets in the recess in the valve stem

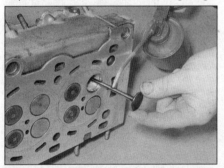
8.1 Lubricate the valve stem with engine oil and insert the valve into the correct guide

8.2b ... pressing it onto the valve guide with a suitable socket

8.2a Fit the valve stem oil seal and spring seat ...

8.3 Refit the valve spring and fit the spring cap

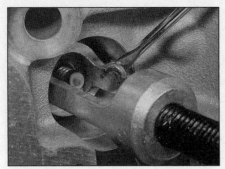

8.4 Compress the valve and locate the collets in the recess on the valve stem

(see illustration and Haynes Hint). Release the compressor, then repeat the procedure on the remaining valves.

5 With all the valves installed, support the cylinder head on blocks on the bench and, using a hammer and interposed block of wood, tap the end of each valve stem to settle the components.

6 Refit the components removed in Section 6, paragraph 1.

9 Pistons/connecting rods – removal

Note: New connecting rod big-end cap bolts will be needed on refitting.

1 Referring to Chapter 2A, Chapter, Chapter 2C or Chapter 2D clean away all external dirt, and remove the following components as ap remove the cylinder head and sump. Where fitted, unbolt the pick-up/strainer from the base of the oil pump.

2 On all models, if there is a pronounced wear ridge at the top of any bore, it may be necessary to remove it with a scraper or ridge reamer, to avoid piston damage during removal. Such a ridge indicates excessive wear of the cylinder bore.

3 If the connecting rods and big-end caps are not marked to indicate their positions in the cylinder block (ie, marked with cylinder numbers), suitably mark both the rod and cap with quick-drying paint or similar. Note which side of the engine the marks face and

Use a little dab of grease to hold the collets in position on the valve stem while the spring compressor is released.

accurately record this also. There may not be any other way of identifying which way round the cap fits on the rod, when refitting.

4 Turn the crankshaft to bring pistons 1 and 4 to BDC (bottom dead centre).

5 Unscrew the bolts from No 1 piston big-end bearing cap, then take off the cap and recover the bottom half-bearing shell. If the bearing shells are to be re-used, tape the cap and the shell together.

Caution: On some engines, the connecting rod/bearing cap mating surfaces are not machined flat; the big-end bearing caps are 'cracked' off from the rod during production and left untouched to ensure the cap and rod mate perfectly. Where this type of connecting rod is fitted, great care must be taken to ensure the mating surfaces of the cap and rod are not marked or damaged in any way. Any damage to the mating surfaces will adversely affect the strength of the connecting rod and could lead to premature failure.

6 Using a hammer handle, push the piston up through the bore, and remove it from the top of the cylinder block. Recover the bearing shell, and tape it to the connecting rod for safe-keeping.

7 Loosely refit the big-end cap to the connecting rod, and secure with the bolts – this will help to keep the components in their correct order.

8 Remove No 4 piston assembly in the same way.

9 Turn the crankshaft through 180° to bring pistons 2 and 3 to BDC, and remove them in the same way.

10 Crankshaft – removal

Note: New main bearing cap bolts will be required on refitting.

Petrol engines

1 Working as described in Chapter 2A, remove the flywheel and the oil pump.

2 Remove the piston and connecting rod assemblies as described in Section 9. If no work is to be done on the pistons and connecting rods, unbolt the caps and push the pistons far enough up the bores that the connecting rods are positioned clear of the crankshaft journals.

3 Before removing the crankshaft, check the endfloat using a dial gauge in contact with the end of the crankshaft. Push the crankshaft fully one way, and then zero the gauge. Push the crankshaft fully the other way, and check the endfloat (see illustration). The result should be compared with the specified limit, and will give an indication as to the size of the main bearing shell thrust journal width which will be required for reassembly.

4 If a dial gauge is not available, a feeler gauge can be used to measure crankshaft endfloat. Push the crankshaft fully towards one end of the crankcase, and insert a feeler gauge between the thrust flange of the main bearing shell and the machined surface of the crankshaft web (see illustration). Before measuring, ensure that the crankshaft is fully forced towards one end of the crankcase, to give the widest possible gap at the measuring location. Note: Measure at the bearing with the thrustwasher (see Section 17).

5 The main bearing caps should be numbered 1 to 5 from the timing belt end of the engine and all identification numbers should be the right way up when read from the rear of the cylinder block (see illustration). If the bearing caps are not marked, using a hammer and

10.3 Check the crankshaft endfloat using a dial gauge ...

10.4 ... or a feeler gauge

10.5 Main bearing cap identification markings – petrol engines

punch or a suitable marker pen, number the caps from 1 to 5 from the timing belt end of the engine and mark each cap to indicate its correct fitted direction to avoid confusion on refitting.

6 Working in a diagonal sequence, evenly and progressively slacken the ten main bearing cap retaining bolts by half a turn at a time until all bolts are loose. Remove all the bolts.

7 Carefully remove each cap from the cylinder block, ensuring that the lower main bearing shell remains in position in the cap.

8 Carefully lift out the crankshaft, taking care not to displace the upper main bearing shells **(see illustration)**. Remove the oil seal and discard it.

9 Recover the upper bearing shells from the cylinder block, and tape them to their respective caps for safe-keeping.

Diesel engines

10 Working as described in Chapter (1.6 litre engine) Chapter 2C (2.0 litre A20 engine) or Chapter 2D (2.0 litre B20 engine) remove the flywheel/driveplate, oil pump and the crankshaft left-hand oil seal housing.

11 Remove the piston and connecting rod assemblies as described in Section 9. If no work is to be done on the pistons and connecting rods, unbolt the caps and push the pistons far enough up the bores that the connecting rods are positioned clear of the crankshaft journals.

12 Before removing the crankshaft, check the endfloat as described in paragraphs 3 and 4.

13 Check the main bearing caps for identification markings. Normally, No 1 bearing cap (timing belt end) is not marked and the remaining caps are numbered I, II, III, IIII. The lug at the base of the cap is used to identify the inlet manifold side of the engine **(see illustrations)**. If the bearing caps are not marked, using a hammer and punch or a suitable marker pen, number the caps from 1 to 5 from the timing belt end of the engine and mark each cap to indicate its correct fitted direction to avoid confusion on refitting.

14 Working in a diagonal sequence, evenly and progressively slacken the ten main bearing cap retaining bolts by half a turn at a time until all bolts are loose. Remove all the bolts.

10.8 Removing the crankshaft – petrol engines

15 Carefully remove each cap from the cylinder block, ensuring that the lower main bearing shell remains in position in the cap.

16 Carefully lift out the crankshaft, taking care not to displace the upper main bearing shells.

17 Recover the upper bearing shells and the thrustwashers from the cylinder block, and tape them to their respective caps for safe-keeping.

---

11 Cylinder block –
  cleaning and inspection

Cleaning

1 For complete cleaning, remove all external components (senders, sensors, brackets, oil pipes, coolant pipes, etc) from the cylinder block.

2 Scrape all traces of gasket and/or sealant from the cylinder block and lower casing (where applicable), taking particular care not to damage the cylinder head and sump mating faces.

3 Remove all oil gallery plugs, where fitted. The plugs are usually very tight – they may have to be drilled out and the holes retapped. Use new plugs when the engine is reassembled. Where fitted, undo the retaining bolts and remove the piston oil spray nozzles from inside the cylinder block **(see illustration)**.

4 If the block is extremely dirty, it should be steam-cleaned.

5 If the block has been steam-cleaned, clean all oil holes and oil galleries one more time on completion. Flush all internal passages with warm water until the water runs clear. Dry the block thoroughly and wipe all machined surfaces with a light oil. If you have access to compressed air, use it to speed-up the drying process, and to blow out all the oil holes and galleries.

⚠ **Warning: Wear eye protection when using compressed air.**

6 If the block is relatively clean, an adequate cleaning job can be achieved with hot soapy water and a stiff brush. Take plenty of time, and do a thorough job. Regardless of the cleaning method used, be sure to clean all oil holes and galleries very thoroughly, dry everything completely, and coat all cast-iron machined surfaces with light oil.

7 The threaded holes in the cylinder block must be clean, to ensure accurate torque readings when tightening fixings during reassembly. Run the correct-size tap (which can be determined from the size of the relevant bolt) into each of the holes to remove rust, corrosion, thread sealant or other contamination, and to restore damaged threads. If possible, use compressed air to clear the holes of debris produced by this operation. Do not forget to clean the threads of all bolts and nuts which are to be re-used, as well.

8 Where applicable, apply suitable sealant to the new oil gallery plugs, and insert them into the relevant holes in the cylinder block. Tighten the plugs securely. Refit the oil spray nozzles into the block and secure with the retaining bolts tightened securely.

9 If the engine is to be left dismantled for some time, cover the cylinder block with a large plastic bag to keep it clean and prevent corrosion.

Inspection

10 Visually check the block for cracks, rust and corrosion. Look for stripped threads in the threaded holes. It's also a good idea to have the block checked for hidden cracks by an engine reconditioning specialist that has the equipment to do this type of work, especially if the vehicle had a history of overheating or using coolant. If defects are found, have the block repaired, if possible, or renewed.

10.13a Main bearing cap identification marks ...

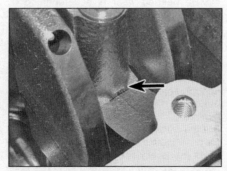

10.13b ... and the lug at the base of the cap is used to identify the inlet manifold side of the engine – diesel engines

11.3 Unscrew the retaining bolts and remove the piston oil spray nozzles from the cylinder block

11 If in any doubt as to the condition of the cylinder block, have it inspected and measured by an engine reconditioning specialist. If the bores are worn or damaged, they will be able to carry out any necessary reboring (where possible), and supply appropriate oversized pistons, etc.

12 Pistons/connecting rods – inspection

1 Before the inspection process can begin, the piston/connecting rod assemblies must be cleaned, and the original piston rings removed from the pistons. **Note:** *Always use new piston rings when the engine is reassembled.*
2 Carefully expand the old rings over the top of the pistons. The use of two or three old feeler gauges will be helpful in preventing the rings dropping into empty grooves **(see illustration)**. Take care, however, as piston rings are sharp.
3 Scrape away all traces of carbon from the top of the piston. A hand-held wire brush, or a piece of fine emery cloth, can be used once the majority of the deposits have been scraped away.
4 Remove the carbon from the ring grooves in the piston, using an old ring. Break the ring in half to do this (be careful not to cut your fingers – piston rings are sharp). Be very careful to remove only the carbon deposits – do not remove any metal, and do not nick or scratch the sides of the ring grooves.
5 Once the deposits have been removed, clean the piston/connecting rod assembly with paraffin or a suitable solvent, and dry thoroughly. Make sure that the oil return holes in the ring grooves are clear.
6 If the pistons and cylinder bores are not damaged or worn excessively, and if the cylinder block does not need to be rebored, the original pistons can be refitted. Normal piston wear shows up as even vertical wear on the piston thrust surfaces, and slight looseness of the top ring in its groove. New piston rings should always be used when the engine is reassembled.
7 Carefully inspect each piston for cracks around the skirt, at the gudgeon pin bosses, and at the piston ring lands (between the ring grooves).

12.2 Using a feeler blade to remove a piston ring

8 Look for scoring and scuffing on the thrust faces of the piston skirt, holes in the piston crown, and burned areas at the edge of the crown. If the skirt is scored or scuffed, the engine may have been suffering from overheating, and/or abnormal combustion ('pinking') which caused excessively-high operating temperatures. The cooling and lubrication systems should be checked thoroughly. A hole in the piston crown, or burned areas at the edge of the piston crown indicates that abnormal combustion (pre-ignition, 'pinking', knocking or detonation) has been occurring. If any of the above problems exist, the causes must be investigated and corrected, or the damage will occur again.
9 Corrosion of the piston, in the form of pitting, indicates that coolant has been leaking into the combustion chamber and/or the crankcase. Again, the cause must be corrected, or the problem may persist in the rebuilt engine.
10 If in any doubt as to the condition of the pistons and connecting rods, have them inspected and measured by an engine reconditioning specialist. If new parts are required, they will be able to supply and fit appropriate-sized pistons/rings, and rebore (where possible) or hone the cylinder block.

13 Crankshaft – inspection

1 Clean the crankshaft using paraffin or a suitable solvent, and dry it, preferably with compressed air if available. Be sure to clean the oil holes with a pipe cleaner or similar probe, to ensure that they are not obstructed.

⚠️ *Warning: Wear eye protection when using compressed air.*

2 Check the main and big-end bearing journals for uneven wear, scoring, pitting and cracking.
3 Big-end bearing wear is accompanied by distinct metallic knocking when the engine is running (particularly noticeable when the engine is pulling from low revs), and some loss of oil pressure.
4 Main bearing wear is accompanied by severe engine vibration and rumble – getting progressively worse as engine revs increase – and again by loss of oil pressure.
5 Check the bearing journal for roughness by running a finger lightly over the bearing surface. Any roughness (which will be accompanied by obvious bearing wear) indicates that the crankshaft requires regrinding.
6 If the crankshaft has been reground, check for burrs around the crankshaft oil holes (the holes are usually chamfered, so burrs should not be a problem unless regrinding has been carried out carelessly). Remove any burrs with a fine file or scraper, and thoroughly clean the oil holes as described previously.

13.8 Transfer the crankshaft speed/position sensor pulse pick-up ring to the new crankshaft

7 Have the crankshaft journals measured by an engine reconditioning specialist. If the crankshaft is worn or damaged, they may be able to regrind the journals and supply suitable undersize bearing shells. If no undersize shells are available and the crankshaft has worn beyond the specified limits, it will have to be renewed. Consult your Vauxhall/Opel dealer or engine reconditioning specialist for further information on parts availability.
8 If a new crankshaft is to be fitted, undo the screws securing the crankshaft speed/position sensor pulse pick-up ring to the crankshaft, and transfer the ring to the new crankshaft **(see illustration)**.

14 Main and big-end bearings – inspection

1 Even though the main and big-end bearings should be renewed during the engine overhaul, the old bearings should be retained for close examination, as they may reveal valuable information about the condition of the engine.
2 Bearing failure occurs because of lack of lubrication, the presence of dirt or other foreign particles, overloading the engine, or corrosion **(see illustration)**. If a bearing fails, the cause must be found and eliminated before the engine is reassembled, to prevent the failure from happening again.
3 To examine the bearing shells, remove them from the cylinder block, the main bearing caps, the connecting rods and the big-end bearing caps, and lay them out on a clean surface in the same order as they were fitted to the engine. This will enable any bearing problems to be matched with the corresponding crankshaft journal.
4 Dirt and other foreign particles can enter the engine in a variety of ways. Contamination may be left in the engine during assembly, or it may pass through filters or the crankcase ventilation system. Normal engine wear produces small particles of metal, which can eventually cause problems. If particles find their way into the lubrication system, it is likely that they will eventually be carried to the bearings. Whatever

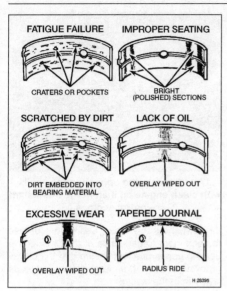

14.2 Typical bearing failures

the source, these foreign particles often end up embedded in the soft bearing material, and are easily recognised. Large particles will not embed in the bearing, and will score or gouge the bearing and journal. To prevent possible contamination, clean all parts thoroughly, and keep everything spotlessly-clean during engine assembly. Once the engine has been installed in the vehicle, ensure that engine oil and filter changes are carried out at the recommended intervals.

5 Lack of lubrication (or lubrication breakdown) has a number of interrelated causes. Excessive heat (which thins the oil), overloading (which squeezes the oil from the bearing face), and oil leakage (from excessive bearing clearances, worn oil pump or high engine speeds) all contribute to lubrication breakdown. Blocked oil passages, which may be the result of misaligned oil holes in a bearing shell, will also starve a bearing of oil and destroy it. When lack of lubrication is the cause of bearing failure, the bearing material is wiped or extruded from the steel backing of the bearing. Temperatures may increase to the point where the steel backing turns blue from overheating.

6 Driving habits can have a definite effect on bearing life. Full-throttle, low-speed operation (labouring the engine) puts very high loads on bearings, which tends to squeeze out the oil film. These loads cause the bearings to flex, which produces fine cracks in the bearing face (fatigue failure). Eventually the bearing material will loosen in places, and tear away from the steel backing. Regular short journeys can lead to corrosion of bearings, because insufficient engine heat is produced to drive off the condensed water and corrosive gases which form inside the engine. These products collect in the engine oil, forming acid and sludge. As the oil is carried to the bearings, the acid attacks and corrodes the bearing material.

7 Incorrect bearing installation during engine assembly will also lead to bearing failure. Tight-fitting bearings leave insufficient bearing lubrication clearance, and will result in oil starvation. Dirt or foreign particles trapped behind a bearing shell results in high spots on the bearing which can lead to failure.

8 Do not touch any shell's bearing surface with your fingers during reassembly; there is a risk of scratching the delicate surface, or of depositing particles of dirt on it.

9 As mentioned at the beginning of this Section, the bearing shells should be renewed as a matter of course during engine overhaul; to do otherwise is false economy.

15 Engine overhaul – reassembly sequence

1 Before reassembly begins, ensure that all necessary new parts have been obtained (particularly gaskets, and various bolts which must be renewed), and that all the tools required are available. Read through the entire procedure to familiarise yourself with the work involved, and to ensure that all items necessary for reassembly of the engine are to hand. In addition to all normal tools and materials, a thread-locking compound will be required. A tube of suitable sealant will be required to seal certain joint faces which are not fitted with gaskets.

2 In order to save time and avoid problems, engine reassembly can be carried out in the following order:

Petrol engines

a) Piston rings (see Section 16).
b) Crankshaft (see Section 17).
c) Piston/connecting rod assemblies (see Section 18).
d) Oil pump (see Chapter 2A, Section 15).
e) Sump (see Chapter 2A, Section 14).
f) Flywheel (see Chapter 2A, Section 16).
g) Cylinder head (see Chapter 2A, Section 13).
h) Coolant pump (see Chapter 3, Section 7).
i) Timing belt and sprockets (see Chapter 2A, Section 8).
j) Inlet and exhaust manifolds (see Chapter 4A, Section 12 and 13).

16.4 Measuring a piston ring end gap using a feeler gauge

Diesel engines

a) Piston rings (see Section 16).
b) Crankshaft (see Section 17).
c) Pistons/connecting rod assemblies (see Section 18).
d) Cylinder head (see Chapter 2B Section 11, Chapter 2C Section 12 or Chapter 2D Section 11).
e) Oil pump (see Chapter 2B Section 13, Chapter 2C Section 14 or Chapter 2D Section 13).
f) Sump (see Chapter 2B Section 12, Chapter 2C Section 13 or Chapter 2D Section 12).
g) Flywheel/driveplate (see Chapter 2B Section 17, Chapter 2C Section 17 or Chapter 2D Section 17).
h) Coolant pump (see Chapter 3, Section 7).
i) Timing belt/chain, sprockets, tensioner and idler pulleys (see Chapter 2B, Chapter 2C or Chapter 2D.
j) Inlet and exhaust manifolds (see Chapter 4B, Section 12 and Chapter 4B Section 17).

3 At this stage, all engine components should be absolutely clean and dry, with all faults repaired. The components should be laid out (or in individual containers) on a completely clean work surface.

16 Piston rings – refitting

1 Before refitting the new piston rings, the ring end gaps must be checked as follows.
2 Lay out the piston/connecting rod assemblies and the new piston ring sets, so that the ring sets will be matched with the same piston and cylinder during the end gap measurement and subsequent engine reassembly.
3 Insert the top ring into the first cylinder, and push it down the bore slightly using the top of the piston. This will ensure that the ring remains square with the cylinder walls. Push the ring down into the bore until it is positioned 15 to 20 mm down from the top edge of the bore, then withdraw the piston.
4 Measure the end gap using feeler gauges, and compare the measurements with the figures given in the Specifications **(see illustration)**.
5 If the gap is too small (unlikely if genuine Vauxhall/Opel parts are used), it must be enlarged or the ring ends may contact each other during engine operation, causing serious damage. Ideally, new piston rings providing the correct end gap should be fitted, but as a last resort, the end gap can be increased by filing the ring ends very carefully with a fine file. Mount the file in a vice equipped with soft jaws, slip the ring over the file with the ends contacting the file face, and slowly move the ring to remove material from the ends – take care, as piston rings are sharp, and are easily broken.

16.9 Fitting the oil control spreader ring

17.6 Fitting a main bearing shell to the cylinder block

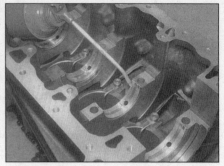

17.7 Lubricate the upper bearing shells with clean engine oil then fit the crankshaft – petrol engines

6 With new piston rings, it is unlikely that the end gap will be too large. If they are too large, check that you have the correct rings for your engine and for the particular cylinder bore size.

7 Repeat the checking procedure for each ring in the first cylinder, and then for the rings in the remaining cylinders. Remember to keep rings, pistons and cylinders matched up.

8 Once the ring end gaps have been checked and if necessary corrected, the rings can be fitted to the pistons.

9 The oil control ring (lowest one on the piston) is composed of three sections, and should be installed first. Fit the lower steel ring, then the spreader ring, followed by the upper steel ring **(see illustration)**.

10 With the oil control ring components installed, the second (middle) ring can be fitted. It is usually stamped with a mark (TOP) which must face up, towards the top of the piston. **Note:** *Always follow the instructions supplied with the new piston ring sets – different manufacturers may specify different procedures. Do not mix up the top and middle rings, as they have different cross-sections.* Using two or three old feeler blades, as for removal of the old rings, carefully slip the ring into place in the middle groove.

11 Fit the top ring in the same manner, ensuring that, where applicable, the mark on the ring is facing up. If a stepped ring is being fitted, fit the ring with the smaller diameter of the step uppermost.

12 Repeat the procedure for the remaining pistons and rings.

17 Crankshaft – refitting

Note: *It is recommended that new main bearing shells are fitted regardless of the condition of the original ones.*

1 Refitting the crankshaft is the first step in the engine reassembly procedure. It is assumed at this point that the cylinder block, cylinder block lower casing (where applicable) and crankshaft have been cleaned, inspected and repaired or reconditioned as necessary.

2 Position the cylinder block with the sump mating face uppermost.

3 Clean the bearing shells and the bearing recesses in both the cylinder block and the bearing caps. If new shells are being fitted, ensure that all traces of the protective grease are cleaned off using paraffin. Wipe the shells dry with a clean lint-free cloth.

4 Note that the crankshaft endfloat is controlled by thrustwashers located on one of the main bearing shells. The thrustwashers may be separate or incorporated into, or attached to, the bearing shells themselves.

5 If the original bearing shells are being re-used, they must be refitted to their original locations in the block or caps.

6 Fit the upper main bearing shells in place in the cylinder block, ensuring that the tab on each shell engages in the notch in the cylinder block **(see illustration)**. Where separate

thrustwashers are fitted, use a little grease to stick them to each side of their respective bearing upper location; ensure that the oilway grooves on each thrustwasher face outwards (away from the block).

Petrol engines

7 Liberally lubricate each bearing shell in the cylinder block, and lower the crankshaft into position **(see illustration)**.

8 If necessary, seat the crankshaft using light taps from a soft-faced mallet on the crankshaft balance webs.

9 Fit the bearing shells into the bearing caps.

10 Lubricate the bearing shells in the bearing caps, and the crankshaft journals, then fit Nos 1, 2, 3 and 4 bearing caps, and tighten the new bolts as far as possible by hand **(see illustration)**.

11 Ensure the rear (No 5) bearing cap is clean and dry then fill the groove on each side of the cap with sealing compound (Vauxhall/Opel recommend the use of sealant, part no 90485251, available from your dealer) **(see illustration)**. Fit the bearing cap to the engine, ensuring it is fitted the correct way around, and tighten the new bolts as far as possible by hand.

12 Working in a diagonal sequence from the centre outwards, tighten the main bearing cap bolts to the specified Stage 1 torque setting **(see illustration)**.

13 Once all bolts are tightened to the specified Stage 1 torque, go around again and tighten all bolts through the specified Stage 2

17.10 Lubricate the crankshaft journals then refit bearing caps Nos 1 to 4 – petrol engines

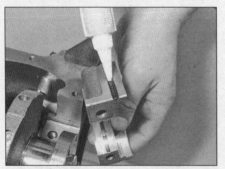

17.11 Fill the side grooves of the rear (No 5) bearing cap with sealant prior to refitting it to the engine – petrol engines

17.12 Tighten the bolts to the specified Stage 1 torque setting ...

angle then go around once more and tighten all bolts through the specified Stage 3 angle. It is recommended that an angle-measuring gauge is used during the final stages of the tightening, to ensure accuracy **(see illustration)**. If a gauge is not available, use white paint to make alignment marks between the bolt head and cap prior to tightening; the marks can then be used to check that the bolt has been rotated through the correct angle.

14 Once all the bolts have been tightened, inject more sealant down the grooves in the rear main bearing cap until sealant is seen to be escaping through the joints. Once you are sure the cap grooves are full of sealant, wipe off all excess sealant using a clean cloth.

15 Check that the crankshaft is free to rotate smoothly; if excessive pressure is required to turn the crankshaft, investigate the cause before proceeding further.

16 Check the crankshaft endfloat with reference to Section 10.

17 Refit/reconnect the piston connecting rod assemblies to the crankshaft as described in Section 18.

18 Referring to Chapter 2A, fit a new left-hand crankshaft oil seal, then refit the oil pump, sump, flywheel, cylinder head, timing belt sprocket(s) and fit a new timing belt.

Diesel engines

19 Liberally lubricate each bearing shell in the cylinder block, and lower the crankshaft into position.

20 If necessary, seat the crankshaft using light taps from a soft-faced mallet on the crankshaft balance webs.

21 Fit the bearing shells into the bearing caps.

22 Lubricate the bearing shells in the bearing caps, and the crankshaft journals, then fit the caps ensuring they are fitted to their correct locations and the right way around. Fit and tighten the new bolts as far as possible by hand.

23 Working in a spiral pattern from the centre outwards, tighten the main bearing cap bolts to the specified Stage 1 torque setting.

24 Once all bolts are tightened to the specified Stage 1 torque, go around again and tighten all bolts through the specified Stage 2 angle. It is recommended that an angle-measuring gauge is used during the final stages of the tightening, to ensure accuracy. If a gauge is not available, use white paint to make alignment marks between the bolt head and cap prior to tightening; the marks can then be used to check that the bolt has been rotated through the correct angle.

25 Check that the crankshaft is free to rotate smoothly; if excessive pressure is required to turn the crankshaft, investigate the cause before proceeding further.

26 Check the crankshaft endfloat with reference to Section 10.

27 Refit/reconnect the piston connecting rod assemblies to the crankshaft as described in Section 18.

17.13 ... and then through the specified Stages 2 and 3 angles – petrol engines

28 Referring to the relevant Chapter, fit a new left-hand crankshaft oil seal/housing, then refit the oil pump, sump, flywheel/driveplate, cylinder head, timing belt sprocket(s) and fit a new timing belt or chain.

18 Pistons/connecting rods – refitting

Note: *It is recommended that new big-end bearing shells are fitted regardless of the condition of the original ones.*

1 Clean the backs of the big-end bearing shells and the recesses in the connecting rods and big-end caps. If new shells are being fitted, ensure that all traces of the protective grease are cleaned off using paraffin. Wipe the shells, caps and connecting rods dry with a

18.2 Fit the bearing shells making sure their tabs are correctly located in the connecting rod/cap groove

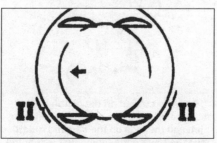

18.4 Piston ring end gap positions – petrol engines

I Top and second compression rings
II Oil control ring side rails

lint-free cloth.

2 Press the bearing shells into their locations, ensuring that the tab on each shell engages in the notch in the connecting rod and cap **(see illustration)**. If there is no tab on the bearing shell (and no notch in the rod or cap) position the shell equidistant from each side of the rod and cap. If the original bearing shells are being used ensure they are refitted in their original locations.

3 Lubricate the bores, the pistons and piston rings then lay out each piston/connecting rod assembly in its respective position **(see illustration)**.

Petrol engines

4 Lubricate No 1 piston and piston rings, and check that the ring gaps are correctly positioned. The gaps in the upper and lower steel rings of the oil control ring should be offset by 25 to 50 mm to the right and left of the spreader ring gap. The two upper compression ring gaps should be offset by 180° to each other **(see illustration)**.

5 Fit a ring compressor to No 1 piston, then insert the piston and connecting rod into the cylinder bore so that the base of the compressor stands on the block. With the crankshaft big-end bearing journal positioned at its lowest point, tap the piston carefully into the cylinder bore with the wooden handle of a hammer, and at the same time guide the connecting rod onto the bearing journal. Note that the arrow on the piston crown must point towards the timing belt end of the engine **(see illustrations)**.

18.3 Lubricate the piston rings with clean engine oil

18.5a Ensure the piston ring end gaps are correctly spaced then fit the ring compressor – petrol engines

18.5b Ensuring the arrow on the piston crown is pointing towards the timing belt end of the engine – petrol engines

18.5c Tap the piston gently into the bore using handle of a hammer – petrol engines

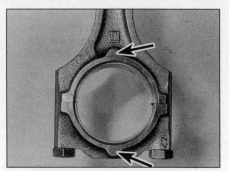

18.6 Make sure the lug is facing the flywheel/driveplate end of the engine – petrol engines

6 Liberally lubricate the bearing journals and bearing shells, and fit the bearing cap in its original location (the lug on the bearing cap base should be facing the flywheel end of the engine) **(see illustration)**.

7 Screw in the new bearing cap retaining bolts, and tighten both bolts to the specified Stage 1 torque setting then tighten them through the specified Stage 2 angle, and finally through the specified Stage 3 angle. It is recommended that an angle-measuring gauge is used during the final stages of the tightening, to ensure accuracy. If a gauge is not available, use white paint to make alignment marks between the bolt head and cap prior to tightening; the marks can then be used to check that the bolt has been rotated through the correct angle.

8 Refit the remaining three piston and connecting rod assemblies in the same way.

9 Rotate the crankshaft, and check that it turns freely, with no signs of binding or tight spots.

10 Refit the oil pump pick-up/strainer, sump and the cylinder head as described in Chapter 2A.

Diesel engines

11 Lubricate No 1 piston and piston rings, and space the ring gaps uniformly around

the piston at 120° intervals **(see illustration)**.

12 Fit a ring compressor to No 1 piston, then insert the piston and connecting rod into the cylinder bore so that the base of the compressor stands on the block. Ensure that the piston/connecting rod assembly is positioned with the cut-out on the piston skirt on the same side as the the oil spray jet, and the lugs on the cap and rod are be toward the timing belt end of the engine **(see illustration)**.

13 With the crankshaft big-end bearing journal positioned at its lowest point, tap the piston carefully into the cylinder bore with the wooden handle of a hammer, and at the same time guide the connecting rod onto the bearing journal.

14 Liberally lubricate the bearing journals and bearing shells, and fit the bearing cap in its original location.

15 Screw in the new bearing cap retaining bolts, and tighten both bolts to the specified Stage 1 torque setting then tighten them through the specified Stage 2 angle. It is recommended that an angle-measuring gauge is used during the final stages of the tightening, to ensure accuracy. If a gauge is not available, use white paint to make alignment marks between the bolt head and

cap prior to tightening; the marks can then be used to check that the bolt has been rotated through the correct angle.

16 Refit the remaining three piston and connecting rod assemblies in the same way.

17 Rotate the crankshaft, and check that it turns freely, with no signs of binding or tight spots.

18 Refit the oil pump pick-up/strainer, sump and the cylinder head as described in Chapter 2A Section 15, Chapter 2B Section 13, Chapter 2C Section 14 or Chapter 2D Section 13.

19 Engine – initial start-up after overhaul

1 With the engine refitted in the vehicle, double-check the engine oil and coolant levels. Make a final check that everything has been reconnected, and that there are no tools or rags left in the engine compartment.

2 On diesel engines, prime and bleed the fuel system as described in Chapter 4B, Section 5.

3 Start the engine, noting that this may take a little longer than usual. Make sure that the oil pressure warning light goes out.

4 While the engine is idling, check for fuel, water and oil leaks. Don't be alarmed if there are some odd smells and smoke from parts getting hot and burning off oil deposits.

5 Assuming all is well, run the engine until it reaches normal operating temperature, then switch off the engine.

6 After a few minutes, recheck the oil and coolant levels as described in *Weekly checks* and top-up as necessary.

7 Note that there is no need to retighten the cylinder head bolts once the engine has first run after reassembly.

8 If new pistons, rings or crankshaft bearings have been fitted, the engine must be treated as new, and run-in for the first 600 miles. Do not operate the engine at full-throttle, or allow it to labour at low engine speeds in any gear. It is recommended that the oil and filter be changed at the end of this period.

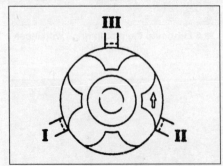

18.11 Piston ring end gap positions – diesel engines

I Top compression ring
II Second compression ring
III Oil control ring

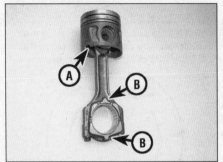

18.12 The cut-out on the piston skirt (A) must be on the same side as the oil spray jet, and the lugs on the cap and rod (B) must be toward the timing belt end of the engine – diesel engines

Chapter 3
Cooling, heating and air conditioning systems

Contents

Degrees of difficulty

Easy, suitable for novice with little experience 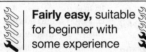	Fairly easy, suitable for beginner with some experience 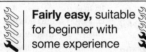	Fairly difficult, suitable for competent DIY mechanic 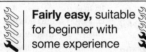	Difficult, suitable for experienced DIY mechanic 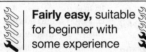	Very difficult, suitable for expert DIY or professional

Specifications

Thermostat

Opening temperatures:

Petrol engines:
Electric element	90°C
Wax capsule	105°C
Diesel engines	88°C

Air conditioning system

Refrigerant	R134a
Refrigerant quantity	600g

Torque wrench settings

	Nm	lbf ft
Petrol engine models		
Air conditioning compressor mounting bolts	22	16
Air conditioning refrigerant pipe block connections	20	15
Coolant pump retaining bolts	8	6
Coolant pump pulley bolts	20	15
Thermostat housing/cover	8	6
Diesel engine models		
Auxiliary drivebelt tensioner bolts	22	16
Air conditioning compressor mounting bolts	22	16
Air conditioning refrigerant pipe block connections	20	15
Coolant pump retaining bolts:		
1.6 litre engine	25	18
2.0 litre (A20) engine	20	15
2.0 litre (B20) engine:		
M6 bolts	10	7
M10 bolts	58	43
Coolant temperature sensor:		
1.6 litre engine	33	24
2.0 litre (A20) engine	22	16
2.0 litre (B20) engine	33	24
Thermostat bypass pipe bolts	10	7
Thermostat housing/cover	10	7
Turbocharger coolant pipe banjo bolt	25	18

1 General information and precautions

General information

1 The cooling system is of pressurised type, comprising a coolant pump, a crossflow radiator, electric cooling fan, and thermostat. The coolant pump is driven by the auxiliary drivebelt on all petrol engines. The B20 (2.0 litre) and B16 (1.6 litre) diesel engines also have an auxiliary belt driven coolant pump. On the A20 (2.0 litre) diesel engine the pump is driven by the timing belt.

2 The system functions as follows. Cold coolant from the radiator passes through the bottom hose to the coolant pump, where it is pumped around the cylinder block, head passages and heater matrix. After cooling the cylinder bores, combustion surfaces and valve seats, the coolant reaches the underside of the thermostat, which is initially closed. The coolant passes through the heater, and is returned to the coolant pump.

3 When the engine is cold, the coolant circulates only through the cylinder block, cylinder head and heater. When the coolant reaches a predetermined temperature, the thermostat opens and the coolant also passes through to the radiator. As the coolant circulates through the radiator, it is cooled by the inrush of air when the car is in forward motion. Airflow is supplemented by the action of the electric cooling fan when necessary. Once the coolant has passed through the radiator, and has cooled, the cycle is repeated.

4 On petrol engines, an electrically assisted thermostat is fitted. Engine coolant temperature is monitored by the engine management system electronic control unit, via the coolant temperature sensor. In conjunction with information received from various other engine sensors, the thermostat opening temperature can be controlled according to engine speed and load. During normal engine operation the thermostat operates conventionally. Under conditions of high engine speed and load, an electric heating element within the thermostat is energised, to cause the thermostat to open at a lower temperature (typically 90°).

5 The electric cooling fan, mounted on the rear of the radiator, is controlled by the engine management system electronic control unit, in conjunction with a cooling fan module. A single fan is used on petrol engines and twin fans are used on diesel engines. At a predetermined coolant temperature, the fan is actuated.

6 An expansion tank is fitted to the left-hand side of the engine compartment to accommodate expansion of the coolant when hot.

Precautions

⚠️ **Warning: Do not attempt to remove the expansion tank filler cap, or disturb any part of the** cooling system, while the engine is hot; there is a high risk of scalding. If the cap must be removed before the engine and radiator have fully cooled (even though this is not recommended) the pressure in the cooling system must first be relieved. Cover the cap with a thick layer of cloth, to avoid scalding, and slowly unscrew the filler cap until a hissing sound can be heard. When the hissing has stopped, indicating that the pressure has reduced, slowly unscrew the filler cap until it can be removed; if more hissing sounds are heard, wait until they have stopped before unscrewing the cap completely. At all times, keep well away from the filler cap opening.

⚠️ **Warning: Do not allow antifreeze to come into contact with the skin, or with the painted surfaces of the vehicle. Rinse off spills immediately, with plenty of water. Never leave antifreeze lying around in an open container, or in a puddle on the driveway or garage floor. Children and pets are attracted by its sweet smell, but antifreeze can be fatal if ingested.**

⚠️ **Warning: If the engine is hot, the electric cooling fan may start rotating even if the engine is not running; be careful to keep hands, hair and loose clothing well clear when working in the engine compartment.**

⚠️ **Warning: Refer to Section 10 for precautions to be observed when working on models equipped with air conditioning.**

2 Cooling system hoses – disconnection and renewal

Note: *Refer to the warnings given in Section 1 of this Chapter before proceeding. Do not attempt to disconnect any hose while the system is still hot.*

1 If the checks described in Chapter 1A, Section 6 or Chapter 1B, Section 6 reveal a faulty hose, it must be renewed as follows.

2 First drain the cooling system (see Chapter 1A, Section 24 or Chapter 1B, Section 26). If the coolant is not due for renewal, it may be re-used if it is collected in a clean container.

3 Before disconnecting a hose, first note its routing in the engine compartment, and whether it is secured by any additional retaining clips or cable ties. Use a pair of pliers to release the clamp-type clips, or a screwdriver to slacken the screw-type clips, then move the clips along the hose, clear of the relevant inlet/outlet union. Carefully work the hose free.

4 Depending on engine, some of the hose attachments may be of the quick-release type. Where this type of hose is encountered, lift the ends of the wire retaining clip, to spread the ends of the wire retaining clip, to spread the

2.4 Pull up the spring to release the hose

clip, then withdraw the hose from the inlet/outlet union **(see illustration)**.

5 Note that the radiator inlet and outlet unions are fragile; do not use excessive force when attempting to remove the hoses. If a hose proves to be difficult to remove, try to release it by rotating the hose ends before attempting to free it.

6 When fitting a hose, first slide the clips onto the hose, then work the hose into position. If clamp-type clips were originally fitted, it is a good idea to use screw-type clips when refitting the hose. If the hose is stiff, use a little soapy water (washing-up liquid is ideal) as a lubricant, or soften the hose by soaking it in hot water.

7 Work the hose into position, checking that it is correctly routed and secured. Slide each clip along the hose until it passes over the flared end of the relevant inlet/outlet union, before tightening the clips securely.

8 Refill the cooling system with reference to Chapter 1A, Section 24 or Chapter 1B, Section 26.

9 Check thoroughly for leaks as soon as possible after disturbing any part of the cooling system.

3 Radiator – removal, inspection and refitting

Note: *The radiator is removed from below, complete with the cooling fan assembly.*

Removal

Petrol engine models

1 Disconnect the battery negative terminal (refer to Chapter 5A, Section 4).

2 Apply the handbrake, then jack up the front of the vehicle and support it on axle stands (see *Jacking and vehicle support*).

3 Remove the front bumper as described in Chapter 11, Section 6.

4 Drain the cooling system as described in Chapter 1A, Section 24.

5 Undo the screw securing the underside of the power steering fluid reservoir to the fan housing.

6 On models fitted with hydraulic power

steering, release the retaining clip and free the power steering fluid pipe from the fan housing **(see illustration)**.

7 Release the retaining clips and lift the coolant expansion tank hose out of the supports on top of the fan housing **(see illustration)**.

8 Disconnect the top and bottom coolant hoses from the radiator.

9 Disconnect the electric cooling fan wiring harness connector **(see illustration)**. Release the wiring harness from the clips on the fan housing.

10 Disconnect the wiring connector from the coolant temperature sensor located on the right-hand side of the radiator.

11 Where fitted, release the power steering fluid cooler pipes from the clips above the air conditioning condenser.

12 Using a screwdriver, depress the tab each side and pull the air conditioning condenser upper mountings out of the radiator.

13 Lift the condenser up to disengage the lower mountings from the radiator, then secure the condenser to the upper body panel with cable ties.

14 Check that all hoses, and connections are released from the radiator in the engine compartment, then engage the help of an assistant to support the radiator.

15 Undo the retaining bolt and remove the radiator upper mounting bracket on each side **(see illustration)**.

16 Lift the radiator up to disengage the lower mounting pegs from the support brackets, then lower the radiator down and remove it from under the car **(see illustration)**.

Diesel engine models

Note: *There are minor differences to the radiator removal procedure depending on the diesel engine fitted. Removal and refitting is essentially the same for all engines.*

17 Disconnect the battery negative terminal (refer to Chapter 5A, Section 4).

18 Remove the cover from the top of the engine.

19 Apply the handbrake, then jack up the front of the vehicle and support it on axle stands (see *Jacking and vehicle support*).

20 Remove the front bumper and the engine undertray as described in Chapter 11, Section 6 and Chapter 11 Section 6.

21 Drain the cooling system as described in Chapter 1B, Section 26.

22 Remove the intercooler as described in Chapter 4B, Section 13.

23 On 2.0 litre (A20) engines undo the two bolts securing the turbocharger wastegate (charge pressure) solenoid valve to the upper body panel. Withdraw the solenoid valve and release the vacuum pipe support clip from the fan housing **(see illustrations)**.

24 Release the retaining clips and lift the coolant expansion tank hose out of the

3.6 Release the retaining clip and free the power steering fluid pipe from the fan housing

3.7 Release the retaining clips and lift the expansion tank hose out of the fan housing supports

3.9 Disconnect the electric cooling fan wiring harness connector

3.15 Undo the retaining bolt and remove the radiator upper mounting bracket on each side

3.16 Disengage the lower mounting pegs, then lower the radiator and remove it from under the car

3.23a Undo the two bolts securing the turbocharger wastegate solenoid valve to the body panel

3.23b Withdraw the solenoid valve …

3.23c … and release the vacuum pipe support clip from the fan housing

3.24 Lift the coolant expansion tank hose out of the supports on the fan housing

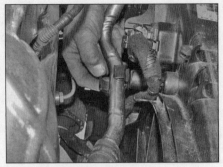

3.26 Release the retaining clip and free the power steering fluid pipe from the fan housing

supports on top of the fan housing **(see illustration)**.

25 Undo the screw securing the underside of the power steering fluid reservoir to the fan housing.

26 Release the retaining clip and free the power steering fluid pipe from the fan housing **(see illustration)**.

27 Disconnect the top and bottom coolant hoses from the radiator.

28 Lift up the locking catch and disconnect the electric cooling fan wiring harness from the upper and lower connectors **(see illustrations)**. Release the wiring harness from the clips on the fan housing.

29 On models with automatic transmission, detach the protective ring (where fitted) over the fluid cooler pipe unions at the radiator. Using a small screwdriver, release the quick-release fitting retaining lugs and disconnect the fitting from the radiator. Suitably cover the open unions after disconnection.

30 Check that all hoses, and connections are released from the radiator in the engine compartment, then engage the help of an assistant to support the radiator.

31 Undo the retaining bolt and remove the radiator upper mounting bracket on each side **(see illustration 3.15)**.

32 Lift the radiator up to disengage the lower mounting pegs from the support brackets, then lower the radiator down and remove it from under the car **(see illustration 3.16)**.

Inspection

33 If the radiator has been removed due to suspected blockage, reverse-flush it as described in Chapter 1A, Section 24 or Chapter 1B, Section 26.

34 Clean dirt and debris from the radiator fins, using an air line (in which case, wear eye protection) or a soft brush.

Caution: Be careful, as the fins are easily damaged, and are sharp.

35 If necessary, a radiator specialist can perform a 'flow test' on the radiator, to establish whether an internal blockage exists.

36 A leaking radiator must be referred to a specialist for permanent repair. Do not attempt to weld or solder a leaking radiator.

37 In an emergency, minor leaks from the radiator can be cured by using a suitable radiator sealant (in accordance with its manufacturer's instructions) with the radiator fitted in the vehicle.

38 Inspect the radiator mounting rubbers, and renew them if necessary.

Refitting

39 Refitting is a reversal of removal, bearing in mind the following points.

a) Ensure that the intercooler or condenser (as applicable) lower mountings are correctly engaged with the radiator when refitting.

b) Ensure that all hoses are correctly reconnected, and their retaining clips securely tightened.

c) On completion, refill the cooling system as described in Chapter 1A, Section 24 or Chapter 1B, Section 26.

d) On models with automatic transmission, check and if necessary top-up the automatic transmission fluid level with reference to the procedures contained in Chapter 7B, Section 2.

4 Thermostat –
removal and refitting

Removal

All engines

1 Remove the cover from the top of the engine.

2 Disconnect the battery negative terminal (refer to Chapter 5A, Section 4).

3 Apply the handbrake, then jack up the front of the vehicle and support it on axle stands (see *Jacking and vehicle support*).

4 Where fitted remove the undershield.

5 Drain the cooling system as described in Chapter 1A, Section 24 (petrol engines) or as described in Chapter 1B Section 22 (diesel engines).

Petrol engine models

6 The thermostat is located in a housing attached to the left-hand side of the cylinder head, and is integral with the housing cover.

7 Disconnect the thermostat wiring connector.

8 Release the clips and disconnect the radiator hose from the thermostat cover.

9 Unscrew the four bolts and remove the thermostat cover from the housing. Recover the O-ring seal.

10 Thoroughly clean the housing and cover contact surfaces.

Diesel engine models

1.6 litre (B16) diesel engines

11 Remove the air filter outlet duct as described in Chapter 4B Section 3.

12 Release the spring retainers and remove the radiator outlet hose.

13 Remove the intercooler inlet hose.

14 Remove the catalytic converter/particulate filter as described in Chapter 4B Section 18.

15 Disconnect the coolant by pass hose at the the thermostat and where fitted disconnect the wiring plug.

16 Remove the front lower bolts form the coolant pump. Access can be improved if the auxiliary drivebelt is removed first (see Chapter 1B Section 22).

17 Working at the rear remove the two upper bolts and lift off the complete thermostat housing **(see illustration)**. Recover the seal and dispose of it.

18 Remove the bolts and lift out the thermostat. The thermostat may be fitted to the top or bottom of the housing. Note that this part has been modified several times.

3.28a Lift up the locking catch ...

3.28b ... and disconnect the electric cooling fan wiring harness connectors

4.17 Remove the complete thermostat housing

4.18 Remove the seals from the thermostat

4.22 Thermostat cover retaining bolts – A20 diesel engine models

4.26 Remove the bolts

4.27a On the 1.6 litre diesel engine fit a new gasket

4.27b Fit a new seal (B20 engine)

The replacement may not be exactly the same as the one removed. Recover the seals and dispose of them **(see illustration)**.

2.0 litre (A20) diesel engines

19 The thermostat is located in a housing attached to the left-hand side of the cylinder head, and is integral with the housing cover.
20 Remove the throttle housing intake duct as described in Chapter 4B, Section 3.
21 Release the clips and disconnect the hoses from the thermostat housing cover.
22 Unscrew the three bolts and remove the thermostat cover from the housing **(see illustration)**. Recover the O-ring seal.
23 Thoroughly clean the housing and cover contact surfaces.

2.0 litre (B20) diesel engine

24 Remove the air filter outlet duct and then remove the top radiator hose.
25 Disconnect the wiring plug and remove the by pass hose.
26 Remove the fixing bolts **(see illustration)** and pull off the housing complete with the thermostat. Recover the seal.

Refitting

27 Refitting is a reversal of removal, but fit a new O-ring seal and tighten the mounting bolts securely **(see illustrations)**. Refill the cooling system as described in Chapter 1A, Section 24 or Chapter 1B, Section 26.

5 Electric cooling fan – removal and refitting

Warning: If the engine is hot, the cooling fan may start up at any time. Take extra precautions when working in the vicinity of the fan.

Removal

1 Remove the radiator as described in Section 3.
2 Depress the tab on the radiator lower guide each side and slide the fan housing up and out of the radiator guides **(see illustrations)**.
3 To remove the fan motor(s), unclip the fan motor resistor and unclip the wiring harness from the fan housing. Undo the three retaining

5.2a Depress the tab on the radiator lower guide each side …

bolts and remove the fan motor from the housing.

Refitting

4 Refitting is a reversal of removal.

6 Coolant temperature sensor – testing, removal and refitting

Testing

1 Testing of the coolant temperature sensor is possible using diagnostic test equipment. The performance of the sensor can also be tested using a multi-meter (set on the Ohms scale) a thermometer and a pan of water. The resistance of the sensor changes according to the temperature of the coolant (or water). The

5.2b … and slide the fan housing up and out of the radiator guides

6.6a The sensor on the 1.6 litre engine

**6.6b Coolant temperature sensor –
2.0 litre (A20 engine)**

**6.6c Coolant temperature sensor –
2.0 litre (B20 engine)**

table below gives the approximate resistance of the sensor for a given temperature **(see illustration)**. Note that the sensor is not an expensive item and it should be replaced if there is any doubt about its performance.

Temperature (Degrees centigrade)	Resistance (in Ohms)
130	85
120	110
110	142
100	186
90	246
80	329
70	446
60	612
50	851
40	1200
30	1715
20	2511
10	3791
0	5887
-10	9426

Removal

2 Partially drain the cooling system with reference to Chapter 1A, Section 24 or Chapter 1B, Section 26. Alternatively, it is possible to change the sensor quickly with minimal loss of coolant by first releasing any pressure from the cooling system. With the engine cold, temporarily remove the expansion tank cap.
3 Remove the cover from the top of the engine.

Petrol engine models

4 On petrol engine models, two temperature sensors are fitted; one located in the side of the thermostat housing at the left-hand end of the cylinder head, and one located in the radiator right-hand side tank. The removal and refitting procedures are the same for both sensors.
5 Disconnect the wiring connector, then extract the wire retaining clip. Remove the sensor from the thermostat housing or radiator. If the cooling system has not been drained, either insert the new sensor or fit a blanking plug to prevent further loss of coolant.

Diesel engine models

6 The coolant temperature sensor is located on the thermostat housing on the left-hand

end of the cylinder head **(see illustrations)** on the 2.0 litre (A20) engine, behind the inlet manifold on the 2.0 litre (B20) engine and next to the alternator on the 1.6 litre engine.
7 On the 1.6 litre engine remove the exhaust front pipe to access the sensor as described in Chapter 4B Section 18.
8 On the 2.0 litre (B20) engine reach around the transmission to access the sensor.
9 On the 2.0 litre (A20) engine, remove the throttle housing intake duct as described in Chapter 4B, Section 3.
10 Disconnect the wiring connector, then unscrew and remove the sensor. If the cooling system has not been drained, either insert the new sensor or fit a blanking plug to prevent further loss of coolant.

Refitting

11 Fit the new sensor using a reversal of the removal procedure. Tighten the sensor to the specified torque (diesel engine models) and refill the cooling system with reference to Chapter 1A, Section 24 or Chapter 1B, Section 26.

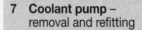

**7 Coolant pump –
removal and refitting**

Removal

1 Disconnect the battery negative terminal (refer to Chapter 5A, Section 4).
2 Drain the cooling system as described in Chapter 1A Section 24 (petrol engines) or Chapter 1B Section 26 (diesel engines).

7.13 Remove the charge air cooler ducting

3 On diesel engine models, remove the cover from the top of the engine.

Petrol engine models

4 Remove the air filter assembly and air intake duct as described in Chapter 4A, Section 2.
5 Slacken the three coolant pump pulley retaining bolts.
6 Remove the auxiliary drivebelts as described in Chapter 1A, Section 20.
7 Unscrew the previously slackened coolant pump pulley retaining bolts and remove the pulley from the pump flange.
8 Undo the five retaining bolts and remove the pump from the oil pump housing.
9 Note that it is not possible to overhaul the pump. If it is faulty, the unit must be renewed complete.

Diesel engine models

1.6 litre engines

10 Remove the auxiliary drivebelt as described in Chapter 1B Section 22.
11 Remove the air filter outlet duct as described in Chapter 4B Section 3.
12 Remove the catalytic converter/particulate filter as described in Chapter 4B Section 18.
13 Remove the charge air duct from the turbocharger **(see illustration)**.
14 Lever up the spring clip and remove the coolant hose from the thermostat housing. Secure the hose to the side or remove it completely.
15 Remove the bolt and move the cable and bracket to the side **(see illustration)**.
16 Unbolt the turbocharger coolant feed pipe. Pull out the banjo bolt and recover the sealing washers. Dispose of the washers – they must be replaced.

7.15 Remove the wiring loom support bracket

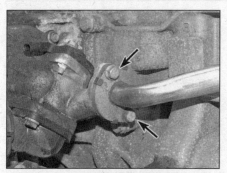

7.18 Remove the pipe

7.19 Remove the bolts (one hidden)

7.22 Unbolt and remove the tensioner

7.24a Disconnect the wiring plug …

7.24b … and unbolt the wiring loom

7.25 Remove the coolant pipe

17 Disconnect the wiring connector from the coolant pump and (where fitted), from the thermostat housing.

18 Unbolt the bypass pipe from the coolant pump **(see illustration)**.

19 Unbolt the coolant pump and recover the gasket **(see illustration)**. A new gasket will be needed.

2.0 litre (B20) engine

20 Remove the auxiliary drivebelt as described in Chapter 1B Section 22.

21 Remove the air filter outlet duct as described in Chapter 4B Section 3.

22 Remove the auxiliary drivebelt tensioner **(see illustration)**.

23 Remove the timing belt upper cover as described in Chapter 2D Section 5.

24 Disconnect the wiring plug from the pump **(see illustrations)**.

25 Unbolt the turbocharger coolant feed pipe. Pull out the banjo bolt and recover the sealing washers**(see illustration)**. Dispose of the washers – they must be replaced.

26 Unbolt the pump from the thermostat housing. Recover the gasket and dispose of it **(see illustrations)**.

2.0 litre (A20) engine

27 Remove the timing belt as described in Chapter 2C, Section 6. **Note:** *The timing belt must not come into contact with coolant.*

28 Unscrew and remove the three coolant pump securing bolts **(see illustration)**.

29 Withdraw the coolant pump from the cylinder block, noting that it may be necessary to tap the pump lightly with a soft-faced mallet to free it from the cylinder block **(see illustration)**.

30 Recover the pump sealing ring, and discard it; a new one must be used on refitting.

31 Note that it is not possible to overhaul the pump. If it is faulty, the unit must be renewed complete.

7.26a Remove the bolts (in reverse order)

7.28 Undo the three coolant pump securing bolts …

Refitting

Petrol engine models

32 Ensure that the pump and pump housing mating surfaces are clean and dry.

33 Place the pump in position and refit

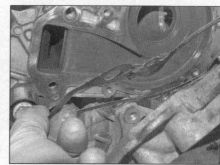

7.26b Recover the gasket

7.29 … and withdraw the coolant pump from the cylinder block

the retaining bolts. Tighten the bolts to the specified torque.

34 Refit the coolant pump pulley and secure with the three retaining bolts moderately tightened at this stage.

35 Refit the auxiliary drivebelts as described in Chapter 1A, Section 20.

36 With the drivebelts refitted, tighten the pump pulley retaining bolts to the specified torque.

37 Refit the air cleaner assembly and air intake duct as described in Chapter 4A, Section 2.

38 Reconnect the battery negative terminal, then refill the cooling system as described in Chapter 1A, Section 24.

Diesel engine models

39 Ensure that the pump and cylinder block/thermostat housing mating surfaces are clean and dry.

40 Fit a new gasket/seal to the pump, and locate the pump in the cylinder block or thermostat housing.

41 Insert the securing bolts and tighten to the specified torque. On the B20 engine tighten the bolts in the order shown **(see illustration 7.26a)**

42 On the 2.0 litre A20 engine, refit the timing belt as described in Chapter 2C, Section 6.

43 On the 2.0 litre B20 engine refit the belt tensioner.

44 On both the 1.6 litre and 2.0 litre (B20) engine refit the auxiliary drivebelt.

45 Reconnect the battery negative terminal, then refill the cooling system as described in Chapter 1B, Section 26.

---

8 Heating and ventilation system – general information

1 The heater/ventilation system consists of a four-speed blower motor (housed behind the facia), face-level vents in the centre and at each end of the facia, and air ducts to the front and rear footwells.

2 The heater controls are located in the centre of the facia, and the controls operate flap valves to deflect and mix the air flowing through the various parts of the heater/ventilation system. The flap valves are contained in the air distribution housing, which acts as a central distribution unit, passing air to the various ducts and vents.

3 Cold air enters the system through the grille at the rear of the engine compartment. A pollen filter is fitted to the ventilation intake, to filter out dust, soot, pollen and spores from the air entering the vehicle.

4 The air (boosted by the blower fan if required) then flows through the various ducts, according to the settings of the controls. Stale air is expelled through ducts at the rear of the vehicle. If warm air is required, the cold air is passed through the heater matrix, which is heated by the engine coolant.

5 A recirculation switch enables the outside air supply to be closed off, while the air inside the vehicle is recirculated. This can be useful to prevent unpleasant odours entering from outside the vehicle, but should only be used briefly, as the recirculated air inside the vehicle will soon deteriorate.

---

9 Heater/ventilation system components – removal and refitting

Air vents

Removal

1 To remove the air vents from the centre of the facia, remove the facia upper centre panel as described in Chapter 11, Section 30.

2 Carefully spread the four tabs securing each vent and withdraw the relevant vent from the facia upper centre panel.

3 To remove the vents from the side of the facia, carefully prise free the relevant facia outer trim panel using a plastic spatula or similar tool **(see illustration)**.

4 Reach in behind the facia and push the vent out from its location.

5 To remove the rear passenger's air vents, carefully prise the vent housing from the centre console using a plastic spatula inserted at the bottom of the housing.

Refitting

6 Refitting is a reversal of removal.

Heater blower motor

Removal

7 Remove the glovebox as described in Chapter 11, Section 30.

8 Extract the centre pin and remove the plastic rivet securing the footwell air duct to the facia crossmember. Detach the air duct from the air distribution housing and remove it from the car **(see illustration)**.

9 Disconnect the wiring connector at the blower motor, and release the wiring harness from the clips on the blower motor housing **(see illustration)**.

10 Undo the three bolts and remove the blower motor down and out from under the facia.

Refitting

11 Refitting is a reversal of removal.

Heater blower motor resistor

Removal

12 Carry out the operations described in paragraphs 7 and 8.

13 Disconnect the wiring connector at the blower motor resistor at the side of the blower motor housing.

14 Undo the two screws and remove the blower motor resistor.

Refitting

15 Refitting is a reversal of removal.

Heater matrix

Removal

16 Working in the engine compartment, use two hose clamps to clamp the hoses leading to the heater matrix. The hoses are located on the bulkhead, just above the steering gear. Alternatively, drain the cooling system completely as described in Chapter 1A, Section 24, or Chapter 1B, Section 26.

17 Carry out the operations described in paragraphs 7 and 8.

18 Undo the retaining bolt and lower the

9.3 Carefully prise free the relevant facia outer trim panel

9.8 Remove the plastic rivet and detach the air duct from the air distribution housing

9.9 Disconnect the wiring connector and release the wiring harness from the blower motor housing

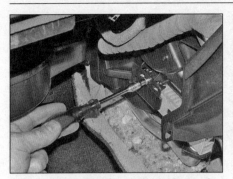

9.18 Undo the retaining bolt and lower the cover panel over the heater matrix

9.27a Lift the control module from its location ...

9.27b ... disconnect the wiring connectors

cover panel over the heater matrix **(see illustration)**.

19 Extract the two plastic clips securing the heater pipes to the matrix **(see illustration)**. Be prepared for coolant spillage as the pipes are disconnected, and place some cloths or absorbent material over the carpet. Recover the seals on the heater pipes.

20 Pull the heater matrix out of the air distribution housing and remove it from the car.

Refitting

21 Refitting is a reversal of removal, bearing in mind the following:
a) Use new seals when refitting the heater pipes to the matrix.
b) If the cooling system was completely drained, refill as described in Chapter 1A, Section 24 or Chapter 1B, Section 26. If the heater hoses were clamped prior to removal, top-up the cooling system as described in Weekly checks.

Heater/air conditioning control unit

Removal

22 Remove the facia lower centre panel as described in Chapter 11, Section 30.

23 Undo the five screws securing the mounting frame to the rear of the facia lower centre panel and remove the frame.

24 Using a plastic spatula or similar tool, carefully prise free the control unit and remove it from the facia lower centre panel.

Refitting

25 Refitting is a reversal of removal.

Heater/air conditioning control module

Removal

26 Remove the facia lower centre panel as described in Chapter 11, Section 30.

27 Lift the module from its location, disconnect the wiring connectors and remove the control module **(see illustrations)**.

Refitting

28 Refitting is a reversal of removal.

Air distribution housing

Note: *It is not possible to remove the air distribution housing without opening the*

refrigerant circuit (see Sections 10 and 11). Have the refrigerant discharged at a dealer service department or an automotive air conditioning repair facility before proceeding.
Note: *This is an involved and complex operation and it is suggested that the contents of this Section, and the relevant Sections in Chapter 11 are studied carefully to gain an understanding of the work involved, before proceeding.*

29 Drain the cooling system as described in Chapter 1A, Section 24, or Chapter 1B, Section 26.

30 Remove the complete facia assembly and the facia crossmember as described in Chapter 11 Section 30 and Chapter 11 Section 31 respectively.

31 Using a small screwdriver, lift up the wire clip securing the left-hand and right-hand heater hoses to the heater matrix pipe stubs, and disconnect the hoses from the stubs **(see illustration)**. Be prepared for some loss of

9.31 Disconnect the coolant hoses from the heater matrix pipe stubs

9.34a Disconnect the condensation drain tube from the base of the housing ...

coolant as the hoses are released, by placing cloth rags beneath them.

32 Undo the nut securing the refrigerant pipe block connection to the expansion valve, then unscrew the retaining stud from the valve. Withdraw the refrigerant pipes from the valve **(see illustration)**. Note that new seals for the refrigerant pipes will be required for refitting. Suitably plug or cover the disconnected pipes.

33 Release the expansion valve rubber seal from the bulkhead by pushing it inward (the seal remains on the valve).

34 Working inside the vehicle, disconnect the condensation drain tube from the base of the housing, then withdraw the air distribution housing from the bulkhead **(see illustrations)**.
Note: *Keep the matrix unions uppermost as the housing is removed, to prevent coolant spillage. Mop up any spilt coolant immediately, and wipe the affected area with a damp cloth to prevent staining.*

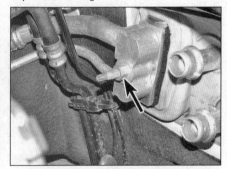

9.32 Refrigerant pipe block connection retaining nut

9.34b ... then withdraw the air distribution housing from the bulkhead

10.6 Air conditioning high-pressure service port ...

10.7 ... and low-pressure service port

Refitting

35 Refitting is the reverse of removal. On completion, refill the cooling system as described in Chapter 1A, Section 24 or Chapter 1B, Section 26. Have the air conditioning system evacuated, charged and leak-tested by the specialist who discharged it.

10 Air conditioning system – general information and precautions

General information

1 Air conditioning is standard on top of the range models, and optional on certain other models. It enables the temperature of incoming air to be lowered, and also dehumidifies the air, which makes for rapid demisting and increased comfort.

2 The cooling side of the system works in the same way as a domestic refrigerator. Refrigerant gas is drawn into a belt-driven compressor, and passes into a condenser mounted in front of the radiator, where it loses heat and becomes liquid. The liquid passes through an expansion valve to an evaporator, where it changes from liquid under high pressure to gas under low pressure. This change is accompanied by a drop in temperature, which cools the evaporator. The refrigerant returns to the compressor, and the cycle begins again.

3 Air blown through the evaporator passes to the heater assembly, where it is mixed with hot air blown through the heater matrix, to achieve the desired temperature in the passenger compartment.

4 The heating side of the system works in the same way as on models without air conditioning (see Section 8).

5 The operation of the system is controlled electronically. Any problems with the system should be referred to a Vauxhall/Opel dealer or an air conditioning specialist.

Air conditioning service ports

6 The high-pressure service port is located behind the air cleaner housing (see illustration).
7 The low-pressure service port is located at the rear right-hand side of the engine compartment, below the brake master cylinder (see illustration).

Precautions

8 It is necessary to observe special precautions whenever dealing with any part of the system, its associated components, and any items which necessitate disconnection of the system.

⚠ Warning: The refrigeration circuit contains a liquid refrigerant. This refrigerant is potentially dangerous, and should only be handled by qualified persons. If it is splashed onto the skin, it can cause frostbite. It is not itself poisonous, but in the presence of a naked flame it forms a poisonous gas; inhalation of the vapour through a lighted cigarette could prove fatal. Uncontrolled discharging of the refrigerant is dangerous, and potentially damaging to the environment. Do not disconnect any part of the system unless it has been discharged by a Vauxhall/Opel dealer or an air conditioning specialist.

Caution: Do not operate the air conditioning system if it is known to be short of refrigerant, as this may damage the compressor.

11 Air conditioning system components – removal and refitting

⚠ Warning: The air conditioning system is under high pressure. Do not loosen any fittings or remove any components until after the system has been discharged. Air conditioning refrigerant should be properly discharged into an approved type of container at a dealer service department or an automotive air conditioning repair facility capable of handling R134a refrigerant. Cap or plug the pipe lines as soon as they are disconnected, to prevent the entry of moisture. Always wear eye protection when disconnecting air conditioning system fittings.

Note: This Section refers to the components of the air conditioning system itself – refer to Sections 8 and 9 for details of components common to the heating/ventilation system.

Compressor

Removal

1 Have the refrigerant discharged at a dealer service department or an automotive air conditioning repair facility.
2 Disconnect the battery negative terminal (refer to Chapter 5A, Section 4).
3 Firmly apply the handbrake, then jack up the front of the car and support it securely on axle stands (see Jacking and vehicle support).
4 On diesel engine models, remove the engine undertray as described in Chapter 11, Section 24.
5 Remove the auxiliary drivebelt as described in Chapter 1A, Section 20, or Chapter 1B, Section 22.
6 With the system discharged, undo the retaining bolt and disconnect the refrigerant pipe block connector from the compressor (see illustration). Discard the O-ring seals – new ones must be used when refitting. Suitably cap the open fittings immediately to keep moisture and contamination out of the system.
7 Disconnect the compressor wiring connector.
8 Unbolt the compressor from the cylinder block/crankcase/sump (see illustration), then withdraw the compressor downwards from under the vehicle.

Refitting

9 Refit the compressor in the reverse order of removal; renew all seals disturbed.
10 If you are installing a new compressor, refer to the compressor manufacturer's instructions for adding refrigerant oil to the system.

11.6 Remove the bolt

11.8 Remove the bolts

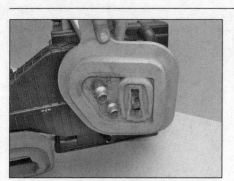

11.15 Remove the bulkhead rubber seal from the expansion valve and heater matrix pipe stubs

11.16 Disconnect the wiring connectors from the two flap valve actuators

11.17 Undo the two bolts securing the matrix pipe support bracket to the side of the air distribution housing

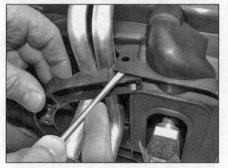

11.18a Lift the edge of the housing and ease out the pipe support bracket ...

11.18b ... then disengage the other end of the bracket from the slot in the housing

11.19 Undo the retaining bolt and lift up the cover panel over the heater matrix

11 Have the system evacuated, charged and leak-tested by the specialist that discharged it.

12 After installing a new compressor, always observe the following running-in procedure:

a) *Open all instrument panel air outlet flaps.*

b) *Start vehicle engine and stabilise idle speed for approximately 5 seconds.*

c) *Switch fan to maximum speed.*

d) *Switch on the air conditioning and let it run for at least 2 minutes without interruption at engine speed under 1500 rpm.*

Evaporator

Removal

13 Have the refrigerant discharged at a dealer service department or an automotive air conditioning repair facility.

14 Remove the air distribution housing as described in Section 9.

15 Remove the bulkhead rubber seal from the expansion valve and heater matrix pipe stubs **(see illustration)**.

16 Disconnect the wiring connectors from the two flap valve actuators **(see illustration)**.

17 Undo the two bolts securing the heater matrix pipe support bracket to the side of the air distribution housing **(see illustration)**.

18 Using a screwdriver, lift the edge of the air distribution housing and ease out the pipe support bracket. Disengage the other end of the bracket from the slot in the housing and remove the bracket **(see illustrations)**.

19 Undo the retaining bolt and lift up the cover panel over the heater matrix **(see illustration)**.

20 Withdraw the heater matrix and pipe assembly from the air distribution housing **(see illustration)**.

21 Disconnect the wiring connector, undo the two retaining screws and remove the blower motor resistor **(see illustrations)**.

11.20 Withdraw the heater matrix and pipe assembly from the air distribution housing

11.21a Disconnect the wiring connector ...

11.21b ... undo the two retaining screws ...

11.21c ... and remove the blower motor resistor

11.22a Undo the four retaining screws ...

11.22b ... and remove the air inlet housing

11.23a Undo the retaining screws ...

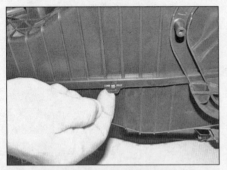

11.23b ... lift the retaining tabs ...

11.23c ... and separate the two halves of the air distribution housing

22 Undo the four retaining screws and remove the air inlet housing **(see illustrations)**.
23 Undo the eleven retaining screws, lift the retaining tabs and separate the two halves of the air distribution housing **(see illustrations)**.
24 Carefully lift the evaporator out of the air distribution housing **(see illustration)**.

Refitting

25 Refitting is the reverse of removal ensuring that all disturbed pipe seals are renewed.
26 Have the system evacuated, charged and leak-tested by the specialist who discharged it.

Condenser

Removal

27 Have the refrigerant discharged at a dealer service department or an automotive air conditioning repair facility.
28 Disconnect the battery negative terminal (refer to Chapter 5A, Section 4).
29 Remove the front bumper as described in Chapter 11, Section 6.
30 Disconnect the wiring connector from the pressure sensor on the right-hand side of the condenser **(see illustration)**.
31 Undo the retaining nuts and disconnect the upper and lower refrigerant pipe connector blocks from the condenser **(see illustrations)**. Discard the seals – new ones

11.24 Carefully lift the evaporator out of the air distribution housing

11.30 Disconnect the wiring connector from the pressure sensor on the condenser

11.31a Undo the retaining nuts and disconnect the upper ...

11.31b ... and lower refrigerant pipe connector blocks from the condenser

must be used when refitting. Suitably cap the open fittings immediately to keep moisture and contamination out of the system.

32 On petrol engine models, release the power steering fluid cooler pipes from the clips above the condenser. Secure the fluid cooler to the upper body panel with cable ties.

33 On diesel engine models, release the power steering fluid cooler pipes from the clips at the upper left-hand side of the intercooler. Slide the fluid cooler to the left to disengage the other end of the cooler from the intercooler bracket **(see illustrations)**. Secure the fluid cooler to the upper body panel with cable ties.

34 Using a screwdriver, depress the tab each side and pull the condenser upper mountings out of the radiator or intercooler **(see illustrations)**.

35 Lift the condenser up to disengage the lower mountings from the radiator or intercooler, and remove the condenser from the car. **(see illustrations)**.

Refitting

36 Refitting is the reverse of removal ensuring that all disturbed pipe seals are renewed.

37 Have the system evacuated, charged and leak-tested by the specialist who discharged it.

Receiver-dryer

Removal

38 Remove the condenser as described previously in this Section.

39 Remove the cap from the base of the condenser on the left-hand side and extract the snap-ring.

40 Unscrew the retaining plug, collect the O-ring seals and remove the receiver-dryer from the condenser.

Refitting

41 Refitting is the reverse of removal, using new O-ring seals and a new snap-ring.

42 On completion, refit the condenser as described previously in this Section.

11.33a Release the power steering fluid cooler pipes from the clips on the intercooler …

11.33b … then disengage the other end of the cooler from the intercooler bracket

11.34a Depress the tab each side …

11.34b … and pull the condenser upper mountings out of the radiator or intercooler

11.35a Lift the condenser up to disengage the right-hand …

11.35b … and left-hand lower mountings

Notes

Chapter 4 Part A
Fuel and exhaust systems – petrol engines

Contents

Degrees of difficulty

Easy, suitable for novice with little experience	**Fairly easy,** suitable for beginner with some experience	**Fairly difficult,** suitable for competent DIY mechanic	**Difficult,** suitable for experienced DIY mechanic	**Very difficult,** suitable for expert DIY or professional

Specifications

System type . . . . AC Delco/Hitachi E83 sequential multi-point fuel injection

Fuel system data
Fuel supply pump type . . . . Electric, immersed in tank
Fuel pump regulated constant pressure . . . . 3.8 bar
Specified idle speed . . . . Not adjustable – controlled by ECU
Idle mixture CO content . . . . Not adjustable – controlled by ECU

Recommended fuel
Minimum octane rating . . . . 95 RON unleaded (UK premium unleaded) Leaded fuel or LRP must NOT be used

Torque wrench settings	**Nm**	**lbf ft**
Camshaft sensor	10	7
Crankshaft position sensor bolt	10	7
Exhaust front pipe-to-main section nuts*	25	18
Exhaust front pipe-to-manifold nuts*	23	17
Exhaust manifold nuts*	20	15
Exhaust manifold heat shield bolts	10	7
Inlet manifold nuts	20	15
Knock sensor bolt	25	18
Throttle housing bolts	10	7

*Use new nut/bolts

2.2 Disconnect the wiring connector from the side of the airflow meter

2.3 Unclip the wiring harness from the side of the air cleaner housing

2.4 Lift up the housing to disengage the front and rear mounting rubbers

1 General information and precautions

1 The fuel system consists of a fuel tank (which is mounted under the rear of the car, with an electric fuel pump immersed in it), and the fuel feed lines. The fuel pump supplies fuel to the fuel rail, which acts as a reservoir for the four fuel injectors which inject fuel into the inlet tracts.

2 The electronic control unit controls both the fuel injection system and the ignition system, integrating the two into a complete engine management system. Refer to Section 9 for further information on the operation of the fuel system and to Chapter 5B for details of the ignition side of the system.

Precautions

Note: *Refer to Chapter 4C for general information and precautions relating to the catalytic converter.*

3 Before disconnecting any fuel lines, or working on any part of the fuel system, the system must be depressurised as described in Section 5.

4 Care must be taken when disconnecting the fuel lines. When disconnecting a fuel union or hose, loosen the union or clamp screw slowly, to avoid sudden uncontrolled fuel spillage. Take adequate fire precautions.

5 When working on fuel system components, scrupulous cleanliness must be observed, and care must be taken not to introduce any foreign matter into fuel lines or components.

6 After carrying out any work involving disconnection of fuel lines, it is advisable to check the connections for leaks; pressurise the system by switching the ignition on and off several times.

7 Electronic control units are very sensitive components, and certain precautions must be taken to avoid damage to these units as follows.

a) *When carrying out welding operations on the vehicle using electric welding equipment, the battery and alternator should be disconnected.*

b) *Although the underbonnet-mounted control units will tolerate normal underbonnet conditions, they can be adversely affected by excess heat or moisture. If using welding equipment or pressure-washing equipment in the vicinity of an electronic control unit, take care not to direct heat, or jets of water or steam, at the unit. If this cannot be avoided, remove the control unit from the vehicle, and protect its wiring plug with a plastic bag.*

c) *Before disconnecting any wiring, or removing components, always ensure that the ignition is switched off.*

d) *After working on fuel injection/engine management system components, ensure that all wiring is correctly reconnected before reconnecting the battery or switching on the ignition.*

⚠ *Warning: Many of the procedures in this Chapter require the removal of fuel lines and connections, which may result in some fuel spillage. Before carrying out any operation on the fuel system, refer to the precautions given in, at the beginning of this manual, and follow them implicitly. Petrol is a highly-dangerous and volatile liquid, and the precautions necessary when handling it cannot be overstressed.*

Note: *Residual pressure will remain in the fuel lines long after the vehicle was last used. Before disconnecting any fuel line, first depressurise the fuel system as described in Section 5.*

2 Air cleaner assembly and intake duct – removal and refitting

Removal

1 Slacken the retaining clip securing the air intake duct to the throttle housing and detach the duct.

2 Disconnect the wiring connector from the side of the airflow meter **(see illustration)**.

3 Unclip the wiring harness from the side of the air cleaner housing **(see illustration)**.

4 Lift up the air cleaner housing to disengage the front and rear mounting rubbers and release it from the air intake duct at the front **(see illustration)**. Lift the air cleaner housing and intake duct out from the engine compartment.

Refitting

5 Refitting is the reverse of removal, making sure the air intake duct is securely reconnected.

3 Accelerator pedal/position sensor – removal and refitting

Removal

1 Disconnect the battery negative terminal (refer to Chapter 5A, Section 4).

2 Remove the facia right-hand lower trim panel as described in Chapter 11, Section 30.

3 Working in the driver's footwell under the facia, disconnect the wiring from the top of the accelerator pedal/position sensor.

4 Unscrew the retaining bolt and withdraw the sensor from the brake pedal mounting bracket **(see illustrations)**.

3.4a Unscrew the retaining bolt ...

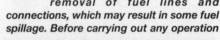

3.4b ... and withdraw the accelerator pedal/position sensor from the brake pedal mounting bracket

Refitting

5 Refitting is a reversal of removal.

4 Unleaded petrol – general information and usage

1 All petrol models are designed to run on fuel with a minimum octane rating of 95 RON. However, if unavailable, 91 octane may be used although a reduction in engine power and torque will be noticed.
2 All models have a catalytic converter, and so must be run on unleaded fuel only. Under no circumstances should leaded fuel or LRP be used, as this will damage the converter.
3 Super unleaded petrol (98 octane) can also be used in all models if wished, though there is no advantage in doing so.

5 Fuel injection system – depressurisation

⚠ **Warning: Refer to the warning note in Section 1 before proceeding. The following procedure will merely relieve the pressure in the fuel system – remember that fuel will still be present in the system components, and take precautions accordingly before disconnecting any of them.**

1 The fuel system referred to in this Section is defined as the tank-mounted fuel pump, the fuel injectors, and the metal pipes and flexible hoses of the fuel lines between these components. All these contain fuel which will be under pressure while the engine is running, and/or while the ignition is switched on. The pressure will remain for some time after the ignition has been switched off, and it must be relieved in a controlled fashion when any of these components are disturbed for servicing work.
2 Locate the fuel pressure connection valve which is fitted to the top, left-hand end of the fuel rail **(see illustration)**.
3 Unscrew the cap from the valve and position a container beneath the valve. Hold a wad of rag over the valve and relieve the pressure in the

5.2 Fuel pressure connection valve

fuel system by depressing the valve core with a suitable screwdriver. Be prepared for the squirt of fuel as the valve core is depressed and catch it with the rag. Hold the valve core down until no more fuel is expelled from the valve.
4 Once all pressure is relieved, securely refit the valve cap.

6 Fuel pump/fuel gauge sender unit – removal and refitting

Note: *Refer to the warning note in Section 1 before proceeding. Vauxhall/Opel specify the use of their service tool EN-48279 to remove and refit the fuel pump/fuel gauge sender unit locking ring. Suitable alternatives to this tool are readily available from accessory stores and motor factor outlets.*

Removal

1 A combined fuel pump and fuel gauge sender unit is located in the top face of the fuel tank. The combined unit can only be detached and withdrawn from the tank after the tank is released and lowered from under the car. Refer to Section 7 and remove the fuel tank, then proceed as follows.
2 With the fuel tank removed, disconnect the fuel supply pipe from the stub by squeezing the quick-release lugs.
3 Unscrew and remove the fuel pump/fuel gauge sender unit locking ring, by unscrewing it with the Vauxhall/Opel tool or a suitable alternative **(see illustration)**.

4 Check that alignment marks are visible on the fuel pump/gauge sender unit and fuel tank. If no marks are visible, suitably mark the tank and sender unit with paint.
5 Carefully lift out the fuel pump/gauge sender unit from the tank. Take care that the sender unit float and arm are not damaged as the unit is removed.
6 Lift out the rubber seal and obtain a new seal for refitting **(see illustration)**.
7 At the time of writing it was not clear whether the fuel gauge sender unit was available separately. If a replacement part can be sourced, the sender unit can be removed from the pump by disconnecting the wiring connector, releasing the retaining catch and withdrawing the unit from the side of the pump.

Refitting

8 Refitting is a reversal of removal, but fit a new rubber seal and tighten the retaining ring securely. Refit the fuel tank as described in Section 7.

7 Fuel tank – removal and refitting

⚠ **Warning: Refer to the warning note in Section 1 before proceeding.**

Removal

1 Disconnect the battery negative terminal (refer to Chapter 5A, Section 4).
2 Depressurise the fuel system as described in Section 5.
3 Before removing the fuel tank, all fuel must be drained from the tank. Since a fuel tank drain plug is not provided, it is therefore preferable to carry out the removal operation when the tank is nearly empty. The remaining fuel can then be siphoned or hand-pumped from the tank.
4 Remove the complete exhaust system as described in Section 13.
5 Disconnect the fuel supply line and the evaporative vent line at the underbody quick-release connectors on the right-hand side of the tank **(see illustration)**. Be prepared for some loss of fuel. A Vauxhall/

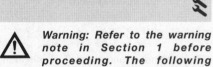

6.3 Using the Vauxhall/Opel special tool, unscrew the locking ring and remove it from the tank

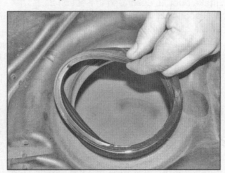
6.6 Renew the rubber seal

7.5 Disconnect the fuel feed line and the evaporative vent line at the underbody quick-release connectors

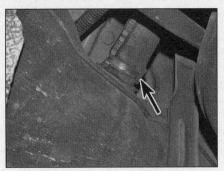

7.6 Slacken the clip and disconnect the fuel filler hose from the fuel tank

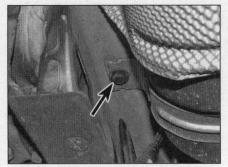

7.9a Undo the bolt securing each fuel tank retaining strap to the underbody ...

7.9b ... then disengage the straps from the underbody at the rear

Opel special tool is available to release the fuel line connectors, but provided care is taken, the connectors can be released using a pair of long-nosed pliers, or a similar tool, to depress the retaining tangs. Suitably plug the disconnected fuel and vent hoses to prevent entry of dust and dirt.

6 Place a suitable container under the tank, then slacken the clip and disconnect the fuel filler hose from the fuel tank **(see illustration)**. Collect the escaping fuel in the container.

7 Disconnect the fuel tank filler vent pipe at the quick-release connector.

8 Support the weight of the fuel tank on a jack with interposed block of wood.

9 Undo the bolts securing the front of each fuel tank retaining strap to the underbody. Disengage the straps from the underbody at the rear and remove the straps **(see illustrations)**.

10 Taking care not to damage the charcoal canister, slowly lower the tank and move it forwards. When sufficient clearance exists, disconnect the wiring connector from the fuel pump/fuel gauge sender unit on the top of the tank.

11 Continue to lower the tank until it can be removed from under the vehicle.

12 If necessary, remove the charcoal canister, fuel lines and hoses, heat shield and wiring from the tank for transfer to the new tank.

13 If the tank contains sediment or water, it may cleaned out with two or three rinses of clean fuel. Remove the fuel pump/fuel gauge sender unit as described in Section 6. Shake the tank vigorously, and change the fuel as

necessary to remove all contamination from the tank. *This procedure should be carried out in a well-ventilated area, and it is vital to take adequate fire precautions.*

14 Any repairs to the fuel tank should be carried out by a professional. Do not under any circumstances attempt any form of DIY repair to a fuel tank.

Refitting

15 Refitting is the reverse of the removal procedure, noting the following points:

a) *When lifting the tank back into position, take care to ensure that none of the hoses become trapped between the tank and vehicle body. Refit the retaining straps and tighten the bolts securely.*

b) *Ensure all pipes and hoses are correctly routed and all hoses unions are securely joined.*

c) *On completion, refill the tank with a small amount of fuel, and check for signs of leakage prior to taking the vehicle out on the road.*

8 Throttle housing – removal and refitting

Removal

1 Disconnect the battery negative terminal (refer to Chapter 5A, Section 4).

2 Remove the air cleaner assembly and intake duct as described in Section 2.

3 Disconnect the crankcase ventilation hose at the quick-release connector on the throttle housing.

4 Disconnect the wiring connector from the throttle housing.

5 Clamp the coolant hoses to minimise coolant loss, then release the retaining clip and disconnect the two coolant hose from the throttle housing.

6 Undo the four bolts and lift the throttle housing off the inlet manifold **(see illustration)**. Recover the gasket.

7 It is not possible to obtain the throttle valve control motor or throttle valve position sensor separately, so if either is faulty, the complete throttle housing must be renewed.

Refitting

8 Refitting is a reversal of removal, but thoroughly clean the mating faces and use a new gasket. Tighten the bolts progressively and securely. On completion, top-up the coolant level as described in *Weekly checks.*

9 Fuel Injection system – general information

1 The engine management (fuel injection/ ignition) systems incorporate a closed-loop catalytic converter, an evaporative emission control system and an exhaust gas recirculation system. The fuel injection side of the systems operate as follows; refer to Chapter 5B for information on the ignition system.

2 The fuel supply pump, immersed in the fuel tank, pumps fuel from the fuel tank to the fuel rail. Fuel supply pressure is controlled by the pressure regulator located in the fuel tank.

3 The electrical control system consists of the ECU, along with the following sensors.

a) *Throttle potentiometer (integral with the throttle housing) – informs the ECU of the throttle position, and confirms the signals received from the accelerator pedal position sensor.*

b) *Accelerator pedal position sensor – informs the ECU of accelerator pedal position, and the rate of throttle opening/ closing.*

c) *Coolant temperature sensor (two) – informs the ECU of engine temperature.*

d) *Airflow meter – informs the ECU of the load on the engine (expressed in terms of the mass of air passing from the air cleaner to the throttle housing).*

e) *Manifold absolute pressure sensor – informs the ECU of the engine load by monitoring the pressure in the inlet manifold.*

f) *Oxygen sensors (two) – inform the ECU of the oxygen content of the exhaust gases (explained in greater detail in Chapter 4C).*

g) *Crankshaft sensor – informs the ECU of engine speed and crankshaft position.*

h) *Camshaft sensors (two) – inform the ECU of speed and position of the camshaft(s).*

8.6 Throttle housing retaining bolts

i) *Knock sensor – informs the ECU when pre-ignition ('pinking') is occurring.*
j) *ABS control unit – informs the ECU of the vehicle speed, based on wheel speed sensor signals (explained in greater detail in Chapter 9, Section 20).*

4 All the above information is analysed by the ECU and, based on this, the ECU determines the appropriate ignition and fuelling requirements for the engine. The ECU controls the fuel injector by varying its pulse width – the length of time the injector is held open – to provide a richer or weaker mixture, as appropriate. The mixture is constantly varied by the ECU, to provide the best setting for cranking, starting (with either a hot or cold engine), warm-up, idle, cruising, and acceleration.

5 Idle speed and throttle position is controlled by the throttle valve control motor, which is an integral part of the throttle housing. The motor is controlled by the ECU, in conjunction with signals received from the accelerator pedal position sensor.

6 The systems incorporate a variable tract inlet manifold to help increase torque output at low engine speeds. Each inlet manifold tract is fitted with a valve. The valve is controlled by the ECU via a solenoid valve and vacuum diaphragm unit.

7 At low engine speeds (below approximately 3600 rpm) the valves remain closed. The air entering the engine is then forced to take the long inlet path through the manifold which leads to an increase in the engine torque output.

8 At higher engine speeds, the ECU switches the solenoid valve which then allows vacuum to act on the diaphragm unit. The diaphragm unit is linked to the valve assemblies and opens up each of the four valves allowing the air passing through the manifold to take the shorter inlet path which is more suited to higher engine speeds.

9 The ECU also controls the exhaust and evaporative emission control systems, which are described in detail in Chapter 4C.

10 If certain sensors fail, and send abnormal signals to the ECU, the ECU has a back-up programme. In this event, the abnormal signals are ignored, and a pre-programmed value is substituted for the sensor signal, allowing the engine to continue running,

albeit at reduced efficiency. If the ECU enters its back-up mode, a warning light on the instrument panel will illuminate, and a fault code will be stored in the ECU memory. This fault code can be read using suitable specialist test equipment.

10 Fuel injection system components – testing

1 If a fault appears in the engine management system, first ensure that all the system wiring connectors are securely connected and free of corrosion. Ensure that the fault is not due to poor maintenance; ie, check that the air cleaner filter element is clean, the spark plugs are in good condition and correctly gapped, the cylinder compression pressures are correct and that the engine breather hoses are clear and undamaged, referring to Chapter 1A, 2A and for further information.

2 If these checks fail to reveal the cause of the problem, the vehicle should be taken to a suitably-equipped Vauxhall/Opel dealer or engine management diagnostic specialist for testing. A diagnostic socket is located at the base of the facia, on the driver's side, to which a fault code reader or other suitable test equipment can be connected **(see illustration)**. By using the code reader or test equipment, the engine management ECU can be interrogated, and any stored fault codes can be retrieved. Live data can also be captured from the various system sensors and actuators, indicating their operating parameters. This will allow the fault to be quickly and simply traced, alleviating the need to test all the system components individually, which is a time-consuming operation that carries a risk of damaging the ECU.

11 Fuel injection system components – removal and refitting

Airflow meter

1 Disconnect the wiring connector from the airflow meter **(see illustration 2.2)**.

10.2 The vehicle diagnostic socket is located at the base of the facia on the driver's side

2 Slacken the retaining clamps and remove the intake duct from the airflow meter, then remove the airflow meter from the air cleaner assembly **(see illustration)**.

3 Refitting is a reversal of removal, but ensure that the arrow on the airflow meter body points toward the throttle housing when fitted.

Fuel rail and injectors

Note: *Refer to the precautions given in Section 1 before proceeding. The seals at both ends of the fuel injectors must be renewed on refitting.*

4 Disconnect the battery negative terminal (refer to Chapter 5A, Section 4).

5 Depressurise the fuel system as described in Section 5.

6 Remove the air cleaner assembly and intake duct as described in Section 2.

7 Unclip the wiring harness trough from the rear of the camshaft cover **(see illustration)**.

8 Pull out the retaining wire clip and disconnect the breather hose from the camshaft cover **(see illustration)**.

9 Disconnect the wiring connectors from the following components, labelling each connector to avoid confusion when refitting:
a) *Evaporative emission control system purge valve.*
b) *Throttle housing.*
c) *Inlet camshaft VVT oil control valve.*
d) *Fuel injectors.*

10 Unclip the wiring harness from the support brackets and move the harness to one side.

11 Disconnect the fuel feed hose

11.2 Slacken the clamps and remove the airflow meter from the air cleaner and intake duct

11.7 Unclip the wiring harness trough from the rear of the camshaft cover

11.8 Pull out the retaining wire clip and disconnect the breather hose from the camshaft cover

11.11 Disconnect the fuel feed hose quick-release connector at the fuel rail

quick-release connector at the fuel rail **(see illustration)**. Be prepared for some loss of fuel. A Vauxhall/Opel special tool is available to release the connector, but provided care is taken, it can be released using a pair of long-nosed pliers, or a similar tool, to depress the retaining tangs. Clamp or plug the open end of the hose, to prevent dirt ingress and further fuel spillage.

12 Unscrew the two mounting bolts, then lift the fuel rail complete with the injectors off of the inlet manifold.

13 To remove an injector from the fuel rail, prise out the metal securing clip using a screwdriver or a pair of pliers, and pull the injector from the fuel rail. Remove and discard the injector sealing rings; new ones must be fitted on refitting.

14 Overhaul of the fuel injectors is not possible, as no spares are available. If faulty, an injector must be renewed.

15 Commence refitting by fitting new O-ring seals to both ends of the fuel injectors. Coat the seals with a thin layer of petroleum jelly before fitting.

16 Refitting is a reversal of removal, bearing in mind the following points:

a) When refitting the injectors to the fuel rail, note that the groove in the metal securing clip must engage with the lug on the injector body.

b) Make sure that the quick-release connector audibly engages on the fuel rail.

c) Ensure that all wiring connectors are

securely reconnected, and that the wiring is secured in the relevant clips and brackets.

Crankshaft position sensor

Note: A new O-ring seal must be used on refitting.

17 The crankshaft sensor is located at the rear left-hand end of the cylinder block, below the starter motor

18 Apply the handbrake, then jack up the front of the vehicle and support it on axle stands (see Jacking and vehicle support).

19 Remove the starter motor as described in Chapter 5A, Section 11.

20 Disconnect the sensor wiring connector, then undo the retaining bolt and withdraw the sensor from the cylinder block.

21 Refitting is a reversal of removal, but ensure that the mating surfaces of the sensor and baseplate are clean and fit a new O-ring seal to the sensor before refitting. Tighten the bolt to the specified torque.

Camshaft sensor

22 Two sensors are fitted, one for each camshaft. Both sensors are located at the left-hand end of the cylinder head.

23 Disconnect the wiring connector from the relevant sensor **(see illustration)**.

24 Undo the retaining bolt and remove the sensor from the cylinder head.

25 Refitting is a reversal of removal, tightening the sensor retaining bolt to the specified torque.

Coolant temperature sensor

26 Refer to Chapter 3, Section 6 for removal and refitting details.

Manifold absolute pressure sensor

27 The manifold absolute pressure sensor is located on the top of the inlet manifold at the rear **(see illustration)**.

28 Disconnect the wiring connector, then undo the retaining bolt and remove the sensor from the inlet manifold.

29 Refit the sensor to the manifold, then refit the retaining bolt and tighten it securely.

30 Reconnect the sensor wiring connector.

Knock sensor

31 The knock sensor is located on the rear of the cylinder block, behind the alternator.

32 Remove the alternator as described in Chapter 5A, Section 8.

33 Disconnect the oxygen sensor wiring connector, then unclip the connector from the support bracket.

34 Unscrew the two retaining bolts and remove the inlet manifold support bracket.

35 Disconnect the knock sensor wiring connector, then unscrew the retaining bolt and remove the sensor from the cylinder block.

36 Clean the contact surfaces of the sensor and block. Also clean the threads of the sensor mounting bolt.

37 Locate the sensor on the block and insert the mounting bolt. Tighten the bolt to the specified torque. Note that the torque setting is critical for the sensor to function correctly.

38 Refit the inlet manifold support bracket and oxygen sensor wiring connector, then refit the alternator as described in Chapter 5A, Section 8.

Electronic control unit (ECU)

Note: If a new ECU is to be fitted, this work must be entrusted to a Vauxhall/Opel dealer or suitably-equipped specialist as it is necessary to program the new ECU after installation. This work requires the use of dedicated Vauxhall/Opel diagnostic equipment or a compatible alternative.

39 The ECU is located on the left-hand side of the engine compartment, attached to the front of the battery box **(see illustration)**.

40 Disconnect the battery negative terminal (refer to Chapter 5A, Section 4).

41 Release the retaining tab and carefully lift the ECU mounting bracket off the front of the battery box.

42 Lift up the locking bars and disconnect the two ECU wiring connectors.

43 If required, undo the four retaining bolts and remove the ECU from the mounting bracket.

44 Refitting is a reversal of removal.

Oxygen sensors

45 Refer to Chapter 4C Section 2 for removal and refitting details.

11.23 Disconnect the wiring connector from the camshaft sensor (exhaust sensor shown)

11.27 The manifold absolute pressure sensor is located on the top of the inlet manifold at the rear

11.39 The ECU is attached to the front of the battery box

12 Inlet manifold –
removal and refitting

Removal

1 Disconnect the battery negative terminal (refer to Chapter 5A, Section 4).
2 Firmly apply the handbrake, then jack up the front of the car and support it securely on axle stands (see *Jacking and vehicle support*).
3 Drain the cooling system as described in Chapter 1A, Section 24.
4 Remove the air cleaner assembly and air intake duct as described in Section 2.
5 Depressurise the fuel system as described in Section 5.
6 Remove the throttle housing as described in Section 8.
7 From under the car, disconnect the oxygen sensor wiring connector, then unclip the connector from the support bracket.
8 Unscrew the two retaining bolts and remove the inlet manifold support bracket.
9 Unclip the wiring harness from the base of the inlet manifold.
10 Disconnect the wiring connector from the evaporative emission control system purge valve **(see illustration)**.
11 Slide the purge valve rubber mounting off the mounting bracket, then disconnect the vapour hoses and remove the valve.
12 Unclip the wiring harness trough from the rear of the camshaft cover **(see illustration 11.7)**.
13 Pull out the retaining wire clip and disconnect the breather hose from the camshaft cover **(see illustration 11.8)**.
14 Disconnect the wiring connectors from the inlet camshaft VVT oil control valve and the four fuel injectors. Release the wiring harness from the support brackets and place it to one side.
15 Disconnect the wiring harness block connector on the left-hand side of the inlet manifold.
16 Release the throttle housing coolant hoses from their clips and supports on the inlet manifold and disconnect the hoses from the coolant expansion tank and thermostat housing. Move the hoses to one side.
17 Disconnect the wiring connectors at the

12.10 Disconnect the wiring connector from the evaporative emission system purge valve

manifold switchover valve diaphragm and solenoid.
18 Undo the retaining bolt and detach the wiring harness support bracket from the engine lifting bracket.
19 Disconnect the fuel feed hose quick-release connector at the fuel rail **(see illustration 11.11)**. Be prepared for some loss of fuel. A Vauxhall/Opel special tool is available to release the connector, but provided care is taken, it can be released using a pair of long-nosed pliers, or a similar tool, to depress the retaining tangs. Clamp or plug the open end of the hose, to prevent dirt ingress and further fuel spillage.
20 Disconnect the quick-release fitting and detach the brake servo vacuum hose from the inlet manifold.
21 Slacken and remove the seven retaining bolts and manoeuvre the manifold assembly away from the cylinder head. Remove the gasket and discard it. **Note:** *The manifold assembly must be treated as a sealed unit; do not attempt to dismantle it as no components, other than the switchover diaphragm and solenoid, are available separately.*

Refitting

22 Refitting is the reverse of removal noting the following.
a) *Ensure the manifold and cylinder head mating surfaces are clean and dry and fit the new gasket. Refit the manifold and tighten the retaining bolts evenly and progressively to the specified torque.*

b) *Ensure that all relevant hoses are reconnected to their original positions, and are securely held (where necessary) by their retaining clips.*
c) *On completion, refill the cooling system as described in Chapter 1A, Section 24.*

13 Exhaust manifold –
removal and refitting

Note: *New manifold and exhaust front pipe retaining nuts, a new manifold gasket, exhaust front pipe gasket and oil dipstick guide tube O-rings must be used on refitting.*

Removal

1 Disconnect the battery negative terminal (refer to Chapter 5A, Section 4).
2 Unbolt and remove the oil dipstick guide tube, and withdraw it from the cylinder block. Remove and discard the O-ring seals.
3 Trace the wiring back from the manifold oxygen sensor and disconnect its wiring connector **(see illustration)**. Free the wiring from the support bracket so the sensor is free to be removed with the manifold.
4 Apply the handbrake, then jack up the front of the vehicle and support it on axle stands (see *Jacking and vehicle support*).
5 Unbolt the air conditioning compressor from the front of the engine with reference to Chapter 3, Section 11 and support it to one side. **Do not** disconnect the refrigerant lines from the compressor.
6 Undo the three nuts securing the exhaust front pipe to the manifold **(see illustration)**. Separate the joint taking care to support the flexible section. **Note:** *Angular movement in excess of 10° can cause permanent damage to the flexible section.* Recover the gasket.
7 Release the mounting rubbers and support the front of the exhaust pipe to one side.
8 Undo the two lower bolts securing the heat shield to the exhaust manifold **(see illustration)**.
9 Undo the two bolts securing the manifold to the lower support bracket, and the two bolts securing the support bracket to the cylinder block. Remove the bracket.

13.3 Disconnect the oxygen sensor wiring connector

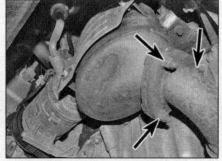

13.6 Undo the three nuts securing the exhaust front pipe to the manifold

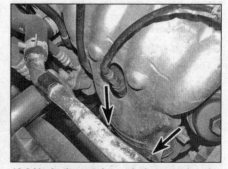

13.8 Undo the two lower bolts securing the heat shield to the exhaust manifold

10 Unbolt the two engine lifting brackets from the exhaust manifold.

11 Undo the bolt securing the wiring harness support bracket, then remove the bracket and the exhaust manifold heat shield.

12 Slacken and remove the nine retaining nuts, and manoeuvre the manifold out of the engine compartment. Recover the gasket.

Refitting

13 Examine all the exhaust manifold studs for signs of damage and corrosion; remove all traces of corrosion, and repair or renew any damaged studs.

14 Ensure that the manifold and cylinder head sealing faces are clean and flat, and fit the new gasket.

15 Refit the manifold then fit the new retaining nuts and tighten them progressively, in a diagonal sequence, to the specified torque.

16 Align the heat shield with the manifold, then refit the wiring harness support bracket and tighten the retaining bolt securely.

17 Refit the air conditioning compressor with reference to Chapter 3, Section 11.

18 Refit the lower support bracket to the cylinder block and manifold and tighten the retaining bolts securely.

19 Refit and tighten the two lower bolts securing the heat shield to the exhaust manifold.

20 Reconnect the exhaust front pipe, using a new gasket. Tighten the new nuts to the specified torque.

21 Reconnect the exhaust manifold oxygen sensor wiring connector making sure the wiring is correctly routed and retained by the support bracket.

22 Fit the new O-ring seals to the oil dipstick guide tube, then insert the tube in the cylinder block. Insert and tighten the retaining bolt.

23 Lower the vehicle to the ground, then reconnect the battery negative terminal.

14 Exhaust system – general information, removal and refitting

Caution: Any work on the exhaust system should only be attempted once the system is completely cool – this may take several hours, especially in the case of the forward sections, such as the manifold and catalytic converter.

General information

1 The exhaust system consists of three main components: the exhaust manifold with integral catalytic converter, the front pipe which incorporates the oxygen sensor (catalytic converter control), and the main section which incorporates the front and rear silencers.

2 A flexible ('mesh') section is fitted to the front pipe to allow for engine movement.

3 The front pipe is attached to the exhaust

manifold (catalytic converter) by a flange joint secured by three nuts. The main section is similarly attached to the front pipe by a flange joint secured by two nuts.

4 When fitted in the factory, the exhaust system from the front pipe flange joint to the end of the system is one piece. However, if the rear silencer is to be renewed, new silencers should be available – check with your parts supplier. It will be necessary to cut through the main section using a hacksaw if a new rear silencer is to be fitted.

5 The system is suspended throughout its entire length by rubber mountings.

Removal

6 To remove a part of the system, first jack up the front or rear of the car, and support it on axle stands (see *Jacking and vehicle support*). Alternatively, position the car over an inspection pit, or on car ramps.

Manifold and catalytic converter

7 Refer to Section 13.

Front pipe

8 Trace the wiring back from the oxygen sensor, noting its correct routing, and disconnect its wiring connector. Free the wiring from any clips so the sensor is free to be removed with the front pipe.

9 Undo the three nuts securing the exhaust front pipe to the manifold **(see illustration 13.6)**. Separate the joint taking care to support the flexible section. **Note:** *Angular movement in excess of 10° can cause permanent damage to the flexible section.* Recover the gasket.

10 Undo the two bolts securing the front pipe support brace to the underbody **(see illustration)**.

11 Undo the nuts securing the front pipe to the main section. Separate the joint and recover the gasket, then remove the front pipe from under the car.

Main section

12 Undo the nuts securing the main section to the front pipe. Separate the joint and recover the gasket

13 Unhook the main section's rubber mountings, and remove it from under the car.

Complete system

14 Trace the wiring back from the front pipe oxygen sensor, noting its correct routing, and disconnect its wiring connector. Free the wiring from any clips so the sensor is free to be removed with the exhaust system.

15 Undo the three nuts securing the exhaust front pipe to the manifold **(see illustration 13.6)**. Separate the joint taking care to support the flexible section. **Note:** *Angular movement in excess of 10° can cause permanent damage to the flexible section.* Recover the gasket.

16 Undo the two bolts securing the front pipe support brace to the underbody **(see illustration 14.10)**.

17 Unhook the main section's rubber mountings, and remove it from under the car.

14.10 Undo the two bolts securing the front pipe support brace to the underbody

Rear silencer

Note: *If a new rear silencer is to be fitted, it will be necessary to obtain a connecting sleeve from your Vauxhall/Opel parts supplier.*

18 If the original one-piece exhaust system is still fitted, it will be necessary to cut off the old rear silencer to enable fitment of the new unit. Using the new silencer as a pattern, mark the exhaust main section to determine the cut point.

19 Using a hacksaw, cut through the main section at the marked cut point. Unhook the silencer's rubber mountings, and remove it from under the car.

20 Fit the new silencer and connect it to the main section using the connecting sleeve. Tighten the connecting sleeve retaining bolt nut securely.

Heat shields

21 The heat shields are secured to the underside of the body by special nuts. Each shield can be removed separately, but note that they may overlap, making it necessary to loosen another section first. If a shield is being removed to gain access to a component located behind it, it may prove sufficient in some cases to remove the retaining nuts and/ or bolts, and simply lower the shield, without disturbing the exhaust system. Otherwise, remove the exhaust section as described earlier.

Refitting

22 In all cases, refitting is a reversal of removal, but note the following points:

a) *Always use new gaskets, nuts and clamps (as applicable), and coat all threads with copper grease.*

b) *If any of the exhaust mounting rubbers are in poor condition, fit new ones.*

c) *Make sure that the exhaust is suspended properly on its mountings, and will not come into contact with the floor or any suspension parts. The rear silencer especially must be aligned correctly before tightening the connecting sleeve retaining bolt nut.*

d) *Tighten all nuts/bolts to the specified torque, where given.*

Chapter 4 Part B
Fuel and exhaust systems – diesel engines

Contents

Degrees of difficulty

Easy, suitable for novice with little experience	**Fairly easy,** suitable for beginner with some experience	**Fairly difficult,** suitable for competent DIY mechanic	**Difficult,** suitable for experienced DIY mechanic	**Very difficult,** suitable for expert DIY or professional

Specifications

Fuel system data

System type:	
1.6 litre engine and 2.0 litre B20 (LFS)	Denso E98 D1P
2.0 litre engine (A20)	Bosch EDC 17 high-pressure direct injection 'common-rail' system, electronically controlled
Firing order	1–3–4–2
Fuel system operating pressure	
1.6 litre engine	2000 bar at 2,000 rpm (approximately)
2.0 litre engine	1400 bar (approx) at 2200 rpm
Idle speed	Controlled by ECU
Maximum speed	Controlled by ECU
High-pressure fuel pump type:	
1.6 litre engine	Denso D1P
2.0 litre engine	Bosch CP1H
Fuel supply pump:	
Type	Electric, mounted in fuel tank
Delivery pressure	3.3 bar (maximum)
Injectors:	
1.6 litre engine	Denso G3.5S
2.0 litre engine (A20)	Bosch CRIP 2-MI
2.0 litre (B20)	Bosch CR12.20

Torque wrench settings

	Nm	lbf ft
Camshaft sensor bolt:		
1.6 litre engine	10	7
2.0 litre B20 engine	8	6
2.0 litre A20 engine	15	11
Catalytic converter clamp bolt:		
1.6 litre engine	15	11
2.0 litre engine	20	15
Crankshaft sensor retaining bolt:		
1.6 and 2.0 litre (B20) engine	10	7
2.0 litre engine	15	11
Exhaust manifold bolts (1.6 litre engines)**	27	20
Exhaust manifold bolts (2.0 litre, B20 engine)	27	20
Exhaust manifold nuts (2.0 litre, A20 engine)	20	15
Exhaust front pipe-to-catalytic converter nuts	23	17
EGR pipe to cooler bolts	10	7
EGR pipe to manifold bolts*	10	7
EGR cooler bolts (2.0 litre B20 engine):		
At the manifold	25	18
At the valve	10	7
Fuel injector clamp bracket (1.6 litre engine): *		
Stage 1	10	7
Stage 2	Angle-tighten a further 60°	
Fuel injector clamp bracket (2.0 litre engines)	25	18
Fuel pressure sensor to fuel rail (A20 engine only)	70	52
Fuel pressure sensor to fuel rail (B20 engine only)	30	22
Fuel pressure regulator (A20 engine):		
Stage 1	50	37
Stage 2	Slacken 90°	
Stage 3	60	45
Fuel pressure regulator (B20 engine):		
Stage 1	60	45
Stage 2	Slacken 90°	
Stage 3	85	63
Fuel rail retaining bolts	25	18
High-pressure fuel pipe unions:		
To fuel rail (1.6 litre engine)	30	22
To fuel rail (2.0 litre engines)	20	15
To injectors and fuel pump	25	18
High-pressure fuel pump mounting bolts	25	18
High-pressure fuel pump sprocket nut:		
1.6 and 2.0 (A20) litre engines	64	47
2.0 litre (B20) engines	80	59
Inlet manifold bolts (1.6 and B20 2.0 litre engines)	12	9
Inlet manifold nuts (2.0 litre engine)	22	16
Subframe rear mounting reinforcement plates-to-underbody*:		
Stage 1	60	45
Stage 2	Angle-tighten a further 30°	
Subframe rear mounting reinforcement plates-to-subframe*	160	118
Throttle body housing bolts	10	7
Turbocharger oil supply pipe banjo union bolt:		
1.6 litre engine	25	18
2.0 litre engine	30	22
2.0 litre (B20) engine		
At the turbocharger	25	18
At the oil filter housing	35	26
Turbocharger oil drain bolts (1.6 litre engine):		
Engine block end	25	18
Turbocharger end	10	7
Turbocharger oil drain bolts (2.0 litre B20 engine)	10	7
Turbocharger mounting nuts/bolts:		
1.6 litre and 2.0 litre (B20) engine	30	22
2.0 litre (A20) engine	25	18

* Use new fasteners
**Use new fasteners and repeat tightening sequence 3 times to the same torque

1 General information and precautions

General information

1 The engines are equipped with a high-pressure direct injection system which incorporates the very latest in diesel injection technology. On this system, a high-pressure fuel pump is used purely to provide the pressure required for the injection system and has no control over the injection timing (unlike conventional diesel injection systems). The injection timing is controlled by the electronic control unit (ECU) via the electrically-operated injectors. The system operates as follows.

2 The fuel system consists of a fuel tank (which is mounted under the rear of the car, with an electric fuel supply pump immersed in it), a fuel filter with integral water separator, a high-pressure fuel pump, injectors and associated components.

3 Fuel is supplied to the fuel filter housing which is attached to the side of the fuel tank. The fuel filter removes all foreign matter and water and ensures that the fuel supplied to the pump is clean.

4 The fuel is heated to ensure no problems occur when the ambient temperature is very low. This is achieved by an electrically-operated fuel heater incorporated in the filter housing, the heater is controlled by the ECU.

5 The high-pressure fuel pump is driven at half-crankshaft speed by the timing chain on the 1.6 litre engine and by the timing belt on the 2.0 litre engine. The high pressure required in the system (up to 2000 bar on the 1.6 litre engine and up to 1400 bar on the 2.0 litre engine) is produced by the three pistons in the pump. The high-pressure pump supplies high pressure fuel to the fuel rail, which acts as a reservoir for the four injectors.

6 The electrical control system consists of the ECU, along with the following sensors:

a) *Accelerator pedal position sensor – informs the ECU of the accelerator pedal position, and the rate of throttle opening/ closing.*

b) *Coolant temperature sensor – informs the ECU of engine temperature.*

c) *Airflow meter (with inlet air temperature sensor) – informs the ECU of the temperature and amount of air passing through the intake duct.*

d) *Crankshaft sensor – informs the ECU of the crankshaft position and speed of rotation.*

e) *Camshaft sensor – informs the ECU of the positions of the pistons.*

f) *Charge (boost) pressure sensor – informs ECU of the pressure in the inlet manifold.*

g) *Fuel pressure sensor – informs the ECU of the fuel pressure present in the fuel rail.*

h) *ABS control unit – informs the ECU of the vehicle speed.*

7 All the above signals are analysed by the ECU which selects the fuelling response appropriate to those values. The ECU controls the fuel injectors (varying the pulse width – the length of time the injectors are held open – to provide a richer or weaker mixture, as appropriate). The mixture is constantly varied by the ECU, to provide the best setting for cranking, starting (with either a hot or cold engine), warm-up, idle, cruising and acceleration.

8 The ECU also has full control over the fuel pressure present in the fuel rail via the high-pressure fuel regulator and third piston deactivator solenoid valve which are fitted to the high-pressure pump. To reduce the pressure, the ECU opens the high-pressure fuel regulator which allows the excess fuel to return direct to the tank from the pump. The third piston deactivator is used mainly to reduce the load on the engine, but can also be used to lower the fuel pressure. The deactivator solenoid valve relieves the fuel pressure from the third piston of the pump which results in only two of the pistons pressurising the fuel system.

9 The ECU also controls the exhaust gas recirculation (EGR) system, described in detail in, the pre/post heating system (see Chapter 5A, Section 16), the engine cooling fan and on later models the addition of 'Adblue' for the SCR (Selective Catalytic Reduction) system.

10 The inlet manifold is fitted with a butterfly valve arrangement to improve efficiency at low engine speeds. Each cylinder has two intake tracts in the manifold, one of which is fitted with a valve; the operation of the valve is controlled by the ECU via an electric motor actuator drive arrangement. At low engine speeds (below approximately 1500 rpm) the valves remain closed, meaning that air entering each cylinder is passing through only one of the two manifold tracts. At higher engine speeds, the ECU opens up each of the four valves allowing the air passing through the manifold to pass through both inlet tracts.

11 A variable-vane turbocharger is fitted to increases engine efficiency. It does this by raising the pressure in the inlet manifold above atmospheric pressure. Instead of the air simply being sucked into the cylinders, it is forced in.

12 Between the turbocharger and the inlet manifold, the compressed air passes through an intercooler. This is an air-to-air heat exchanger, mounted in front of the radiator, and supplied with cooling air from the front of the vehicle. The purpose of the intercooler is to remove some of the heat gained in being compressed from the inlet air. Because cooler air is denser, removal of this heat further increases engine efficiency.

13 Energy for the operation of the turbocharger comes from the exhaust gas. The gas flows through a specially-shaped housing (the turbine housing) and in so doing, spins the turbine wheel. The turbine wheel is attached to a shaft, at the end of which is another vaned wheel known as the compressor wheel. The compressor wheel

1.14 The vehicle diagnostic socket is located at the base of the facia on the driver's side

spins in its own housing, and compresses the inlet air on the way to the inlet manifold. The turbo shaft is pressure-lubricated by an oil feed pipe from the main oil gallery. The shaft 'floats' on a cushion of oil. A drain pipe returns the oil to the sump.

14 If certain sensors fail, and send abnormal signals to the ECU, the ECU has a back-up programme. In this event, the abnormal signals are ignored, and a pre-programmed value is substituted for the sensor signal, allowing the engine to continue running, albeit at reduced efficiency. If the ECU enters its back-up mode, a warning light on the instrument panel will illuminate, and a fault code will be stored in the ECU memory. This fault code can be read using suitable specialist test equipment plugged into the system's diagnostic socket. The diagnostic socket is located at the base of the facia, on the driver's side **(see illustration)**.

Precautions

⚠️ *Warning: It is necessary to take certain precautions when working on the fuel system components, particularly the high-pressure side of the system. Before carrying out any operations on the fuel system, refer to the precautions given in 'Safety first!' at the beginning of this manual, and to any additional warning notes at the start of the relevant Sections. Also refer to the additional information contained in Section 2.*

Caution: Do not operate the engine if any of air intake ducts are disconnected or the filter element is removed. Any debris entering the engine will cause severe damage to the turbocharger.

Caution: To prevent damage to the turbocharger, do not race the engine immediately after start-up, especially if it is cold. Allow it to idle smoothly to give the oil a few seconds to circulate around the turbocharger bearings. Always allow the engine to return to idle speed before switching it off – do not blip the throttle and switch off, as this will leave the turbo spinning without lubrication.

Caution: Observe the recommended intervals for oil and filter changing, and

2.10 Typical plastic plug and cap set for sealing disconnected fuel pipes and components

2.12 Two crow-foot adaptors will be necessary for tightening the fuel pipe unions

use a reputable oil of the specified quality. Neglect of oil changing, or use of inferior oil, can cause carbon formation on the turbo shaft, leading to subsequent failure.

2 High pressure Diesel injection system – special information

Warnings and precautions

It is essential to observe strict precautions when working on the fuel system components, particularly the high pressure side of the system. Before carrying out any operations on the fuel system, refer to the precautions given in *Section* at the beginning of this manual, and to the following additional information.

● Do not carry out any repair work on the high pressure fuel system unless you are competent to do so, have all the necessary tools and equipment required, and are aware of the safety implications involved.
● Before starting any repair work on the fuel system, wait at least 30 seconds after switching off the engine to allow the fuel circuit to return to atmospheric pressure.
● Never work on the high pressure fuel system with the engine running.
● Keep well clear of any possible source of fuel leakage, particularly when starting the engine after carrying out repair work. A leak in the system could cause an extremely high pressure jet of fuel to escape, which could result in severe personal injury.
● Never place your hands or any part of your body near to a leak in the high pressure fuel system.
● Do not use steam cleaning equipment or compressed air to clean the engine or any of the fuel system components.

Repair procedures and general information

Strict cleanliness must be observed at all times when working on any part of the fuel system. This applies to the working area in general, the person doing the work, and the components being worked on.

Before working on the fuel system components, they must be thoroughly cleaned with a suitable degreasing fluid. Cleanliness is particularly important when working on the fuel system connections at the following components:
a) Fuel filter.
b) High-pressure fuel pump.
c) Fuel rail.
d) Fuel injectors.
e) High pressure fuel pipes.

After disconnecting any fuel pipes or components, the open union or orifice must be immediately sealed to prevent the entry of dirt or foreign material. Plastic plugs and caps in various sizes are available in packs from motor factors and accessory outlets, and are particularly suitable for this application **(see illustration)**. Fingers cut from disposable latex gloves should be used to protect components such as fuel pipes, fuel injectors and wiring connectors, and can be secured in place using elastic bands.

Whenever any of the high pressure fuel pipes are disconnected or removed, a new pipe(s) must be obtained for refitting.

The torque wrench settings given in the Specifications must be strictly observed when tightening component mountings and connections. This is particularly important when tightening the high pressure fuel pipe unions. To enable a torque wrench to be used on the fuel pipe unions, two crow-foot adaptors are required. Suitable types are available from motor factors and accessory outlets **(see illustration)**.

3.1a Slacken the retaining clip securing the airflow meter to the air cleaner lid and detach the meter

3.1b Alternatively, disconnect the airflow sensor …

3.1c … and remove the complete inlet duct at the turbocharger (I.6 litre engine shown)

3.2 Unclip the wiring harness from the side of the air cleaner lid

3 Air filter assembly and intake ducts – removal and refitting

Removal

Air filter assembly

Note: *Removal of the air filter housing and associated pipework is essentially the same for both the 1.6 and 2.0 litre engines.*

1 Slacken the retaining clip securing the airflow meter to the air cleaner lid and detach the meter **(see illustrations)**.

2 Unclip the wiring harness from the side of the air cleaner lid **(see illustration)**.

3.3 Disconnect the drain tube from the front of the air cleaner housing

3.4a Lift up the air cleaner housing to disengage the rear mounting rubber …

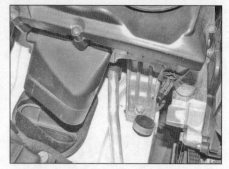

3.4b … and release it from the front mounting rubber and air intake duct

3 Disconnect the drain tube from the front of the air cleaner housing **(see illustration)**.

4 Lift up the air cleaner housing to disengage the rear mounting rubber and release it from the front mounting rubber and air intake duct **(see illustrations)**. Lift the air cleaner housing out from the engine compartment.

Turbocharger intake duct

5 Remove the plastic cover over the top of the engine.

6 Slacken the retaining clips securing the intake duct to the turbocharger and airflow meter **(see illustrations)**.

7 Disconnect the wiring connector at the crankcase ventilation hose heating element **(see illustration)**.

8 Disconnect the crankcase ventilation hose from the heating element **(see illustration)**.

9 Release the intake duct from the turbocharger and airflow meter and remove it from the car.

Throttle housing intake duct

10 Remove the plastic cover over the top of the engine.

11 Where fitted, release the brake servo vacuum hose from the clips on the intake air duct **(see illustration)**.

12 On A20 engines, release the upper coolant hose from the clip on the intake air duct **(see illustration)**.

13 Undo the bolt securing the intake air duct **(see illustration)**.

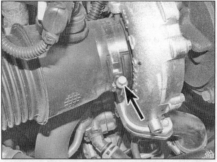

3.6a Slacken the retaining clip securing the intake duct to the turbocharger …

3.6b … and airflow meter

3.7 Disconnect the wiring connector at the crankcase ventilation hose heating element (where fitted)

3.8 Disconnect the crankcase ventilation hose from the heating element (where fitted)

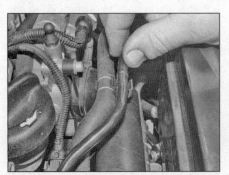

3.11 Release the brake servo vacuum hose from the clips on the intake air duct

3.12 Release the upper coolant hose from the clip on the intake air duct

3.13 Undo the bolt securing the intake air duct

3.14a Undo the three bolts and release the air duct from the throttle housing

3.14b On later models rotate the locking collar ...

3.14c ... and remove the air duct

14 Undo the three bolts securing the intake air duct to the throttle housing and release the duct from the housing **(see illustrations)**.
15 Spread the sides of the wire retaining clip and lift the forward end of the intake air

duct out of the intercooler elbow **(see illustration)**.
16 Release the lower coolant hose from the clips on the intake air duct and remove the duct from the engine **(see illustrations)**.

Intercooler air ducts

17 Remove the front bumper as described in Chapter 11, Section 6.
18 Slacken the retaining clip securing the relevant air duct elbow to the intercooler **(see illustration)**.
19 Disengage the retaining clip (a worm drive clip on some models and a spring clip on others) and detach the elbow from the intercooler **(see illustrations)**.
20 Disconnect the other end of the duct either by slackening the retaining clip, or releasing the wire retaining clip and remove the air duct from the car.

Refitting

21 Refitting is the reverse of removal, making sure all the air intake ducts/hoses are securely reconnected.

3.15 Spread the sides of the wire retaining clip and lift the intake air duct out of the intercooler elbow

3.16a Release the lower coolant hose from the clips on the intake air duct ...

4 Accelerator pedal/position sensor – removal and refitting

1 Refer to Chapter 4A, Section 3.

5 Fuel system – priming and bleeding

3.16b ... and remove the duct from the engine

3.18 Slacken the retaining clip securing the air duct elbow to the intercooler

1 After disconnecting part of the fuel supply system or running out of fuel, it is necessary to prime the fuel system and bleed off any air which may have entered the system components, as follows.
2 Prime the system by switching on the ignition three times for approximately 15 seconds each time. Operate the starter for a maximum of 30 seconds. If the engine does not start within this time, wait 5 seconds and repeat the procedure.
3 When the engine starts, run it at a fast idle speed for a minute or so to purge any trapped air from the fuel lines. After this time the engine should idle smoothly at a constant speed.
4 If the engine idles roughly, then there is still some air trapped in the fuel system. Increase the engine speed again for another minute or so then allow it to idle. Repeat this procedure as necessary until the engine is idling smoothly.

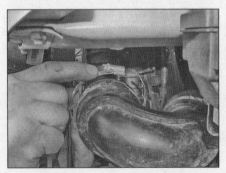

3.19a Disengage the retaining clip ...

3.19b ... and detach the elbow from the intercooler

6 Fuel pump/fuel gauge sender unit – removal and refitting

Note: *Refer to the warnings and precautions in Section 2 before proceeding.*

1 Removal and refitting of the combined fuel pump and fuel gauge sender unit is the same as described Chapter 4A, Section 6, for petrol engines.

2 On completion, prime the fuel system as described in Section 5.

7 Fuel tank – removal and refitting

Note: *Refer to the warnings and precautions in Section 2 before proceeding.*

1 Refer to Chapter 4A, Section 7. Fuel tank removal and refitting is the same as for petrol engines, with the exception that the fuel filter takes the place of the evaporative emissions charcoal canister. Note also that it will be necessary to disconnect the fuel supply and return lines at the quick-release connectors, rather than the fuel supply line and the evaporative vent line.

2 On completion, prime the fuel system as described in Section 5.

8 Injection system electrical components – removal and refitting

Airflow meter

1 Disconnect the airflow meter wiring connector **(see illustration)**.
2 Slacken the retaining clip securing the air intake duct to the airflow meter and disconnect the duct.
3 Slacken the retaining clip and remove the airflow meter from the air cleaner housing lid.
4 Refitting is a reversal of removal, but ensure that the arrow on the airflow meter points toward the turbocharger when fitted.

Throttle body

5 Remove the throttle body intake duct as described in Section 3.

8.1 Disconnect the airflow meter wiring connector

8.6b On some models disconnect the wiring after removing the throttle body

6 Disconnect the wiring connector from the throttle housing **(see illustrations)**.
7 Undo the retaining bolts **(see illustration)** (noting the different bolt lengths on some models) and remove the throttle housing from the inlet manifold. Recover the gasket and dispose of it – a new one must be fitted. Note the location of any wiring harness support brackets also secured by the retaining bolts.
8 Refitting is a reversal of removal, but thoroughly clean the mating faces and use a new gasket/seal. Tighten the retaining bolts to the specified torque.

Crankshaft sensor

9 The sensor is located at the front of the engine cylinder block on the 1.6 litre engine and at the rear of the cylinder block (below the starter motor) on the 2.0 litre engine **(see illustrations)**. To gain access, firmly apply the handbrake, then jack up

8.6a Disconnect the wiring connector from the throttle housing (A20 engine)

8.7 Remove the bolts

the front of the car and support it securely on axle stands (see *Jacking and vehicle support*).
10 Disconnect the battery (as described in Chapter 5A Section 4) and then remove the undertray as described in Chapter 11, Section 24.
11 On models fitted with an automatic transmission remove the catalytic converter as described in Chapter 4C Section 3.
12 On 1.6 litre engines remove the charge air outlet hose and unclip the wiring loom. Release the hose clips from the particulate filter pressure sensor pipes and disconnect the pipes. Unbolt the fixing bracket and move the pipes to the side.
13 Wipe clean the area around the crankshaft sensor then disconnect the wiring connector.
14 Slacken and remove the retaining bolt and slide out the retaining clip (where fitted) **(see illustration)**. Remove the sensor from

8.9a The crankshaft sensor is below the starter motor on the 2.0 litre A20 engine ...

8.9b ... and in a similar position on the 2.0 litre B20 engine

8.14 The mounting bolt and bracket fitted to the 1.6 litre engine

8.17a Disconnect the camshaft sensor wiring connector (2.0 litre A20 engine shown)

8.17b The camshaft sensor on the 1.6 (LVL) engine …

8.17c … and on the 2.0 litre B20 engine

the cylinder block and recover the sealing ring (where fitted).

15 Refitting is the reverse of removal, using a new sealing ring. Tighten the sensor retaining bolt to the specified torque.

Camshaft sensor

16 The camshaft sensor is located at the right-hand end of the camshaft housing or cylinder head. To gain access, remove the cover from the top of the engine.

17 Wipe clean the area around the camshaft sensor then disconnect the wiring connector **(see illustrations)**.

18 Slacken and remove the retaining bolt and remove the sensor from the camshaft cover. Recover the sealing ring.

19 Refitting is the reverse of removal, using a

new sealing ring. Tighten the sensor retaining bolt to the specified torque.

Coolant temperature sensor

20 The coolant temperature sensor is located behind the alternator on the 1.6 litre engine and on the thermostat housing (on the left-hand end of the cylinder head) on the 2.0 litre engine. Refer to Chapter 3, Section 6 for removal and refitting details.

Charge (boost) pressure sensor

21 Remove the plastic cover from the top of the engine.

22 Disconnect the wiring connector **(see illustrations)** from the charge (boost) pressure sensor located on the inlet manifold.

23 Slacken and remove the retaining bolt and remove the sensor from the manifold.

24 Refitting is the reverse of removal.

Fuel pressure sensor and fuel pressure regulator

25 A pressure regulator and a fuel pressure sensor are fitted to the fuel rail on most models. Some versions of the A20 diesel engine only have a regulator fitted to the fuel rail. The removal and refitting of the sensor or regulator is only applicable to 2.0 litre engines. If the sensor is faulty on the 1.6 litre engine the fuel rail must be replaced.

26 On the 2.0 litre, B20 (LFS) diesel engine the fuel pressure regulator can only be removed after the fuel rail has been removed. On these engines follow the procedure for fuel rail removal in Section 10 and remove the regulator on the bench.

27 Disconnect the battery negative terminal (refer to Chapter 5A, Section 4).

28 Remove the cover from the top of the engine.

29 Disconnect the wiring connector at the fuel pressure sensor **(see illustration)**.

30 Unscrew the regulator and remove it from the fuel rail. Be prepared for some loss of fuel.

31 Refitting is the reverse of removal, tightening the sensor to the specified torque. Note the tightening procedure for the regulator involves tightening and then slackening the regulator, before fully tightening to the specified torque.

Electronic control unit (ECU)

Note: If a new ECU is to be fitted, this work must be entrusted to a Vauxhall/Opel dealer or suitably-equipped specialist as it is necessary to program the new ECU after installation. This work requires the use of dedicated Vauxhall/Opel diagnostic equipment or a compatible alternative.

32 Disconnect the battery negative terminal (refer to Chapter 5A, Section 4).

33 Lift the wiring loom support bracket from its location on the front of the battery box **(see illustration)**.

34 Using a small screwdriver, depress the retaining tab and lift the ECU mounting

8.29 Disconnect the wiring connector at the fuel pressure regulator (A20 engine shown)

8.22a The boost pressure sensor on the 1.6 litre engine

8.22b The boost pressure sensor on the 2.0 litre (B20) engine

8.33 Lift the wiring loom support bracket from its location on the battery box

8.34a Depress the retaining tab ...

8.34b ... and lift the ECU mounting bracket off the side of the battery box

8.35a Open the locking bar ...

8.35b ... and disconnect the wiring connectors from the ECU

8.36a Remove the ECU

8.36b Release the retaining catch and remove the ECU from the mounting bracket

bracket off the side of the battery box **(see illustrations)**.

35 Open the locking bar and disconnect the wiring connectors from the ECU. The number will vary depending on the model **(see illustrations)**.

36 Remove the ECU and on some models, release the retaining catch and remove the ECU from the mounting bracket **(see illustrations)**.

37 Refitting is the reverse of removal.

Turbocharger wastegate solenoid

Note: *The B20 (LFS) engine uses an electronic control system (with position feedback) to operate the wastegate and control the vane position on the turbocharger.*

38 The wastegate (charge pressure) solenoid valve is located above the starter motor on the 1.6 litre engine and at the front of the engine compartment above the radiator on the 2.0 litre (A20) engine **(see illustrations)**.

39 Disconnect the wiring connector and the two vacuum hoses from the valve then undo the retaining nuts (or bolts) and remove the valve from its mounting bracket.

40 Refitting is the reverse of removal.

9 High-pressure fuel pump – removal and refitting

⚠ **Warning: Refer to the information contained in Section 2 before proceeding.**

Note: *A new fuel pump-to-fuel rail high pressure fuel pipe will be required for refitting.*

1.6 litre engine
Removal

Note: *If the transmission and timing chain are removed, then the pump can be removed after the removal of the fuel pump sprocket*

(as described in Chapter 2B Section 8). If the transmission and timing chain are in position then the fuel pump can only be removed with the Vauxhall special tools (EN-50885-1 and EN-50885-2). The special tool supports the fuel pump sprocket and keeps the timing chain in position whilst the pump is removed.

1 Remove the inlet manifold as described in Section 12.

2 Remove the battery and battery tray as described in Chapter 5A Section 4.

3 Disconnect the following attachments at the high-pressure fuel pump **(see illustration)**:

a) Fuel supply pipe.
b) Fuel return pipe.
c) Fuel injector return hose.
d) Wiring connector.

4 Release the fuel pipes and hoses from any support clips and move them to one side. Plug or cover the pump unions, hoses and pipes to prevent dirt entry.

8.38a The control solenoid on the 1.6 litre engine

8.38b The wastegate solenoid valve on the 2.0 litre (A20) engine

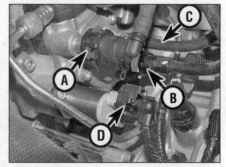

9.3 Wiring, hose and pipe attachments at the high-pressure fuel pump

9.6 Remove the vacuum hose

9.8 Remove the selector shaft housing

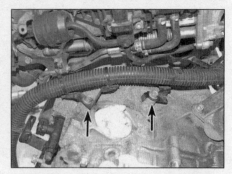

9.10a Remove the loom support bracket bolts ...

9.10b ... and the bell housing bolt to release the rear bracket

9.11a Install the tool. Note the piercing spike

9.11b The tool removed with the blanking plug

5 If the transmission and timing chain are already removed, then unscrew the two mounting bolts and withdraw the pump from its location. Recover the sealing O-ring. If the special tool is available and the gearbox and

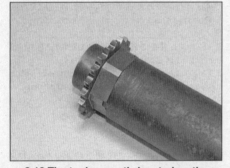

9.13 The tool correctly located on the sprocket (shown removed for clarity)

timing chain are in position, then proceed as follows:

6 Disconnect the wiring plug and vacuum hose from the boost pressure control solenoid (see illustration).

7 Remove the gear selector cable(s) as described in Chapter 7A Section 4 (manual transmission) or Chapter 7B Section 4(automatic transmission).

8 On manual transmissions unbolt and remove the selector housing (see illustration). Seal the opening.

9 Unclip and unbolt the diesel particulate pressure sensors form the EGR cooler.

10 Unbolt the wiring loom and disconnect the wiring plugs from below the EGR cooler and control valve (see illustrations). Move the loom to the side.

11 Fit the piercing spike to the tool. Align the tool with the plastic blanking plug and drive

the spike through the plastic plug. Turn the spike through 90 degrees and pull out the blanking plug (see illustrations).

12 Remove the spike and blanking plug from the main body of the tool. Discard the blanking plug. A new one must be fitted.

13 Fit the second part of the special tool (EN-50885-2) ensuring that the lugs engage with the slots on the fuel pump sprocket (see illustration). The outer ring of the tool must be positioned so that the socket square drive is accessible.

14 Screw the inner section of the tool into the inner threaded section of the fuel pump sprocket. Counter hold the main body of the tool with a socket extension and using a socket through the centre of the inner body, locate and release the sprocket nut. Remove the nut (see illustrations).

9.14a Screw the tool into the pump sprocket

9.14b Fit a socket with an extension bar ...

9.14c ... counterhold the tool and unbolt the sprocket nut

9.14d Recover the sprocket nut

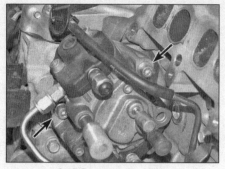

9.15 Remove the bolts

9.16 Fit the forcing screw

Caution: Do not attempt to turn the engine with the special tool installed.

15 Remove the fuel injection pump mounting bolts **(see illustration)** and loosen the fuel pump. Tapping the pump gently with a wood block is permissible. Do not attempt to fully remove the pump at this stage.

16 Screw the pressure spindle tool (EN-50885-2) into the main body of the tool and using a hex key push the sprocket off the pump taper **(see illustration)**. Note that using the tool to force the sprocket off the taper if the pump body is not first loosed will damage the pump internals.

17 Remove the pump and then remove the pressure spindle from the tool. Do not remove the main body of the tool.

Caution: The high-pressure fuel pump is manufactured to extremely close tolerances and must not be dismantled in any way. No parts for the pump are available separately and if the unit is in any way suspect, it must be renewed.

Refitting

18 Thoroughly clean the fuel pump and engine mating faces.

19 Locate a new sealing O-ring on the pump flange **(see illustration)** and lubricate the O-ring with clean oil.

20 Mark the position of the woodruff key on the shaft with paint **(see illustration)**.

21 Rotate the pump shaft so that the marked position of the woodruff key aligns with the slot in the fuel pump sprocket. A mirror and pen light will be helpful here.

22 Push the pump home, fit and then tighten the pump mounting bolts to the specified torque.

23 Reversing the removal procedure install and tighten the sprocket retaining nut to the specified torque setting.

24 Remove the special tool and then fit a new blanking plug to the tool. Hold the tool firmly against the timing chain cover and then using a hammer drive the blanking plug into the housing on the timing chain cover **(see illustrations)**. Remove the tool and check that the new blanking plug is correctly seated.

25 Reconnect the pipe, hose and wiring

connections previously removed from the rear of the pump.

26 Refit the wiring loom electrical connectors and support brackets.

27 Refit the selector cables and selector shaft (where removed) and refit the vacuum hose to the boost control solenoid.

28 Refit the inlet manifold as described in Section 12.

29 Refit the battery tray and battery as described in Chapter 5A Section 4.

30 Observing the precautions listed in Section 2, prime the fuel system as described in Section 5, then start the engine and allow it to idle. Check for leaks at the high-pressure fuel pipe unions with the engine idling. If satisfactory, increase the engine speed to 4000 rpm and check again for leaks. If any

leaks are detected, obtain and fit a new high-pressure fuel pipe.

2.0 litre (A20) engine

Removal

31 Disconnect the battery negative terminal (refer to Chapter 5A, Section 4).

32 Remove the cover from the top of the engine.

33 Remove the timing belt and the high-pressure fuel pump sprocket as described in Chapter 2C, Section 6 and Chapter 2C Section 7 respectively.

34 Disconnect the crankcase ventilation hose from the heating element **(see illustration 3.8)**.

35 Unclip the wiring harness from the crankcase ventilation pipe, then undo the two

9.19 Fit a new O-ring to the pump

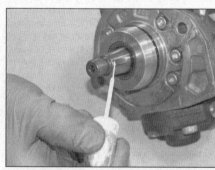

9.20 Mark the position of the key way

9.24a Fit a new blanking plug and ...

9.24b ... then use the tool to drive the plug into the timing chain cover

9.35a Unclip the wiring harness from the crankcase ventilation pipe ...

9.35b ... then undo the upper bolt ...

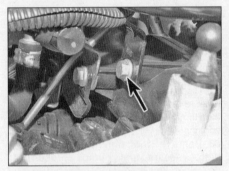

9.35c ... and lower bolt at the rear ...

9.35d ... and move the crankcase ventilation pipe to one side

bolts and move the crankcase ventilation pipe to one side **(see illustrations)**.

36 Disconnect the fuel return hose quick-release fitting, then undo the bolts securing the engine lifting eye and hose/cable support bracket and move the bracket clear of the fuel pump **(see illustrations)**. Unbolt and remove any additional support brackets over the top of the fuel pump as necessary for access.

37 Release the retaining clips and disconnect the two fuel hoses from the top of the fuel pump. Suitably plug or cover the open unions to prevent dirt entry.

38 Disconnect the wiring connector from the high-pressure fuel pump.

39 Thoroughly clean the fuel pipe unions on the fuel pump and fuel rail. Using an open-ended spanner, unscrew the union nuts securing the high-pressure fuel pipe to

the fuel pump and fuel rail. Counterhold the union on the pump with a second spanner, while unscrewing the union nut. Withdraw the high-pressure fuel pipe and plug or cover the open unions to prevent dirt entry.

40 Unscrew the three retaining nuts and remove the pump from the engine bracket **(see illustration)**.

Caution: The high-pressure fuel pump is manufactured to extremely close tolerances and must not be dismantled in any way. No parts for the pump are available separately and if the unit is in any way suspect, it must be renewed.

Refitting

41 Refit the pump to the engine bracket and tighten the retaining bolts to the specified torque.

42 Remove the blanking plugs from the fuel

pipe unions on the pump and fuel rail. Locate a new high-pressure fuel pipe over the unions and screw on the union nuts finger tight at this stage.

43 Using a torque wrench and crow-foot adaptor, tighten the fuel pipe union nuts to the specified torque. Counterhold the unions on the pump with an open-ended spanner, while tightening the union nuts.

44 Reconnect the pump wiring connector and the two fuel hoses on top of the pump.

45 Refit the hose/cable support bracket and the engine lifting eye and securely tighten the retaining bolts. Refit any additional support brackets removed for access, then reconnect the fuel return hose quick-release fitting.

46 Refit the crankcase ventilation pipe and secure with the three bolts.

47 Refit the high-pressure fuel pump sprocket and the timing belt as described in Chapter 2C, Section 6 and Chapter 2D Section 6.

48 Reconnect the battery negative terminal.

49 Observing the precautions listed in Section 2, prime the fuel system as described in Section 5, then start the engine and allow it to idle. Check for leaks at the high-pressure fuel pipe unions with the engine idling. If satisfactory, increase the engine speed to 4000 rpm and check again for leaks. If any leaks are detected, obtain and fit a new high-pressure fuel pipe.

50 Refit the engine cover on completion.

2.0 litre (B20) engine

Note: *Special tools (EN-51413, EN-51420 and EN-51585) are available that allow the pump to be removed with the timing belt still in place. These tools (at the time of writing) are not available in the aftermarket. It is more than likely that an engine that requires attention to the fuel pump will have covered a reasonable mileage and will be due a timing belt replacement regardless of the pump condition.*

Removal

51 Disconnect the battery negative terminal (refer to Chapter 5A, Section 4).

52 Remove the cover from the top of the engine and air filter housing as described in Section 3.

53 Remove the timing belt and the high-pressure fuel pump sprocket as

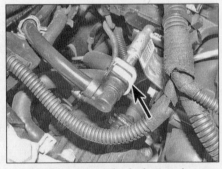

9.36a Disconnect the fuel return hose quick-release fitting ...

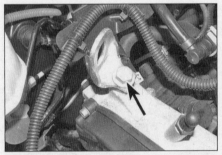

9.36b ... then undo the bolt and move the engine lifting eye and support bracket clear of the fuel pump

9.40 High-pressure fuel pump retaining nuts

9.57a High pressure pump mounting bolts

9.57b Remove the pump

10 Fuel rail –
removal and refitting

Removal

  Warning: Refer to the information contained in Section 2 before proceeding.

Note: A complete new set of high-pressure fuel pipes will be required for refitting.

1 Disconnect the battery negative terminal (refer to Chapter 5A, Section 4).

2 Remove the cover from the top of the engine.

3 On the 1.6 litre engine remove the fuel return line from the pump and fuel injectors (as described in Section 11) and then remove the insulation **(see illustration)**.

4 Thoroughly clean all the high pressure fuel pipe unions on the fuel rail, fuel pump and injectors. Using two spanners, hold the unions and unscrew the union nuts securing the high pressure fuel pipes to the fuel injectors. Unscrew the union nuts securing the high pressure fuel pipes to the fuel rail, withdraw the pipes and plug or cover the open unions to prevent dirt entry **(see illustration)**.

5 Using an open-ended spanner, unscrew the union nuts securing the high-pressure fuel pipe to the fuel pump and fuel rail. Counterhold the unions on the pump with a second spanner, while unscrewing the union nuts. Withdraw the high-pressure fuel pipe and plug or cover the open unions to prevent dirt entry.

6 Disconnect the wiring connector at the fuel pressure sensor, then undo the two bolts and remove the fuel rail **(see illustrations)**.

described in Chapter 2D Section 5 and Chapter 2D Section 6 respectively.

54 At the rear of the pump disconnect the fuel return pipe and unbolt the three way distribution fitting. Seal the pipes and openings in the pump and fuel rail.

55 Disconnect the high pressure fuel line from the pump and fuel rail. Anticipate some loss of diesel fuel as the pipe is disconnected.

56 Lift up the safety lock and disconnect the wiring plug from the pump.

57 Remove the three pump mounting bolts and remove the pump **(see illustrations)**.

Refitting

58 Refit the pump to the engine and tighten the retaining bolts to the specified torque.

59 Remove the blanking plugs from the fuel pipe unions on the pump and fuel rail. Locate a new high-pressure fuel pipe over the unions and screw on the union nuts finger tight at this stage.

60 Using a torque wrench and crow-foot adaptor, tighten the fuel pipe union nuts to the specified torque. Counterhold the unions on the pump with an open-ended spanner, while tightening the union nuts.

61 Refit the fuel return pipe and distribution pipe.

62 Refit the high-pressure fuel pump sprocket and the timing belt as described in Chapter 2D Section 6 and Chapter 2D Section 5.

63 Reconnect the battery negative terminal.

64 Refit the air filter housing and pipework

65 Observing the precautions listed in Section 2, prime the fuel system as described in Section 5, then start the engine and allow it to idle. Check for leaks at the high-pressure fuel pipe unions with the engine idling. If satisfactory, increase the engine speed to 4000 rpm and check again for leaks. If any leaks are detected, obtain and fit a new high-pressure fuel pipe.

66 Refit the engine cover.

10.3 Remove the sound proof insulation

10.4 Unscrew the union nuts securing the high pressure fuel pipes to the fuel rail (A20 engine)

10.6a On the 1.6 litre engines remove the fuel return line

10.6b The fuel rail bolts on the A20 engine

10.6c Removing the fuel rail on the B20 engine

10.6d Removing the fuel rail from the 1.6 litre engine

10.8 Tighten the fuel pipe union nuts using a torque wrench and crow-foot adaptor

Refitting

7 Refit the fuel rail and tighten the retaining bolts to the specified torque. Reconnect the fuel pressure sensor wiring connector.

8 Working on one fuel injector at a time, remove the blanking plugs from the fuel pipe unions on the fuel rail and the relevant injector. Locate the new high pressure fuel pipe over the unions and screw on the union nuts finger tight. Tighten the union nuts to the specified torque using a torque wrench and crow-foot adaptor **(see illustration)**. Counterhold the union on the injector with an open-ended spanner, while tightening the union nut. Repeat this operation for the remaining three injectors.

9 Similarly, fit the new high pressure fuel pipe to the fuel pump and fuel rail, and tighten the union nuts to the specified torque.

Counterhold the union on the pump with an open-ended spanner, while tightening the union nut.

10 Reconnect the battery negative terminal.

11 Observing the precautions listed in Section 2, prime the fuel system as described in Section 5, then start the engine and allow it to idle. Check for leaks at the high-pressure fuel pipe unions with the engine idling. If satisfactory, increase the engine speed to 4000 rpm and check again for leaks. If any leaks are detected, obtain and fit a new high-pressure fuel pipe.

12 Refit the engine cover on completion.

11 Fuel injectors – removal and refitting

> ⚠️ **Warning: Refer to the information contained in Section 2 before proceeding.**

Note: *A new copper washer, retaining nut and high-pressure fuel pipe will be required for each injector when refitting.*

Note: *The injectors can be an extremely tight fit in the cylinder head, and it is likely that the special Vauxhall/Opel slide hammer (EN-51146-1-3) and puller (EN-51187) will be required for the 1.6 litre engine. The 2.0 litre A20 engine requires slide hammer DT-49407, adaptor EN-32025012 and puller EN-46786. For the 2.0 litre B20 engine, slide hammer*

EN51146-1-3 and puller EN-51187 will be required. Suitable universal alternatives are available in the aftermarket.

Removal

1 Disconnect the battery negative terminal (refer to Chapter 5A, Section 4).

2 Remove the cover cover from the top of the engine.

3 On the 2.0 litre A20 engine, disconnect the crankcase ventilation hose from the heating element **(see illustration 3.8)**.

4 On the 2.0 litre A20 engine, unclip the wiring harness from the crankcase ventilation pipe, then undo the two bolts and move the crankcase ventilation pipe to one side **(see illustrations 9.35a to 9.35d)**.

5 On the 2.0 litre A20 engine, undo the two ball-studs securing the injector wiring harness plastic conduit to the camshaft housing **(see illustration)**.

6 Pull out the locking catch, depress the retainer and disconnect the wiring plug at each injector **(see illustrations)**.

7 On the 2.0 litre (A20) engine, undo the two bolts securing the plastic conduit to the camshaft housing and move the conduits and injector wiring harness to one side **(see illustration)**.

8 Disconnect the fuel leak-off hose connection at each injector by either pushing in the locking clip and lifting out the hose fitting, or by removing the locking clip (1.6 litre engines). Suitably plug or cap the

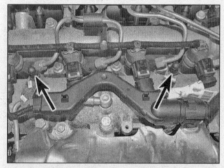

11.5 Undo the two ball-studs securing the plastic conduit to the camshaft housing

11.6a Pull out the yellow locking catch ...

11.6b ... depress the retainer ...

11.6c ... and disconnect the wiring plug at each injector

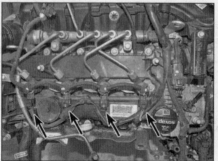

11.6d A slightly different locking plug system is used on the 2.0 litre (B20) engine

11.7 Undo the two bolts and move the plastic conduits and wiring harness to one side

leak-off hose union on each injector, and slip a plastic bag over the disconnected leak-off hose to prevent dirt entry **(see illustrations)**. Remove the o-ring seals and dispose of them – new ones must be used. On the 1.6 litre engine the locking clips must also be replaced.

9 Move the bleed off (return) hose to the side and then on the 1.6 litre engine remove the noise insulator **(see illustration 10.3)**.

10 Thoroughly clean the fuel pipe unions on the fuel rail and injector. Using two spanners, hold the unions and unscrew the union nut securing the high pressure fuel pipe to the fuel injector. Unscrew the union nut securing the high pressure fuel pipe to the fuel rail, withdraw the pipe and plug or cover the open unions to prevent dirt entry **(see illustrations)**. Blanking plugs for the injectors and fuel rail can be made from old fuel lines with the pipe cut off and bolt heads glued over the opening.

11 Starting with injector No 1, unscrew the retaining nut (A20 engines) or bolt (all other engines) On the A20 engine remove the washer from the injector clamp bracket **(see illustrations)**.

12 Withdraw the injector together with the clamp bracket from the cylinder head. If difficulty is experienced removing the injector, liberally apply penetrating oil to the base of the injector and allow time for the oil to penetrate. If the injector is still reluctant to free, it will be necessary to use a small slide hammer engaged under the flange of the injector body casting, and gently tap it free **(see illustration)**. If available, use Vauxhall/ Opel special tools for this purpose. Note that it is not possible to twist the injectors from side-to-side on the A20 engine to free them, due to the design of the clamp bracket.

13 Once the injector has been removed, where required, separate it from the clamp bracket and remove the copper washer from the injector base. The copper washer may have remained in place at the base of the injector orifice in the cylinder head. If so, hook it out with a length of wire.

14 Remove the remaining injectors in the same way. If the original injectors are to be refitted, it is absolutely essential that they

11.8a Disconnect the fuel leak-off hose connection at each injector …

11.8b … then plug or cap the leak-off hose union on each injector

11.8c On the 1.6 litre engine remove (and discard) the locking clips

11.8d On the 2.0 litre (B20) engine depress the wings of the connector to release the hose

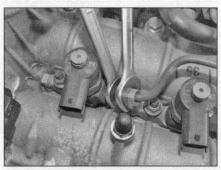

11.10a Counterhold the injector union when unscrewing the high-pressure fuel pipe unions

11.10b The injectors and fuel rail ports all sealed

11.11a Unscrew the injector clamp bracket retaining nut then remove the washer (A20 engine)

11.11b On the 2.0 litre (B20) engine remove the bolt and clamp

11.12 Using a small slide hammer to free the injector body from the cylinder head

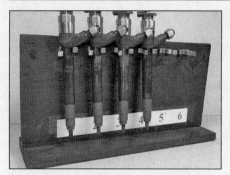

11.14 Keep the injectors upright at all times. Store them in order

11.19 A simple bore cleaning tool. Note the lower nut is filed to fit in the injector nozzle opening in the cylinder head

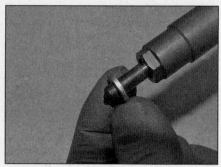

11.20 Fit a new sealing washer to each injector

are refitted in to their original positions **(see illustration)**.

15 Examine the injector visually for any signs of obvious damage or deterioration. If any defects are apparent, renew the injector.

Caution: The injectors are manufactured to extremely close tolerances and must not be dismantled in any way. Do not unscrew the fuel pipe union on the side of the injector, or separate any parts of the injector body. Do not attempt to clean carbon deposits from the injector nozzle or carry out any form of ultra-sonic or pressure testing.

16 If the injectors are in a satisfactory condition, plug the fuel pipe union (if not already done) and suitably cover the electrical element and the injector nozzle.

17 Prior to refitting, obtain a new set of copper washers and high-pressure fuel pipes. The retaining nuts must be replaced on the A20 engine. The bolts can be reused on the 1.6 and 2.0 B20 engines.

Refitting

18 If new injectors are being fitted, take of note of the identification numbers. These need to be uploaded into the ECU on completion of the work.

19 Thoroughly clean the injector seat in the cylinder head, ensuring all traces of carbon and other deposits are removed. Special tools are available for this purpose, but a simple cleaning tool can be fabricated from a length of threaded bar and one of the old injector washers with some fine emery cloth (or wet and dry paper) glued to the copper washer **(see illustration)**.

20 Starting with injector No 4, locate a new copper washer on the base of the injector **(see illustration)**.

21 Place the injector clamp bracket in the slot on the injector body and refit the injector to the cylinder head.

22 Fit the washer and the injector clamp bracket retaining nut on the A20 engine. On all other engines fit the retaining bolt. Do not fully tighten the bolts at this stage

23 Slacken the mounting bolts on the fuel rail and then remove the blanking plug from the fuel pipe union on the fuel rail and the injector. Locate the new high pressure fuel pipe over

the unions and screw on the union nuts. Having the fuel rail and injectors loose at this stage will help to locate the new high pressure fuel pipes on the injectors and fuel rail. Hand tighten the new high pressure fuel pipes.

24 Tighten the fuel injectors and fuel rail bolts/nuts to the specified torque.

25 Tighten the fuel pipe union nuts to the specified torque using a torque wrench and crow-foot adaptor **(see illustration 10.7)**. Counterhold the union on the injector with an open-ended spanner, while tightening the union nut.

26 Repeat this procedure for the remaining injectors.

27 Fit new seals to the leak-off hose fittings and refit them to the injectors by pushing in the locking clip, attaching the fitting, then releasing the locking clip. Ensure that each fitting is securely connected and retained by the clip. On the 1.6 litre engines fit new spring clips.

28 Reconnect the wiring connectors to the fuel injectors, then secure the plastic conduit to the camshaft housing.

29 Where removed, refit the crankcase ventilation pipe and secure with the three bolts.

30 Reconnect the battery negative terminal.

31 If new injectors have been fitted, their classification numbers must be programmed into the engine management ECU using dedicated diagnostic equipment. If this equipment is not available, entrust this task to a Vauxhall/Opel dealer or suitably-equipped repairer. Note that it should be possible to drive the vehicle, albeit with reduced

12.6 Move the disconnected wiring harness clear of the inlet manifold

performance/increased emissions, to a repairer for the numbers to be programmed.

32 Observing the precautions listed in Section 2, prime the fuel system as described in Section 5, then start the engine and allow it to idle. Check for leaks at the high-pressure fuel pipe unions with the engine idling. If satisfactory, increase the engine speed to 4000 rpm and check again for leaks. If any leaks are detected, obtain and fit a new high-pressure fuel pipe.

33 Refit the engine cover on completion.

12 Inlet manifold – removal and refitting

1.6 litre engines

Removal

1 Remove the battery and battery tray as described in Chapter 5A Section 4.

2 Lift off the engine cover.

3 Remove the air cleaner assembly as described in Section 3.

4 Undo the three bolts securing the wiring harness trough to the inlet manifold.

5 Disconnect the wiring connectors at the following components:

a) Inlet manifold actuator.
b) The camshaft sensor.
c) Inlet air pressure and temperature sensor.
d) Fuel rail pressure sensor.
e) The exhaust temperature sensor
f) The fuel injectors
g) Glow plugs.

6 Undo the remaining wiring trough retaining bolts and support bracket retaining bolts, release the retaining clips and move the wiring harness clear of the inlet manifold **(see illustration)**.

7 Working at the left-hand end of the engine, disconnect the wiring connectors at the following components **(see illustrations)** :

a) Exhaust pressure sensor.
b) EGR vacuum solenoid.
c) EGR valve.
d) Oxygen sensor.
e) Throttle body.

8 Release the wiring harness from the retaining clips and move it to one side.

12.7a Disconnect the wiring connector at the exhaust pressure sensor ...

12.7b ... EGR vacuum solenoid ...

12.7c ... EGR valve ...

12.7d ... oxygen sensor ...

12.7e ... and throttle housing

12.9 Disconnect the fuel return hose from the fuel rail

9 Release the retaining clip and disconnect the fuel return hose from the fuel rail **(see illustration)**, then release the fuel return hose from the clips on the inlet manifold support bracket

10 Undo the bolt securing the upper section of the intercooler outlet air duct to the EGR cooler.

11 Rotate the locking collar and disconnect the intercooler outlet air duct from the throttle housing **(see illustration 3.14c)**.

12 Disconnect the brake servo vacuum hose at the quick-release connector above the inlet manifold.

13 Undo the four bolts securing the EGR pipe to the inlet manifold and EGR cooler. Lift away the pipe and collect the gasket and rubber seal **(see illustrations)**.

14 Release the wiring harness retaining clip from the inlet manifold brace, then undo the four bolts and remove the brace **(see illustrations)**.

15 Using an open-ended spanner, unscrew the union nuts securing the high-pressure fuel pipe to the fuel pump and fuel rail. Counterhold the union on the pump with a second spanner, while unscrewing the union nut. Undo the bolt securing the high-pressure fuel pipe to the inlet manifold bracket, then withdraw the pipe and plug or cover the open unions to prevent dirt entry.

16 Remove the engine wiring harness bracket from the engine lifting bracket.

17 Undo the four retaining bolts and remove the wiring harness bracket and fuel return

hose bracket from the inlet manifold **(see illustrations)**.

18 Remove the throttle housing as described in Section.

12.13a Undo the EGR pipe retaining bolts ...

12.14a Release the wiring harness retaining clip ...

19 Work around the manifold and release any remaining wiring harness retaining clips and mounting brackets likely to impede removal of the manifold.

12.13b ... then remove the pipe and collect the gasket and seal

12.14b ... then undo the four bolts and remove the inlet manifold brace

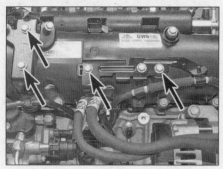

12.17a Undo the retaining bolts …

12.17b … then remove the wiring harness bracket …

12.17c … and fuel return hose bracket from the manifold

12.20a Lift the inlet manifold off the cylinder head …

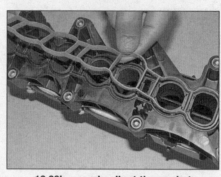

12.20b … and collect the gasket

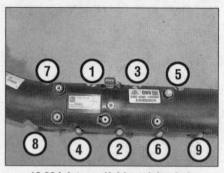

12.22 Inlet manifold retaining bolt tightening sequence

20 Working in the reverse of the tightening sequence **(see illustration 12.22)** slacken, then remove the nine inlet manifold retaining bolts. Lift the manifold off the cylinder head and collect the gasket **(see illustrations)**.

Refitting

21 Thoroughly clean the inlet manifold and cylinder head mating faces, then locate a new rubber gasket on the inlet manifold flange.
22 Locate the manifold in position and refit the retaining bolts. Tighten the bolts in the sequence shown to the specified torque **(see illustration)**.
23 The remainder of refitting is the reverse of removal, bearing in mind the following points:
a) Use new gaskets and seals at all disturbed connections.
b) Refit the throttle housing as described in Section 8.

c) Refit the air cleaner assembly as described in Section 3.
d) Refit the battery tray and battery as described in Chapter 5A Section 4.
e) Observing the precautions listed in Section 1, prime the fuel system as described in Section 5, then start the engine and allow it to idle. Check for leaks at the high-pressure fuel pipe unions with the engine idling. If satisfactory, increase the engine speed to 4000 rpm and check again for leaks. If any leaks are detected, obtain and fit a new high-pressure fuel pipe.
f) Refit the engine cover on completion.

2.0 litre A20 engine

Removal

24 Disconnect the battery negative terminal (refer to Chapter 5A, Section 4).

25 Remove the cover from top of the engine.
26 Drain the cooling system as described in Chapter 1B, Section 26.
27 Remove the high-pressure fuel pump as described in Section 9.
28 Remove the exhaust gas recirculation (EGR) valve cooler as described in Chapter 4C Section 3.
29 Remove the charge (boost) pressure sensor as described in Section 8.
30 Disconnect the throttle housing wiring connector **(see illustration)**.
31 Disconnect the wiring connectors from the four glow plugs **(see illustration)**.
32 Disconnect the wiring harness connector above the inlet manifold, then undo the retaining bolts and move the wiring harness support bracket and the harness to one side **(see illustrations)**.

12.30 Disconnect the throttle housing wiring connector

12.31 Disconnect the wiring connectors from the four glow plugs

12.32a Disconnect the wiring harness connector above the inlet manifold …

12.32b ... then undo the retaining bolts and move the wiring harness and support bracket to one side

33 Disconnect the coolant hose at the quick-release fitting at the rear of the manifold.
34 Release the clips and disconnect the crankcase breather hoses from the top and bottom of the oil separator.
35 Undo the retaining bolts and remove the oil separator from the inlet manifold.
36 Disconnect the wiring connector from the changeover flap actuator drive on the underside of the inlet manifold.
37 Screw two nuts onto the inner high-pressure fuel pump mounting stud. Lock the two nuts together and unscrew the stud from the engine bracket **(see illustration)**.
38 Work around the manifold and release any remaining wiring harness retaining clips and mounting brackets likely to impede removal of the manifold.
39 Undo the nine retaining nuts and remove the inlet manifold from the cylinder head studs. Recover the gaskets.
40 With the manifold removed, if required, remove the throttle housing with reference to Section 8.

Refitting
41 If removed, refit the throttle housing with reference to Section 8.
42 Thoroughly clean the inlet manifold and cylinder head mating faces, then locate the new gaskets on the inlet manifold flange.
43 Locate the manifold in position and refit the retaining nuts. Diagonally and progressively, tighten the nuts to the specified torque.
44 The remainder of refitting is the reverse of removal, bearing in mind the following points:
a) Refit the charge (boost) pressure sensor as described in Section 8.
b) Refit the exhaust gas recirculation (EGR) valve cooler as described in Chapter 4C Section 3.
c) Refit the high-pressure fuel pump as described in Section 9.
d) Refill the cooling system as described in Chapter 1B, Section 26.
e) Observing the precautions listed in Section 2, prime the fuel system as described in Section 5, then start the engine and allow it to idle. Check for leaks at the high-pressure fuel pipe unions with the engine idling. If satisfactory, increase the engine speed to 4000 rpm and check again for leaks. If any

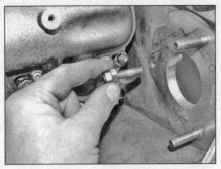

12.37 Lock two nuts together and unscrew the fuel pump stud from the engine bracket

leaks are detected, obtain and fit a new high-pressure fuel pipe.
f) Refit the engine cover on completion.

2.0 litre B20 engine
Removal
45 Disconnect the battery negative terminal (refer to Chapter 5A, Section 4).
46 Remove the cover from top of the engine.
47 Remove the throttle body as described in Section 8.
48 Observing the precautions given (Section 1) remove the high pressure fuel line from between the fuel rail and fuel pump.
49 Disconnect the wiring plugs from the fuel injectors, glow plugs, boost pressure sensor, oil pressure sensor, fuel pump, alternator, fuel rail, camshaft sensor and inlet manifold flap control motor. Unbolt the wiring loom conduit and move it to the side **(see illustration)**.
50 Remove the fuel return line and separator from the cylinder head.

12.49 Remove the conduit and wiring loom

12.52a Remove the bolts and ...

51 Unbolt and remove the EGR pipe **(see illustration)**. Recover the seal and dispose of it – a new one must be fitted.
52 Slacken each manifold bolt in turn. Note that the bolts are captive in the manifold. Remove the manifold, recover the gasket and dispose of it **(see illustrations)**.

Refitting
53 Thoroughly clean the inlet manifold and cylinder head mating faces, then locate the new gaskets on the inlet manifold flange.
54 Fit a new gasket to the manifold and tighten the bolts in a diagonal sequence, starting from the centre and working outwards.
55 The remainder of refitting is the reverse of removal.
56 Observing the precautions listed in Section 2, prime the fuel system as described in Section 5, then start the engine and allow it to idle. Check for leaks at the high-pressure fuel pipe unions with the engine idling. If satisfactory, increase the engine speed to 4000 rpm and check again for leaks. If any leaks are detected, obtain and fit a new high-pressure fuel pipe.

---

13 Intercooler – removal and refitting

Removal
1 Disconnect the battery negative terminal (refer to Chapter 5A, Section 4).
2 Remove the cover from the top of the engine.

12.51 Remove the EGR pipe

12.52b ... lift off the manifold

13.5a Release the power steering fluid cooler pipes from the clips on the intercooler …

13.5b … then disengage the other end of the cooler from the intercooler bracket

13.6a Depress the tab each side …

13.6b … and pull the air conditioning condenser upper mountings out of the intercooler

13.7a Lift the condenser up to disengage the right-hand …

13.7b … and left-hand lower mountings from the intercooler

3 Apply the handbrake, then jack up the front of the vehicle and support it on axle stands (see *Jacking and vehicle support*).

4 Remove the front bumper cover as described in Chapter 11, Section 6.

5 On models fitted with hydraulic power steering, release the power steering fluid cooler pipes (where fitted) from the clips at the upper left-hand side of the intercooler. Slide the fluid cooler to the left to disengage the other end of the cooler from the intercooler bracket (see illustrations). Secure the fluid cooler to the upper body panel with cable ties.

6 Using a screwdriver, depress the tab each side and pull the air conditioning condenser upper mountings out of the intercooler (see illustrations).

7 Lift the condenser up to disengage the lower mountings from the intercooler, then secure the condenser to the upper body panel with cable ties (see illustrations).

8 Slacken the retaining clip securing the air duct elbows to the intercooler on both sides (see illustration 3.18).

9 Disengage the retaining clips and detach the elbows from the intercooler (see illustrations 3.19a and 3.19b).

10 Using a screwdriver, depress the tab each side and pull the intercooler upper mountings out of the radiator (see illustrations).

11 Lift the intercooler up to disengage the lower mountings from the radiator, then lower the intercooler down and remove it from under the car (see illustrations).

Refitting

12 Refitting is the reverse of removal.

14 Turbocharger – description and precautions

Description

1 The turbocharger increases engine efficiency by raising the pressure in the

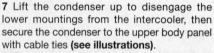

13.10a Depress the tab on each side …

13.10b … and pull the intercooler upper mountings out of the radiator

13.11a Lift the intercooler up to disengage the lower mountings …

13.11b … then lower the intercooler down and remove it from under the car

inlet manifold above atmospheric pressure. Instead of the air simply being sucked into the cylinders, it is forced in.

2 Energy for the operation of the turbocharger comes from the exhaust gas. The gas flows through a specially-shaped housing (the turbine housing) and, in so doing, spins the turbine wheel. The turbine wheel is attached to a shaft, at the end of which is another vaned wheel known as the compressor wheel. The compressor wheel spins in its own housing, and compresses the inlet air on the way to the intercooler and inlet manifold.

3 The turbocharger operates on the principle of variable vane geometry. The vanes on most models are swivelled by a vacuum unit on the turbocharger, controlled by a vane position actuator, which is in turn controlled by the engine management ECU. On some later models the position of the vanes is controlled by an electric motor. The position of the eleven controllable vanes is altered to vary the amount of boost pressure. The boost pressure can be controlled independent of engine speed. The vanes mount to a drive ring which is rotated to change the vane angle. The ECU will vary the boost dependent upon the load requirements of the engine.

4 The turbo shaft is pressure-lubricated by an oil feed pipe from the main oil gallery. The shaft 'floats' on a cushion of oil. A drain pipe returns the oil to the sump.

Precautions

5 The turbocharger operates at extremely high speeds and temperatures. Certain precautions must be observed, to avoid premature failure of the turbo, or injury to the operator.

6 Do not operate the turbo with any of its parts exposed, or with any of its hoses removed. Foreign objects falling onto the rotating vanes could cause excessive damage, and (if ejected) personal injury.

7 Do not race the engine immediately after start-up, especially if it is cold. Give the oil a few seconds to circulate.

8 Always allow the engine to return to idle speed before switching it off – do not blip the throttle and switch off, as this will leave the turbo spinning without lubrication.

9 Allow the engine to idle for several minutes before switching off after a high-speed run.

10 Observe the recommended intervals for

15.6 Undo the retaining bolt and withdraw the turbocharger oil return pipe end fitting from the block

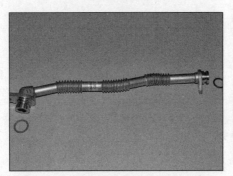

15.7b ... then remove the pipe and collect the O-ring seals

oil and filter changing, and use a reputable oil of the specified quality. Neglect of oil changing, or use of inferior oil, can cause carbon formation on the turbo shaft, leading to subsequent failure.

15 Turbocharger – removal and refitting

1.6 litre engine

Removal

1 Disconnect the battery negative lead as described in Chapter 5A Section 4.

2 Lift off the engine cover.

3 Drain the cooling system as described in Chapter 1B Section 26.

4 Remove the air cleaner outlet air duct and intercooler inlet air duct as described in

15.7a Undo the bolt and withdraw the oil return pipe from the turbocharger ...

15.8 Release the retaining clips and remove the crankcase ventilation hose

Section 3.

5 Remove the diesel particulate filter as described in Section 18.

6 Undo the bolt securing the turbocharger oil return pipe to the cylinder block and withdraw the end fitting from the block **(see illustration)**.

7 Undo the bolt securing the oil return pipe to the turbocharger, then remove the pipe and collect the two O-ring seals **(see illustrations)**.

8 Release the two clips securing the positive crankcase ventilation hose to the camshaft cover and turbocharger and remove the hose **(see illustration)**.

9 Undo the bolts securing the turbocharger wastegate actuator pipe and turbocharger coolant pipe support brackets to their attachments. Disconnect the pipe hose ends from the vacuum pipe and wastegate actuator and remove the pipe **(see illustrations)**.

15.9a Undo the turbocharger coolant pipe bracket bolt ...

15.9b ... and wastegate actuator pipe bracket bolt at the left-hand end of the engine ...

15.9c ... at the centre of the engine ...

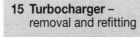

15.9d ... and at the turbocharger ...

15.9e ... then disconnect the hose ends
and remove the wastegate actuator pipe

15.10 Disconnect the wastegate actuator
wiring connector

15.11 Unscrew the turbocharger oil supply
pipe banjo union bolt and collect the two
sealing washers

15.12a Unscrew the turbocharger oil
supply pipe banjo union bolt from the
cylinder block ...

15.12b Unbolt the oil supply pipe from
the turbocharger and remove it from the
engine

10 Disconnect the turbocharger wastegate actuator wiring connector **(see illustration)**.
11 Unscrew the turbocharger oil supply pipe banjo union bolt from the top of the

turbocharger and collect the two sealing washers **(see illustration)**.
12 Similarly, unscrew the turbocharger oil supply pipe banjo union bolt from the cylinder

block and collect the two sealing washers. Undo the bolt securing the oil supply pipe to the turbocharger and remove the pipe **(see illustrations)**.
13 Undo the two bolts and remove the turbocharger inner heat shield **(see illustration)**.
14 Slacken the retaining clip and disconnect the turbocharger coolant return pipe from the thermostat bypass pipe hose connection **(see illustration)**.
15 Remove the wiring harness bracket from the coolant pump.
16 Unscrew the turbocharger coolant feed pipe banjo union bolt from the coolant pump and collect the two sealing washers **(see illustration)**.
17 Undo the three nuts (one from above and two from below) securing the turbocharger to the exhaust manifold **(see illustrations)**.

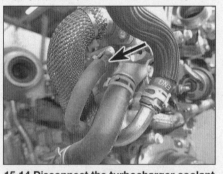

15.13 Unbolt and remove the turbocharger
inner heat shield

15.14 Disconnect the turbocharger coolant
return pipe from the thermostat bypass
pipe hose

15.16 Unscrew the turbocharger coolant feed
pipe banjo union bolt from the coolant pump

15.17a Undo the upper retaining nut ...

15.17b ... and two lower retaining nuts ...

15.17c ... then lift the turbocharger off the exhaust manifold ...

15.17d ... and recover the gasket

15.18a Undo the two retaining bolts ...

Lift off the turbocharger and recover the gasket.

18 With the turbocharger on the bench, undo the two retaining bolts, remove the coolant feed and return pipe and collect the gasket **(see illustrations)**.

Refitting

19 Refitting is the reverse of removal, noting the following points:

a) *Ensure all mating surfaces are clean and dry and renew all gaskets and sealing washers.*
b) *Tighten all retaining nuts and bolts to the specified torque (where given).*
c) *Refit the diesel particulate filter as described in Section 18.*
d) *Refit the air cleaner outlet air duct and intercooler inlet air duct as described in Section 3.*
e) *Refill the cooling system as described in Chapter 1B Section 26.*

2.0 litre (A20) engine

Removal

20 Disconnect the battery negative terminal (refer to Chapter 5A, Section 4).
21 Remove the catalytic converter as described in Section 18.
22 Unscrew the two bolts securing the oil return pipe to the underside of the turbocharger. Separate the flange joint and recover the gaskets. Dispose of the gaskets.
23 Unscrew the turbocharger oil supply pipe banjo union from the top of the turbocharger and collect the two copper washers **(see illustration)**.

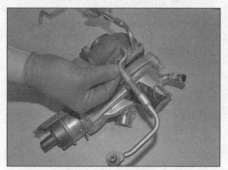

15.18b ... remove the coolant feed and return pipe from the turbocharger ...

24 Undo the two bolts securing the intercooler intake duct to the underside of the turbocharger **(see illustration)**. Separate the flange joint and recover the gasket.
25 Remove the turbocharger intake duct as described in Section 3.
26 Disconnect the wiring connector and vacuum hose from the vane position actuator on the underside of the turbocharger.
27 Undo the three nuts (one from above and two from below) securing the turbocharger to the exhaust manifold. Lift off the turbocharger and recover the gasket.

Refitting

28 Refitting is the reverse of removal, noting the following points:

a) *Ensure all mating surfaces are clean and dry and renew all gaskets, seals and copper washers.*

15.18c ... and collect the gasket

b) *Where possible fill the turbocharger and oil feed pipe with fresh oil before installing the turbocharger.*
c) *Tighten all retaining nuts and bolts to the specified torque (where given).*
d) *Refit the catalytic converter as described in Section 18.*

2.0 litre (B20) engine

Removal

29 Disconnect the battery negative terminal (refer to Chapter 5A, Section 4) and remove the air filter housing as described in Section 3.
30 Drain the coolant as described in Chapter 1B Section 26.
31 Remove the crankcase ventilation and oil separator hose **(see illustration)**.
32 Remove the catalytic converter as described in Section 18.

15.23 Unscrew the turbocharger oil supply pipe banjo union and collect the two copper washers

15.24 Undo the two bolts securing the intercooler intake duct to the underside of the turbocharger

15.31 Remove the breather hose (A) and note the oil feed line (B)

15.35 Disconnect the wiring plug

15.37 Remove the turbocharger. Not that the coolant lines (A) are still attached as the turbocharger is removed

33 Anticipate some loss of engine oil and remove the turbocharger oil feed line **(see illustration 15.31)**. Disconnect the oil return line at the engine block. Dispose of the gaskets – they must be replaced.

34 Remove the intercooler inlet hose.

35 Disconnect the control unit wiring plug **(see illustration)**.

36 Anticipate some loss of coolant and disconnect the turbocharger coolant hoses where accessible. The remaining hoses can be removed from the turbocharger after the turbocharger is removed from the vehicle.

37 Unbolt and remove the turbocharger **(see illustration)**. Recover the gasket and dispose of it. A new one must be used.

Refitting

38 Refitting is the reverse of removal, noting the following points:

a) *Ensure all mating surfaces are clean and dry and renew all gaskets, seals and copper washers.*

b) *Where possible fill the turbocharger and oil feed pipe with fresh oil before installing the turbocharger.*

c) *Tighten all retaining nuts and bolts to the specified torque (where given).*

d) *Refit the catalytic converter as described in Section 18.*

e) *Refill the cooling system as described in Chapter 1B Section 26.*

16 Turbocharger – examination and overhaul

1 With the turbocharger removed, inspect the housing for cracks or other visible damage.

2 Spin the turbine or the compressor wheel to verify that the shaft is intact and to feel for excessive shake or roughness. Some play is normal since in use the shaft is 'floating' on a film of oil. Check that the wheel vanes are undamaged.

3 The vane position actuator is integral with the turbocharger, and cannot be checked or renewed separately. Consult a Vauxhall/Opel dealer or other specialist if it is thought that the actuator may be faulty.

4 If the exhaust or induction passages are oil-contaminated, the turbocharger shaft oil seals have probably failed. (On the induction side, this will also have contaminated the intercooler, which if necessary should be flushed with a suitable solvent.)

5 No DIY repair of the turbocharger is possible. A new unit may be available on an exchange basis.

17 Exhaust manifold – removal and refitting

1.6 litre engines

Removal

Note: *New exhaust manifold retaining bolts will be required for refitting.*

1 Remove the turbocharger as described in Section 15.

2 Undo the two bolts securing the manifold EGR pipe to the EGR cooler **(see illustration)**.

3 Undo the eight retaining bolts and remove the manifold, together with the gasket, from the cylinder head **(see illustration)**.

Refitting

4 Using a suitable tap, recut the exhaust manifold retaining bolt threads in the cylinder head **(see illustration)**.

5 Thoroughly clean the mating surfaces of the cylinder head, exhaust manifold, EGR pipe and EGR cooler.

6 Locate a new gasket on the EGR pipe and bend over the tabs to retain the gasket in position.

7 Place a new gasket on the manifold, fit the manifold to the cylinder head and screw in the new retaining bolts.

8 Working in the sequence shown, tighten the manifold retaining bolts to the specified torque in the three stages given in the Specifications **(see illustration)**.

9 Attach the EGR pipe to the EGR cooler and tighten the two retaining bolts to the specified torque.

10 Refit the turbocharger as described in Section 15

2.0 litre engines

Removal

11 Remove the turbocharger as described in Section 15.

12 On 2.0 litre, A20 engines, undo the oil dipstick guide tube retaining bolt.

17.2 Undo the bolts securing the EGR pipe to the EGR cooler

17.3 Undo the retaining bolts and remove the exhaust manifold from the cylinder head

17.4 Recut the manifold retaining bolt threads in the cylinder head using a suitable tap

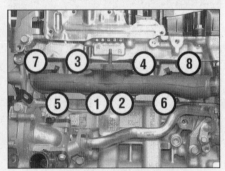

17.8 Exhaust manifold retaining bolt tightening sequence

13 On the 2.0 litre B20 engines, remove the EGR pipe bolts first and then remove the manifold bolts. Recover the gaskets **(see illustrations)**.

14 Unscrew the nuts securing the exhaust manifold to the cylinder head and (where fitted) collect the spacers. Withdraw the manifold from the mounting studs and remove it from the engine **(see illustrations)**. Recover the gasket.

Refitting

15 Refitting is the reverse of removal, noting the following points.

a) *Ensure all mating surfaces are clean and dry and renew the manifold gasket.*

b) *Tighten the manifold retaining nuts evenly and progressively to the specified torque, working in a diagonal sequence from the centre outwards (see illustration 17.8).*

c) *Refit the turbocharger as described in Section 15.*

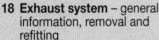

18 Exhaust system – general information, removal and refitting

Caution: Any work on the exhaust system should only be attempted once the system is completely cool – this may take several hours, especially in the case of the forward sections, such as the manifold and catalytic converter.

General information

1 The exhaust system consists of the catalytic converter (incorporating the particulate filter on later models) the front pipe and the main section which incorporates the silencer.

2 A flexible ('mesh') section is fitted to the front pipe to allow for engine movement.

3 The front pipe is attached to the catalytic converter/particulate filter by a flange joint secured by three nuts. The main section is similarly attached to the front pipe by a flange joint secured by two nuts.

4 When fitted in the factory, the exhaust system from the front pipe flange joint to the end of the system is one piece. However, if the silencer is to be renewed, new silencers should be available – check with your parts supplier. It will be necessary to cut through the main section using a hacksaw if a new silencer is to be fitted.

5 The system is suspended throughout its entire length by rubber mountings.

Removal

6 To remove a part of the system, first jack up the front or rear of the car, and support it on axle stands (see *Jacking and vehicle support*). Alternatively, position the car over an inspection pit, or on car ramps. Where fitted remove the engine under shield.

17.13a Remove the bolts …

17.13b … and remove the pipe

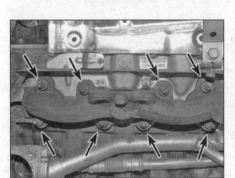
17.14a Remove the bolts (B20 engine shown)

17.14b Pull off the manifold and recover the gasket

Catalytic converter/diesel particulate filter – 1.6 litre engines

7 Disconnect the battery negative lead as described in Chapter 5A Section 4.

8 Remove the cover from the top of the engine.

9 Remove the engine undertray as described in Chapter 11 Section 24.

10 Remove the upstream oxygen sensor (position 1) from the top of the diesel particulate filter as described in Chapter 4C Section 3.

11 Undo the nut and four bolts securing the upper heat shield to the turbocharger. Remove the washer from the particulate filter stud, then lift off the heat shield **(see illustrations)**.

12 Remove the two exhaust temperature

18.11a Undo the nut and four bolts …

18.11b … and lift off the turbocharger upper heat shield

18.14a Undo the four bolts …

18.14b … and remove the particulate filter heat shield

18.15 Release the retaining clips and disconnect the two exhaust pressure sensor hoses

18.16a Undo the three retaining nuts …

18.16b … then separate the front pipe flange and collect the gasket

18.17a Undo the right-hand retaining nut …

sensors (positions 1 and 2) from the left-hand side of the diesel particulate filter as described in Chapter 4C Section 3.

18.17b … and left-hand retaining nut securing the particulate filter to the cylinder block studs

13 Where fitted, remove the downstream oxygen sensor (position 2) from the left-hand side of the diesel particulate filter as described in Chapter 4C Section 3.

14 Undo the four bolts and remove the particulate filter heat shield **(see illustrations)**.

15 Release the retaining clips and disconnect the two exhaust pressure sensor hoses from the pressure sensor pipes **(see illustration)**.

16 Undo the three nuts and separate the exhaust front pipe from the particulate filter, taking care to support the flexible section. Collect the flange joint gasket noting that a new gasket and three new nuts will be required for refitting **(see illustrations)**.

17 Undo the two nuts securing the particulate filter to the cylinder block studs **(see illustrations)**.

18 Slacken the particulate filter clamp bolt

nut. Expand the clamp and disconnect the particulate filter from the exhaust manifold. Lift the filter up and out of the engine compartment and collect the particulate filter-to-manifold gasket **(see illustrations)**. Note that a new clamp and new gasket will be required for refitting.

Catalytic converter/diesel particulate filter – 2.0 litre (A20) engines

19 Remove the engine cover by pulling it up.

20 Disconnect the battery negative lead as described in Chapter 5A Section 4.

21 Remove the engine undertray as described in Chapter 11 Section 24.

22 Undo the nut and three bolts securing the exhaust manifold heat shield to the manifold and camshaft housing, and lift off the shield **(see illustrations)**.

18.18a Expand the clamp and disconnect the particulate filter from the exhaust manifold …

18.18b … then remove the particulate filter and collect the gasket

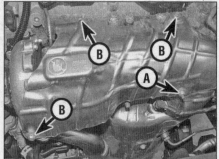

18.22a Undo the exhaust manifold heat shield nut (A) and three bolts (B) …

18.22b ... and lift off the shield

18.24 Undo the nut and five bolts and lift the heat shield up and off the catalytic converter

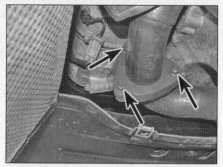

18.26 Undo the nuts securing the exhaust system front pipe to the catalytic converter

23 Remove the oxygen sensor and the diesel particulate filter temperature sensor as described in Chapter 4C.

24 Undo the nut and five bolts securing the heat shield to the catalytic converter. Lift the heat shield up and off the catalytic converter **(see illustration)**.

25 Release the retaining clip and disconnect the pressure sensor hose from the pipe stub at the rear of the catalytic converter.

26 Undo the three nuts securing the exhaust system front pipe to the catalytic converter **(see illustration)**. Separate the joint taking care to support the flexible section. **Note:** *Angular movement in excess of 10° can cause permanent damage to the flexible section.* Recover the gasket.

27 Undo the two nuts securing the catalytic converter to the support bracket, and the two bolts securing the catalytic converter lower mounting bracket to the sump **(see illustration)**.

28 Slacken the catalytic converter clamp bolt nut **(see illustration)**. Expand the clamp and disconnect the catalytic converter from the exhaust manifold. Either lift the catalytic converter up and out of the engine compartment or lower down and out.

Catalytic converter/particulate filter 2.0 litre (B20) engines

29 Removal and refiiting of the combined catalytic converter and particulate filter on the 2.0 litre B20 engine is essentially the same as the removal procedure for the 1.6 litre (LVL) described above. Note that on models fitted

18.27 Undo the two bolts securing the catalytic converter mounting bracket to the sump

with the 'Adblue' emissions reduction system an additional catalytic converter is fitted to the system after the primary filter and converter

Front pipe (all models)

30 Remove the engine undertray as described in Chapter 11 Section 24.

31 On models fitted with the 'Adblue' diesel exhaust fluid (DEF) system, disconnect (and seal) the fluid supply pie and then release the electrical connector. To avoid damage to the fluid injector, remove the injector as described in Chapter 4C Section 5. Where required disconnect the wiring connectors from the nitrogen oxides sensor and the exhaust gas temperature sensor.

32 Undo the three nuts securing the exhaust

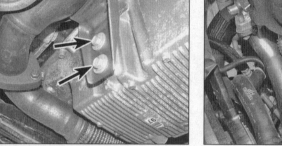

18.28 Slacken the catalytic converter clamp bolt nut

front pipe to the catalytic converter **(see illustration 18.26)**. Separate the joint taking care to support the flexible section. **Note:** *Angular movement in excess of 10° can cause permanent damage to the flexible section.* Recover the gasket.

33 Undo the nuts securing the front pipe to the main section. Separate the joint and recover the gasket.

34 Undo the two bolts each side securing the subframe rear mountings and the reinforcement plates to the underbody **(see illustration)**. Note that new bolts will be required for refitting. Remove the reinforcement plates and remove the front pipe from under the car.

Main section

35 Undo the nuts securing the main section to the front pipe **(see illustration)**. Separate the joint and recover the gasket

36 Unhook the main section's rubber mountings, and remove it from under the car.

Complete system

37 Undo the nuts securing the exhaust front pipe to the catalytic converter. Separate the joint taking care to support the flexible section. **Note:** *Angular movement in excess of 10° can cause permanent damage to the flexible section.* Recover the gasket.

38 Undo the two bolts each side securing the subframe rear mountings and the reinforcement plates to the underbody **(see illustration 18.34)**. Remove the reinforcement plates.

18.34 Undo the bolts securing the subframe rear mountings and the reinforcement plates to the underbody

18.35 The front pipe to main section (1.6 litre shown)

39 Unhook the main section's rubber mountings, and remove it from under the car.

Rear silencer

Note: *If a new rear silencer is to be fitted, it will be necessary to obtain a connecting sleeve from your Vauxhall/Opel parts supplier.*

40 On models fitted with the 2.0 litre B20 (LFS) engine disconnect the Nox sensor before removing the rear exhaust section. A rear silencer is not fitted to the 2.0 litre B20 (LFS) engine.

41 If the original one-piece exhaust system is still fitted, it will be necessary to cut off the old rear silencer to enable fitment of the new unit. Using the new silencer as a pattern, mark the exhaust main section to determine the cut point.

42 Using a hacksaw, cut through the main section at the marked cut point. Unhook the silencer's rubber mountings, and remove it from under the car.

43 Fit the new silencer and connect it to the main section using the connecting sleeve. Tighten the connecting sleeve retaining bolt nut securely.

Heat shields

44 The heat shields are secured to the underside of the body by special nuts. Each shield can be removed separately, but note that they may overlap, making it necessary to loosen another section first. If a shield is being removed to gain access to a component located behind it, it may prove sufficient in some cases to remove the retaining nuts and/or bolts, and simply lower the shield, without disturbing the exhaust system. Otherwise, remove the exhaust section as described earlier.

Refitting

45 In all cases, refitting is a reversal of removal, but note the following points:

a) *Always use new gaskets, nuts and clamps (as applicable), and coat all threads with copper grease.*

b) *If any of the exhaust mounting rubbers are in poor condition, fit new ones.*

c) *Make sure that the exhaust is suspended properly on its mountings, and will not come into contact with the floor or any suspension parts. The rear silencer especially must be aligned correctly before tightening the connecting sleeve retaining bolt nut.*

d) *Tighten all nuts/bolts to the specified torque, where given.*

Chapter 4 Part C
Emission control systems

Contents

Degrees of difficulty

Easy, suitable for novice with little experience	**Fairly easy,** suitable for beginner with some experience	**Fairly difficult,** suitable for competent DIY mechanic	**Difficult,** suitable for experienced DIY mechanic	**Very difficult,** suitable for expert DIY or professional

Specifications

Diesel emissions fluid
Fluid tank capacity . . . .   7.5 litres

Torque wrench settings

	Nm	lbf ft
Petrol engines		
Oxygen sensor	40	30
Diesel engines		
EGR cooler mounting bolts/nuts	25	18
Emissions reduction fluid tank bolts	22	18
Emissions reduction fluid tank bracket bolt (front)	45	33
Emissions reduction fluid tank bracket bolt (rear)	22	18
Emissions reduction injector nuts	22	16
Exhaust temperature sensor	45	33
Oxygen sensor	45	33

1 General Information

1 All petrol engine models use unleaded petrol and also have various other features built into the fuel system to help minimise harmful emissions. These include a crankcase emission control system, a catalytic converter, an evaporative emission control system and, on certain models, an exhaust gas recirculation (EGR) system to keep fuel vapour/exhaust gas emissions down to a minimum.

2 All diesel engine models are also designed to meet strict emission requirements. The engines are fitted with a crankcase emission control system, a catalytic converter and (on later models), a diesel particulate filter to keep exhaust emissions down to a minimum.

An exhaust gas recirculation (EGR) system is also fitted to further decrease exhaust emissions. Some very late models also have a Diesel Exhaust Fluid (DEF) system fitted that injects a urea based fluid into the exhaust gas stream. The fluid is commonly referred to as a 'AdBlue'.

3 The emission control systems function as follows.

Petrol engines

Crankcase emission control

4 To reduce the emission of unburned hydrocarbons from the crankcase into the atmosphere, the engine is sealed and the blow-by gases and oil vapour are drawn from inside the crankcase, through an oil separator, into the inlet tract to be burned by the engine during normal combustion.

5 Under all conditions the gases are forced out of the crankcase by the (relatively) higher crankcase pressure; if the engine is worn, the raised crankcase pressure (due to increased blow-by) will cause some of the flow to return under all manifold conditions.

Exhaust emission control

6 To minimise the amount of pollutants which escape into the atmosphere, all models are fitted with a catalytic converter in the exhaust system. The system is of the closed-loop type, in which the oxygen sensors in the exhaust system provides the fuel injection/ignition system ECU with constant feedback, enabling the ECU to adjust the mixture to provide the best possible conditions for the converter to operate.

7 Two heated oxygen sensors are fitted to the exhaust system. The sensor in the exhaust manifold (before the catalytic converter) determines the residual oxygen content of

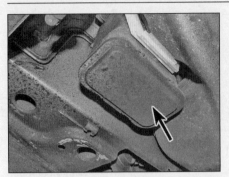

2.3 Charcoal canister location on the side of the fuel tank

the exhaust gasses for mixture correction. The sensor in the exhaust front pipe (after the catalytic converter) monitors the function of the catalytic converter to give the driver a warning signal if there is a fault.

8 The oxygen sensor's tip is sensitive to oxygen and sends the ECU a varying voltage signal depending on the amount of oxygen in the exhaust gases. Peak conversion efficiency of all major pollutants occurs if the intake air/ fuel mixture is maintained at the chemically-correct ratio for the complete combustion of petrol of 14.7 parts (by weight) of air to 1 part of fuel (the 'stoichiometric' ratio). The sensor output voltage alters in a large step at this point, the ECU using the signal change as a reference point and correcting the intake air/ fuel mixture accordingly by altering the fuel injector pulse width.

Evaporative emission control

9 To minimise the escape into the atmosphere of unburned hydrocarbons, an evaporative emissions control system is also fitted to all models. The fuel tank filler cap is sealed and a charcoal canister is mounted on the fuel tank. The canister collects the petrol vapours generated in the tank when the car is parked and stores them until they can be cleared from the canister (under the control of the fuel injection/ignition system ECU) via the purge valve into the inlet tract to be burned by the engine during normal combustion.

10 To ensure that the engine runs correctly when it is cold and/or idling and to protect the catalytic converter from the effects of an over-rich mixture, the purge control valve is not opened by the ECU until the engine has warmed-up, and the engine is under load; the valve solenoid is then modulated on and off to allow the stored vapour to pass into the inlet tract.

Diesel engines

Crankcase emission control

11 Refer to paragraphs 4 and 5.

Exhaust emission control

12 To minimise the level of exhaust pollutants released into the atmosphere, a catalytic converter incorporating a diesel particulate filter is fitted in the exhaust system.

13 The catalytic converter consists of a canister containing a fine mesh impregnated with a catalyst material, over which the hot exhaust gases pass. The catalyst speeds up the oxidation of harmful carbon monoxide and unburned hydrocarbons, effectively reducing the quantity of harmful products released into the atmosphere via the exhaust gases.

14 The diesel particle filter (integral with the catalytic converter) contains a silicon carbide honeycomb block containing microscopic channels in which the exhaust gasses flow. As the gasses flow through the honeycomb channels, soot particles are deposited on the channel walls. To prevent clogging of the honeycomb channels, the soot particles are burned off at regular intervals during what is known as a 'regeneration phase'. Under the control of the injection system ECU, the injection characteristics are altered to raise the temperature of the exhaust gasses to approximately 600°C. At this temperature, the soot particles are effectively burned off the honeycomb walls as the exhaust gasses pass through. A differential pressure sensor and a temperature sensor are used to inform the ECU of the condition of the particulate filter, and the temperature of the exhaust gasses during the regeneration phase. When the ECU detects that soot build-up is reducing the efficiency of the particulate filter, it will instigate the regeneration process. This occurs at regular intervals under certain driving conditions and will normally not be detected by the driver.

Exhaust gas recirculation (EGR) system

15 This system is designed to recirculate small quantities of exhaust gas into the inlet tract, and therefore into the combustion process. This process reduces the level of unburnt hydrocarbons present in the exhaust gas before it reaches the catalytic converter. The system is controlled by the injection system ECU, using the information from its various sensors, via the electrically-operated EGR valve.

Diesel exhaust fluid

16 In order to comply with the Euro 6 diesel emissions standard, many passenger cars manufactured after 2015 will have an additional emissions control system fitted. For the majority of vehicles this will be the addition of a urea based fluid (most often referred to as 'AdBlue') injection system where fluid is injected into the exhaust gas stream.

17 The addition of the fluid reduces the nitrogen oxides produced by the combustion process by breaking them down into water and nitrogen. The addition of the fluid is carefully controlled by the engine management system and the effectiveness of the process is monitored by a downstream NOx sensor. The system requires no maintenance other than the replacement of the injection fluid which is widely available.

2 Petrol engine emission control systems – testing and component renewal

Crankcase emission control

1 The components of this system require no attention other than to check that the hose(s) are clear and undamaged at regular intervals.

Evaporative emission control system

Testing

2 If the system is thought to be faulty, disconnect the hoses from the charcoal canister and purge control valve and check that they are clear by blowing through them. Full testing of the system can only be carried out using specialist electronic equipment which is connected to the engine management system diagnostic connector. If the purge control valve or charcoal canister are thought to be faulty, they must be renewed.

Charcoal canister renewal

3 The charcoal canister is located on the side of the fuel tank (see illustration). To gain access to the canister, remove the fuel tank as described in Chapter 4A Section 7.

4 With the fuel tank removed, disconnect the vapour hose quick-release fittings at the charcoal canister.

5 Detach the locking clamp and release the canister from its mounting bracket on the fuel tank. Remove the canister from the tank.

6 Refitting is a reverse of the removal procedure, ensuring the hoses are correctly and securely reconnected.

Purge valve renewal

7 The purge valve is mounted on the inlet manifold (see illustration).

8 To renew the valve, ensure the ignition is switched off then depress the retaining clip and disconnect the wiring connector from the valve.

9 Disconnect the hoses from the valve, noting their correct fitted locations then unclip and remove the valve from the engine.

10 Refitting is a reversal of the removal procedure, ensuring the valve is fitted the correct way around and the hoses are securely connected.

Exhaust emission control

Testing

11 The performance of the catalytic converter can be checked only by measuring the exhaust gases using a good-quality, carefully-calibrated exhaust gas analyser.

12 If the CO level at the tailpipe is too high, the vehicle should be taken to a Vauxhall/ Opel dealer or engine diagnostic specialist so that the complete fuel injection and ignition systems, including the oxygen sensors, can be thoroughly checked using diagnostic equipment. This equipment will give an

2.7 Purge valve location on the inlet manifold

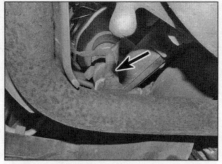

2.17a Oxygen sensors are located in the exhaust system front pipe …

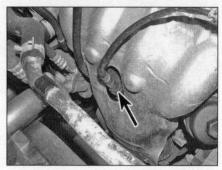

2.17b … and in the exhaust manifold

indication as to where the fault lies and the necessary components can then be renewed.

Catalytic converter renewal

13 The catalytic converter is an integral part of the exhaust manifold. Exhaust manifold removal and refitting procedures are contained in Chapter 4A Section 13.

Oxygen sensor renewal

Note: *There are two heated oxygen sensors fitted to the exhaust system. The sensor in the exhaust manifold is for mixture regulation and the sensor in the exhaust front pipe is to check the operation of the catalytic converter (see Section 1).*

Note: *The oxygen sensor is delicate and will not work if it is dropped or knocked, if its power supply is disrupted, or if any cleaning materials are used on it.*

14 Warm the engine up to normal operating temperature then stop the engine and

disconnect the battery negative terminal (refer to Chapter 5A Section 4).

15 For the sensor fitted in the exhaust front pipe, firmly apply the handbrake, then jack up the front of the car and support it securely on axle stands (see *Jacking and vehicle support*).

16 Trace the wiring back from the oxygen sensor which is to be replaced, and disconnect its wiring connector, freeing the wiring from any relevant retaining clips or ties and noting its correct routing.

Caution: Take great care not burn yourself on the hot manifold/sensor.

17 Unscrew the sensor and remove it from the exhaust system front pipe/manifold **(see illustrations)**. Where applicable recover the sealing washer and discard it; a new one should be used on refitting.

18 Refitting is a reverse of the removal procedure, using a new sealing washer (where applicable). Prior to installing the sensor,

apply a smear of high temperature grease to the sensor threads (Vauxhall/Opel recommend the use of special grease available from your dealer). Tighten the sensor to the specified torque and ensure that the wiring is correctly routed and in no danger of contacting either the exhaust system or engine.

3 Diesel engine emission control systems – testing and component renewal

Crankcase emission control

1 The components of this system require no attention other than to check that the hose(s) are clear and undamaged at regular intervals.

Exhaust emission control

Testing

2 The performance of the catalytic converter and diesel particulate filter can only be checked using special diagnostic equipment. If a system fault is suspected, the vehicle should be taken to a Vauxhall/Opel dealer so that the complete fuel injection system can be thoroughly checked.

Catalytic converter/diesel particulate filter renewal

3 Refer to Chapter 4B Section 18 for removal and refitting details.

Oxygen sensor renewal

Note: *On later models, a second oxygen sensor, located near the base of the diesel particulate filter, may be fitted. Removal and refitting procedures are similar to those for the upper sensor described below, but access is from under the car.*

4 Warm the engine up to normal operating temperature then stop the engine and disconnect the battery negative terminal (refer to Chapter 5A Section 4). Remove the plastic cover from the top of the engine.

5 Using a screwdriver, ease the wiring connector out of the support bracket. Open the locking catch and disconnect the wiring connector **(see illustrations)**. Release the wiring from the clip on the support bracket.

Caution: Take great care not burn yourself on the hot manifold/sensor.

3.5a Using a screwdriver, ease the wiring connector out of the support bracket (A20 engine) …

3.5b … open the locking catch …

3.5c … and disconnect the wiring connector

3.5d On the 1.6 litre engine and the B20 engine the electrical connector is close to the throttle body

3.6 Unscrew the oxygen sensor and remove it from the exhaust manifold

3.9a Ease the wiring connector out of the support bracket ...

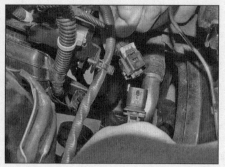

3.9b ... then open the locking catch and disconnect the wiring connector

3.10 Unscrew the sensor and remove it from the exhaust manifold

3.12 The DPF sensor on the 2.0 litre (B20) engine

6 Unscrew the sensor and remove it from the exhaust manifold **(see illustration)**.
7 Refitting is a reverse of the removal procedure. Prior to installing the sensor, apply a smear of high temperature grease to the sensor threads (Vauxhall/Opel recommend the use of a special grease available from your dealer). Tighten the sensor to the specified torque and ensure that the wiring is correctly routed and in no danger of contacting either the exhaust system or engine.

Particulate filter temperature sensor renewal

Note: *On later models, a second temperature sensor, (located near the base of the diesel particulate filter) may be fitted. Removal and refitting procedures are similar to those for the upper sensor described below.*

8 Warm the engine up to normal operating temperature then stop the engine and disconnect the battery negative terminal (refer to Chapter 5A Section 4). Remove the plastic cover from the top of the engine.
9 Using a screwdriver, ease the wiring connector out of the support bracket. Open the locking catch and disconnect the wiring connector **(see illustrations)**.
Caution: Take great care not burn yourself on the hot manifold/sensor.
10 Unscrew the sensor and remove it from the exhaust manifold **(see illustration)**.
11 Refitting is a reverse of the removal procedure. Prior to installing the sensor, apply a smear of high temperature grease to the

sensor threads (Vauxhall/Opel recommend the use of a special grease available from your dealer). Tighten the sensor to the specified torque and ensure that the wiring is correctly routed and in no danger of contacting either the exhaust system or engine.

Differential pressure sensor renewal

12 The differential pressure sensor is either attached to a bracket located above the centre of the inlet manifold or mounted next to the EGR by-pass control solenoid on the left-hand end of the engine **(see illustration)**.
13 Remove the cover from the top of the engine.
14 Disconnect the pressure hose and the sensor wiring connector.
15 Undo the retaining bolt and remove the sensor from the mounting bracket.
16 Refitting is the reverse of removal.

3.23a Disconnect the vacuum solenoid valve wiring connector (A20 engine)

Exhaust gas recirculation (EGR) system

Testing

17 Comprehensive testing of the system can only be carried out using specialist electronic equipment which is connected to the injection system diagnostic wiring connector.

EGR valve renewal

18 Disconnect the battery negative terminal (refer to Chapter 5A Section 4). Remove the cover from the top of the engine.
19 Disconnect the EGR valve wiring connector.
20 Unscrew the two bolts and remove the valve from the EGR cooler.
21 Refitting is the reverse of removal using a new O-ring and tightening the retaining bolts securely.

EGR valve vacuum solenoid renewal

Note: *On the 1.6 litre and 2.0 litre (B20) engines the solenoid is part of the EGR cooler. If faulty on these engines the complete EGR cooler must be replaced.*

22 Disconnect the battery negative terminal (refer to Chapter 5A Section 4). Remove the plastic cover over the top of the engine.
23 Disconnect the vacuum solenoid valve wiring connector **(see illustrations)**.
24 Disconnect the two vacuum hoses from the valve.
25 If required, unscrew the retaining bolts and remove the valve from the top of the EGR cooler.
26 Refitting is the reverse of removal.

3.23b The by-pass vacuum control solenoid on the 1.6 litre engine ...

3.23c … and on the 2.0 litre B20 engine

EGR valve cooler

27 The EGR valve cooler is a major assembly attached to the left-hand end of the cylinder head, and containing many engine, cooling system and emission system components **(see illustration)**.

28 Remove the cover from the top of the engine.

29 Drain the cooling system as described in Chapter 1B Section 26.

30 Remove the battery and battery tray as described in Chapter 5A Section 4.

31 Remove the throttle housing intake duct as described in Chapter 4B Section 8.

32 Where necessary remove the EGR valve as described previously in this Section.

33 Disconnect the wiring connector at the

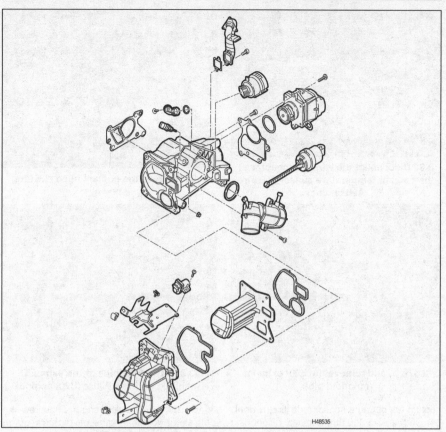

3.27a EGR valve cooler components and attachments (A20 engine)

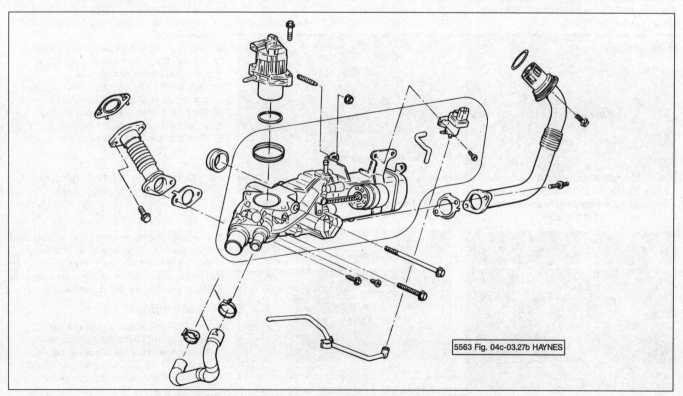

3.27b EGR valve and cooler components and attachments (B20 engine)

3.33 Disconnect the wiring connector at the coolant temperature sensor (2.0 litre A20 engine)

3.34 Remove the coolant hose (1.6 litre shown)

3.37a Remove the flexible EGR pipe from the inlet manifold ...

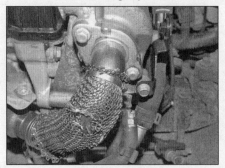

3.37b ... and remove the EGR exhaust manifold pipe

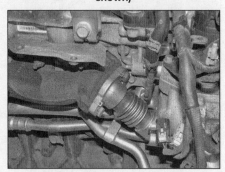

3.37c The EGR pipe at the exhaust manifold on the 2.0 litre (B20) engine

3.39a On the 2.0 (B20) engine the coolant by-pass pipe must be removed with the EGR cooler

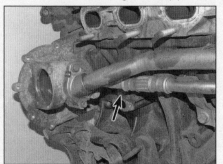

3.39b The by-pass pipe at the thermostat housing on the 2.0 litre (B20) engine

3.40 Removing the complete EGR cooler and control valve from the 1.6 litre engine

3.41 All traces of oil and carbon must be removed. This EGR pipe was nearly completely blocked

coolant temperature sensor **(see illustration)**.
34 On the early 2.0 litre engines, disconnect the coolant hoses at the thermostat housing. On later models remove the coolant hoses at the EGR cooler **(see illustration)**. Remove the remaining coolant hoses.

35 On the 2.0 litre A20 engine, unscrew the bolt securing the engine oil dipstick guide tube to the front of the EGR valve cooler.
36 Disconnect the vacuum hose at the EGR valve vacuum actuator.
37 Undo the bolts securing the EGR pipe to the

EGR cooler, and the bolts securing the pipe to the inlet manifold **(see illustrations)**. Remove the pipe and recover the gasket(s) where fitted.
38 Disconnect the vacuum pipes from the vacuum reservoir at the front of the EGR cooler.
39 Disconnect any remaining support brackets, wiring harness clips and additional fasteners as necessary to allow removal of the EGR cooler. On the 2.0 litre B20 engine the coolant by-pass pipe must be removed with the EGR cooler and because this runs behind the DPF, the DPF must be removed first to access the fitting at the rear of the thermostat housing **(see illustrations)**.
40 Undo the fixings securing the EGR cooler to the cylinder head. Remove the cooler and recover the gasket **(see illustration)**.
41 Refitting is the reverse of removal, bearing in mind the following points:
a) Clean all traces of oil and carbon from the cooler and associated pipe work **(see illustration)**.
b) Renew all disturbed gaskets and seals.
c) Tighten the retaining bolts/nuts to the specified torque (where given).
d) Refit the throttle housing intake duct as described in Chapter 4B Section 3.
e) Refit the battery tray and battery as described in Chapter 5A Section 4.
f) Refill the cooling system as described in Chapter 1B Section 26.

4 Catalytic converter – general information and precautions

1 The catalytic converter is a reliable and simple device which needs no maintenance in itself, but there are some facts of which an owner should be aware if the converter is to function properly for its full service life.

Petrol engines
a) DO NOT use leaded petrol in a car equipped with a catalytic converter – the lead will coat the precious metals, reducing their converting efficiency and will eventually destroy the converter.
b) Always keep the ignition and fuel systems well-maintained in accordance with the manufacturer's schedule.

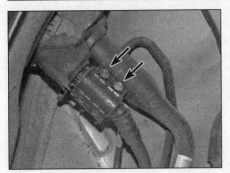

5.7 Remove the bolts

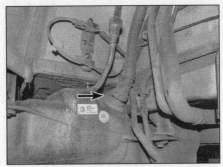

5.8 Release and remove the filler neck

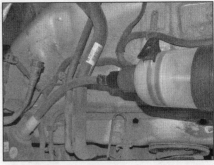

5.9 Remove as much fluid as possible from the tank

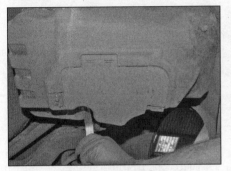

5.10a Release and …

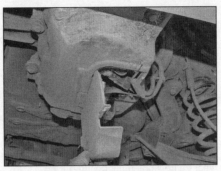

5.10b … remove the cover

5.10c Disconnect the wiring plugs

c) If the engine develops a misfire, do not drive the car at all (or at least as little as possible) until the fault is cured.

d) DO NOT push- or tow-start the car – this will soak the catalytic converter in unburned fuel, causing it to overheat when the engine does start.

e) DO NOT switch off the ignition at high engine speeds.

f) DO NOT use fuel or engine oil additives – these may contain substances harmful to the catalytic converter.

g) DO NOT continue to use the car if the engine burns oil to the extent of leaving a visible trail of blue smoke.

h) Remember that the catalytic converter operates at very high temperatures. DO NOT, therefore, park the car in dry undergrowth, over long grass or piles of dead leaves after a long run.

i) Remember that the catalytic converter is FRAGILE – do not strike it with tools during servicing work.

j) In some cases a sulphurous smell (like that of rotten eggs) may be noticed from the exhaust. This is common to many catalytic converter-equipped cars and once the car has covered a few thousand miles the problem should disappear.

k) The catalytic converter on a well-maintained and well-driven car should last for between 50 000 and 100 000 miles – if the converter is no longer effective it must be renewed.

Diesel engines

2 Refer to the information given in parts f, g,

h, i and k of the petrol engines information given above.

5 Diesel exhaust additive system components – removal and refitting

Caution: Always wear suitable gloves and eye protection when handling the additive fluid and immediately mop up/wash off spills with clean water.

1 Models built after 2015 may have a emissions reduction system fitted that injects a urea based liquid (AdBlue) into the exhaust stream. Vehicles fitted with the system can easily be identified by the blue additive filler cap next to the fuel filler neck.

2 When the fluid level is low a warning message will be displayed on the instrument panel and/or the driver information display. Fluid should then be added to the separate tank. Note that the vehicle will not start if the diesel exhaust fluid tank is empty.

Fluid reservoir

Removal

3 Disconnect the battery as described in Chapter 5A Section 4.

4 Remove the filler cap, and remove as much fluid as possible from the tank using a vacuum pump or similar. The angle of the filler pipe makes this difficult.

5 Firmly apply the handbrake, chock the front wheels and then jack up the rear of the vehicle and support it securely on axle stands (see Jacking and vehicle support 13 Section 5).

6 Remove the right rear wheel and then remove the wing liner as described in Chapter 11 Section 24.

7 Clean the inner wing and all the area around the fuel filler neck and then release the additive filler neck by removing the bolts **(see illustration)**.

8 Release the connector at the fluid tank and remove the filler neck **(see illustration)**.

9 With the neck removed use a vacuum pump or similar to remove any remaining fluid from the fluid tank **(see illustration)**. Seal the tank opening after removing the fluid.

10 Release and remove the protective cover from the fluid tank and disconnect the wiring plugs **(see illustrations)**.

11 Anticipating some fluid spillage, release the fluid outlet pipe at the quick release connector. Seal the pipe and the outlet at the fluid pump.

12 Remove the large protective shield from the fluid tank **(see illustrations)**.

5.12a Release the clips and …

5.12b ... remove the main cover

5.12c To avoid any damage to the control module remove it

5.13 Remove the fluid tank

13 Remove the now exposed mounting bolts and remove the complete fluid tank and pump assembly from the vehicle **(see illustration)**.

Refitting

14 Refitting is a reversal of removal. Tighten the tank bolts to the specified torque and refill the tank with exhaust fluid (AdBlue).

Pump

Removal

15 The pump is located beneath the additive tank. Remove the fluid tank (as described in this section). Place it on a clean work surface and invert the tank.

16 Disconnect the wiring plug from the pump. If not already done so, to avoid damaging the control module remove it from the tank **(see illustration)**.

17 Note the position of the locking ring and pump outlet pipe on the fluid tank **(see illustrations)**.

18 Remove the pump locking ring **(see illustration)**. A special tool is available (EN-48378) but similar tools are widely available in the aftermarket. Have an assistant restrain the fluid tank and then remove the locking collar. Note that the locking ring can be a tight fit on the tank and may have to be carefully cut off.

19 Pull out the pump module and remove the sealing ring **(see illustrations)**. Dispose of the seal – a new one must be fitted.

Refitting

20 Refitting is a reversal of removal. Fit a new seal and if required a new locking ring. Align the outlet pipe with the mark on the tank and tighten the locking ring until the arrow aligns with the mark on the tank **(see illustrations 5.17a and 5.17b)**.

Fluid injector

Removal

21 Firmly apply the handbrake, then jack up the front of the vehicle and support it securely on axle stands (see Jacking and vehicle support 13 Section 5).

22 Remove the engine undershield.

23 Disconnect the wiring plug from the injector.

24 Have a suitable plug ready and then (anticipating some fluid spillage) disconnect the fluid supply pipe from the injector. Seal the supply pipe.

25 Remove the injector mounting bolts, pull out the injector and discard the gasket. A new one must be fitted.

Refitting

26 Refitting is a reversal of removal, but install a new gasket.

5.16 Disconnect the wiring plug from the pump module

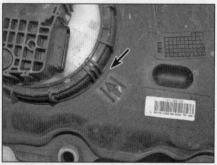

5.17a The locking ring alignment marks ...

5.17b ... and the outlet pipe alignment mark on the tank

5.18 Remove the locking collar

5.19a Remove the pump ...

5.19b ... and recover the seal

Chapter 5 Part A
Starting and charging systems

Contents

Degrees of difficulty

| Easy, suitable for novice with little experience | | Fairly easy, suitable for beginner with some experience | | Fairly difficult, suitable for competent DIY mechanic | | Difficult, suitable for experienced DIY mechanic | | Very difficult, suitable for expert DIY or professional | |

Specifications

General
Electrical system type .... 12 volt negative earth

Battery
Type .... Lead-acid, 'maintenance-free' (sealed for life)
Charge condition:
  Poor .... 12.5 volts
  Normal .... 12.6 volts
  Good .... 12.7 volts

Torque wrench settings

	Nm	lbf ft
Alternator bolts:		
Petrol engine models	35	26
Diesel engine models:		
1.6 litre engines	22	16
2.0 litre (A20) engines	60	44
2.0 litre (B20) engines:		
Lower bolts	22	16
Upper bolt	58	43
Auxiliary drivebelt tensioner:		
Petrol engine models	55	41
Diesel engine models	22	16
Glow plugs:		
1.6 litre and 2.0 litre (A20) engine	10	7
2.0 litre (B20) engine	16.5	12
Oil pressure warning light switch:		
Petrol engine models	20	15
Diesel engine models	30	22
Roadwheel nuts	150	111
Starter motor:		
Petrol engine models:		
Inlet manifold support bracket bolts	8	6
Starter motor mounting bolts	25	18
Diesel engine models	22	16

3.2 Battery charge condition indicator – 'Delco' type battery

1 General information and precautions

General information

1 The engine electrical system consists mainly of the charging and starting systems, and the diesel engine pre/post-heating system. Because of their engine-related functions, these components are covered separately from the body electrical devices such as the lights, instruments, etc (which are covered in Chapter 12). On petrol engine models refer to Chapter 5B for information on the ignition system.

2 The electrical system is of 12 volt negative earth type.

3 The battery is of the maintenance-free (sealed for life) type, and is charged by the alternator, which is belt-driven from the crankshaft pulley.

4 The starter motor is of pre-engaged type incorporating an integral solenoid. On starting, the solenoid moves the drive pinion into engagement with the flywheel/driveplate ring gear before the starter motor is energised. Once the engine has started, a one-way clutch prevents the motor armature being driven by the engine until the pinion disengages.

5 Further details of the various systems are given in the relevant Sections of this Chapter. While some repair procedures are given, the usual course of action is to renew the component concerned.

3.6 A modern 'intelligent' battery charger, capable of charging all types of battery

Precautions

6 It is necessary to take extra care when working on the electrical system to avoid damage to semi-conductor devices (diodes and transistors), and to avoid the risk of personal injury. In addition to the precautions given in *Safety first!* at the beginning of this manual, observe the following when working on the system:

● Always remove rings, watches, etc before working on the electrical system. Even with the battery disconnected, capacitive discharge could occur if a component's live terminal is earthed through a metal object. This could cause a shock or nasty burn.

● Do not reverse the battery connections. Components such as the alternator, electronic control units, or any other components having semi-conductor circuitry could be irreparably damaged.

● If the engine is being started using jump leads and a slave battery, connect the batteries positive-to-positive and negative-to-negative (see *Jump starting*). This also applies when connecting a battery charger but in this case both of the battery terminals should first be disconnected.

● Never disconnect the battery terminals, the alternator, any electrical wiring or any test instruments when the engine is running.

● Do not allow the engine to turn the alternator when the alternator is not connected.

● Never test for alternator output by flashing the output lead to earth.

● Never use an ohmmeter of the type incorporating a hand-cranked generator for circuit or continuity testing.

● Always ensure that the battery negative lead is disconnected when working on the electrical system.

● Before using electric-arc welding equipment on the car, disconnect the battery, alternator and components such as the fuel injection/ ignition electronic control unit to protect them from the risk of damage.

2 Electrical fault finding – general information

1 Refer to Chapter 12, Section 2.

3 Battery – testing and charging

Testing

1 All models are fitted with a 'sealed for life' maintenance-free battery, topping-up and testing of the electrolyte in each cell is not possible. The condition of the battery can therefore only be tested using a battery condition indicator or a voltmeter. Note that some later models may also have a battery condition indicator fitted as part of the engine electrical system. On these models a warning

message will be displayed on the instrument panel if a problem is detected with either the battery or the charging system.

2 Some models are fitted with a maintenance-free battery with a built-in 'magic-eye' charge condition indicator. The indicator is located in the top of the battery casing, and indicates the condition of the battery from its colour **(see illustration)**. If the indicator shows green, then the battery is in a good state of charge. If the indicator turns darker, eventually to black, then the battery requires charging, as described later in this Section. If the indicator shows clear/yellow, then the electrolyte level in the battery is too low to allow further use, and the battery should be renewed. Do not attempt to charge, load or jump start a battery when the indicator shows clear/yellow.

3 If testing the battery using a voltmeter, connect the voltmeter across the battery and compare the result with those given in the Specifications under 'charge condition'. The test is only accurate if the battery has not been subjected to any kind of charge for the previous six hours. If this is not the case, switch on the headlights for 30 seconds, then wait four to five minutes before testing the battery after switching off the headlights. All other electrical circuits must be switched off, so check that the doors and tailgate are fully shut when making the test.

4 If the voltage reading is less than 12.2 volts, then the battery is discharged, whilst a reading of 12.2 to 12.4 volts indicates a partially-discharged condition.

5 If the battery is to be charged, remove it from the vehicle (Section 4) and charge it as described later in this Section. Note that most modern 'intelligent' battery chargers can be used with the battery connected. Always read the instructions that came with the battery charger before charging the battery.

Charging

Note: *The following is intended as a guide only. Always refer to the manufacturer's recommendations (often printed on a label attached to the battery) before charging a battery.*

6 If the battery is to be recharged, we recommend that you use an 'intelligent' charger **(see illustration)**. Whilst some chargers are capable of safely charging the battery with the battery connected to the vehicle, if you are unsure, always disconnect the battery. If the battery is disconnected (e.g. if it is to be removed and recharged on the bench), note that certain 'learned' values will be lost from the engine management ECU memory, requiring the car to be driven over a short distance after refitting the battery. Also, when the battery is reconnected, the warning lights for the ESP and electro-mechanical steering may light up and stay on. They will extinguish if you drive briefly in a straight line at a speed of 9 to 13 mph.

7 On stop/start models fitted with a battery sensor (attached to the battery ground/ earth cable) to avoid the need to calibrate the sensor using a diagnostic scan tool the

battery must be charged with the negative cable of the battery charger connected to a suitable engine ground. Battery chargers that are capable of charging the battery with the battery connected should only be used. Check with the manufacturer of the battery charger if in any doubt.

4 Battery and battery tray – disconnecting, reconnecting, removal and refitting

Note: *Refer to Section 1 before proceeding.*

Battery

Disconnection

1 Numerous systems fitted to the vehicle require battery power to be available at all times, either to ensure their continued operation (such as the clock) or to maintain control unit memories which would be erased if the battery were to be disconnected. Whenever the battery is to be disconnected therefore, first note the following, to ensure that there are no unforeseen consequences of this action:

a) *Lower the drivers window. Remove the key from the ignition, and to keep it with you, so that it does not get locked in, if the central locking should engage accidentally when the battery is reconnected.*

b) *Depending on model and specification, the Vauxhall anti-theft alarm system may be of the type which is automatically activated when the vehicle battery is disconnected and/or reconnected. To prevent the alarm sounding on models so equipped, switch the ignition on, then off, and disconnect the battery within 15 seconds. If the alarm is activated when the battery is reconnected, switch the ignition on then off to deactivate the alarm.*

c) *If a security-coded audio unit is fitted, and the unit and/or the battery is disconnected, the unit will not function again on reconnection until the correct security code is entered. Details of this procedure, which varies according to the unit fitted, are given in the vehicle audio system operating instructions. Ensure you have the correct code before you disconnect the battery. If you do not have the code or*

4.3a Depress the tab at the left-hand side ...

details of the correct procedure, but can supply proof of ownership and a legitimate reason for wanting this information, a Vauxhall dealer may be able to help.

d) *The engine management electronic control unit is of the ' self-learning' type, meaning that as it operates, it also monitors and stores the settings which give optimum engine performance under all operating conditions. When the battery is disconnected, these settings are lost and the ECU reverts to the base settings programmed into its memory at the factory. On restarting, this may lead to the engine running/idling roughly for a short while, until the ECU has re-learned the optimum settings. This process is best accomplished by taking the vehicle on a road test (for approximately 15 minutes), covering all engine speeds and loads, concentrating mainly in the 2500 to 3500 rpm region.*

e) *On models equipped with automatic transmission, the transmission selector lever assembly incorporates an electrically-operated selector lever lock mechanism that prevents the lever being moved out of the P position unless the ignition is switched on and the brake pedal is depressed. If the selector lever is in the P position and the battery is disconnected, it will not be possible to move the selector lever out of position P by the normal means. Although it is possible to manually override the system (see Chapter 7B, Section 3), it is sensible to move the selector lever to the N position before disconnecting the battery.*

4.3b ... and right-hand side and lift up the battery box lid at the rear

f) *On models with electric windows, it will be necessary to reprogramme the motors to restore the one-touch function of the buttons, after reconnection of the battery. To do this, fully close both front windows. With the windows closed, depress the up button of the driver's side window for approximately 5 seconds, then release it and depress the passenger side window up button for approximately 5 seconds.*

g) *On models with an electric sliding sunroof, it will be necessary to fully open and fully close the sunroof after battery reconnection, to recalibrate the sensors.*

h) *On all models, when reconnecting the battery after disconnection, switch on the ignition and wait 10 seconds to allow the electronic vehicle systems to stabilise and re-initialise.*

2 The battery is located at the front, left-hand side of the engine compartment, housed in a protective plastic box.

3 Depress the tab at the rear of the battery box lid on both sides and lift up the lid at the rear **(see illustrations)**.

4 Disengage the hooks at the front of the battery box lid and remove the lid **(see illustration)**.

5 Disconnect the lead at the negative (–) terminal by unscrewing the retaining nut and removing the terminal clamp **(see illustration)**.

Removal

6 Lift open the junction box lid on the top of the battery. Undo the retaining nut and disconnect the positive lead from the junction box terminal **(see illustration)**.

4.4 Disengage the hooks at the front of the battery box lid and remove the lid

4.5 Disconnect the lead at the battery negative (–) terminal by unscrewing the nut and removing the terminal clamp

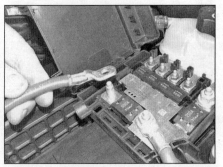

4.6 Undo the retaining nut and disconnect the positive lead from the junction box terminal

4.7 Disconnect the lead at the battery positive (+) terminal by unscrewing the retaining nut and removing the clamp

4.8a Release the retaining clip on the left-hand side ...

4.8b ... and right-hand side and lift the junction box up and off the battery

4.9 Lift the safety strap up and off the battery positive terminal

4.10a Undo the retaining bolt ...

4.10b ... and remove the battery retaining clamp

7   Disconnect the lead at the battery positive (+) terminal by unscrewing the retaining nut and removing the terminal clamp **(see illustration)**.
8   Release the retaining clip each side and lift the junction box up and off the battery **(see illustrations)**. Move the junction box to the

rear and rest it on the coolant expansion tank.
9   Lift the safety strap up and off the battery positive terminal **(see illustration)**.
10   Undo the retaining bolt and remove the battery retaining clamp **(see illustrations)**.
11   Carefully lift the battery from its location

and remove it from the car. Make sure the battery is kept upright at all times.

Refitting and reconnection

Note: *As a precaution, before refitting the battery check that all doors are unlocked.*
12   Refitting is a reversal of removal, but smear petroleum jelly on the terminals after reconnecting the leads to reduce corrosion, and always reconnect the POSITIVE leads first, followed by the negative lead.

Battery box

Removal – petrol engine models

13   Remove the battery as described previously.
14   Release the cable clip securing the battery positive lead to the front of the battery box.
15   Release the retaining tab and carefully lift the engine management ECU mounting bracket off the front of the battery box. Position the ECU and mounting bracket to one side.
16   Release the cable clip securing the wiring loom to the side of the battery box.

Removal – diesel engine models

17   Remove the battery as described previously.
18   Release the cable clip securing the battery positive lead to the front of the battery box **(see illustration)**.
19   Lift the wiring loom support bracket from its location on the front of the battery box **(see illustration)**.
20   Using a small screwdriver, depress the retaining tab and lift the engine management ECU mounting bracket off the side of the battery box **(see illustrations)**. Position the ECU and mounting bracket to one side.

4.18 Release the cable clip securing the battery positive lead to the front of the battery box

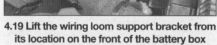

4.19 Lift the wiring loom support bracket from its location on the front of the battery box

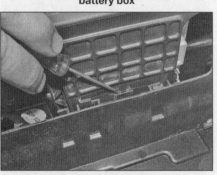

4.20a Using a small screwdriver, depress the retaining tab ...

4.20b ... and lift the engine management ECU mounting bracket off the side of the battery box

4.21a Depress the retaining tab ...

4.21b ... and lift the pre/post-heating system control unit off the front of the battery box

4.22a Open the plastic retainers ...

21 Where fitted, depress the retaining tab and lift the pre/post-heating system control unit off the front of the battery box **(see illustrations)**. Position the control unit to one side.

Removal – all models

22 Open the plastic retainers and release the power steering fluid pipe from the side of the battery box **(see illustrations)**.

23 Working between the battery box and the coolant expansion tank, undo the positive terminal safety strap retaining bolt **(see illustration)**.

24 Undo the three retaining bolts and lift the battery box up and out of the engine compartment **(see illustrations)**.

Refitting

25 Refitting is a reversal of removal.

4.22b ... and release the power steering fluid pipe from the side of the battery box

4.23 Undo the battery positive terminal safety strap retaining bolt

5 Charging system – testing

Note: *Refer to the precautions given in 'Safety first!' and in Section 1 of this Chapter before starting work.*

1 If the ignition no-charge warning light fails to illuminate when the ignition is switched on, first check the alternator wiring connections for security. If satisfactory, check the condition of all related fuses, fusible links, wiring connections and earthing points. If this fails to reveal the fault, the vehicle should be taken to a Vauxhall/Opel dealer or auto-electrician, as further testing entails the use of specialist diagnostic equipment.

2 If the ignition warning light illuminates when the engine is running, stop the engine and check the condition of the auxiliary drivebelt (see Chapter 1A, Section 20 or Chapter 1B, Section 22) and the security of the alternator wiring connections. If satisfactory, have the alternator checked by a Vauxhall/Opel dealer or auto-electrician.

3 If the alternator output is suspect even though the warning light functions correctly, the regulated voltage may be checked as follows.

4 Connect a voltmeter across the battery terminals, and start the engine.

5 Increase the engine speed until the

4.24a Undo the three retaining bolts ...

4.24b ... and lift the battery box up and out of the engine compartment

voltmeter reading remains steady; the reading should be approximately 12 to 14.8 volts, and no more than 15.8 volts **(see illustrations)**.

6 Switch on as many electrical accessories (eg, the headlights, heated rear window and heater blower) as possible. Slowly increase the engine speed to 2,500 rpm. Check that the alternator maintains the regulated voltage at around 12.6 to 15.8 volts.

7 If the regulated voltage is not as stated, the

5.5a The battery voltage with the engine off and with no load (12.28 volts)

5.5b The battery voltage with the engine running (14.69 volts)

7.3 Auxiliary drivebelt tensioner mounting bolt – petrol engines

fault may be due to worn brushes, weak brush springs, a faulty voltage regulator, a faulty diode, a severed phase winding, or worn or damaged slip rings. The alternator should be renewed or taken to a Vauxhall/Opel dealer or auto-electrician for testing and repair.

6 Auxiliary drivebelt – removal and refitting

1 Refer to Chapter 1A, Section 20, or Chapter 1B, Section 22, as applicable.

7 Auxiliary drivebelt tensioner – removal and refitting

Removal

1 Firmly apply the handbrake, then jack up the front of the car and support it securely on axle stands (see *Jacking and vehicle support*). Remove the right-hand front roadwheel.
2 Remove the auxiliary drivebelt as described in Chapter 1A, Section 20, or Chapter 1B, Section 22, as applicable.
3 Undo the central mounting bolt (petrol engines) or the two retaining bolts (diesel engines) and remove the tensioner assembly from the engine **(see illustration)**.

Refitting

4 Place the tensioner assembly in position ensuring that the locating pegs on the

8.11a Alternator lower front mounting bolt – A20 diesel engines

tensioner mounting surface engage correctly with the corresponding holes in the mounting bracket. Tighten the tensioner retaining bolts, or the central mounting bolt to the specified torque.
5 Refit the auxiliary drivebelt as described in Chapter 1A, Section 20 or Chapter 1B, Section 22 as applicable.
6 Refit the roadwheel then lower the car to the ground. Tighten the roadwheel nuts to the specified torque.

8 Alternator – removal and refitting

Removal

Petrol engine models

1 Disconnect the battery negative terminal (refer to Section 4).
2 Firmly apply the handbrake, then jack up the front of the car and support it securely on axle stands (see *Jacking and vehicle support*). Remove the right-hand front roadwheel.
3 Remove the auxiliary drivebelt as described in Chapter 1A, Section 20.
4 Remove the rubber covers (where fitted) from the alternator terminals, then unscrew the two retaining nuts and disconnect the wiring from the rear of the alternator.
5 Unscrew the upper and lower mounting bolts and withdraw the alternator upwards from the block.

Diesel engine models

6 Disconnect the battery negative terminal (refer to Section 4).
7 Firmly apply the handbrake, then jack up the front of the car and support it securely on axle stands (see *Jacking and vehicle support*). Remove the right-hand front roadwheel.
8 Remove the auxiliary drivebelt as described in Chapter 1B, Section 22.
9 On 2.0 litre B20 diesel engines remove the right-hand driveshaft as described in Chapter 8 Section 2.
10 Unscrew the retaining nut and disconnect the wiring terminal, then unplug the wiring block connector from the rear of the alternator.
11 Undo the alternator lower front mounting bolt **(see illustrations)**.

8.11b Alternator mounting bolts (1.6 litre engine)

12 Undo the alternator upper rear mounting bolts, collect the support bracket, and manoeuvre the alternator upwards and out of position.

Refitting

Petrol engine models

13 Manoeuvre the alternator into position and refit the upper and lower mounting bolts. Tighten the bolts to the specified torque.
14 Reconnect the wiring to the alternator terminals and tighten the retaining nuts securely. Where applicable, refit the rubber covers to the alternator terminals.
15 Refit the auxiliary drivebelt as described in Chapter 1A, Section 20.
16 Refit the roadwheel then lower the car to the ground. Tighten the roadwheel nuts to the specified torque.
17 On completion, reconnect the battery negative terminal.

Diesel engine models

18 Manoeuvre the alternator into position and refit the upper rear retaining bolts. Tighten the bolts finger tight only at this stage.
19 Refit the alternator lower front mounting bolt, then tighten the upper and lower mounting bolts to the specified torque.
20 Reconnect the alternator wiring block connector and the terminal wiring, tightening the retaining nut securely.
21 Refit the auxiliary drivebelt as described in Chapter 1B, Section 22.
22 Where removed refit the driveshaft (Chapter 8 Section 2).
23 Refit the roadwheel then lower the car to the ground. Tighten the roadwheel nuts to the specified torque.
24 On completion, reconnect the battery negative terminal.

9 Alternator – testing and overhaul

1 If the alternator is thought to be suspect, it should be removed from the vehicle and taken to an auto-electrician for testing. Most auto-electricians will be able to supply and fit brushes at a reasonable cost. However, check on the cost of repairs before proceeding as it may prove more economical to obtain a new or exchange alternator.

10 Starting system – testing

Note: *Refer to the precautions given in 'Safety first!' and in Section 1 of this Chapter before starting work.*

1 If the starter motor fails to operate when the ignition key is turned to the appropriate position, the possible causes are as follows:
a) *The engine immobiliser is faulty.*

b) *The battery is faulty.*
c) *The electrical connections between the switch, solenoid, battery and starter motor are somewhere failing to pass the necessary current from the battery through the starter to earth.*
d) *The solenoid is faulty.*
e) *The starter motor is mechanically or electrically defective.*

2 To check the battery, switch on the headlights. If they dim after a few seconds, this indicates that the battery is discharged – recharge (see Section 3) or renew the battery. If the headlights glow brightly, operate the starter switch while watching the headlights. If they dim, then this indicates that current is reaching the starter motor, therefore the fault must lie in the starter motor. If the lights continue to glow brightly (and no clicking sound can be heard from the starter motor solenoid), this indicates that there is a fault in the circuit or solenoid – see the following paragraphs. If the starter motor turns slowly when operated, but the battery is in good condition, then this indicates either that the starter motor is faulty, or there is considerable resistance somewhere in the circuit.

3 If a fault in the circuit is suspected, disconnect the battery leads (including the earth connection to the body), the starter/solenoid wiring and the engine/transmission earth strap. Thoroughly clean the connections, and reconnect the leads and wiring. Use a voltmeter or test light to check that full battery voltage is available at the battery positive lead connection to the solenoid. Smear petroleum jelly around the battery terminals to prevent corrosion – corroded connections are among the most frequent causes of electrical system faults.

4 If the battery and all connections are in good condition, check the circuit by disconnecting the ignition switch supply wire from the solenoid terminal. Connect a voltmeter or test lamp between the wire end and a good earth (such as the battery negative terminal), and check that the wire is live when the ignition switch is turned to the 'start' position. If it is, then the circuit is sound – if not the circuit wiring can be checked as described in Chapter 12, Section 2.

5 The solenoid contacts can be checked by connecting a voltmeter or test light between the battery positive feed connection on the starter side of the solenoid and earth. When the ignition switch is turned to the 'start' position, there should be a reading or lighted bulb, as applicable. If there is no reading or lighted bulb, the solenoid is faulty and should be renewed.

6 If the circuit and solenoid are proved sound, the fault must lie in the starter motor. In this event, it may be possible to have the starter motor overhauled by a specialist, but check on the cost of spares before proceeding, as it may prove more economical to obtain a new or exchange motor.

11 Starter motor – removal and refitting

Removal

Petrol engine models

1 Disconnect the battery negative terminal (refer to Section 4).
2 Firmly apply the handbrake, then jack up the front of the car and support it securely on axle stands (see *Jacking and vehicle support*).
3 Disconnect the oxygen sensor wiring at the cable connector below the inlet manifold.
4 Undo the two retaining bolts and remove the support bracket from the underside of the inlet manifold.
5 Slacken and remove the two retaining nuts and disconnect the wiring from the starter motor solenoid. Recover the washers under the nuts.
6 Where applicable, unscrew the retaining nut and disconnect the earth lead from the starter motor upper bolt.
7 Slacken and remove the retaining bolts then manoeuvre the starter motor out from underneath the engine.

Diesel engine models

8 Disconnect the battery negative terminal (refer to Section 4).
9 Firmly apply the handbrake, then jack up the front of the car and support it securely on axle stands (see *Jacking and vehicle support*).
10 Remove the engine cover by pulling it upwards off the mounting studs.
11 Remove the engine undertray as described in Chapter 11, Section 24.
12 Slacken and remove the two retaining nuts and disconnect the wiring from the starter motor solenoid. Recover the washers under the nuts.
13 Unscrew the retaining nut and disconnect the earth lead from the starter motor lower stud bolt.
14 On some models, open the retaining clips and release the two heater hoses from the coolant pipe support bracket. Do not disconnect the coolant hoses.
15 Undo the two nuts and release the wiring harness from the support bracket above the starter motor.
16 To improve access, carefully lift the cooling system expansion tank out of its mounting bracket and place the tank to one side.
17 Unscrew the starter motor lower bolt and the one (or two) upper mounting bolts **(see illustration)**. Collect the wiring harness support bracket then manoeuvre the starter motor upwards and out of position.

Refitting

18 Refitting is a reversal of removal tightening the retaining bolts to the specified torque. Ensure all wiring is correctly routed and its retaining nuts are securely tightened.

11.17 Access to the upper bolt on the 1.6 litre engine is difficult – lower bolt arrowed

12 Starter motor – testing and overhaul

1 If the starter motor is thought to be suspect, it should be removed from the vehicle and taken to an auto-electrician for testing. Most auto-electricians will be able to supply and fit brushes at a reasonable cost. However, check on the cost of repairs before proceeding as it may prove more economical to obtain a new or exchange motor.

13 Ignition switch – removal and refitting

1 The switch is integral with the steering column lock, and removal and refitting is described in Chapter 10, Section 20.

14 Oil pressure warning light sensor – removal and refitting

Removal

Petrol engine models

1 The oil pressure warning light sensor screwed into the front of the cylinder block.
2 Firmly apply the handbrake, then jack up the front of the car and support it securely on axle stands (see *Jacking and vehicle support*).
3 Refer to Chapter 3, Section 11 and unbolt the air conditioning compressor from the cylinder block without disconnecting the refrigerant lines. Support the compressor to one side for access to the oil pressure warning light switch.
4 Disconnect the wiring connector then unscrew the switch and recover the sealing washer. Be prepared for oil spillage, and if the switch is to be left removed from the engine for any length of time, plug the switch aperture.

Diesel engine models

5 On the 1.6 litre engine the sensor is fitted

14.5 The sensors at the rear of the block on the 1.6 litre engine

A Oil pressure sensor
B Piston cooling jets control
   solenoid
C Oil pressure switch
D Coolant temperature
   sensor
E Cylinder head
   temperature sensor

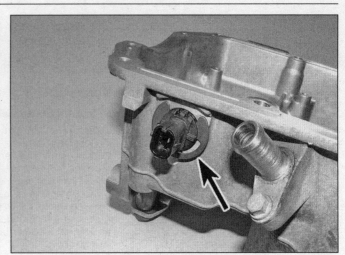

15.2 Slide off the retaining clip and free the oil level sensor wiring connector from the sump

in the engine block above the oil cooler **(see illustration)**. On all 2.0 litre engines the sensor is screwed into the oil filter housing at the rear of the engine.
6 Firmly apply the handbrake, then jack up the front of the car and support it securely on axle stands (see *Jacking and vehicle support*).
7 Remove the engine undertray as described in Chapter 11, Section 24.
8 On 1.6 litre engines remove the front exhaust pipe as described in Chapter 4B Section 18.
9 Disconnect the wiring connector then unscrew the sensor and recover the sealing washer. Be prepared for oil spillage, and if the switch is to be left removed from the engine for any length of time, plug the switch aperture.

Refitting

10 Examine the sealing washer for signs of damage or deterioration and if necessary renew.
11 Refit the switch and washer, tightening it to the specified torque, and reconnect the wiring connector.
12 On diesel engine models, refit the engine undertray and the exhaust front pipe (where removed).

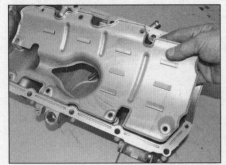

15.3 Where fitted, undo the retaining bolts and remove the oil baffle plate

13 Lower the vehicle to the ground then check and, if necessary, top-up the engine oil as described in *Weekly checks*.

15 Oil level sensor – removal and refitting

Removal

1 The oil level sensor is located inside the sump which must first be removed (see Chapter 2A, Section 14, Chapter 2B Section 12, Chapter 2C Section 13 or Chapter 2D Section 12).
2 With the sump removed, slide off the retaining clip and free the sensor wiring connector from the sump **(see illustration)**.
3 Where fitted, undo the retaining bolts and remove the oil baffle plate from inside the sump **(see illustration)**.
4 Note the correct routing of the wiring then undo the retaining bolts and remove the sensor assembly from the sump **(see illustration)**. Check the wiring connector seal for signs or damage and renew if necessary.

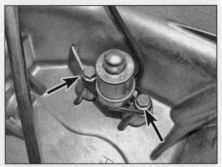

15.4 Undo the two bolts and remove the oil level sensor from the sump

Refitting

5 Prior to refitting remove all traces of locking compound from the sensor retaining bolt and sump threads. Apply a drop of fresh locking compound to the bolt threads and lubricate the wiring connector seal with a smear of engine oil.
6 Fit the sensor, making sure the wiring is correctly routed, and securely tighten its retaining bolts. Ease the wiring connector through the sump, taking care not to damage its seal, and secure it in position with the retaining clip.
7 Ensure the sensor is correctly refitted then, where applicable, refit the oil baffle plate.
8 Refit the sump as described in Chapter 2A, Section 14, Chapter 2C, Section 13 or Chapter 2D Section 12.

16 Pre/post-heating system (diesel models) – description and testing

Description

1 Each cylinder of the engine is fitted with a heater plug (commonly called a glow plug) screwed into it. The plugs are electrically-operated before and during start-up when the engine is cold. Electrical feed to the glow plugs is controlled via the pre/post-heating system control unit.
2 A warning light in the instrument panel tells the driver that pre/post-heating is taking place. When the light goes out, the engine is ready to be started. The voltage supply to the glow plugs continues for several seconds after the light goes out. If no attempt is made to start, the timer then cuts off the supply, in order to avoid draining the battery and overheating the glow plugs.
3 The glow plugs also provide a 'post-

heating' function, whereby the glow plugs remain switched on after the engine has started. The length of time 'post-heating' takes place is also determined by the control unit, and is dependant on engine temperature.

4 The fuel filter is fitted with a heating element to prevent the fuel 'waxing' in extreme cold temperature conditions and to improve combustion. The heating element is an integral part of the fuel filter housing and is controlled by the pre/post-heating system control unit.

Testing

Caution: Do not apply a 12 volt (battery) supply to the glow plugs. All the diesel engines covered in this manual feature glow plugs that operate with a 4.4 volt supply. Applying 12 volts directly to the glow plugs will destroy them.

5 If the system malfunctions, testing is ultimately by substitution of known good units, but some preliminary checks may be made as follows.

6 Connect a voltmeter between the glow plug supply cable and earth (engine or vehicle metal). Make sure that the live connection is kept clear of the engine and bodywork.

7 Have an assistant switch on the ignition, and check that voltage is applied to the glow plugs. Note the time for which the warning light is lit, and the total time for which voltage is applied before the system cuts out. Switch off the ignition.

8 At an underbonnet temperature of 20°C (68°F), typical times noted should be approximately 3 seconds for warning light operation. Warning light time will increase with lower temperatures and decrease with higher temperatures.

9 If there is no supply at all, the control unit or associated wiring is at fault.

10 The factory diagnostic tool is capable of logging a fault code for each individual glow plug. Many after market tools will also have this facility. If there is any concern about the operation of the glow plugs then connecting the engine management system to a diagnostic tool will be the most cost effective way of checking the glow plugs.

11 As a final check, the glow plugs can be removed and inspected as described in the following Section.

---

17 Glow plugs (diesel models) – removal, inspection and refitting

Caution: If the pre/post-heating system has just been energised, or if the engine has been running, the glow plugs will be very hot.

Removal

1 The glow plugs are located at the rear of the cylinder head above the inlet manifold.

2 Remove the engine cover by pulling it upwards off the mounting studs.

3 Disconnect the wiring from the glow plugs by squeezing the connectors with thumb and forefinger, and pulling them from the plugs.
Note: *The glow plugs are fragile and snapping them in half them whilst trying to remove them is not uncommon. Soak them with penetrating oil before attempting to remove them. Removing them when the engine is warm also helps.*

4 Unscrew the glow plugs and remove them from the cylinder head **(see illustration)**.

Inspection

5 Inspect each glow plug for physical damage. Burnt or eroded glow plug tips can be caused by a bad injector spray pattern. Have the injectors checked if this type of damage is found.

6 The glow plugs have a very low resistance and unless an expensive low resistance measuring multi-meter is available the plug resistance can not be measured accurately. However a standard multi-meter can be used to test for an open circuit.
Caution: Do not apply battery voltage to the glow plugs to test them. The glow plugs are designed to operate on a 4.4 volt supply.

7 The glow plugs can be energised by applying a 4 volt supply to them to verify that they heat up evenly and in the required time. Observe the following precautions:

a) *Support the glow plug by clamping it carefully in a vice or self-locking pliers. Remember it will become hot.*

b) *Connect 3 AA cells together in series to supply the correct voltage to the glow plug. Check that the output of the AA cells does not exceed 4.4 volts.*

c) *Briefly apply current to the glow plug under test. A small drop of oil on the plug will confirm the plug is heating. Note that the use of AA batteries as a power source will not necessarily heat the glow plug fully, but it will confirm that the plug draws current.*

d) *After testing, allow the glow plug to cool for several minutes before attempting to handle it.*

8 A glow plug in good condition will start to heat the tip after drawing current for 5 seconds or less. Any plug which takes much longer to start glowing, or which starts glowing in the middle instead of at the tip, is defective.

17.4 Unscrew the glow plugs and remove them from the cylinder head (A20 engine shown)

Refitting

9 Carefully refit the plugs and tighten to the specified torque. Do not overtighten, as this can damage the glow plug element. Push the electrical connectors firmly onto the glow plugs.

10 The remainder of refitting is a reversal of removal, checking the operation of the glow plugs on completion.

---

18 Pre/post-heating system control unit (diesel models) – removal and refitting

Note: *On later models the control unit is integrated into the main engine management control module (ECU).*

Removal

1 The pre/post-heating system control unit is located on the left-hand side of the engine compartment where it is mounted onto the front of the battery box.

2 Disconnect the battery negative terminal (refer to Section 4).

3 Unclip the control unit and slide it up and off the battery box **(see illustration)**.

4 Disconnect the wiring connectors from the base of the control unit and remove the unit from the engine compartment **(see illustration)**.

Refitting

5 Refitting is a reversal of removal.

18.3 Unclip the control unit and slide it up and off the battery box

18.4 Disconnect the wiring connectors from the base of the control unit

Chapter 5 Part B
Ignition system – petrol engines

Contents

Degrees of difficulty

Easy, suitable for novice with little experience		**Fairly easy,** suitable for beginner with some experience		**Fairly difficult,** suitable for competent DIY mechanic		**Difficult,** suitable for experienced DIY mechanic		**Very difficult,** suitable for expert DIY or professional	

Specifications

General

System type	Distributorless ignition system
Location of No 1 cylinder	Timing belt end of engine
Firing order	1-3-4-2

Torque wrench setting	**Nm**	**lbf ft**
Ignition module retaining bolts.	8	6

1 Ignition system – general information

1 The ignition system is integrated with the fuel injection system to form a combined engine management system under the control of one electronic control unit (ECU) – see Chapter 4A, Section 9 for further information. The ignition side of the system is of the distributorless type, and consists of the ignition module and the knock sensor.

2 The ignition module consists of four ignition coils, one per cylinder, in one casing mounted directly above the spark plugs. This module eliminates the need for any HT leads as the coils locate directly onto the relevant spark plug. The ECU uses its inputs from the various sensors to calculate the required ignition advance setting and coil charging time.

3 The knock sensor is mounted onto the cylinder block and informs the ECU when the engine is 'pinking' under load. The sensor is sensitive to vibration and detects the knocking which occurs when the engine starts to 'pink' (pre-ignite). The knock sensor sends an electrical signal to the ECU which in turn retards the ignition advance setting until the 'pinking' ceases.

4 The ignition system operates under the overall control of the engine management ECU. The system comprises various sensors (whose inputs also provide data to control the fuel injection system), and the ECU, in addition to the ignition module and spark plugs. Further details of the system sensors and the ECU are given in Chapter 4A, Section 2.

5 The ECU selects the optimum ignition advance setting based on the information received from the various sensors, and fires the relevant ignition coil accordingly. The degree of advance can thus be constantly varied to suit the prevailing engine operating conditions.

 Warning: Due to the high voltages produced by the electronic ignition system, extreme care must be taken when working on the system with the ignition switched on. Persons with surgically-implanted cardiac pacemaker devices should keep well clear of the ignition circuits, components and test equipment.

2.2 The vehicle diagnostic socket is located at the base of the facia on the driver's side

3.1 Remove the ignition module cover by sliding it towards the transmission and lifting off

3.2 Disconnect the ignition module wiring connector

3.3 Undo the retaining bolts and pull the ignition module up and off the spark plugs

3.4 Check the condition of the sealing grommets and renew if necessary

2 Ignition system – testing

1 If a fault appears in the engine management system, first ensure that all the system wiring connectors are securely connected and free of corrosion. Ensure that the fault is not due to poor maintenance; ie, check that the air cleaner filter element is clean, the spark plugs are in good condition and correctly gapped, the cylinder compression pressures are correct and that the engine breather hoses are clear and undamaged.

2 If these checks fail to reveal the cause of the problem, the vehicle should be taken to a suitably-equipped Vauxhall/Opel dealer or engine management diagnostic specialist for testing. A diagnostic socket is located at the base of the facia, on the driver's side, to which a fault code reader or other suitable test equipment can be connected **(see illustration)**. By using the code reader or test equipment, the engine management ECU can be interrogated, and any stored fault codes

can be retrieved. This will allow the fault to be quickly and simply traced, alleviating the need to test all the system components individually, which is a time-consuming operation that carries a risk of damaging the ECU.

3 The only ignition system checks which can be carried out by the home mechanic are those described in Chapter 1A, Section 26 relating to the spark plugs. If necessary, the system wiring and wiring connectors can be checked as described in Chapter 12, Section 2, ensuring that the ECU wiring connector(s) have first been disconnected.

3 Ignition module – removal and refitting

Removal

1 Unclip the wiring trough from the left-hand end of the cylinder head, then remove the cover from the ignition module by sliding it towards the transmission and lifting off **(see illustration)**.

2 Disconnect the wiring connector at the

left-hand end of the ignition module **(see illustration)**.

3 Undo the retaining bolts, and lift the module up and out of position **(see illustration)**. If the module proves reluctant to separate from the spark plugs, insert two long 8 mm bolts into the threaded holes in the top of the module, and pull up on the bolts to free the module from the plugs.

4 With the module removed, check the condition of the sealing grommets and renew if necessary **(see illustration)**.

Refitting

5 Refitting is the reversal of removal, tightening the retaining bolts to the specified torque.

4 Ignition timing – checking and adjustment

1 Due to the nature of the ignition system, the ignition timing is constantly being monitored and adjusted by the engine management ECU.

2 The only way in which the ignition timing can be checked is by using specialist diagnostic test equipment, connected to the engine management system diagnostic socket. No adjustment of the ignition timing is possible. Should the ignition timing be incorrect, then a fault is likely to be present in the engine management system.

5 Knock sensor – removal and refitting

1 Refer to the procedures contained in Chapter 4A, Section 11.

Chapter 6
Clutch

Contents

Degrees of difficulty

Easy, suitable for novice with little experience	Fairly easy, suitable for beginner with some experience	Fairly difficult, suitable for competent DIY mechanic	Difficult, suitable for experienced DIY mechanic	Very difficult, suitable for expert DIY or professional

Specifications

Type . . . . Single dry plate with diaphragm spring, hydraulically-operated

Friction disc
Diameter . . . . 240 mm

Torque wrench settings	Nm	lbf ft
Clutch master cylinder retaining nuts.	22	16
Pressure plate retaining bolts*:		
M7 bolts	15	11
M8 bolts	22	16
1.6 litre diesel	28	21
2.0 litre diesel (LFS)	25	18

*Use new bolts

1 General Information

1 The clutch consists of a friction disc, a pressure plate assembly, and the hydraulic release cylinder (which incorporates the release bearing); all of these components are contained in the large cast-aluminium alloy bellhousing, sandwiched between the engine and the transmission.

2 The friction disc is fitted between the engine flywheel and the clutch pressure plate, and is allowed to slide on the transmission input shaft splines.

3 The pressure plate assembly is bolted to the engine flywheel. When the engine is running, drive is transmitted from the crankshaft, via the flywheel, to the friction disc (these components being clamped securely together by the pressure plate assembly) and from the friction disc to the transmission input shaft.

4 To interrupt the drive, the spring pressure must be relaxed. This is achieved using a hydraulic release mechanism which consists of the master cylinder, the release cylinder and the pipe/hose linking the two components. Depressing the pedal pushes on the master cylinder pushrod which hydraulically forces the release cylinder piston against the pressure plate spring fingers. This causes the springs to deform and releases the clamping force on the friction disc.

5 The clutch is self-adjusting and requires no manual adjustment.

2 Clutch hydraulic system – bleeding

Warning: Hydraulic fluid is poisonous; wash off immediately and thoroughly in the case of skin contact, and seek immediate medical advice if any fluid is swallowed or gets into the eyes. Certain types of hydraulic fluid are flammable, and may ignite when allowed into contact with hot components; when servicing any hydraulic system, it is safest to assume that the fluid is flammable, and to take precautions against the risk of fire as though it is petrol that is being handled. Hydraulic fluid is also an

2.8 Clutch bleed screw

effective paint stripper, and will attack plastics; if any is spilt, it should be washed off immediately, using copious quantities of fresh water. Finally, it is hygroscopic (it absorbs moisture from the air) – old fluid may be contaminated and unfit for further use. When topping-up or renewing the fluid, always use the recommended type, and ensure that it comes from a freshly-opened sealed container.

General information

1 The correct operation of any hydraulic system is only possible after removing all air from the components and circuit; this is achieved by bleeding the system.

2 The manufacturer's stipulate that the system must be initially bled by the 'back-bleeding' method using Vauxhall/Opel special bleeding equipment. This entails connecting a pressure bleeding unit containing fresh brake fluid, to the release cylinder bleed screw, with a collecting vessel connected to the brake fluid master cylinder reservoir. The pressure bleeding unit is then switched on, the bleed screw is opened and hydraulic fluid is delivered under pressure, backwards, to be expelled from the reservoir into the collecting vessel. Final bleeding is then carried out in the conventional way.

3 In practice, this method would normally only be required if new hydraulic components have been fitted, or if the system has been completely drained of hydraulic fluid. If the system has only been disconnected to allow component removal and refitting procedures to be carried out, such as removal and refitting of the transmission (for example for clutch replacement) or engine removal and refitting, then it is quite likely that normal bleeding will be sufficient.

4 Our advice would therefore be as follows:

a) *If the hydraulic system has only been partially disconnected, try bleeding by the conventional methods described in paragraphs 10 to 15, or 16 to 19.*

b) *If the hydraulic system has been completely drained and new components have been fitted, try bleeding by using the pressure bleeding method described in paragraphs 20 to 22.*

c) *If the above methods fail to produce a firm*

pedal on completion, it will be necessary to 'back-bleed' the system using Vauxhall/Opel bleeding equipment, or suitable alternative equipment as described in paragraphs 23 to 28.

5 During the bleeding procedure, add only clean, unused hydraulic fluid of the recommended type; never re-use fluid that has already been bled from the system. Ensure that sufficient fluid is available before starting work.

6 If there is any possibility of incorrect fluid being already in the system, the hydraulic circuit must be flushed completely with uncontaminated, correct fluid.

7 If hydraulic fluid has been lost from the system, or air has entered because of a leak, ensure that the fault is cured before continuing further.

8 The bleed screw is located in the hose end fitting which is situated on the top of the transmission housing **(see illustration)**. On some models access to the bleed screw is limited and it may be necessary to jack up the front of the vehicle and support it on axle stands so that the screw can be reached from below, or remove the battery and battery box as described in Chapter 5A, Section 4, so that the screw can be reached from above.

9 Check that all pipes and hoses are secure, unions tight and the bleed screw is closed. Clean any dirt from around the bleed screw.

Bleeding procedure

Conventional method

10 Collect a clean glass jar, a suitable length of plastic or rubber tubing which is a tight fit over the bleed screw, and a ring spanner to fit the screw. The help of an assistant will also be required.

11 Unscrew the master cylinder fluid reservoir cap (the clutch shares the same fluid reservoir as the braking system), and top the master cylinder reservoir up to the upper (MAX) level line. Ensure that the fluid level is maintained at least above the lower level line in the reservoir throughout the procedure.

12 Remove the dust cap from the bleed screw. Fit the spanner and tube to the screw, place the other end of the tube in the jar, and pour in sufficient fluid to cover the end of the tube.

13 Have the assistant fully depress the clutch pedal several times to build-up pressure, then maintain it on the final down stroke.

14 While pedal pressure is maintained, unscrew the bleed screw (approximately one turn) and allow the compressed fluid and air to flow into the jar. The assistant should maintain pedal pressure and should not release it until instructed to do so. When the flow stops, tighten the bleed screw again, have the assistant release the pedal slowly, and recheck the reservoir fluid level.

15 Repeat the steps given in paragraphs 13 and 14 until the fluid emerging from the bleed screw is free from air bubbles. If the master

cylinder has been drained and refilled allow approximately five seconds between cycles for the master cylinder passages to refill.

Conventional method using a one-way valve kit

16 As their name implies, these kits consist of a length of tubing with a one-way valve fitted, to prevent expelled air and fluid being drawn back into the system; some kits include a translucent container, which can be positioned so that the air bubbles can be more easily seen flowing from the end of the tube.

17 The kit is connected to the bleed screw, which is then opened.

18 The user returns to the driver's seat, depresses the clutch pedal with a smooth, steady stroke, and slowly releases it; this is repeated until the expelled fluid is clear of air bubbles.

19 Note that these kits simplify work so much that it is easy to forget the clutch fluid reservoir level; ensure that this is maintained at least above the lower level line at all times.

Pressure-bleeding method

20 These kits are usually operated by the reservoir of pressurised air contained in the spare tyre. However, note that it will probably be necessary to reduce the pressure to a lower level than normal; refer to the instructions supplied with the kit.

21 By connecting a pressurised, fluid-filled container to the clutch fluid reservoir, bleeding can be carried out simply by opening the bleed screw and allowing the fluid to flow out until no more air bubbles can be seen in the expelled fluid.

22 This method has the advantage that the large reservoir of fluid provides an additional safeguard against air being drawn into the system during bleeding.

'Back-bleeding' method

23 The following procedure describes the bleeding method using Vauxhall/Opel equipment. Alternative equipment is available and should be used in accordance with the maker's instructions.

24 Connect the pressure hose of the bleeding kit (DT-6174-A) to the bleed screw located in the hose end fitting situated on the top of the transmission housing **(see illustration 2.8)**. Connect the other end of the hose to a suitable pressure bleeding device set to operate at approximately 2.0 bar.

25 Attach the cap of the bleeding kit to the master cylinder reservoir, and place the hose in a collecting vessel.

26 Switch on the pressure bleeding equipment, open the bleed screw, and allow fresh hydraulic fluid to flow from the pressure bleeding unit, through the system and out through the top of the reservoir and into the collecting vessel. When fluid, free from air bubbles appears in the reservoir, close the bleed screw and switch off the bleeding equipment.

3.5 Extract the retaining clip and disconnect the hydraulic pipe from the master cylinder connector

3.6 Fluid supply hose connection at the brake/clutch hydraulic fluid reservoir

3.11 Clutch master cylinder retaining nuts

27 Disconnect the bleeding equipment from the bleed screw and reservoir.

28 Carry out a final conventional bleeding procedure as described in paragraphs 10 to 15, or 16 to 19.

All methods

29 When bleeding is complete, no more bubbles appear and correct pedal feel is restored, tighten the bleed screw securely (do not overtighten). Remove the tube and spanner, and wash off any spilt fluid. Refit the dust cap to the bleed screw.

30 Check the hydraulic fluid level in the master cylinder reservoir, and top-up if necessary (see *Weekly checks*).

31 Discard any hydraulic fluid that has been bled from the system; it will not be fit for re-use.

32 Check the operation of the clutch pedal. If the clutch is still not operating correctly, air must still be present in the system, and further bleeding is required. Failure to bleed satisfactorily after a reasonable repetition of the bleeding procedure may be due to worn master cylinder/release cylinder seals.

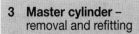

3 Master cylinder – removal and refitting

Removal

1 Where fitted, remove the plastic cover over the top of the engine.

2 Release the clutch hydraulic pipe from the support clip(s) on the bulkhead.

3 Unscrew the brake/clutch hydraulic fluid reservoir filler cap, and top-up the reservoir to the MAX mark (see *Weekly checks*). Place a piece of polythene over the filler neck, and secure the polythene with the filler cap. This will minimise brake fluid loss during subsequent operations.

4 Remove all traces of dirt from the outside of the master cylinder and the brake/clutch hydraulic fluid reservoir, then position some cloth beneath the cylinder to catch any spilt fluid.

5 Extract the retaining clip and disconnect the hydraulic pipe from the connector on the end of the master cylinder (see illustration).

Plug the pipe end and master cylinder port to minimise fluid loss and prevent the entry of dirt.

6 Release the retaining clip (where fitted) and disconnect the fluid supply hose from the brake/clutch hydraulic fluid reservoir (see illustration).

7 From inside the car, remove the facia right-hand lower trim panel as described in Chapter 11, Section 30.

8 Disconnect the wiring connector, undo the retaining bolt, and remove the clutch switch from the pedal mounting bracket.

9 Release the return spring from the underside of the clutch pedal.

10 Separate the clutch pedal from the master cylinder piston rod by releasing the retaining clip at the pedal. Vauxhall technicians use a special tool to do this, however, the clip may be released by pressing the retaining tabs together using screwdrivers, while at the same time pulling the clutch pedal rearwards. **Note:** *Do not remove the clip from the master cylinder piston rod, just release it from the pedal.*

11 Unscrew the two nuts securing the master cylinder to the bulkhead, then return to the engine compartment and remove the master cylinder from the vehicle (see illustration). If the master cylinder is faulty it must be renewed; overhaul of the unit is not possible.

Refitting

12 Manoeuvre the master cylinder into position whilst ensuring that the piston rod and its retaining clip align correctly with the pedal. Fit the two master cylinder retaining nuts and tighten them to the specified torque.

13 Push the master cylinder piston rod retaining clip into the clutch pedal, ensuring that the two lugs on the clip fully engage.

14 Refit the clutch switch to the pedal mounting bracket.

15 Reposition the return spring to the underside of the clutch pedal.

16 Refit the facia lower trim panel as described in Chapter 11, Section 30.

17 Connect the fluid supply hose to the master cylinder and, where applicable, secure with the retaining clip.

18 Press the hydraulic pipe back into the connector on the end of the master cylinder and refit the retaining clip. Ensure that the

retaining clip engages fully and the pipe is securely retained. Secure the pipe with the support clip(s).

19 Bleed the clutch hydraulic system as described in Section 2, then refit the engine cover (where applicable).

4 Release cylinder – removal and refitting

Note: *Due to the amount of work necessary to remove and refit clutch components, it is usually considered good practice to renew the clutch friction disc, pressure plate assembly and release cylinder as a matched set, even if only one of these is actually worn enough to require renewal. It is also worth considering the renewal of the clutch components on a preventative basis if the engine and/or transmission have been removed for some other reason.*

Note: *Refer to the warning concerning the dangers of asbestos dust at the beginning of Section 6.*

Petrol engine models

Removal

1 Unless the complete engine/transmission unit is to be removed from the car and separated for major overhaul (see Chapter 2E, Section 4), the clutch release cylinder can be reached by removing the transmission only, as described in Chapter 7A, Section 8.

2 Depress the two tabs on the hydraulic pipe fastening sleeve and draw the sleeve out of the transmission slightly.

3 Depress the two lugs on the hydraulic pipe retainer and remove the retainer from the transmission.

4 Unscrew the three retaining bolts and slide the release cylinder off from the transmission input shaft. Whilst the cylinder is removed, take care not to allow any debris to enter the transmission unit.

5 The release cylinder is a sealed unit and cannot be overhauled. If the cylinder seals are leaking or the release bearing is noisy or rough in operation, then the complete unit must be renewed.

4.13 Clutch release cylinder hydraulic pipe union nut

Refitting

6 Ensure the release cylinder and transmission mating surfaces are clean and dry.

7 Lubricate the release cylinder seal with a smear of transmission oil then carefully ease the cylinder along the input shaft and into position.

8 Locate the hydraulic pipe in position and refit the retainer and fastening sleeve.

9 Refit the release cylinder retaining bolts and tighten them securely.

10 Refit the transmission unit as described in Chapter 7A, Section 8.

11 Bleed the clutch hydraulic system as described in Section 2.

Diesel engine models

Removal

12 Unless the complete engine/transmission unit is to be removed from the car and separated for major overhaul (see Chapter 2E, Section 4), the clutch release cylinder can be reached by removing the transmission only, as described in Chapter 7A, Section 8.

13 Wipe clean the outside of the release cylinder then slacken the union nut and disconnect the hydraulic pipe **(see illustration)**. Wipe up any spilt fluid with a clean cloth.

14 Unscrew the three retaining bolts and slide the release cylinder off from the transmission input shaft **(see illustration)**. Remove the sealing ring which is fitted between the cylinder and transmission housing and discard it; a new one must be used on refitting. Whilst

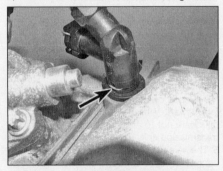

4.16 Extract the retaining clip and remove the hydraulic hose end fitting from the fastening sleeve

4.14 Clutch release cylinder retaining bolts

the cylinder is removed, take care not to allow any debris to enter the transmission unit.

15 The release cylinder is a sealed unit and cannot be overhauled. If the cylinder seals are leaking or the release bearing is noisy or rough in operation, then the complete unit must be renewed.

16 To remove the hydraulic pipe, extract the retaining clip and remove the hydraulic hose end fitting from the fastening sleeve on top of the transmission housing **(see illustration)**. Gently squeeze the legs of the retaining clip together and re-insert the clip back into position in the end fitting.

17 Using a small screwdriver, carefully spread the retaining lugs of the fastening sleeve to release the hydraulic pipe connection, and remove the pipe from inside the transmission housing. Check the condition of the sealing ring on the hydraulic pipe and renew if necessary.

18 If required, the fastening sleeve can be removed by squeezing the lower retaining lugs together with pointed-nose pliers, then withdrawing the sleeve upwards and out of the transmission. Note that if the fastening sleeve is removed, a new one must be obtained for refitting.

Refitting

19 Ensure the release cylinder and transmission mating surfaces are clean and dry and fit the new sealing ring to the transmission recess.

20 Lubricate the release cylinder seal with a smear of transmission oil then carefully

4.21 Make sure the lug on the fastening sleeve is located correctly in the transmission housing

ease the cylinder along the input shaft and into position. Ensure the sealing ring is still correctly seated in its groove then refit the release cylinder retaining bolts and tighten them securely.

21 If removed, fit the new fastening sleeve, engaging the lug on the sleeve with the cut-out in the housing **(see illustration)**. Ensure that the sleeve can be felt to positively lock in position.

22 Insert the hydraulic pipe into the fastening sleeve until the end fitting can be felt to positively lock in position.

23 Reconnect the hydraulic pipe to the release cylinder, tightening its union nut securely.

24 Refit the hydraulic hose end fitting to the fastening sleeve ensuring that it is positively retained by its clip.

25 Refit the transmission unit as described in Chapter 7A, Section 8.

26 Bleed the clutch hydraulic system as described in Section 2.

---

5 Clutch pedal – removal and refitting

1 The clutch pedal is an integral part of the brake pedal and mounting bracket assembly and cannot be individually removed. Removal and refitting details for the brake pedal and mounting bracket assembly are contained in Chapter 9, Section 10.

---

6 Clutch assembly – removal, inspection and refitting

⚠ **Warning: Dust created by clutch wear and deposited on the clutch components may contain asbestos, which is a health hazard. DO NOT blow it out with compressed air, or inhale any of it. DO NOT use petrol or petroleum-based solvents to clean off the dust. Brake system cleaner or methylated spirit should be used to flush the dust into a suitable receptacle. After the clutch components are wiped clean with rags, dispose of the contaminated rags and cleaner in a sealed, marked container.**

Note: *To prevent possible damage to the ends of the pressure plate diaphragm spring fingers, Vauxhall/Opel recommend the use of a special jig (DT-6263) to remove the clutch assembly, however, with care it is possible to carry out the work without the jig.*

Removal

1 Unless the complete engine/transmission unit is to be removed from the car and separated for major overhaul (see Chapter 2E, Section 4), the clutch can be reached by removing the transmission as described in Chapter 7A, Section 8.

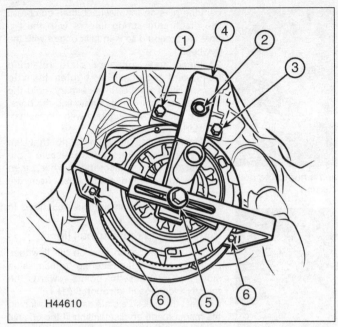

6.3a Vauxhall special jig DT-6263 for removing the clutch pressure plate and friction disc

1, 3 and 6   Bolts securing the jig to the engine
2 and 5   Bolts for adjusting the jig to the centre of the crankshaft
4   Special tool

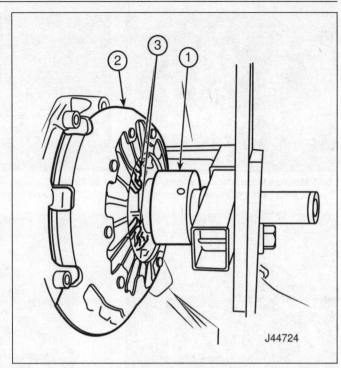

6.3b Thrust piece (1) in contact with the diaphragm spring fingers (3) of the pressure plate (2)

2 Before disturbing the clutch, use chalk or a marker pen to mark the relationship of the pressure plate assembly to the flywheel.

3 At this stage, Vauxhall technicians fit the special jig DT-6263 to the rear of the engine and compress the diaphragm spring fingers until the friction disc is released **(see illustrations)**. The pressure plate mounting bolts are then unscrewed, and the jig spindle backed off.

4 If the jig is not available, progressively unscrew the pressure plate retaining bolts in diagonal sequence by half a turn at a time, until spring pressure is released and the bolts can be unscrewed by hand.

5 Remove the pressure plate assembly and collect the friction disc, noting which way round the disc is fitted. It is recommended that new pressure plate retaining bolts are obtained.

Inspection

Note: *Due to the amount of work necessary to remove and refit clutch components, it is usually considered good practice to renew the clutch friction disc, pressure plate assembly and release cylinder as a matched set, even if only one of these is actually worn enough to require renewal. It is also worth considering the renewal of the clutch components on a preventative basis if the engine and/or trans-mission have been removed for some other reason.*

6 When cleaning clutch components, read first the warning at the beginning of this Section; remove dust using a clean, dry cloth, and working in a well-ventilated atmosphere.

7 Check the friction disc facings for signs of wear, damage or oil contamination. If the friction material is cracked, burnt, scored or damaged, or if it is contaminated with oil or grease (shown by shiny black patches), the friction disc must be renewed.

8 If the friction material is still serviceable, check that the centre boss splines are unworn, that the torsion springs are in good condition and securely fastened, and that all the rivets are tight. If any wear or damage is found, the friction disc must be renewed.

9 If the friction material is fouled with oil, this must be due to an oil leak from the crankshaft oil seal, from the sump-to-cylinder block joint, or from the release cylinder assembly (either the main seal or the sealing ring). Renew the crankshaft oil seal or repair the sump joint as described in the Chapter 2A or 2C, before installing the new friction disc. The clutch release cylinder is covered in Section 4.

10 Check the pressure plate assembly for obvious signs of wear or damage; shake it to check for loose rivets, or worn or damaged fulcrum rings, and check that the drive straps securing the pressure plate to the cover do not show signs of overheating (such as a deep yellow or blue discoloration). If the diaphragm spring is worn or damaged, or if its pressure is in any way suspect, the pressure plate assembly should be renewed.

11 Examine the machined bearing surfaces of the pressure plate and of the flywheel; they should be clean, completely flat, and free from scratches or scoring. If either is discoloured from excessive heat, or shows signs of cracks, it should be renewed – although minor

damage of this nature can sometimes be polished away using emery paper.

12 Check that the release cylinder bearing rotates smoothly and easily, with no sign of noise or roughness. Also check that the surface itself is smooth and unworn, with no signs of cracks, pitting or scoring. If there is any doubt about its condition, the clutch release cylinder should be renewed (it is not possible to renew the bearing separately).

Refitting

13 On diesel engine models, the clutch pressure plate is unusual, as there is a pre-adjustment mechanism to compensate for wear in the friction disc (this is termed by Vauxhall/Opel as a self-adjusting clutch (SAC), which is slightly ambiguous as all clutches fitted to these models are essentially self-adjusting). However, this mechanism must be reset before refitting the pressure plate. A new plate may be supplied preset, in which case this procedure can be ignored.

14 A large diameter bolt (M14 at least) long enough to pass through the pressure plate, a matching nut, and several large diameter washers, will be needed for this procedure. Mount the bolt head in the jaws of a sturdy bench vice, with one large washer fitted.

15 Offer the plate over the bolt, friction disc surface facing down, and locate it centrally over the bolt and washer – the washer should bear on the centre hub **(see illustration)**.

16 Fit several further large washers over the bolt, so that they bear on the ends of the spring fingers, then add the nut and tighten by hand to locate the washers **(see illustration)**.

6.15 Mount a large bolt and washer into a vice, then fit the pressure plate over it

6.16 Fit large washers and a nut to the bolt and hand-tighten

6.17a Tighten the nut until the spring adjuster is free to turn ...

6.17b ... then open up the jaws of suitable pliers to compress the springs

17 The purpose of the procedure is to turn the plate's internal adjuster disc so that the small coil springs visible on the plate's outer surface are fully compressed. Tighten the nut just fitted until the adjuster disc is free to turn. Using a pair of thin-nosed, or circlip pliers, in one of the windows in the top surface, open the jaws of the pliers to turn the adjuster disc anti-clockwise, so that the springs are fully compressed **(see illustrations)**.

18 Hold the pliers in this position, then unscrew the centre nut. Once the nut is released, the adjuster disc will be gripped in position, and the pliers can be removed. Take the pressure plate from the vice, and it is ready to fit.

19 On reassembly, ensure that the friction surfaces of the flywheel and pressure plate are completely clean, smooth, and free from oil or grease. Use solvent to remove any protective grease from new components.

20 Lightly grease the teeth of the friction disc hub with high melting-point grease. Do not apply too much, otherwise it may eventually contaminate the friction disc linings.

Using the Vauxhall jig

21 Fit the special Vauxhall guide bush to the centre of the crankshaft, and locate the friction disc on it, making sure that the lettering 'transmission side' or 'Getriebeseite' points towards the transmission **(see illustration)**.

22 Locate the pressure plate on the special

centring pins on the flywheel, then compress the diaphragm spring fingers with the jig, until the friction disc is in full contact with the flywheel.

23 Insert new pressure plate retaining bolts, and progressively tighten them to the specified torque. If necessary, hold the flywheel stationary while tightening the bolts, using a screwdriver engaged with the teeth of the starter ring gear.

24 Back off the jig spindle so that the diaphragm spring forces the pressure plate against the friction disc and flywheel, then remove the jig and guide bush from the engine.

25 Refit the transmission as described in Chapter 7A, Section 8.

Without using the Vauxhall jig

26 Locate the friction disc on the flywheel, making sure that the lettering 'transmission side' or 'Getriebeseite' points towards the transmission **(see illustration 6.21)**.

27 Refit the pressure plate assembly, aligning the marks made on dismantling (if the original pressure plate is re-used). Fit new pressure plate bolts, but tighten them only finger-tight so that the friction disc can still be moved **(see illustration)**.

28 The friction disc must now be centralised so that, when the transmission is refitted, its input shaft will pass through the splines at the centre of the friction disc.

29 Centralisation can be achieved by passing a screwdriver or other long bar through the friction disc and into the hole in the crankshaft. The friction disc can then be moved around until it is centred on the crankshaft hole. Alternatively, a clutch-aligning tool can be used to eliminate the guesswork; these can be obtained from most accessory shops **(see illustration)**.

30 When the friction disc is centralised, tighten the pressure plate bolts evenly and in a diagonal sequence to the specified torque setting.

31 Refit the transmission as described in Chapter 7A, Section 8.

6.21 The lettering 'transmission side' or 'Getriebeseite' on the friction disc must point towards the transmission

6.27 Fit the pressure plate assembly over the friction disc

6.29 Centralise the friction disc using a clutch aligning tool or similar

Chapter 7 Part A
Manual transmission

Contents

Degrees of difficulty

Easy, suitable for novice with little experience	**Fairly easy,** suitable for beginner with some experience	**Fairly difficult,** suitable for competent DIY mechanic	**Difficult,** suitable for experienced DIY mechanic	**Very difficult,** suitable for expert DIY or professional

Specifications

General

Type	Six forward speeds and reverse. Synchromesh on all forward speeds and reverse
Manufacturer's designation:	
Petrol engine models	M32
Diesel engine models	M32 or F40

Lubrication

Lubricant type	See *Lubricants and fluids*
Lubricant capacity	See Chapter 1A or 1B

Torque wrench settings

	Nm	lbf ft
Engine/transmission mountings.	See Chapter 2B. 2C or 2D Specifications	
Engine-to-transmission bolts	See Chapter 2B. 2C or 2D Specifications	
Gearchange lever assembly mounting bolts	10	7
Oil drain plug:		
M32 transmissions	20	15
F40 transmissions	30	22
Oil filler plug:		
M32 transmissions	30	22
F40 transmissions	30	22
Oil seal carrier-to-differential (M32 transmissions).	20	15
Reversing light switch	20	15
Roadwheel nuts	150	111

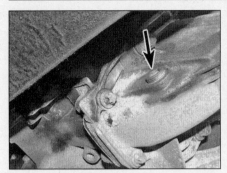

2.3a Transmission oil drain plug – M32 transmissions

2.3b Transmission oil drain plug – F40 transmissions

2.6 Transmission oil filler plug

1 General Information

1 The transmission is contained in a cast-aluminium alloy casing bolted to the engine's left-hand end, and consists of the gearbox and final drive differential – often called a transaxle.

2 Drive is transmitted from the crankshaft via the clutch to the input shaft, which has a splined extension to accept the clutch friction disc, and rotates in tapered roller bearings. From the input shaft, drive is transmitted to the upper and lower main shafts, which also rotate in tapered roller bearings. From the lower main shaft, the drive is transmitted to the differential crown-wheel, which rotates with the differential case and planetary gears, thus driving the sun gears and driveshafts. The rotation of the planetary gears on their shaft allows the inner roadwheel to rotate at a slower speed than the outer roadwheel when the car is cornering.

3 The input shaft and main shafts are arranged side-by-side, so that their gear pinion teeth are in constant mesh. In the neutral position, the main shaft gear pinions rotate freely, so that drive cannot be transmitted to the crownwheel.

4 Gear selection is via a floor-mounted lever and cable-operated selector linkage mechanism. The selector linkage causes the appropriate selector fork to move its

respective synchro-sleeve along the shaft, to lock the gear pinion to the synchro-hub. Since the synchro-hubs are splined to the main shafts, this locks the pinion to the shaft, so that drive can be transmitted. To ensure that gearchanging can be made quickly and quietly, a synchromesh system is fitted to all gears, consisting of baulk rings and spring-loaded fingers, as well as the gear pinions and synchro-hubs. The synchro-mesh cones are formed on the mating faces of the baulk rings and gear pinions.

2 Transmission oil – draining and refilling

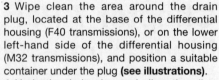

1 This operation is much more efficient if the car is first taken on a journey of sufficient length to warm the engine/transmission up to normal operating temperature.
Caution: Caution: If the procedure is to be carried out on a hot transmission unit, take care not to burn yourself on the hot exhaust or the transmission/engine unit.

2 Position the vehicle over an inspection pit, on vehicle ramps, or jack it up and support it securely on axle stands (see *Jacking and vehicle support*), but make sure that it is level. On diesel engine models, remove the engine undertray as described in Chapter 11, Section 24.

Draining

Note: *A new transmission oil drain plug will be required.*

3 Wipe clean the area around the drain plug, located at the base of the differential housing (F40 transmissions), or on the lower left-hand side of the differential housing (M32 transmissions), and position a suitable container under the plug **(see illustrations)**.
4 Undo the drain plug and allow the oil to drain.
5 Once the oil has finished draining, fit the new drain plug and tighten the plug to the specified torque.

Refilling

6 The transmission is refilled via the oil filler plug on the top of the casing **(see illustration)**. To gain access to the plug, remove the battery, battery box and battery tray as described in Chapter 5A, Section 4.
7 Wipe clean the area around the plug and unscrew it. Refill the transmission with *exactly* 2.2 litres (M32 transmissions) or 1.8 litres (F40 transmissions) of the specified grade of oil given in *Lubricants and fluids,* then refit and tighten the oil filler plug to the specified torque (see illustration).
8 Refit the engine undertray (where applicable), then lower the vehicle to the ground.
9 Refit the battery tray, battery box and battery as described in Chapter 5A, Section 4.

3 Selector cables – adjustment

Note: *A 5 mm drill bit or dowel rod will be required to carry out this procedure.*
1 Position the gear lever in the 'neutral' position.
2 Remove the centre console as described in Chapter 11, Section 29.
3 Push the black sliding collars on the end of each selector cable back against spring pressure until they lock in the released position **(see illustration)**.
4 Using a screwdriver, depress the two tabs and push the blue gear lever locking ring upwards **(see illustration)**. Lift the gear lever knob up and off the gear lever.
5 Turn the gear lever knob through 180° and place it back on the gear lever. Slide the knob down the lever and engage the two lugs on

2.7 Use a graduated container to fill the transmission with the correct quantity of oil

3.3 Push the black sliding collars on the selector cables, against spring pressure, until they lock in the released position

the reverse detent block with the two holes in the gear lever housing **(see illustration)**. The gear lever is now locked in the adjustment position.

6 On diesel engine models, remove the engine management ECU from the battery box with reference to the procedures contained in Chapter 4B, Section 8. Place the ECU to one side without disconnecting the wiring connectors.

7 Set the gearchange selector on the transmission to the 'neutral' position. Pull the selector up and lock it in the adjustment position by inserting a 5 mm drill bit or dowel rod through the hole in the side of the housing **(see illustration)**. Ensure that the drill bit or dowel rod fully engages with the selector.

8 Working back inside the car, release the black sliding collars on the selector cables by pressing the blue release button on the cable end fitting **(see illustration)**. There should be an audible click as the sliding collars release, indicating that the cables are now locked.

9 Lift off the gear lever, turn it back through 180° to its original position and refit it to the gear lever. Push the knob down as far as it will go, then lock it in place by pushing the blue locking ring down.

10 Remove the drill bit or dowel rod used to lock the gearchange selector on the transmission.

11 Check the gearchange mechanism for correct operation and if necessary, repeat the adjustment procedure.

12 When all is satisfactory, refit the centre console as described in Chapter 11, Section 29.

13 On diesel engine models, refit the engine management ECU to the battery tray.

4 Selector cables – removal and refitting

Removal

1 Remove the battery and battery tray as described in Chapter 5A, Section 4.

2 Working in the engine compartment, note the fitted locations of the cables at their transmission attachments.

3 Using a large screwdriver, prise the inner cable end fittings from the transmission selector lever ballpins **(see illustrations)**.

4 Push the retaining sleeves toward the rear of the car and detach the outer cables from the mounting bracket on the transmission **(see illustration)**.

5 Release the rubber grommet at the cable entry point on the engine compartment bulkhead.

6 Remove the centre console as described in Chapter 11, Section 29.

7 Push the black sliding collars on the end of each selector cable back against spring pressure until they lock in the released position **(see illustration 3.3)**.

8 Note the fitted locations of the two cables,

then depress the lugs on the sides of the outer cable ends and lift the outer cables from the gear lever housing **(see illustration)**.

9 Move the two selector cables forward to disengage the inner cables from the gear lever clamping pieces.

3.4 Depress the two tabs and push the blue gear lever locking ring upwards

3.5 Engage the two lugs on the reverse detent block with the two holes in the gear lever housing

3.7 Using a 5 mm drill bit to lock the selector mechanism in the adjustment position

3.8 Press the blue release buttons to release the black sliding collars on the selector cables

4.3a Prise the inner cable end fittings from the transmission selector lever ballpins ...

4.3b ... then lift the end fittings off the ballpins

4.4 Push the retaining sleeves rearward and detach the outer cables from the transmission bracket

4.8 Depress the lugs on the sides of the outer cable ends and lift the outer cables from the gear lever housing

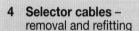

5.4 Release the wiring harness retaining clips from the side of the gear lever housing base

5.5a Undo the two retaining bolts each side ...

5.5b ... and lift the gear lever housing from the floor

10 Pull the two cables (complete with grommet) out of the bulkhead and into the engine compartment.

Refitting

11 Push the selector cables through the bulkhead from the engine compartment and locate the rubber grommet back into position in the bulkhead. Ensure that the cable with the white markings is uppermost.

12 Engage the selector inner cables with the clamping pieces on the gear lever, then refit the outer cables to the gear lever housing. Do not lock the clamping pieces at this stage.

13 Refit the outer cables to the mounting bracket on the transmission.

14 Engage the inner cable end fittings with the transmission selector lever ballpins, squeezing them together with pliers if necessary.

15 Carry out the selector cable adjustment procedure, as described in Section 3.

16 Refit the centre console as described in Chapter 11, Section 29.

17 Refit the battery tray and battery as described in Chapter 5A, Section 4.

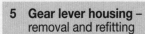

5 Gear lever housing – removal and refitting

Removal

1 Remove the centre console as described in Chapter 11, Section 29.

2 Push the black sliding collars on the end of each selector cable back against spring pressure until they lock in the released position **(see illustration 3.3)**.

3 Note the fitted locations of the two cables, then depress the lugs on the sides of the outer cable ends and lift the outer cables from the gear lever housing **(see illustration 4.8)**.

4 Release the wiring harness retaining clips from the side of the gear lever housing base **(see illustration)**.

5 Undo the four retaining bolts and lift the gear lever housing from the floor **(see illustrations)**.

Refitting

6 Position the gear lever housing on the floor, insert the securing bolts and tighten them securely.

7 Engage the selector inner cables with the clamping pieces, then refit the outer cables to the gear lever housing. Do not lock the clamping pieces at this stage.

8 Carry out the selector cable adjustment procedure, as described in Section 3.

9 Refit the centre console as described in Chapter 11, Section 29.

6 Oil seals – renewal

Driveshaft oil seals

F40 transmissions

1 Firmly apply the handbrake, then jack up the front of the car and support it securely on axle stands (see *Jacking and vehicle support*).

2 Drain the transmission oil as described in Section 2.

3 Remove the driveshaft/intermediate shaft as described in Chapter 8, Section 2.

4 Note the correct fitted depth of the seal in its housing then carefully prise it out of position using a large flat-bladed screwdriver **(see illustration)**.

5 Remove all traces of dirt from the area around the oil seal aperture, then lubricate the

outer lip of the new oil seal with transmission oil. Ensure the seal is correctly positioned, with its sealing lip facing inwards, and tap it squarely into position, using a suitable tubular drift (such as a socket) which bears only on the hard outer edge of the seal **(see illustration)**. Ensure the seal is fitted at the same depth in its housing that the original was.

6 Refit the driveshaft/intermediate shaft as described in Chapter 8, Section 2 and 3.

7 Refill the transmission with the specified type and amount of oil, as described in Section 2.

M32 transmissions – right-hand oil seal

8 Proceed as described above in paragraphs 1 to 7.

M32 transmissions – left-hand oil seal

Note: *A hydraulic press, together with tubes and mandrels of suitable diameters will be needed for this operation.*

9 Firmly apply the handbrake, then jack up the front of the car and support it securely on axle stands (see *Jacking and vehicle support*).

10 Drain the transmission oil as described in Section 2.

11 Remove the driveshaft as described in Chapter 8, Section 2.

12 Undo the four bolts and remove the oil seal carrier from the side of the differential housing.

13 Place the oil seal carrier on the press bed with its outer surface facing down. Using a

6.4 Prising out a driveshaft oil seal

6.5 Fitting a new driveshaft oil seal using a socket as a tubular drift

suitable mandrel, press the oil seal out of the carrier.

14 Using a small screwdriver, remove the sealing O-ring from the oil seal carrier.

15 Support the inner surface of the oil seal carrier on the press bed. Lubricate the new oil seal with transmission oil, then press it fully into position in the carrier using a suitable tube which bears only on the hard outer edge of the seal.

16 Fit a new O-ring to the oil seal carrier, then refit the carrier to the differential housing, tightening the retaining bolts to the specified torque.

17 Refit the driveshaft as described in Chapter 8, Section 2.

18 Refill the transmission with the specified type and amount of oil, as described in Section 2.

Input shaft oil seal

19 The input shaft oil seal is an integral part of the clutch release cylinder; if the seal is leaking the complete release cylinder assembly must be renewed. Before condemning the release cylinder, check that the leak is not coming from the sealing ring which is fitted between the cylinder and the transmission housing; the sealing ring can be renewed once the release cylinder assembly has been removed. Refer to Chapter 6, Section 6 for removal and refitting details.

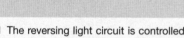

7 Reversing light switch –
testing, removal and refitting

1 The reversing light circuit is controlled by a plunger-type switch screwed into the front of the transmission casing **(see illustration)**.

Testing

2 If a fault develops in the circuit, first ensure that the circuit fuse has not blown and that the reversing light bulbs are sound.

3 To test the switch, disconnect the wiring connector. Use a multimeter (set to the resistance function) or a battery-and-bulb test circuit to check that there is continuity between the switch terminals only when reverse gear is selected. If this is not the case, and there are no obvious breaks or other damage to the wires, the switch is faulty, and must be renewed.

Removal

4 Disconnect the wiring connector, then unscrew the switch and remove it from the transmission casing along with its sealing washer.

Refitting

5 Fit a new sealing washer to the switch, then screw it back into position in the transmission casing and tighten it to the specified torque. Reconnect the wiring connector, then test the operation of the circuit.

8 Transmission –
removal and refitting

Removal

1 Apply the handbrake, then jack up the front of the vehicle and support it on axle stands (see *Jacking and vehicle support*). Allow sufficient working room to remove the transmission from under the left-hand side of the engine compartment. Remove both front roadwheels. Also remove the engine top cover where fitted.

2 On diesel engine models, remove the engine undertray as described in Chapter 11, Section 24.

3 Remove the battery, battery box and battery tray (Chapter 5A Section 4) and the starter motor as described in Chapter 5A Section 11.

4 For improved access, remove the air intake ducts over the top of the transmission as described in Chapter 4A, Section 2 or Chapter 4B, Section 3.

5 Drain the transmission oil as described in Section 2.

6 Remove the filler cap from the brake/clutch fluid reservoir on the bulkhead, then tighten it onto a piece of polythene. This will reduce the loss of fluid when the clutch hydraulic hose is disconnected. Alternatively, fit a hose clamp to the flexible hose next to the clutch hydraulic connection on the transmission housing.

7 Place some cloth rags beneath the hose, then prise out the retaining clip securing the clutch hydraulic hose to the end fitting on top of the transmission bellhousing. Detach the hose from the end fitting **(see illustrations)**. Gently squeeze the two legs of the retaining clip together and re-insert the retaining clip back into position in the end fitting. Discard the sealing ring from the hose end; a new sealing ring must be used on refitting. Plug/cover both the end fitting and hose end to minimise fluid loss and prevent the entry of dirt into the hydraulic system. **Note:** *Whilst the hose is disconnected, do not depress the clutch pedal.*

8 Note the fitted locations of the gearchange selector cables at their transmission attachments. Using a large screwdriver, prise the inner cable end fittings from the transmission selector lever ballpins **(see illustrations 4.3a and 4.3b)**.

9 Push the retaining sleeves toward the rear of the car and detach the outer cables from the mounting bracket on the transmission **(see illustration 4.4)**. Undo the retaining bolts and remove the cable mounting bracket(s) from the transmission.

10 Disconnect the wiring connector from the reversing light switch and free the wiring from the transmission unit and retaining brackets.

11 Remove both driveshafts as described in Chapter 8, Section 2.

12 Unscrew and remove the upper bolts securing the transmission to the rear of the engine.

13 Remove the front subframe assembly as described in Chapter 10, Section 6, ensuring that the engine unit is securely supported by connecting a hoist to the engine assembly. If available, the type of support bar which locates in the engine compartment side channels is to be preferred.

14 Unbolt and remove the front and rear engine/transmission mounting torque link brackets with reference to Chapter 2A, Section 18 or Chapter 2C, Section 18.

15 Place a jack with a block of wood beneath the transmission, and raise the jack to take the weight of the transmission.

16 Unbolt and remove the left-hand engine/transmission mounting bracket from the transmission with reference to Chapter 2A, Section 18 or Chapter 2C, Section 18.

7.1 The reversing light switch is screwed into the front of the transmission casing

8.7a Using a small screwdriver, prise out the retaining clip ...

8.7b ... and disconnect the clutch hydraulic hose from the end fitting on the transmission bellhousing

17 Lower the engine and transmission by approximately 5 cm making sure that the coolant hoses and wiring harnesses are not stretched.

18 Slacken and remove the remaining bolts securing the transmission to the engine and sump flange. Note the correct fitted positions of each bolt, and the relevant brackets, as they are removed to use as a reference on refitting. Make a final check that all components have been disconnected, and are positioned clear of the transmission so that they will not hinder the removal procedure.

19 With the bolts removed, move the trolley jack and transmission, to free it from its locating dowels. Once the transmission is free, lower the jack and manoeuvre the unit out from under the car. Remove the locating dowels from the transmission or engine if they are loose, and keep them in a safe place.

Refitting

20 The transmission is refitted by a reversal of the removal procedure, bearing in mind the following points.

a) *Ensure the locating dowels are correctly positioned prior to installation.*

b) *Tighten all nuts and bolts to the specified torque (where given).*

c) *Renew the driveshaft oil seals (see Section 6) before refitting the driveshafts/ intermediate shaft.*

d) *Refit the front subframe assembly as described in Chapter 10, Section 6.*

e) *Fit a new sealing ring to the clutch hydraulic hose before clipping the hose into the end fitting. Ensure the hose is securely retained by its clip then bleed the hydraulic system as described in Chapter 6, Section 2.*

f) *Refill the transmission with the specified type and quantity of oil, as described in Section 2.*

g) *On completion, adjust the selector cables as described in Section 3.*

9 Transmission overhaul – general information

1 Overhauling a manual transmission unit is a difficult and involved job for the DIY home mechanic. In addition to dismantling and reassembling many small parts, clearances must be precisely measured and, if necessary, changed by selecting shims and spacers. Internal transmission components are also often difficult to obtain, and in many instances, extremely expensive. Because of this, if the transmission develops a fault or becomes noisy, the best course of action is to have the unit overhauled by a specialist repairer, or to obtain an exchange reconditioned unit.

10 Transmission oil level check

1 There is no provision for oil level checking once the transmission has been initially filled. If for any reason it is thought that the oil level may be low, the transmission oil must be completely drained, then refilled with an exact specified quantity of oil as described in Section 2.

Chapter 7 Part B
Automatic transmission

Contents

Degrees of difficulty

Easy, suitable for novice with little experience	Fairly easy, suitable for beginner with some experience	Fairly difficult, suitable for competent DIY mechanic	Difficult, suitable for experienced DIY mechanic	Very difficult, suitable for expert DIY or professional

Specifications

General

Type . . . . Electronically-controlled adaptive automatic, six forward speeds and reverse, with sequential manual gear selection capability

Manufacturer's designation AF40

Lubrication

Lubricant type . . . . See *Lubricants and fluids*
Lubricant capacity . . . . See Chapter 1B, Specifications

Torque wrench settings

	Nm	lbf ft
Automatic transmission fluid drain/filler plugs:		
Drain plug	50	37
Filler plug	40	30
Level checking plug	8	6
Electronic control unit mounting bolts	25	18
Engine/transmission mountings	See Chapter 2B. 2C or 2D Specifications	
Engine-to-transmission bolts	See Chapter 2B. 2C or 2D Specifications	
Fluid cooler pipes-to-transmission	7	5
Roadwheel nuts	150	111
Selector lever-to-transmission selector shaft	15	11
Torque converter-to-driveplate bolts*	60	44

*Use new nuts/bolts

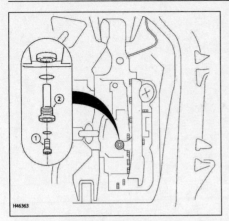

2.2 Transmission fluid level checking plug (1) and drain plug (2)

1 General Information

1 Diesel engine models are optionally available with a six-speed, electronically-controlled automatic transmission. The transmission consists of a torque converter, an epicyclic geartrain, and hydraulically-operated clutches and brakes. The unit is controlled by the electronic control unit (ECU) via electrically-operated solenoid valves. In addition to the fully automatic operation, the transmission can also be operated manually with a six-speed sequential gear selection.

2 The torque converter provides a fluid coupling between engine and transmission, which acts as an automatic clutch, and also provides a degree of torque multiplication when accelerating. The torque converter incorporates a lock-up function whereby the engine and transmission can be directly coupled by means of a clutch unit inside the torque converter. The lock-up function is controlled by the ECU according to operating conditions.

3 The epicyclic geartrain provides either of the six forward or one reverse gear ratios, according to which of its component parts are held stationary or allowed to turn. The

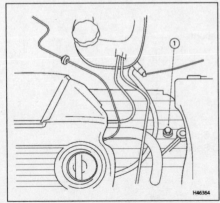

2.5 Transmission fluid filler plug (1)

components of the geartrain are held or released by hydraulically actuated brakes and clutches. A fluid pump within the transmission provides the necessary hydraulic pressure to operate the brakes and clutches.

4 In automatic mode, the transmission is fully adaptive, whereby the shift points are dependant on driver input, road speed, engine speed and vehicle operating conditions. The ECU receives inputs from various engine and drive train related sensors, and determines the appropriate shift point for each gear.

5 Driver control of the transmission is by a four-position selector lever. The drive D position, allows automatic changing throughout the range of forward gear ratios. An automatic kickdown facility shifts the transmission down a gear if the accelerator pedal is fully depressed. If the selector lever is moved to the left from the D position, the transmission enters manual mode. In manual mode the gear selector lever can be used to shift the transmission up or down each gear sequentially.

6 Due to the complexity of the automatic transmission, any repair or overhaul work must be left to a Vauxhall/Opel dealer or transmission specialist with the necessary special equipment for fault diagnosis and repair. The contents of the following Sections are therefore confined to supplying general information, and any service information and instructions that can be used by the owner.

2 Automatic transmission fluid – draining and refilling

Draining

1 Position the vehicle over an inspection pit, on vehicle ramps, or jack it up and support it securely on axle stands (see *Jacking and vehicle support*), but make sure that it is level. Remove the engine undertray as described in Chapter 11, Section 24.

2 Position a container under the combined drain plug/level checking plug at the base of the transmission. Note that the drain plug and level checking plug are incorporated into one unit – the drain plug is the larger of the two plugs, with the level checking plug screwed into the centre of it **(see illustration)**.

3 Unscrew the level checking plug and remove it, along with its sealing washer, from the centre of the drain plug. Now unscrew the drain plug and remove it, along with its sealing washer, from the transmission. Allow the fluid to drain completely into the container.

4 When the fluid has finished draining, clean the drain plug threads and those of the transmission casing, fit a new sealing washer and refit the drain plug, tightening it to the specified torque.

Refilling

5 Wipe clean the area around the transmission fluid filler plug, located on the top of the

transmission housing, adjacent to the selector cable **(see illustration)**. Unscrew and remove the filler plug along with its sealing washer.

6 Slowly refill the transmission with the specified type of fluid, via the filler plug aperture until fluid just starts to drip out of the level checking plug aperture. Use a funnel with a fine mesh gauze, to avoid spillage, and to ensure that no foreign matter enters the transmission.

7 Once the level is correct, refit the level checking plug and fluid filler plug and tighten both securely.

8 Lower the vehicle to the ground and take it on a short journey to warm the transmission up to normal operating temperature. On your return, park the vehicle on a level surface.

9 Unscrew and remove the fluid filler plug once more.

10 With the engine running at idle, and the footbrake firmly applied, slowly move the selector lever from position P to position D and back to position P, stopping at each position for at least two seconds. Repeat this procedure twice.

11 With the engine still idling, once again unscrew the fluid level checking plug. Allow the excess fluid to run from the level checking plug aperture until it is only dripping out. Refit the level checking plug with a new sealing washer, and tighten the plug to the specified torque.

12 If no fluid runs from the level checking plug aperture, add further fluid until it does.

13 Add a further 0.4 litres of fluid, then refit the filler plug with a new sealing washer. Tighten the plug to the specified torque.

14 On completion, refit the engine undertray.

3 Selector cable – adjustment

Note: *If the battery is disconnected with the selector lever in the P (park) position, the lever will be locked in position. To manually release the lever, carefully release the selector lever trim from the centre console and fold it upwards. Insert the release tool (located in the glovebox lid) into the hole in the selector lever base to release the selector lever lock, then move the selector lever to the N (neutral) position (see illustrations).*

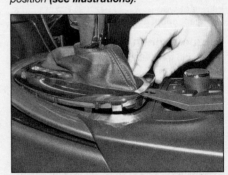

3.0a Carefully release the selector lever trim from the centre console

3.0b Insert the release tool into the hole in the selector lever base to release the selector lever lock

1 Operate the selector lever throughout its entire range and check that the transmission engages the correct gear indicated on the selector lever position indicator. If adjustment is necessary, continue as follows.

2 Position the selector lever in the P (park) position.

3 Carefully release the selector lever trim from the centre console and fold it upwards **(see illustration 3.0a)**.

4 Working in the centre console aperture, lift up the yellow clamping piece on the selector cable adjuster to unlock the cable **(see illustration)**.

5 Working in the engine compartment, move the transmission selector lever fully forwards so that the transmission is also positioned in the P position. With both the selector lever and transmission correctly positioned, lock the clamping piece on the selector cable by pushing it down until it clicks in position.

6 Check the operation of the selector lever and, if necessary, repeat the adjustment procedure. On completion, refit the selector lever trim to the centre console.

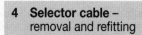

4 Selector cable – removal and refitting

Removal

1 Remove the centre console as described in Chapter 11, Section 29.

2 Position the selector lever in the P (park) position.

3 Lift up the yellow clamping piece on the selector cable adjuster to unlock the cable **(see illustration 3.4)**.

4 Using pointed nose pliers, compress the selector outer cable retaining clip, and lift the outer cable up and out of its support in the selector lever housing **(see illustrations)**.

5 Move the selector cable forward to disengage the inner cable from the selector lever clamping piece.

6 Working in the engine compartment, remove the battery and battery box as described in Chapter 5A, Section 4. Depress the tab and

3.4 Lift up the yellow clamping piece on the selector cable adjuster to unlock the cable

lift the selector inner cable end fitting off the balljoint on the transmission selector lever.

7 Using pointed nose pliers, compress the selector outer cable retaining clip, and lift the outer cable up and out of the support bracket on the transmission. Release the outer cable from the retaining clip on the transmission.

8 Release the rubber grommet at the cable entry point on the engine compartment bulkhead, then pull the cable (complete with grommet) out of the bulkhead and into the engine compartment.

Refitting

9 Push the selector cable through the bulkhead passage from the engine compartment and locate the rubber grommet back into position in the bulkhead.

10 Refit the outer cable to the mounting

4.4a Compress the selector outer cable retaining clip ...

5.2a Pull the selector lever knob upward and off the selector lever ...

bracket and retaining clip on the transmission.

11 Engage the inner cable end fitting with the balljoint on the selector lever position switch, and push the end fitting fully onto the balljoint.

12 Move the transmission selector lever fully forwards so that the transmission is positioned in the P position.

13 From inside the car, position the selector lever in the P position and guide the cable back into its location in the selector lever housing, engaging the inner cable with the clamping piece. Engage the outer cable with the selector lever housing, then push down the inner cable clamping piece to lock the cable in position.

14 Refit the centre console as described in Chapter 11, Section 29.

15 Refit the battery box and battery as described in Chapter 5A, Section 4.

5 Selector lever assembly – removal and refitting

Removal

1 Carefully release the selector lever trim from the centre console and fold it upwards **(see illustration 3.0a)**.

2 Pull the selector lever knob upward and off the selector lever. Disconnect the wiring connector, then remove the selector lever knob, gaiter and trim **(see illustrations)**.

3 Remove the centre console as described in Chapter 11, Section 29.

4.4b ... and lift the outer cable up and out of its support in the selector lever housing

5.2b ... then disconnect the wiring connector and remove the selector lever knob, gaiter and trim

4 Lift up the yellow clamping piece on the selector cable adjuster to unlock the cable **(see illustration 3.4)**.

5 Using pointed nose pliers, compress the selector outer cable retaining clip, and lift the outer cable up and out of its support in the selector lever housing **(see illustrations 4.4a and 4.4b)**.

6 Move the selector cable forward to disengage the inner cable from the selector lever clamping piece.

7 Disconnect the selector lever assembly wiring connector and release the wiring harness from the retaining clips and ties.

8 Undo the four mounting bolts and lift the selector lever assembly from the floor **(see illustration)**.

Refitting

9 Manoeuvre the selector lever assembly into place, engaging it with the selector cable. Refit the mounting bolts and tighten them securely.

10 Engage the selector outer cable with the selector lever housing.

11 Reconnect the selector lever assembly wiring connector and secure the wiring harness with the retaining clips and ties.

12 Adjust the selector cable as described in Section 3.

13 Refit the centre console as described in Chapter 11, Section 29.

14 Reconnect the wiring connector, then refit the selector lever knob, gaiter and trim.

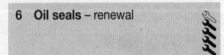

6 Oil seals – renewal

Driveshaft oil seals

1 Remove the driveshaft/intermediate shaft as described in Chapter 8, Section 2.

2 Note the correct fitted depth of the seal in its housing then carefully prise it out of position using a large flat-bladed screwdriver.

3 Remove all traces of dirt from the area around the oil seal aperture, then lubricate the new oil seal with automatic transmission fluid. Ensure the seal is correctly positioned, with its sealing lip facing inwards, and tap it squarely into position, using a suitable tubular drift (such as a socket) which bears only on the hard outer edge of the seal. Ensure the seal is fitted at the same depth in its housing that the original was.

4 Refit the driveshaft/intermediate shaft as described in Chapter 8, Section 2 and 3.

5 Refill the transmission with the specified type and amount of oil, as described in Section 2.

Torque converter oil seal

6 Remove the transmission as described in Section 10.

7 Carefully slide the torque converter off of the transmission shaft whilst being prepared for fluid spillage.

8 Note the correct fitted position of the seal in

5.8 Selector lever assembly left-hand mounting bolts

the oil pump housing then carefully lever the seal out of position taking care not to mark the housing or input shaft.

9 Remove all traces of dirt from the area around the oil seal aperture then press the new seal into position, ensuring its sealing lip is facing inwards.

10 Lubricate the seal with clean transmission fluid then carefully ease the torque converter into position. Slide the torque converter onto the transmission shaft by turning it until it fully engages with the oil pump.

11 Refit the transmission as described in Section 10.

7 Fluid cooler – general information

1 The transmission fluid cooler is an integral part of the radiator assembly. Refer to Chapter 3, Section 3 for removal and refitting details, if the cooler is damaged the complete radiator assembly must be renewed.

8 Transmission input/output speed sensors – removal and refitting

1 The input and output shaft speed sensors are located internally within the transmission and are not individually available. If one or

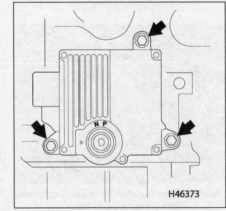

9.8 Electronic control unit mounting bolts

both speed sensors are diagnosed as faulty, it will be necessary to obtain a complete new transmission.

9 Electronic control unit – removal and refitting

Note: *If a new ECU is to be fitted, this work must be entrusted to a Vauxhall/Opel dealer or suitably-equipped specialist. It is necessary to reset the transmission electronic control system prior to removal, and to program the new ECU after installation. This work requires the use of dedicated Vauxhall/Opel diagnostic equipment or a compatible alternative.*

Removal

1 The combined ECU and selector lever position switch are located on the top of the transmission housing.

2 Ensure the handbrake is fully applied, then move the gear selector lever to the N (neutral) position.

3 Remove the battery and battery box as described in Chapter 5A, Section 4.

4 Release the ECU wiring harness from its retaining clips, then disconnect the wiring harness connector from the ECU.

5 Depress the tab and lift the selector inner cable end fitting off the balljoint on the transmission selector lever.

6 Using pointed nose pliers, compress the selector outer cable retaining clip, and lift the outer cable up and out of the support bracket on the transmission.

7 Unscrew the retaining nut and remove the lever from the transmission selector shaft.

8 Unscrew and remove the three mounting bolts, then carefully lift the ECU upwards and remove it from the transmission **(see illustration)**.

Refitting

9 Prior to refitting, first make sure that the transmission selector shaft is still in the N (neutral) position. If there is any doubt, temporarily engage the selector shaft lever with the transmission selector shaft and move the lever fully forwards (to the P position) then move it two notches backwards.

10 Set the selector lever position switch on the ECU to the N position by turning the switch until the two arrows are aligned.

11 Check that the transmission wiring harness is correctly located, then carefully place the ECU in position. Take great care not to damage the wiring connector pins as the ECU is fitted.

12 Refit the three bolts and tighten to the specified torque.

13 Refit the selector lever to the shaft and tighten its retaining nut to the specified torque.

14 Reconnect the selector cable end fitting to the transmission selector shaft lever balljoint.

15 Reconnect the ECU wiring harness connector, then secure the harness in its retaining clips.

16 Refit the battery box and battery as described in Chapter 5A, Section 4.

17 Adjust the selector cable as described in Section 3.

10 Automatic transmission – removal and refitting

Note: *New torque converter-to-driveplate bolts will be required for refitting.*

Removal

1 Apply the handbrake, then jack up the front of the vehicle and support it on axle stands (see *Jacking and vehicle support*). Allow sufficient working room to remove the transmission from under the left-hand side of the engine compartment. Remove both front roadwheels. Remove the engine top cover.

2 Drain the transmission fluid as described in Section 2, then refit the drain plug and tighten it to the specified torque.

3 Remove the battery and battery box as described in Chapter 5A, Section 4.

4 Release the transmission ECU wiring harness from its retaining clips, then disconnect the wiring harness connector from the ECU.

5 Depress the tab and lift the selector inner cable end fitting off the balljoint on the transmission selector lever.

6 Using pointed nose pliers, compress the selector outer cable retaining clip, and lift the outer cable up and out of the support bracket on the transmission.

7 Release the battery wiring harness from the clips or ties securing it to the engine/transmission unit.

8 Remove both driveshafts as described in Chapter 8, Section 2.

9 Unscrew and remove the upper bolts securing the transmission to the rear of the engine.

10 Remove the front subframe assembly as described in Chapter 10, Section 6, ensuring that the engine unit is securely supported by connecting a hoist to the engine assembly. If available, the type of support bar which locates in the engine compartment side channels is to be preferred.

11 Undo the three retaining bolts and remove the engine/transmission rear mounting/torque link from the rear of the transmission housing.

12 Unscrew the central retaining nut and detach the fluid cooler pipes from the transmission. Suitably cover the pipe ends and plug the transmission orifices to prevent dirt entry.

13 Undo the two retaining bolts and remove the engine/transmission front mounting/torque link from the front of the transmission housing.

14 Remove the starter motor as described in Chapter 5A, Section 11.

15 Using a socket and extension bar, turn the crankshaft pulley until one of the bolts securing the torque converter to the driveplate becomes accessible through the starter motor aperture. Slacken and remove the bolt, then turn the crankshaft pulley as necessary, and undo the remaining bolts as they become accessible. There are six securing bolts in total. Discard the bolts, new ones must be used on refitting.

16 Disconnect the breather hose from the top of the transmission.

17 Place a jack with a block of wood beneath the transmission, and raise the jack to take the weight of the transmission.

18 Mark the bolt positions for correct refitting, then unscrew the three bolts securing the left-hand engine/transmission mounting to the transmission casing.

19 By manipulating the engine hoist and the jack under the transmission, lower the engine/transmission approximately 50mm. Ensure that the various coolant hoses and wiring harnesses are not stretched.

20 Slacken and remove the remaining bolts securing the transmission to the engine and sump flange. Note the correct fitted positions of each bolt, and the relevant brackets, as they are removed to use as a reference on refitting. Make a final check that all components have been disconnected, and are positioned clear of the transmission so that they will not hinder the removal procedure.

21 With all the bolts removed, move the trolley jack and transmission, to free it from its locating dowels. Once the transmission is free, lower the jack and manoeuvre the unit out from under the car, taking care to ensure that the torque converter does not fall off. Remove the locating dowels from the transmission or engine if they are loose, and keep them in a safe place. Retain the torque converter while the transmission is removed by bolting a strip of metal across the transmission bellhousing end face.

Refitting

22 The transmission is refitted by a reversal of the removal procedure, bearing in mind the following points.

a) Prior to refitting, remove all traces of old locking compound from the torque converter threads by running a tap of the correct thread diameter and pitch down the holes. In the absence of a suitable tap, use one of the old bolts with slots cut in its threads.

b) Ensure the engine/transmission locating dowels are correctly positioned and apply a smear of molybdenum disulphide grease to the torque converter locating pin and its centering bush in the crankshaft end.

c) Check that the torque converter is fully entered inside the transmission bellhousing by measuring the distance from the flange to the bolt holes in the torque converter, using a straight-edge and vernier calipers(see illustration). The distance must measure approximately 15.0 mm.

d) Once the transmission and engine are correctly joined, refit the securing bolts, tightening them to the specified torque setting.

e) Fit the new torque converter to driveplate bolts and tighten them lightly only to start, then go around and tighten them to the specified torque setting in a diagonal sequence.

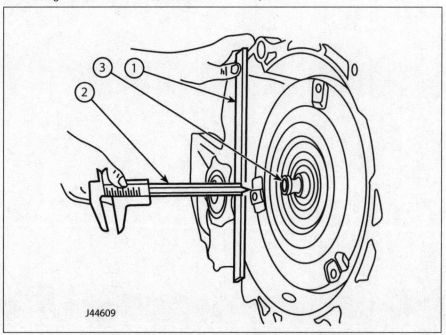

10.22a Check that the torque converter is fully entered

1 Straight edge
2 Vernier calipers on bolt hole
3 Torque converter centre stub

J44609

f) Tighten all nuts and bolts to the specified torque (where given).

g) Renew the driveshaft oil seals (see Section 6) and refit the driveshafts/intermediate shaft to the transmission as described in Chapter 8, Section 2 and 3.

h) Refit the front subframe assembly as described in Chapter 10, Section 6.

i) On completion, refill the transmission with the specified type and quantity of fluid as described in Section 2 and adjust the selector cable as described in Section 3.

11 Automatic transmission overhaul – general information

1 In the event of a fault occurring with the transmission, it is first necessary to determine whether it is of a mechanical, electrical or hydraulic nature, and to do this, special test equipment is required. It is therefore essential to have the work carried out by a Vauxhall/Opel dealer or suitably equipped specialist if a transmission fault is suspected.

2 Do not remove the transmission from the car for possible repair before professional fault diagnosis has been carried out, since most tests require the transmission to be in the vehicle.

Chapter 8
Driveshafts

Contents

Degrees of difficulty

Easy, suitable for novice with little experience	**Fairly easy,** suitable for beginner with some experience	**Fairly difficult,** suitable for competent DIY mechanic	**Difficult,** suitable for experienced DIY mechanic	**Very difficult,** suitable for expert DIY or professional

Specifications

General

Driveshaft type	Solid steel shafts with inner and outer constant velocity (CV) joints. Right-hand driveshaft incorporating intermediate shaft on diesel engine models

Constant velocity joint type:
  Manual transmission models:

Inner and outer joints	Ball-and-cage

  Automatic transmission models:

Inner joints	Tripod
Outer joints	Ball-and-cage

Lubrication (overhaul only – see text)

Lubricant type/specification	Use only special grease supplied in sachets with gaiter kits – joints are otherwise pre-packed with grease and sealed

Torque wrench settings

	Nm	lbf ft
Driveshaft retaining nut*:		
Stage 1	150	110
Stage 2	Slacken the nut by 45°	
Stage 3	250	185
Intermediate shaft bearing housing-to-support bracket	22	16
Lower arm balljoint clamp bolt nut*:		
Stage 1	50	37
Stage 2	Slacken 120°	
Stage 3	50	37
Stage 4	Angle-tighten a further 30°	
Roadwheel nuts	150	111
Track rod end-to-swivel hub*:		
Stage 1	35	26
Stage 2	Angle-tighten through a further 30°	

*Use new nuts/bolts

2.1 Remove the protective cap

1 General Information

1 Drive is transmitted from the differential to the front wheels by means of two, unequal-length driveshafts.

2 Both driveshafts are splined at their outer ends to accept the wheel hubs, and are threaded so that each hub can be fastened by a large nut. The inner end of each driveshaft is splined to accept the intermediate shaft or differential sun gear and is held in place by an internal circlip.

3 Constant velocity (CV) joints are fitted to each end of the driveshafts, to ensure the smooth and efficient transmission of drive at all the angles possible as the roadwheels move up-and-down with the suspension, and as they turn from side-to-side under steering. On manual transmission models,

the inner and outer constant velocity joints are of the ball-and-cage type. On automatic transmission models, the outer constant velocity joints are of the ball-and-cage type and the inner joints are of the tripod type.

4 The right-hand driveshaft on diesel engine models has an intermediate shaft attached to the rear of the cylinder block.

2 Driveshaft – removal and refitting

Note: *A new driveshaft retaining nut, inner joint circlip, lower arm balljoint clamp bolt and nut, and a new track rod end retaining nut will be needed for refitting. The driveshaft outer joint splines may be a tight fit in the hub and it is possible that a puller/extractor will be required to draw the hub assembly off the driveshaft during removal.*
Note: On diesel engine models, the right-hand driveshaft must be removed together with the intermediate shaft as an assembly. The driveshaft is bonded to the intermediate shaft with a special adhesive and the two components cannot be separated.

Removal

1 Firmly apply the handbrake, then jack up the front of the car and support it securely on axle stands (see *Jacking and vehicle support*). Remove the relevant front wheel and where fitted remove the protective cap from the nut **(see illustration)**.

2 On diesel engine models, remove the

A tool to hold the wheel hub stationary whilst the driveshaft retaining nut is slackened can be fabricated from a length of square-sectionsteel tube, a short length of steel strip and a nut and bolt; the nut and bolt forming the pivot of a forked tool.

engine undertray as described in Chapter 11, Section 24.

3 Drain the transmission oil/fluid as described in Chapter 7A, Section 2 or Chapter 7B, Section 2.

4 To prevent rotation of the wheel hub as the driveshaft retaining nut is slackened, make up a holding tool and attach the tool to the wheel hub using two wheel nuts **(see Tool Tip)**.

5 With the holding tool in place, slacken and remove the driveshaft retaining nut using a socket and long bar. Where necessary, support the socket on an axle stand to prevent it slipping off the nut. This nut is very tight; make sure that there is no risk of pulling the car off the axle stands as the nut is slackened.

6 Slacken the nut securing the track rod end to the steering arm on the swivel hub then use a two-legged puller to separate the track rod end balljoint taper. Unscrew the securing nut completely and remove the track rod end from the steering arm **(see illustrations)**. Note that a new nut will be required for refitting.

7 Unscrew the nut and remove the clamp bolt securing the front suspension lower arm to the swivel hub. Note that the bolt head faces the front of the vehicle **(see illustrations)**.

8 Using a lever, push down on the suspension lower arm to free the balljoint from the swivel hub, then move the swivel hub to one side and release the arm, taking care not to damage the balljoint rubber boot **(see illustration)**. It is

2.6a Use a two-legged puller to separate the track rod end balljoint taper ...

2.6b ... and remove the track rod end from the steering arm

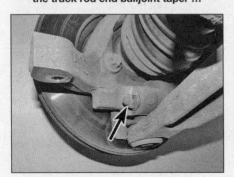

2.7a Unscrew the retaining nut ...

2.7b ... and withdraw the clamp bolt from the swivel hub

2.8 Push down the lower suspension arm to free the balljoint from the swivel hub

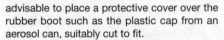

2.9 Pull the swivel hub outwards then withdraw the driveshaft from the hub splines

2.10 Collect the spacer from the end of the driveshaft constant velocity joint

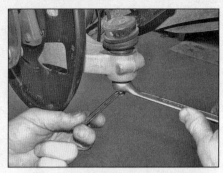

2.27 Countrehold the track rod end balljoint shank using a second spanner as the nut is tightened

advisable to place a protective cover over the rubber boot such as the plastic cap from an aerosol can, suitably cut to fit.

9 The hub must now be freed from the end of the driveshaft **(see illustration)**. It may be possible to pull the hub off the driveshaft, but if the end of the driveshaft is tight in the hub, temporarily refit the driveshaft retaining nut to protect the driveshaft threads, then tap the end of the driveshaft with a soft-faced hammer while pulling outwards on the swivel hub. Alternatively, use a suitable puller to press the driveshaft through the hub.

10 Collect the spacer from the end of the constant velocity joint **(see illustration)**.

11 With the driveshaft detached from the swivel hub, tie the suspension strut to one side and support the driveshaft on an axle stand.

Petrol engine models

12 Place a suitable container beneath the differential, to collect escaping transmission oil when the driveshaft is withdrawn.

13 Using a stout bar, release the inner end of the driveshaft from the differential. Lever between the constant velocity joint and differential housing to release the driveshaft retaining circlip.

Diesel engine models

14 Place a suitable container beneath the differential, to collect escaping transmission oil/fluid when the driveshaft/intermediate shaft is withdrawn.

15 If working on the left-hand driveshaft, use a stout bar to release the inner end of the driveshaft from the differential. Lever between the constant velocity joint and differential housing to release the driveshaft retaining circlip.

16 If working on the right-hand driveshaft, undo the three bolts securing the intermediate shaft bearing housing to the support bracket on the cylinder block.

All models

17 Withdraw the driveshaft/intermediate shaft, ensuring that the constant velocity joints are not placed under excessive strain, and remove the driveshaft from beneath the vehicle. Whilst the driveshaft is removed, plug or tape over the differential aperture to prevent dirt entry.

18 Caution: Do not allow the vehicle to rest on its wheels with one or both driveshafts removed, as damage to the wheel bearings(s) may result. If the vehicle must be moved on its wheels, clamp the wheel bearings using spacers and a long threaded rod to take the place of the driveshaft.

Refitting

19 Before refitting the driveshaft, examine the oil seal in the differential housing and renew it if necessary as described in Chapter 7A, Section 6 or Chapter 7B, Section 6.

20 Remove the circlip from the end of the driveshaft inner joint splines and discard it. Fit a new circlip, making sure it is correctly located in the groove.

21 Thoroughly clean the driveshaft splines, intermediate shaft splines (where applicable), and the apertures in the transmission and hub assembly. Apply a thin film of grease to the oil seal lips, and to the driveshaft splines and shoulders. Check that all gaiter clips are securely fastened.

22 Offer up the driveshaft, and engage the inner joint splines, or intermediate shaft splines with those of the differential sun gear, taking care not to damage the oil seal. Push the inner joint fully into position, then check that the circlip is correctly located and securely holds the joint in position. If necessary, use a soft-faced mallet or drift to drive the driveshaft inner joint fully home.

23 If working on the right-hand driveshaft on diesel engine models, refit the three bolts securing the intermediate shaft bearing housing to the support bracket on the cylinder block and tighten the bolts to the specified torque.

24 Ensure that he spacer is in position on the constant velocity joint, then align the outer constant velocity joint splines with those of the hub, and slide the joint back into position in the hub.

25 Using a lever, push down on the lower suspension arm, then relocate the balljoint and release the arm. Make sure that the balljoint stub is fully entered in the swivel hub.

26 Insert a new lower arm balljoint clamp bolt with its head facing the front of the vehicle, fit a new retaining nut and tighten the nut to

the specified torque in the stages given in the Specifications.

27 Engage the track rod end in the swivel hub, then fit the new retaining nut and tighten it to the specified torque and through the specified angle given in the Specifications, using a torque wrench and angle-tightening gauge. Countrehold the balljoint shank using a second spanner to prevent rotation as the nut is tightened **(see illustration)**.

28 Lubricate the inner face and threads of the new driveshaft retaining nut with clean engine oil, and refit it to the end of the driveshaft. Use the method employed on removal to prevent the hub from rotating, and tighten the driveshaft retaining nut to the specified torque in the stages given in the Specifications. Check that the hub rotates freely.

29 Refill the transmission with oil/fluid as described in Chapter 7A, Section 2 or Chapter 7B, Section 2.

30 On diesel engine models, refit the engine undertray.

31 Refit the roadwheel, lower the vehicle to the ground and tighten the roadwheel nuts to the specified torque.

3 Intermediate shaft – renewal

Note: *An intermediate shaft is not fitted to petrol engine models.*

Note: *A hydraulic press, together with tubes and mandrels of suitable diameters will be needed for this operation.*

1 The right-hand driveshaft inner constant velocity joint is bonded to the intermediate shaft with a special adhesive and the two components cannot be separated. If renewal of the intermediate shaft, or intermediate shaft bearing is required, it will be necessary to obtain a new inner constant velocity joint and gaiter kit, rubber dust cover, intermediate shaft, intermediate shaft bearing, bearing housing, bearing retaining circlips and a tube of the special adhesive (Vauxhall/Opel part No. 90542117). The renewal procedure is as follows.

5.2 Release the rubber gaiter retaining clips by cutting through them using a hacksaw

5.3 Cut the gaiter open using a suitable knife and remove it from the driveshaft

5.5 Sharply strike the edge of the outer joint to drive it off the end of the shaft

5.6 Removing the circlip from the groove in the driveshaft splines

2 Remove the right-hand driveshaft and intermediate shaft assembly as described in Section 2.

3 Working as described in Section 5, remove the inner CV joint, together with the intermediate shaft, from the driveshaft.

4 Again, working as described in Section 5, fit the new rubber gaiter and inner CV joint to the existing driveshaft, then slide the new rubber dust cover into position on the end of the CV joint. Fit a new circlip, making sure it is correctly located in the groove.

5 Using circlip pliers, fit the inner circlip to the new intermediate shaft.

6 Locate the new intermediate shaft bearing in the housing and press it fully into position using a suitable tube in contact with the bearing outer race.

7 Position the bearing and housing assembly on the end of the intermediate shaft and press

the bearing onto the shaft using a suitable tube in contact with the bearing inner race. Fit the outer circlip to the intermediate shaft.

8 Ensure that the splines in the intermediate shaft and on the inner CV joint are clean and free from any oil or grease contamination.

9 Using a small clean paint brush, apply a liberal quantity of the special adhesive to the end of the inner CV joint, from the edge of the rubber dust cover to the end of the splines.

10 Suitably support the driveshaft and inner CV joint and engage the intermediate shaft with the joint splines. Using a soft-faced mallet, tap the other end of the intermediate shaft until it is fully engaged with the CV joint.

11 Refit the driveshaft and intermediate shaft assembly as described in Section 2. Note that the special adhesive must be allowed to cure for 12 hours at room temperature before the car is driven.

4 Intermediate shaft bearing – renewal

1 Refer to the procedures contained in Section 3.

5 Driveshaft joint gaiters – renewal

Note: *On automatic transmission models the inner tripod type CV joint cannot be detached from the driveshaft. If inner CV joint gaiter renewal is required, it will be necessary to remove the outer CV joint and slide the inner joint gaiter off the outer end of the driveshaft.*

1 Remove the driveshaft from the car as described in Section 2, then secure the shaft in a vice equipped with soft jaws.

2 Release the rubber gaiter inner and outer retaining clips by cutting through them using a junior hacksaw **(see illustration)**. Spread the clips and remove them from the gaiter.

3 Slide the rubber gaiter down the shaft to expose the CV joint or, alternatively, cut the gaiter open using a suitable knife and remove it from the driveshaft **(see illustration)**.

4 Using old rags, clean away as much of the old grease as possible from the CV joint. It is advisable to wear disposable rubber gloves during this operation.

5 The CV joints are retained on the driveshaft by an internal circlip. Using a mallet, sharply strike the edge of the outer joint to compress the circlip and drive the joint off the end of the shaft **(see illustration)**.

6 Once the joint has been removed, extract the circlip from the groove in the driveshaft splines **(see illustration)**. A new circlip must be fitted on reassembly.

7 If still in place, withdraw the rubber gaiter from the driveshaft.

8 With the CV joint removed from the driveshaft, wipe away the remaining grease (do not use any solvent) to allow the joint components to be inspected.

9 Move the inner splined driving member from side-to-side, to expose each ball in turn at the top of its track. Examine the balls for cracks, flat spots, or signs of surface pitting.

10 Inspect the ball tracks on the inner and outer members. If the tracks have widened, the balls will no longer be a tight fit. At the same time, check the ball cage windows for wear or cracking between the windows.

11 If on inspection any of the constant velocity joint components are found to be worn or damaged, it will be necessary to renew the complete joint assembly. If the joint is in satisfactory condition, obtain a repair kit consisting of a new gaiter and retaining clips, a constant velocity joint circlip, and the correct type and quantity of grease **(see illustration)**.

12 Slide the new rubber gaiter and retaining clips onto the driveshaft **(see illustration)**.

5.11 Components required for driveshaft gaiter renewal

5.12 Slide the new rubber gaiter and retaining clips onto the driveshaft

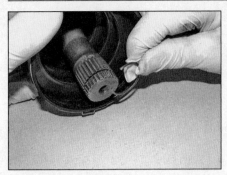

5.13 Fit a new circlip to the groove in the driveshaft

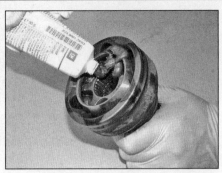

5.14 Pack the joint with the grease supplied in the repair kit

5.15 Tap the joint onto the driveshaft until the circlip engages in its groove

13 Fit a new circlip to the groove in the driveshaft **(see illustration)**.

14 Pack the joint with the grease supplied in the repair kit **(see illustration)**. Work the grease well into the bearing tracks whilst twisting the joint, and fill the rubber gaiter with any excess.

15 Engage the joint with the driveshaft splines. Using a soft-faced mallet, tap the joint onto the driveshaft until the circlip engages in its groove **(see illustration)**. Make sure that the joint is securely retained, by pulling on the joint, not the shaft.

16 Ease the gaiter over the joint, and ensure that the gaiter lips are correctly located in the grooves on both the driveshaft and constant velocity joint. Lift the outer sealing lip of the gaiter, to equalise air pressure within the gaiter.

17 Pull the large gaiter retaining clip as tight as possible, and locate the hooks on the clip in their slots. Remove any slack in the gaiter retaining clip by carefully compressing the raised section of the clip. In the absence of the special tool, a pair of side-cutters may be used. Secure the small retaining clip using the same procedure **(see illustrations)**.

18 Check that the constant velocity joint moves freely in all directions, then refit the driveshaft to the car as described in Section 2.

5.17a Secure the large gaiter retaining clip in position by compressing the raised section of the clip

5.17b The small inner retaining clip is secured in the same way

6 Driveshaft overhaul – general information

1 If any of the checks described in Chapter 1A, Section 10 or Chapter 1B, Section 11 reveal possible wear in any driveshaft joint, carry out the following procedures to identify the source of the problem.

2 Firmly apply the handbrake, then jack up the front of the vehicle and support it securely on axle stands (see *Jacking and vehicle support*).

3 Referring to the information contained in Section 2, make up a tool to hold the wheel hub, and attach the tool to the hub using two wheel nuts. Use a torque wrench to check that the driveshaft retaining nut is securely fastened, then repeat this check on the remaining driveshaft nut.

4 Road test the vehicle, and listen for a metallic clicking from the front as the vehicle is driven slowly in a circle on full-lock. If a clicking noise is heard, this indicates wear in the outer constant velocity joint.

5 If vibration, consistent with road speed, is felt through the car when accelerating, there is a possibility of wear in the inner constant velocity joints.

6 To check the joints for wear, remove the driveshafts, then dismantle them as described in Section 3 ; if any wear or free play is found, the affected joint must be renewed.

Chapter 9
Braking system

Contents

Degrees of difficulty

Easy, suitable for novice with little experience	Fairly easy, suitable for beginner with some experience	Fairly difficult, suitable for competent DIY mechanic	Difficult, suitable for experienced DIY mechanic	Very difficult, suitable for expert DIY or professional

Specifications

Front brakes

Type	Ventilated disc, with single- or twin-piston sliding caliper
Disc diameter.................................	296.0 mm, 321.0 mm or 337.0 mm according to model
Disc thickness:	
New	30.0 mm
Minimum.....................................	27.0 mm
Maximum disc thickness variation............................	0.025 mm
Maximum disc run-out..................................	0.05 mm
Minimum brake pad friction material thickness...................	2.0 mm

Rear brakes

Type	Solid disc, with single-piston sliding caliper
Disc diameter.................................	292.0 mm or 315.0 mm according to model
Disc thickness:	
New:	
With 292.0 mm diameter disc............................	12.0 mm
With 315 mm diameter disc	23.0 mm
Minimum:	
With 292.0 mm diameter disc............................	10.0 mm
With 315.0 mm diameter disc............................	21.0 mm
Maximum disc run-out	0.05 mm
Minimum brake pad friction material thickness...................	2.0 mm

Handbrake

Type	Self-adjusting cable-operated, acting on rear brake calipers. Electronically operated on later models

Torque wrench settings

	Nm	lbf ft
ABS hydraulic modulator mounting bracket bolts	20	15
ABS hydraulic modulator-to-mounting bracket	10	7
ABS wheel speed sensor retaining bolts	10	7
Brake caliper bleed screws	10	7
Brake caliper guide pin bolts:		
Single piston calipers	28	21
Twin piston calipers	32	24
Brake caliper mounting bracket bolts:		
Front caliper mounting bracket bolts: *		
Stage 1	150	111
Stage 2	Angle-tighten a further 45°	
Stage 3	Angle-tighten a further 15°	
Rear caliper mounting bracket bolts:		
Stage 1	100	74
Stage 2	Angle-tighten a further 60°	
Brake fluid pipe union nuts.	18	13
Brake hydraulic hose banjo union bolts	40	30
Brake pedal mounting bracket nuts*	22	16
Handbrake lever retaining nuts	10	7
Master cylinder retaining nuts*	50	37
Roadwheel nuts	150	111
Vacuum pump mounting bolts/nuts:		
Petrol engine models	10	7
A20 Diesel engine models: *		
Stage 1	5	4
Stage 2	Angle-tighten a further 50°	
B20 diesel engine models*	25	18
Vacuum servo unit stud bolts*	20	15

*Use new fasteners

1 General Information

1 The braking system is of servo-assisted, dual-circuit hydraulic type split diagonally. The arrangement of the hydraulic system is such that each circuit operates one front and one rear brake from a tandem master cylinder. Under normal circumstances, both circuits operate in unison. However, in the event of hydraulic failure in one circuit, full braking force will still be available at two wheels.

2 All models are fitted with front and rear disc brakes. The disc brakes are actuated by single- or twin-piston sliding type calipers, which ensure that equal pressure is applied to each disc pad.

3 An Anti-lock Braking System (ABS) is fitted as standard equipment to all vehicles covered in this manual. On higher specification models, the ABS may also incorporate traction control or an electronic stability program. Refer to Section 20 for further information on ABS operation.

4 The self-adjusting, cable-operated handbrake provides an independent mechanical means of rear brake application. On later models, the handbrake is electronically operated by an electric motor located under the left-hand rear wheel arch.

5 On petrol engine models, to ensure that an adequate source of vacuum to operate the vacuum servo unit under all engine operating conditions is available (particularly during cold start, high engine RPM and high altitude) an auxiliary vacuum pump is fitted. The pump is located on the front subframe on the right-hand side and is driven by an integral electric motor. The pump only operates on demand and is controlled by a vacuum switch located on the vacuum servo unit.

6 On diesel engine models, since there is no throttling as such of the inlet manifold, the manifold is not a suitable source of vacuum to operate the vacuum servo unit. The servo unit is therefore connected to a separate vacuum pump bolted to the left-hand end of the cylinder head (driven by the camshaft) or incorporated into the oil pump (1.6 litre diesel engines).

⚠ *Warning: When servicing any part of the system, work carefully and methodically; also observe scrupulous cleanliness when overhauling any part of the hydraulic system. Always renew components (in axle sets, where applicable) if in doubt about their condition, and use only genuine Vauxhall/Opel replacement parts, or at least those of known good quality. Note the warnings given in 'Safety first!' and at relevant points in this Chapter concerning the dangers of asbestos dust and hydraulic fluid.*

2 Hydraulic system – bleeding

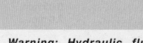

⚠ *Warning: Hydraulic fluid is poisonous; wash off immediately and thoroughly in the case of skin contact, and seek immediate medical advice if any fluid is swallowed or gets into the eyes. Certain types of hydraulic fluid are inflammable, and may ignite when allowed into contact with hot components; when servicing any hydraulic system, it is safest to assume that the fluid is inflammable, and to take precautions against the risk of fire as though it is petrol that is being handled. Hydraulic fluid is also an effective paint stripper, and will attack plastics; if any is spilt, it should be washed off immediately, using copious quantities of fresh water. Finally, it is hygroscopic (it absorbs moisture from the air) – old fluid may be contaminated and unfit for further use. When topping-up or renewing the fluid, always use the recommended type, and ensure that it comes from a freshly-opened sealed container.*

General

1 The correct operation of any hydraulic system is only possible after removing all air from the components and circuit; this is achieved by bleeding the system.

2 During the bleeding procedure, add only clean, unused hydraulic fluid of the recommended type; never re-use fluid that has already been bled from the system. Ensure that sufficient fluid is available before starting work.

3 If there is any possibility of incorrect fluid being already in the system, the brake components and circuit must be flushed completely with uncontaminated, correct fluid, and new seals should be fitted to the various components.

4 If hydraulic fluid has been lost from the system, or air has entered because of a leak, ensure that the fault is cured before proceeding further.

5 Park the vehicle over an inspection pit or on car ramps. Alternatively, apply the handbrake then jack up the front and rear of the vehicle and support it on axle stands (see *Jacking and vehicle support*). For improved access with the vehicle jacked up, remove the roadwheels.

6 Check that all pipes and hoses are secure, unions tight and bleed screws closed. Clean any dirt from around the bleed screws.

7 Unscrew the master cylinder reservoir cap, and top the master cylinder reservoir up to the MAX level line; refit the cap loosely, and remember to maintain the fluid level at least above the MIN level line throughout the procedure, otherwise there is a risk of further air entering the system.

8 There are a number of one-man, do-it-yourself brake bleeding kits currently available from motor accessory shops. It is recommended that one of these kits is used whenever possible, as they greatly simplify the bleeding operation, and also reduce the risk of expelled air and fluid being drawn back into the system. If such a kit is not available, the basic (two-man) method must be used, which is described in detail below.

Caution: Vauxhall/Opel recommend using a pressure bleeding kit for this operation (see paragraphs 24 to 27).

9 If a kit is to be used, prepare the vehicle as described previously, and follow the kit manufacturer's instructions, as the procedure may vary slightly according to the type being used; generally, they are as outlined below in the relevant sub-section.

10 Whichever method is used, the same sequence should be followed (paragraphs 11 and 12) to ensure the removal of all air from the system.

Bleeding sequence

11 If the system has been only partially disconnected, and suitable precautions were taken to minimise fluid loss, it should only be necessary to bleed that part of the system (ie, the primary or secondary circuit). If the master cylinder or main brake lines have been disconnected, then the complete system must be bled.

12 If the complete system is to be bled, then it should be done working in the following sequence:

a) Left-hand front brake.
b) Right-hand rear brake.
c) Right-hand front brake.
d) Left-hand rear brake.

Bleeding

Basic (two-man) method

13 Collect together a clean glass jar, a suitable length of plastic or rubber tubing which is a tight fit over the bleed screw, and

2.14a Front brake caliper bleed screw ...

2.14b ... and rear brake caliper bleed screw

a ring spanner to fit the screw. The help of an assistant will also be required.

14 Remove the dust cap from the first bleed screw in the sequence **(see illustrations)**. Fit the spanner and tube to the screw, place the other end of the tube in the jar, and pour in sufficient fluid to cover the end of the tube.

15 Ensure that the master cylinder reservoir fluid level is maintained at least above the MIN level line throughout the procedure.

16 Have the assistant fully depress the brake pedal several times to build-up pressure, then maintain it on the final downstroke.

17 While pedal pressure is maintained, unscrew the bleed screw (approximately one turn) and allow the compressed fluid and air to flow into the jar. The assistant should maintain pedal pressure, following it down to the floor if necessary, and should not release it until instructed to do so. When the flow stops, tighten the bleed screw again, have the assistant release the pedal slowly, and recheck the reservoir fluid level.

18 Repeat the steps given in paragraphs 16 and 17 until the fluid emerging from the bleed screw is free from air bubbles. If the master cylinder has been drained and refilled, and air is being bled from the first screw in the sequence, allow approximately five seconds between cycles for the master cylinder passages to refill.

19 When no more air bubbles appear, securely tighten the bleed screw, remove the tube and spanner, and refit the dust cap. Do not overtighten the bleed screw.

20 Repeat the procedure on the remaining screws in the sequence, until all air is removed from the system and the brake pedal feels firm again.

Using a one-way valve kit

21 As the name implies, these kits consist of a length of tubing with a one-way valve fitted, to prevent expelled air and fluid being drawn back into the system; some kits include a translucent container, which can be positioned so that the air bubbles can be more easily seen flowing from the end of the tube.

22 The kit is connected to the bleed screw, which is then opened. The user returns to the driver's seat, depresses the brake pedal with a

smooth, steady stroke, and slowly releases it; this is repeated until the expelled fluid is clear of air bubbles.

23 Note that these kits simplify work so much that it is easy to forget the master cylinder reservoir fluid level; ensure that this is maintained at least above the MIN level line at all times.

Using a pressure-bleeding kit

24 These kits are usually operated by a reservoir of pressurised air contained in the spare tyre. However, note that it will probably be necessary to reduce the pressure to a lower level than normal; refer to the instructions supplied with the kit. Note also that if the car is equipped with a puncture repair kit instead of a spare tyre, it will be necessary to borrow a friend's spare wheel and tyre.

25 By connecting a pressurised, fluid-filled container to the master cylinder reservoir, bleeding can be carried out simply by opening each screw in turn (in the specified sequence), and allowing the fluid to flow out until no more air bubbles can be seen in the expelled fluid.

26 This method has the advantage that the large reservoir of fluid provides an additional safeguard against air being drawn into the system during bleeding.

27 Pressure-bleeding is particularly effective when bleeding 'difficult' systems, or when bleeding the complete system at the time of routine fluid renewal.

All methods

28 When bleeding is complete, and firm pedal feel is restored, wash off any spilt fluid, securely tighten the bleed screws, and refit the dust caps.

29 Check the hydraulic fluid level in the master cylinder reservoir, and top-up if necessary (see *Weekly checks*.

30 Discard any hydraulic fluid that has been bled from the system; it will not be fit for re-use.

31 Check the feel of the brake pedal. If it feels at all spongy, air must still be present in the system, and further bleeding is required. Failure to bleed satisfactorily after a reasonable repetition of the bleeding procedure may be due to worn master cylinder seals.

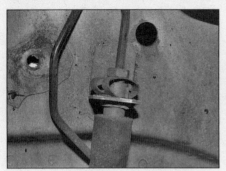

3.2a Front flexible brake hose attachment at the mounting bracket ...

3.2b ... and at the brake caliper

3 Hydraulic pipes and hoses – renewal

Note: *Before starting work, refer to the note at the beginning of Section 2 concerning the dangers of hydraulic fluid.*

1 If any pipe or hose is to be renewed, minimise fluid loss by first removing the master cylinder reservoir cap and screwing it down onto a piece of polythene. Alternatively, flexible hoses can be sealed, if required, using a proprietary brake hose clamp. Metal brake pipe unions can be plugged (if care is taken not to allow dirt into the system) or capped immediately they are disconnected. Place a wad of rag under any union that is to be disconnected, to catch any spilt fluid.

2 If a flexible hose is to be disconnected, unscrew the brake pipe union nut before removing the spring clip which secures the hose to its mounting bracket. Where applicable, unscrew the banjo union bolt securing the hose to the caliper and recover the copper washers **(see illustrations)**. When removing the front flexible hose, withdraw the hose and grommet from the bracket on the suspension strut.

3 To unscrew union nuts, it is preferable to obtain a brake pipe spanner of the correct size; these are available from most motor accessory shops. Failing this, a close-fitting open-ended spanner will be required, though if the nuts are tight or corroded, their flats may be rounded-off if the spanner slips. In such a case, a self-locking wrench is often the only way to unscrew a stubborn union, but it follows that the pipe and the damaged nuts must be renewed on reassembly. Always clean a union and surrounding area before disconnecting it. If disconnecting a component with more than one union, make a careful note of the connections before disturbing any of them.

4 If a brake pipe is to be renewed, it can be obtained, cut to length and with the union nuts and end flares in place, from Vauxhall/Opel dealers. All that is then necessary is to bend it to shape, following the line of the original, before fitting it to the car. Alternatively, most motor accessory shops can make up brake pipes from kits, but this requires very careful measurement of the original, to ensure that the replacement is of the correct length. The safest answer is usually to take the original to the shop as a pattern.

5 On refitting, do not overtighten the union nuts.

6 When refitting hoses to the calipers, always use new copper washers and tighten the banjo union bolts to the specified torque. Make sure that the hoses are positioned so that they will not touch surrounding bodywork or the roadwheels.

7 Ensure that the pipes and hoses are correctly routed, with no kinks, and that they are secured in the clips or brackets provided. After fitting, remove the polythene from the reservoir, and bleed the hydraulic system as described in Section 2. Wash off any spilt fluid, and check carefully for fluid leaks.

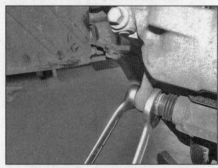

4.3a Unscrew the lower guide pin bolt while counter-holding the guide pin with a second spanner ...

4.3c Lift the caliper upwards to gain access to the brake pads ...

4 Front brake pads – renewal

Warning: Renew BOTH sets of front brake pads at the same time – NEVER renew the pads on only one wheel, as uneven braking may result. Note that the dust created by wear of the pads may contain asbestos, which is a health hazard. Never blow it out with compressed air, and do not inhale any of it. An approved filtering mask should be worn when working on the brakes. DO NOT use petroleum-based solvents to clean brake parts – use brake cleaner or methylated spirit only.

Note: *The photos in this Section depict the renewal of brake pads fitted to single-piston front brake calipers. The pad renewal procedures for twin-piston calipers are similar.*

1 Apply the handbrake, then jack up the front of the vehicle and support it on axle stands (see *Jacking and vehicle support*). Remove the front roadwheels.

2 Push in the caliper piston(s) by sliding the caliper body towards the outside of the vehicle by hand.

3 Follow the accompanying photos **(illustrations 4.3a to 4.3p)** for the actual pad renewal procedure, bearing in mind the additional points listed below. Be sure to stay in order and read the caption under each illustration. Note that if the old pads are to be

4.3b ... then remove the guide pin bolt from the caliper

4.3d Lift out the outer brake pad ...

4.3e … and the inner brake pad …

4.3f Remove the anti-rattle springs from the caliper mounting bracket, noting their fitted position

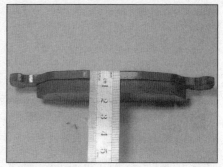

4.3g Measure the thickness of the pad friction material. If any are worn down to the specified minimum, or fouled with oil or grease, all four pads must be renewed

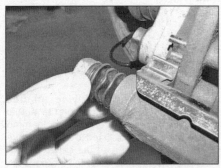

4.3h Check the condition of the guide pin rubber gaiters and check that the guide pins are a snug fit in the caliper bracket

4.3i If new pads are to be fitted, before refitting the caliper, push back the caliper piston whilst opening the bleed screw.

4.3j Refit the anti-rattle springs to the caliper mounting bracket

4.3k Ensure that the anti-squeal shim is in place on the inner pad

4.3l Place the inner pad in position …

4.3m … followed by the outer pad

4.3n Ensure that the pads are fully engaged with the anti-rattle springs

4.3o Lower the caliper back into position over the brake pads

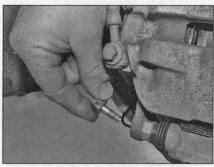

4.3p Refit the guide pin bolt and tighten it to the specified torque

refitted, ensure that they are identified so that they can be returned to their original positions.

4 If the original brake pads are still serviceable, carefully clean them using a clean, fine wire brush or similar, paying particular attention to the sides and back of the metal backing plate. Clean out the grooves in the friction material, and pick out any large embedded particles of dirt or debris. Carefully clean the pad locations in the caliper mounting bracket.

5 Prior to fitting the pads, check that the guide pins are a snug fit in the caliper mounting bracket. Brush the dust and dirt from the caliper and piston, but do not inhale it, as it is injurious to health. Inspect the dust seal around the piston for damage, and the piston for evidence of fluid leaks, corrosion or damage. If attention to any of these components is necessary, refer to Section 7.

6 If new brake pads are to be fitted, the caliper piston must be pushed back into the cylinder to allow for the extra pad thickness. Either use a G-clamp or similar tool, or use suitable pieces of wood as levers. Clamp off the flexible brake hose leading to the caliper then connect a brake bleeding kit to the caliper bleed screw. Open the bleed screw as the piston is retracted, the surplus brake fluid will then be collected in the bleed kit vessel **(see illustration 4.3i)**. Close the bleed screw just before the caliper piston is pushed fully into the caliper. This should ensure no air enters the hydraulic system.

Note: *The ABS unit contains hydraulic components that are very sensitive to impurities in the brake fluid. Even the smallest particles can cause the system to fail through blockage. The pad retraction method described here prevents any debris in the brake fluid expelled from the caliper from being passed back to the ABS hydraulic unit, as well as preventing any chance of damage to the master cylinder seals.*

7 Note that the inner brake pads are fitted with mechanical brake pad wear warning indicators. The warning indicators consist of a metal strip riveted to the backing plate. When the pad friction material reaches the minimum thickness, the metal strip contacts the disc causing a squeaking noise audible to the driver.

8 With the brake pads installed, depress the brake pedal repeatedly, until normal (non-assisted) pedal pressure is restored, and the pads are pressed into firm contact with the brake disc.

9 Repeat the above procedure on the remaining front brake caliper.

10 Refit the roadwheels, then lower the vehicle to the ground and tighten the roadwheel nuts to the specified torque setting.

11 Check the hydraulic fluid level as described in *Weekly checks*.

Caution: New pads will not give full braking efficiency until they have bedded-in. Be prepared for this, and avoid hard braking as far as possible for the first hundred miles or so after pad renewal.

5 Rear brake pads – renewal

⚠ *Warning: Renew BOTH sets of rear brake pads at the same time – NEVER renew the pads on only one wheel, as uneven braking may result. Note that the dust created by wear of the pads may contain asbestos, which is a health hazard. Never blow it out with compressed air, and do not inhale any of it. An approved filtering mask should be worn when working on the brakes. DO NOT use petroleum-based solvents to clean brake parts – use brake cleaner or methylated spirit only.*

1 On models with an electronic handbrake, set the mechanism in the service mode as described in Section 14. Chock the front wheels then jack up the rear of the car and securely support it on axle stands (see *Jacking and vehicle support*). Remove the rear roadwheels.

2 Follow the accompanying photos **(illustrations 5.2a to 5.2t)** for the actual pad renewal procedure, bearing in mind the additional points listed below. Be sure to stay in order and read the caption under each illustration. Note that if the old pads are to be refitted, ensure that they are identified so that they can be returned to their original positions.

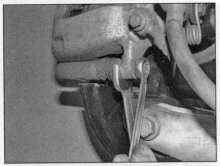

5.2a Unscrew the lower guide pin bolt while counter-holding the guide pin with a second spanner ...

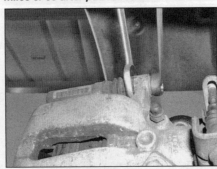

5.2b ... then unscrew the upper guide pin bolt in the same way

5.2c Withdraw the caliper from the brake pads and mounting bracket and suspend it from a convenient place under the wheel arch using wire or cable ties

5.2d Unscrew the lower caliper mounting bracket bolt ...

5.2e ... and the upper mounting bracket bolt ...

5.2f ... and withdraw the mounting bracket, together with the brake pads, from the hub carrier

5.2g Lift out the inner brake pad ...

5.2h ... and the outer brake pad from the caliper mounting bracket

5.2i Remove the anti-rattle springs from the caliper mounting bracket, noting their fitted position

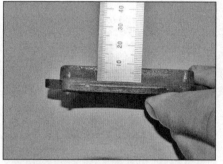

5.2j Measure the thickness of the pad friction material. If any are worn down to the specified minimum, or fouled with oil or grease, all four pads must be renewed

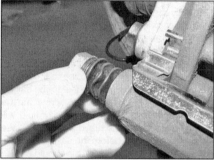

5.2k Check the condition of the guide pin rubber gaiters and check that the guide pins are a snug fit in the caliper bracket

5.2l Using a caliper retracting tool to rotate the piston whilst at the same time pushing it in

5.2m Refit the anti-rattle springs to the caliper mounting bracket

5.2n Place the inner pad in position ...

5.2o ... followed by the outer pad ...

5.2p ... then place the caliper mounting bracket in position over the brake disc

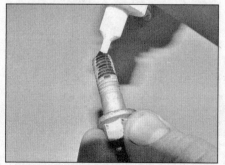

5.2q Apply thread locking compound to the mounting bracket retaining bolts ...

5.2r ... then refit the bolts and tighten them to the specified torque

5.2s Place the caliper back into position over the brake pads

5.2t Refit the upper and lower guide pin bolts and tighten them to the specified torque

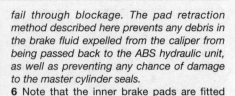

3 If the original brake pads are still serviceable, carefully clean them using a clean, fine wire brush or similar, paying particular attention to the sides and back of the metal backing plate. Clean out the grooves in the friction material, and pick out any large embedded particles of dirt or debris. Carefully clean the pad locations in the caliper body/mounting bracket.

4 Prior to fitting the pads, check that the guide pins are a snug fit in the caliper mounting bracket. Brush the dust and dirt from the caliper and piston, but do not inhale it, as it is injurious to health. Inspect the dust seal around the piston for damage, and the piston for evidence of fluid leaks, corrosion or damage. If attention to any of these components is necessary, refer to Section 8.

5 If new brake pads are to be fitted, it will be necessary to retract the piston fully into the caliper bore by rotating it in a clockwise direction. Special tools are readily available at moderate cost to achieve this **(see illustration 5.2l)**. While the caliper is being retracted, clamp off the flexible brake hose leading to the caliper then connect a brake bleeding kit to the caliper bleed screw. Open the bleed screw as the piston is retracted, the surplus brake fluid will then be collected in the bleed kit vessel. Close the bleed screw just before the caliper piston is pushed fully into the caliper. This should ensure no air enters the hydraulic system.

Note: *The ABS unit contains hydraulic components that are very sensitive to impurities in the brake fluid. Even the smallest particles can cause the system to*

fail through blockage. The pad retraction method described here prevents any debris in the brake fluid expelled from the caliper from being passed back to the ABS hydraulic unit, as well as preventing any chance of damage to the master cylinder seals.

6 Note that the inner brake pads are fitted with mechanical brake pad wear warning indicators. The warning indicators consist of a metal strip riveted to the backing plate. When the pad friction material reaches the minimum thickness, the metal strip contacts the disc causing a squeaking noise audible to the driver.

7 With the brake pads installed, depress the brake pedal repeatedly, until normal (non-assisted) pedal pressure is restored, and the pads are pressed into firm contact with the brake disc.

8 Repeat the above procedure on the remaining rear brake caliper.

9 Refit the roadwheels, then lower the vehicle to the ground and tighten the roadwheel nuts to the specified torque setting.

10 Check the hydraulic fluid level as described in *Weekly checks*.

11 On models with an electronic handbrake, reset the mechanism as described in Section 14.

Caution: New pads will not give full braking efficiency until they have bedded-in. Be prepared for this, and avoid hard braking as far as possible for the first hundred miles or so after pad renewal.

---

6 Front/rear brake disc – inspection, removal and refitting

Note: *Before starting work, refer to the warning at the beginning of Section 4 or 5 concerning the dangers of asbestos dust. If either disc requires renewal, both should be renewed at the same time together with new pads, to ensure even and consistent braking.*

Inspection

Front disc

1 Firmly apply the handbrake, then jack up the front of the vehicle and support it securely on axle stands (see *Jacking and vehicle support*). Remove the roadwheel.

2 Release the brake hydraulic hose from the suspension strut bracket **(see illustration)**.

3 Unscrew the two bolts securing the brake caliper mounting bracket to the swivel hub, noting that new bolts will be required for refitting. Slide the caliper/bracket assembly from the swivel hub and brake disc (there is no need to remove the brake pads). Suspend the caliper/bracket assembly from the strut coil spring using wire or a cable tie – do not allow the caliper to hang on the brake hose **(see illustrations)**.

Rear disc

4 Chock the front wheels, then jack up the rear of the vehicle, and support it securely on axle stands (see *Jacking and vehicle support*).

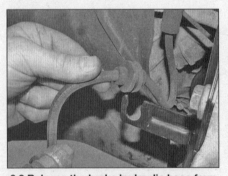

6.2 Release the brake hydraulic hose from the suspension strut bracket

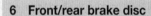

6.3a Unscrew the two bolts securing the front brake caliper mounting bracket to the swivel hub …

6.3b … slide the caliper/bracket assembly from the swivel hub and brake disc …

6.3c … and suspend the caliper/bracket assembly from the strut coil spring using wire or a cable tie

Remove the roadwheel, then ensure that the handbrake is released.

5 Unscrew the two bolts securing the brake caliper mounting bracket to the hub carrier. Slide the caliper/bracket assembly from the hub carrier and brake disc (there is no need to remove the brake pads) **(see illustrations)**. Suspend the caliper/bracket assembly from a convenient place under the wheel arch using wire or a cable tie – do not allow the caliper to hang on the brake hose.

Front and rear discs

6 Temporarily refit two of the wheel nuts to diagonally-opposite studs, with the flat sides of the nuts against the disc. Tighten the nuts progressively, to hold the disc firmly.

7 Scrape any corrosion from the disc. Rotate the disc, and examine it for deep scoring, grooving or cracks. Using a micrometer, measure the thickness of the disc in several places **(see illustration)**. The minimum thickness is given in the Specifications. Light wear and scoring is normal, but if excessive, the disc should be removed, and either reground by a specialist, or renewed. If regrinding is undertaken, the minimum thickness must be maintained. Obviously, if the disc is cracked, it must be renewed.

8 Using a dial gauge, check that the disc run-out 10 mm from the outer edge does not exceed the limit given in the Specifications. To do this, fix the measuring equipment, and rotate the disc, noting the variation in measurement as the disc is rotated **(see illustration)**. The difference between the minimum and maximum measurements recorded is the disc run-out.

9 If the run-out is greater than the specified amount, check for variations of the disc thickness as follows. Mark the disc at eight positions 45° apart then, using a micrometer, measure the disc thickness at the eight positions, 15 mm in from the outer edge. If the variation between the minimum and maximum readings is greater than the specified amount, the disc should be renewed.

Removal

10 If not already done, remove the brake caliper and mounting bracket as described in paragraph 3 (front disc) or 5 (rear disc). Where applicable, remove the two wheel nuts used when checking the disc.

11 Undo the securing screw and withdraw the disc from the hub **(see illustrations)**.

Refitting

12 Refit the disc, making sure that the mating faces of the disc and hub are perfectly clean, then refit and tighten the securing screw.

13 Refit the caliper mounting bracket, together with the caliper and brake pads and tighten the retaining bolts to the specified torque. Ensure that new bolts are used if refitting the front caliper mounting bracket, and apply thread locking compound to the

6.5a Unscrew the two bolts securing the rear brake caliper mounting bracket to the hub carrier …

6.7 Using a micrometer to measure the thickness of the brake disc

retaining bolts if refitting the rear caliper mounting bracket.

14 Where applicable refit the brake hydraulic hose to the suspension strut bracket.

15 Refit the roadwheel, then lower the vehicle to the ground and tighten the roadwheel nuts to the specified torque.

---

7 Front brake caliper – removal, overhaul and refitting

Note: *New brake hose copper washers will be required when refitting. Before starting work, refer to the note at the beginning of Section 2 concerning the dangers of hydraulic fluid, and to the warning at the beginning of Section 4 concerning the dangers of asbestos dust.*

6.11a Undo the securing screw …

6.5b … and slide the caliper/bracket assembly from the hub carrier and brake disc

6.8 Using a dial gauge to measure the brake disc run-out

Removal

1 Firmly apply the handbrake, then jack up the front of the car and support it securely on axle stands (see *Jacking and vehicle support*). Remove the appropriate roadwheel.

2 Minimise fluid loss by first removing the master cylinder reservoir cap, then tightening it down onto a piece of polythene to obtain an airtight seal.

3 Clean the area around the caliper brake hose union. Unscrew and remove the union bolt, and recover the copper sealing washer from each side of the hose union. Discard the washers; new ones must be used on refitting. Plug the hose end and caliper hole, to minimise fluid loss and prevent the ingress of dust and dirt into the hydraulic system.

4 Slacken and remove the lower and upper caliper guide pin bolts, while counter-holding

6.11b … and withdraw the brake disc from the hub

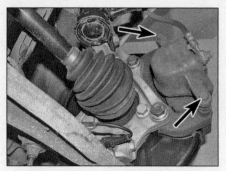

7.4 Front brake caliper guide pin bolts

the guide pins with a second spanner, and remove the brake caliper from the mounting bracket **(see illustration)**. Note that the brake pads need not be disturbed, and can be left in position in the caliper mounting bracket.

5 If required, the caliper mounting bracket can be unbolted from the swivel hub. Discard the bolts as new ones must be fitted.

Overhaul

Note: *Before starting work, check with your local dealer for the availability of parts to overhaul the caliper.*

6 With the caliper on the bench, wipe away all traces of dust and dirt, but *avoid inhaling the dust, as it is a health hazard.*

7 Withdraw the partially-ejected piston from the caliper body, and remove the dust seal. The piston can be withdrawn by hand, or if necessary pushed out by applying compressed air to the brake hose union hole. Only low pressure should be required, such as is generated by a foot pump, and as a precaution a block of wood should be positioned to prevent any damage to the piston.

8 Using a small screwdriver, carefully remove the piston seal from the caliper, taking great care not mark the bore **(see illustration)**.

9 Thoroughly clean all components, using only methylated spirit, isopropyl alcohol or clean hydraulic fluid as a cleaning medium. Never use mineral-based solvents such as petrol or paraffin, which will attack the hydraulic system's rubber components. Dry the components immediately, using compressed air or a clean, lint-free cloth. If compressed air is available, use it to blow through the fluid passages to make sure they are clear

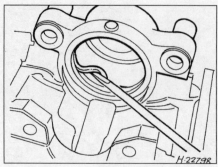

7.8 Removing the piston seal from the caliper body

> ⚠️ *Warning: Always wear eye protection when using compressed air.*

10 Check all components, and renew any that are worn or damaged. Check particularly the cylinder bore and piston; these should be renewed (note that this means the renewal of the complete body assembly) if they are scratched, worn or corroded in any way. Similarly check the condition of the guide pin rubber gaiters and check that the guide pins are a snug fit in the caliper mounting bracket. If there is any doubt about the condition of any component, renew it.

11 If the assembly is fit for further use, obtain the necessary components from your Vauxhall/Opel dealer. Renew the caliper seals as a matter of course; these should never be re-used.

12 On reassembly, ensure that all components are absolutely clean and dry.

13 Soak the piston and the new piston (fluid) seal in clean hydraulic fluid. Smear clean fluid on the cylinder bore surface.

14 Fit the new piston (fluid) seal, using only the fingers to manipulate it into the cylinder bore groove.

15 Fit the new dust seal to the piston, refit it to the cylinder bore using a twisting motion, and ensure that the piston enters squarely into the bore. Press the dust seal fully into the caliper body, and push the piston fully into the caliper bore.

Refitting

17 If previously removed, refit the caliper mounting bracket to the swivel hub, and tighten the new bolts to the specified torque.

18 Refit the brake pads as described in Section 4, together with the caliper which at this stage will not have the hose attached.

19 Position a new copper sealing washer on each side of the hose union, and connect the brake hose to the caliper. Ensure that the hose is correctly positioned against the caliper body lug, then install the union bolt and tighten it to the specified torque setting.

20 Remove the brake hose clamp or polythene, and bleed the hydraulic system as described in Section 2. Note that, providing the precautions described were taken to minimise brake fluid loss, it should only be necessary to bleed the relevant front brake circuit.

21 Refit the roadwheel, then lower the vehicle to the ground and tighten the roadwheel nuts to the specified torque.

8 Rear brake caliper – removal, overhaul and refitting

Note: *Before starting work, refer to the note at the beginning of Section 2 concerning the dangers of hydraulic fluid, and to the warning at the beginning of Section 5 concerning the dangers of asbestos dust.*

Removal

1 Chock the front wheels, then jack up the rear of the vehicle and support on axle stands (see *Jacking and vehicle support*). Remove the roadwheel.

2 Minimise fluid loss by first removing the master cylinder reservoir cap and screwing it down onto a piece of polythene. Alternatively, use a brake hose clamp to clamp the flexible hose leading to the brake caliper.

3 Clean the area around the caliper brake hose union. Unscrew and remove the union bolt, and recover the copper sealing washer from each side of the hose union. Discard the washers; new ones must be used on refitting. Plug the hose end and caliper hole, to minimise fluid loss and prevent the ingress of dust and dirt into the hydraulic system.

4 Disengage the handbrake inner cable from the caliper lever. Extract the retaining circlip then pull the outer cable out of the caliper bracket **(see illustrations)**.

8.4a Disengage the handbrake inner cable from the caliper lever …

8.4b … extract the retaining circlip …

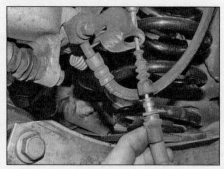

8.4c … then pull the outer cable out of the caliper bracket

5 Slacken and remove the lower and upper caliper guide pin bolts, while counter-holding the guide pins with a second spanner, and remove the brake caliper from the mounting bracket **(see illustration)**. Note that the brake pads need not be disturbed, and can be left in position in the caliper mounting bracket.

6 If required, the caliper mounting bracket can be unbolted and removed from the hub carrier.

Overhaul

7 No overhaul procedures, or parts, were available at the time of writing. Check the availability of spares before dismantling the caliper. Do not attempt to dismantle the handbrake mechanism inside the caliper; if the mechanism is faulty, the complete caliper assembly must be renewed.

Refitting

8 If previously removed, refit the brake pads as described in Section 5, together with the caliper which at this stage will not have the hose attached.

9 Position a new copper sealing washer on each side of the hose union, and connect the brake hose to the caliper. Ensure that the hose is correctly positioned against the caliper body lug, then install the union bolt and tighten it to the specified torque setting.

10 Engage the handbrake outer cable with the caliper bracket and refit the circlip. Pull back the operating lever and reconnect the handbrake inner cable.

11 Remove the brake hose clamp or polythene, and bleed the hydraulic system as described in Section 2. Note that, providing the precautions described were taken to minimise brake fluid loss, it should only be necessary to bleed the relevant rear brake circuit.

12 Refit the roadwheel, then lower the vehicle to the ground and tighten the roadwheel nuts to the specified torque.

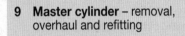

9 Master cylinder – removal, overhaul and refitting

Note: *Before starting work, refer to the*

8.5 Remove the lower and upper caliper guide pin bolts and remove the brake caliper from the mounting bracket

warning at the beginning of Section 2 concerning the dangers of hydraulic fluid.
Note: *New master cylinder retaining nuts will be required for refitting.*

Removal

1 Remove the master cylinder reservoir cap, and siphon the hydraulic fluid from the reservoir. **Note:** *Do not siphon the fluid by mouth, as it is poisonous; use a syringe or an old hydrometer.* Alternatively, open any convenient bleed screw in the system, and gently pump the brake pedal to expel the fluid through a plastic tube connected to the screw (see Section 2).

2 Disconnect the wiring connector from the brake fluid level sensor on the top of the reservoir **(see illustration)**.

3 On models with manual transmission, release the clip (if fitted) and disconnect the clutch hydraulic pipe from the fluid reservoir **(see illustration)**. Tape over or plug the outlet.

4 Place cloth rags beneath the master cylinder to collect escaping brake fluid. Identify the brake lines for position, then unscrew the union nuts and move the lines to one side. Tape over or plug the line outlets.

5 Unscrew the mounting nuts and withdraw the master cylinder from the vacuum servo unit **(see illustration)**. Recover the seal. Take care not to spill fluid on the vehicle paintwork. Note that new retaining nuts will be required for refitting.

Overhaul

6 At the time of writing, master cylinder overhaul is not possible as no spares are available.

7 The only parts available individually are the fluid reservoir, its mounting seals, the filler cap and the master cylinder mounting seal.

8 If the master cylinder is worn excessively, it must be renewed.

9 To remove the fluid reservoir, undo the retaining bolt and pull the reservoir out of the rubber seals in the master cylinder body. Place absorbent rags under the master cylinder as you do this to catch the escaping hydraulic fluid.

10 Remove the reservoir seals from the master cylinder body and obtain new seals for reassembly.

11 Lubricate the new seals with clean brake hydraulic fluid and push the new seals into position.

12 Refit the reservoir and secure with the retaining bolt.

Refitting

13 Ensure that the mating surfaces are clean and dry then fit the new seal to the rear of the master cylinder.

14 Fit the master cylinder to the servo unit, ensuring that the servo unit pushrod enters the master cylinder piston centrally. Fit the new retaining nuts and tighten them to the specified torque setting.

15 Refit the brake lines and tighten the union nuts securely.

16 On manual transmission models, reconnect the clutch hydraulic pipe and secure with the clip (where fitted).

17 Reconnect the wiring connector to the brake fluid level sensor.

18 Remove the reservoir filler cap and polythene, then top-up the reservoir with fresh hydraulic fluid to the MAX mark (see *Weekly checks*).

19 Bleed the hydraulic systems as described in Section 2 and Chapter 6, Section 2 then refit the filler cap. Thoroughly check the operation of the brakes and clutch before using the vehicle on the road.

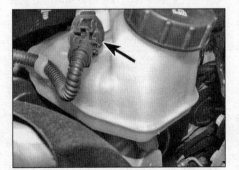

9.2 Disconnect the wiring connector from the brake fluid level sensor

9.3 On manual transmission models disconnect the clutch hydraulic pipe from the fluid reservoir

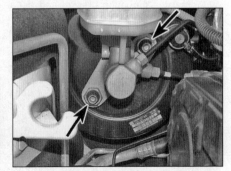

9.5 Master cylinder mounting nuts

10 Brake pedal – removal and refitting

Note: *The brake pedal mounting bracket, the brake pedal and, on manual transmission models, the clutch pedal are one assembly and must be renewed as a complete unit. In the event of a frontal collision, the brake pedal is released from its bearing in the mounting bracket to prevent injury to the driver's feet and legs (this also applies to the clutch pedal). If an airbag has been deployed, inspect the pedal and mounting bracket assembly and if necessary renew the complete unit.*

Removal

1 Disconnect the battery negative terminal (refer to Chapter 5A, Section 4).
2 On manual transmission models, remove the clutch master cylinder as described in Chapter 6, Section 3.
3 Remove the steering column as described in Chapter 10, Section 21.
4 Remove the complete facia assembly and the facia crossmember as described in Chapter 11, Sections 30 and 31 respectively.
5 Remove the brake light switch from the pedal mounting bracket as described in Section 17.
6 Refer to Chapter 4A, Section 2 and 3 or Chapter 4B, Section 3 and 4 as applicable and remove the air cleaner assembly and the accelerator pedal/position sensor. Where fitted, remove the clutch switch from the pedal mounting bracket.
7 Working in the engine compartment, unscrew the two nuts securing the brake master cylinder to the vacuum servo unit **(see illustration 9.5)**. Now unscrew the two stud bolts securing the vacuum servo unit to the bulkhead. Note that new master cylinder retaining nuts will be required for refitting.
8 Pull the brake pedal upward, away from the bulkhead to release the pedal connector from the servo unit pushrod. Note that a new connector will be required for refitting.
9 From within the engine compartment, unscrew the four nuts securing the mounting bracket and pedal assembly to the bulkhead. Withdraw the mounting bracket and pedal assembly and remove it from inside the car.

Refitting

10 Manoeuvre the mounting bracket and pedal assembly into position, whilst ensuring that the vacuum servo unit pushrod locates in the brake pedal connector. Fit the four pedal mounting bracket new retaining nuts and tighten them to the specified torque.
11 Working in the engine compartment, fit the two stud bolts securing the vacuum servo unit to the bulkhead and tighten the bolts to the specified torque. Fit the two new brake master cylinder retaining nuts and tighten the nuts to the specified torque.
12 Refer to Chapter 4A, Section 2 and 3 or

Chapter 4B, Section 3 and 4 as applicable and refit the air cleaner assembly and the accelerator pedal/position sensor. Where fitted, refit the clutch switch to the pedal mounting bracket.
13 Refit the brake light switch to the pedal mounting bracket as described in Section 17.
14 Refit the facia crossmember and facia assembly as described in Chapter 11, Section 30 and 31.
15 Refit the steering column as described in Chapter 10, Section 21.
16 On manual transmission models, refit the clutch master cylinder as described in Chapter 6, Section 3.
17 Reconnect the battery negative terminal on completion.

11 Vacuum servo unit – testing, removal and refitting

Testing

1 To test the operation of the servo unit, with the engine off, depress the footbrake several times to exhaust the vacuum. Now start the engine, keeping the pedal firmly depressed. As the engine starts, there should be a noticeable 'give' in the brake pedal as the vacuum builds-up. Allow the engine to run for at least two minutes, then switch it off. The brake pedal should now feel normal, but further applications should result in the pedal feeling firmer, the pedal stroke decreasing with each application.
2 If the servo does not operate as described, first inspect the servo unit check valve as described in Section 12.
3 If the servo unit still fails to operate satisfactorily, the fault lies within the unit itself. Repairs to the unit are not possible; if faulty, the servo unit must be renewed.

Removal

Right-hand drive models

4 It will first be necessary to remove the engine and transmission assembly as described in Chapter 2E, Section 4 to obtain the necessary clearance for removal of the servo unit.
5 Remove the brake master cylinder as described in Section 9.
6 Remove the facia footwell trim panel on the driver's side as described in Chapter 11, Section 30.
7 Pull the brake pedal upward, away from the bulkhead to release the pedal connector from the servo unit pushrod. Note that a new connector will be required for refitting.
8 Pull out the vacuum hose from the rubber grommet in the vacuum servo.
9 Unscrew the two stud bolts securing the vacuum servo unit to the bulkhead, and remove the servo unit from the engine compartment.

Left-hand drive models

10 Remove the battery and battery box as described in Chapter 5A, Section 4.
11 Remove the retaining clip, lift up the cooling system expansion tank and remove it from the mounting bracket. Place the tank to one side.
12 Remove the ABS hydraulic modulator together with its mounting bracket as described in Section 21.
13 Remove the brake master cylinder as described in Section 9.
14 Remove the facia footwell trim panel on the driver's side as described in Chapter 11, Section 30.
15 Pull the brake pedal upward, away from the bulkhead to release the pedal connector from the servo unit pushrod. Note that a new connector will be required for refitting.
16 Pull out the vacuum hose from the rubber grommet in the vacuum servo.
17 Unscrew the two stud bolts securing the vacuum servo unit to the bulkhead, and remove the servo unit from the engine compartment.

Refitting

Right-hand drive models

18 Locate the vacuum servo unit in position on the bulkhead ensuring that the servo unit pushrod locates correctly in the brake pedal connector. Refit the two new retaining stud bolts and tighten them to the specified torque.
19 Refit the vacuum hose to the servo grommet, ensuring that the hose is correctly seated.
20 Refit the brake master cylinder as described in Section 9.
21 Refit the engine and transmission assembly as described in Chapter 2E, Section 4.
22 Refit the facia footwell trim panel as described in Chapter 11, Section 30.
23 On completion, reconnect the battery negative terminal.

Left-hand drive models

24 Locate the vacuum servo unit in position on the bulkhead ensuring that the servo unit pushrod locates correctly in the brake pedal connector. Refit the two new retaining stud bolts and tighten them to the specified torque.
25 Refit the vacuum hose to the servo grommet, ensuring that the hose is correctly seated.
26 Refit the brake master cylinder as described in Section 9, but don't bleed the hydraulic circuits at this stage.
27 Refit the ABS hydraulic modulator and mounting bracket as described in Section 21.
28 Refit the cooling system expansion tank to the mounting bracket.
29 Refit the battery box and battery as described in Chapter 5A, Section 4.
30 Refit the facia footwell trim panel on the driver's side as described in Chapter 11, Section 30.
31 Remove the master cylinder reservoir filler

12.3 Disconnect the secondary vacuum hose quick-release fitting from the vacuum pump

12.6 Disconnect the wiring connector from the vacuum switch on the servo unit

12.11 Disconnect the hose quick-release fitting from the vacuum pump (2.0 litre model)

cap and polythene, then top-up the reservoir with fresh hydraulic fluid to the MAX mark (see *Weekly checks*).

32 Bleed the hydraulic systems as described in Section 2 and Chapter 6, Section 2 (where applicable) then refit the filler cap. Thoroughly check the operation of the brakes and clutch before using the vehicle on the road.

12 Vacuum servo unit check valve and hose – removal, testing and refitting

Removal

Petrol engine models

1 Firmly apply the handbrake, then jack up the front of the vehicle and support it securely on axle stands (see *Jacking and vehicle support*). Remove the right-hand front roadwheel.

2 Undo the screws, release clips and remove the right-hand front wheel arch liner.

3 Working under the wheel arch, disconnect the secondary vacuum hose quick-release fitting from the vacuum pump **(see illustration)**.

4 Unclip the secondary vacuum hose from its supports under the wheel arch and in the engine compartment.

5 Disconnect the primary vacuum hose quick-release fitting from the inlet manifold.

6 Disconnect the wiring connector from the vacuum switch on the servo unit **(see illustration)**.

7 Pull out the vacuum hose adaptor from the rubber grommet in the servo unit.

8 Unclip the primary vacuum hose from its supports on the bulkhead and engine, then remove the adaptor, hoses and check valve assembly from the car.

Diesel engine models

9 Pull out the vacuum hose from the rubber grommet in the vacuum servo unit.

10 Remove the plastic cover over the top of the engine.

11 Disconnect the hose quick-release fitting from the vacuum pump **(see illustration)**.

12 Unclip the vacuum hose from its supports on the bulkhead and engine, then remove the

hose and check valve from the car.

Testing

13 Examine the check valve and hose for signs of damage, and renew if necessary. The valve may be tested by blowing through it in both directions. Air should flow through the valve in one direction only – when blown through from the servo unit end. If air flows in both directions, or not at all, renew the valve and hose as an assembly.

14 Examine the servo unit rubber sealing grommet for signs of damage or deterioration, and renew as necessary.

Refitting

15 Refitting is a reversal of removal ensuring that the quick-release connectors audibly lock in position, and that the hose/adaptor is correctly seated in the servo grommet.

16 On completion, start the engine and check that there are no air leaks.

13 Handbrake lever (mechanical handbrake) – removal and refitting

Removal

1 Remove the centre console as described in Chapter 11, Section 29.

2 Ensure that the handbrake lever is released (off).

3 Set the handbrake cable self-adjusting

13.3 Push the piston rod and spring rearward with a suitable tool, then press down the transport fixing to lock the mechanism

mechanism to the fully released position as follows. Push the piston rod and spring rearward with a suitable tool. Hold them in this position and press down the transport fixing to lock the mechanism in the released position **(see illustration)**.

4 Rotate the front handbrake cable end to release it from the equalizer.

5 Disconnect the wiring connector from the handbrake lever warning light switch.

6 Undo the four retaining nuts and remove the handbrake lever assembly from inside the car.

Refitting

7 Locate the handbrake lever assembly in position over the mounting studs. Refit the four retaining nuts and tighten to the specified torque.

8 Reconnect the handbrake lever warning light switch wiring connector.

9 Reconnect the front handbrake cable to the equalizer.

10 Pull the handbrake lever up to release the transport fixing and automatically adjust the handbrake cable.

11 Refit the centre console as described in Chapter 11, Section 29.

14 Handbrake motor (electronic handbrake) – removal and refitting

Removal

1 Set the electronic handbrake in the service mode as follows:

a) *Chock the front wheels and place the gear lever in neutral (manual transmission) or PARK (automatic transmission).*

b) *Pull the hand brake switch up to apply the handbrake.*

c) *Turn the ignition switch to the RUN position and depress the footbrake.*

d) *Press and hold the the handbrake switch down for for approximately 5 seconds.*

e) *When a flashing yellow telltale appears on the instrument panel, release the switch, then immediately press and release the switch again.*

f) *Turn the ignition off.*

2 Chock the front wheels, then jack up the

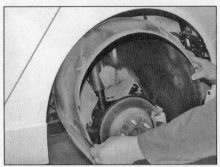

14.3 Undo the screws, release clips and remove the left-hand rear wheel arch liner

14.4 Disconnect the wiring connector, then release the wiring harness clips from the handbrake motor mounting bracket

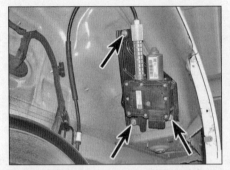

14.5a Undo the three retaining nuts ...

14.5b ... and withdraw the motor and mounting bracket from the wheel arch

rear of the vehicle, and support it securely on axle stands (see *Jacking and vehicle support*). Remove the left-hand rear roadwheel.
3 Undo the screws, release clips and remove

the left-hand rear wheel arch liner **(see illustration)**.
4 Disconnect the handbrake motor wiring connector, then release the two wiring harness

14.6a Unscrew the knurled nut securing the handbrake cable to the motor ...

14.6b ... then disengage the handbrake inner cable from the motor operating shaft

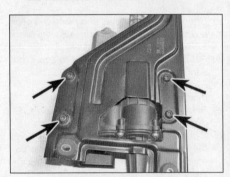

14.7 Handbrake motor-to-mounting bracket retaining bolts

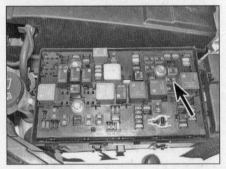

14.14 Electronic handbrake control unit fuse

retaining clips from the motor mounting bracket **(see illustration)**.
5 Undo the three retaining nuts and withdraw the motor and mounting bracket from the wheel arch **(see illustrations)**.
6 Unscrew the knurled nut securing the handbrake cable to the motor, then disengage the handbrake inner cable from the motor operating shaft **(see illustrations)**.
7 Remove the motor and mounting bracket from under the wheel arch then, if required, undo the four retaining bolts and separate the motor from the mounting bracket **(see illustration)**.

Refitting

8 Where applicable, place the motor in position on the mounting bracket and secure with the four retaining bolts, tightened securely.
9 Connect the handbrake inner cable to the motor operating shaft, then screw on the knurled nut to secure the outer cable to the motor.
10 Locate the motor and mounting bracket in position under the wheel arch and refit the three retaining nuts. Tighten the nuts securely.
11 Reconnect the motor wiring connector and refit the two wiring harness retaining clips.
12 Refit the wheel arch liner and the roadwheel, then lower the vehicle to the ground and tighten the wheel nuts to the specified torque.
13 If the original handbrake motor has been refitted, carry out the following procedure to adjust the handbrake cables and calibrate the motor.

a) *Chock the front wheels and place the gear lever in neutral (manual transmission) or PARK (automatic transmission).*
b) *Turn the ignition switch to the RUN position and depress the footbrake.*
c) *Briefly lift, then release the handbrake switch to apply the handbrake.*
d) *Briefly press, then release the handbrake switch to release the handbrake.*
e) *Repeat steps c and d four more times.*
f) *Turn the ignition off.*

14 If a new handbrake motor has been fitted, the handbrake electronic control unit must be programmed using the procedures described below.

a) *Chock the front wheels and place the gear lever in neutral (manual transmission) or PARK (automatic transmission).*
b) *Turn the ignition switch to the RUN position and depress the footbrake.*
c) *Press and hold the the handbrake switch down for 5 to 6 seconds, then release it.*
d) *Briefly press the handbrake switch down again.*
e) *Lift off the engine compartment fuse/relay box cover and remove the electronic handbrake control unit fuse (fuse 27) (see illustration).*
f) *Refit the fuse and apply the handbrake, then release the handbrake.*
g) *Apply and release the handbrake a further four times.*
h) *Turn the ignition off.*

16.4 Disconnect the handbrake inner cable end fitting from the caliper operating lever

16.5a Extract the circlip securing the handbrake outer cable to the bracket on the brake caliper ...

16.5b ... then withdraw the cable from the caliper

15 Handbrake cable (mechanical handbrake) – removal and refitting

Removal

1 The handbrake cable consists of three parts, a short front connecting cable which connects the lever to the equalizer plate, and the two main cables which link the equalizer plate to the left-hand and right-hand rear brake calipers. The connecting cable is an integral part of the handbrake lever assembly and cannot be separated. The main cables are available individually.

2 Carry out the operations described in Section 13, paragraphs 1 to 3.

3 From inside the car, disconnect the handbrake inner cable from the equalizer plate at the rear of the handbrake lever.

4 Chock the front wheels, then jack up the rear of the vehicle, and support it securely on axle stands (see *Jacking and vehicle support*).

5 Push down on the handbrake operating lever on the relevant rear brake caliper and slip the inner cable end fitting out of the lever **(see illustration 16.4)**.

6 Extract the circlip securing the handbrake outer cable to the bracket on the brake caliper, then withdraw the cable from the caliper **(see illustrations 16.5a and 16.5b)**.

7 Release the cable from the support brackets and clips on the underbody and suspension arms, then pull the cable out of the entry point on the underbody. Remove the cable from under the car.

Refitting

8 Feed the cable through the entry point on the underbody, then locate the cable in position in the underbody support clips and brackets.

9 Engage the handbrake outer cable with the caliper bracket and secure with the circlip. Pull back the caliper operating lever and reconnect the handbrake inner cable.

10 From inside the car, reconnect the handbrake inner cable to the equalizer plate.

11 Pull the handbrake lever up to release the transport fixing and automatically adjust the handbrake cable.

12 Lower the car to the ground, then refit the centre console as described in Chapter 11, Section 29.

16 Handbrake cable (electronic handbrake) – removal and refitting

Removal

1 Carry out the operations described in Section 14, paragraphs 1 to 3.

2 Unscrew the knurled nut securing the handbrake cable to the motor, then disengage the handbrake inner cable from the motor operating shaft **(see illustrations 14.6a and14.6b)**.

3 Release the outer cable from the retaining clip under the wheel arch.

16.7a Extract the circlip ...

16.7c ... and slide the cable grommet out of the other subframe bracket

4 Push down on the handbrake operating lever on the left-hand rear brake caliper and slip the inner cable end fitting out of the lever **(see illustration)**.

5 Extract the circlip securing the handbrake outer cable to the bracket on the brake caliper, then withdraw the cable from the caliper **(see illustrations)**.

6 Repeat paragraphs 4 and 5 to disconnect the handbrake cable from the right-hand rear brake caliper.

7 Extract the circlip and withdraw the right-hand (main) cable from the subframe support bracket. Slide the cable grommet out of the other subframe bracket **(see illustrations)**.

8 Extract the circlip, withdraw the left-hand cable from the subframe support bracket and disconnect the inner cable end fitting from the cable compensator **(see illustrations)**. Remove the cables from under the car.

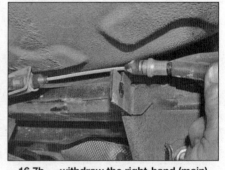

16.7b ... withdraw the right-hand (main) cable from the subframe support bracket ...

16.8a Extract the circlip ...

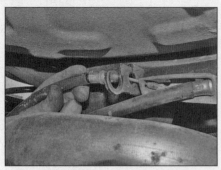

16.8b ... withdraw the left-hand cable from the subframe support bracket ...

16.8c ... and disconnect the inner cable end fitting from the cable compensator

Refitting

9 Engage the left-hand cable end fitting with the cable compensator, then locate the outer cable in the subframe support bracket and secure with the circlip.

10 Locate the right-hand outer cable in the subframe support bracket and secure with the circlip. Fit the cable grommet to the other subframe support bracket.

11 Engage the handbrake outer cables with the caliper brackets and secure with the circlips. Pull back the caliper operating levers and reconnect the handbrake inner cables.

12 Refit the outer cable to the retaining clip under the wheel arch.

13 Connect the handbrake inner cable to the motor operating shaft, then screw on the knurled nut to secure the outer cable to the motor.

19.2a Undo the centre retaining screw ...

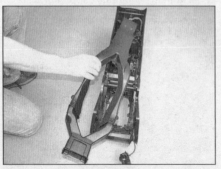

19.2c ... then remove the footwell air duct from the underside of the centre console

14 Refit the wheel arch liner and the roadwheel, then lower the vehicle to the ground and tighten the wheel nuts to the specified torque.

15 Carry out the following procedure to adjust the handbrake cables and calibrate the handbrake motor.

a) *Chock the front wheels and place the gear lever in neutral (manual transmission) or PARK (automatic transmission).*

b) *Turn the ignition switch to the RUN position and depress the footbrake.*

c) *Briefly lift, then release the handbrake switch to apply the handbrake.*

d) *Briefly press, then release the handbrake switch to release the handbrake.*

e) *Repeat steps c and d four more times.*

f) *Turn the ignition off.*

19.2b ... and the rear retaining screw ...

19.3 From the underside of the console, release the retaining tabs, then lift off the switch upper trim panel

17 Brake light switch – removal and refitting

Removal

Note: *The brake light switch is also a brake pedal position sensor. The body control module (BCM) uses the switch/sensor signal to determine brake pedal position and rate of brake application. If a new brake light switch is to be fitted, this work must be entrusted to a Vauxhall/Opel dealer or suitably-equipped specialist as it is necessary to calibrate the BCM after installation. This work requires the use of dedicated Vauxhall/Opel diagnostic equipment or a compatible alternative.*

1 The brake light switch is located on the brake pedal mounting bracket in the driver's footwell, behind the facia.

2 Remove the facia footwell trim panel on the driver's side as described in Chapter 11, Section 30.

3 Disconnect the wiring connector from the brake light switch.

4 Undo the retaining bolt and remove the switch from the pedal mounting bracket.

Refitting

5 Refitting is a reversal of removal.

18 Handbrake warning light switch (mechanical handbrake) – removal and refitting

Removal

1 Remove the centre console as described in Chapter 11, Section 29.

2 Disconnect the wiring connector from the warning light switch on the side of the handbrake lever.

3 Unscrew the mounting bolt and remove the switch from the handbrake lever bracket.

Refitting

4 Refitting is a reversal of removal.

19 Handbrake operating switch (electronic handbrake) – removal and refitting

Removal

1 Remove the centre console as described in Chapter 11, Section 29.

2 Undo the three screws and remove the footwell air duct from the underside of the console **(see illustrations)**.

3 From the underside of the console, release the retaining tabs using a small screwdriver and lift off the switch upper trim panel **(see illustration)**.

4 Undo the retaining screw, withdraw the handbrake operating switch from the console and disconnect the wiring connector **(see illustrations)**.

Refitting

5 Refitting is a reversal of removal.

20 Anti-lock braking and stability control systems – general information

1 ABS is fitted as standard to all models. On higher specification models, the ABS may also incorporate traction control, an electronic stability program and various other additional safety features.

2 The ABS system comprises a hydraulic modulator and electronic control unit together with four wheel speed sensors. The hydraulic modulator contains the electronic control unit (ECU), the hydraulic solenoid valves (one set for each brake) and the electrically-driven pump. The purpose of the system is to prevent the wheel(s) locking during heavy braking. This is achieved by automatic release of the brake on the relevant wheel, followed by re-application of the brake.

3 The solenoid valves are controlled by the ECU, which itself receives signals from the four wheel speed sensors which monitor the speed of rotation of each wheel. By comparing these signals, the ECU can determine the speed at which the vehicle is travelling. It can then use this speed to determine when a wheel is decelerating at an abnormal rate, compared to the speed of the vehicle, and therefore predicts when a wheel is about to lock. During normal operation, the system functions in the same way as a conventional braking system.

4 If the ECU senses that a wheel is about to lock, it operates the relevant solenoid valve(s) in the hydraulic modulator, which then isolates from the master cylinder the relevant brake(s) on the wheel(s) which is/are about to lock, effectively sealing-in the hydraulic pressure.

5 If the speed of rotation of the wheel continues to decrease at an abnormal rate, the ECU operates the electrically-driven pump which pumps the hydraulic fluid back into the master cylinder, releasing the brake. Once the speed of rotation of the wheel returns to an acceptable rate, the pump stops, and the solenoid valves switch again, allowing the hydraulic master cylinder pressure to return to the caliper, which then re-applies the brake. This cycle can be carried out many times a second.

6 The action of the solenoid valves and return pump creates pulses in the hydraulic circuit. When the ABS system is functioning, these pulses can be felt through the brake pedal.

7 On models with traction control, the ABS hydraulic modulator incorporates an additional set of solenoid valves which operate the traction control system. The system operates using the signals supplied by the wheel speed sensors. If the ECU senses

19.4a Undo the retaining screw ...

that a driving wheel is about to lose traction, the ECU communicates with the engine management ECU which will reduce engine power. In severe cases of traction loss the ABS ECU will momentarily apply the relevant front brake to assist with traction recovery.

8 The electronic stability program (ESP) is a further development of ABS and traction control. Using additional sensors to monitor steering wheel position, vehicle yaw rate, acceleration and deceleration, in conjunction with the ABS sensors, the ECU can intervene under conditions of vehicle instability. Using the signals from the various sensors, the ECU can determine driver intent (steering wheel position, throttle position, vehicle speed and engine speed). From the sensor inputs from the wheel speed sensors, yaw rate sensors and acceleration sensors the ECU can calculate whether the vehicle is responding to driver input, or whether an unstable driving situation is occurring. If instability is detected, the ECU will intervene by applying or releasing the relevant front or rear brake, in conjunction with a power reduction, until vehicle stability returns.

9 The operation of the ABS, traction control, and stability programs is entirely dependent on electrical signals. To prevent the system responding to any inaccurate signals, a built-in safety circuit monitors all signals received by the ECU. If an inaccurate signal or low battery voltage is detected, the system is automatically shut down, and the relevant warning light on the instrument panel is illuminated, to inform the driver that the

21.5 Brake pipe connections at the ABS hydraulic modulator

19.4b ... then withdraw the handbrake operating switch and disconnect the wiring connector

system is not operational. Normal braking is still available, however.

10 If a fault develops in the ABS/traction control/ESP system, the vehicle must be taken to a Vauxhall/Opel dealer for fault diagnosis and repair.

21 Anti-lock braking and stability control system components – removal and refitting

Note: *Faults on the ABS system can only be diagnosed using Vauxhall/Opel diagnostic equipment or compatible alternative equipment.*

Note: *Before starting work, refer to the note at the beginning of Section 2 concerning the dangers of hydraulic fluid.*

Hydraulic modulator and ECU

Removal

1 Remove the battery, battery box and battery tray as described in Chapter 5A, Section 4.

2 Release the coolant expansion tank from its mountings and move it to one side.

3 Minimise fluid loss by first removing the master cylinder reservoir cap and screwing it down onto a piece of polythene.

4 Pull out the locking bar and disconnect the wiring harness plug from the ECU.

5 Note and record the fitted position of the brake pipes at the modulator, then unscrew the union nuts and release the pipes **(see illustration)**. As a precaution, place absorbent rags beneath the brake pipe unions when unscrewing them. Suitably plug or cap the disconnected unions to prevent dirt entry and fluid loss.

6 Unscrew the bolt and two nuts securing the hydraulic modulator mounting bracket, then remove the modulator and mounting bracket from the engine compartment.

7 Undo the three bolts and separate the modulator from the mounting bracket.

Refitting

8 Refitting is a reversal of removal, noting the following points:

a) *Tighten the modulator retaining bolts and*

21.16 Undo the screws, release clips and remove the front wheel arch liner

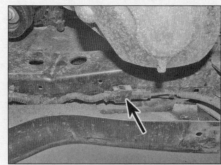

21.17 Disconnect the front wheel speed sensor wiring at the connector at the base of the wheelarch

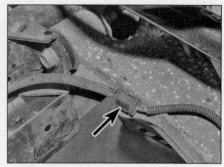

21.18a Free the sensor wiring harness inner clip ...

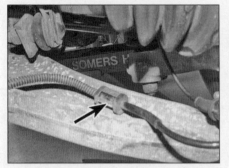

21.18b ... and outer clip on the lower suspension arm ...

21.18c ... then release the clip securing the harness to the base of the swivel hub

modulator mounting bracket retaining bolts to the specified torque.

b) Refit the brake pipes to their respective locations, and tighten the union nuts to the specified torque.

c) Ensure that the wiring is correctly routed, and that the ECU wiring harness plug is firmly pressed into position and secured with the locking bar.

d) Refit the battery tray, battery box and battery as described in Chapter 5A, Section 4.

e) On completion, bleed the complete hydraulic system as described in Section 2. Ensure that the system is bled in the correct order, to prevent air entering the modulator return pump.

Electronic control unit (ECU)

Note: *If a new electronic control unit is to*

be fitted, this work must be entrusted to a Vauxhall/Opel dealer or suitably-equipped specialist as it is necessary to calibrate the unit after installation. This work requires the use of dedicated Vauxhall/Opel diagnostic equipment or a compatible alternative.

Removal

9 Remove the hydraulic modulator from the car as described previously in this Section.

10 Undo the four retaining bolts and carefully withdraw the ECU upwards and off the hydraulic modulator.

Refitting

11 Prior to refitting, clean and then carefully inspect, the condition of the gasket sealing surfaces on the ECU and hydraulic modulator. If the surfaces are in any way deformed, damaged, or rough to the extent that a perfect gasket seal cannot be maintained, the

complete modulator and ECU assembly must be renewed.

12 Holding the ECU by the outer edges, carefully lower it over the solenoid valves on the modulator, keeping it square and level. Ensure that the wiring connectors correctly engage.

13 Fit the four retaining bolts and tighten securely.

14 On completion, refit the hydraulic modulator as described previously in this Section.

Front wheel speed sensors

Removal

15 Firmly apply the handbrake, then jack up the front of the vehicle and support it securely on axle stands (see *Jacking and vehicle support*). Remove the relevant front roadwheel.

16 Undo the screws, release clips and remove the relevant front wheel arch liner **(see illustration)**.

17 Disconnect the wheel speed sensor wiring at the connector at the base of the wheel arch **(see illustration)**. Release the wiring harness clips from the front subframe.

18 Free the wiring harness clips from the lower suspension arm and release the clip securing the harness to the base of the swivel hub **(see illustrations)**.

19 Undo the retaining bolt and withdraw the sensor from the swivel hub **(see illustrations)**. Remove the sensor and wiring harness from under the wheel arch.

Refitting

20 Refitting is a reversal of removal. Tighten the sensor retaining bolt to the specified torque and ensure that the wiring harness is correctly routed and secured by the retaining clips.

Rear wheel speed sensors

Removal

21 Chock the front wheels, then jack up the rear of the vehicle, and support it securely on axle stands (see *Jacking and vehicle support*). Remove the relevant rear roadwheel.

22 Disconnect the wheel speed sensor wiring at the connector under the wheel arch.

21.19a Undo the retaining bolt ...

21.19b ... and withdraw the sensor from the swivel hub

21.23 Free the rear wheel speed sensor wiring harness from the clips on the suspension arm and underbody

21.24a Undo the retaining bolt ...

21.24b ... and withdraw the sensor from the hub carrier

23 Free the wiring harness from the two clips on the suspension arm and the two clips on the underbody (see illustration).
24 Undo the retaining bolt and withdraw the sensor from the hub carrier (see illustrations). Remove the sensor and wiring harness from under the wheel arch.

Refitting

25 Refitting is a reversal of removal. Tighten the sensor retaining bolt to the specified torque and ensure that the wiring harness is correctly routed and secured by the retaining clips.

Steering angle sensor

Note: *If a new steering angle sensor is to be fitted, this work must be entrusted to a Vauxhall/Opel dealer or suitably-equipped specialist as it is necessary to calibrate the unit after installation. This work requires the use of dedicated Vauxhall/Opel diagnostic equipment or a compatible alternative.*

Removal

26 The steering angle sensor is fitted to the rear of the airbag rotary connector. Remove the airbag rotary connector as described in Chapter 12, Section 23.
27 Press the retaining clips on the rear of the airbag rotary connector and slide the steering angle sensor off the rotary connector boss.

Refitting

28 Refitting is a reversal of removal.

Yaw rate sensor

Note: *If a new yaw rate sensor is to be fitted, this work must be entrusted to a Vauxhall/Opel dealer or suitably-equipped specialist as it is necessary to calibrate the unit after installation. This work requires the use of dedicated Vauxhall/Opel diagnostic equipment or a compatible alternative.*

Removal

29 The yaw rate sensor is located under the centre console, beneath the gearchange lever or selector lever.
30 Remove the gearchange lever or selector lever as described in Chapter 7A, Section 5 or Chapter 7B, Section 5 as applicable.
31 Lift up the sound deadening material, then undo the two nuts and withdraw the sensor from the floor.
32 Disconnect the sensor wiring connector and remove the sensor from the car.

Refitting

33 Refitting is a reversal of removal.

22 Vacuum pump – removal and refitting

Removal

Petrol engine models

1 Firmly apply the handbrake, then jack up the front of the vehicle and support it securely on axle stands (see *Jacking and vehicle support*). Remove the right-hand front roadwheel.
2 Undo the screws, release clips and remove the right-hand front wheel arch liner.
3 Working under the wheel arch, disconnect the secondary vacuum hose quick-release fitting from the vacuum pump (see illustration 12.3).
4 Disconnect the vacuum pump motor wiring connector and release the wiring harness from the support clips (see illustration).
5 Undo the two retaining nuts and remove the vacuum pump from under the wheel arch (see illustration).

Diesel engine models

Note: *On model fitted with the 1.6 litre diesel engine, the vacuum pump is part of the oil pump. Refer to Chapter 2B Section 13 for the removal and refitting procedure.*
6 Remove the plastic cover over the top of the engine.

2.0 litre (A20) engines

7 Disconnect the quick-release fitting and detach the vacuum servo unit vacuum hose from the pump (see illustration 12.11). Disconnect the smaller vacuum hose from the outlet on the side of the pump.
8 Release the vacuum hose from the clips on the intake air duct and move the vacuum hose to one side (see illustration).

22.4 Disconnect the vacuum pump motor wiring connector and release the harness from the support clips

22.5 Vacuum pump retaining nuts

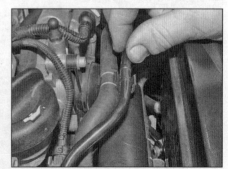

22.8 Release the vacuum hose from the clips on the intake air duct

22.9 Release the upper coolant hose from the clip on the intake air duct

22.10 Undo the bolt securing the intake air duct to the camshaft housing

22.11 Undo the three bolts and release the intake air duct from the throttle housing

22.12 Spread the sides of the retaining clip and lift the forward end of the intake air duct out of the intercooler elbow

22.13a Release the lower coolant hose from the clips on the intake air duct ...

22.13b ... and remove the duct from the engine

9 Release the upper coolant hose from the clip on the intake air duct (see illustration).
10 Undo the bolt securing the intake air duct to the camshaft housing (see illustration).
11 Undo the three bolts securing the intake air duct to the throttle housing and release the duct from the housing (see illustration).
12 Spread the sides of the wire retaining clip and lift the forward end of the intake air duct out of the intercooler elbow (see illustration).
13 Release the lower coolant hose from the clips on the intake air duct and remove the duct from the engine (see illustrations).
14 Undo the four mounting bolts and remove the vacuum pump from the camshaft housing

(see illustration). Recover the gasket. Note that new bolts will be required for refitting.

2.0 litre (B20) engines

15 Drain the cooling system as described in Chapter 1B Section 26.
16 Remove the throttle body and associated pipe work as described in Chapter 4B Section 8.
17 Remove the camshaft cover as described in Chapter 2D Section 8.
18 Remove the EGR cooler and control valve assembly as described in Chapter 4C Section 3.
19 Remove the coolant hoses and the vacuum pump outlet pipe.
20 Anticipate some oil spillage by placing

a shop towel beneath the vacuum pump. Remove the mounting bolts and release the vacuum pump from the cylinder head (see illustrations).
21 Recover the seals from the pump and dispose of them. New ones should be fitted.

Refitting

22 Refitting is a reversal of removal. On diesel engine models, clean the mating faces of the pump and camshaft housing, and fit a new gasket (A20 engines). On B20 engines fit new O-ring seals and apply a bead of sealing compound (see illustrations). Tighten the new mounting bolts to the specified torque.

22.14 Vacuum pump mounting bolts

22.20a Remove the bolts ...

22.20b ... and lift off the vacuum pump

22.22a Fit new seals

22.22b Apply a 3-4 mm bead of sealant ...

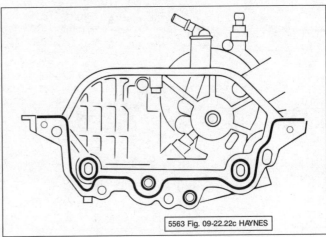

22.22c ... to the area shown.

Chapter 10
Suspension and steering

Contents

Degrees of difficulty

Easy, suitable for novice with little experience 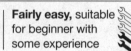	Fairly easy, suitable for beginner with some experience 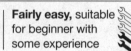	Fairly difficult, suitable for competent DIY mechanic 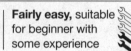	Difficult, suitable for experienced DIY mechanic	Very difficult, suitable for expert DIY or professional

Specifications

Front suspension
Type . . . . Independent, with MacPherson struts and anti-roll bar

Rear suspension
Type . . . . Independent multilink with coil springs, telescopic shock absorbers and anti-roll bar

Steering
Type . . . . Hydraulic power-assisted rack and pinion or electric power steering

Wheel alignment and steering angles
Note: *The following data applies to vehicles with standard suspension.*
Front wheel: . . . .

	Saloon and Hatchback models	Estate models
Camber angle:		
Nominal setting	-0.42° ± 0.75°	-0.45° ± 0.75°
Maximum permitted variation side-to-side	1°	1°
Castor angle:		
Nominal setting	4.72° ± 0.75°	4.62° ± 0.75°
Maximum permitted variation side-to-side	1°	1°
Toe setting	0.26° ± 0.17° toe-in	0.22° ± 0.17° toe-in
Rear wheel:		
Camber angle:		
Nominal setting	-0.74° ± 0.25°	-1.03° ± 0.25°
Maximum permitted variation side-to-side	1°	1°
Toe setting	0.20° ± 0.17° toe-in	0.21° ± 0.17° toe-in

Tyres
Tyre pressures . . . . See sticker attached to the front door pillar on the left-hand side.

Torque wrench settings	Nm	lbf ft
Front suspension		
Anti-roll bar link	50	37
Anti-roll bar-to-subframe*:		
Stage 1	22	16
Stage 2	Angle-tighten a further 30°	
Driveshaft retaining nut*:		
Stage 1	150	110
Stage 2	Slacken the nut by 45°	
Stage 3	250	185
Hub bearing assembly-to-swivel hub*:		
Stage 1	100	74
Stage 2	Angle-tighten a further 75°	
Lower arm balljoint clamp bolt nut*:		
Stage 1	50	37
Stage 2	Slacken 120°	
Stage 3	50	37
Stage 4	Angle-tighten a further 30°	
Lower arm front pivot bolt*:		
Stage 1	100	74
Stage 2	Angle-tighten a further 90°	
Lower arm rear mounting bush-to-lower arm*:		
Stage 1	55	41
Stage 2	Angle-tighten a further 100°	
Lower arm rear mounting bush-to-subframe*:		
Stage 1	100	74
Stage 2	Angle-tighten a further 90°	
Subframe:		
Front engine mounting/torque link-to-subframe*	100	74
Rear engine mounting/torque link-to-transmission bracket*	100	74
Front mounting bolts*	160	118
Rear mounting reinforcement plates-to-underbody*:		
Stage 1	60	44
Stage 2	Angle-tighten a further 30°	
Rear mounting reinforcement plates-to-subframe*	160	118
Suspension strut piston rod nut	70	52
Suspension strut-to-swivel hub*:		
Stage 1	85	63
Stage 3	Angle-tighten a further 60°	
Stage 4	Angle-tighten a further 15°	
Suspension strut upper mounting nut	45	33
Rear suspension		
Anti-roll bar clamp bolts*:		
Stage 1	22	16
Stage 2	Angle-tighten a further 30°	
Anti-roll bar link rod nut/bolt	50	37
Auxiliary control arm-to-hub carrier*:		
Stage 1	115	85
Stage 2	Angle-tighten a further 90°	
Auxiliary control arm-to-subframe*:		
Stage 1	90	66
Stage 2	Angle-tighten a further 60°	
Hub bearing assembly-to-hub carrier*:		
Stage 1	90	66
Stage 2	Angle-tighten a further 75°	
Lower control arm-to-hub carrier*:		
Stage 1	90	66
Stage 2	Angle-tighten a further 90°	
Lower control arm-to-subframe*:		
Stage 1	90	66
Stage 2	Angle-tighten a further 60°	
Shock absorber lower mounting bolt*:		
Stage 1	150	111
Stage 2	Angle-tighten a further 70°	
Shock absorber upper mounting bolts*	100	74
Shock absorber upper mounting nut	20	15

Rear suspension (continued)

Subframe mounting bolts*:
Stage 1	90	66
Stage 2	Angle-tighten a further 120°	
Stage 3	Angle-tighten a further 15°	

Trailing arm front mounting bracket bolts*:
Stage 1	150	111
Stage 2	Angle-tighten a further 30°	

Trailing arm-to-hub carrier*:
Stage 1	150	111
Stage 2	Angle-tighten a further 30°	

Upper control arm-to-hub carrier*:
Stage 1	115	85
Stage 2	Angle-tighten a further 90°	
Stage 3	Angle-tighten a further 15°	

Upper control arm-to-subframe*:
Stage 1	70	52
Stage 2	Angle-tighten a further 90°	
Stage 3	Angle-tighten a further 15°	

Steering

Hydraulic fluid pipes-to-steering gear	19	7

Intermediate shaft-to-steering column*:
Stage 1	25	18
Stage 2	Angle-tighten a further 170°	

Intermediate shaft-to-steering gear pinion*:
Stage 1	25	18
Stage 2	Angle-tighten a further 185°	

Power steering pump high-pressure pipe union	38	28
Power steering pump mounting bolts	22	16

Steering column mounting nuts*:
Stage 1	22	16
Stage 2	Angle-tighten a further 30°	

Steering gear-to-subframe*:
Stage 1	110	81
Stage 2	Angle-tighten a further 150°	

Steering wheel bolt	30	22
Track rod inner balljoint-to-steering rack	60	44

Track rod end-to-swivel hub*:
Stage 1	35	26
Stage 2	Angle-tighten a further 30°	
Roadwheel nuts	150	111

*Use new nuts/bolts

1 General Information

1 The independent front suspension is of the MacPherson strut type, incorporating coil springs and integral telescopic shock absorbers. The MacPherson struts are located by transverse lower suspension arms, which utilise rubber inner mounting bushes, and incorporate a balljoint at the outer ends. The front swivel hubs, which carry the hub bearings, brake calipers and disc assemblies, are bolted to the MacPherson struts, and connected to the lower arms via the balljoints. A front anti-roll bar is fitted, which has link rods with balljoints at each end to connect it to the strut. High performance models feature Vauxhall's 'Hiper strut' front suspension system. These models and the Hiper strut suspension are not covered in this manual.

2 The rear suspension is of fully independent multilink type, with a central subframe, telescopic shock absorbers, coil springs, trailing arms, upper and lower transverse control arms, auxiliary transverse control arms and an anti-roll bar. The shock absorbers are attached at their upper ends to the vehicle underbody and at their lower ends to the hub carriers. The rear hub carriers are attached to the trailing arms, upper and lower control arms and auxiliary control arms by means of flexible rubber bushes. The anti-roll bar is mounted on the subframe and is connected to the hub carriers by drop links.

3 The steering system is of the conventional rack-and-pinion type mounted on the front subframe, with variable hydraulic power assistance or (on later models) electrical power steering. Power assistance for the hydraulic power steering is derived from a hydraulic pump driven by the coolant pump pulley via a secondary auxiliary drivebelt (petrol engines) or driven by the crankshaft pulley via the main auxiliary drivebelt (diesel engines). Models with electric power steering (EPS) have a motor attached to the steering rack. The motor either drives a belt which powers the steering rack or the steering rack is driven directly from the motor via a reduction gear. Note that on models fitted with EPS the steering rack and motor are a single assembly and must be replaced as such in the event of a fault.

4 The steering column is linked to the steering gear by an intermediate shaft. The intermediate shaft has a universal joint fitted at each end, and is secured to the column and to the steering gear pinion shaft by means of clamp bolts.

HAYNES HINT

A tool to hold the wheel hub stationary whilst the driveshaft retaining nut is slackened can be fabricated from a length of square-sectionsteel tube, a short length of steel strip and a nut and bolt; the nut and bolt forming the pivot of a forked tool.

2 Front swivel hub – removal and refitting

Note: *A new driveshaft retaining nut, lower arm balljoint clamp bolt and nut, swivel hub-to-suspension strut bolts and nuts, brake caliper mounting bracket bolts and a new track rod end retaining nut will be needed for refitting. The driveshaft outer joint splines may be a tight fit in the hub and it is possible that a puller/extractor will be required to draw*

2.3 With the holding tool in place, slacken and remove the driveshaft retaining nut

the hub assembly off the driveshaft during removal.

Removal

1 Firmly apply the handbrake, then jack up the front of the car and support it securely on axle stands (see *Jacking and vehicle support*). Remove the relevant front roadwheel.
2 To prevent rotation of the wheel hub as the driveshaft retaining nut is slackened, make up a holding tool and attach the tool to the wheel hub using two wheel nuts **(see Tool Tip)**.
3 With the holding tool in place, slacken and remove the driveshaft retaining nut using a socket and long bar **(see illustration)**. This nut is very tight; make sure that there is no risk of pulling the car off the axle stands as the nut is slackened.
4 Release the brake hydraulic hose from the suspension strut bracket **(see illustration)**.

2.4 Release the brake hydraulic hose from the suspension strut bracket

5 Unscrew the two bolts securing the brake caliper mounting bracket to the swivel hub, noting that new bolts will be required for refitting. Slide the caliper/bracket assembly from the swivel hub and brake disc (there is no need to remove the brake pads). Suspend the caliper/bracket assembly from the strut coil spring using wire or a cable tie – do not allow the caliper to hang on the brake hose **(see illustrations)**.
6 Undo the securing screw and remove the brake disc from the wheel hub **(see illustration)**.
7 Slacken the nut securing the track rod end to the steering arm on the swivel hub then use a two-legged puller to separate the track rod end balljoint taper. Unscrew the securing nut completely and remove the track rod end from the steering arm **(see illustrations)**. Note that a new nut will be required for refitting.

2.5a Unscrew the two bolts securing the brake caliper mounting bracket to the swivel hub ...

2.5b ... slide the caliper/bracket assembly from the swivel hub and brake disc ...

2.5c ... and suspend the caliper/bracket assembly from the strut coil spring using wire or a cable tie

2.6 Undo the securing screw and remove the brake disc

2.7a Use a two-legged puller to separate the track rod end balljoint taper ...

2.7b ... and remove the track rod end from the steering arm

2.8a Release the wheel speed sensor wiring harness clip from the swivel hub ...

2.8b ... then undo the retaining bolt ...

2.8c ... and withdraw the sensor from the hub

8 Release the ABS wheel speed sensor wiring harness clip from the base of the swivel hub, then undo the retaining bolt and withdraw the sensor from the hub **(see illustrations)**.

9 Slacken and remove the two nuts and bolts securing the suspension strut to the swivel hub, noting that new nuts and bolts will be required for refitting **(see illustration)**. Disengage the swivel hub from the strut and pull the upper end outward.

10 The hub must now be freed from the end of the driveshaft **(see illustration)**. It may be possible to pull the hub off the driveshaft, but if the end of the driveshaft is tight in the hub, temporarily refit the driveshaft retaining nut to protect the driveshaft threads, then tap the end of the driveshaft with a soft-faced hammer while pulling outwards on the swivel hub. Alternatively, use a suitable puller to press the driveshaft through the hub.

11 Unscrew the nut and remove the clamp bolt securing the suspension lower arm balljoint to the swivel hub **(see illustration)**. Note that a new clamp bolt and nut will be required for refitting.

12 Support the swivel hub, then push down on the suspension lower arm to free the balljoint from the hub. Lift the swivel hub up and remove it from the car **(see illustration)**.

Refitting

13 Locate the lower arm balljoint in the swivel hub. Insert the new clamp bolt from the front of the swivel hub, so that its threads are facing to the rear. Fit the new nut to the clamp bolt, and tighten it to the specified torque and through the specified angle given in the Specifications, using a torque wrench and angle-tightening gauge.

14 Ensure that the driveshaft outer constant velocity joint and hub splines are clean, and make sure that, where fitted, the spacer washer is in place on the end of the constant velocity joint **(see illustration)**.

15 Engage the driveshaft splines with the hub and push the driveshaft through until sufficient threads are exposed to allow the nut to be fitted. Fit the new driveshaft retaining nut, tightening it by hand only at this stage.

16 Engage the swivel hub with the suspension strut, and insert the new bolts from the front of the strut so that their threads

2.9 Remove the two nuts and bolts securing the suspension strut to the swivel hub

2.10 Pull the swivel hub outward and disengage the driveshaft

2.11 Unscrew the nut and remove the clamp bolt securing the lower arm balljoint to the swivel hub

2.12 Lift the swivel hub up and disengage the lower arm balljoint

are facing to the rear. Fit the new nuts and tighten them to the specified torque and through the specified angle given in the

2.14 Ensure that the spacer washer (where fitted) is in place on the end of the constant velocity joint

Specifications, using a torque wrench and angle-tightening gauge **(see illustrations)**.

17 Refit the ABS wheel speed sensor to

2.16a Tighten the strut-to-swivel hub nuts to the specified torque using a torque wrench ...

2.16b ... and through the specified angle using an angle-tightening gauge

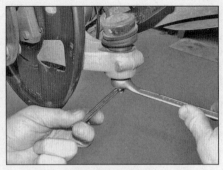

2.18 Counterhold the track rod end balljoint shank using a second spanner as the nut is tightened

the swivel hub, refit the bolt and tighten it to the specified torque (see Chapter 9, Specifications). Refit the wheel speed sensor wiring harness clip to the base of the swivel hub.

18 Engage the track rod end in the swivel hub, then fit the new retaining nut and tighten it to the specified torque and through the specified angle given in the Specifications, using a torque wrench and angle-tightening gauge. Counterhold the balljoint shank using a second spanner to prevent rotation as the nut is tightened **(see illustration)**.

19 Refit the brake disc and tighten its retaining screw securely.

20 Slide the brake pads, caliper and mounting bracket over the disc and into position on the swivel hub. Fit the two new caliper mounting bracket retaining bolts and

tighten them to the specified torque (see Chapter 9, Specifications).

21 Refit the brake hydraulic hose to the suspension strut.

22 Using the method employed on removal to prevent rotation, tighten the driveshaft retaining nut through the stages given in the Specifications.

23 Refit the roadwheel, then lower the vehicle to the ground and tighten the roadwheel nuts to the specified torque.

3 Front hub bearing – removal and refitting

Note: *The front hub bearing is a sealed unit and no repairs are possible. If the bearing*

is worn, a new bearing assembly must be obtained.

Note: *New hub bearing retaining bolts will be required for refitting.*

Removal

1 Remove the swivel hub as described in Section 2.

2 Slacken the three bolts securing the bearing assembly to the swivel hub approximately two to three turns **(see illustration)**.

3 Support the swivel hub then, using a medium hammer, sharply strike the bolt heads to drive the hub bearing out of the swivel hub **(see illustration)**. The bearing is flanged into the swivel hub by approximately 20 mm and is likely to be very tight; particularly on older vehicles where the effects of corrosion will be a factor.

4 Once the hub bearing begins to free, liberally lubricate the flange with penetrating oil. Slacken the bolts a few more turns and continue to drive out the hub bearing.

5 When the hub bearing has released from the swivel hub, unscrew and remove the bolts. Lift away the hub bearing, followed by the brake disc shield, noting the fitted position of the shield **(see illustrations)**.

Refitting

6 Thoroughly clean the swivel hub and place the disc shield in position.

7 Locate the hub bearing over the disc shield and into the swivel hub. Align the retaining bolt holes and fit the three new bolts. Progressively and evenly tighten the bolts to draw the hub bearing into the swivel hub.

8 Tighten the retaining bolts progressively to the specified Stage 1 torque setting using a torque wrench, and then through the specified Stage 2 angle, using an angle tightening gauge.

9 Refit the swivel hub as described in Section 2.

4 Front suspension strut – removal, overhaul and refitting

Note: *New strut-to-swivel hub bolts and nuts will be required for refitting. Ideally, both front suspension struts should be renewed at the same time in order to maintain good steering and suspension characteristics.*

Removal

1 Apply the handbrake, then jack up the front of the vehicle and support it on axle stands (see *Jacking and vehicle support*). Remove the front roadwheel.

2 Release the brake hydraulic hose from the suspension strut bracket **(see illustration 2.4)**.

3 Unscrew the nut and disconnect the anti-roll bar link rod from the strut. Use a suitable Torx key inserted into the link to hold the link while the nut is being loosened **(see illustrations)**.

4 Slacken and remove the two nuts and bolts securing the suspension strut to the

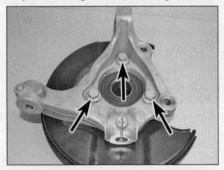

3.2 Slacken the three hub bearing bolts approximately two to three turns

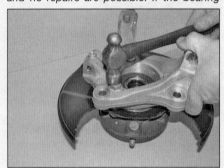

3.3 Support the swivel hub then sharply strike the bolt heads to drive out the hub bearing

3.5a Lift away the hub bearing ...

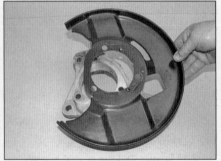

3.5b ... followed by the brake disc shield

4.3a Unscrew the anti-roll bar link rod nut while using a Torx key to hold the link …

4.3b … then disconnect the link rod from the strut

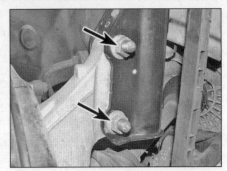

4.4a Undo the two nuts …

4.4b … then remove the bolts securing the suspension strut to the swivel hub

4.5a Lift off the plastic cap …

4.5b … and unscrew the strut upper mounting nut

swivel hub, noting that new nuts and bolts will be required for refitting (see illustrations). Disengage the top of the swivel hub from the strut.

5 Engage the help of an assistant to support the strut beneath the front wing. From within the engine compartment, lift off the plastic cap and unscrew the strut upper mounting nut (see illustrations).

6 Lift off the upper mounting plate, then lower the strut and withdraw it from under the front wing (see illustrations).

Overhaul

Note: A spring compressor tool will be required for this operation. Before overhaul, mark the position of each component in relationship with each other for reassembly.

7 With the suspension strut resting on a bench, or clamped in a vice, fit a spring compressor

tool, and compress the coil spring to relieve the pressure on the spring seats (see illustration). Ensure that the compressor tool is securely located on the spring, in accordance with the tool manufacturer's instructions.

8 Mark the position of the spring relevant to the top and bottom mountings, then counter-hold the strut piston rod with a Torx key or suitable bit, and unscrew the piston rod nut (see illustrations).

4.6a Lift off the upper mounting plate …

4.6b … then withdraw the strut from under the front wing

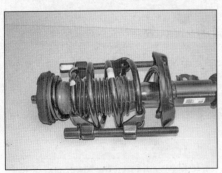

4.7 Fit a spring compressor tool, and compress the coil spring

4.8a Counter-hold the strut piston rod with a Torx key or suitable bit …

4.8b … and unscrew the piston rod nut

4.9a Remove the washer ...

4.9b ... strut upper mounting ...

4.9c ... upper spring seat ...

4.9d ... spring ...

4.9e ... rubber gaiter upper cover ...

4.9f ... rubber gaiter ...

9 Remove the washer, strut upper mounting, upper spring seat, spring, rubber gaiter upper cover, rubber gaiter, buffer and lower spring seat from the strut **(see illustrations)**.

10 With the strut assembly now completely dismantled, examine all the components for wear, damage or deformation. Renew any of the components as necessary.

11 Examine the strut for signs of fluid leakage. Check the strut piston for signs of pitting along its entire length, and check the strut body for signs of damage. While holding it in an upright position, test the operation of the strut by moving the piston through a full stroke, and then through short strokes of 50 to 100 mm. In both cases, the resistance felt should be smooth and continuous. If the resistance is jerky or uneven or if there is any visible sign of wear or damage to the strut, renewal is necessary.

12 If any doubt exists as to the condition of the coil spring, carefully remove the spring

compressors and check the spring for distortion and signs of cracking. Renew the spring if it is damaged or distorted, or if there is any doubt as to its condition.

13 Inspect all other components for damage or deterioration, and renew any that are suspect.

14 Begin reassembly by placing the lower spring seat in position on the strut, ensuring that the end of the seat locates in the depression in the strut plate.

15 Refit the buffer, rubber gaiter and rubber gaiter upper cover. Locate the lower end of the rubber gaiter over the buffer, and fit the upper end around the upper cover.

16 With the spring compressed with the compressor tool, locate the spring on the strut making sure that it is correctly seated with its lower end against the raised stop on the lower spring seat **(see illustration)**.

17 Refit the upper spring seat, upper mounting and washer, then screw on the

piston rod nut. Tighten the nut to the specified torque while counterholding the piston rod.

18 Slowly slacken the spring compressor tool to relieve the tension in the spring. Check that the end of the spring locates correctly against the stop on the lower spring seat. If necessary, turn the spring so that it locates correctly before the compressor tool is completely slackened. Remove the compressor tool when the spring is fully seated.

Refitting

19 Locate the strut in position under the front wing and place the upper mounting plate in position. Refit the upper mounting nut and tighten it to the specified torque. Refit the plastic cap to the strut piston rod.

20 Engage the swivel hub with the suspension strut, and insert the new bolts from the front of the strut so that their threads are facing to the rear. Fit the new nuts and tighten them to

4.9g ... buffer ...

4.9h ... and lower spring seat from the strut

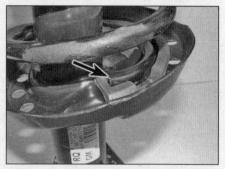

4.16 Make sure that the lower end of the spring is against the raised stop on the lower spring seat

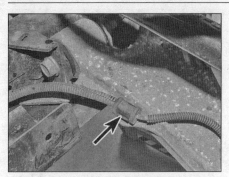

5.3a Free the wheel speed sensor wiring harness from the inner clip ...

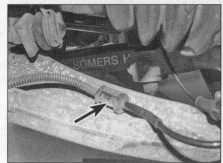

5.3b ... and outer clip on the lower suspension arm

5.5 Push down the lower suspension arm to free the balljoint from the swivel hub

the specified torque and through the specified angle given in the Specifications, using a torque wrench and angle-tightening gauge **(see illustrations 2.16a and 2.16b)**.

21 Connect the anti-roll bar link rod to the strut and use a Torx key to hold the link while tightening the nut to the specified torque.

22 Refit the brake hydraulic hose to the suspension strut bracket.

23 Refit the roadwheel, then lower the vehicle to the ground and tighten the roadwheel nuts to the specified torque.

5 Front lower arm – removal, overhaul and refitting

Note: *New lower arm pivot bolts, and new lower arm balljoint nut/bolt, will be required.*

Removal

1 Firmly apply the handbrake, then jack up the front of the car and support it securely on axle stands (see *Jacking and vehicle support*). Remove the appropriate front roadwheel.

2 On diesel engine models, remove the engine undertray as described in Chapter 11, Section 24.

3 Free the ABS wheel speed sensor wiring harness from the two clips on the lower suspension arm **(see illustrations)**.

4 Unscrew the nut and remove the clamp bolt securing the lower arm balljoint to the swivel hub **(see illustrations 2.11)**. Note that a new bolt and nut will be required for refitting.

5 Using a lever, push down on the lower arm to free the balljoint from the swivel hub, then move the swivel hub to one side and release the arm, taking care not to damage the balljoint rubber boot **(see illustration)**. It is advisable to place a protective cover over the rubber boot such as the plastic cap from an aerosol can, suitably cut to fit.

6 Unscrew the nut and remove the pivot bolt securing the lower arm front mounting to the subframe **(see illustration)**. Note that a new nut and bolt will be required for refitting.

7 Undo the two nuts and remove the two bolts securing the lower arm rear mounting bush to the subframe **(see illustration)**. Note that new nuts and bolts will be required for refitting.

8 Disengage the front mounting from the subframe and remove the lower arm from under the car.

Overhaul

9 Thoroughly clean the lower arm and the area around the arm mountings, removing all traces of dirt and underseal if necessary. Check carefully for cracks, distortion, or any other signs of wear or damage, paying particular attention to the mounting bushes and lower arm balljoint. If the front mounting bush or the balljoint are worn, the lower arm must be renewed as these components are not available separately.

10 To renew the rear mounting bush, undo the retaining bolt and remove the bush from the arm. Fit the new bush together with a new retaining bolt. Tighten the bolt just sufficiently to retain the bush. Final tightening is carried out with the car on its roadwheels.

Refitting

11 Offer up the lower arm, aligning the front end of the arm with its subframe bracket. Insert the new front pivot bolt, and secure the rear mounting with two new retaining bolts. Tighten the rear mounting bush retaining bolts to the specified torque and through the specified angles given in the Specifications. Only tighten the pivot bolts hand tight at this stage.

12 Locate the lower arm balljoint in the swivel hub. Insert the new clamp bolt from the front of the swivel hub, so that its threads are facing to the rear. Fit the new nut to the clamp

5.6 Unscrew the nut and remove the pivot bolt securing the lower arm front mounting to the subframe

bolt, and tighten it to the specified torque and through the specified angle given in the Specifications, using a torque wrench and angle-tightening gauge.

13 Attach the ABS wheel speed sensor wiring harness clips to the lower suspension arm.

14 On diesel engine models, refit the engine undertray as described in Chapter 11, Section 24.

15 Refit the roadwheel, lower the car to the ground, and tighten the roadwheel nuts to the specified torque.

16 Push the car forwards and backwards slightly to settle the suspension and allow the car to adopt its normal ride height. Now tighten the lower arm front pivot bolt to the specified torque and through the specified angle given in the Specifications. If the rear mounting bush has been renewed, tighten its mounting bolt to the specified torque and through the specified angle also.

6 Front subframe – removal and refitting

Note: *Vauxhall/Opel technicians use special jigs to ensure that the subframe is correctly aligned. Without the use of these tools it is important to note the position of the subframe accurately before removal.*

Note: *New subframe mounting bolts, new lower arm balljoint clamp bolts and nuts and new track rod end retaining nuts will be needed for refitting.*

5.7 Undo the two nuts and remove the bolts securing the lower arm rear mounting bush to the subframe

6.6 Unscrew the bolt securing the steering column intermediate shaft to the steering gear pinion

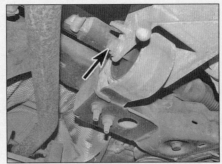

6.9 Undo and remove the through-bolt securing the rear engine mounting/torque link to the transmission bracket

6.10 Undo the through-bolt securing the front engine mounting/torque link to the subframe bracket

Removal

1 Jack up the front and rear of the car and support it securely on axle stands (see *Jacking and vehicle support*). Preferably, position the car over an inspection pit, or on a lift. The help of an assistant will be needed for this procedure.

2 Set the front wheels in the straight-ahead position, then remove the ignition key and lock the column by turning the steering wheel as required. Remove both front roadwheels.

3 On diesel engine models, remove the engine undertray as described in Chapter 11, Section 24.

4 Remove the front bumper as described in Chapter 11, Section 6.

5 Remove the facia footwell trim panel on the driver's side as described in Chapter 11, Section 30.

6 In the driver's footwell, unscrew the bolt securing the bottom of the steering column intermediate shaft to the steering gear pinion **(see illustration)**. Use paint or a suitable marker pen to make alignment marks between the intermediate shaft and the steering gear pinion, then pull the shaft from the pinion and position to one side.

7 Remove the exhaust system front pipe as described in Chapter 4A, Section 14, or Chapter 4B, Section 18, as applicable.

8 Use cable-ties or suitable straps to secure the radiator on each side to prevent the radiator dropping when the subframe is removed.

9 Undo and remove the through-bolt securing the rear engine mounting/torque link to the transmission bracket **(see illustration)**.

10 Similarly, undo the through-bolt securing the front engine mounting/torque link to the subframe bracket. Withdraw the through-bolt **(see illustration)**.

11 Disconnect the ABS wheel speed sensor wiring at the connector at the base of the wheel arch on both sides **(see illustration)**. Release the wiring harness clips from the front subframe and from the lower suspension arm.

12 Disconnect the steering track rod ends from the swivel hubs by slackening the nuts securing the track rod ends to the steering arms on the swivel hub then use a two-legged puller to separate each track rod end balljoint taper. Unscrew the securing nuts completely and remove the track rod ends from the steering arm **(see illustrations 2.7a and 2.7b)**. Note that new nuts will be required for refitting.

13 Unscrew the nut and remove the clamp bolt each side securing the lower arm balljoint to the swivel hub **(see illustrations)**. Note that new bolts and nuts will be required for refitting.

14 Working on one side at a time, use a lever to push down on the lower arm to free the balljoint from the swivel hub, then move the swivel hub to one side and release the arm, taking care not to damage the balljoint rubber boot **(see illustration 5.5)**. It is advisable to place a protective cover over the rubber boot

such as the plastic cap from an aerosol can, suitably cut to fit.

15 Unscrew the nuts and disconnect the anti-roll bar link rods from the anti-roll bar on both sides. Use a suitable Torx key inserted into the link to hold the link while the nut is being loosened.

16 Place a suitable container beneath the hydraulic supply and return pipes on the steering gear and be prepared for escaping hydraulic fluid. Undo the bolt securing the hydraulic supply and return pipe retaining plate to the steering gear. Withdraw the pipes from the steering gear and collect the escaping fluid in the container. Note that new sealing O-rings will be required for the hydraulic pipes for refitting. Suitably cover or plug the disconnected unions to prevent dirt entry.

17 Release the wiring harness, fluid pipes and hoses from the various clips around the subframe.

18 Accurately mark the position of the subframe and mounting bolts to ensure correct refitting. Note that Vauxhall/Opel technicians use a special jig with guide pins located through the alignment holes in the subframe and underbody.

19 Support the subframe with a cradle across a trolley jack. Alternatively, two trolley jacks and the help of an assistant will be required.

20 Undo the two bolts each side securing the subframe rear mountings and the reinforcement plates (where fitted) to the

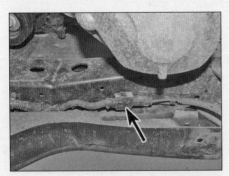

6.11 Disconnect the wheel speed sensor wiring at the connector at the base of the wheel arch

6.13a Unscrew the retaining nut …

6.13b … and withdraw the clamp bolt from the swivel hub

underbody **(see illustration)**. Remove the reinforcement plates.

21 Undo the subframe front mounting bolt on each side.

22 Slowly and carefully lower the subframe to the ground. As the subframe is lowered, make sure there are no cables or wiring still attached.

23 Remove the lower suspension arms from the subframe with reference to Section 5, the anti-roll bar with reference to Section 7, the rear engine mounting/torque link with reference to Chapter 2A or 2C, and the steering gear with reference to Section 25.

Refitting

24 Refitting is a reversal of removal, bearing in mind the following points:

a) *Ensure that the radiator lower mounting pegs engage correctly in the subframe brackets as the subframe is refitted.*

b) *Tighten all nuts and bolts to the specified torque and, where necessary, through the specified angle. Note that new nuts/bolts should be used on all disturbed fittings.*

c) *Make sure that the subframe is correctly aligned with the underbody before fully tightening the mounting bolts.*

d) *On completion, bleed the power steering hydraulic system as described in Section 24.*

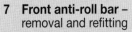

7 Front anti-roll bar –
removed and refitting

Note: *It is recommended that all mounting nuts and bolts are renewed when refitting.*

Removal

1 Remove the front subframe assembly as described in Section 6.

2 Unscrew the two bolts from each anti-roll bar mounting clamp, and remove the anti-roll bar from the subframe **(see illustration)**.

3 If any damage or deterioration of the mounting clamp rubber bushes is detected, the complete anti-roll bar must be renewed; the rubber bushes are not available separately and must not be disturbed.

Refitting

4 Refit the anti-roll bar to the subframe, and

8.3 Undo the securing screw and withdraw the brake disc from the hub

6.20 Undo the bolts securing the subframe rear mountings and the reinforcement plates to the underbody

fit the mounting clamp retaining bolts. Tighten the retaining bolts to the specified torque.

5 Refit the front subframe assembly as described in Section 6.

6 Refit the roadwheels if not already done, then lower the vehicle to the ground and tighten the roadwheel nuts to the specified torque.

8 Rear hub carrier –
removal and refitting

Note: *It is recommended that all mounting nuts and bolts are renewed when refitting.*

Removal

1 Chock the front wheels, then jack up the rear of the vehicle, and support it securely on axle stands (see *Jacking and vehicle support*).

8.2a Unscrew the two bolts securing the brake caliper mounting bracket to the hub carrier …

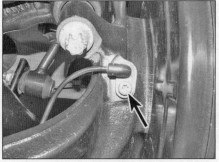

8.4a Undo the retaining bolt …

7.2 Anti-roll bar clamp mounting bolts

Remove the roadwheel, then ensure that the handbrake is released.

2 Unscrew the two bolts securing the brake caliper mounting bracket to the hub carrier. Slide the caliper/bracket assembly from the hub carrier and brake disc (there is no need to remove the brake pads) **(see illustrations)**. Suspend the caliper/bracket assembly from a convenient place under the wheel arch using wire or a cable tie – do not allow the caliper to hang on the brake hose.

3 Undo the securing screw and withdraw the brake disc from the hub **(see illustration)**.

4 Undo the retaining bolt and withdraw the ABS wheel speed sensor from the hub carrier **(see illustrations)**. Release the sensor wiring harness retaining clip from the hub carrier.

5 Remove the rear coil spring as described in Section 10.

8.2b … then slide the caliper/bracket assembly from the hub carrier and brake disc

8.4b … and withdraw the wheel speed sensor from the hub carrier

8.6 Unscrew the shock absorber lower mounting bolt

8.7 Undo the bolt and detach the anti-roll bar link rod from the hub carrier

8.8 Undo the nut and remove the bolt securing the auxiliary control arm to the hub carrier

8.9 Undo the two bolts securing the trailing arm to the hub carrier

8.10a Undo the nut …

8.10b … and remove the bolt securing the upper control arm to the hub carrier

6 Unscrew the shock absorber lower mounting bolt and detach the shock absorber from the hub carrier **(see illustration)**.

7 Undo the bolt and detach the anti-roll bar link rod from the hub carrier **(see illustration)**.

8 Undo the nut and remove the bolt securing the auxiliary control arm to the hub carrier **(see illustration)**.

9 Undo the two bolts securing the trailing arm to the hub carrier **(see illustration)**.

10 Undo the nut and remove the bolt securing the upper control arm to the hub carrier, then remove the hub carrier from the car **(see illustrations)**.

Refitting

11 Refitting is a reversal of removal, bearing in mind the following points:

a) *New nuts/bolts should be used on all disturbed fittings, tightened to the specified torque and, where necessary, through the specified angle.*

b) *When attaching the auxiliary control arm and the upper control arm to the hub carrier, do not fully tighten the nuts until the rest of the refitting procedure has been carried out. Set the rear suspension to its normal running height using a jack under the lower control arm, then tighten the control arm nuts to the specified torque and through the specified angle.*

c) *Refit the rear coil spring as described in Section 10.*

9 Rear hub bearing – removal and refitting

Note: *The rear hub bearing is a sealed unit and no repairs are possible. If the bearing is worn, a new bearing assembly must be obtained.*

Note: *New hub bearing retaining bolts will be required for refitting.*

Removal

1 Remove the hub carrier (see Section 8).

2 Slacken the three bolts securing the bearing assembly to the hub carrier approximately two to three turns **(see illustration)**.

3 Support the hub carrier then, using a medium hammer, sharply strike the bolt heads to drive the hub bearing out of the hub carrier. The bearing is flanged into the hub carrier by approximately 20 mm and is likely to be very tight; particularly on older vehicles where the effects of corrosion will be a factor.

4 Once the hub bearing begins to free, liberally lubricate the flange with penetrating oil. Slacken the bolts a few more turns and continue to drive out the hub bearing.

5 When the hub bearing has released from the hub carrier, unscrew and remove the bolts. Lift away the hub bearing, followed by the brake disc shield, noting the fitted position of the shield **(see illustrations)**.

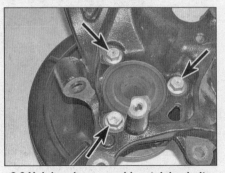

9.2 Hub bearing assembly retaining bolts

9.5a Lift away the hub bearing …

9.5b … followed by the brake disc shield

10.3 Fit a spring compressor tool to the coil spring, and compress the spring

10.5 Undo the nut and remove the bolt securing the lower control arm to the hub carrier

10.6 Remove the spring together with the upper and lower spring seats

Refitting

6 Thoroughly clean the hub carrier and place the disc shield in position.

7 Locate the hub bearing over the disc shield and into the hub carrier. Align the retaining bolt holes and fit the three new bolts. Progressively and evenly tighten the bolts to draw the hub bearing into the swivel hub.

8 Tighten the retaining bolts progressively to the specified Stage 1 torque setting using a torque wrench, and then through the specified Stage 2 angle, using an angle tightening gauge.

9 Refit the hub carrier as described in Section 8.

10 Rear coil spring – removal and refitting

Note: *Always renew coil springs in pairs and the correct version for model, to maintain good handling.*
Note: *Suitable coil spring compressors will be required for this operation.*

Removal

1 Chock the front wheels then jack up the rear of the car and securely support it on axle stands (see *Jacking and vehicle support*). Remove the roadwheel.

2 Unscrew the two bolts securing the brake caliper mounting bracket to the hub carrier. Slide the caliper/bracket assembly from the hub carrier and brake disc (there is no need to remove the brake pads) **(see illustrations 8.2a and 8.2b)**. Suspend the caliper/bracket assembly from a convenient place under the wheel arch using wire or a cable tie – do not allow the caliper to hang on the brake hose.

3 Fit a spring compressor tool to the coil spring, and compress the spring to relieve the pressure on the spring seats **(see illustration)**. Ensure that the compressor tool is securely located on the spring, in accordance with the tool manufacturer's instructions.

4 Position a trolley jack under the lower control arm and raise the jack until the control arm is firmly supported.

5 Undo the nut and remove the bolt securing

the lower control arm to the hub carrier **(see illustration)**. Note that a new nut and bolt will be required for refitting.

6 Slowly lower the jack and lower control arm, then remove the spring together with the upper and lower spring seats **(see illustration)**.

Refitting

7 Locate the compressed spring in position ensuring that the upper and lower spring seats are correctly located.

8 Raise the lower control arm using the trolley jack, then fit the new lower control arm-to-hub carrier retaining bolt. Screw on the new nut, but do not fully tighten the nut at this stage.

9 Release the tension on the spring compressor and remove the compressor from the spring.

10 Slide the brake pads, caliper and mounting bracket over the disc and into position on the hub carrier. Apply thread locking compound to the threads of the caliper bracket retaining bolts, then refit the bolts and tighten them to the specified torque, then through the specified angle.

11 Using the trolley jack positioned under the lower control arm, set the rear suspension to its normal running height, then tighten the control arm retaining nut to the specified torque and through the specified angle.

12 Refit the roadwheel, then lower the vehicle to the ground and tighten the roadwheel nuts to the specified torque.

11 Rear suspension upper control arm – removal and refitting

Note: *It is recommended that all mounting nuts and bolts are renewed when refitting.*

Removal

1 Chock the front wheels then jack up the rear of the car and securely support it on axle stands (see *Jacking and vehicle support*). Remove the roadwheel.

2 Position a trolley jack under the lower control arm and raise the jack until the control arm is firmly supported.

3 Undo the nut and remove the bolt securing

the upper control arm to the hub carrier **(see illustrations 8.10a and 8.10b)**.

4 Undo the nut and remove the bolt securing the upper control arm to the rear subframe and remove the control arm from the car **(see illustration)**.

Refitting

5 Refitting is a reversal of removal, bearing in mind the following points:
a) New nuts/bolts should be used on all disturbed fittings.
b) Set the rear suspension to its normal running height using a jack under the lower control arm, then tighten the control arm nuts to the specified torque and through the specified angles in the stages given.

12 Rear suspension lower control arm – removal and refitting

Note: *It is recommended that all mounting nuts and bolts are renewed when refitting.*

Removal

1 Chock the front wheels then jack up the rear of the car and securely support it on axle stands (see *Jacking and vehicle support*). Remove the roadwheel.

2 Remove the rear coil spring as described in Section 10.

3 Accurately mark the position of the camber

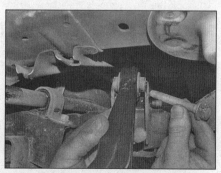

11.4 Undo the nut and remove the bolt securing the upper control arm to the subframe

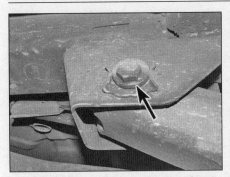

12.3 Mark the position of the camber adjustment eccentric disc on the control arm inner mounting bolt

adjustment eccentric disc on the lower control arm inner mounting bolt **(see illustration)**. Undo the nut and remove the bolt securing the lower control arm to the rear subframe, then remove the control arm from the car.

Refitting

4 Refitting is a reversal of removal, bearing in mind the following points:

a) *Tighten all nuts and bolts to the specified torque and through the specified angles in the stages given. Note that new nuts/bolts should be used on all disturbed fittings.*

b) *Set the rear suspension to its normal running height using a jack under the lower control arm, prior to tightening the control arm inner mounting nut.*

c) *Align the camber adjustment eccentric disc with the marks made on removal when tightening the control arm inner mounting nut.*

d) *Refit the rear coil spring as described in Section 10.*

e) *Have the rear wheel toe setting and camber angle checked and if necessary adjusted at the earliest opportunity.*

13 Rear suspension auxiliary control arm – removal and refitting

Note: *It is recommended that all mounting nuts and bolts are renewed when refitting.*

Removal

1 Chock the front wheels then jack up the

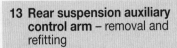

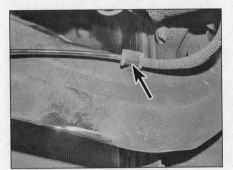

14.2 Unclip the wheel speed sensor wiring harness from the trailing arm

13.3 Undo the nut and remove the bolt securing the auxiliary control arm to the subframe

rear of the car and securely support it on axle stands (see *Jacking and vehicle support)*. Remove the roadwheel.

2 Undo the nut and remove the bolt securing the auxiliary control arm to the hub carrier **(see illustration 8.8)**.

3 Accurately mark the position of the toe-in adjustment eccentric disc on the auxiliary control arm inner mounting bolt. Undo the nut and remove the bolt securing the auxiliary control arm to the rear subframe and remove the control arm from the car **(see illustration)**.

Refitting

4 Refitting is a reversal of removal, bearing in mind the following points:

a) *Tighten all nuts and bolts to the specified torque and through the specified angles in the stages given. Note that new nuts/bolts should be used on all disturbed fittings.*

b) *Align the toe-in adjustment eccentric disc with the marks made on removal when tightening the control arm inner mounting nut.*

c) *Have the rear wheel toe setting and camber angle checked and if necessary adjusted at the earliest opportunity.*

14 Rear suspension trailing arm – removal and refitting

Note: *It is recommended that all mounting bolts are renewed when refitting.*

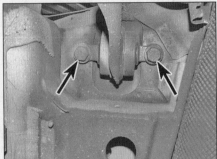

14.3 Undo the two bolts securing the trailing arm front mounting to the underbody

Removal

1 Chock the front wheels then jack up the rear of the car and securely support it on axle stands (see *Jacking and vehicle support)*. Remove the roadwheel.

2 Unclip the ABS wheel speed sensor wiring harness from the trailing arm **(see illustration)**.

3 Undo the two bolts securing the trailing arm front mounting to the underbody **(see illustration)**.

4 Undo the two bolts securing the trailing arm to the hub carrier and remove the trailing arm from the car **(see illustration 8.9)**.

Refitting

5 Refitting is a reversal of removal, tightening the new retaining bolts to the specified torque and through the specified angle.

15 Rear shock absorber – removal, testing and refitting

Note: *Always renew shock absorbers in pairs and the correct version for model, to maintain good handling.*
Note: *It is recommended that the shock absorber mounting bolts are renewed when refitting.*

Removal

1 Chock the front wheels then jack up the rear of the car and securely support it on axle stands (see *Jacking and vehicle support)*. Remove the roadwheel.

2 Position a trolley jack under the lower control arm and raise the jack until the control arm is firmly supported.

3 Unscrew the shock absorber lower mounting bolt and detach the shock absorber from the hub carrier **(see illustration 8.6)**.

4 Unscrew the shock absorber upper mounting bracket bolts and remove the shock absorber from the car **(see illustration)**.

5 If required, unscrew the upper retaining nut and remove the upper mounting bracket from the shock absorber body.

Testing

6 Examine the shock absorber for signs of

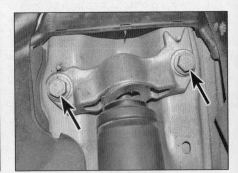

15.4 Shock absorber upper mounting bracket retaining bolts

16.3a Extract the circlip ...

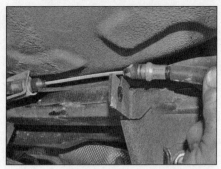

16.3b ... withdraw the right-hand (main) cable from the subframe support bracket ...

16.3c ... and slide the cable grommet out of the other subframe bracket

16.4a Extract the circlip ...

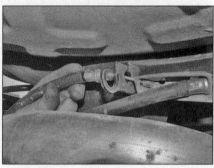

16.4b ... and withdraw the left-hand cable from the subframe support bracket

fluid leakage or damage. Test the operation of the shock absorber, while holding it in an upright position, by moving the piston through a full stroke, and then through short strokes of 50 to 100 mm. In both cases, the resistance felt should be smooth and continuous. If the resistance is jerky, or uneven, or if there is any visible sign of wear or damage, renewal is necessary. Also check the rubber mounting bush(es) for damage and deterioration. If the lower bush is damaged or worn, the complete shock absorber will have to be renewed, as the mounting bush is not available separately. If the upper mounting bush is damaged or worn, obtain a new upper mounting bracket.

Refitting

7 Refitting is a reversal of removal, tightening the new mounting bolts to the specified torque and, where applicable, through the specified angle.

16 Rear subframe – removal and refitting

Note: *It is recommended that all mounting nuts and bolts are renewed when refitting.*

Removal

1 Chock the front wheels then jack up the rear of the car and securely support it on axle stands (see *Jacking and vehicle support*). Remove both rear the roadwheels.
2 Remove the complete exhaust system as described in Chapter 4A, Section 14, or Chapter 4B, Section 18, as applicable.
3 Extract the circlip and withdraw the right-hand (main) handbrake cable from the subframe support bracket. Slide the cable grommet out of the other subframe bracket **(see illustrations)**.
4 Extract the circlip and withdraw the left-hand handbrake cable from the subframe support bracket **(see illustrations)**.
5 Remove the rear coil spring on each side as described in Section 10.
6 Undo the bolt and detach the anti-roll bar link rod from the hub carrier on each side **(see illustration 8.7)**.
7 Undo the nut and remove the bolt securing

the auxiliary control arm to the hub carrier **(see illustration 8.8)**.
8 Undo the nut and remove the bolt securing the upper control arm to the hub carrier **(see illustrations 8.10a and 8.10b)**.
9 Accurately mark the position of the subframe and mounting bolts to ensure correct refitting.
10 Support the rear subframe with a cradle across a trolley jack. Alternatively, two trolley jacks and the help of an assistant will be required.
11 Undo the four bolts securing the rear subframe to the vehicle underbody **(see illustrations)**.
12 Slowly and carefully lower the subframe to the ground. As the assembly is lowered, make sure there are no cables or wiring still attached.

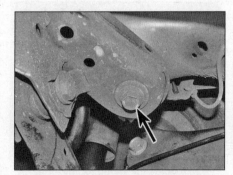

16.11a Rear subframe front mounting bolt ...

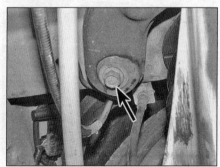

16.11b ... and rear mounting bolt

13 With the subframe removed from the car, if required, carry out further dismantling to remove the attached components, with reference to the applicable Sections of this Chapter.

Refitting

14 Refitting is a reversal of removal, bearing in mind the following points:
a) Tighten all nuts and bolts to the specified torque and, where necessary, through the specified angles in the stages given. Note that new nuts/bolts should be used on all disturbed fittings.
b) Make sure that the subframe is correctly aligned with the vehicle underbody before fully tightening the mounting bolts.

17 Rear anti-roll bar – removal and refitting

Note: *It is recommended that all mounting nuts and bolts are renewed when refitting.*

Removal

1 Remove the rear subframe as described in Section 16.
2 Prior to removal of the anti-roll bar, mark the position of each anti-roll bar mounting clamp rubber.
3 Unscrew the two bolts from each mounting clamp, and remove the clamp. As the last clamp is removed, support the anti-roll bar and remove it from the rear subframe.
4 Inspect the mounting clamp rubbers for signs of damage and deterioration, and renew if necessary.

Refitting

5 Align the mounting rubbers with the marks made on the anti-roll bar prior to removal.
6 Refit the anti-roll bar to the rear subframe and fit the mounting clamps with new retaining bolts. Ensure that the clamp half is correctly engaged with the anti-roll bar rubbers, then tighten each clamp retaining bolt, by hand only at this stage.
7 With the two clamps loosely installed, check the position of the anti-roll bar to the marks made on removal, then tighten the clamp bolts to the specified torque and through the specified angle.
8 Refit the rear subframe as described in Section 16.

19.4 Disconnect the wiring harness connector for the steering wheel switches

19.7 Alignment marks between the steering column shaft and steering wheel

18.4 Using a bush renewal tool to renew the rear suspension arm bushes

18 Rear suspension arm bushes – renewal

1 The mounting bushes in the rear suspension upper and lower control arms, auxiliary control arm and trailing arm can be renewed by pressing them out using a hydraulic press and mandrels of suitable diameter or, alternatively, by using a commercially available bush renewal tool. The new bushes are then pressed into place in the same way. The following procedure describes the use of a typical bush renewal tool. If using a press, the same basic procedure applies. Note that if a new bush is being fitted to the trailing arm, a hydraulic press will definitely be needed.
2 Begin by removing the relevant suspension arm as described in the previous Sections of this Chapter.

19.5 Steering wheel retaining bolt

19.8 Guide the wiring for the airbag through the aperture in the wheel, taking care not to damage the wiring connectors

3 If a bush renewal tool is being used, select an adaptor that will bear against the bush location in the arm, but with a large enough internal diameter for the bush to be drawn through it. Select a second adaptor to bear against the steel outer casing of the bush, but with a small enough external diameter to enable it to pass through the bush location in the suspension arm.
4 Fit the threaded bar of the renewal tool through the centre of the old bush then assemble the adaptors and nuts to the threaded bar. Tighten the nuts to draw the old bush out of the arm **(see illustration)**.
5 Locate the new bush in position and draw it into the arm using the same method as for removal. Ensure that the bush is fitted centrally in its location, with the same amount of steel outer casing visible on each side when the bush is fitted.
6 If a new bush is being fitted to the trailing arm, initially position the bush as follows. Place a straight edge on the flat underside of the mounting arm. Position the bush so that the top of the straight edge is approximately 19 mm below the trailing arm upper front mounting hole. Maintain this position as the bush is fitted.
7 On completion, refit the suspension arm as described in the previous Sections of this Chapter.

19 Steering wheel – removal and refitting

⚠ Warning: Make sure that the airbag safety recommendations given in Chapter 12, Section 22 are followed, to prevent personal injury.

Removal

1 Remove the airbag as described in Chapter 12, Section 23.
2 Remove the steering column shrouds as described in Chapter 11, Section 30.
3 Set the front wheels in the straight-ahead position, then lock the column in position after removing the ignition key.
4 Disconnect the wiring harness connector for the steering wheel switches **(see illustration)**.
5 Slacken the Torx retaining bolt securing the steering wheel to the column until two or three threads are left engaged **(see illustration)**.
6 Grip the steering wheel with both hands and carefully rock it from side-to-side to release it from the splines on the steering column. Once the wheel is free, remove the retaining bolt.
7 Check that there are alignment marks between the steering column shaft and steering wheel **(see illustration)**. If no marks are visible, centre punch the wheel and column shaft to ensure correct alignment when refitting.
8 Lift the steering wheel up and off the column. As the wheel is being removed, guide the wiring for the airbag through the aperture in the wheel, taking care not to damage the wiring connectors **(see illustration)**.
9 With the steering wheel removed, place

a strip of adhesive tape across the side and front of the airbag rotary connector to prevent the connector rotating **(see illustration)**.

Refitting

10 Remove the adhesive tape used to prevent the airbag rotary connector rotating. If there is any doubt about the position of the rotary connector with regard to its centred position, centre the unit as described in Chapter 12, Section 23.

11 Refit the steering wheel, aligning the marks made prior to removal. Route the airbag wiring connectors through the steering wheel aperture.

12 Clean the threads on the retaining bolt and the threads in the steering column. Coat the retaining bolt with locking compound, then fit the retaining bolt and tighten it to the specified torque **(see illustration)**.

13 Reconnect the wiring connector for the steering wheel switches.

14 Release the steering lock, and refit the airbag as described in Chapter 12, Section 23.

15 Refit the steering column shrouds as described in Chapter 11, Section 30.

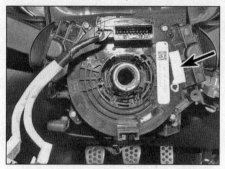

19.9 Place a strip of adhesive tape across the airbag rotary connector to prevent the connector rotating

8 Refit steering column shrouds as described in Chapter 11, Section 30, then reconnect the battery.

21 Steering column – removal and refitting

Warning: Make sure that the airbag safety recommendations given in Chapter 12, Section 22 are followed, to prevent personal injury.

Note: *It is recommended that all mounting nuts and bolts are renewed when refitting.*

Removal

1 Set the front wheels in the straight-ahead position, then lock the column in position after removing the ignition key.

2 Remove the facia right-hand lower trim panel and the steering column shrouds as described in Chapter 11, Section 30.

3 Disconnect the wiring connectors at the steering column multi-function switches, ignition switch, airbag rotary connector, immobiliser transponder and any other electrical components according to equipment fitted. Release the wiring harness retaining clips and free the harness from the column.

4 Unscrew the bolt securing the bottom of the steering column intermediate shaft to the steering gear pinion **(see illustration 6.6)**. Use paint or a suitable marker pen to make alignment marks between the intermediate

19.12 Apply thread locking compound to the steering wheel retaining bolt

shaft and the steering gear pinion, then pull the shaft from the pinion and position to one side.

5 Suitably support the steering column and unscrew the four mounting nuts. Withdraw the steering column from the facia crossmember, and remove the column from inside the vehicle.

Refitting

6 Refitting is a reversal of removal, bearing in mind the following points:
a) *Tighten all nuts and bolts to the specified torque and, where necessary, through the specified angle. Note that new nuts/bolts should be used on all disturbed fittings.*
b) *Ensure that the marks made on the intermediate shaft and steering gear pinion are correctly aligned.*
c) *Refit the steering column shrouds and facia lower trim panel as described in Chapter 11, Section 30.*

22 Steering column intermediate shaft – removal and refitting

Note: *It is recommended that the intermediate shaft clamp bolts are renewed when refitting.*

Removal

1 Set the front wheels in the straight-ahead position, then lock the column in position after removing the ignition key.

2 Remove the facia right-hand lower trim panel as described in Chapter 11, Section 30.

20 Ignition switch/steering column lock – removal and refitting

Removal

1 Disconnect the battery negative terminal (refer to Chapter 5A, Section 4).

2 Remove the steering column shrouds as described in Chapter 11, Section 30.

3 Undo the three screws and remove the security shield from the lock housing **(see illustrations)**.

4 Insert the ignition key into the ignition switch/lock, and turn it to position I.

5 Insert a thin rod into the hole in the top of the lock housing. Press the rod to release the detent spring, turn the key to the START position and pull out the lock cylinder using the key **(see illustration)**.

Refitting

6 Insert the ignition switch/lock into the lock housing, while the key is in the START position. Remove the rod from the lock housing.

7 Refit the security shield and tighten the retaining screws securely.

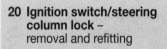

20.3a Undo the three retaining screws ...

20.3b ... and remove the security shield from the lock housing

20.5 Insert a thin rod into the lock housing hole, press the rod to release the detent spring, and pull out the lock cylinder

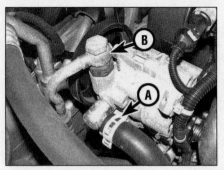

23.5 Power steering pump reservoir fluid supply hose (A) and high-pressure pipe union (B)

3 Using paint or similar, make alignment marks between the steering column and intermediate shaft, then slacken and remove the clamp bolt securing the intermediate shaft to the steering column. Separate the intermediate shaft from the steering column shaft.

4 Similarly, make alignment marks between the intermediate shaft and the steering gear pinion. Unscrew the bolt securing the intermediate shaft to the steering gear pinion, then pull the shaft from the pinion and remove it from the car **(see illustration 6.6)**.

Refitting

5 Refitting is a reversal of removal, bearing in mind the following points:
a) *Tighten the intermediate shaft clamp bolts to the specified torque and through the specified angle. Note that new bolts should be used.*
b) *Ensure that the marks made on the intermediate shaft, steering column shaft and steering gear pinion are correctly aligned.*
c) *Refit the facia lower trim panel as described in Chapter 11, Section 30.*

23 Hydraulic power steering pump – removal and refitting

Removal

1 On diesel engine models, remove the plastic cover over the top of the engine.

2 Remove the air cleaner assembly as described in Chapter 4A, Section 2, or Chapter 4B, Section 3 as applicable.

3 Remove the auxiliary drivebelt as described in Chapter 1A, Section 20, or Chapter 1B, Section 22 as applicable. Note that on petrol engine models it is only necessary to remove the secondary (power steering pump) drivebelt.

4 Wipe clean the area around the power steering pump reservoir filler neck, and unscrew the filler cap. Siphon as much of the power steering fluid from the reservoir as possible. **Note:** *Do not siphon the fluid by mouth, as it is poisonous; use a syringe or an old hydrometer.*

5 Position a suitable container beneath the power steering pump, then release the retaining clip and disconnect the reservoir supply hose from the pump outlet **(see illustration)**. Allow the fluid to drain into the container, then cover or seal the hose end and pump outlet.

6 Undo the banjo union bolt and withdraw the high-pressure pipe from the top of the pump. Recover the sealing washer from each side of the pipe union. Discard the washers; new ones must be used on refitting. Cover or seal the hose end and pump outlet.

7 Undo the three mounting bolts and remove the pump from the engine.

Refitting

8 Refitting is a reversal of removal, bearing in mind the following points:
a) *Use a new sealing washer on each side of the high-pressure pipe union.*
b) *Tighten the mounting bolts and high-pressure banjo union bolt to the specified torque.*
c) *Refit (or renew) the auxiliary drivebelt as described in Chapter 1A, Section 20 or Chapter 1B, Section 22 as applicable.*
d) *Refit the air cleaner assembly as described in Chapter 4A, Section 2 or Chapter 4B, Section 3 as applicable.*
e) *Refill/top-up the fluid reservoir, and bleed the system as described in Section 24.*

24 Power steering hydraulic system – filling and bleeding

1 Wipe clean the area around the reservoir filler neck, and unscrew the filler cap from the reservoir.

2 If topping-up is necessary, use clean fluid of the specified type (see *Weekly checks*). Check for leaks if frequent topping-up is required. Do not run the engine without fluid in the reservoir.

3 After component renewal, or if the fluid level has been allowed to fall so low that air has entered the hydraulic system, bleeding must be carried out as follows.

4 Fill the reservoir to the MAX mark as described in Weekly checks. Note that the power steering fluid should be cold, and

25.2 Steering gear mounting bolt retaining nut

poured slowly into the reservoir to minimise aeration. Leave the filler cap off at this stage.

5 Start the engine and immediately top-up the reservoir to maintain the level above the MIN mark.

6 With the engine still running, slowly turn the steering wheel two to three times approximately 45° to the left and right. Now turn the steering wheel from lock to lock twice, holding it at each full lock position for approximately 10 seconds. Add power steering fluid until the fluid level ceases to drop.

7 Switch off the engine and check the fluid level. Top-up if necessary and refit the filler cap.

8 Start the engine and turn the steering from lock to lock. If excessive noise is still apparent (indicating air in the system), leave the vehicle overnight, then try again.

9 If the steering is still noisy, it may be that the pump is faulty. Consult a Vauxhall/Opel dealer or specialist.

10 On completion, stop the engine and recheck the fluid level.

25 Steering gear assembly – removal, inspection and refitting

Note: *It is recommended that all mounting nuts and bolts are renewed when refitting.*

Hydraulic power steering

Removal

1 Remove the front subframe as described in Section 6.

2 Undo the nuts from the two steering gear mounting bolts, while counter-holding the bolts from under the subframe **(see illustration)**. Lift off the two washers then remove the bolts. Note that new nuts and bolts will be required for refitting.

3 Twist the anti-roll bar upwards, then lift the steering gear off the subframe.

4 If a new steering gear assembly is to be fitted, then the track rod ends will need to be removed from each end of the steering track rods (see Section 27).

Inspection

5 Examine the steering gear assembly for signs of wear or damage, and check that the rack moves freely throughout the full length of its travel, with no signs of roughness or excessive free play between the steering gear pinion and rack. If any problems of this nature are noted, renewal of the steering gear will be necessary. The only components which can be renewed separately are the steering gear gaiters, the track rod ends and the track rods. Steering gear gaiter, track rod end and track rod renewal procedures are covered in Sections 26, 27 and 28 respectively.

Refitting

6 Refitting is a reverse of the removal

25.9 Disconnect the wiring plugs.

procedure, bearing in mind the following points:

a) Tighten the steering gear mounting bolt nuts to the specified torque, then through the specified angle. Note that new nuts/bolts should be used.

b) Set the steering gear in the straight-ahead position prior to refitting the front subframe.

c) Refit the front subframe as described in Section 6.

d) Where applicable, fit new track rod ends as described in Section 27.

e) On completion, fill and bleed the power steering system as described in Section 24.

f) Have the front wheel toe setting checked and if necessary adjusted at the earliest opportunity.

Electric power steering

Removal

7 Disconnect the battery as described in Chapter 5A Section 4.

8 Jack up and support the front of the vehicle (see *Jacking and vehicle support*).

9 Note the exact position of the wiring loom on the subframe and then disconnect the wiring plugs from the steering rack and motor assembly **(see illustration)**.

10 Disconnect the steering column at the pinch bolt and then remove the front subframe as described in Section 6.

11 Undo the nuts from the two steering gear mounting bolts, while counter-holding the bolts from under the subframe. Lift off the two washers then remove the bolts. Note that new nuts and bolts will be required for refitting.

Refitting

12 Refitting is a reverse of the removal procedure, bearing in mind the following points:

a) Tighten the steering gear mounting bolt nuts to the specified torque, then through the specified angle. Note that new nuts/bolts should be used.

b) Set the steering gear in the straight-ahead position prior to refitting the front subframe.

c) Refit the front subframe as described in Section 6.

d) Where applicable, fit new track rod ends as described in Section 27.

e) Have the front wheel toe setting checked and if necessary adjusted at the earliest opportunity.

f) If a new steering rack has been fitted it will require programming using a diagnostic tool (Tech2, Vaux Com or similar).

26 Steering gear rubber gaiters – renewal

1 Remove the track rod end as described in Section 27.

2 Mark the correct fitted position of the gaiter on the track rod, then release the retaining clips, and slide the gaiter off the steering gear housing and track rod.

3 Thoroughly clean the track rod and the steering gear housing, clean off any corrosion, burrs or sharp edges which might damage the new gaiter's sealing lips on installation.

4 Carefully slide the new gaiter onto the track rod end, and locate it on the steering gear housing. Align the outer edge of the gaiter with the mark made on the track rod prior to removal, then secure it in position with new retaining clips.

5 Refit the track rod end as described in Section 27.

27 Track rod end – removal and refitting

Note: *A new track rod end-to-swivel hub retaining nut will be required when refitting.*

Removal

1 Firmly apply the handbrake, then jack up the front of the car and support it securely on axle stands (see *Jacking and vehicle support*). Remove the appropriate front roadwheel.

2 If the track rod end is to be re-used, use a scriber, or similar, to mark its relationship to the track rod.

3 Hold the track rod arm, and unscrew the track rod end locknut by a quarter of a turn.

4 Slacken the nut securing the track rod end to the steering arm on the swivel hub then use a two-legged puller to separate the track rod end balljoint taper. Unscrew the securing nut completely and remove the track rod end from the steering arm **(see illustrations 2.7a and 2.7b)**. Note that a new nut will be required for refitting.

5 Counting the exact number of turns necessary to do so, unscrew the track rod end from the track rod.

6 Count the number of exposed threads between the end of the track rod and the locknut, and record this figure. If a new gaiter is to be fitted, unscrew the locknut from the track rod.

7 Carefully clean the track rod end and the track rod threads. Renew the track rod end if there is excessive free play of the balljoint

shank, or if the shank is excessively stiff. If the balljoint gaiter is damaged, the complete track rod end assembly must be renewed; it is not possible to obtain the gaiter separately.

Refitting

8 If it was removed, screw the locknut onto the track rod threads, and position it so that the same number of exposed threads are visible as was noted prior to removal.

9 Screw the track rod end on to the track rod by the number of turns noted on removal. This should bring the track rod end to within approximately a quarter of a turn from the locknut, with the alignment marks that were noted on removal.

10 Refit the track rod end balljoint shank to the swivel hub, then fit a new retaining nut and tighten it to the specified torque setting. If the balljoint shank turns as the nut is being tightened, counterhold the balljoint shank using a second spanner to prevent rotation **(see illustration 2.18)**.

11 Tighten the track rod end securing locknut on the track rod while holding the track rod stationary with a second spanner on the flats provided.

12 Refit the roadwheel, then lower the vehicle to the ground and tighten the roadwheel nuts to the specified torque.

13 Have the front wheel toe setting checked and if necessary adjusted at the earliest opportunity.

28 Track rod – renewal

Note: *When refitting, a new track rod end-to-swivel hub nut and new gaiter retaining clips will be required. Vauxhall/Opel special tool KM-6321, or a suitable equivalent, will be required to unscrew the track rod inner balljoint from the end of the steering rack.*

1 Remove the track rod end as described in Section 27.

2 Release the retaining clips, and slide the steering gear gaiter off the end of the track rod as described in Section 26.

3 If the track rod on the passenger's side is being removed, it will be necessary to release the clip and fold back the gaiter on the driver's side also. A flat is provided on the rack, on the driver's side, to enable the rack to be held stationary while the track rod is unscrewed.

4 Turn the steering on full lock, so that the rack protrudes from the steering gear housing on the relevant side, slide the cover (where fitted) off the inner balljoint.

5 Engage the help of an assistant, if necessary, and prevent the rack from rotating using an open-ended spanner located on the rack flat on the driver's side. Unscrew and remove the track rod inner balljoint from the end of the steering rack using the special tool or suitable equivalent.

6 Remove the track rod assembly, and examine the track rod inner balljoint for signs of slackness or tight spots. Check that the track rod itself is straight and free from damage. If necessary, renew the track rod; it is also recommended that the steering gear gaiter/dust cover is renewed.

7 Screw the balljoint into the end of the steering rack. Tighten the track rod inner balljoint to the specified torque, whilst retaining the steering rack with an open-ended spanner.

8 Install the steering gaiter(s) and track rod end as described in Sections 26 and 27.

29 Wheel alignment and steering angles – general information

Definitions

1 A car's steering and suspension geometry is defined in four basic settings – all angles are expressed in degrees (toe settings are also sometimes expressed as a measurement); the steering axis is defined as an imaginary line drawn through the axis of the suspension strut, extended where necessary to contact the ground.

2 Camber is the angle between each roadwheel and a vertical line drawn through its centre and tyre contact patch, when viewed from the front or rear of the car. Positive camber is when the roadwheels are tilted outwards from the vertical at the top; negative camber is when they are tilted inwards. The front camber angle is not adjustable. The rear camber angle can be adjusted by altering the position of the eccentric disc on the lower control arm inner mounting.

3 Castor is the angle between the steering axis and a vertical line drawn through each roadwheel's centre and tyre contact patch, when viewed from the side of the car. Positive castor is when the steering axis is tilted so that it contacts the ground ahead of the vertical; negative castor is when it contacts the ground behind the vertical. The castor angle is not adjustable.

4 Toe is the difference, viewed from above, between lines drawn through the roadwheel centres and the car's centre-line. 'Toe-in' is when the roadwheels point inwards, towards each other at the front, while 'toe-out' is when they splay outwards from each other at the front.

5 The front wheel toe setting is adjusted by screwing the track rods in or out of the track rod ends, to alter the effective length of the track rod assembly. The rear wheel toe setting can be adjusted by altering the position of the eccentric disc on the auxiliary control arm inner mounting.

Checking and adjustment

6 Due to the special measuring equipment necessary to check the wheel alignment and steering angles, and the skill required to use it properly, the checking and adjustment of these settings is best left to a Vauxhall/Opel dealer or similar expert. Note that most tyre-fitting shops now possess sophisticated checking equipment.

Chapter 11
Bodywork and fittings

Contents

Degrees of difficulty

Easy, suitable for novice with little experience	Fairly easy, suitable for beginner with some experience	Fairly difficult, suitable for competent DIY mechanic	Difficult, suitable for experienced DIY mechanic	Very difficult, suitable for expert DIY or professional

Specifications

Torque wrench settings	Nm	lbf ft
Front bumper lower impact bar	25	18
Facia crossmember centre brace retaining bolts	22	16
Facia crossmember mounting bolts	22	16
Front seat mounting bolts	45	30
Seat belt component mountings	45	30

1 General Information

1 The bodyshell is of four-door Saloon or five-door Hatchback and Estate configurations, and is made of pressed-steel sections. The bodyshell and underframe feature variable thickness steel, achieved by laser-welded technology, used to join steel panels of different gauges. This gives a stiffer structure, with mounting points being more rigid, which gives an improved crash performance.

2 An additional safety crossmember is incorporated between the A-pillars in the upper area of the bulkhead, and the facia and steering column are secured to it. The lower bulkhead area is reinforced by additional systems of members connected to the front of the vehicle. The body side rocker panels (sills) have been divided along the length of the vehicle by internal reinforcement, this

functions like a double tube which increases its strength. All doors are reinforced and incorporate side impact protection, which is secured in the door structure. There are additional impact absorbers to the front and rear of the vehicle, behind the bumper assemblies.

3 All sheet metal surfaces which are prone to corrosion are galvanised. The painting process includes a base colour which closely matches the final topcoat, so that any stone damage is not as noticeable. The front wings are of a bolt-on type to ease their renewal if required.

4 Extensive use is made of plastic materials, mainly in the interior, but also in exterior components. The front and rear bumpers and the front grille are injection-moulded from a synthetic material which is very strong, and yet light. Plastic components such as wheel arch liners are fitted to the underside of the car, to improve the body's resistance to corrosion.

2 Maintenance – bodywork and underframe

1 The general condition of a vehicle's body-work is the one thing that significantly affects its value. Maintenance is easy, but needs to be regular. Neglect, particularly after minor damage, can lead quickly to further deterioration and costly repair bills. It is important also to keep watch on those parts of the vehicle not immediately visible, for instance the underside, inside all the wheel arches, and the lower part of the engine compartment.

2 The basic maintenance routine for the bodywork is washing – preferably with a lot of water, from a hose. This will remove all the loose solids which may have stuck to the vehicle. It is important to flush these off in such a way as to prevent grit from scratching the finish. The wheel arches and underframe

need washing in the same way, to remove any accumulated mud, which will retain moisture and tend to encourage rust. Paradoxically enough, the best time to clean the underframe and wheel arches is in wet weather, when the mud is thoroughly wet and soft. In very wet weather, the underframe is usually cleaned of large accumulations automatically, and this is a good time for inspection.

3 Periodically, except on vehicles with a wax-based underbody protective coating, it is a good idea to have the whole of the underframe of the vehicle steam-cleaned, engine compartment included, so that a thorough inspection can be carried out to see what minor repairs and renovations are necessary. Steam-cleaning is available at many garages, and is necessary for the removal of the accumulation of oily grime, which sometimes is allowed to become thick in certain areas. If steam-cleaning facilities are not available, there are some excellent grease solvents available which can be brush-applied; the dirt can then be simply hosed off. Note that these methods should not be used on vehicles with wax-based underbody protective coating, or the coating will be removed. Such vehicles should be inspected annually, preferably just prior to Winter, when the underbody should be washed down, and any damage to the wax coating repaired. Ideally, a completely fresh coat should be applied. It would also be worth considering the use of such wax-based protection for injection into door panels, sills, box sections, etc, as an additional safeguard against rust damage, where such protection is not provided by the vehicle manufacturer.

4 After washing paintwork, wipe off with a chamois leather to give an unspotted clear finish. A coat of clear protective wax polish will give added protection against chemical pollutants in the air. If the paintwork sheen has dulled or oxidised, use a cleaner/polisher combination to restore the brilliance of the shine. This requires a little effort, but such dulling is usually caused because regular washing has been neglected. Care needs to be taken with metallic paintwork, as special non-abrasive cleaner/polisher is required to avoid damage to the finish. Always check that the door and ventilator opening drain holes and pipes are completely clear, so that water can be drained out. Brightwork should be treated in the same way as paintwork. Windscreens and windows can be kept clear of the smeary film which often appears, by the use of proprietary glass cleaner. Never use any form of wax or other body or chromium polish on glass.

3 Maintenance of upholstery and carpets – general

1 Mats and carpets should be brushed or vacuum-cleaned regularly, to keep them free of grit. If they are badly stained, remove them

from the vehicle for scrubbing or sponging, and make quite sure they are dry before refitting. Seats and interior trim panels can be kept clean by wiping with a damp cloth. If they do become stained (which can be more apparent on light-coloured upholstery), use a little liquid detergent and a soft nail brush to scour the grime out of the grain of the material. Do not forget to keep the headlining clean in the same way as the upholstery. When using liquid cleaners inside the vehicle, do not over-wet the surfaces being cleaned. Excessive damp could get into the seams and padded interior, causing stains, offensive odours or even rot.

2 If the inside of the vehicle gets wet accidentally, it is worthwhile taking some trouble to dry it out properly, particularly where carpets are involved. Do not leave oil or electric heaters inside the vehicle for this purpose.

4 Minor body damage – repair

Minor scratches

1 If the scratch is very superficial, and does not penetrate to the metal of the bodywork, repair is very simple. Lightly rub the area of the scratch with a paintwork renovator, or a very fine cutting paste, to remove loose paint from the scratch, and to clear the surrounding bodywork of wax polish. Rinse the area with clean water.

2 Apply touch-up paint to the scratch using a fine paint brush; continue to apply fine layers of paint until the surface of the paint in the scratch is level with the surrounding paintwork. Allow the new paint at least two weeks to harden, then blend it into the surrounding paintwork by rubbing the scratch area with a paintwork renovator or a very fine cutting paste. Finally, apply wax polish.

3 Where the scratch has penetrated right through to the metal of the bodywork, causing the metal to rust, a different repair technique is required. Remove any loose rust from the bottom of the scratch with a penknife, then apply rust-inhibiting paint to prevent the formation of rust in the future. Using a rubber or nylon applicator, fill the scratch with bodystopper paste. If required, this paste can be mixed with cellulose thinners to provide a very thin paste which is ideal for filling narrow scratches. Before the stopper-paste in the scratch hardens, wrap a piece of smooth cotton rag around the top of a finger. Dip the finger in cellulose thinners, and quickly sweep it across the surface of the stopper-paste in the scratch; this will ensure that the surface of the stopper-paste is slightly hollowed. The scratch can now be painted over as described earlier in this Section.

Dents

4 When deep denting of the vehicle's

bodywork has taken place, the first task is to pull the dent out, until the affected bodywork almost attains its original shape. There is little point in trying to restore the original shape completely, as the metal in the damaged area will have stretched on impact, and cannot be reshaped fully to its original contour. It is better to bring the level of the dent up to a point which is about 3 mm below the level of the surrounding bodywork. In cases where the dent is very shallow anyway, it is not worth trying to pull it out at all. If the underside of the dent is accessible, it can be hammered out gently from behind, using a mallet with a wooden or plastic head. Whilst doing this, hold a suitable block of wood firmly against the outside of the panel, to absorb the impact from the hammer blows and thus prevent a large area of the bodywork from being 'belled-out'.

5 Should the dent be in a section of the bodywork which has a double skin, or some other factor making it inaccessible from behind, a different technique is called for. Drill several small holes through the metal inside the area – particularly in the deeper section. Then screw long self-tapping screws into the holes, just sufficiently for them to gain a good purchase in the metal. Now the dent can be pulled out by pulling on the protruding heads of the screws with a pair of pliers.

6 The next stage of the repair is the removal of the paint from the damaged area, and from an inch or so of the surrounding 'sound' bodywork. This is accomplished most easily by using a wire brush or abrasive pad on a power drill, although it can be done just as effectively by hand, using sheets of abrasive paper. To complete the preparation for filling, score the surface of the bare metal with a screwdriver or the tang of a file, or alternatively, drill small holes in the affected area. This will provide a really good 'key' for the filler paste.

7 To complete the repair, see the Section on filling and respraying.

Rust holes or gashes

8 Remove all paint from the affected area, and from an inch or so of the surrounding 'sound' bodywork, using an abrasive pad or a wire brush on a power drill. If these are not available, a few sheets of abrasive paper will do the job most effectively. With the paint removed, you will be able to judge the severity of the corrosion, and therefore decide whether to renew the whole panel (if this is possible) or to repair the affected area. New body panels are not as expensive as most people think, and it is often quicker and more satisfactory to fit a new panel than to attempt to repair large areas of corrosion.

9 Remove all fittings from the affected area, except those which will act as a guide to the original shape of the damaged bodywork (eg headlight shells etc). Then, using tin snips or a hacksaw blade, remove all loose metal and any other metal badly affected by corrosion. Hammer the edges of the hole inwards, in order to create a slight depression for the filler paste.

10 Wire-brush the affected area to remove the powdery rust from the surface of the remaining metal. Paint the affected area with rust-inhibiting paint, if the back of the rusted area is accessible, treat this also.

11 Before filling can take place, it will be necessary to block the hole in some way. This can be achieved by the use of aluminium or plastic mesh, or aluminium tape.

12 Aluminium or plastic mesh, or glass-fibre matting, is probably the best material to use for a large hole. Cut a piece to the approximate size and shape of the hole to be filled, then position it in the hole so that its edges are below the level of the surrounding bodywork. It can be retained in position by several blobs of filler paste around its periphery.

13 Aluminium tape should be used for small or very narrow holes. Pull a piece off the roll, trim it to the approximate size and shape required, then pull off the backing paper (if used) and stick the tape over the hole; it can be overlapped if the thickness of one piece is insufficient. Burnish down the edges of the tape with the handle of a screwdriver or similar, to ensure that the tape is securely attached to the metal underneath.

Filling and respraying

14 Before using this Section, see the Sections on dent, deep scratch, rust holes and gash repairs.

15 Many types of bodyfiller are available, but generally speaking, those proprietary kits which contain a tin of filler paste and a tube of resin hardener are best for this type of repair. A wide, flexible plastic or nylon applicator will be found invaluable for imparting a smooth and well-contoured finish to the surface of the filler.

16 Mix up a little filler on a clean piece of card or board – measure the hardener carefully (follow the maker's instructions on the pack), otherwise the filler will set too rapidly or too slowly. Using the applicator, apply the filler paste to the prepared area; draw the applicator across the surface of the filler to achieve the correct contour and to level the surface. As soon as a contour that approximates to the correct one is achieved, stop working the paste – if you carry on too long, the paste will become sticky and begin to 'pick-up' on the applicator. Continue to add thin layers of filler paste at 20-minute intervals, until the level of the filler is just proud of the surrounding bodywork.

17 Once the filler has hardened, the excess can be removed using a metal plane or file. From then on, progressively-finer grades of abrasive paper should be used, starting with a 40-grade production paper, and finishing with a 400-grade wet-and-dry paper. Always wrap the abrasive paper around a flat rubber, cork, or wooden block – otherwise the surface of the filler will not be completely flat. During the smoothing of the filler surface, the wet-and-dry paper should be periodically rinsed in water. This will ensure that a very smooth finish is imparted to the filler at the final stage.

18 At this stage, the 'dent' should be surrounded by a ring of bare metal, which in turn should be encircled by the finely 'feathered' edge of the good paintwork. Rinse the repair area with clean water, until all of the dust produced by the rubbing-down operation has gone.

19 Spray the whole area with a light coat of primer – this will show up any imperfections in the surface of the filler. Repair these imperfections with fresh filler paste or bodystopper, and once more smooth the surface with abrasive paper. Repeat this spray-and-repair procedure until you are satisfied that the surface of the filler, and the feathered edge of the paintwork, are perfect. Clean the repair area with clean water, and allow to dry fully.

20 The repair area is now ready for final spraying. Paint spraying must be carried out in a warm, dry, windless and dust-free atmosphere. This condition can be created artificially if you have access to a large indoor working area, but if you are forced to work in the open, you will have to pick your day very carefully. If you are working indoors, dousing the floor in the work area with water will help to settle the dust which would otherwise be in the atmosphere. If the repair area is confined to one body panel, mask off the surrounding panels; this will help to minimise the effects of a slight mis-match in paint colours. Bodywork fittings (eg chrome strips, door handles etc) will also need to be masked off. Use genuine masking tape, and several thicknesses of newspaper, for the masking operations.

21 Before commencing to spray, agitate the aerosol can thoroughly, then spray a test area (an old tin, or similar) until the technique is mastered. Cover the repair area with a thick coat of primer; the thickness should be built up using several thin layers of paint, rather than one thick one. Using 400-grade wet-and-dry paper, rub down the surface of the primer until it is really smooth. While doing this, the work area should be thoroughly doused with water, and the wet-and-dry paper periodically rinsed in water. Allow to dry before spraying on more paint.

22 Spray on the top coat, again building up the thickness by using several thin layers of paint. Start spraying at one edge of the repair area, and then, using a side-to-side motion, work until the whole repair area and about 2 inches of the surrounding original paintwork is covered. Remove all masking material 10 to 15 minutes after spraying on the final coat of paint.

23 Allow the new paint at least two weeks to harden, then, using a paintwork renovator, or a very fine cutting paste, blend the edges of the paint into the existing paintwork. Finally, apply wax polish.

Plastic components

24 With the use of more and more plastic body components by the vehicle manufacturers (eg bumpers. spoilers, and in some cases major body panels), rectification of more serious damage to such items has become a matter of either entrusting repair work to a specialist in this field, or renewing complete components. Repair of such damage by the DIY owner is not really feasible, owing to the cost of the equipment and materials required for effecting such repairs. The basic technique involves making a groove along the line of the crack in the plastic, using a rotary burr in a power drill. The damaged part is then welded back together, using a hot-air gun to heat up and fuse a plastic filler rod into the groove. Any excess plastic is then removed, and the area rubbed down to a smooth finish. It is important that a filler rod of the correct plastic is used, as body components can be made of a variety of different types (eg polycarbonate, ABS, polypropylene).

25 Damage of a less serious nature (abrasions, minor cracks etc) can be repaired by the DIY owner using a two-part epoxy filler repair material. Once mixed in equal proportions, this is used in similar fashion to the bodywork filler used on metal panels. The filler is usually cured in twenty to thirty minutes, ready for sanding and painting.

26 If the owner is renewing a complete component himself, or if he has repaired it with epoxy filler, he will be left with the problem of finding a suitable paint for finishing which is compatible with the type of plastic used. At one time, the use of a universal paint was not possible, owing to the complex range of plastics encountered in body component applications. Standard paints, generally speaking, will not bond to plastic or rubber satisfactorily. However, it is now possible to obtain a plastic body parts finishing kit which consists of a pre-primer treatment, a primer and coloured top coat. Full instructions are normally supplied with a kit, but basically, the method of use is to first apply the pre-primer to the component concerned, and allow it to dry for up to 30 minutes. Then the primer is applied, and left to dry for about an hour before finally applying the special-coloured top coat. The result is a correctly-coloured component, where the paint will flex with the plastic or rubber, a property that standard paint does not normally possess.

5 Major body damage repair – general

1 Where serious damage has occurred, or large areas need renewal due to neglect, it means that complete new panels will need welding-in, and this is best left to professionals. If the damage is due to impact, it will also be necessary to check completely the alignment of the bodyshell, and this can only be carried out accurately by a Vauxhall/ Opel dealer, or accident repair specialist, using special jigs. If the body is left misaligned, it is primarily dangerous as the car will not handle properly, and secondly, uneven stresses will be imposed on the steering, suspension and possibly transmission, causing abnormal wear, or complete failure, particularly to such items as the tyres.

6.1 Undo the three screws each side securing the wheel arch liner to the bumper

6.2 Slacken the bolt each side securing the bumper lower side mounting brackets to the subframe

6.3a Extract the centre pin ...

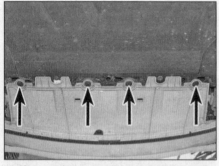

6.3b ... and remove the four plastic rivets securing the lower centre of the bumper to the subframe

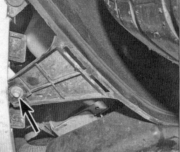

6.4 Undo the bolt each side securing the wheel arch liner to the base of the bumper

6 Front bumper – removal and refitting

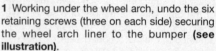

Removal

1 Working under the wheel arch, undo the six retaining screws (three on each side) securing the wheel arch liner to the bumper **(see illustration)**.

2 From under the front of the bumper, slacken (but do not remove) the bolt each side securing the lower side mounting brackets to the subframe **(see illustration)**.

3 Extract the centre pin and remove the four plastic rivets securing the lower centre of the bumper to the subframe **(see illustrations)**.

4 Undo the bolt each side securing the wheel arch liner to the base of the bumper **(see illustration)**.

5 From within the engine compartment, undo the six screws securing the upper edge of the bumper to the support **(see illustrations)**.

6 With the aid of an assistant, pull the bumper out at the sides to disengage the bumper from the guide rails then pull the bumper forward **(see illustration)**.

7 Where applicable, disconnect the foglight, exterior temperature sensor and parking distance sensor wiring connectors, and the headlight washer hoses **(see illustration)**. Carefully remove the bumper from the car.

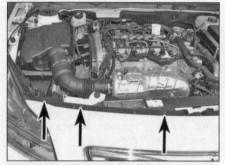

6.5a Undo the three right-hand screws ...

6.5b ... and three left hand screws securing the upper edge of the bumper to the support

Refitting

8 Refitting is a reversal of the removal procedure, ensuring that all bumper fasteners are securely tightened.

7 Rear bumper – removal and refitting

Removal
Saloon and Hatchback models

1 Remove the rear light cluster each side and the rear number plate lights as described in Chapter 12, Section 7.

2 Working under the wheel arch, undo the six retaining screws (three on each side) securing

6.6 Pull the bumper out at the sides to disengage the bumper from the guide rails

6.7 Disconnect the wiring connectors, and headlight washer hoses, then remove the bumper

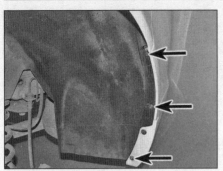

7.2 Undo the three screws each side securing the wheel arch liner to the bumper

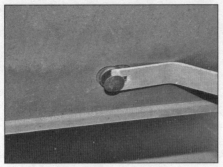

7.3a Extract the centre pin …

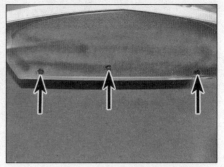

7.3b … and remove the three plastic rivets securing the bumper to the underbody

the wheel arch liner to the bumper **(see illustration)**.

3 Extract the centre pin and remove the three plastic rivets securing the lower centre of the bumper to the underbody **(see illustrations)**.

4 With the aid of an assistant, pull the bumper out at the sides to disengage the support bracket. Disengage the bumper rear locating pegs from the guides on each side and carefully pull the bumper rearwards **(see illustrations)**.

5 Where applicable, disconnect the parking distance sensor wiring connectors, then remove the bumper from the car.

Estate models

6 Remove the rear light cluster each side as described in Chapter 12, Section 7.

7 Undo the two screws each side and remove the tailgate closure guides from each side of the tailgate aperture.

8 Working under the wheel arch, undo the six retaining screws (three on each side) securing the wheel arch liner to the bumper **(see illustration 7.2)**.

9 Extract the centre pin and remove the three plastic rivets securing the lower centre of the bumper to the underbody **(see illustrations 7.3a and 7.3b)**.

10 With the aid of an assistant, pull the bumper out at the sides to disengage the support bracket. Disengage the bumper from the guides on each side and carefully pull the bumper rearwards.

11 Where applicable, disconnect the parking distance sensor wiring connectors, then remove the bumper from the car.

Refitting

12 Refitting is a reversal of the removal procedure, ensuring that all bumper fasteners are securely tightened.

---

8 Bonnet and support strut – removal, refitting and adjustment

Bonnet

Removal

1 Open the bonnet, and have an assistant support it.

2 Using a marker pen or paint, mark around the hinge positions on the bonnet.

3 Using a small screwdriver, prise the spring clip from the top of the support strut and disconnect it from the ball on the bonnet.

4 With the aid of the assistant, unscrew the two nuts securing the bonnet to the hinges on both sides.

5 Lift off the bonnet taking care not to damage the vehicle paintwork.

Refitting

6 Align the marks made on the bonnet before removal with the hinges, then refit and tighten the bonnet securing nuts.

7 Reconnect the support strut and secure with the retaining clip.

8 Check the bonnet adjustment as follows.

Adjustment

9 Close the bonnet, and check that there is an equal gap (approximately 4.0 mm) at each side, between the bonnet and the wing panels. Check also that the bonnet sits flush in relation to the surrounding body panels.

10 The bonnet should close smoothly and positively without excessive pressure. If this is not the case, adjustment will be required.

11 To adjust the bonnet alignment, loosen the bonnet-to-hinge mounting nuts, and move the bonnet on the studs as required (the holes in the hinges are enlarged). If necessary, the scissor-type hinge mounting bolts may be loosened as well. To adjust the bonnet front height in relation to the front wings, adjustable rubber bump stops are fitted to the front corners of the bonnet. These may be screwed in or out as necessary.

Support strut

Removal

12 Open the bonnet and have an assistant support the bonnet in its open position.

13 Using a small screwdriver, prise the spring clip from the top of the support strut and disconnect it from the ball on the bonnet.

14 Similarly prise the spring clip from the bottom of the strut and disconnect it from the ball on the body. Withdraw the strut.

Refitting

15 Refitting is a reversal of removal.

---

9 Bonnet lock – removal and refitting

Removal

1 Remove the front bumper as described in Section 6.

2 Undo the two bolts each side securing the bumper upper support to the front

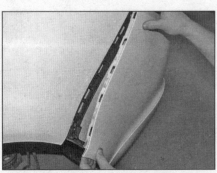

7.4a Pull the bumper out at the sides to disengage the support bracket …

7.4b … then disengage the rear locating pegs from the guides on each side

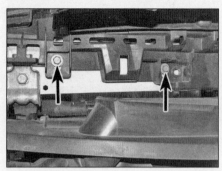

9.2a Undo the two right-hand retaining bolts ...

9.2b ... and two left-hand retaining bolts ...

9.2c ... then disengage the two catches and remove the bumper upper support

crossmember. Disengage the two catches and remove the upper support **(see illustrations)**.

3 Release the bonnet lock wiring connector

from the front crossmember and disconnect the connector **(see illustrations)**.

4 Using a marker pen or paint, mark around the bonnet lock position on the front crossmember.

5 Undo the two bonnet lock retaining bolts and withdraw the lock from the crossmember **(see illustration)**.

6 Disengage the bonnet release cable end fitting from the lock lever, then depress the tabs and withdraw the outer cable from the lock **(see illustration)**. Remove the lock from the car.

Refitting

7 Refitting is a reversal of removal, aligning the lock with the marks made on the crossmember before removal.

9.3a Release the bonnet lock wiring connector from the front crossmember ...

9.3b ... and disconnect the connector

10 Bonnet release cable – removal and refitting

Removal

1 Remove the facia right-hand lower trim panel as described in Section 30.

2 Remove the bonnet lock as described in Section 9.

3 Insert a small screwdriver between the body of the bonnet release handle and the facia crossmember to free the detent lugs, then pull the handle downward to disengage it from the crossmember **(see illustration)**.

4 Disengage the outer cable from the release handle, then slide the inner cable end fitting out of the handle **(see illustrations)**.

5 Release the cable from the support clips and brackets in the engine compartment, then withdraw the cable through the rubber grommet and into the passenger compartment.

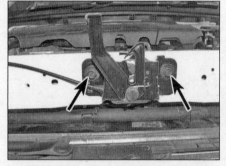

9.5 Undo the two retaining bolts and withdraw the bonnet lock from the crossmember

9.6 Disengage the release cable end fitting, then depress the tabs and withdraw the outer cable from the lock

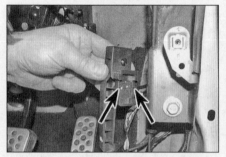

10.3 Use a small screwdriver to free the detent lugs and then pull the release handle downward

10.4a Disengage the outer cable from the release handle ...

10.4b ... then slide the inner cable end fitting out of the handle

11.2 Carefully prise free the wiring harness rubber boot and the boot frame from the door pillar

11.3a Open the locking bar …

11.3b … and disconnect the wiring harness connector from the door pillar socket

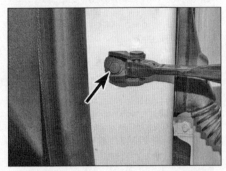

11.5 Undo the door check strap retaining bolt

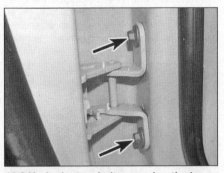

11.6 Undo the two bolts securing the lower hinge to the door …

11.7 … then undo the clamping bolt securing the two parts of the upper hinge together

As an aid to refitting, tie a length of string to the cable before removing it and leave the string in position ready for refitting.

Refitting

6 Refitting is a reversal of removal, but tie the string to the end of the cable, and use the string to pull the cable into position. Ensure that the cable is routed as noted before removal, and make sure that the grommet is correctly seated. On completion, refit the bonnet lock as described in Section 9 and the interior trim panels as described in Section 30.

11 Door – removal, refitting and adjustment

Removal

1 Open the door and support it under its lower edge on a trolley jack covered with pads of rags.
2 Carefully prise free the wiring harness rubber boot and the boot frame from the door pillar **(see illustration)**. Refit the boot to the frame allowing the frame (and boot) to be simply pushed back into position when refitting.
3 Open the locking bar and disconnect the wiring harness connector from the door pillar socket **(see illustrations)**.
4 Using a marker pen or paint, mark around the lower door hinge position on the door.
5 Undo the bolt securing the door check

strap to the vehicle body **(see illustration)**.
6 Ensure that the door is well supported, then undo the two bolts securing the lower hinge to the door **(see illustration)**.
7 Undo the upper clamping bolt securing the two parts of the hinge together **(see illustration)**.
8 With the aid of an assistant, lower the jack, disengage the upper hinge from the hinge pin, and lift away the door.

Refitting and adjustment

9 Refit the door using the reverse of the removal procedure, then close the door and check that it fits correctly in its aperture, with equal gaps at all points between it and the surrounding bodywork.
10 If adjustment is required, slacken the bolts securing the hinges to the door and reposition the door as required. Securely tighten the

12.2a Carefully prise off the door mirror interior trim panel …

bolts after completing the adjustment.
11 The striker alignment should be checked after either the door or the lock has been disturbed. To adjust a striker, slacken its screws, reposition it and securely tighten the screws.

12 Door inner trim panel – removal and refitting

Front door
Removal

1 Open the door window.
2 Using a plastic wedge or similar tool, carefully prise off the door mirror interior trim panel. Disconnect the speaker wiring connector and remove the panel **(see illustrations)**.

12.2b … then disconnect the speaker wiring connector and remove the panel

12.3a Insert a small screwdriver into the upper corner of the interior handle trim plate ...

12.3b ... and carefully prise off the plate

12.4 Undo the inner trim panel upper retaining screw

3 Insert a small screwdriver into the upper corner of the interior handle trim plate and carefully prise off the plate **(see illustrations)**.
4 Undo the screw now exposed after removal of the trim plate **(see illustration)**.

5 Insert a screwdriver into the slot at the lower front of the door grab handle plastic cover. Carefully prise free the cover to disengage the three retaining clips and remove the cover **(see illustrations)**.

6 Undo the two screws now exposed after removal of the cover **(see illustration)**.
7 Using a wide-bladed screwdriver or removal tool, carefully prise the bottom and sides of the panel away from door to release the eight internal clips. Lift the panel upward to release it from the window aperture **(see illustrations)**.
8 Once the panel is free, reach behind, and using a small screwdriver, lift the front edge of the door lock operating cable retainer. Slide the outer cable to the rear and disengage the inner cable end from the interior handle **(see illustrations)**.
9 Disconnect the wiring connectors from the mirror control switch (driver's door), window control switch, auxiliary connector, and courtesy light, then remove the panel from the door **(see illustrations)**.
10 Check the condition of the panel retaining clips and renew any that are broken or

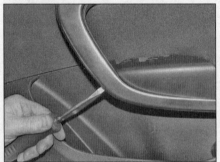
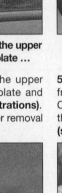

12.5a Insert a screwdriver into the slot at the lower front of the door grab handle plastic cover ...

12.5b ... then carefully prise free the cover

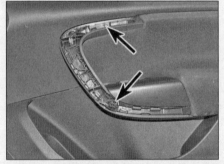

12.6 Undo the two screws now exposed after removal of the cover

12.7a Carefully prise the bottom and sides of the panel away from door ...

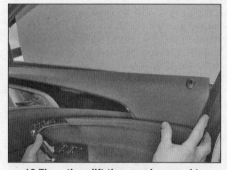

12.7b ... then lift the panel upward to release it from the window aperture

12.8a Lift the front edge of the door lock operating cable retainer and slide the outer cable to the rear ...

12.8b ... then disengage the inner cable end from the interior handle

12.9a Disconnect the wiring connectors from the mirror control switch (driver's door) ...

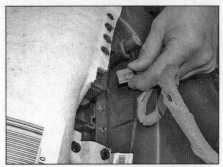

12.9b … window control switch …

12.9c … auxiliary connector …

12.9d … and courtesy light

12.13a Where a manual regulator is fitted, use a cloth rag to release the handle spring clip …

12.13b … remove the handle from the splined shaft …

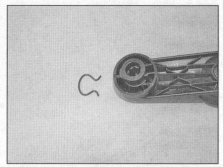

12.13c … and refit the spring clip to the handle

distorted. There are five blue clips and three green clips. Ensure that any new clips are fitted to their correct locations.

Refitting

11 Refitting is a reversal of removal.

Rear door

Removal

12 Open the door window.
13 Where a manual window regulator is fitted, locate a cloth rag between the handle and the trim panel and pull it back and forth to release the spring clip. Alternatively use a proprietary regulator spring clip removal tool. Remove the handle from the splined shaft then remove the circular spacer **(see illustrations)**. Refit the spring clip to the handle.
14 Insert a small screwdriver into the upper corner of the interior handle trim plate

and carefully prise off the plate **(see illustration)**.
15 Undo the screw now exposed after removal of the trim plate **(see illustration)**.
16 Insert a screwdriver into the slot at the

12.14 Insert a small screwdriver into the upper corner of the interior handle trim plate and carefully prise off the plate

lower front of the door grab handle plastic cover. Carefully prise free the cover to disengage the three retaining clips. Disengage the lug at the rear of the cover and remove the cover **(see illustrations)**.

12.15 Undo the inner trim panel upper retaining screw

12.16a Insert a screwdriver into the slot at the lower front of the door grab handle cover and carefully prise free the cover …

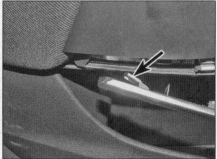

12.16b … disengage the lug at the rear of the cover …

12.16c … and remove the cover

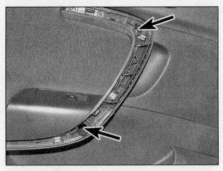

12.17 Undo the two screws now exposed after removal of the cover

12.18 Carefully prise off the circular trim cap around the interior lock button

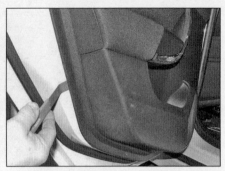

12.19a Carefully prise the bottom and sides of the panel away from door ...

12.19b ... then lift the panel upward to release it from the window aperture

12.20 Release the door lock operating cable retainer, slide the outer cable to the rear and disengage the inner cable end fitting

13.2 Prise out the blanking cap from the rear edge of the door to gain access to the handle locking screw

17 Undo the two screws now exposed after removal of the cover **(see illustration)**.

18 Carefully prise off the circular trim cap around the interior lock button **(see illustration)**.

19 Using a wide-bladed screwdriver or removal tool, carefully prise the bottom and sides of the panel away from door to release the six internal clips. Lift the panel upward to release it from the window aperture **(see illustrations)**.

20 Once the panel is free, reach behind, and using a small screwdriver, lift the front edge of the door lock operating cable retainer. Slide the outer cable to the rear and disengage the inner cable end from the interior handle **(see illustration)**.

21 Disconnect the wiring connectors from the window control switch (where applicable) then remove the panel from the door.

22 Check the condition of the panel retaining clips and renew any that are broken or distorted. There are four blue clips and two green clips. Ensure that any new clips are fitted to their correct locations.

Refitting

23 Refitting is a reversal of removal.

13 Door handles and lock components – removal and refitting

Door interior handle

Removal

1 The door interior handle is an integral part of the door inner trim panel and cannot be individually removed. If there are any problems with the interior handle, a new inner trim panel will be required.

Front door exterior handle
Removal

2 Open the door and carefully prise out the blanking cap from the rear edge of the door to gain access to the handle locking screw **(see illustration)**.

3 Pull the exterior door handle outwards and hold it in that position. With the exterior door handle held in the open position, turn the handle locking screw anti-clockwise until it reaches its stop **(see illustration)**. The exterior door handle should now be fixed in the open position.

4 Withdraw the fixed part of the handle, containing the lock cylinder, from the door **(see illustration)**.

5 Slide the exterior door handle to the rear, disengage the front pivot from the handle frame and remove the handle from the door **(see illustration)**.

13.3 Turn the handle locking screw anti-clockwise until it reaches its stop

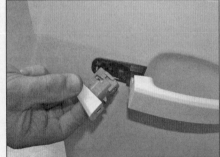

13.4 Withdraw the fixed part of the handle, containing the lock cylinder, from the door

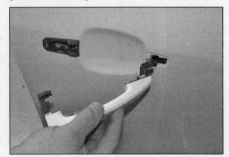

13.5 Slide the handle to the rear, disengage the front pivot from the frame and remove the handle

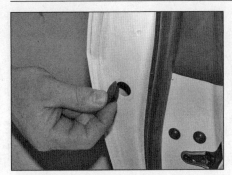

13.10 Prise out the blanking cap from the rear edge of the door to gain access to the handle locking screw

13.11 Turn the handle locking screw anti-clockwise until it reaches its stop

13.12 Withdraw the fixed part of the handle from the door

Refitting

6 Engage the handle front pivot with the frame and move the handle back into position.
7 Refit the fixed part of the handle with the lock cylinder to the door.
8 Hold the exterior handle and turn the handle locking screw clockwise to retain the handle.
9 Check the operation of the handle then refit the blanking cap to the edge of the door.

Rear door exterior handle

Removal

10 Open the door and carefully prise out the blanking cap from the rear edge of the door to gain access to the handle locking screw **(see illustration)**.
11 Pull the exterior door handle outwards and hold it in that position. With the exterior door handle held in the open position, turn the handle locking screw anti-clockwise until it reaches its stop **(see illustration)**. The exterior door handle should now be fixed in the open position.
12 Withdraw the fixed part of the handle from the door **(see illustration)**.
13 Slide the exterior door handle to the rear, disengage the front pivot from the handle frame and remove the handle from the door **(see illustration)**.

Refitting

14 Engage the handle front pivot with the frame and move the handle back into position.
15 Refit the fixed part of the handle to the door.

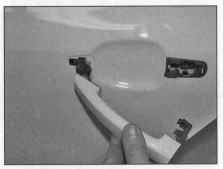

13.13 Slide the handle to the rear, disengage the front pivot from the frame and remove the handle

16 Hold the exterior handle and turn the handle locking screw clockwise to retain the handle.
17 Check the operation of the handle then refit the blanking cap to the edge of the door.

Front door lock cylinder

Removal

18 Remove the exterior handle as described previously in this Section.
19 Unclip the trim cap and remove the cap from the lock cylinder housing **(see illustration)**.
20 The lock cylinder body is an integral part of the housing and no further dismantling is possible.

Refitting

21 Refitting is a reversal of removal.

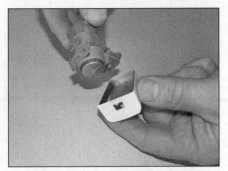

13.19 Unclip the trim cap and remove the cap from the lock cylinder housing

Front door lock

Removal

22 Remove the exterior handle as described previously in this Section.
23 Remove the door inner trim panel as described in Section 12.
24 Carefully peel back the protective plastic sheet from the door, starting at the top. When sufficient clearance exists, reach in through the door aperture and push out the clips securing the wiring harness to the door, then completely remove the plastic sheet **(see illustrations)**.
25 Undo the three screws securing the security cover to the exterior handle frame, door lock and door, and remove the cover through the door aperture **(see illustrations)**.
26 Reach in through the door aperture and

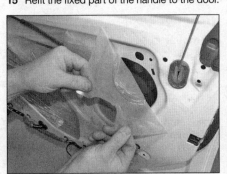

13.24a Carefully peel back the protective plastic sheet from the door, starting at the top

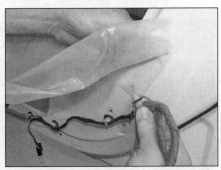

13.24b When sufficient clearance exists, push out the wiring harness clips and completely remove the plastic sheet

13.25a Undo the upper screw ...

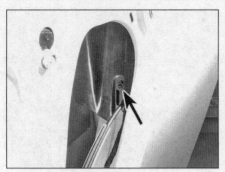

13.25b … the lower screw …

13.25c … and the outer screw …

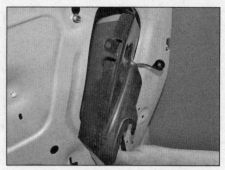

13.25d … then remove the security cover through the door aperture

13.26 Open the exterior handle operating rod clamp at the lock lever

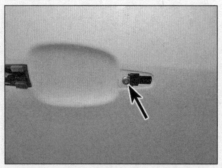

13.27 Slacken the exterior handle frame front retaining screw approximately five turns

13.28 Release the interior lock button operating rod grommet from the door panel

open the exterior handle operating rod clamp at the lock lever **(see illustration)**.

27 Slacken the exterior handle frame front retaining screw approximately five turns **(see illustration)**. Slide the handle frame forward

to release the rear locating lugs and free the frame from the door.

28 Release the interior lock button operating rod grommet from the door panel **(see illustration)**.

29 Undo the three screws securing the lock to the door **(see illustration)**.

30 Withdraw the lock from its location and remove the plastic cover over the lock wiring connector. Lift the locking bar and disconnect the wiring connector **(see illustrations)**.

31 Lower the lock assembly together with the exterior handle frame down into the door, bringing the interior lock button and rod in through the hole provided. Now remove the lock assembly and exterior handle frame through the upper door aperture **(see illustration)**.

32 If required, disconnect the operating cable and rods from the lock linkage and bracket.

Refitting

33 Refitting is a reversal of removal. Ensure that the protective plastic sheet is firmly stuck with no air bubbles. If the sheet was damaged during removal it should be renewed.

Rear door lock

Removal

34 Remove the exterior handle as described previously in this Section.

35 Remove the door inner trim panel as described in Section 12.

36 Carefully peel back the protective plastic sheet from the door, starting at the top **(see illustration)**. When sufficient clearance exists, reach in through the door aperture and push out the clips securing the wiring harness to the door, then completely remove the plastic sheet.

37 Reach in through the door aperture and open the exterior handle operating rod clamp at the lock lever **(see illustration)**.

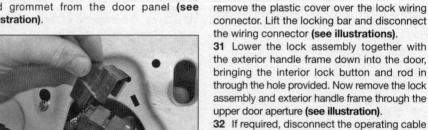

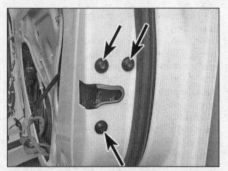

13.29 Undo the three screws securing the lock to the door

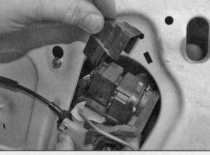

13.30a Remove the plastic cover over the lock wiring connector …

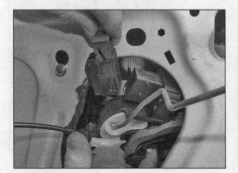

13.30b … then lift the locking bar and disconnect the wiring connector

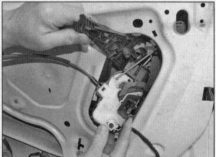

13.31 Remove the lock assembly and exterior handle frame through the upper door aperture

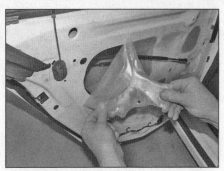

13.36 Carefully peel back the protective plastic sheet from the door, starting at the top

13.37 Open the exterior handle operating rod clamp at the lock lever (shown with lock removed)

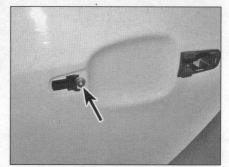

13.38 Slacken the exterior handle frame front retaining screw approximately five turns

13.39 Undo the three screws securing the lock to the door

13.40 Lower the lock assembly down into the door, bringing the interior lock button and rod in through the grommet

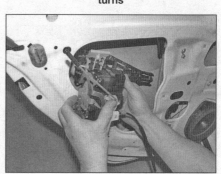

13.41 Remove the lock assembly and exterior handle frame through the door aperture

38 Slacken the exterior handle frame front retaining screw approximately five turns **(see illustration)**. Slide the handle frame forward to release the rear locating lugs and free the frame from the door.

39 Undo the three screws securing the lock to the door **(see illustration)**.

40 Lower the lock assembly together with the exterior handle frame down into the door, bringing the interior lock button and rod in through the grommet **(see illustration)**.

41 Remove the lock assembly and exterior handle frame through the door aperture **(see illustration)**.

42 Remove the plastic cover over the lock wiring connector. Lift the locking bar and disconnect the wiring connector, then remove the lock and exterior handle frame from the door **(see illustrations)**.

43 If required, disconnect the operating cable and rods from the lock linkage and bracket.

Refitting

44 Refitting is a reversal of removal. Ensure that the protective plastic sheet is firmly stuck with no air bubbles. If the sheet was damaged during removal it should be renewed.

14 Door window glass and regulator – removal and refitting

Front door window glass

Removal

1 Remove the door inner trim panel as described in Section 12.

2 Carefully peel back the protective plastic sheet from the door, starting at the top. When sufficient clearance exists, reach in through the door aperture and push out the clips securing the wiring harness to the door, then completely remove the plastic sheet **(see illustrations 13.24a and 13.24b)**.

3 Release the retaining clip at the front and rear of the window aperture trim surround, then remove the trim surround from the door **(see illustrations)**.

4 Reconnect the wiring connector to the window control switch and position the window glass so that the two retainers securing the glass to the regulator are accessible through the door aperture.

5 Using a screwdriver, press the centre of the window glass retainer while at the same time pulling up on the glass to disengage it from

13.42a Remove the plastic cover over the lock wiring connector ...

13.42b ... then lift the locking bar and disconnect the wiring connector

14.3a Release the retaining clip at the front ...

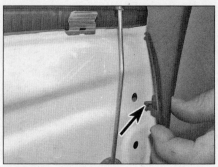

14.3b … and rear of the window aperture trim surround …

14.3c … then remove the trim surround from the door

14.5a Press the centre of the window glass rear retainer while at the same pulling up on the glass …

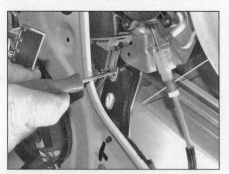

14.5b … then release the front retainer in the same way

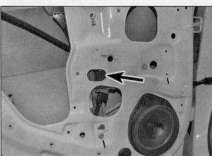

14.9 Position the window so that the fixing clip is accessible through the small opening in the door

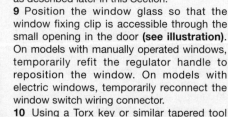

the regulator. Release the other retainer in the same way **(see illustrations)**.

6 Lower the regulator, then tilt the window glass down at the front, lift it upwards and remove it from the outside of the door.

Refitting

7 Refitting is a reversal of removal. Ensure that the retainers on the regulator positively lock in position on the window glass.

Rear door window glass
Removal

8 Remove the rear door fixed window glass as described later in this Section.

9 Position the window glass so that the window fixing clip is accessible through the small opening in the door **(see illustration)**. On models with manually operated windows, temporarily refit the regulator handle to reposition the window. On models with electric windows, temporarily reconnect the window switch wiring connector.

10 Using a Torx key or similar tapered tool with approximately a 4.0 mm shaft diameter, push the tool through the centre of the two-part window fixing clip to expand the internal locking lugs and separate the clip **(see illustrations)**. Disengage the window from the regulator lifting block and recover the two parts of the fixing clip.

11 Move the window and regulator to the fully open position, then carefully lift the window glass upwards at the rear, and remove it from the outside of the door **(see illustration)**.

Refitting

12 Refitting is a reversal of removal.

Rear door fixed window glass
Removal

13 Fully lower the rear door window.

14 Remove the door inner trim panel as described in Section 12.

15 Carefully peel back the protective plastic sheet from the door, starting at the top **(see illustration 13.36)**. When sufficient clearance exists, reach in through the door aperture and push out the clips securing the wiring harness to the door, then completely remove the plastic sheet.

16 Using a plastic wedge or similar tool, tap up the window outer waist seal from the door

14.10a Push the tool through the centre of the two-part window fixing clip …

14.10b … to expand the internal locking lugs (shown with clip removed) …

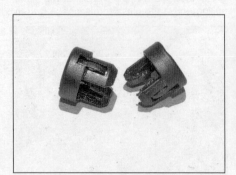

14.10c … and separate the clip

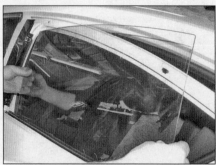

14.11 Lift the window glass upwards at the rear, and remove it from the outside of the door

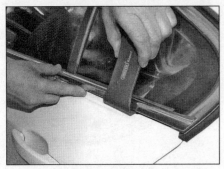

14.16a Lift the window outer waist seal up ...

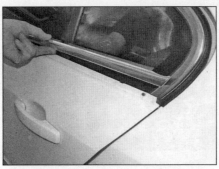

14.16b ... and remove it from the door

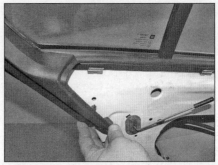

14.17a Pull the window aperture inner trim away from the door at the lower front and rear edges ...

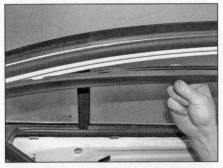

14.17b ... then pull the surround away from the door frame at the top

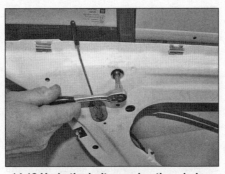

14.18 Undo the bolt securing the window rear guide rail to the door

14.19 Pull the guide rail down and out of the rubber window channel

aperture. Lift the seal up and remove it from the door **(see illustrations)**.

17 Pull the window aperture inner trim away from the door at the lower front and rear edges to release the two clips, then pull the surround away from the door frame at the top to remove **(see illustrations)**.

18 Undo the bolt securing the window rear guide rail to the door **(see illustration)**.

19 Pull the guide rail down and out of the rubber window channel, then remove the guide rail through the door aperture **(see illustration)**.

20 Using a plastic wedge or similar tool, carefully prise up the window inner waist seal from the door aperture. Lift the seal up and remove it from the door **(see illustration)**.

21 Extract the plastic retaining clip securing the upper and lower front corners of the weatherstrip to the outer door frame. Pull the

14.20 Prise up and remove the window inner waist seal from the door aperture

weatherstrip forward to release it from the door **(see illustrations)**.

22 Pull the rubber window channel up and out of the door frame at the front to gain

14.21a Extract the plastic retaining clip securing the upper ...

access to the three screws securing window frame front cover to the door. Undo the three screws and remove the window frame front cover **(see illustration)**.

14.21b ... and lower front corners of the weatherstrip to the outer door frame ...

14.21c ... then pull the weatherstrip forward to release it from the door

14.22 Undo the three screws and remove the window frame front cover

23 Release the fixed window glass upper moulding and weatherstrip from the top of the door frame and remove it, together with the fixed window glass from the door **(see illustration)**.
24 If required, ease the weatherstrip away from the fixed window glass and remove the glass from the upper moulding **(see illustration)**.

Refitting

25 Refitting is a reversal of removal.

Front door window regulator

Removal

26 Remove the door inner trim panel as described in Section 12.
27 Carefully peel back the protective plastic sheet from the door, starting at the top. When sufficient clearance exists, reach in through the door aperture and push out the clips securing the wiring harness to the door, then completely remove the plastic sheet **(see illustrations 13.24a and 13.24b)**.
28 Release the window glass from the regulator as described previously in paragraphs 4 and 5. Slide the window glass to the fully closed position. Retain the window glass in the closed position using adhesive tape over the top of the door frame.
29 Disconnect the wiring connector from the window regulator motor **(see illustration)**.
30 Undo the five bolts securing the regulator to the door, then manipulate the regulator out through the door aperture **(see illustrations)**.

Refitting

31 Refitting is a reversal of removal.

14.23 Release the upper moulding and weatherstrip from the door frame and remove it together with the fixed window glass

Rear door window regulator

Removal

32 Remove the door inner trim panel as described in Section 12.
33 Carefully peel back the protective plastic sheet from the door, starting at the top **(see illustration 13.36)**. When sufficient clearance exists, reach in through the door aperture and push out the clips securing the wiring harness to the door, then completely remove the plastic sheet.
34 Release the window glass from the regulator as described previously in paragraphs 9 and 10. Slide the window glass to the fully closed position. Retain the window glass in the closed position using adhesive tape over the top of the door frame.
35 On models with electric windows,

14.24 Ease the weatherstrip away from the fixed window glass and remove the glass from the upper moulding

disconnect the window regulator motor wiring connector **(see illustration)**.
36 Undo the three bolts (electric windows) or four bolts (manual windows) securing the regulator to the door, then manipulate the regulator out through the door aperture **(see illustrations)**.

Refitting

37 Refitting is a reversal of removal.

15 Bootlid – removal, refitting and adjustment

Removal

1 Remove the bootlid trim panel as described in Section 28.

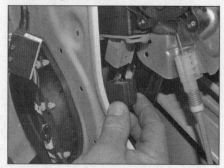

14.29 Disconnect the wiring connector from the window regulator motor

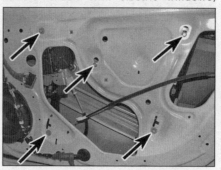

14.30a Undo the five bolts securing the regulator to the door ...

14.30b ... then manipulate the regulator out through the door aperture

14.35 On models with electric windows, disconnect the window regulator motor wiring connector

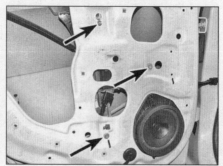

14.36a Undo the bolts securing the regulator to the door (electric regulator shown) ...

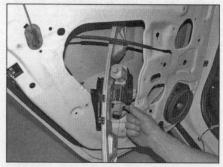

14.36b ... then manipulate the regulator out through the door aperture

2 Disconnect the wiring connectors at all the bootlid components and release the wiring harness from the bootlid clips.

3 Using a pencil or marker pen, mark around the hinges on the bootlid as a guide for refitting.

4 Unscrew the mounting bolts then lift the bootlid from the hinges.

5 The hinges can be removed if required by unbolting the hinges from the body.

Refitting and adjustment

6 Refitting is a reversal of removal, but make sure that the bootlid is positioned on the hinges as noted on removal and tighten the mounting bolts securely. With the bootlid closed, check that it is positioned centrally within the body aperture. If adjustment is necessary, loosen the bootlid mounting bolts, reposition the bootlid, then retighten the bolts. Check that the striker enters the lock centrally, and if necessary adjust the striker position by loosening the mounting bolts. Tighten the bolts on completion.

16 Bootlid lock components – removal and refitting

Lock assembly

Removal

1 Remove the bootlid trim panel as described in Section 28.

2 Disconnect the lock wiring connector.

3 Undo the two lock assembly retaining screws.

4 Push the lock to the left, slide it forward and withdraw it from the bootlid.

5 Disconnect the lock cable and remove the lock.

Refitting

6 Refitting is a reversal of removal. Check that when closed the bootlid lock engages the lock striker centrally. If necessary loosen the bolts and adjust the position of the striker, then tighten the bolts.

Release switch

Removal

7 Remove the bootlid trim panel as described in Section 28.

8 Disconnect the release switch wiring connector.

17.8 Hinge-to-tailgate retaining bolts – Hatchback models

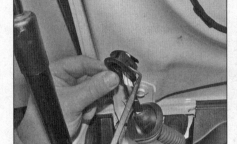

17.2 Disconnect the tailgate washer hose at the connector on the tailgate – Hatchback models

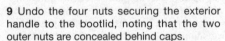

17.3b ... depress the retaining tabs and release the plastic frames from the tailgate ...

9 Undo the four nuts securing the exterior handle to the bootlid, noting that the two outer nuts are concealed behind caps.

10 Remove the exterior handle from the bootlid, then using a small screwdriver, release the four tabs and remove the release switch from the exterior handle.

Refitting

11 Refitting is a reversal of removal.

17 Tailgate and support struts – removal, refitting and adjustment

Tailgate

Removal – Hatchback models

1 Remove the tailgate trim panel as described in Section 28.

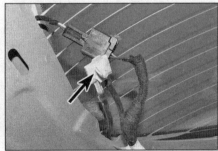

17.10 Disconnect the tailgate washer hose at the connector on the tailgate – Estate models

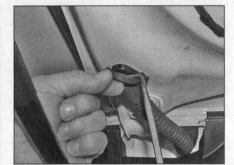

17.3a Carefully release the rubber gaiters at the top of the tailgate from their plastic frames ...

17.3c ... then refit the gaiter to the frame – Hatchback models

2 Disconnect the tailgate washer hose at the connector on the tailgate **(see illustration)**.

3 Using a hooked tool, carefully release the rubber gaiters at the top of the tailgate from their plastic frames. Depress the retaining tabs and release the plastic frames from the tailgate. Refit the gaiter to the frame allowing the frame (and gaiter) to be simply pushed back into position when refitting **(see illustrations)**.

4 Disconnect the wiring connectors at all the tailgate components and release the wiring harness from the tailgate clips.

5 Carefully start to pull the wiring harness and washer hose out of the tailgate. If the same tailgate is being refitted, tie on a length of string to the wiring harness and washer hose beforehand – the string can then be untied when it emerges from the top of the tailgate, and left in place to pull the harness and washer hose back through.

6 Using a pencil or marker pen, mark the position of the hinges on the tailgate to aid refitting.

7 Engage the help of an assistant to support the tailgate, then disconnect the support struts as described later in this Section.

8 Unscrew the four bolts securing the hinges to the tailgate, and lift the tailgate from the car **(see illustration)**.

Removal – Estate models

9 Remove the tailgate trim panel as described in Section 28.

10 Disconnect the tailgate washer hose at the connector on the tailgate **(see illustration)**.

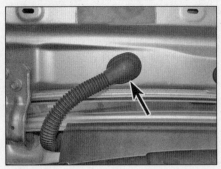

17.11 Carefully release the rubber gaiters at the top of the tailgate from their plastic frames

17.16 Hinge-to-tailgate retaining bolts – Estate models

17.19 Prise off the spring clips from the top and bottom of the support strut

11 Using a hooked tool, carefully release the rubber gaiters at the top of the tailgate from their plastic frames **(see illustration)**. Depress the retaining tabs and release the plastic frames from the tailgate. Refit the gaiter to the frame allowing the frame (and gaiter) to be simply pushed back into position when refitting.

12 Disconnect the wiring connectors at all the tailgate components and release the wiring harness from the tailgate clips.

13 Carefully start to pull the wiring harness and washer hose out of the tailgate. If the same tailgate is being refitted, tie on a length of string to the wiring harness and washer hose beforehand – the string can then be untied when it emerges from the top of the tailgate, and left in place to pull the harness and washer hose back through.

14 Using a pencil or marker pen, mark the position of the hinges on the tailgate to aid refitting.

15 Engage the help of an assistant to support the tailgate, then disconnect the support struts as described later in this Section.

16 Unscrew the four bolts securing the hinges to the tailgate, and lift the tailgate from the car **(see illustration)**.

Refitting

17 Refitting is a reversal of removal, but make sure that the tailgate is positioned on the hinges as noted on removal and tighten the mounting bolts securely. With the tailgate closed, check that it is positioned centrally within the body aperture. If adjustment is necessary, loosen the tailgate mounting bolts, reposition the tailgate, then retighten the bolts. Check that the striker enters the lock centrally, and if necessary adjust the striker position by loosening the mounting bolts. Tighten the bolts on completion.

Support struts

Note: *On Estate models equipped with a power tailgate, refer to Section 19 if removing the right-hand support strut.*

Removal

18 Open the tailgate and note which way round the struts are fitted. Have an assistant support the tailgate in its open position.

19 Using a small screwdriver, prise the spring clip from the top of the strut and disconnect it from the ball on the tailgate **(see illustration)**.

20 Similarly prise the spring clip from the bottom of the strut and disconnect it from the ball on the body. Withdraw the strut.

Refitting

21 Refitting is a reversal of removal.

18 Tailgate lock components – removal and refitting

Lock assembly

Removal – Hatchback models

1 Remove the tailgate trim panel as described in Section 28.

2 Disconnect the lock wiring connector **(see illustration)**.

3 Undo the two lock assembly retaining screws and remove the lock from the tailgate **(see illustration)**.

Refitting – Hatchback models

4 Refitting is a reversal of removal. Check that when closed the tailgate lock engages the lock striker centrally. If necessary loosen the bolts and adjust the position of the striker, then tighten the bolts.

Removal – Estate models

5 Remove the tailgate trim panel as described in Section 28.

6 Disconnect the lock wiring connector **(see illustration)**.

7 Undo the three lock assembly retaining screws and remove the lock from the tailgate **(see illustration)**.

Refitting – Estate models

8 Refitting is a reversal of removal. Check that when closed the tailgate lock engages

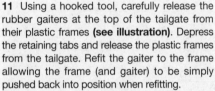

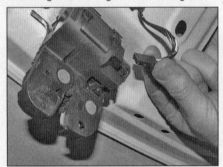

18.2 Disconnect the tailgate lock wiring connector – Hatchback models

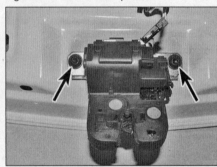

18.3 Undo the retaining screws and remove the lock from the tailgate – Hatchback models

18.6 Disconnect the tailgate lock wiring connector – Estate models

18.7 Undo the retaining screws and remove the lock from the tailgate – Estate models

18.10 Disconnect the tailgate release switch wiring connector – Hatchback models

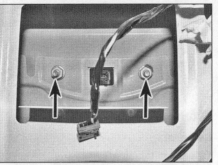

18.11a Undo the two inner nuts securing the exterior handle to the tailgate ...

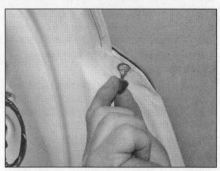

18.11b ... and the two outer nuts which are concealed behind caps – Hatchback models

the lock striker centrally. If necessary loosen the bolts and adjust the position of the striker, then tighten the bolts.

Release switch

Removal – Hatchback models

9 Remove the tailgate trim panel as described in Section 28.
10 Disconnect the release switch wiring connector **(see illustration)**.
11 Undo the four nuts securing the exterior handle to the tailgate, noting that the two outer nuts are concealed behind caps **(see illustrations)**.
12 Remove the exterior handle from the tailgate, then using a small screwdriver, release the four tabs and remove the release switch from the exterior handle **(see illustration)**.

Refitting – Hatchback models

13 Refitting is a reversal of removal.

Removal – Estate models

14 Remove the tailgate trim panel as described in Section 28.
15 Remove the number plate light units and the tailgate wiper motor as described in Chapter 12, Section 7 and 14.
16 Disconnect the release switch wiring connector.
17 Undo the eight nuts securing the exterior handle to the tailgate **(see illustration)**.
18 Pull the exterior handle away from the tailgate to release the internal retaining clips and remove the handle from the tailgate.

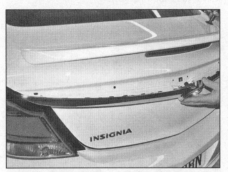

18.12 Remove the exterior handle from the tailgate, then remove the release switch from the handle – Hatchback models

19 Using a small screwdriver, release the four tabs and remove the release switch from the exterior handle.

Refitting – Estate models

20 Refitting is a reversal of removal.

---

19 Power tailgate components (Estate models) – removal and refitting

Tailgate hydraulic actuator strut

Removal

1 Remove the luggage compartment lower side trim panel on the right-hand side as described in Section 28.
2 Release the hydraulic pump wiring

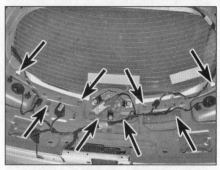

18.17 Exterior handle retaining nuts – Estate models

connector from the pump cover and disconnect the connector **(see illustration)**.
3 Cut off the two cable ties securing the hydraulic pump outer cover to the inner cover and remove the outer cover **(see illustration)**.
4 Ensure that the tailgate is adequately supported in the open position with a suitable additional prop.
5 Disconnect the two hydraulic hoses at the quick-release connectors on the top of the hydraulic pump. Do not close the tailgate with the hydraulic hoses disconnected.
6 Prise out the rubber grommet from the hydraulic hose entry point in the D-pillar **(see illustration)**. Release the hoses from the retaining clips inside the pillar.
7 Using a small screwdriver, prise the spring clip from the top of the strut and disconnect it from the ball on the tailgate **(see illustration 17.19)**.

19.2 Release the hydraulic pump wiring connector from the pump cover and disconnect the connector

19.3 Cut off the two cable ties securing the hydraulic pump outer cover to the inner cover

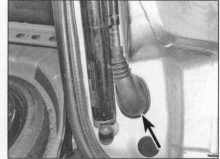

19.6 Prise out the rubber grommet from the hydraulic hose entry point in the D-pillar

8 Similarly prise the spring clip from the bottom of the strut and disconnect it from the ball on the body. Withdraw the strut and guide the hydraulic hoses out through the D-pillar opening.

Refitting

9 Refitting is a reversal of removal, using new cable ties to secure the hydraulic pump outer cover. Open and close the tailgate several times to bleed the hydraulic system.

Tailgate hydraulic pump

Removal

10 Carry out the operations described previously in paragraphs 1 to 5.
11 Withdraw the hydraulic pump from the inner cover, remove the upper and lower insulators and remove the pump.

Refitting

12 Refitting is a reversal of removal, using new cable ties to secure the hydraulic pump

outer cover. Open and close the tailgate several times to bleed the hydraulic system.

20 Exterior mirrors and associated components – removal and refitting

Exterior mirror

Removal

1 Remove the door inner trim panel as described in Section 12.
2 Disconnect the wiring connector from the mirror **(see illustration)**.
3 Undo the three retaining bolts and remove the mirror assembly from the door **(see illustrations)**.

Refitting

4 Refitting is a reversal of removal.

Mirror glass

Removal

5 Press the top of the glass inwards so that the glass is forced out from the bottom.
6 Using a plastic wedge, prise the lower edge of the glass outwards to release the internal retaining clips **(see illustration)**.
7 Withdraw the mirror glass and disconnect the wiring connectors **(see illustration)**.

Refitting

8 Refitting is a reversal of removal. Carefully press the mirror glass into the housing until the centre retainer clips are engaged.

Mirror motor

Removal

9 Remove the mirror glass as described previously.
10 Undo the three retaining screws and withdraw the motor assembly from the mirror body **(see illustration)**.
11 Disconnect the wiring connector and remove the mirror motor from the mirror body.

Refitting

12 Refitting is a reversal of removal.

Outer cover

Removal

13 Using a plastic wedge, carefully prise the outer cover away from the mirror body to release the inner locating clips. Withdraw the cover from the mirror body. **(see illustrations)**.

Refitting

14 Refitting is a reversal of removal.

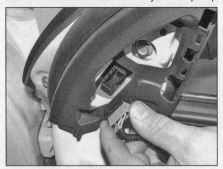

20.2 Disconnect the exterior mirror wiring connector

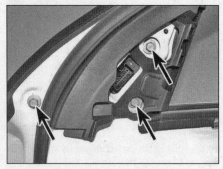

20.3a Undo the three retaining bolts ...

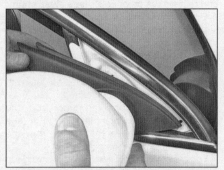

20.3b ... and remove the mirror assembly from the door

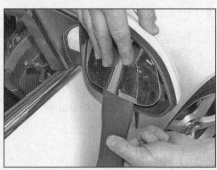

20.6 Prise the lower edge of the glass outwards to release the internal retaining clips

20.7 Withdraw the mirror glass and disconnect the wiring connectors

20.10 Mirror motor retaining screws

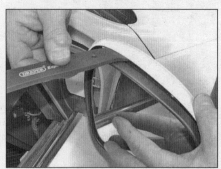

20.13a Using a plastic wedge, carefully prise the outer cover away from the mirror body ...

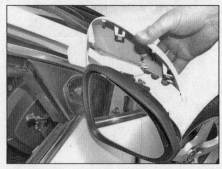

20.13b ... then withdraw the cover from the mirror body

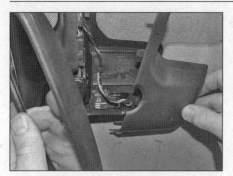

21.1a Using a small screwdriver, carefully ease the right-hand side mirror base trim sideways and lift off the trim …

21.1b … then remove the trim on the left-hand side in the same way

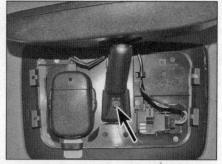

21.2 Undo the screw securing the mirror mount to the mirror base

21 Interior mirror – removal and refitting

Removal

1 Using a small screwdriver, carefully ease the right-hand side mirror base trim sideways and lift off the trim. Remove the trim on the left-hand side in the same way **(see illustrations)**.

2 Undo the screw securing the mirror mount to the mirror base **(see illustration)**.

3 Disconnect the mirror wiring connector.

4 Grasp the mirror in both hands and rock it from side to side while at the same time pushing upwards to release the internal mounting tab.

5 Refitting is the reverse of removal.

22 Windscreen and fixed window glass – general information

1 The windscreen, tailgate, rear window and side window glass are cemented in position with a special adhesive and require the use of specialist equipment for their removal and refitting. Renewal of such fixed glass is considered beyond the scope of the home mechanic. Owners are strongly advised to have the work carried out by one of the many specialist windscreen fitting specialists.

23 Sunroof – general information

1 An electric sunroof is offered as an optional extra on most models, and is fitted as standard equipment on some models.

2 Due to the complexity of the sunroof mechanism, considerable expertise is needed to repair, renew or adjust the sunroof components successfully. Removal of the roof first requires the headlining to be removed, which is a complex and tedious operation in itself, and not a task to be undertaken lightly. Therefore, any problems with the sunroof should be referred to a Vauxhall/Opel dealer.

24 Body exterior fittings – removal and refitting

Radiator grille

1 Remove the front bumper as described in Section 6.

2 The radiator grille panel and the other detachable panels on the bumper are retained by a series of plastic clips, the location of which will become obvious on visual inspection.

3 Carefully disengage all the relevant clips using a small screwdriver, while at the same time pulling the panel from its location.

4 Refit the grille to the bumper ensuring it is

securely held by the retaining tabs, then refit the front bumper as described in Section 6.

Wheel arch liners

5 The plastic wheel arch liners fitted to the underside of the front and rear wings are secured in position by a mixture of screws and plastic rivets, and removal will be fairly obvious on inspection. Work methodically around the liner, removing its retaining screws and plastic rivets until it is free to be removed from under the relevant wheel arch **(see illustration)**. The wheel arch liner plastic rivets are removed by prising out the centre pin using a small screwdriver, then removing the rivet body.

Engine undertray

6 On diesel engine models an undertray is fitted beneath the engine/transmission assembly. The undertray is secured to the front subframe with eight bolts and to the wheel arch liners with two plastic rivets each side **(see illustrations)**. The plastic rivets are removed by prising out the centre pin using a small screwdriver, then removing the rivet body.

7 The undertray incorporates a hinged centre section secured to the main undertray with four screws. After releasing the screws the centre section can be lowered at the rear to provide access for engine oil and filter renewal. There is insufficient clearance to enable this centre section to be lowered if the car is supported on axle stands and, in practice, it can only really be used if the car is positioned on a ramp or over an inspection pit.

24.5 Removing a front wheel arch liner

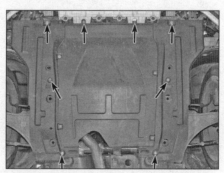

24.6a Engine undertray retaining bolts …

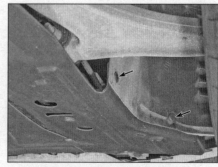

24.6b … and plastic rivets

24.9a Remove the water deflector plastic rivets on the right-hand side ...

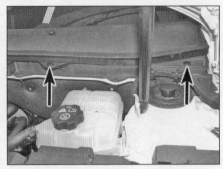

24.9b ... and left-hand side ...

24.9c ... by prising out the centre pin using a small screwdriver ...

24.9d ... then removing the rivet body

Water deflector

8 Remove the windscreen wiper arms as described in Chapter 12, Section 12.
9 Remove the four plastic rivets securing

24.10 Pull the upper edge of the deflector away from the windscreen to release the flange from the windscreen channel

the front edge of the water deflector to the deflector frame by prising out the centre pin using a small screwdriver, then removing the rivet body **(see illustrations)**.
10 Pull the upper edge of the water deflector away from the windscreen to release the flange from the windscreen channel **(see illustration)**.
11 Disconnect the washer hose from the washer jet and remove the water deflector.
12 If necessary the water deflector inner panel can be removed by lifting it from its location and feeding the washer hose through the grommet **(see illustrations)**.
13 Refit the water deflector using a reversal of the removal procedure. Refit the wiper arms as described in Chapter 12, Section 12.

Body trim strips and badges

14 The various body trim strips and badges

24.12a Withdraw the water deflector inner panel ...

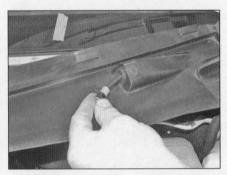

24.12b ... and feed the washer hose through the grommet

are held in position with a special adhesive tape. Removal requires the trim/badge to be heated, to soften the adhesive, and then cut away from the surface. Due to the high risk of damage to the vehicle's paintwork during this operation, it is recommended that this task should be entrusted to a Vauxhall/Opel dealer.

25 Seats – removal and refitting

⚠️ *Warning: The front seats are equipped with seat belt tensioners, and side airbags are incorporated into the outer sides of the seats. Side airbags may also be fitted to the backrest side padding of the rear seats. The seat belt tensioners and side airbags may cause injury if triggered accidentally. If the tensioner has been triggered due to a sudden impact or accident, the unit must be renewed, as it cannot be reset. If a seat is to be disposed of, the tensioner must be triggered before the seat is removed from the vehicle. Due to safety considerations, tensioner or seat disposal must be entrusted to a Vauxhall/Opel dealer. Where side airbags are fitted, refer to Chapter 12, Section 22 for the precautions which should be observed when dealing with an airbag system.*

Front seat removal

1 Set the seat height adjustment to its middle position.
2 Disconnect the battery negative terminal (refer to Chapter 5A, Section 4). Wait 2 minutes for the capacitors to discharge, before working on the seat electrics.
3 Using a small screwdriver, carefully prise off the trim cap on the seat belt tensioner connector. Undo the retaining bolt, lift off the connector cover and separate the seat belt from the tensioner **(see illustrations)**.
4 Slide the seat adjustment fully forward.
5 Slacken and remove the seat retaining bolts from the rear of the guide rails **(see illustration)**.
6 Tip the seat forward, then pull out the locking bar and disconnect the wiring

25.3a Carefully prise off the trim cap on the seat belt tensioner connector and undo the retaining bolt ...

25.3b ... lift off the connector cover ...

25.3c ... and separate the seat belt from the tensioner

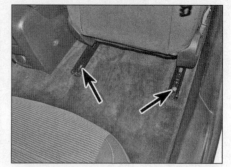

25.5 Remove the front seat retaining bolts from the rear of the guide rails

connector from the under the seat, at the rear **(see illustration)**.

7 Pull the seat backwards to disengage the guide rail front mounting lugs from the floor. The seat can now be lifted out of the vehicle. Note that` seat is very heavy and the help of an assistant may be required.

Rear seat removal

Cushion

8 Pull the front of the rear seat cushion upwards to disengage the front mountings **(see illustration)**.

9 Lift the cushion out of the rear mountings and remove it from the car.

Backrest

10 Remove the rear seat cushion as described previously in this Section.

11 Remove the luggage compartment lower side trim panel as described in Section 28.

12 If the backrest side padding incorporates

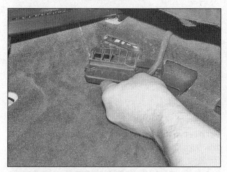

25.6 Pull out the locking bar and disconnect the wiring connector from the under the seat

an airbag, disconnect the battery negative terminal (refer to Chapter 5A, Section 4). Wait 2 minutes for the capacitors to discharge, before continuing.

13 Reach in through the aperture below the seat belt reel and compress the two tabs of

25.8 Pull the front of the rear seat cushion upwards to disengage the front mountings

the backrest side padding upper mounting. Pull the upper portion of the side padding forward, then lift it up to disengage the lower hook **(see illustrations)**. Where applicable, disconnect the airbag wiring connector, then remove the side padding from the car.

14 If removing the right-hand backrest, undo the three nuts securing the hinge centre support to the floor.

15 Unscrew the retaining nut and remove the centre seat belt buckle.

16 Fold the backrest forward, then using a screwdriver, press the outer hinge pin locking collar in, to free the hinge pin, while at the same time pulling upward to release the backrest **(see illustrations)**.

17 Fold the backrest upward, then pull the hinge pin out of the centre support (left-hand side), or pull the backrest off the hinge pin (right-hand side) **(see illustration)**. Remove the backrest from the vehicle.

25.13a Compress the two tabs of the backrest side padding upper mounting ...

25.13b ... then pull the upper portion of the side padding forward and lift it up to disengage the lower hook

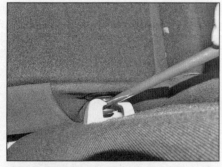

25.16a Press the backrest outer hinge pin locking collar in, to free the hinge pin ...

25.16b ... while at the same time pulling upward to release the backrest

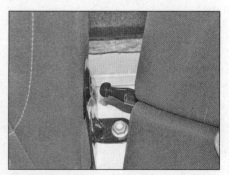

25.17 Pull the backrest hinge pin out of the centre support (left-hand backrest shown)

Front and rear seat refitting

18 Refitting is a reverse of the removal procedure, tightening the retaining bolts (where applicable) to the specified torque.

26 Seat belt tensioning mechanism – general information

1 All models covered in this manual are fitted with a front seat belt pyrotechnic tensioner system. The system is designed to instantaneously take up any slack in the seat belt in the case of a sudden frontal impact, therefore reducing the possibility of injury to the front seat occupants. Each front seat is fitted with its own system, the components of which are mounted on the seat frame.

2 The seat belt tensioner is triggered by a frontal impact causing a deceleration of six times the force of gravity or greater. Lesser impacts, including impacts from behind, will not trigger the system.

3 When the system is triggered, the material within the tensioner canister is ignited, producing a rapid generation of gas. The gas produced from this reaction deploys the seat belt pretensioners which removes all of the slack in the seat belts.

4 There is a risk of injury if the system is triggered inadvertently when working on the vehicle, and it is therefore strongly recommended that any work involving the seat belt tensioner system is entrusted to a Vauxhall/Opel dealer. Refer to the warning

27.2 Undo the front seat belt upper mounting bolt

27 Seat belt components – removal and refitting

Warning: The front seats are fitted with pyrotechnic seat belt tensioners which are triggered by the airbag control system. Before removing a seat belt, disconnect the battery and wait at least 2 minutes to allow the system capacitors to discharge.

Front belt and reel

Removal

1 Remove the B-pillar inner trim panel as described in Section 28.

2 Undo the seat belt upper mounting bolt

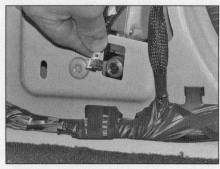

27.3 Disconnect the wiring connector from the seat belt reel

(see illustration).

3 Disconnect the wiring connector from the seat belt reel **(see illustration)**.

4 Release the seat belt guide from the B-pillar.

5 Undo the bolt securing the seat belt reel to the B-pillar, then remove the reel from the inside of the pillar **(see illustration)**.

Refitting

6 Refitting is a reversal of removal, but tighten the mounting bolts to the specified torque.

Front belt stalk

Removal

7 Remove the front seat as described in Section 25.

8 Unclip the cover **(see illustration 27.12)**, then disconnect the wiring connector, then undo the retaining bolt and remove the stalk from the seat **(see illustration)**.

Refitting

9 Refitting is a reversal of removal, but tighten the retaining bolt to the specified torque.

Front belt tensioner

Removal

10 Remove the front seat as described in Section 25.

11 Using a small screwdriver, carefully unclip the trim cover over the tensioner stalk **(see illustration)**.

12 Carefully prise off the seat tilt lever trim cap, undo the lever retaining screw and remove the tilt adjustment lever **(see illustrations)**.

given at the beginning of Section 25 before contemplating any work on the front seats.

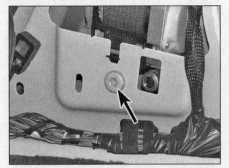

27.5 Undo the bolt and remove the seat belt reel from the inside of the B-pillar

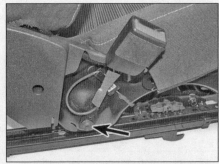

27.8 Disconnect the wiring connector, then undo the seat belt stalk retaining bolt

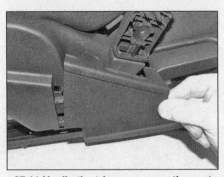

27.11 Unclip the trim cover over the seat belt tensioner stalk

27.12a Carefully prise off the seat tilt adjustment lever trim cap ...

27.12b ... undo the lever retaining screw ...

27.12c ... and remove the tilt adjustment lever

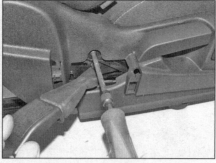

27.13a Undo the retaining screw ...

27.13b ... and remove the seat recliner lever

13 Undo the retaining screw and remove the seat recliner lever **(see illustrations)**.

14 Carefully prise off the trim cap and undo the screw securing the rear of the seat side trim panel **(see illustrations)**.

15 Working behind the seat side trim panel at the front, lift the tab to open the retaining clip, then lift the trim panel up to disengage the lower hook **(see illustrations)**.

16 Lift the trim panel up at the centre to disengage the centre hook and manipulate the trim panel off the seat frame.

17 Disconnect the wiring connectors and remove the trim panel.

18 Undo the screw securing the seat guide rail trim panel to the front of the seat frame. Unclip the trim panel at the rear and remove it from the seat frame **(see illustrations)**.

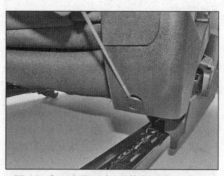

27.14a Carefully prise off the trim cap ...

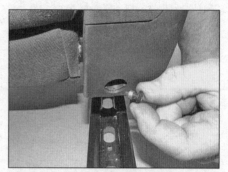

27.14b ... and undo the screw securing the rear of the seat side trim panel

19 Disconnect the tensioner wiring connector and cut off the cable tie securing the wiring to the tensioner body. Undo the retaining bolt

and remove the tensioner from the seat frame **(see illustration)**.

Refitting

20 Refitting is a reverse of the removal procedure, noting the following points:

a) *Tighten the tensioner retaining bolt to the specified torque.*

b) *Secure the tensioner wiring to the tensioner body using a new cable tie.•*

c) *Rear outer belt and reel*

Removal

21 Remove the rear seat cushion as described in Section 25.

22 Remove the luggage compartment upper side trim panel as described in Section 28.

27.15a Lift the tab to open the retaining clip ...

27.15b ... then lift the trim panel up to disengage the lower hook

27.18a Undo the screw securing the seat guide rail trim panel to the front of the seat frame ...

27.18b ... then unclip the trim panel at the rear and remove it from the seat frame

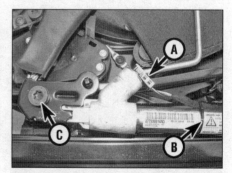

27.19 Seat belt tensioner wiring connector (A), cable tie (B) and retaining bolt (C)

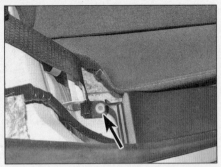

27.23 Rear outer seat belt lower mounting bolt

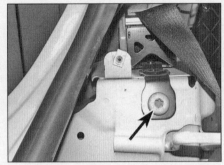

27.24 Rear outer seat belt reel mounting bolt

27.28 Rear seat belt stalk retaining nut

23 Undo the seat belt lower mounting bolt **(see illustration)**.

24 Undo the seat belt reel mounting bolt and remove the reel and belt from the car **(see illustration)**.

Refitting

25 Refitting is a reversal of removal, but tighten the mounting bolts to the specified torque.

Rear centre belt and reel

26 The inertia reel for the centre rear seat belt is located internally within the rear seat backrest. To gain access, the backrest must be removed and completely dismantled. This is a complex operation and considerable expertise is needed to remove and refit the seat upholstery and internal components without damage. Therefore, any problems with the centre seat belt and reel should be referred to a Vauxhall/Opel dealer.

Rear belt stalk

Removal

27 Remove the rear seat cushion as described in Section 25.

28 Undo the retaining nut and remove the relevant stalk from the floor **(see illustration)**.

Refitting

29 Refitting is a reversal of removal, but tighten the mounting nuts to the specified torque.

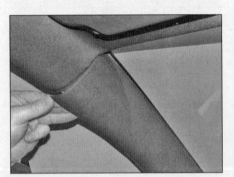

28.2a Pull the trim panel away from the A-pillar at the top …

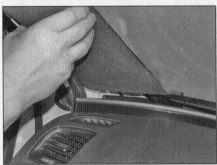

28.2b … then lift it up to disengage it at the bottom

28 Interior trim – removal and refitting

1 The interior trim panels are secured by a combination of clips and screws. Removal and refitting is generally self-explanatory, noting that it may be necessary to remove or loosen surrounding panels to allow a particular panel to be removed. The following paragraphs describe the general removal and refitting details of the major panels.

A-pillar trim panel

2 Pull the trim panel away from the A-pillar at the top then lift it up to disengage it at the bottom **(see illustrations)**.

3 Reach in behind the panel and extract the locking clip from the safety strap catch using a small screwdriver **(see illustration)**.

4 Depress the tabs of the safety strap catch and slide the catch up and out of the trim panel **(see illustrations)**. Remove the panel from the car.

5 Refitting is a reversal of removal ensuring that the safety strap is correctly fitted and secured by the locking clip.

Side sill inner trim panel

6 Starting at the front and working rearwards, pull the panel upward from the sill to release the six retaining clips **(see illustration)**.

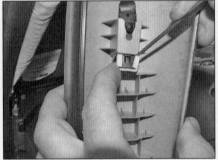

28.3 Extract the locking clip from the safety strap catch using a small screwdriver

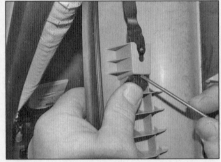

28.4a Depress the tabs of the safety strap catch …

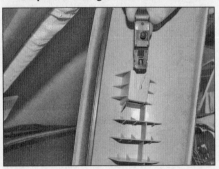

28.4b … and slide the catch up and out of the trim panel

28.6 Pull the side sill trim panel upward from the sill to release the six retaining clips

28.12 Pull the B-pillar trim panel away from the pillar at the bottom to release the lower retaining clips

28.13a Release the centre of the panel from the B-pillar ...

28.13b ... then feed the seat belt through the aperture in the panel

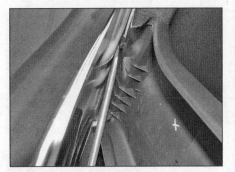

28.14a Using a screwdriver inserted up behind the panel ...

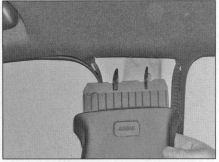

28.14b ... release the two upper tabs and remove the panel from the car

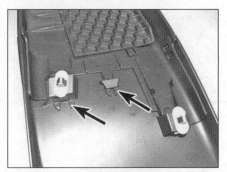

28.15a Compress the locking tabs on the rear of the panel ...

7 Where applicable, disconnect the footwell courtesy light wiring connector, then remove the panel from the car.

8 Refitting is a reversal of removal.

B-pillar trim panel

9 Remove the side sill inner trim panel as described previously in this Section.

10 Move the front seat fully forward.

11 Using a small screwdriver, carefully prise off the trim cap on the seat belt tensioner connector. Undo the retaining bolt, lift off the connector cover and separate the seat belt from the tensioner **(see illustrations 25.3a, b and c)**.

12 Pull the panel away from the B-pillar at the bottom to release the lower retaining clips **(see illustration)**.

13 Release the centre of the panel from the B-pillar then feed the seat belt through the aperture in the panel **(see illustrations)**.

14 Using a screwdriver inserted up behind the panel, release the two upper tabs, then remove the panel from the car **(see illustrations)**.

15 To separate the upper panel from the lower panel, compress the locking tabs on the rear of the panel and pull the panels apart **(see illustrations)**.

16 Refitting is a reversal of removal.

Luggage compartment lower side trim panel

Saloon and Hatchback models

17 On Hatchback models, fold the rear seat backrests forward.

18 Remove the tailgate aperture lower centre trim panel as described later in this Section.

19 Unclip and remove the cover over the luggage retaining lug, then undo the retaining bolt and remove the luggage retaining lug **(see illustrations)**.

20 On Saloon models, extract the centre pins

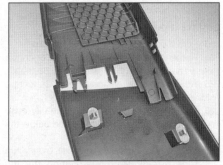

28.15b ... and pull the panels apart

and remove the three plastic rivets securing the trim panel to the body.

21 Manipulate the panel from its location and remove it from the luggage compartment **(see illustration)**.

22 Refitting is a reversal of removal.

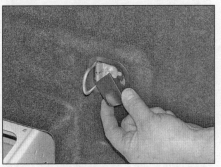

28.19a Unclip and remove the cover over the luggage retaining lug ...

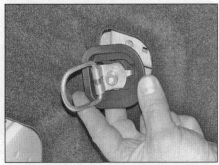

28.19b ... then undo the retaining bolt and remove the luggage retaining lug

28.21 Manipulate the lower side trim panel out of the luggage compartment – Saloon and Hatchback models

28.25 Remove the access cover from the centre of the trim panel – Estate models

28.26 Prise out the two plastic retainers located below the access cover – Estate models

28.27a Unclip and remove the cover over each luggage retaining lug ...

28.27b ... undo the lug retaining bolt ...

28.27c ... remove the luggage retaining lug ...

28.27d ... followed by the plastic insert – Estate models

Estate models

23 Fold the rear seat backrests forward.

24 Remove the tailgate aperture lower centre trim panel, as described later in this Section.

25 Remove the access cover from the centre of the trim panel **(see illustration)**.

26 Using a small screwdriver, carefully prise out the two plastic retainers located below the access cover **(see illustration)**.

27 Unclip and remove the cover over each luggage retaining lug, then undo the lug retaining bolt. Remove the luggage retaining lug followed by the plastic insert **(see illustrations)**.

28 Remove the auxiliary rear light cluster as described in Chapter 12, Section 7.

29 Pull the panel away at the bottom, disengage it from the upper trim panel and remove the panel from the car **(see illustration)**.

30 Refitting is a reversal of removal.

Luggage compartment upper side trim panel

Hatchback models

31 Remove the luggage compartment lower side trim panel as described previously in this Section.

32 If the rear seat backrest side padding incorporates an airbag, disconnect the battery negative terminal (refer to Chapter 5A, Section 4). Wait 2 minutes for the capacitors to discharge, before continuing.

33 Reach in through the aperture below the rear seat belt reel and compress the two tabs of the backrest side padding upper mounting. Pull the upper portion of the side padding forward, then lift it up to disengage the lower hook **(see illustrations 25.13a and 25.13b)**. Where applicable, disconnect the airbag wiring connector, then remove the side padding from the car.

34 Undo the screw securing the front of the upper side trim panel to the C-pillar **(see illustration)**.

35 Undo the screw securing the rear of the upper side trim panel to the D-pillar **(see illustration)**.

36 Using a small screwdriver prise free the

28.29 Manipulate the lower side trim panel out of the luggage compartment – Estate models

28.34 Undo the screw securing the front of the upper side trim panel to the C-pillar – Hatchback models

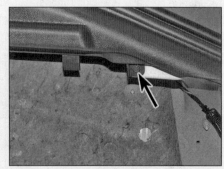

28.35 Undo the screw securing the rear of the upper side trim panel to the D-pillar – Hatchback models

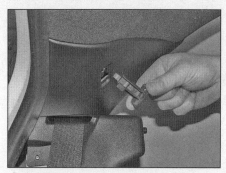

28.36 Prise free the curtain airbag positioning clip from the front of the trim panel – Hatchback models

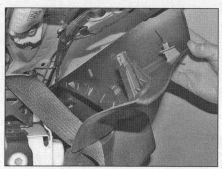

28.37a Pull the panel away to release the internal clips …

28.37b … then slide the seat belt webbing out through the slot in the panel – Hatchback models

28.40a Undo the retaining screw at the front …

28.40b … and at the rear of the upper side trim panel – Estate models

28.41 Carefully prise out the two plastic retainers at the front and rear of the panel – Estate models

curtain airbag positioning clip from the front of the trim panel **(see illustration)**.

37 Pull the panel away to release the internal clips. Slide the seat belt webbing out through the slot in the panel and remove the panel from the car **(see illustrations)**.

38 Refitting is a reversal of removal.

Estate models

39 Remove the luggage compartment lower side trim panel as described previously in this Section.

40 Undo the retaining screw at the front and rear of the panel **(see illustrations)**.

41 Using a small screwdriver, carefully prise out the two plastic retainers at the front and rear of the panel **(see illustration)**.

42 Pull the panel away to release the internal clips and slide the seat belt webbing out through the slot in the panel. Disconnect the accessory socket wiring connector and remove the panel from the car **(see illustrations)**.

43 Refitting is a reversal of removal.

C-pillar trim panel

44 On Estate models, remove the luggage compartment upper side trim panel as described previously.

45 Using a small screwdriver prise free the curtain airbag positioning clip from the top of the trim panel.

46 Pull the panel away to release the internal clips, and remove the panel from the car.

47 Refitting is a reversal of removal.

D-pillar trim panel – Estate models

48 Remove the C-pillar trim panel as described previously.

49 Pull the panel away to release the internal clips, and remove the panel from the car.

50 Refitting is a reversal of removal.

Bootlid trim panel

51 Open the bootlid, and remove the trim cover from the bootlid lock using a small screwdriver.

52 Undo the two screws and remove the bootlid pull handle from the bootlid inner trim panel.

53 Using a forked tool carefully prise out the inner trim panel stud retainers and remove the trim panel.

54 Refitting is a reversal of removal.

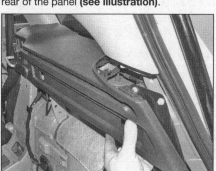

28.42a Pull the panel away to release the internal clips …

28.42b … slide the seat belt webbing out through the slot in the panel …

28.42c … then disconnect the accessory socket wiring connector and remove the panel from the car – Estate models

28.55 Unscrew the parcel shelf lifting pins from the tailgate on each side – Hatchback models

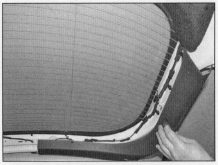

28.56 Prise free the upper side trim panel on each side to release the four retaining clips – Hatchback models

28.57 Undo the screw in the tailgate pull handle aperture – Hatchback models

Tailgate trim panel

Hatchback models

55 Remove the parcel shelf, then unscrew the parcel shelf lifting pins from the tailgate on each side **(see illustration)**.

56 Carefully prise free the upper side trim panel on each side to release the four retaining clips **(see illustration)**.

57 Undo the screw in the tailgate pull handle aperture **(see illustration)**.

58 Using a small screwdriver, remove the trim cover from the tailgate lock **(see illustration)**.

59 Pull the main panel away from the tailgate to release the internal clips and remove the panel from the tailgate **(see illustration)**.

60 Refitting is a reversal of removal.

Estate models

61 Carefully prise free the centre of the upper side trim panel on the right-hand side to disengage it from the left-hand side panel **(see illustration)**.

62 Pull the panel away from the tailgate to release the retaining clips, disengage the four tabs from the main panel and remove the right-hand side trim panel **(see illustration)**.

63 Repeat paragraph 62 to remove the left-hand upper side trim panel **(see illustration)**.

64 Undo the screw in the tailgate pull handle aperture **(see illustration)**.

65 Undo the two screws located behind the elastic restraining straps **(see illustration)**.

66 Using a small screwdriver carefully prise out the centre of the two trim panel plastic

28.58 Remove the trim cover from the tailgate lock – Hatchback models

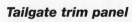

28.59 Pull the main panel away from the tailgate to release the internal clips – Hatchback models

28.61 Carefully prise free the centre of the tailgate upper side trim panel on the right-hand side – Estate models

28.62 Pull the panel away from the tailgate and remove the right-hand side trim panel – Estate models

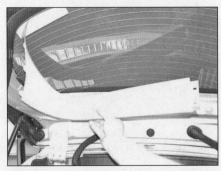

28.63 Remove the tailgate left-hand upper side trim panel in the same way – Estate models

28.64 Undo the screw in the tailgate pull handle aperture – Estate models

28.65 Undo the two screws located behind the elastic restraining straps – Estate models

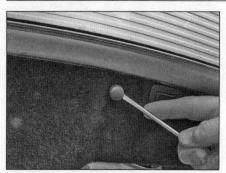

28.66a Carefully prise out the centre of the two trim panel plastic rivets ...

28.66b ... and remove the rivet bodies – Estate models

28.67 Where fitted, carefully prise out the tailgate closing switch and disconnect the wiring connector – Estate models

rivets and remove the rivet bodies **(see illustrations)**.

67 Where fitted, carefully prise out the tailgate closing switch, disconnect the wiring connector and remove the switch **(see illustration)**.

68 Pull the main panel away from the tailgate to release the internal clips and remove the panel from the tailgate **(see illustration)**.

69 Refitting is a reversal of the removal procedure.

Boot lid/tailgate aperture lower centre trim panel

70 Open the bootlid or tailgate.

71 Remove the luggage compartment floor covering.

72 Pull the weatherstrip away at the base of the boot lid/tailgate aperture **(see illustration)**.

73 On Estate models, undo the two panel retaining screws **(see illustration)**.

74 Pull the panel away to release the internal clips, and remove the panel from the car **(see illustration)**.

75 Refitting is a reversal of removal.

28.68 Pull the main panel away from the tailgate and remove the panel – Estate models

28.72 Pull the weatherstrip away at the base of the boot lid/tailgate aperture

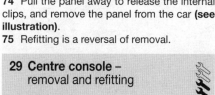

28.73 On Estate models, undo the two panel retaining screws

28.74 Pull the panel away to release the internal clips, and remove the panel from the car

29 Centre console – removal and refitting

Removal

1 Disconnect the battery negative terminal (refer to Chapter 5A, Section 4).

2 Remove the centre console front side panel on each side by carefully pulling them away from the console to release the internal retaining clips **(see illustration)**.

3 Open the ashtray housing door and take out the ashtray insert.

4 Using a plastic spatula or similar tool, carefully prise up the lower corners of the ashtray housing to release the internal clips, then disengage the upper retaining tangs from the facia. Disconnect the wiring connector, then remove the ashtray housing **(see illustrations)**.

29.2 Remove the centre console front side panels by carefully pulling them away from the console to release the retaining clips

29.4a Prise up the lower corners of the ashtray housing to release the internal clips, then disengage the upper retaining tangs

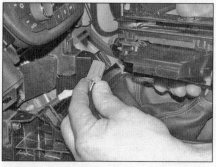

29.4b Disconnect the wiring connector and remove the ashtray housing

29.5a Prise up the gearshift/selector lever gaiter frame at the rear and disengage it at the front ...

29.5b ... then turn the gaiter and frame around, so it can be fed through the console aperture when the console is removed

29.6 Undo the three bolts and remove the facia crossmember centre brace on the right-hand side

29.7a Lift the locking bar and disconnect the main wiring harness connector ...

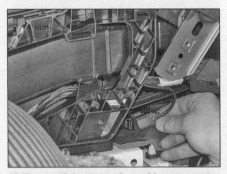

29.7b ... and the secondary wiring connector located behind the centre brace location

29.8 Undo the centre console rear retaining screw each side

29.9a Undo the centre console upper front ...

29.9b ... and lower front retaining bolts on each side

29.10 Lift the console up and slide it to the rear, then remove the console from the car

5 Again using a plastic spatula or similar tool, carefully prise up the gearshift/selector lever gaiter frame at the rear and disengage it at the front. Turn the gaiter and frame around, so it can be fed through the console aperture when the console is removed **(see illustrations)**.

6 Undo the three bolts and remove the facia crossmember centre brace on the right-hand side **(see illustration)**.

7 Disconnect the two centre console wiring harness connectors located behind the centre brace location **(see illustrations)**.

8 Position the front seats as necessary to gain access to the centre console rear retaining screws, then undo the screw each side **(see illustration)**.

9 Undo the centre console upper front and lower front retaining bolts on each side **(see illustrations)**.

10 Lift the console up and slide it to the rear, then remove the console from the car **(see illustration)**.

Refitting

11 Refitting is a reversal of removal, tightening the facia crossmember centre brace retaining bolts to the specified torque.

30 Facia panel components – removal and refitting

Facia left-hand footwell trim panel

Removal

1 Working under the glovebox, extract the centre pin and remove the three plastic rivets securing the footwell trim panel to the underside of the glovebox **(see illustrations)**.

2 Lower the panel at the rear, disengage

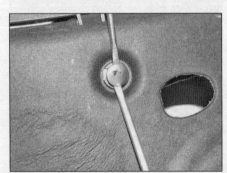

30.1a Extract the centre pin ...

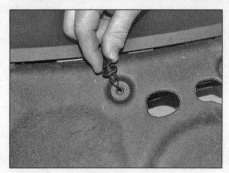

30.1b ... and remove the plastic rivets ...

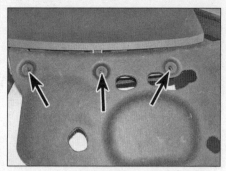

30.1c ... from the locations securing the footwell trim panel to the underside of the glovebox

30.2 Lower the panel at the rear, disengage it at the front, and remove it from under the glovebox

it at the front and remove it from under the glovebox (see illustration).

Refitting

3 Refitting is a reversal of removal.

Glovebox

Removal

4 Remove the facia left-hand footwell trim panel as described previously.

5 Open the glovebox lid, then using a plastic spatula or similar tool, carefully prise free the facia outer trim panel (see illustration).

6 Undo the upper and lower screw each side securing the glovebox to the facia (see illustration).

7 Withdraw the glovebox from the facia, disconnect the glovebox light wiring connector and remove the glovebox from the car (see illustration).

Refitting

8 Refitting is a reversal of removal.

30.5 Carefully prise free the facia outer trim panel

Facia right-hand footwell trim panel

Removal

9 Working under the steering column, extract

30.6 Undo the upper and lower screw each side securing the glovebox to the facia

the centre pin and remove the two plastic rivets securing the footwell trim panel to the lower trim panel. Lower the panel at the rear, disengage it at the front and remove it from the footwell (see illustrations).

Refitting

10 Refitting is a reversal of removal.

Facia right-hand lower trim panel

Removal

11 Remove the facia right-hand footwell trim panel as described previously.

12 Using a plastic spatula or similar tool, carefully prise free the facia outer trim panel. Disconnect the airbag disable switch wiring connector and remove the panel (see illustrations).

13 Remove the steering column shrouds as described later in this Section.

30.7 Withdraw the glovebox and disconnect the glovebox light wiring connector

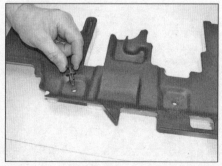

30.9a Extract the centre pin and remove the two plastic rivets ...

30.9b ... then disengage the footwell trim at the front and remove it from under the facia

30.12a Prise free the facia outer trim panel ...

30.12b ... disconnect the airbag disable switch wiring connector and remove the panel

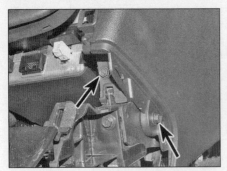

30.14a Undo the two left-hand screws ...

30.14b ... and one right-hand screw securing right-hand lower trim panel to the facia

30.15a Lower the panel and unclip the diagnostic socket ...

30.15b ... then remove the panel from the facia

14 Undo the two screws on the left-hand side, and one screw on the right-hand side securing right-hand lower trim panel to the facia **(see illustrations)**.

15 Lower the panel and unclip the diagnostic

socket, then remove the panel from the facia **(see illustrations)**.

Refitting

16 Refitting is a reversal of removal.

Facia left-hand lower trim panel

Removal

17 Remove the glovebox as described previously.

18 Remove the centre console front side panel on each side by carefully pulling them away from the console to release the internal retaining clips **(see illustration 29.2)**.

19 Open the ashtray housing door and take out the ashtray insert.

20 Using a plastic spatula or similar tool, carefully prise up the lower corners of the ashtray housing to release the internal clips, then disengage the upper retaining tangs from the facia. Disconnect the wiring connector,

then remove the ashtray housing **(see illustrations 29.4a and 29.4b)**.

21 Again, using a plastic spatula or similar tool, carefully prise out the facia side moulding, starting at the left-hand side and moving toward the centre, then remove the moulding from the facia **(see illustration)**.

22 Undo the upper screw and two lower screws securing the lower trim panel to the facia. Pull the panel away to release the retaining clip and remove the panel from the facia **(see illustrations)**.

Refitting

23 Refitting is a reversal of removal.

Facia upper centre panel

Removal

24 Using a plastic spatula or similar tool, carefully ease the panel away from the facia to release the two upper and two lower retaining clips **(see illustrations)**.

30.21 Carefully prise out the facia side moulding, starting at the left-hand side and moving toward thecentre

30.22a Undo the upper screw ...

30.22b ... and two lower screws securing the lower trim panel to the facia ...

30.22c ... then pull the panel away to release the retaining clip and remove the panel

30.24a Carefully ease the facia upper centre panel away from the facia to release the upper and lower retaining clips

30.24b On later models lever the panel free at the lower edge first

30.25a Withdraw the panel from the facia ...

30.25b ... and disconnect the wiring connectors

30.31a Carefully prise out the facia side moulding on the driver's side, starting at the top corner ...

30.31b ... then remove the moulding from the facia

30.33a Undo the four screws securing the lower centre panel to the facia

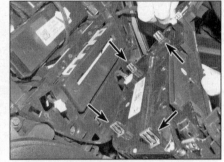

30.33b On later models the panel is clip to a support panel

25 Withdraw the panel from the facia, disconnect the wiring connectors and remove the panel **(see illustrations)**.

Refitting

26 Refitting is a reversal of removal.

Facia lower centre panel

Removal

27 Remove the facia upper centre panel as described previously.
28 Remove the centre console front side panel on each side by carefully pulling them away from the console to release the internal retaining clips **(see illustration 29.2)**.
29 Open the ashtray housing door and take out the ashtray insert.
30 Using a plastic spatula or similar tool, carefully prise up the lower corners of the ashtray housing to release the internal clips,

then disengage the upper retaining tangs from the facia. Disconnect the wiring connector, then remove the ashtray housing **(see illustrations 29.4a and 29.4b)**.
31 Again, using a plastic spatula or similar tool, carefully prise out the facia side moulding on the driver's side, starting at the top corner, then remove the moulding from the facia **(see illustrations)**.
32 Similarly, carefully prise out the facia side moulding on the passenger's side, starting at the left-hand side and moving toward the centre, then remove the moulding from the facia **(see illustration 30.21)**.
33 Undo the four screws securing the lower centre panel to the facia **(see illustrations)**.
34 Withdraw the panel from the facia, disconnect the wiring connectors and remove the panel **(see illustration)**. On later models remove the support panel.

Refitting

35 Refitting is a reversal of removal.

Steering column shrouds

Note: *There are small differences in the removal procedure between early and later models. Removal and refitting is essentially the same. See also steering column switch removal as described in Chapter 12 Section 4 for further details.*

Removal

36 Fully extend the steering column using the telescopic function.
37 Unclip the upper shroud from the lower shroud and fold it back toward the instrument panel **(see illustration)**.
38 Turn the steering wheel as necessary for access and unscrew the lower shroud retaining screw on each side **(see illustration)**.

30.34 Withdraw the panel from the facia and disconnect the wiring connectors

30.37 Unclip the upper steering column shroud from the lower shroud and fold it back toward the instrument panel

30.38 Unscrew the lower shroud retaining screw on each side

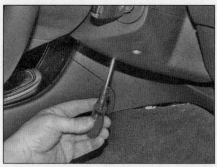

30.39 Undo the screw securing the shroud to the underside of the steering column

30.40a Lift off the ignition switch lock cylinder bezel ...

30.40b ... then remove the lower shroud from the steering column

30.41 Undo the two headlight switch bezel retaining screws

30.42a Carefully prise the headlight switch bezel out of the facia ...

30.42b ... then disconnect the wiring connector and remove the headlight switch and bezel

39 Undo the retaining screw securing the lower shroud to the underside of the steering column **(see illustration)**.

40 Lift off the ignition switch lock cylinder bezel, then remove the lower shroud from the steering column **(see illustrations)**.

41 Open the driver's side stowage compartment in the facia and undo the two headlight switch bezel retaining screws **(see illustration)**.

42 Using a plastic spatula or similar tool, carefully prise the headlight switch bezel out of the facia. Disconnect the wiring connector and remove the headlight switch and bezel **(see illustrations)**.

43 Remove the centre console front side panel on each side by carefully pulling them away from the console to release the internal retaining clips **(see illustration 29.2)**.

44 Open the ashtray housing door and take out the ashtray insert.

45 Using a plastic spatula or similar tool, carefully prise up the lower corners of the ashtray housing to release the internal clips, then disengage the upper retaining tangs from the facia. Disconnect the wiring connector, then remove the ashtray housing **(see illustrations 29.4a and 29.4b)**.

46 Again, using a plastic spatula or similar tool, carefully prise out the facia side moulding, starting at the top corner, then remove the moulding from the facia **(see illustrations 30.31a and 30.31b)**.

47 Undo the screw each side securing the upper steering column shroud to the facia and remove the shroud **(see illustrations)**.

Refitting

48 Refitting is a reversal of removal.

Complete facia assembly

Note: *This is an involved operation entailing*

the removal of numerous components and assemblies, and the disconnection of a multitude of wiring connectors. Make notes on the location of all disconnected wiring, or attach labels to the connectors, to avoid confusion when refitting. Taking a series of photographs throughout the removal procedure will prove invaluable when refitting, particularly as an aid to the routing and location of the various wiring looms.

Removal

49 Disconnect the battery negative terminal (refer to Chapter 5A, Section 4).

50 Remove the A-pillar trim panel and side sill inner trim panel on both sides as described in Section 28.

51 Remove the centre console as described in Section 29.

52 Remove the following facia panels as described previously in this Section:

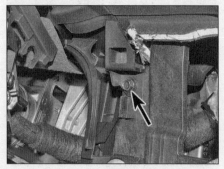

30.47a Undo the right-hand retaining screw ...

30.47b ... and left-hand retaining screw ...

30.47c ... then remove the upper shroud from the steering column

a) *Facia left-hand and right-hand footwell trim panels.*
b) *Glovebox.*
c) *Facia right-hand and left-hand lower trim panels.*
d) *Facia upper and lower centre panels.*
e) *Steering column shrouds.*

53 Remove the audio unit (Chapter 12 Section 16), communication interface module (Chapter 12 Section 17), facia centre speaker (Chapter 12 Section 18), and instrument panel (Chapter 12 Section 9).

54 Remove the heater/air conditioning control module as described in Chapter 3, Section 9.

55 Lift out the auxiliary control module from behind the instrument panel aperture **(see illustration)**. Disconnect the wiring connector and remove the module.

56 Undo the following fasteners securing the facia to the mounting bracket **(see illustrations)** :

a) *1 bolt at the left-hand and right-hand end.*
b) *1 lower centre bolt each side.*
c) *Two lower front centre bolts.*
d) *One upper centre bolt.*

57 With the help of an assistant, carefully lift the facia from its location. Check that all wiring has been disconnected, then remove the facia from the car **(see illustration)**.

Refitting

58 Refitting is a reversal of removal ensuring that all wiring is correctly reconnected and all mountings securely tightened.

31 Facia crossmember – removal and refitting

Removal

1 Remove the facia assembly as described in Section 30.

2 Remove the steering column as described in Chapter 10, Section 21.

3 Extract the centre pin and remove the plastic rivet securing the footwell air duct to the facia crossmember. Detach the air duct

30.55 Lift out the auxiliary control module from behind the instrument panel aperture

30.56b ... the lower centre bolt each side ...

30.56d ... and the upper centre bolt

from the air distribution housing and remove it from the car **(see illustrations)**.

4 Insert a small screwdriver between the body of the bonnet release handle and the

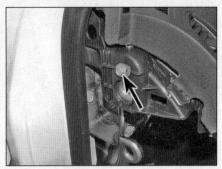

30.56a Undo the facia retaining bolt at the left-hand and right-hand end ...

30.56c ... the two lower front centre bolts ...

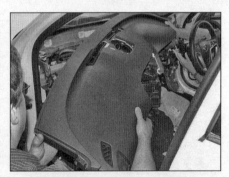

30.57 With the help of an assistant, carefully lift the facia from its location

facia crossmember to free the detent lugs, then pull the handle downward to disengage it from the crossmember **(see illustration)**.

5 Undo the retaining nut and detach the earth

31.3a Remove the plastic rivet securing the footwell air duct to the facia crossmember ...

31.3b ... then detach the air duct from the air distribution housing3

31.4 Use a small screwdriver to free the detent lugs, then pull the bonnet release handle downward

31.5 Undo the retaining nut and detach the earth lead from the stud on the right-hand side sill

31.6 Disconnect the wiring connector at the base of the right-hand side A-pillar

31.7a Disconnect the wiring connectors at the accelerator pedal position sensor ...

31.7b ... and at the brake and clutch pedal position switches

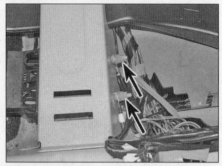

31.8 Undo the nuts and detach the earth leads from the studs at the right-hand side of the floor crossmember

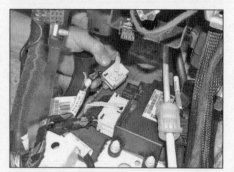

31.9 Lift the locking bars and disconnect the wiring connectors at the airbag control unit

31.10 Disconnect the wiring connectors at the left-hand side of the air distribution housing

31.11 Disconnect the lower three wiring connectors at the body control module

8 Undo the retaining nuts and detach the earth leads from the studs at the right-hand side of the floor crossmember **(see illustration)**.

9 Lift the locking bars and disconnect the wiring connectors at the airbag control unit **(see illustration)**.

10 Disconnect the heater/air conditioning wiring connectors at the left-hand side of the air distribution housing **(see illustration)**.

11 Disconnect the lower three wiring connectors at the body control module **(see illustration)**.

12 Undo the retaining nut and detach the upper earth lead from the stud on the left-hand side sill **(see illustration)**.

13 Lift the locking bar and disconnect the main wiring harness connector at the base of the left-hand side A-pillar **(see illustrations)**.

14 Undo the three bolts and remove the facia

lead from the stud on the right-hand side sill **(see illustration)**.

6 Disconnect the wiring connector at the base of the right-hand side A-pillar **(see illustration)**.

7 Disconnect the wiring connectors at the accelerator pedal position sensor, and at the brake and clutch pedal position switches **(see illustrations)**.

31.12 Undo the retaining nut and detach the upper earth lead from the stud on the left-hand side sill

31.13a Lift the locking bar ...

31.13b ... and disconnect the main wiring harness connector at the base of the left-hand side A-pillar

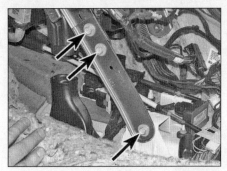

31.14 Undo the three bolts and remove the facia crossmember centre brace

31.15a Undo the bolts securing the facia crossmember to the pedal mounting brackets ...

31.15b ... then rotate the plastic guide bushes through 90° and remove the bushes

31.16 Undo the nut securing the heater blower motor housing to the facia crossmember bracket

31.17a Undo the two upper nuts ...

31.17b ... and the lower bolt securing the air distribution housing to the facia crossmember

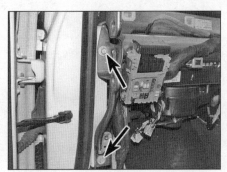

31.18 Undo the two bolts each side securing the facia crossmember to the A-pillars

31.19 Check that all wiring has been disconnected, then remove the facia crossmember from the car

crossmember centre brace on the left-hand side **(see illustration)**.

15 Undo the four bolts securing the facia crossmember to the brake and clutch pedal mounting brackets. Rotate the two plastic guide bushes through 90° and remove the guide bushes **(see illustrations)**.

16 Undo the nut securing the heater blower motor housing to the facia crossmember bracket **(see illustration)**.

17 Undo the two upper nuts and the lower bolt securing the air distribution housing to the facia crossmember **(see illustrations)**.

18 Undo the two bolts each side securing the facia crossmember to the A-pillars **(see illustration)**.

19 With the help of an assistant, carefully withdraw the facia crossmember from the bulkhead and air distribution housing. Check that all wiring has been disconnected, then remove the facia crossmember from the car **(see illustration)**.

Refitting

20 Refitting is a reversal of removal ensuring that all wiring is correctly reconnected and all mountings securely tightened.

Chapter 12
Body electrical systems

Contents

Degrees of difficulty

| **Easy,** suitable for novice with little experience | | **Fairly easy,** suitable for beginner with some experience | | **Fairly difficult,** suitable for competent DIY mechanic | | **Difficult,** suitable for experienced DIY mechanic | | **Very difficult,** suitable for expert DIY or professional | |

Specifications

General

System type . . . .   12 volt, negative earth

Fuses

Refer to the labels on the fuse/relay box covers and to the wiring diagrams at the end of this Chapter

Bulbs

Bulb	Type	Wattage
Front direction indicator light (Type 1)	PY21W	21
Front direction indicator light (Type 2)	PSY24W	24
Front direction indicator side repeater light	W5W	5
Front foglight	H10	42
Front sidelight (daytime running)*	W21/5	21/5
Glovebox light	Festoon	10
Headlight cornering light (xenon type headlight)	H11	55
Headlight dipped beam (halogen type headlight)	H1	55
Headlight dipped/main beam (xenon type headlight)	D1S	35
Headlight main beam (halogen type headlight)	H7	55
Headlight dipped beam (models with adaptive lighting)	H1R2	55
Interior light	Festoon	10
Number plate light	W5W	5
Rear light cluster (Saloon and Hatchback models):		
Rear direction indicator light	PY21W	21
Rear foglight.	P25	21
Reversing light	P25	21
Brake light.	P25	21
Tail light	R10W	10
Tailgate/auxiliary light cluster (Estate models):		
Rear direction indicator light	PY21W	21
Rear foglight.	H21W	21
Reversing light	H21W	21
Brake light.	P21W	21
Tail light.	W5W	5

Later models are fitted with non-replaceable LED bulbs

1 General information and precautions

⚠ **Warning: Before carrying out any work on the electrical system, read through the precautions given in 'Safety first! at the beginning of this manual, and in Chapter 5A, Section 1.**

1 The electrical system is of the 12 volt negative earth type. Power for the lights and all electrical accessories is supplied by a lead-acid type battery, which is charged by the engine-driven alternator.

2 This Chapter covers repair and service procedures for the various electrical components not associated with the engine. Information on the battery, alternator and starter motor can be found in Chapter 5A.

3 It should be noted that, prior to working on any component in the electrical system, the battery negative terminal should first be disconnected, to prevent the possibility of electrical short-circuits and/or fires.

Caution: Before proceeding, refer to 'Disconnecting the battery' in Chapter 5A Section 4 for further information.

2 Electrical fault finding – general information

Note: *Refer to the precautions given in 'Safety first!' and in Section 1 before starting work. The following tests relate to testing of the main electrical circuits, and should not be used to test delicate electronic circuits (such as the anti-lock braking system or fuel injection system), particularly where an electronic control unit is used.*

General

1 A typical electrical circuit consists of an electrical component, any switches, relays, motors, fuses, fusible links or circuit breakers related to that component, and the wiring and connectors which link the component to both the battery and the vehicle body. To help to pinpoint a problem in an electrical circuit, wiring diagrams are shown at the end of this Chapter.

2 Before attempting to diagnose an electrical fault, first study the appropriate wiring diagram to obtain a complete understanding of the components included in the particular circuit concerned. The possible sources of a fault can be narrowed down by noting if other components related to the circuit are operating properly. If several components or circuits fail at one time, the problem is likely to be related to a shared fuse or earth connection.

3 Electrical problems usually stem from simple causes, such as loose or corroded connections, a faulty earth connection, a blown fuse, a melted fusible link, or a faulty relay (refer to Section 3 for details of testing relays). Inspect the condition of all fuses, wires and connections in a problem circuit before testing the components. Use the wiring diagrams to determine which terminal connections will need to be checked in order to pinpoint the trouble-spot.

4 The basic tools required for electrical fault finding include a circuit tester or voltmeter (a 12 volt bulb with a set of test leads can also be used for certain tests); a self-powered test light (sometimes known as a continuity tester); an ohmmeter (to measure resistance); a battery and set of test leads; and a jumper wire, preferably with a circuit breaker or fuse incorporated, which can be used to bypass suspect wires or electrical components. Before attempting to locate a problem with test instruments, use the wiring diagram to determine where to make the connections.

5 To find the source of an intermittent wiring fault (usually due to a poor or dirty connection, or damaged wiring insulation), a 'wiggle' test can be performed on the wiring. This involves wiggling the wiring by hand to see if the fault occurs as the wiring is moved. It should be possible to narrow down the source of the fault to a particular section of wiring. This method of testing can be used in conjunction with any of the tests described in the following sub-Sections.

6 Apart from problems due to poor connections, two basic types of fault can occur in an electrical circuit – open-circuit, or short-circuit.

7 Open-circuit faults are caused by a break somewhere in the circuit, which prevents current from flowing. An open-circuit fault will prevent a component from working, but will not cause the relevant circuit fuse to blow.

8 Short-circuit faults are caused by a 'short' somewhere in the circuit, which allows the current flowing in the circuit to 'escape' along an alternative route, usually to earth. Short-circuit faults are normally caused by a breakdown in wiring insulation, which allows a feed wire to touch either another wire, or an earthed component such as the bodyshell. A short-circuit fault will normally cause the relevant circuit fuse to blow.

Finding an open-circuit

9 To check for an open-circuit, connect one lead of a circuit tester or voltmeter to either the negative battery terminal or a known good earth.

10 Connect the other lead to a connector in the circuit being tested, preferably nearest to the battery or fuse.

11 Switch on the circuit, bearing in mind that some circuits are live only when the ignition switch is turned to a particular position.

12 If voltage is present (indicated either by the tester bulb lighting or a voltmeter reading, as applicable), this means that the section of the circuit between the relevant connector and the battery is problem-free.

13 Continue to check the remainder of the circuit in the same fashion.

14 When a point is reached at which no voltage is present, the problem must lie between that point and the previous test point with voltage. Most problems can be traced to a broken, corroded or loose connection.

Finding a short-circuit

15 To check for a short-circuit, first disconnect the load(s) from the circuit (loads are the components which draw current from a circuit, such as bulbs, motors, heating elements, etc).

16 Remove the relevant fuse from the circuit, and connect a circuit tester or voltmeter to the fuse connections.

17 Switch on the circuit, bearing in mind that some circuits are live only when the ignition switch is turned to a particular position.

18 If voltage is present (indicated either by the tester bulb lighting or a voltmeter reading, as applicable), this means that there is a short-circuit.

19 If no voltage is present, but the fuse still blows with the load(s) connected, this indicates an internal fault in the load(s).

Finding an earth fault

20 The battery negative terminal is connected to 'earth' – the metal of the engine/transmission unit and the car body – and most systems are wired so that they only receive a positive feed, the current returning via the metal of the car body. This means that the component mounting and the body form part of that circuit. Loose or corroded mountings can therefore cause a range of electrical faults, ranging from total failure of a circuit, to a puzzling partial fault. In particular, lights may shine dimly (especially when another circuit sharing the same earth point is in operation), motors (eg, wiper motors or the radiator cooling fan motor) may run slowly, and the operation of one circuit may have an apparently-unrelated effect on another. Note that on many vehicles, earth straps are used between certain components, such as the engine/transmission and the body, usually where there is no metal-to-metal contact between components, due to flexible rubber mountings, etc.

21 To check whether a component is properly earthed, disconnect the battery, and connect one lead of an ohmmeter to a known good earth point. Connect the other lead to the wire or earth connection being tested. The resistance reading should be zero; if not, check the connection as follows.

22 If an earth connection is thought to be faulty, dismantle the connection, and clean back to bare metal both the bodyshell and the wire terminal or the component earth connection mating surface. Be careful to remove all traces of dirt and corrosion, then use a knife to trim away any paint, so that a clean metal-to-metal joint is made. On reassembly, tighten the joint fasteners securely; if a wire terminal is being refitted, use serrated washers between the terminal and the bodyshell, to ensure a clean and secure connection. When the connection is

remade, prevent the onset of corrosion in the future by applying a coat of petroleum jelly or silicone-based grease. Alternatively, at regular intervals, spray on a proprietary ignition sealer or a water-dispersant lubricant.

3 Fuses and relays – general information

Fuses

1 The main fuses are located in the fuse/relay box on the left-hand side of the engine compartment, with additional fuses located behind a cover in the glovebox, and in the left-hand side of the luggage compartment.
2 To gain access to the engine compartment fuses, depress the three tabs and lift off the fuse/relay box cover (see illustrations).
3 To gain access to the fuses in the glovebox, open the glovebox and lift off the fusebox cover (see illustration).
4 Access to the fuses in the luggage compartment can be gained by opening the stowage compartment cover (see illustration). Note that only some models have a luggage compartment fuse/relay box.
5 To remove a fuse, first switch off the circuit concerned (or the ignition), then pull the fuse out of its terminals using the plastic removal tool provided. The wire within the fuse is clearly visible; if the fuse is blown, it will be broken or melted (see illustrations).
6 Always renew a fuse with one of an identical rating; never use a fuse with a different rating from the original, nor substitute anything else. Never renew a fuse more than once without tracing the source of the trouble. The fuse rating is stamped on top of the fuse; note that the fuses are also colour-coded for easy recognition.
7 If a new fuse blows immediately, find the cause before renewing it again; a short to earth as a result of faulty insulation is most likely. Where a fuse protects more than one circuit, try to isolate the defect by switching on each circuit in turn (if possible) until the fuse blows again. Always carry a supply of spare fuses of each relevant rating on the vehicle, a spare of each rating should be clipped into the base of the fuse/relay box.

3.2a To gain access to the engine compartment fuses, depress the three tabs …

3.3 To gain access to the fuses in the glovebox, open the glovebox and lift off the fusebox cover

Relays

8 Most of the relays are located in the fuse/relay box in the engine compartment (see illustration).
9 If a circuit or system controlled by a relay develops a fault and the relay is suspect, operate the system; if the relay is functioning, it should be possible to hear it click as it is energised. If this is the case, the fault lies with the components or wiring of the system. If the relay is not being energised, then either the relay is not receiving a main supply or a switching voltage, or the relay itself is faulty. Testing is by the substitution of a known good unit, but be careful; while some relays are identical in appearance and in operation, others look similar but perform different functions.

3.2b … and lift off the fuse/relay box cover

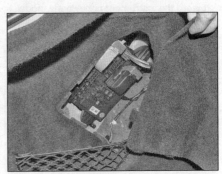
3.4 Access to the fuses in the luggage compartment can be gained by opening the stowage compartment cover

10 To renew a relay, first ensure that the ignition switch is off. The relay can then simply be pulled out from the socket and the new relay pressed in.

4 Switches – removal and refitting

Note: Disconnect the battery negative terminal (refer to Chapter 5A, Section 4) before removing any switch, and reconnect the terminal after refitting.

Ignition switch/ steering column lock

1 Refer to Chapter 10, Section 20.

3.5a Pull the fuse out of its terminals using the plastic removal tool provided …

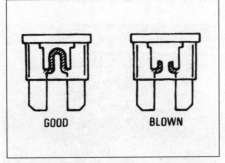
GOOD   BLOWN
3.5b … the wire within the fuse is clearly visible; if the fuse is blown, it will be broken or melted

3.8 Most of the relays are located in the fuse/relay box in the engine compartment

4.3 Unclip the upper steering column shroud from the lower shroud and fold it back toward the instrument panel (early models)

4.4 Turn the steering wheel as necessary and unscrew the lower shroud retaining screw on each side

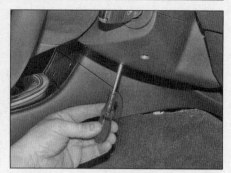

4.5 Undo the screw securing the lower shroud to the underside of the steering column

4.6a Lift off the ignition switch lock cylinder bezel ...

4.6b ... then remove the lower shroud from the steering column

4.7 Disconnect the wiring connector from the rear of the relevant steering column switch

4.8 Depress the tabs on the top and bottom of the switch, then slide the switch from the housing

Steering column switches

2 Fully extend the steering column using the telescopic function.

Early models (up to 2013)

3 Unclip the upper steering column shroud from the lower shroud and fold it back toward the instrument panel (see illustration).

4 Turn the steering wheel as necessary for access and unscrew the lower shroud retaining screw on each side (see illustration).

5 Undo the retaining screw securing the lower shroud to the underside of the steering column (see illustration).

6 Lift off the ignition switch lock cylinder bezel, then remove the lower shroud from the steering column (see illustrations).

7 Disconnect the wiring connector from the rear of the relevant switch (see illustration).

8 Depress the tabs on the top and bottom of the switch, then slide the switch from the housing (see illustration).

9 Refitting is a reversal of removal.

Later models (after 2013)

10 Using a plastic trim tool, release the lower panel from the central switch panel. Disconnect the wiring plugs as the panel is removed (see illustrations).

11 Unclip the drivers side upper section of the central switch panel/information display (see illustration).

12 Open the storage compartment and remove the fixings from the lighting switch panel. Release the switch panel and

4.10a Release the panel ...

4.10b ... and disconnect the wiring plugs

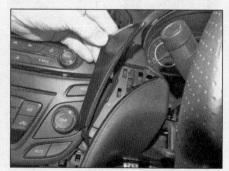

4.11 Remove the upper side trim panel

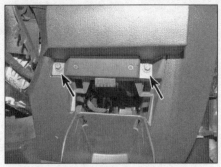

4.12a Remove the fixings …

4.12b … disconnect the wiring plug and remove the switch panel

4.14a Remove the lower shroud upper screws …

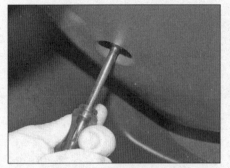

4.14b … and the single screw

4.14c Remove the shroud and …

4.14d … recover the lock bezel

disconnect the wiring plug **(see illustrations)**.
13 Remove the now exposed upper shroud fixings and remove the shroud.
14 Turning the steering wheel as required, remove the upper fixings from the lower shroud. Remove the lower fixing screw, release the shroud and recover the lock bezel **(see illustrations)**.
15 Disconnect the wiring connector from the rear of the relevant switch and release the switch **(see illustrations 4.7 and 4.8)**.
16 Refitting is a reversal of removal.

Exterior light switch

17 Open the driver's side stowage compartment in the facia and undo the two light switch bezel retaining screws **(see illustration)**.
18 Using a plastic trim tool (or similar) carefully prise the light switch bezel out of the facia. Disconnect the wiring connector and remove the light switch and bezel **(see illustrations)**.
19 Depress the three tabs at the rear of the

light switch and remove the switch from the bezel **(see illustration)**.
20 Refitting is a reversal of removal.

Facia upper centre panel switches

21 Remove the facia upper centre panel as described in Chapter 11, Section 30.

4.17 Undo the two exterior light switch bezel retaining screws

22 On early models, using a small screwdriver, carefully ease back the tabs securing the switch block to the facia panel, while at the same time, pushing the switch block out. On later models remove the screws and pull out the switch panel **(see illustration)**.
23 Once the tabs are released, remove

4.18a Carefully prise the light switch bezel out of the facia …

4.18b … then disconnect the wiring connector and remove the light switch and bezel

4.19 Depress the three tabs at the rear of the light switch and remove the switch from the bezel

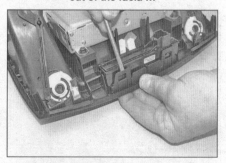

4.22 Ease back the tabs securing the switch block to the facia panel, while pushing the switch block out

4.23 Once the tabs are released, remove the switch block from the facia panel

4.30a Undo the front retaining screw ...

4.30b ... and the two rear retaining screws ...

4.30c ... then remove the footwell air duct from the underside of the centre console

4.31 Release the retaining tabs using a small screwdriver and lift off the switch upper trim panel

4.32 Release the tabs securing the multi-function switch to the underside of the centre console

the switch block from the facia panel **(see illustration)**.

24 Refitting is a reversal of removal.

Facia lower centre panel switches

25 Remove the facia lower centre panel as described in Chapter 11, Section 30.

26 Undo the five screws securing the mounting frame to the rear of the facia lower centre panel and remove the frame.

27 Using a plastic trim tool (or similar) carefully prise free the switch cluster and remove the cluster from the facia lower centre panel.

28 Refitting is a reversal of removal.

Centre console multi-function switch/Infotainment switch

29 Remove the centre console as described in Chapter 11, Section 29.

30 Undo the three screws and remove the footwell air duct from the underside of the console **(see illustrations)**.

31 From the underside of the console, release the retaining tabs using a small screwdriver and lift off the switch upper trim panel **(see illustration)**.

32 Using a small screwdriver, release the tabs securing the switch to the underside of the centre console **(see illustration)**.

33 Withdraw the switch, disconnect the wiring connector and remove the switch **(see illustration)**.

34 Refitting is a reversal of removal.

Heater/air conditioning switches

35 The heater and air conditioning system controls and switches are an integral part of the heater/air conditioning control unit.

Removal and refitting procedures are contained in Chapter 3, Section 9.

Handbrake warning light switch

36 Refer to Chapter 9, Section 18.

Handbrake operating switch

37 Refer to Chapter 9, Section 19.

Brake light switch

38 Refer to Chapter 9, Section 17.

Door mirror switch

39 Remove the front door inner trim panel as described in Chapter 11, Section 12.

40 Using a small screwdriver, carefully lift the three retaining tabs and remove the switch from inside the trim panel **(see illustrations)**.

41 Refitting is the reverse of removal.

4.33 Withdraw the switch, disconnect the wiring connector and remove the switch

4.40a Lift the three retaining tabs ...

4.40b ... and remove the electric mirror switch from inside the trim panel

4.43 Disconnect the electric window switch wiring connector

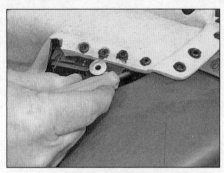

4.44a Using a screwdriver, inserted between the end of the electric window switch and the trim panel …

4.44b … release the retainer and remove the switch

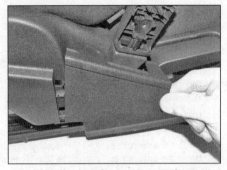

4.47 Unclip the trim cover over the seat belt tensioner stalk

4.48a Carefully prise off the seat tilt adjustment lever trim cap …

4.48b … undo the lever retaining screw …

Power window switches

42 Remove the front door inner trim panel as described in Chapter 11, Section 12.
43 Disconnect the switch wiring connector **(see illustration)**.
44 Using a small screwdriver, inserted between the end of the switch and the trim panel, release the retainer and remove the switch **(see illustrations)**.
45 Refitting is the reverse of removal.

Electric front seat switches

46 Remove the relevant front seat as described in Chapter 11, Section 25.
47 Using a small screwdriver, carefully unclip the trim cover over the seat belt tensioner stalk **(see illustration)**.
48 Carefully prise off the seat tilt adjustment lever trim cap, undo the lever retaining screw

and remove the tilt adjustment lever **(see illustrations)**.
49 Undo the retaining screw and remove the seat recliner lever **(see illustrations)**.

4.48c … and remove the tilt adjustment lever

50 Carefully prise off the trim cap and undo the screw securing the rear of the seat side trim panel **(see illustrations)**.
51 Working behind the seat side trim panel

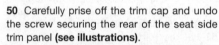

4.49a Undo the retaining screw …

4.49b … and remove the seat recliner lever

4.50a Prise off the trim cap …

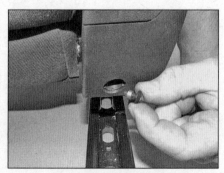

4.50b … and undo the screw securing the rear of the seat side trim panel

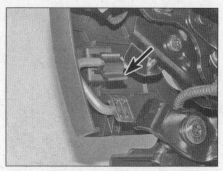

4.51a Lift the tab to open the retaining clip

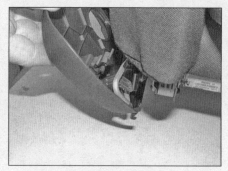

4.51b ... then lift the trim panel up to disengage the lower hook

4.54a Using a thin screwdriver, inserted down the side of the lumbar control switch, spread the retainer ...

4.54b ... and withdraw the switch from inside the trim panel

4.55 Disconnect the switch wiring connector and remove the switch

at the front, lift the tab to open the retaining clip, then lift the trim panel up to disengage the lower hook **(see illustrations)**.
52 Lift the trim panel up at the centre to disengage the centre hook and manipulate the trim panel off the seat frame.
53 Disconnect the wiring connectors and remove the trim panel.

Lumbar control switch

54 Using a thin screwdriver, inserted down the side of the switch, spread the retainer and withdraw the switch from inside the trim panel **(see illustrations)**.
55 Disconnect the switch wiring connector and remove the switch **(see illustration)**.

Height control switch

56 Using a thin screwdriver, inserted down the side of the switch, spread the retainer and withdraw the switch from inside the trim panel **(see illustrations)**.
57 Disconnect the switch wiring connector and remove the switch **(see illustration)**.

Seat adjuster memory switch

58 Using a small screwdriver, release the two retaining tabs and withdraw the switch from the outside of the trim panel.
59 Disconnect the switch wiring connector and remove the switch

All switches

60 Refitting is the reverse of removal.

Roof console switches

61 Using a small screwdriver, carefully prise free the relevant switch panel from the roof console. Withdraw the panel and disconnect the wiring connector(s) **(see illustrations)**.
62 Depress the retaining tabs and remove the relevant switch from the panel.
63 Refitting is the reverse of removal.

4.56a Using a thin screwdriver, inserted down the side of the height control switch, spread the retainer ...

4.56b ... and withdraw the switch from inside the trim panel

4.57 Disconnect the switch wiring connector and remove the switch

4.61a Carefully prise free the relevant switch panel from the roof console ...

4.61b ... then withdraw the panel and disconnect the wiring connector(s)

Steering wheel switches

64 Remove the driver's airbag as described in Section 23.

65 Using a plastic trim tool, carefully prise free the plastic trim surround from the steering wheel **(see illustration)**.

66 Disconnect the two wiring connectors for the steering wheel switches and remove the trim surround **(see illustration)**.

67 Undo the two retaining screws and remove the relevant switch from the trim surround **(see illustrations)**.

68 Refitting is the reverse of removal.

---

5 Bulbs (exterior lights) – renewal

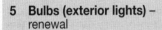

General

1 Whenever a bulb is renewed, note the following points:

a) *Make sure the switch is in the OFF position, for the respective bulb you are working on.*

b) *Remember that if the light has just been in use, the bulb may be extremely hot.*

c) *Always check the bulb contacts and holder, ensuring that there is clean metal-to-metal contact between the bulb and its live(s) and earth. Clean off any corrosion or dirt before fitting a new bulb.*

d) *Wherever bayonet-type bulbs are fitted, ensure that the live contact(s) bear firmly against the bulb contact.*

e) *Always ensure that the new bulb is of the correct rating, and that it is completely clean before fitting it; this applies particularly to headlight/foglight bulbs.*

Note: *Later models have the front sidelight/daytime running light and the rear tail light bulbs replaced with LED (Light Emitting Diode) type bulbs. These are not replaceable. If faulty the complete headlight or light assembly will require replacement.*

Halogen type headlight unit

Note: *Access to the rear of the headlight unit*

4.65 Carefully prise free the plastic trim surround from the steering wheel

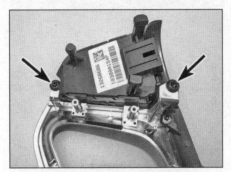

4.67a Undo the two retaining screws ...

4.66 Disconnect the two wiring connectors for the steering wheel switches and remove the trim surround

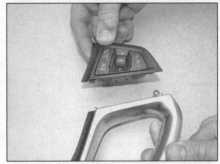

4.67b ... and remove the relevant switch from the trim surround

for bulb renewal is limited. Depending on the bulb being renewed, access can be improved by removing the windscreen washer reservoir filler tube (left-hand light unit), or removing the air cleaner assembly as described in the Chapter 4A, Section 2 or Chapter 4B, Section 3 (right-hand light unit). Alternatively (and preferably) remove the relevant headlight unit from the car as described in Section 7).

Dipped beam

2 Rotate the plastic cover anti-clockwise and remove it from the rear of the headlight unit **(see illustration)**.

3 Rotate the bulbholder anti-clockwise and withdraw it from the light unit **(see illustration)**.

4 Hold the bulb by its base and remove it from the bulbholder **(see illustration)**. When handling the new bulb, use a tissue or clean cloth to avoid touching the glass with the fingers; moisture and grease from the skin can cause blackening and rapid failure of this type of bulb. If the glass is accidentally touched, wipe it clean using methylated spirit.

5 Fit the new bulb to the bulbholder, then refit the bulbholder to the light unit. Turn the bulbholder clockwise to secure.

6 Refit the plastic cover to the rear of the headlight unit.

5.2 Rotate the dipped beam bulb plastic cover anti-clockwise and remove it from the rear of the headlight unit

5.3 Rotate the dipped beam bulbholder anti-clockwise and withdraw it from the light unit

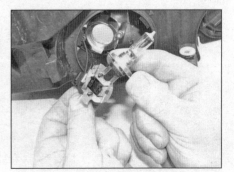

5.4 Hold the bulb by its base and remove it from the bulbholder

5.7 Rotate the main beam bulb plastic cover anti-clockwise and remove it from the rear of the headlight unit

5.8 Disconnect the wiring connector from the rear of the main beam bulb

5.9a Disengage the legs of the retaining spring clip by pushing them down and swivelling them outward ...

5.9b ... then pivoting them away from the bulb

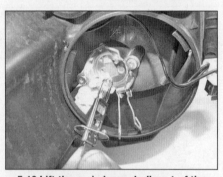

5.10 Lift the main beam bulb out of the headlight unit

the legs down, swivelling them outward, then pivoting them away from the bulb **(see illustrations)**.

10 Lift the bulb out of the headlight unit **(see illustration)**. When handling the new bulb, use a tissue or clean cloth to avoid touching the glass with the fingers; moisture and grease from the skin can cause blackening and rapid failure of this type of bulb. If the glass is accidentally touched, wipe it clean using methylated spirit.

11 Fit the new bulb to the headlight unit and secure with the spring clip. Reconnect the wiring connector, then refit the plastic cover to the rear of the headlight unit.

Main beam

7 Rotate the plastic cover anti-clockwise and remove it from the rear of the headlight unit **(see illustration)**.

8 Disconnect the wiring connector from the rear of the bulb **(see illustration)**.

9 Disengage the legs of the retaining spring clip from the lugs on the light unit by pushing

Front sidelight

12 Rotate the plastic cover anti-clockwise and remove it from the rear of the headlight unit **(see illustration)**.

13 Depress the tabs on the bulbholder and withdraw the bulbholder from the light unit **(see illustrations)**. Model fitted with Daytime Running Lights (DRL) use a different type of bulb.

14 Remove the capless (push fit) bulb from the bulbholder **(see illustration)**.

15 Fit the new bulb to the bulbholder, then refit the bulbholder to the light unit.

16 Refit the plastic cover to the rear of the headlight unit.

Front direction indicator

17 Twist the indicator bulbholder anti-clockwise, and remove it from the rear of the headlight unit **(see illustration)**.

5.12 Rotate the sidelight plastic cover anti-clockwise and remove it from the rear of the headlight unit

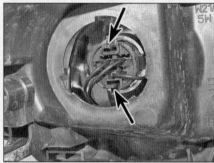
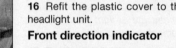

5.13a Depress the tabs on the sidelight bulbholder ...

5.13b ... and withdraw the bulbholder from the light unit

5.14 Remove the sidelight bulb from the bulbholder

5.17 Twist the direction indicator bulbholder anti-clockwise, and remove it from the rear of the headlight unit

5.18 Remove the bayonet-fit bulb from the bulbholder

5.22 Remove the cover

5.23a Remove the bulb and ...

5.23b ... disconnect the wiring plug

5.27 Remove the cover

5.28 Remove the bulb

18 The bulb is a bayonet fit in the holder, and can be removed by pressing it and twisting in an anti-clockwise direction **(see illustration)**.
19 Fit the new bulb to the bulbholder, then refit the bulbholder to the light unit.

Xenon type headlight unit

⚠️ **Warning: Xenon headlights operate at very high voltage. Do not touch the associated wiring when the headlights are switched on.**

Dipped/main beam

20 Disconnect the battery negative terminal (refer to refer to Chapter 5A, Section 4).
21 Disconnect the main wiring connector from the headlight unit.
22 Detach the cover at the rear of the dipped/ main beam bulb aperture and remove it from the headlight unit **(see illustration)**.
23 Rotate the bulb and starter unit anti-

clockwise to remove it. Disconnect the wiring connector as the bulb is removed **(see illustrations)**. Note that the starter unit and bulb are a single unit and cannot be separated.
24 Refitting is the reverse of the removal procedure.

Cornering light

25 Disconnect the battery negative terminal (refer to Chapter 5A, Section 4).
26 Disconnect the main wiring connector from the headlight unit.
27 Detach the cover from the cornering light bulb aperture and remove it from the top of the headlight unit **(see illustration)**.
28 Rotate the bulb holder anti-clockwise, and remove it from the headlight unit **(see illustration)**.
29 Disconnect the wiring plug after removing the bulb. Note that the bulb and bulb holder are a single complete assembly.

30 Refitting is the reverse of the removal procedure.

Front direction indicator

31 Renewal of the front indicator bulb is as described previously in this Section for the halogen type headlight unit.

Indicator side repeater

32 Push the light unit toward the front door, and release the front edge of the unit from the wing. If necessary, assist removal using a small screwdriver or suitable plastic wedge, taking great care not damage the painted finish of the wing **(see illustration)**.
33 Withdraw the light unit from the wing, and pull the bulbholder out of the light unit. The bulb is of the capless (push-fit) type, and can be removed by simply pulling it out of the bulbholder **(see illustrations)**.
34 Refitting is a reverse of the removal procedure.

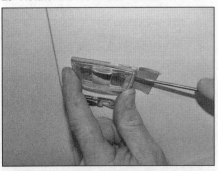

5.32 Push the light unit toward the front door, and release the front edge of the unit from the wing

5.33a Withdraw the light unit from the wing, and pull the bulbholder out of the light unit

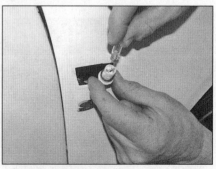

5.33b Remove the push-fit bulb by simply pulling it out of the bulbholder

5.37 Twist the bulbholder anti-clockwise, and remove it from the rear of the unit

5.39 Remove the access cover from the luggage compartment side trim panel

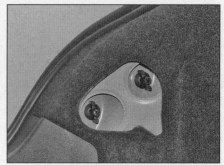

5.40 Unscrew the plastic nuts securing the light unit to the rear wing

Front foglight

35 Remove the front wheel arch liner on the side concerned as described in Chapter 11, Section 24.

36 Disconnect the wiring connector from the bulbholder.

37 Twist the foglight bulbholder anti-clockwise, and remove it from the rear of the foglight unit **(see illustration)**. The bulb and bulbholder are a single unit and cannot be separated. When handling the new bulb, use a tissue or clean cloth to avoid touching the glass with the fingers; moisture and grease from the skin can cause blackening and rapid failure of this type of bulb. If the glass is accidentally touched, wipe it clean using methylated spirit.

38 Refitting is a reverse of the removal procedure.

Rear light cluster

Saloon and Hatchback models

39 Remove the access cover from the luggage compartment side trim panel **(see illustration)**.

40 Reach in through the trim panel aperture and unscrew the two (or three) plastic nuts securing the light unit to the rear wing **(see illustration)**.

41 Lift the front of the light unit and pull it to the rear to release it from the wing **(see illustration)**.

42 Disconnect the wiring connector and remove the light unit **(see illustration)**.

43 Undo the six retaining screws and remove the bulbholder from the rear of the light unit **(see illustrations)**.

44 The relevant bulb can now be renewed **(see illustrations)**.

45 Refitting is a reverse of the removal procedure.

Estate models – tailgate light cluster

46 Open the tailgate and remove the access cover from the tailgate trim panel.

47 Reach in through the trim panel aperture and unscrew the three plastic nuts securing the light unit to the tailgate.

48 Withdraw the light unit from the tailgate, disconnect the wiring connector and remove the light unit **(see illustration)**.

49 To renew the tail light bulbs, turn the

5.41 Lift the front of the light unit and pull it to the rear to release it from the wing

5.42 Disconnect the wiring connector and remove the light unit

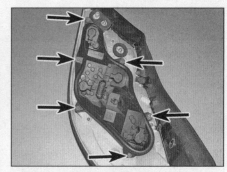

5.43a Undo the six retaining screws ...

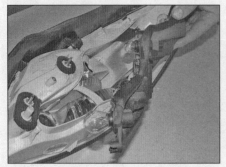

5.43b ... and remove the bulbholder from the rear of the light unit

5.44a The relevant bulb can now be renewed

5.44b Later models use the large capless (wedge) type bulbs

relevant tail light bulbholder anti-clockwise and remove it from the main bulbholder **(see illustration)**.

50 Remove the capless (push fit) bulb from the bulbholder **(see illustration)**.

51 To renew the remainder of the bulbs in the tailgate light cluster, undo the four retaining screws and remove the main bulbholder from the rear of the light unit **(see illustration)**.

52 The relevant bulb can now be renewed; all bulbs have a bayonet fitting **(see illustration)**.

53 Refitting is a reverse of the removal procedure.

Estate models – auxiliary light cluster

54 Remove the access cover from the luggage compartment side trim panel **(see illustration)**.

55 Reach in through the trim panel aperture and push the light unit out from its location **(see illustration)**.

56 Turn the relevant bulbholder anti-clockwise and remove it from the light unit **(see illustration)**.

57 The bulbs are a bayonet fit in the bulbholders, and can be removed by pressing in and twisting in an anti-clockwise direction **(see illustration)**.

58 Refitting is a reverse of the removal procedure.

Number plate light

59 Insert a small flat-bladed screwdriver into the slot on the side of the light unit, depress the tab and carefully prise the light unit out from its location **(see illustration)**.

5.48 Withdraw the light unit from the tailgate and disconnect the wiring connector

5.49 Turn the relevant tail light bulbholder anti-clockwise and remove it from the main bulbholder

5.50 Remove the push-fit bulb by simply pulling it out of the bulbholder

5.51 To renew the remainder of the bulbs, undo the four screws and remove the main bulbholder

5.52 The relevant bulb can now be renewed; all bulbs have a bayonet fitting

5.54 Remove the access cover from the luggage compartment side trim panel

5.55 Push the light unit out from its location

5.56 Turn the relevant bulbholder anti-clockwise and remove it from the light unit

5.57 The bulbs are a bayonet fit in the bulbholders

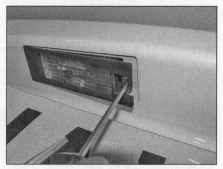

5.59 Carefully prise the light unit out from its location

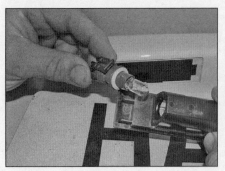

5.60a Twist the bulbholder to remove it from the light unit …

60 Twist the bulbholder to remove it from the light unit and remove the capless (push fit) bulb from the bulbholder **(see illustrations)**.
61 Refitting is a reverse of the removal procedure.

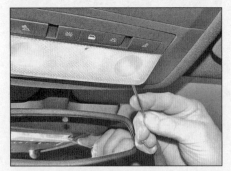

6.2 Carefully prise the light unit lens from the overhead console

6.3 Pull the relevant bulb from its socket

6.8a Carefully prise the light unit out of position …

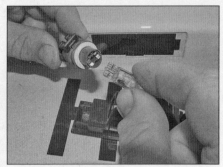

5.60b … and remove the push-fit bulb

High-level brake light

62 The high-level brake light bulbs are of the LED (light emitting diode) type and cannot be individually renewed. Remove the complete light unit as described in Section 7.

---

6 Bulbs (interior lights) – renewal

General

1 Refer to Section 5, paragraph 1.

Front and rear courtesy lights

2 Using a small screwdriver, carefully prise the light unit lens from the overhead console **(see illustration)**.
3 Pull the relevant bulb from its socket **(see illustration)**.

6.5 Fold down the sun visor and carefully prise out the light unit lens

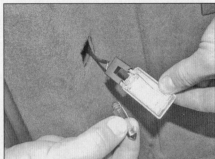

6.8b … and release the bulb from the light unit contacts

4 Install the new bulb, ensuring that it is securely held in position by the contacts, and clip the light unit lens back into position.

Vanity light

5 Fold down the sun visor and carefully prise out the light unit lens **(see illustration)**.
6 Using a small screwdriver, release the bulb from its contacts **(see illustration)**.
7 Install the new bulb, ensuring that it is securely held in position by the contacts, and clip the light unit lens back into position.

Luggage compartment, door and footwell lights

8 Using a suitable screwdriver, carefully prise the light unit out of position, and release the bulb from the light unit contacts **(see illustrations)**.
9 Install the new bulb, ensuring that it is securely held in position by the contacts, and clip the light unit back into position.

Glovebox light

10 Remove the glovebox as described in Chapter 11, Section 30.
11 Release the bulb from its contacts, install the new bulb, ensuring it is securely held in position by the contacts, and refit the glovebox **(see illustration)**.

Switch illumination

12 All the switches are fitted with illumination bulbs; some are also fitted with a bulb to show when the circuit concerned is operating. These bulbs are an integral part of the switch assembly, and cannot be obtained separately.

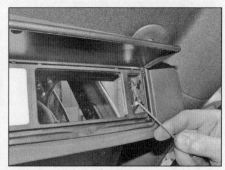

6.6 Using a small screwdriver, release the bulb from its contacts

6.11 Release the glovebox light bulb from its contacts

7.2 Undo the screws securing the plastic moulding to the bumper brace

7 Exterior light units – removal and refitting

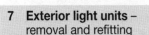

Note: *Disconnect the battery negative terminal (refer to Chapter 5A, Section 4) before removing any light unit, and reconnect the terminal after refitting.*

Headlight

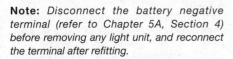

Warning: Xenon dipped beam headlights operate at very high voltage. Do not touch the associated wiring when the headlights are switched on.

1 Remove the front bumper as described in Chapter 11, Section 6.
2 Undo the two screws (left-hand side) or three screws (right-hand side) securing the plastic moulding to the bumper brace **(see illustration)**.

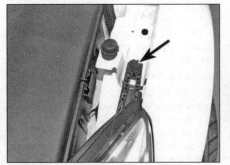

7.5a Undo the upper retaining bolt ...

7.5d ... and the upper front retaining bolt ...

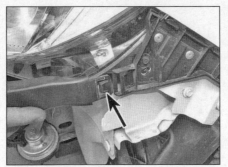

7.3 Release the tab and remove the plastic moulding

3 Disengage the plastic mounting from the headlight unit, then release the tab on the side and remove the moulding **(see illustration)**.
4 Disconnect the wiring connector from the rear of the headlight unit **(see illustration)**.
5 Undo the four retaining bolts and remove the headlight unit from the car **(see illustrations)**.
6 Refitting is a reverse of the removal procedure. On completion, check the headlight beam alignment using the information given in Section 8.

Front direction indicator light

7 The front direction indicator lights are integral with the headlight units. Removal and refitting is as described above.

Indicator side repeater light

8 Push the light unit toward the front door,

7.5b ... the outer retaining bolt ...

7.5e ... then remove the headlight unit from the car

7.4 Disconnect the wiring connector from the rear of the headlight unit

and release the front edge of the unit from the wing. If necessary, assist removal using a small screwdriver or suitable plastic wedge, taking great care not to damage the painted finish of the wing **(see illustration 5.32)**.
9 Withdraw the light unit from the wing, and disconnect its wiring connector. Tie a piece of string to the wiring, to prevent it falling back into the wing.
10 On refitting, connect the wiring connector, and clip the light unit back into position.

Front foglight

11 Remove the front wheel arch liner on the side concerned as described in Chapter 11, Section 24.
12 Disconnect the wiring connector from the bulbholder.
13 Undo the two bolts securing the foglight unit to the front bumper **(see illustration)**.
14 Release the foglight unit from the upper

7.5c ... the lower front retaining bolt ...

7.13 Undo the two bolts securing the foglight unit to the front bumper

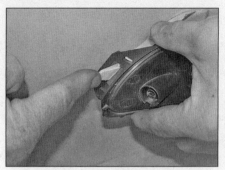

7.14a Release the foglight unit from the upper retaining tabs on the bumper …

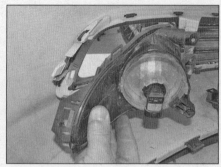

7.14b … and remove the foglight from the car

7.19 Reach in through the trim panel aperture and push the light unit out from its location

retaining tabs on the bumper, and remove the foglight from the car **(see illustrations)**.

15 Refitting is a reverse of the removal procedure.

Rear light cluster

Saloon and Hatchback models

16 The procedure is described as part of the bulb renewal procedure in Section 5.

Estate models – tailgate light cluster

17 The procedure is described as part of the bulb renewal procedure in Section 5.

Estate models – auxiliary light cluster

18 Remove the access cover from the luggage compartment side trim panel **(see illustration 5.54)**.

19 Reach in through the trim panel aperture and push the light unit out from its location **(see illustration)**.

7.23 Lift the tab and disconnect the wiring connector from the number plate bulbholder

20 Disconnect the wiring connector and remove the light unit.

21 Refitting is a reverse of the removal procedure.

Number plate light

22 Insert a small flat-bladed screwdriver into the slot on the side of the light unit, depress the tab and carefully prise the light unit out from its location **(see illustration 5.59)**.

23 Lift the tab and disconnect the wiring connector from the bulbholder **(see illustration)**.

24 Refitting is a reversal of removal.

High-level brake light

Saloon and Hatchback models

25 Remove the bootlid or tailgate trim panel as described in Chapter 11, Section 28.

26 Working through the apertures in the

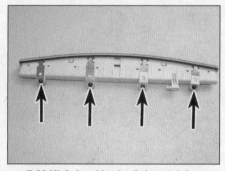

7.26 High-level brake light retaining bracket screws

bootlid or tailgate, slacken the four brake light unit retaining bracket screws **(see illustration)**.

27 Pull the four retaining brackets back using a suitable hooked tool.

28 Using a plastic spatula or similar tool, work around the brake light unit and carefully prise it free from the bootlid or tailgate. Take great care when doing this so as not to scratch the paintwork. Preferably, protect the paint in the area around the light unit using masking tape. Note that in addition to the four retaining brackets, the light unit is also retained by an adhesive seal.

29 Once the light unit is released, disconnect the wiring connector and remove the unit from the car **(see illustration)**.

30 If the original unit is to be refitted, clean off the remains of the old adhesive seal and obtain a new seal. Place the four retaining brackets in their original position and tighten the four screws.

31 Connect the wiring connector and push the light unit into position in the bootlid or tailgate.

Estate models

32 Open the tailgate and carefully prise free the centre of the upper side trim panel on the right-hand side to disengage it from the left-hand side panel **(see illustration)**.

33 Pull the panel away from the tailgate to release the retaining clips, disengage the four tabs from the main panel and remove the right-hand side trim panel **(see illustration)**.

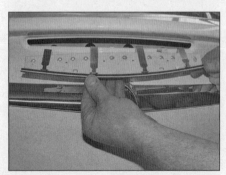

7.29 Disconnect the connector and remove the high-level brake light unit from the car

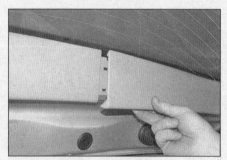

7.32 Carefully prise free the centre of the tailgate upper side trim panel on the right-hand side

7.33 Pull the panel away from the tailgate and remove the right-hand side trim panel

34 Repeat paragraph 33 to remove the left-hand upper side trim panel **(see illustration)**.

35 Disconnect the high-level brake light wiring connector and the tailgate washer hose at the connectors on the left-hand side of the tailgate. Release the wiring and washer hose retaining clips from the tailgate **(see illustrations)**.

36 Extract the rubber grommets and peel back the tape to gain access to the five tailgate spoiler retaining nuts **(see illustrations)**.

37 Undo the five tailgate spoiler retaining nuts and withdraw the spoiler from the tailgate. Feed the wiring and washer hose out through the tailgate opening and remove the spoiler from the car **(see illustrations)**.

38 Disconnect the high-level brake light wiring connector, then undo the two screws and remove the brake light unit from the spoiler **(see illustration)**.

39 Refitting is a reversal of removal.

8 Headlight beam alignment – general information

1 Accurate adjustment of the headlight beam is only possible using optical beam-setting equipment, and this work should therefore be carried out by a Vauxhall/Opel dealer or suitably-equipped workshop. All UK MOT stations have the correct equipment for checking and adjusting the headlight beam.

2 For reference, the headlights can be adjusted using the adjuster assemblies fitted to the top of each light unit. The outer adjuster, alters the vertical position of the beam. The inner adjuster alters the horizontal aim of the beam **(see illustration)**.

3 Most models have an electrically-operated

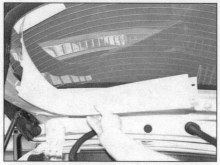

7.34 Remove the tailgate left-hand upper side trim panel in the same way

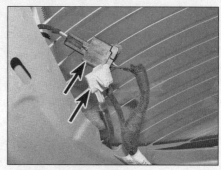

7.35a Disconnect the high-level brake light wiring and the tailgate washer hose at the tailgate connectors ...

7.35b ... then release the wiring and washer hose retaining clips from the tailgate

7.36a Extract the rubber grommet at each side ...

7.36b ... and in the centre ...

7.36c ... then peel back the insulation tape ...

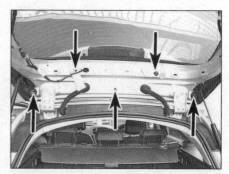

7.36d ... for access to the tailgate spoiler retaining nuts

7.37a Withdraw the spoiler from the tailgate ...

7.37b ... and feed the wiring and washer hose out through the tailgate opening

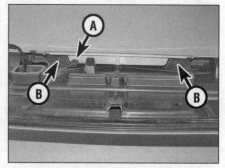

7.38 High-level brake light wiring connector (A) and retaining screws (B)

8.2 The headlight beam adjusters

9.3 Undo the two instrument panel retaining screws

9.4a Disengage the instrument panel from the facia ...

9.4b ... and disconnect the wiring connector

headlight beam adjustment system, controlled via a switch in the facia. The recommended settings are as follows.

a) 0 Front seat(s) occupied
b) 1 All seats occupied
c) 2 All seats occupied, and load in luggage compartment
d) 3 Driver's seat occupied and load in the luggage compartment

Note: *When adjusting the headlight aim, ensure that the switch is set to position 0.*

9 Instrument panel – removal and refitting

Note: *The instrument panel is a complete*

sealed assembly, and no dismantling of the instrument panel is possible.

Removal

1 Disconnect the battery negative terminal (refer to Chapter 5A, Section 4).
2 Remove the steering column shrouds as described in Chapter 11, Section 30 and in this Section 4.
3 Undo the two lower retaining screws, then pull the panel away from the facia at the bottom **(see illustration)**.
4 Disengage the top of the panel from the facia, disconnect the wiring connector and remove the panel from the car **(see illustrations)**.

Refitting

5 Refitting is a reversal of removal.

10 Information display unit – removal and refitting

Removal

1 Disconnect the battery negative terminal (refer to Chapter 5A, Section 4).
2 Remove the facia upper centre panel as described in Chapter 11, Section 30.
3 Undo the two retaining screws, release the clips and remove the information display unit from the facia upper centre panel **(see illustration)**.

Refitting

4 Refitting is a reversal of removal.

11 Horn – removal and refitting

Removal

1 Remove the front bumper as described in Chapter 11, Section 6.
2 Disconnect the wiring connector, undo the retaining nuts and remove both horns from the mounting bracket **(see illustration)**.

Refitting

3 Refitting is the reverse of removal.

12 Wiper arm – removal and refitting

Removal

1 Operate the wiper motor, then switch it off so that the wiper arm returns to the at-rest (parked) position.
2 Stick a piece of masking tape to the windscreen or tailgate glass, then make a mark on the tape, in line with the wiper blade, to use as an alignment aid on refitting **(see illustration)**.
3 Unclip the wiper arm spindle nut cover (windscreen wiper arm), or pivot the cover up

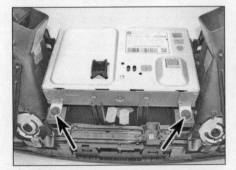

10.3 Undo the two retaining screws and remove the information display unit from the facia upper centre panel (early version)

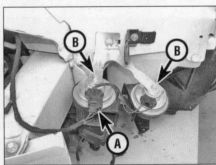

11.2 Disconnect the wiring connector (A) and undo the horn retaining nuts (B)

12.2 Stick a piece of masking tape to the glass, then mark it to use as an alignment aid on refitting

12.3 Unclip the wiper arm spindle nut cover, then slacken and remove the spindle nut and washer

12.4a If removing a windscreen wiper arm, rock the arm from side-to-side to release it from the spindle

12.4b If removing a tailgate wiper arm, use a small puller to release the arm

(tailgate wiper arm), then slacken and remove the spindle nut and washer **(see illustration)**.
4 If removing a windscreen wiper arm, rock the arm from side-to-side to release it from the spindle. If removing a tailgate wiper arm, use a small puller to release the arm **(see illustrations)**.

Refitting

5 Ensure that the wiper arm and spindle splines are clean and dry, then refit the arm to the spindle, aligning the wiper blade with the tape fitted on removal. Refit the spindle nut, tightening it securely, and clip the nut cover back in position.

13 Windscreen wiper motor and linkage – removal and refitting

Removal

1 Remove the wiper arms as described in the Section 12.
2 Remove the water deflector as described in Chapter 11, Section 24.
3 Disconnect the wiring connector from the wiper motor **(see illustration)**.
4 Undo the four retaining bolts, and remove the wiper motor and linkage assembly out from the vehicle **(see illustrations)**.
5 If necessary, mark the relative positions of the motor shaft and linkage arm, then

unscrew the retaining nut from the motor spindle. Free the wiper linkage from the spindle, then remove the three motor retaining bolts, and separate the motor and linkage **(see illustration)**.

Refitting

6 Where necessary, assemble the motor and linkage, and securely tighten the motor retaining bolts. Locate the linkage arm on the motor spindle, aligning the marks made prior to removal, and securely tighten its retaining nut.
7 Manoeuvre the motor assembly back into position in the vehicle. Refit the retaining bolts, and tighten them securely.
8 Reconnect the wiper motor wiring connector.

13.3 Disconnect the wiring connector from the windscreen wiper motor

9 Refit the water deflector as described in Chapter 11, Section 24.
10 Install both the wiper arms as described in Section 12.

14 Tailgate wiper motor – removal and refitting

Removal

1 Remove the wiper arm as described in Section 12.
2 Remove the tailgate trim panel as described in Chapter 11, Section 28.
3 Disconnect the wiring connector, then slacken and remove the wiper motor

13.4a Undo the two centre retaining bolts ...

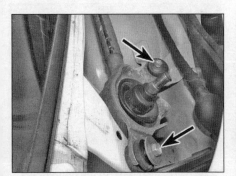

13.4b ... and the two side retaining bolts ...

13.4c ... then remove the wiper motor and linkage assembly

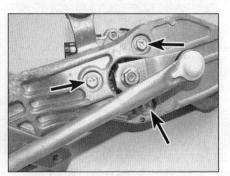

13.5 Windscreen wiper motor retaining bolts

14.3a Disconnect the tailgate wiper motor wiring connector ...

14.3b ... undo the wiper motor mounting bolts on Hatchback models ...

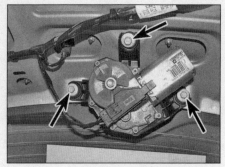

14.3c ... and on Estate models ...

14.3d ... then remove the wiper motor from the tailgate

15.2 Pull up and remove the windscreen washer reservoir filler neck

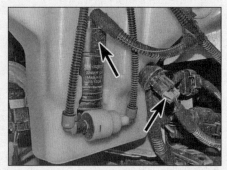

15.3 Disconnect the washer pump and fluid level sensor wiring connectors

mounting bolts and remove the wiper motor **(see illustrations)**.

Refitting

4 Refitting is the reverse of removal, ensuring the wiper motor retaining bolts are securely tightened.

---

15 Windscreen, tailgate and head-light washer system components – removal and refitting

---

Washer system reservoir

1 Remove the front wheel arch liner on the left-hand side as described in Chapter 11, Section 24.
2 From within the engine compartment, pull up and remove the filler neck for the washer reservoir **(see illustration)**.
3 Disconnect the wiring connectors at the washer pump(s) and washer fluid level sensor, and release the wiring from the reservoir **(see illustration)**.
4 Being prepared for fluid spillage, disconnect the washer hoses from the washer pump(s).
5 Undo the three nuts and remove the reservoir from under the car **(see illustration)**.
6 Refitting is the reverse of removal, ensuring that the wiring and washer hoses are securely connected.

Washer pump

7 Remove the front wheel arch liner on the left-hand side as described in Chapter 11, Section 24.

8 Being prepared for fluid spillage, disconnect the washer hoses from the washer pump.
9 Carefully ease the pump out from the reservoir and recover its sealing grommet.
10 Refitting is the reverse of removal, using a new sealing grommet if the original one shows signs of damage or deterioration.

Windscreen washer jets

11 Remove the water deflector as described in Chapter 11, Section 24.
12 Disconnect the washer hose(s) from the washer jet.
13 Using a small screwdriver, depress the catch on the water deflector, while carefully prising up on the jet using a second screwdriver. Remove the jet from the panel **(see illustrations)**.
14 Refitting is the reverse of removal.

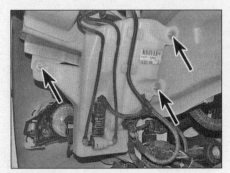

15.5 Washer reservoir retaining nuts

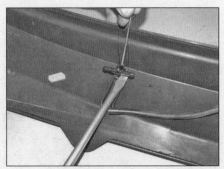

15.13a Depress the catch on the water deflector, while carefully prising up on the jet ...

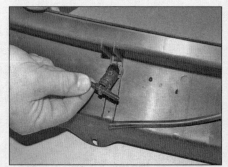

15.13b ... then remove the jet from the water deflector panel

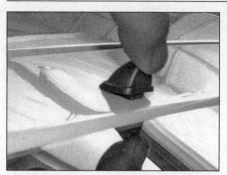

15.15 Push the top of the jet towards the front of the car to release it from the tailgate

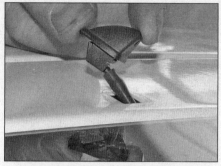

15.16 Lift the jet out of the tailgate and disconnect the washer hose

15.19 Slip the jet out of the slot in the tailgate spoiler and disconnect the washer hose

Tailgate washer jet

Hatchback models

15 Push the top of the jet towards the front of the car to release it from the tailgate **(see illustration)**.
16 Lift the jet out of the tailgate, disconnect the washer hose and remove the jet **(see illustration)**.
17 Refitting is the reverse of removal.

Estate models

18 Remove the tailgate spoiler as described in Section 7, paragraphs 32 to 37.
19 Slip the washer jet out of the slot in the tailgate spoiler and disconnect the washer hose **(see illustration)**.
20 Refitting is the reverse of removal.

Headlight washers

21 Using a plastic trim tool (and protecting the paint work if required) pull the jet assembly forward and remove the cover by unclipping it from the main jet body **(see illustrations)**.
22 Pull the main jet assembly forwards and hold it out using pliers. Protect the tube with a cloth if necessary and then release the jet housing from the main tube with a small screwdriver **(see illustrations)**.
23 If the main body requires replacement then remove the bumper cover as described in Chapter 11 Section 6.
24 With the bumper cover removed, disconnect the washer supply line, depress the locking tabs and remove the main body **(see illustrations)**. Note that the front

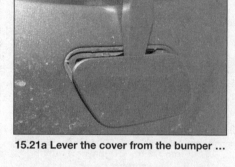

15.21a Lever the cover from the bumper ...

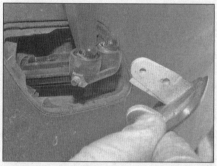

15.21b ... and unclip the cover

15.22a Hold the main assembly in the extended position ...

15.22b ... use a screwdriver to release the jet assembly ...

cosmetic cover and washer jet assembly must be removed first.
25 Refitting is a reversal of removal, but fit

the washer jet and cosmetic cover together before pushing the jet and cover into the main body.

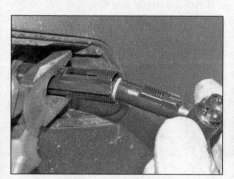

15.22c ... and remove it

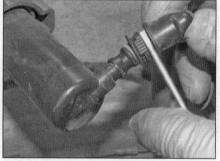

15.24a Remove the supply hose by lifting the locking collar

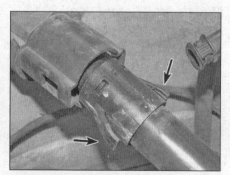

15.24b Depress the tabs to release the main body (shown removed)

16.3 Undo the four bolts securing the radio/CD player to the facia

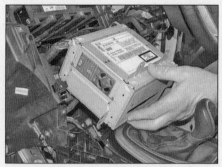

16.4 Withdraw the radio/CD player from the facia and disconnect the wiring and aerial connections

16.8a Remove the AC control panel

16.8b Remove the screws and lift out the support panel

16.8c Remove the CD player mounting screws ...

16.8d ... and pull out the CD player

16 Audio unit – removal and refitting

Note: If a new radio/CD player is to be fitted, the unit must be programmed and configured to the car using Vauxhall/Opel diagnostic equipment. Sound quality may be impaired until this work is carried out.

Note: In June 2013 Vauxhall updated the design of the fascia panel with a central information display that replaced the old audio units and controls. The updated facia is easily recognised by the central display screen. This is a either a four inch display with tactile switches or an eight inch display with a touch screen. The operation of the audio system is controlled via the screen.

Models built before June 2013

Removal

1 Disconnect the battery negative terminal (refer to Chapter 5A, Section 4).
2 Remove the facia lower centre panel as described in Chapter 11, Section 30.
3 Undo the four bolts securing the radio/CD player to the facia **(see illustration)**.
4 Withdraw the radio/CD player from the facia, disconnect the wiring and aerial connections at the rear, and remove the unit from the car **(see illustration)**.

Refitting

5 Refitting is the reverse of removal.

Models built after June 2013

Removal

6 The audio controls and CD player are part of the central information display. Removal and refitting of the display is described in Section 10.
7 The main audio/radio module is mounted behind the glove box. Remove the glovebox as described in Chapter 11 Section 30.
8 Remove the heater/AC control panel (Chapter) and the mounting plate. Remove the bolts, pull out the CD player and disconnect the wiring plugs **(see illustrations)**.
9 Where a DAB radio is fitted there is an additional module located behind the glovebox close to the A-pillar. Slide the module down from the bracket and disconnect the wiring plug.

17.3a Disconnect the wiring connector ...

Refitting

10 Refitting is a reversal of removal.

17 Communication interface module – removal and refitting

Removal

1 Disconnect the battery negative terminal (refer to Chapter 5A, Section 4).
2 Remove the facia lower centre panel as described in Chapter 11, Section 30.
3 Disconnect the wiring connector and remove the unit from the facia. On later models remove the CD player (Section 16) to access the module **(see illustrations)**.

Refitting

4 Refitting is the reverse of removal.

17.3b ... and remove the communication interface module from the facia

17.3c The module on later models

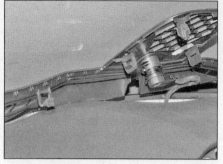

18.1 Carefully prise up the windscreen demister grille from the top of the facia

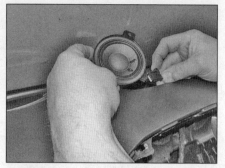

18.2 Undo the two screws then withdraw the speaker and disconnect the wiring connector

18 Speakers –
removal and refitting

Facia centre speaker

1 Using a plastic spatula or similar tool, carefully prise up the windscreen demister grille from the top of the facia **(see illustration)**. Disconnect the sensor wiring connector and remove the grille.

2 Undo the two screws, withdraw the speaker from the facia and disconnect the wiring connector **(see illustration)**.

3 Refitting is the reverse of removal.

Front door upper speaker

4 Using a plastic spatula or similar tool,

carefully prise off the door mirror interior trim panel. Disconnect the speaker wiring connector and remove the panel **(see illustrations)**.

5 Lift out the foam insulation pad from the door mirror interior trim panel **(see illustration)**.

6 Release the retaining tabs and remove the speaker from the mirror interior trim panel **(see illustration)**.

7 Refitting is the reverse of removal.

Front/rear door lower speaker

8 Remove the door inner trim panel as described in Chapter 11, Section 12.

9 Undo the retaining screw, then free the speaker from the door. Disconnect the wiring connector and remove the speaker **(see illustrations)**.

10 Refitting is the reverse of removal.

Rear speaker – Saloon models

11 Extract the three fasteners and remove the rear parcel shelf trim panel.

12 Undo the retaining screw, then lift the speaker from the parcel shelf. Disconnect the wiring connector and remove the speaker.

13 Refitting is the reverse of removal.

19 Radio aerial –
general information

1 Removal of the radio aerial entails removal of the headlining, which is a complicated operation, considered to be outside the scope of this manual. Therefore, any problems relating to the aerial or wiring should be entrusted to a Vauxhall/Opel dealer.

18.4a Carefully prise off the door mirror interior trim panel ...

18.4b ... then disconnect the speaker wiring connector

18.5 Lift out the foam insulation pad from the mirror interior trim panel

18.6 Release the retaining tabs and remove the speaker from the trim panel

18.9a Undo the retaining screw ...

18.9b ... then free the speaker from the door and disconnect the wiring connector

20 Anti-theft alarm system – general information

Note: *This information is applicable only to the anti-theft alarm system fitted by Vauxhall/ Opel as standard equipment.*

1 Most models in the range are fitted with an anti-theft alarm system as standard equipment. The alarm is automatically armed and disarmed when the deadlocks are operated using the driver's door lock or remote control key. The alarm has switches on all the doors (including the bootlid/tailgate), the bonnet, the radio/CD player and the ignition and starter circuits. If the bootlid/tailgate, bonnet or any of the doors are opened whilst the alarm is set, the alarm horn will sound and the hazard warning lights will flash. The alarm also has an immobiliser function which makes the ignition and starter circuits inoperable whilst the alarm is triggered.

2 The alarm system performs a self-test every time it is switched on; this test takes approximately 30 seconds. During the self-test, the LED (light emitting diode) on the top of the facia will come on. If the LED flashes quickly, then either the tailgate, bonnet or one of the doors is open, or there is a fault in the circuit. After the initial 30-second period, the LED will flash slowly to indicate that the alarm is switched on. On unlocking the driver's door lock, the LED will illuminate for approximately 1 second, then go out, indicating that the alarm has been switched off.

3 Should the alarm system develop a fault, the vehicle should be taken to a Vauxhall/ Opel dealer or suitably equipped garage for examination.

21 Heated seat components – general information

1 On models with heated seats, a heater mat is fitted to both the seat back and seat cushion. Renewal of either heater mat involves peeling back the upholstery, removing the old mat, sticking the new mat in position and then refitting the upholstery. Note that upholstery removal and refitting requires considerable skill and experience if it is to be carried out successfully, and is therefore best entrusted to your Vauxhall/Opel dealer. In practice, it will be very difficult for the home mechanic to carry out the job without ruining the upholstery.

22 Airbag system – general information and precautions

General information

1 A driver's airbag is fitted as standard equipment on all models. The airbag is fitted in the steering wheel centre pad. Additionally, a passenger's airbag located in the facia, side airbags located in the front seats, and curtain airbags located in the headlining are optionally available.

2 The system is armed only when the ignition is switched on, however, a reserve power source maintains a power supply to the system in the event of a break in the main electrical supply. The steering wheel and facia airbags are activated by a 'g' sensor (deceleration sensor), and controlled by an electronic control unit located under the centre console. The side airbags and curtain airbags are activated by severe side impact and operate independently of the main system. A separate electrical supply, control unit and sensor is provided for the side/ curtain airbags on each side of the car.

3 The airbags are inflated by a gas generator, which forces the bag out from its location in the steering wheel, facia, seat back frame, or headlining.

Precautions

 Warning: The following pre-cautions must be observed when working on vehicles equipped with an airbag system, to prevent the possibility of personal injury.

General precautions

4 The following precautions **must** be observed when carrying out work on a vehicle equipped with an airbag:

a) *Do not disconnect the battery with the engine running.*
b) *Before carrying out any work in the vicinity of the airbag, removal of any of the airbag components, or any welding work on the vehicle, de-activate the system as described in the following sub-Section.*
c) *Do not attempt to test any of the airbag system circuits using test meters or any other test equipment.*
d) *If the airbag warning light comes on, or any fault in the system is suspected, consult a Vauxhall/Opel dealer without delay.*
e) *Do not attempt to carry out fault diagnosis, or any dismantling of the components.*

Precautions when handling an airbag

a) *Transport the airbag by itself, bag upward.*
b) *Do not put your arms around the airbag.*
c) *Carry the airbag close to the body, bag outward.*
d) *Do not drop the airbag or expose it to impacts.*
e) *Do not attempt to dismantle the airbag unit.*
f) *Do not connect any form of electrical equipment to any part of the airbag circuit.*

Precautions when storing an airbag

a) *Store the unit in a cupboard with the airbag upward.*
b) *Do not expose the airbag to temperatures above 80°C.*
c) *Do not expose the airbag to flames.*
d) *Do not attempt to dispose of the airbag – consult a Vauxhall/Opel dealer.*
e) *Never refit an airbag which is known to be faulty or damaged.*

De-activation of airbag system

5 The system must be de-activated before carrying out any work on the airbag components or surrounding area:

a) *Switch on the ignition and check the operation of the airbag warning light on the instrument panel. The light should illuminate when the ignition is switched on, then extinguish.*
b) *Switch off the ignition.*
c) *Remove the ignition key.*
d) *Switch off all electrical equipment.*
e) *Disconnect the battery negative terminal (refer to Chapter 5A, Section 4).*
f) *Insulate the battery negative terminal and the end of the battery negative lead to prevent any possibility of contact.*
g) *Wait for at least two minutes before carrying out any further work. Wait at least ten minutes if the airbag warning light did not operate correctly.*

Activation of airbag system

6 To activate the system on completion of any work, proceed as follows:

a) *Ensure that there are no occupants in the vehicle, and that there are no loose objects around the vicinity of the steering wheel. Close the vehicle doors and windows.*
b) *Ensure that the ignition is switched off then reconnect the battery negative terminal.*
c) *Open the driver's door and switch on the ignition, without reaching in front of the steering wheel. Check that the airbag warning light illuminates briefly then extinguishes.*
d) *Switch off the ignition.*
e) *If the airbag warning light does not operate as described in paragraph c), consult a Vauxhall/Opel dealer before driving the vehicle.*

23 Airbag system components – removal and refitting

 Warning: Refer to the precautions given in Section 22 before attempting to carry out work on any of the airbag components.

1 De-activate the airbag system as described in the previous Section, then proceed as described under the relevant heading.

Driver's airbag

2 To release the airbag retaining wire spring, make up a removal tool as shown **(see Tool Tip)**.

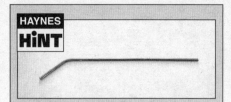

HAYNES HINT

To make an airbag removal tool, use a coat hanger or metal rod 3 to 4 mm in diameter and cut to approximately 180 mm in length. Bend the rod by approximately 30° at a point approximately 30 mm from one end of the rod.

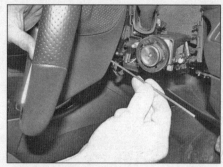

23.3a Insert the bent end of the removal tool into one of the holes on the rear of the steering wheel ...

23.3b ... and bring the tool into contact with the wire spring (shown with airbag removed)

23.3c Pull the tool away from the steering column, and pull the airbag up to release it on that side

23.4 Release the locking clips and then disconnect the airbag wiring connectors

23.7 Passenger's airbag retaining nuts

3 Insert the bent end of the removal tool into one of the holes on the rear of the steering wheel and bring the tool into contact with the wire spring. Pull the other end of the tool away from the steering column, and at the same time pull the airbag away from the steering wheel to release it on that side **(see illustrations)**. Repeat the procedure on the other side of the steering wheel.

4 Release the locking clips, then disconnect the wiring connectors at the rear of the airbag unit **(see illustration)**. Remove the airbag unit. Note that the airbag must not be knocked or dropped, and should be stored the correct way up, with its padded surface uppermost.

5 Refitting is a reversal of the removal procedure.

Passenger's airbag

6 Remove the complete facia assembly as described in Chapter 11, Section 30.

7 Undo the six retaining nuts and remove the airbag from the underside of the facia **(see illustration)**.

8 Disconnect the airbag wiring connector(s) from the side of the unit. Note that the airbag must not be knocked or dropped, and should be stored the correct way up (as mounted in the vehicle).

9 Refitting is a reversal of the removal procedure, tightening the retaining nuts securely.

Side airbags

10 The side airbags are located internally within the front seat back and no attempt

should be made to remove them. Any suspected problems with the side airbag system should be referred to a Vauxhall/Opel dealer.

Curtain airbags

11 The curtain airbags are located behind the headlining above the doors on each side and no attempt should be made to remove them. Any suspected problems with the curtain airbag system should be referred to a Vauxhall/Opel dealer.

Airbag control unit

12 The airbag control unit is located beneath the centre console and no attempt should be made to remove it. Any suspected problems with the control unit should be referred to a Vauxhall/Opel dealer.

Airbag rotary connector

13 Disconnect the battery negative terminal (refer to Chapter 5A, Section 4) and wait for 2 minutes.

14 Fully extend the steering column using the telescopic function.

15 Set the roadwheels in the straight-ahead position and ensure they remain in that position during the removal and refitting procedures.

16 Remove the steering wheel as described in Chapter 10, Section 19.

17 Remove the steering column shrouds as described in Section 4.

18 Disconnect the two upper wiring connectors and, where fitted, the lower wiring connector from the airbag rotary connector **(see illustrations)**.

23.18a Disconnect the two upper wiring connectors ...

23.18b ... and, where fitted, the lower wiring connector from the airbag rotary connector

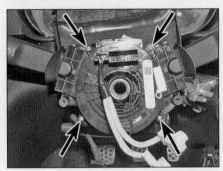

23.19a Undo the four retaining screws ...

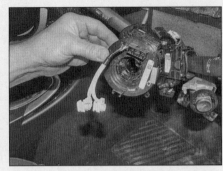

23.19b ... and remove the rotary connector from the steering column

23.23 The rotary connector is centered when the yellow indicator is visible in the connector window

19 Undo the four retaining screws and remove the rotary connector from the steering column **(see illustrations)**.
20 Refitting is a reversal of the removal procedure.
21 Before refitting the steering wheel, the rotary connector should be centralised (unless it is known absolutely that it was centralised before removal, and that the rotary connector has not been turned during or since its removal).
22 Ensure that the roadwheels are in the straight-ahead position and the centering mark on the end of the steering column shaft is in the 6 o'clock position
23 Turn the rotary connector clockwise gently, until resistance is felt. Now turn the rotary connector about three turns anti-clockwise, until the yellow indicator is visible in the connector window **(see illustration)**.

FUSE AND RELAY BOX IN ENGINE COMPARTMENT
(FUSE BLOCK – UNDERHOOD)

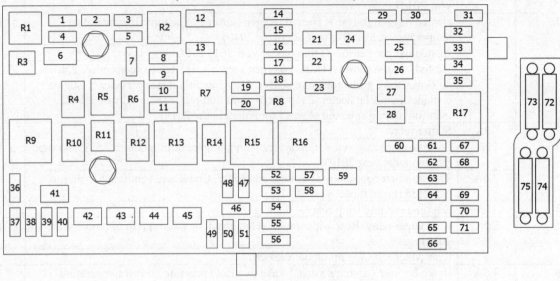

FUSE/RELAY	VALUE	DESCRIPTION	OEM NAME
1	15A	Transmission control module (Up to model year 2013)	F1UA
		Transmission control module (M36 or MDK), Automatic transmission assembly (MJ7, M7U or M7W) (From model year 2014)	
2	15A	Engine control module	F2UA
3	-	Not used	F3UA
4	-	Not used	F4UA
5	15A	Engine control module, Transmission control module (Up to model year 2013)	F5UA
		Engine control module, Transmission control module (M36 or MDK), Automatic transmission assembly (MH7, M7U or M7W) (From model year 2014)	
6	30A	Windshield wiper relay, Windshield wiper speed relay (Up to model year 2010)	F6UA
		Windshield wiper motor (From model year 2011 to 2013)	
		Windshield wiper relay, Windshield wiper speed relay (From model year 2014)	
7	-	Not used	F7UA
8	15A	Fuel injector 2, Fuel injector 4, Fuel injector 6, Ignition coil 2, Ignition coil 4, Ignition coil 6 (Up to model year 2010)	F8UA
		Ignition coils, Fuel injectors, Engine control module (From model year 2011 to 2013)	
		Fuel injector 2, Fuel injector 4, Fuel injector 6, Ignition coil 2, Ignition coil 4, Ignition coil 6 (For model year 2014)	
		Engine control module (From model year 2015)	
9	15A	Ignition coil module, Fuel injector 1, Fuel injector 2, Fuel injector 3, Fuel injector 4, Fuel injector 5, Ignition coil 1, Ignition coil 2, Ignition coil 3, Ignition coil 4 (Up to model year 2010)	F9UA
		Ignition coils, Fuel injectors, Engine control module (From model year 2011 to 2013)	
		Ignition coil module, Fuel injector 1, Fuel injector 2, Fuel injector 3, Fuel injector 4, Fuel injector 5, Ignition coil 1, Ignition coil 2, Ignition coil 3, Ignition coil 4 (For model year 2014)	
		Engine control module, Ignition coil module, Fuel injector 1, Fuel injector 2, Fuel injector 3, Fuel injector 4, Fuel injector 5 (From model year 2015)	

10	20A	Engine control module, 15 A also used (Up to model year 2014)	F10UA
		Engine control module, Glow plug control module, 15A also used (From model year 2015)	
11	10A	Heated oxygen sensor 1, Heated oxygen sensor 2, Mass air flow/intake air temperature sensor (Up to model year 2010)	F11UA
		Heated oxygen sensors (From model year 2011 to 2013)	
		Heated oxygen sensors, Heated oxygen sensor 1, Heated oxygen sensor 2, Mass air flow/intake air temperature sensor, Multifunction intake air sensor, Engine coolant thermostat heater, Evaporative emission purge solenoid valve, Intake manifold tuning solenoid valve (From model year 2014)	
12	30A	Starter relay	F12UA
13	20A	Positive crankcase ventilation heater, Fuel pump control module, 7.5 A also used (Up to model year 2010)	F13UA
	7.5A	Transmission control module, Fuel controller, Crankcase ventilation heater or Not used (From model year 2011)	
14	15A	Daytime running lamp relay – right	F14UA
15	20A	Rear wiper relay, Rear wiper motor (Hatchback or wagon) (Up to model year 2010)	F15UA
		Rear wiper relay (From model year 2011)	
16	7.5A	Brake booster vacuum switch, Intake manifold pressure and air temperature sensor, Mass air flow sensor, Mass air flow/intake air temperature sensor, Water in fuel sensor (Up to model year 2010)	F16UA
		Brake booster vacuum switch, Air quality sensor, Water in fuel sensor (From model year 2011 to 2013)	
		Mass air flow/intake air temperature sensor, Rearview Camera, Water in fuel sensor, Engine coolant thermostat heater, Active grille air shutter actuator, Power supply transformer (KL9), Coolant pump clutch (From model year 2014)	
17	5A	Inflatable restraint sensing and diagnostic module (Up to model year 2013)	F17UA
	-	Not used (From model year 2014 to 2015)	
	5A	Trailer lighting control module (Wagon without VK0, TB5 or KI7) (For model year 2016)	
	-	Not used (For model year 2017)	
18	15A	Headlamp control module	F18UA
19	10A	Headlamp horizontal motor – left, Headlamp horizontal motor – right	F19UA
20	20A	Fuel pump relay	F20UA
21	30A	Window motor – left rear, Window motor- right rear, Window switch – left rear, Window switch – right rear (Up to model year 2010)	F21UA
		Windows motors, Front door (For model year 2011)	
		Windows motors (From model year 2012)	
22	50A	Electronic brake control module, 30A also used	F22UA
23	10A	Power steering control module	F23UA
24	30A	Window motor – driver, Window motor – passenger	F24UA
25	30A	Accessory DC/AC power inverter module (Up to model year 2015)	F25UA
		Trailer lighting control module (Wagon without TB5), Accessory DC/AC power inverter module (KI7) (For model year 2016)	
		Accessory DC/AC power inverter module (KI7) (For model year 2017)	
26	60A	Electronic brake control module	F26UA
27	30A	Parking brake control module	F27UA
28	40A	Rear defogger grid (Up to model year 2015)	F28UA
		Rear defogger grid, Rear window defogger noise filter – right (US3), Fuse F63UA (From model year 2016)	
29	15A	Seat lumbar support switch – left	F29UA
30	15A	Seat lumbar support switch – right	F30UA

31	10A	A/C compressor clutch relay	F31UA
32	20A	Body control module (Up to model year 2013)	F32UA
		Inside rearview mirror (without TQ5 or UFL), Rearview camera (UVC), Turn signal lamp – left rear, Backup lamp – left, Backup lamp – right, Door courtesy lamp – driver, Instrument panel courtesy lamp – left, Instrument panel courtesy lamp – right, Door courtesy lamp – passenger, Body control module (From model year 2014)	
33	25A	Heated seat control module	F33UA
34	25A	Sunroof sunshade motor module, Sunroof control module (Up to model year 2015)	F34UA
		Sunroof sunshade motor module (C3U), Sunroof control module (CF5), Liftgate control module (Without TB5, VK0 or KI7) (For model year 2016)	
		Sunroof sunshade motor module (C3U), Sunroof control module (CF5) (For model year 2017)	
35	30A	Audio amplifier (Up to model year 2015)	F35UA
		Liftgate control module (Without UQA), Audio amplifier (IO3, IO5, IO6, IO7 with UQA) (For model year 2016)	
		Audio amplifier (For model year 2017)	
36	-	Not used	F36UA
37	10A	Headlamp – right high beam (Up to model year 2013)	F37UA
		Headlamp – right high beam (T4A), High beam solenoid actuator – right (T4A) (From model year 2014)	
38	10A	Headlamp – left high beam (Up to model year 2013)	F38UA
		Headlamp – left high beam (T4A), High beam solenoid actuator – left (T4A) (From model year 2014)	
39	-	Not used (Up to model year 2013)	F39UA
	15A	Steering column lock module (From model year 2014)	
40	-	Not used	F40UA
41	30A	Brake booster pump motor (Up to model year 2010)	F41UA
		Remote control door lock receiver or Brake booster pump motor (For model year 2011)	
		Charge air cooler cooling fan relay (From model year 2012 to 2013)	
		Brake booster pump motor relay, Brake booster pump motor (From model year 2014)	
42	60A	Cooling fan left high speed relay, Cooling fan medium speed relay (Up to model year 2010)	F42UA
	50A	Cooling fan medium speed 1 relay, 30A, 40A also used (From model year 2011 to 2013)	
	30A	Cooling fan low speed relay, Cooling fan high speed relay, Cooling fan relay, Cooling fan left medium speed relay, Cooling fan medium speed relay, 40A, 50A also used (From model year 2014)	
43	30A	Power supply transformer, Fuse block – instrument panel (Up to model year 2010)	F43UA
		Heated washer nozzle module, Remote control door lock receiver (For model year 2011)	
		Battery saver relay, Power supply transformer (From model year 2012)	
44	25A	Headlamp washer pump relay	F44UA
45	60A	Cooling fan high speed relay, Cooling fan right high speed relay, Cooling fan medium speed relay, 40A, 50 A also used (Up to model year 2010)	F45UA
		Cooling fan high speed relay, 30A, 40A, 50 A also used (From model year 2011 to 2014)	
		Cooling fan high speed relay, Cooling fan right medium speed relay, 40A, 50A also used (From model year 2015)	

46	10A	Cooling fan high speed relay, Cooling fan relay, Cooling fan left low speed relay, Cooling fan left medium speed relay, Cooling fan medium speed relay (Up to model year 2010)	F46UA
		Cooling fan relay (From model year 2011 to 2013)	
		Cooling fan low speed relay, Cooling fan high speed relay, Cooling fan speed control relay, Cooling fan relay, Cooling fan left medium speed relay, Cooling fan right medium speed relay (From model year 2014)	
47	10A	Engine control module, Intake manifold runner control solenoid valve, Turbocharger vane position control solenoid valve, Turbocharger 1 wastegate solenoid valve, Turbocharger 2 wastegate solenoid valve, Exhaust gas recirculation cooler bypass solenoid valve (Up to model year 2010)	F47UA
		Heated oxygen sensor (From model year 2011 to 2013)	
		Engine coolant thermostat heater, Positive crankcase ventilation heater, Cooling fan left high speed relay, Cooling fan medium speed relay, A/C compressor clutch relay, Intake manifold runner control solenoid valve, Turbocharger vane position control solenoid valve, Turbocharger wastegate solenoid valve, Engine oil pressure control solenoid valve, Exhaust gas recirculation cooler bypass solenoid valve (From model year 2014)	
48	15A	Fog lamp – left front, Fog lamp – right front	F48UA
49	15A	Headlamp – right low beam (Up to model year 2013)	F49UA
		Headlamp ballast – right (From model year 2014)	
50	15A	Headlamp – left low beam (Up to model year 2013)	F50UA
		Headlamp ballast – left (From model year 2014)	
51	15A	Horn – high note, Horn – low note	F51UA
52	5A	Instrument cluster	F52UA
53	10A	Inside rear-view mirror, Tire pressure indicator module, Headlamp levelling actuator – left, Headlamp levelling actuator – right, Seat blower motors	F53UA
54	5A	Headlamp switch (Up to model year 2010)	F54UA
		Headlamp switch, Electrical auxiliary heater (From model year 2011)	
55	7.5A	Outside rear-view mirror, Window switch driver, Window switch passenger (Up to model year 2013)	F55UA
		Mirror control module, Window switch – driver, Window switch – passenger, Outside rearview mirror switch (From model year 2014)	
56	15A	Windshield washer pump	F56UA
57	15A	Steering column lock module	F57UA
58	-	Not used	F58UA
59	50A	Fuel heater relay, 30A, 40A also used (Up to model year 2010)	F59UA
	40A	Fuel heater, Secondary air injection pump, 30A also used (From model year 2011)	
60	7.5A	Outside rearview mirror	F60UA
61	7.5A	Outside rearview mirror	F61UA
62	-	Not used (Up to model year 2011)	F62UA
	10A	Evaporative emission vent solenoid valve (For model year 2012)	
	-	Not used (From model year 2013 to 2015)	
	10A	Steering wheel heater relay or Not used (From model year 2016)	
63	7.5A	Glass breakage sensor – right (wagon) (Up to model year 2010)	F63UA
		Body control module or Glass breakage sensor – right (From model year 2011 to 2013)	
		Glass breakage sensor – right (For model year 2014)	
		Glass breakage sensor – right (UTV), Rear defogger grid (Wagon with UTV) (From model year 2015 to 2016)	
		Glass breakage sensor – right (For model year 2017)	
64	5A	Headlamp control module	F64UA

65	7.5A	Coolant pump – auxiliary (Up to model year 2010)	F65UA
		Theft deterrent alarm siren (From model year 2011 to 2013)	
		Coolant pump – auxiliary or Not used (From model year 2014)	
66	15A	Rear window washer pump relay	F66UA
67	20A	Fuel pump control module or Not used	F67UA
68	-	Not used	F68UA
69	5A	Body control module	F69UA
70	5A	Rain sensor	F70UA
71	-	Not used (Up to model year 2013)	F71UA
	5A	Battery sensor module (KL9) (From model year 2014)	
72	100A	Electrical auxiliary heater (with C32) (Up to model year 2010)	F72UA
	30A	Fuse Holder – Parking heater (with K07) (Up to model year 2010)	
	30A	Parking heater control module, Parking heater control module-auxiliary, Parking heater remote control receiver, Parking heater relay, Parking heater resistor (with K07, From model year 2011 to 2013)	
	30A	Electrical auxiliary heater (with C32), F1UC, F2UC, F3UC fuses (K07), 50A also used (From model year 2014)	
73	80A	Glow plug control module, 60A also used (Up to model year 2015)	F73UA
		Engine control module, Glow plug control module (For model year 2016)	
		Glow plug control module (For model year 2017)	
74	80A	Power steering control module, 100A also used	F74UA
75	-	Not used	F75UA
R1	-	A/C compressor clutch relay	-
R2	-	Starter relay	-
R3	-	Cooling fan relay or Not used	-
R4	-	Windshield wiper speed control relay	-
R5	-	Windshield wiper relay	-
R6	-	Daytime running lamp relay – right	-
R7	-	Powertrain relay	-
R8	-	Fuel pump relay	-
R9	-	Cooling fan low speed relay or Cooling fan left high speed relay or Cooling fan medium speed relay or Not used	-
R10	-	Cooling fan medium speed relay or Cooling fan low speed relay (Up to model year 2011)	-
		Charge air cooler cooling fan relay or Cooling fan low speed relay or Not used (From model year 2012)	
R11	-	Headlamp washer fluid pump relay	-
R12	-	Cooling fan speed control relay or Not used	-
R13	-	Cooling fan high speed relay	-
R14	-	Headlamp low beam relay or Daytime running lamp relay- left	-
R15	-	Ignition main relay	-
R16	-	Fuel heater relay or Secondary air injection pump relay	-
R17	-	Rear window defogger relay	-
R26	-	Door lock security relay (no location information available)	-

Relays listed below are non-serviceable Printed Circuit Board (PCB) relays

RELAY	VALUE	DESCRIPTION	OEM NAME
-	-	Horn relay	-
-	-	Rear window washer pump relay	-
-	-	Rear window wiper relay	-
-	-	Windshield washer pump relay	-

-	-	Front fog lamp relay	-
-	-	Headlamp high beam relay	-
-	-	Door lock relay	-
-	-	Theft deterrent security siren relay	-
-	-	Driver door lock relay	-
-	-	Door lock security relay	-
-	-	Fuel filler door lock relay	-
-	-	Coolant pump relay – auxiliary	-

FUSE BOX ON THE BATTERY
(FUSE BLOCK – BATTERY)

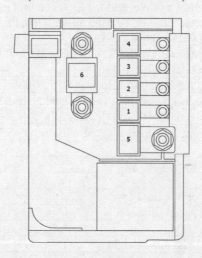

FUSE	VALUE	DESCRIPTION	OEM NAME
1	100A	Fuse block - instrument panel	F1UD/F1UB
2	100A	Fuse block - instrument panel	F2UD/F2UB
3	100A	Fuse block – rear body	F3UD/F3UB
4	100A	Fuse block – rear body	F4UD/F4UB
5	250A	Fuse block – underhood (Petrol engines)	F5UD/F5UB
	300A	Fuse block – underhood (Diesel engines)	
6	500A	Generator, Starter motor (Diesel engines)	F6UD/F6UB
	300A	Generator, Starter motor (Petrol engines), 250 also used	

FUSE AND RELAY BOX IN PASSENGER COMPARTMENT
(FUSE BLOCK – INSTRUMENT PANEL)

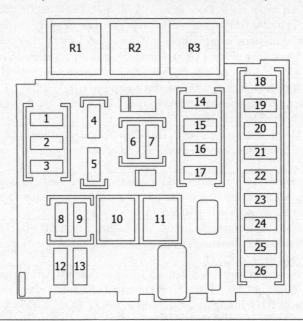

FUSE/RELAY	VALUE	DESCRIPTION	OEM NAME
1	10A	Digital radio receiver control module (U4D) (Up to model year 2011)	F1DA
		Digital radio receiver control module, Mobile telephone control module, Advanced parking assist control module, power sounder content theft deterrent alarm module (UTR) (For model year 2012)	
		Digital radio receiver control module (U4D) (For model year 2013)	
		Side object sensor module – left, Side object sensor module – right, Advanced parking assist control module, Power sounder content theft deterrent alarm module, Power sounder content theft deterrent alarm module, Telematics communication interface control module (From model year 2014)	
2	20A	Body control module (Up to model year 2011)	F2DA
		Body control module: Turn signal lamp – left front, Turn signal lamp – right rear, Turn signal repeater lamp (For model year 2012)	
		Body control module (For model year 2013)	
		Body control module: Sunshade – left (DH6), Sunshade – right (DH6), Turn signal lamp – left front, Turn signal lamp – right rear (C3U), Turn signal repeater lamp – left, Instrument panel compartment lamp, Dome/Reading lamps – front, Dome/Reading lamps – left rear (C3U), Dome/Reading lamps – right rear (C3U) (From model year 2014)	
3	25A	Side marker lamp – Left front, Park/Turn signal lamp – left (T4A), Park/Turn signal lamp – right (T4A), Turn signal lamp – right front, Turn signal repeater lamp – right, Tail lamp- left outer, Tail lamp- left inner, Body control module (Up to model year 2013)	F3DA
		Body control module: Park/Daytime running lamp – left, Turn signal lamp – right front, Turn signal repeater lamp – right, Tail lamp – left, Tail lamp – auxiliary left, Stop lamp – left, Cigarette lighter receptacle, Headlamp washer pump relay (CE4), Rear window washer pump relay, Rear wiper relay, Door dead lock relay (UTT), Fuel fill door lock relay (UTT), Transmission shift lever (MM1) (For model year 2014 and 2015)	

		Body control module: Turn signal lamp – right front (TF4), Turn signal repeater lamp – right, Tail lamp – left outer, Tail lamp – left inner, Cigarette lighter receptacle, Headlamp washer pump relay (CE4), Rear window washer pump relay, Rear wiper relay, Door dead lock relay (UTT), Fuel fill door lock relay (UTT), Transmission shift lever (MM1) (From model year 2016)	
4	20A	Radio, Chime alarm control module (Up to model year 2013)	F4DA
		Radio, Media disc player (TG5), Human machine interface control module (IO5 or O6), Chime alarm control module (KRP) (From model year 2014 to 2015)	
		Radio (IO3, IO5, IO6 or IO7), Media disc player (IO3 or IO7 with TG5), Human machine interface control module (IO5 or O6), Chime alarm control module (KRP) (For model year 2016)	
		Radio, Media disc player (TG5), Human machine interface control module (IO5 or O6), Chime alarm control module (KRP), Auxiliary audio input (For model year 2017)	
5	7.5A	Radio controls, Info display module, Multi-function switch module – center console, Advanced parking assist control module, Power sounder control theft deterrent alarm module (Up to model year 2011)	F5DA
		Radio controls, Instrument cluster, Info display module (UAG, UDK or UFD), Radio control multifunction switch, Multimedia player interface module (From model year 2012 to 2013)	
		Inside rearview mirror (TQ5 without UFL), Advanced parking assist control module (UD5 or UDP), Instrument cluster (KL9), Info display module (IO3, IO5, IO6 or IO7), Infotainment control touchpad (IO5 or IO6 with KOT), Auxiliary audio input (IO3, IO5, IO6 or IO7) (From model year 2014)	
6	20A	Accessory power receptacle – center console (without DUJ), Cigarette lighter receptacle – front (DUJ)	F6DA
7	20A	Accessory power receptacle – center console 1, Accessory power receptacle-center console 2 (KD4)	F7DA
8	30A	Headlamp – left blow beam (TT4), Park lamp – left front (TT6), Body control module (Up to model year 2013)	F8DA
		Body control module: Park/Daytime running lamp – left (T4F) (From model year 2014 to 2015)	
		Body control module: Park/Daytime running lamp – Left (T4F), Daytime running lamp relay – left (T4A), Park/Daytime running lamp – left (T4A), Stop lamp – left (From model year 2016)	
9	30A	Headlamp – right blow beam (TT4), Park lamp – right front (TT6), Body control module (Up to model year 2013)	F9DA
		Body control module: Park/Daytime running lamp – right (T4F) (From model year 2014)	
10	30A	Door latch assembly – driver, Door latch assembly – left rear, Door latch assembly – passenger, Door latch assembly – right rear, Body control module, Fuel door lock actuator	F10DA
11	40A	Blower motor control module	F11DA
12	25A	Seat adjuster switches, Seat memory control module	F12DA
13	25A	Seat adjuster switches, Seat memory control module	F13DA
14	7.5A	Data link connector	F14DA
15	10A	Inflatable restraint sensing and diagnostic module	F15DA
16	10A	Rear compartment Lid release relay	F16DA
17	10A	HVAC controls, HVAC control module	F17DA
18	30A	(Diagnostic Provision) (without logistic mode relay 1) (Up to model year 2011)	F18DA
		Retained accessory power relay, Battery saver relay 1, Power supply transformer (For model year 2012)	
		(Diagnostic Provision) (without logistic mode relay 1) (For model year 2013)	
		F1DA, F4DA, F5DA, Battery saver relay 1 (From model year 2014)	

19	5A	Seat heating control module (KA1), Seat memory control module (A45)	F19DA
20	5A	Passenger presence detection module or Not used (Up to model year 2013)	F20DA
		Keyless entry control module (BTM) (From model year 2014)	
21	10A	Instrument cluster	F21DA
22	2A	Ignition switch (without BTM), Remote control door lock receiver (BTM)	F22DA
23	20A	Ambient light/sunload sensor, Center high mounted stop lamp, License plate lamp– Left, License plate lamp – right, Door courtesy lamp – driver, Instrument panel courtesy lamp – left, Instrument panel courtesy lamp – right, Door courtesy lamp –passenger, Dome/reading lamps -overhead console, Dome/reading lamps -rear, Door compartment flood lamp –driver, Door compartment flood lamp –passenger, Body control module, Windshield washer pump relay, Rear compartment lid release relay, Outside rearview mirror switch, Sunroof switch, Window switch – driver, Window switch - passenger, Sunroof tilt switch (Up to model year 2013)	F23DA
		Ambient light/sunload sensor (UTV), Center high mounted stop lamp, License plate lamp – left, License plate lamp – right, Fog lamp – left rear (without T94), Foglamp – right rear (T94), Dome/Reading lamps – front (C95), Dome/Reading lamps – rear (without C3U), Engine control module, Trailer lighting control module (VK0), Transmission control module (MM1), Windshield washer pump relay , Ignition main relay, Retained accessory power relay, Rear compartment lid release relay, Battery saver relay 1 (V9B), Battery Saver Relay 2 (V9B), Transmission shift lever position indicator (MM1), Transmission shift lever (MM1), Headlamp switch, Ignition mode switch (BTM), Content theft deterrent sensor disable switch (UTV), Liftgate control switch − Interior (TB5), Multifunction switch − instrument panel, Outside rearview mirror switch (without A45), Steering wheel controls switch − left (without W1Y), Sunroof switch (C3U or CF5), Window switch − driver (without AER), Window switch − left rear (AER), Window switch − right rear (AER), Window switch - passenger, Sunroof tilt switch (CF5), Sunroof sunshade switch (C34), Park brake control switch (J71), Fuel type select switch (KL7), Stop/Start select switch (KL9), Accessory power receptacle − 220V AC (KI7) (From model year 2014)	
24	20A	Side marker lamp – right front, Turn signal lamp – left front, Park/turn signal lamp – left (TT4), Park/turn signal lamp – right (TT4), Turn signal repeater lamp – left, Tail lamp – right outer, Tail lamp– right inner, Rear compartment courtesy lamp, Body control module, HVAC control module, Auxiliary power relay, Transmission shift lever position indicator (MDK or MH7), Transmission manual shift switch (MDK or MH7), Headlamp switch, Multi- function switch 1 – instrument panel, Multi-function switch 2 – instrument panel, Steering wheel controls switch – Left, Steering wheel controls switch – right, Park brake control switch, Parking assist on/off switch (UD7), Accessory power receptacle -110V AC (KI6), (Up to model year 2011)	F24DA
		Body control module: Battery saver relay 2, Multifunction switch 1 – instrument panel (For model year 2012)	
		Side marker lamp – right front, Turn signal lamp – left front, Park/turn signal lamp – left (T4A), Park/turn signal lamp – right (T4A), Turn signal repeater lamp – left, Tail lamp – right outer, Tail lamp– right inner, Rear compartment courtesy lamp, Body control module, HVAC control module, Auxiliary power relay, Transmission shift lever position indicator (M36 or MDK), Transmission manual shift switch (M36 or MDK), Headlamp switch, Multi- function switch 1 – instrument panel, Multi-function switch 2 – instrument panel, Steering wheel controls switch – Left, Steering wheel controls switch – right, Park brake control switch, Parking assist on/off switch (UD7), Accessory power receptacle -230V AC (KI7) (For model year 2013)	

		Body control module: Park/daytime running lamp – right (T4A), Tail lamp – right, tail lamp – auxiliary right, Stop lamp – right, Rear compartment courtesy lamp (68 or 69), Cargo lamp (35), HVAC control module, Battery saver relay (V9B), Battery saver relay 2 (V9B), Trailer ignition power relay (UVD or VK0), Key capture solenoid actuator (MM1), Transmission shift lever (MM1), Multifunction switch – instrument panel, Fuel type select switch (KL7), Stop/Start select switch (KL9) (From model year 2014)	
25	20A	Steering column lock control module or Not used (Up to model year 2014)	F25DA
	2A	Steering wheel controls switch – right (W1Y) (From model year 2014)	
26	20A	Accessory power Receptacle – Cargo	F26DA
R1	-	Rear compartment lid release relay	-
R2	-	Logistic mode relay 1 or Battery saver relay 1	-
R3	-	Auxiliary power relay	-

FUSE AND RELAY BOX IN LUGGAGE COMPARTMENT
(FUSE BLOCK – REAR BODY)

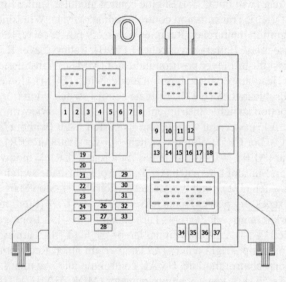

FUSE	VALUE	DESCRIPTION	OEM NAME
1	30A	Liftgate control module (Up to model year 2013)	F1RA
		Keyless entry control module (ATS or BTM) (From model year 2014)	
2	40A	Trailer lighting control module, Audio Amplifier (if fitted)	F2RA
3	40A	Trailer lightning control module or Not used	F3RA
4	-	Not used	F4RA
5	30A	Trailer connector, 20A also used	F5RA
6	7.5A	Heated steering wheel control module (UVD), Steering wheel air bag coil (UVD)	F6RA
7	30A	Reductant control module or Not used	F7RA
8	30A	Trailer connector (VK0)	F8RA
9	30A	Sunroof control module or Not used	F9RA
10	30A	Liftgate control module or Not used	F10RA
11	-	Not used	F11RA
12	10A	Exhaust particulate matter sensor, Nitrogen oxides sensor 1, Nitrogen oxides sensor 2 or Not used	F12RA
13	-	Not used	F13RA

14	-	Not used	F14RA
15	20A	Liftgate control module or Not used	F15RA
16	-	Not used	F16RA
17	5A	Reductant control module or Not used	F17RA
18	20A	Liftgate control module or Not used (Up to model year 2014)	F18RA
	10A	Reductant control module or Not used (From model year 2015)	
19	30A	Fuse F21UA, Battery saver PCB relay 2 or Not used (Up to model year 2013)	F19RA
	30A	Battery saver relay 2 (V9B) (From model year 2014)	
20	-	Not used	F20RA
21	7.5A	Trailer lighting control module (Up to model year 2011)	F21RA
	10A	Inside rearview mirror, Cruise control vehicle distance sensor, Suspension control module, Frontview camera module (From model year 2012)	
22	15A	Content theft deterrent sensor module (UTV) (Up to model year 2010)	F22RA
		Rear window sunshade motor (For model year 2011)	
	5A	Content theft deterrent sensor module (UTV) (From model year 2012 to 2015)	
	-	Not used (For model year 2016)	
	5A	Content theft deterrent sensor module (UTV) (For model year 2017)	
23	5A	Content theft deterrent sensor module (UTV) (Up to model year 2010)	F23RA
	10A	Rear differential clutch control module (From model year 2011)	
24	-	Not used	F24RA
25	-	Not used	F25RA
26	-	Not used	F26RA
27	-	Not used	F27RA
28	-	Not used	F28RA
29	30A	Battery saver PCB relay 2 (Up to model year 2011)	F29RA
	7.5A	Trailer lighting control module or Not used (From model year 2012)	
30	30A	Battery saver fuse (KR104B) or Not used	F30RA
31	10A	Suspension control module, Inside rearview mirror, Cruise control vehicle distance sensor, Frontview camera module or Not used	F31RA
32	-	Not used	F32RA
33	10A	Rear differential clutch control module or Not used	F33RA
34	30A	Sunroof control module or Not used	F34RA
35	30A	Sunroof control module or Not used	F35RA
36	-	Not used	F36RA
37	-	Not used	F37RA

Relays listed below are non-serviceable Printed Circuit Board (PCB) relays

RELAY	VALUE	DESCRIPTION	OEM NAME
-	-	Battery saver relay 2	-
-	-	Ignition 1 relay	-
-	-	Ignition 2 relay	-
-	-	Fuel fill door relay	-

The location for the following relays is not shown (fitted from Model year 2014):

RELAY	VALUE	DESCRIPTION	OEM NAME
-	-	Reductant control module relay 2	-
-	-	Trailer ignition power relay	-
-	-	Reductant control module relay 1	-

ADDITIONAL FUSE BOX IN ENGINE COMPARTMENT
(FUSE HOLDER – PARKING HEATER)

FUSE	VALUE	DESCRIPTION	OEM NAME
1	20A	Parking heater control module	F1
2	5A	Parking heater remote control receiver, Parking heater relay	F2
3	5A	Parking heater resistor, Parking heater control module – auxiliary	F3

ADDITIONAL RELAY BOX IN ENGINE COMPARTMENT
(RELAY BLOCK – UNDERHOOD)

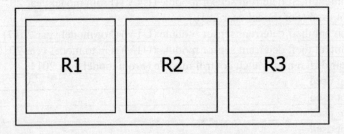

RELAY	VALUE	DESCRIPTION	OEM NAME
R1	-	Cooling fan left low speed relay or Cooling fan left medium speed relay	-
R2	-	Cooling fan right low speed relay or Cooling fan right medium speed relay	-
R3	-	Cooling fan speed control 2 relay or Cooling fan speed control relay	-

FUSE BOX ON THE STEERING COLUMN
(FUSE HOLDER – STEERING COLUMN)
(FROM MODEL YEAR 2012 TO 2013)

FUSE	VALUE	DESCRIPTION	OEM NAME
1	7.5A	Steering wheel heating control module	-

FUSE COLOR CODE INDEX

	5 A
	7.5 A
	10 A
	15 A
	20 A
	25 A
	30 A
	35 A
	40 A

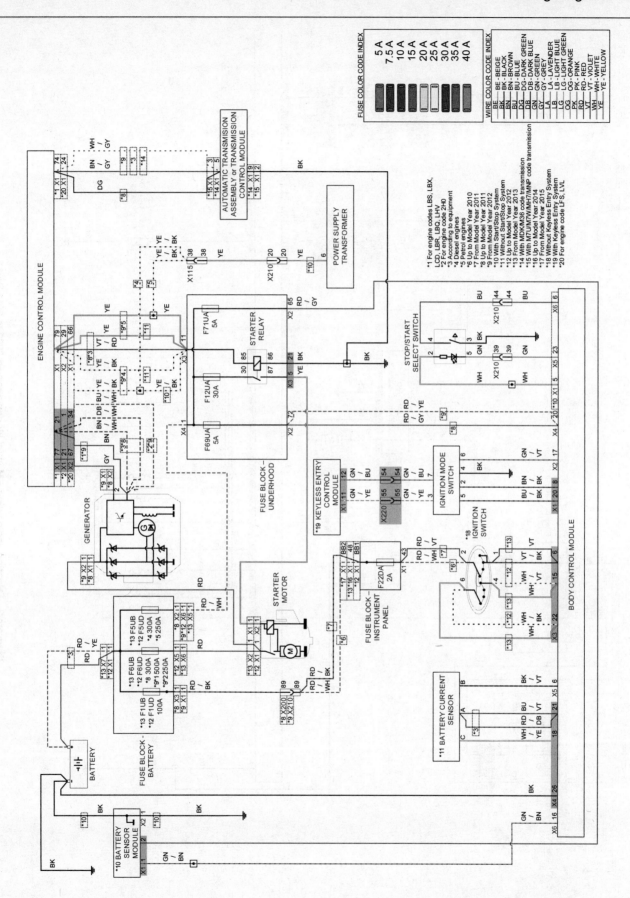

Diagram 1 – Starting and charging

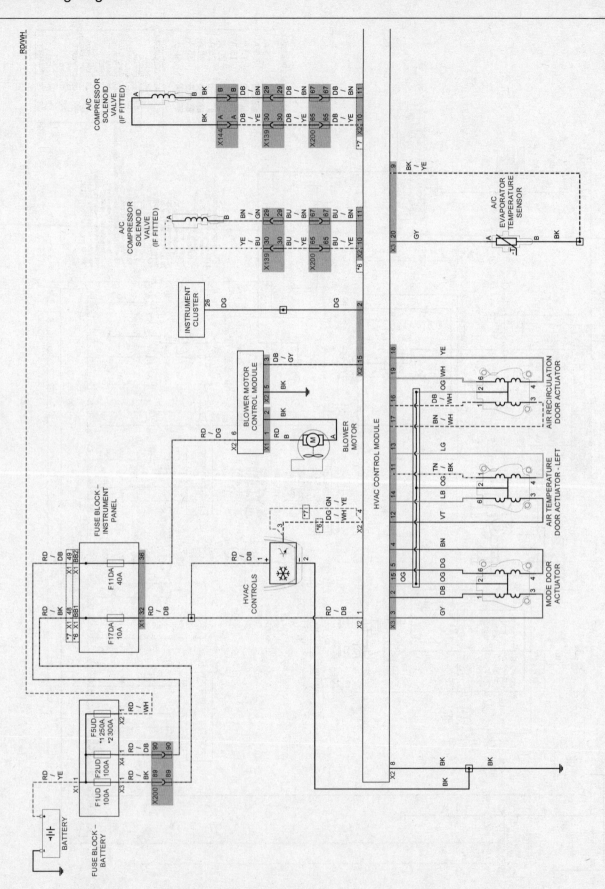

Diagram 2a – Heating and cooling – Manual air conditioning 2009 to 2011 Part 1

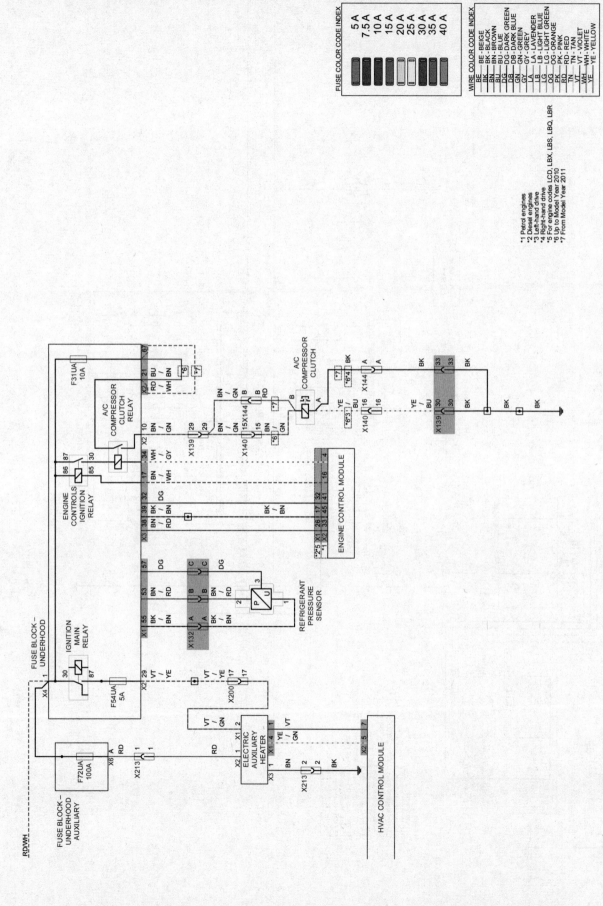

Diagram 2b – Heating and cooling – Manual air conditioning 2009 to 2011 Part 2

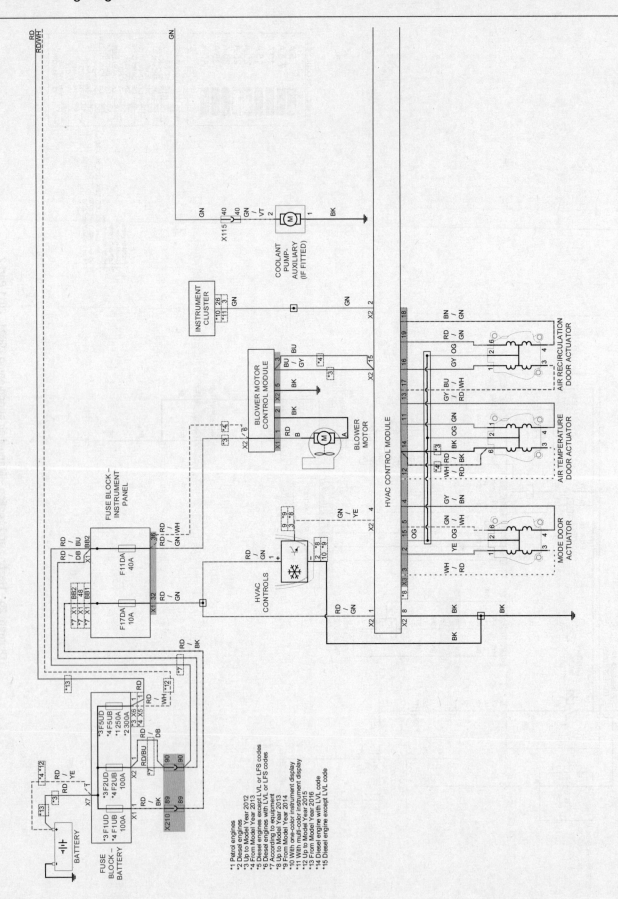

Diagram 3a – Heating and cooling – Manual air conditioning 2012 to 2017 Part 1

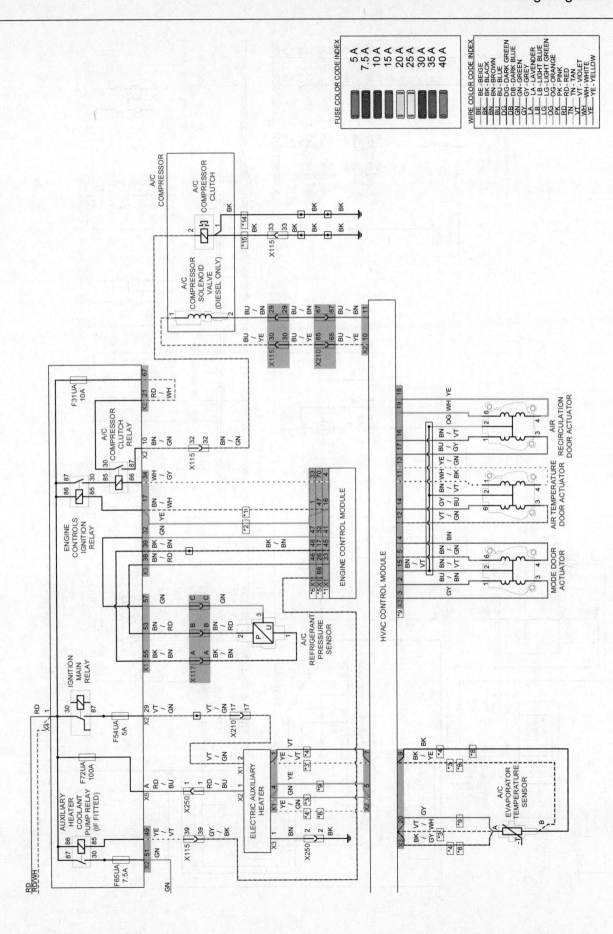

Diagram 3b – Heating and cooling – Manual air conditioning 2012 to 2017 Part 2

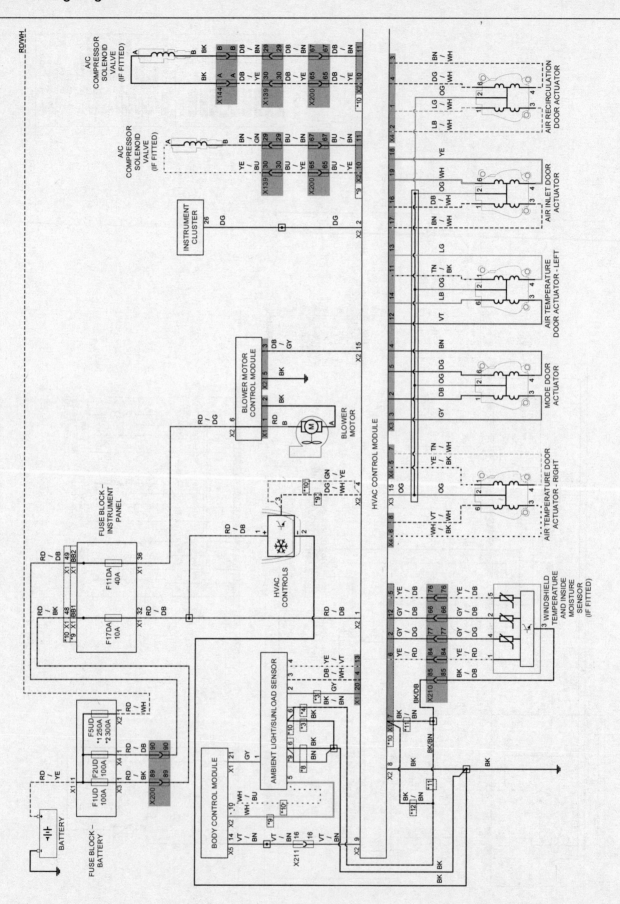

Diagram 4a – Heating and cooling – Automatic air conditioning 2009 to 2011 Part 1

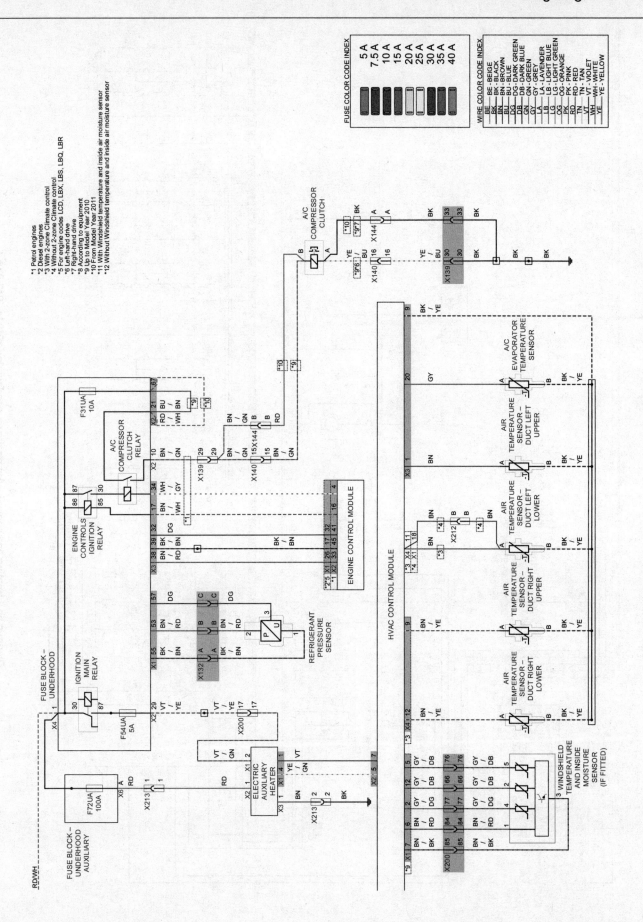

Diagram 4b – Heating and cooling – Automatic air conditioning 2009 to 2011 Part 2

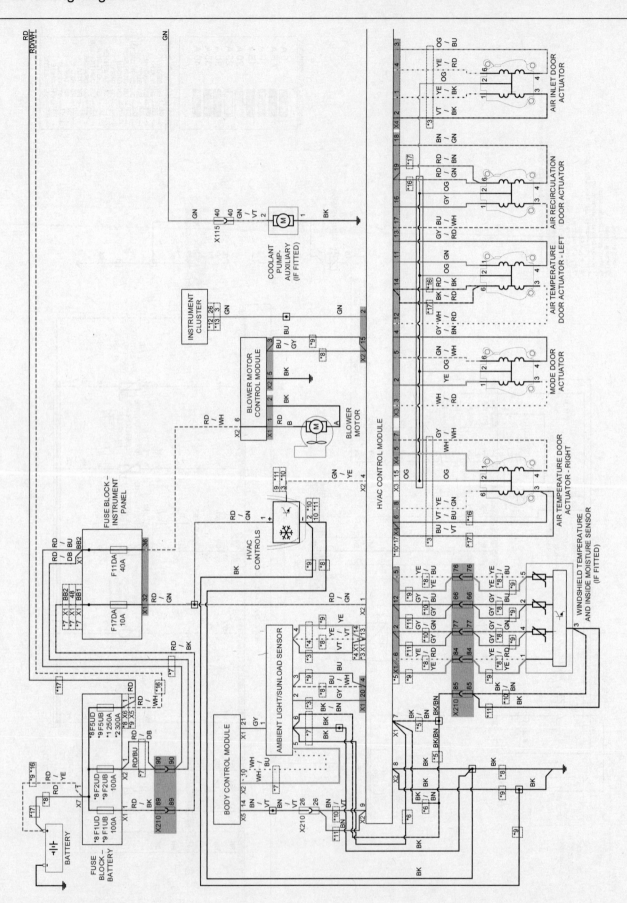

Diagram 5a – Heating and cooling – Automatic air conditioning 2012 to 2017 Part 1

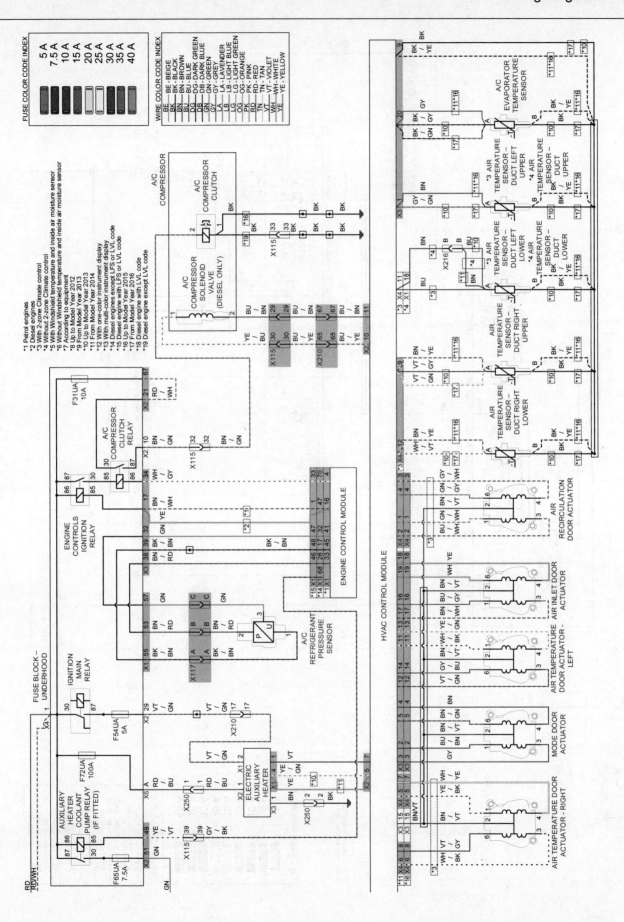

Diagram 5b – Heating and cooling – Automatic air conditioning 2012 to 2017 Part 2

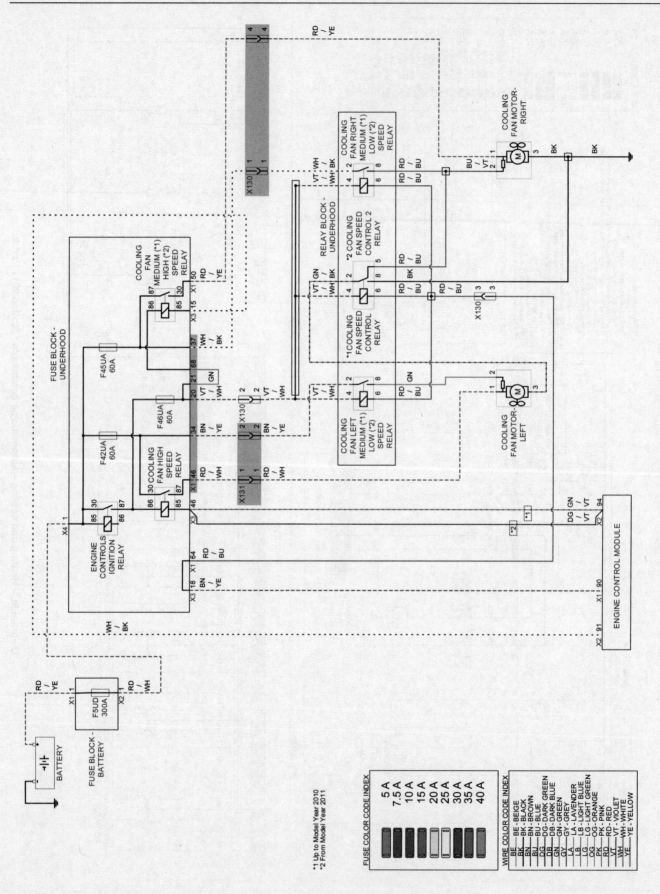

Diagram 6 – Cooling fans 2009 to 2011 Diesel

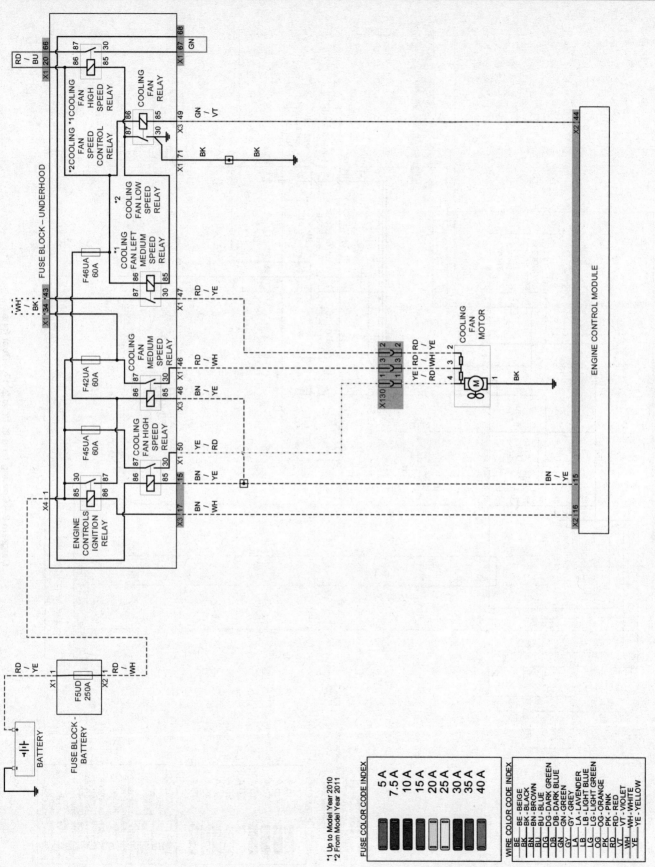

Diagram 7 – Cooling fans 2009 to 2011 Petrol

*1 Up to Model Year 2010
*2 From Model Year 2011

FUSE COLOR CODE INDEX

5 A
7.5 A
10 A
15 A
20 A
25 A
30 A
35 A
40 A

WIRE COLOR CODE INDEX

BE – BEIGE
BK – BLACK
BN – BROWN
BU – BLUE
DG – DARK GREEN
DB – DARK BLUE
GN – GREEN
GY – GREY
LA – LAVENDER
LB – LIGHT BLUE
LG – LIGHT GREEN
OG – ORANGE
PK – PINK
RD – RED
VT – VIOLET
WH – WHITE
YE – YELLOW

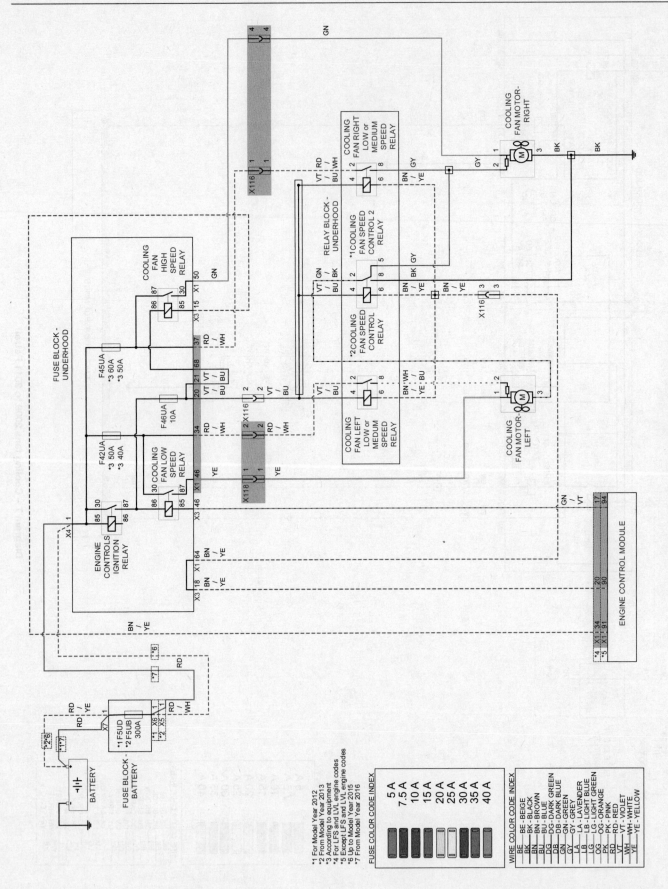

Diagram 8 – Cooling fans 2012 to 2017 – Dual fans

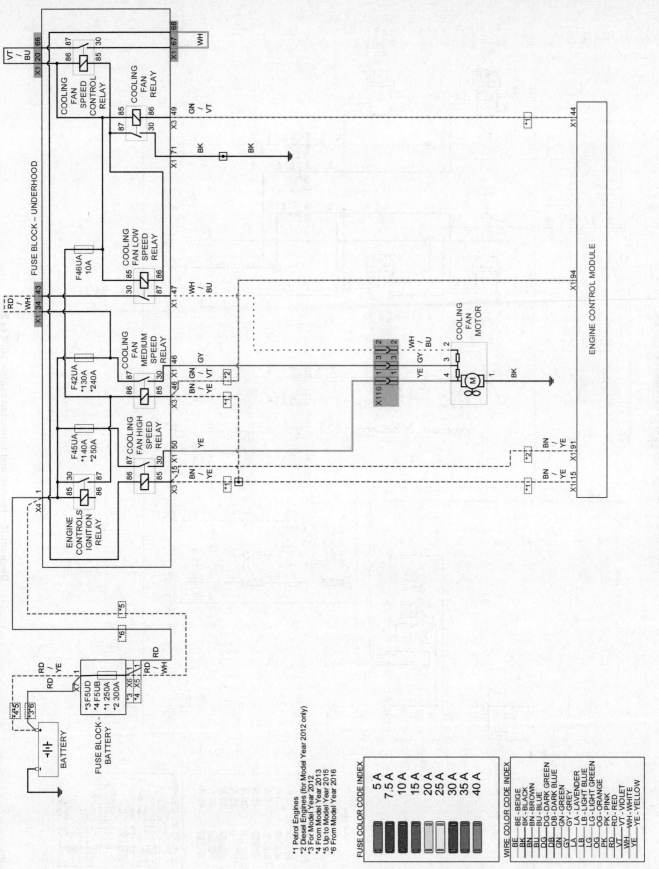

Diagram 9 – Cooling fans 2012 to 2017 – Single fan

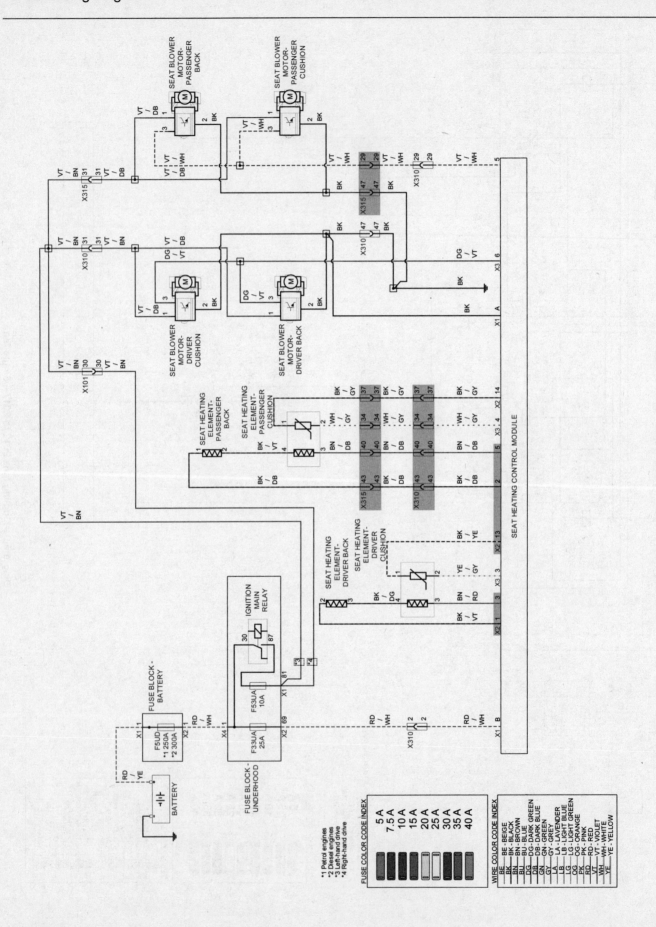

Diagram 10 – Heated and ventilated seats – 2009 to 2010

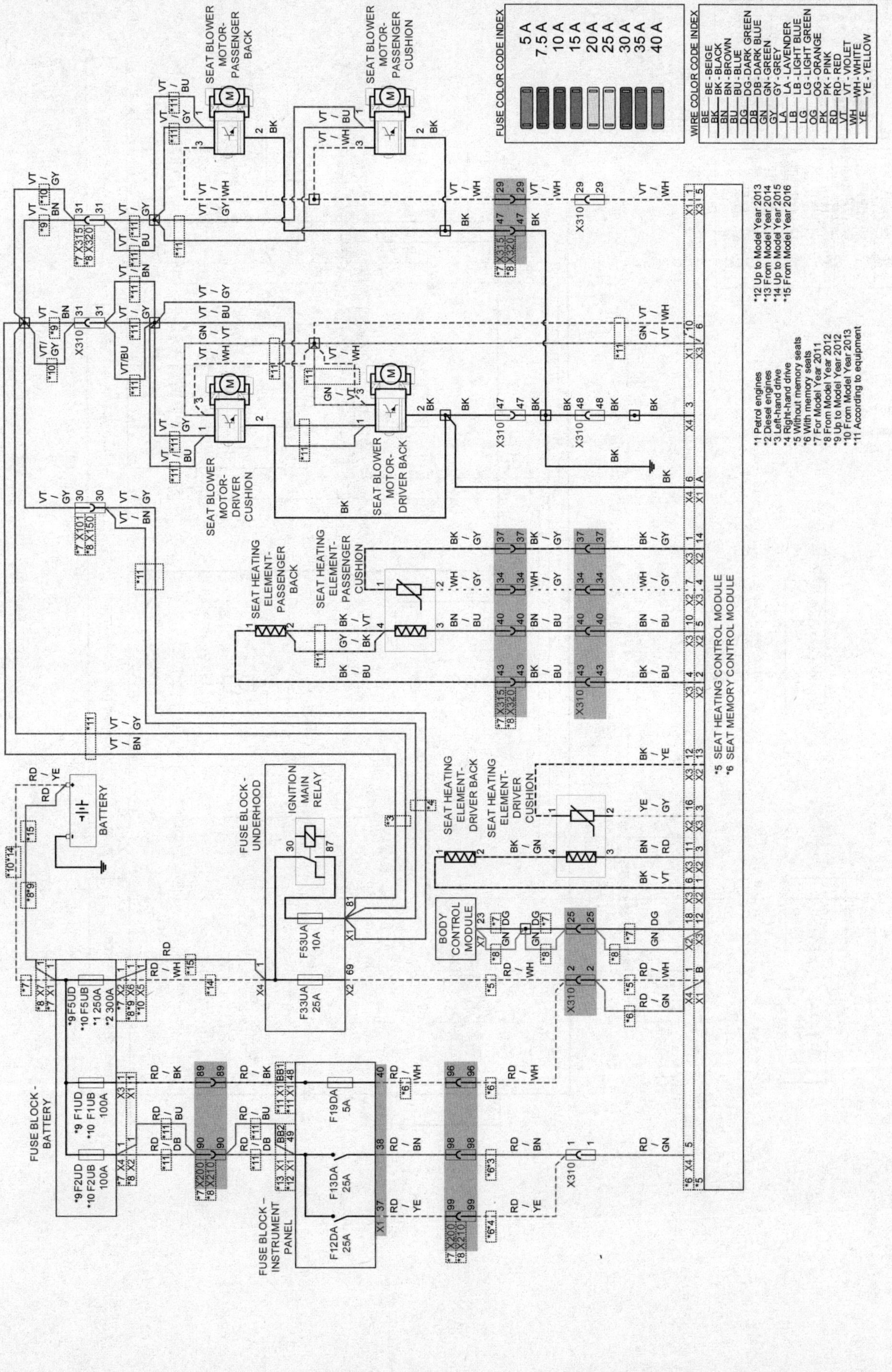
FUSE BLOCK - BATTERY
*9 F2UD
*10 F2UB
100A
*9 F1UD
*10 F1UB
100A
*9 F5UD
*10 F5UB
*1 250A
*2 300A
FUSE BLOCK - INSTRUMENT PANEL
F12DA
25A
F13DA
25A
F19DA
5A
FUSE BLOCK - UNDERHOOD
F33UA
25A
F53UA
10A
IGNITION MAIN RELAY
BATTERY
BODY CONTROL MODULE
SEAT HEATING ELEMENT-DRIVER BACK
SEAT HEATING ELEMENT-DRIVER CUSHION
SEAT HEATING ELEMENT-PASSENGER BACK
SEAT HEATING ELEMENT-PASSENGER CUSHION
SEAT BLOWER MOTOR-DRIVER CUSHION
SEAT BLOWER MOTOR-DRIVER BACK
SEAT BLOWER MOTOR-PASSENGER BACK
SEAT BLOWER MOTOR-PASSENGER CUSHION
*5 SEAT HEATING CONTROL MODULE
*6 SEAT MEMORY CONTROL MODULE
FUSE COLOR CODE INDEX
5 A
7.5 A
10 A
15 A
20 A
25 A
30 A
35 A
40 A
WIRE COLOR CODE INDEX
BE - BEIGE
BK - BLACK
BN - BROWN
BU - BLUE
DG - DARK GREEN
DB - DARK BLUE
GN - GREEN
GY - GREY
LA - LAVENDER
LB - LIGHT BLUE
LG - LIGHT GREEN
OG - ORANGE
PK - PINK
RD - RED
VT - VIOLET
WH - WHITE
YE - YELLOW
*1 Petrol engines
*2 Diesel engines
*3 Left-hand drive
*4 Right-hand drive
*5 Without memory seats
*6 With memory seats
*7 For Model Year 2011
*8 From Model Year 2012
*9 Up to Model Year 2012
*10 From Model Year 2013
*11 According to equipment
*12 Up to Model Year 2013
*13 From Model Year 2014
*14 Up to Model Year 2015
*15 From Model Year 2016

Diagram 11 – Heated and ventilated seats – 2011 to 2017

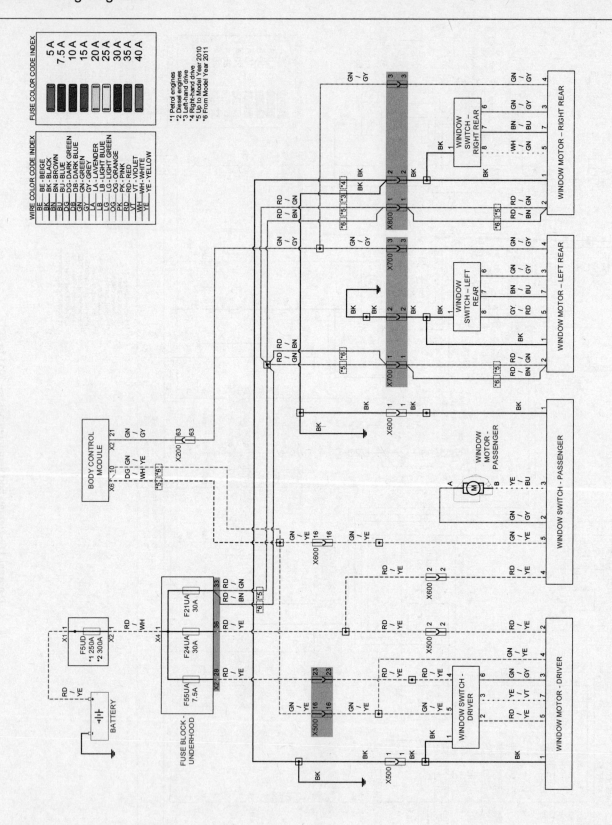

Diagram 12 – Power windows – with power rear windows 2009 to 2011

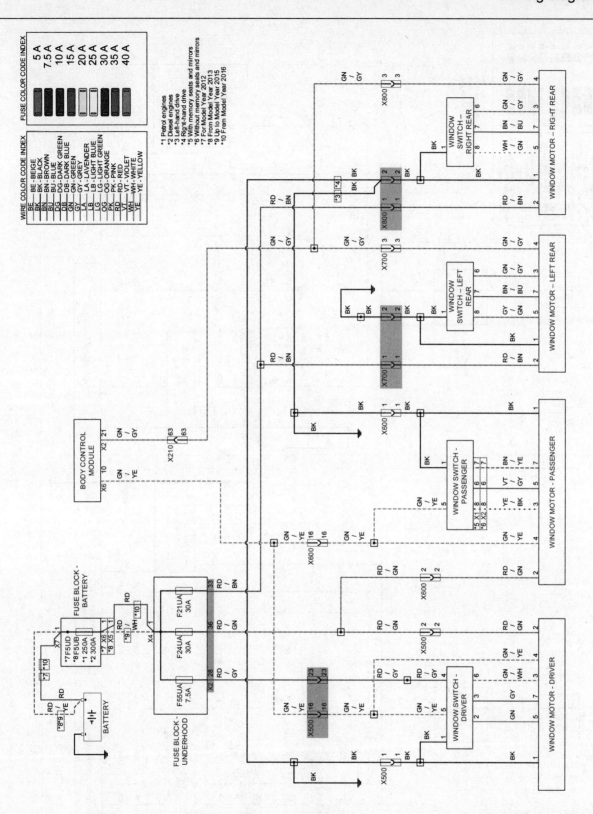

Diagram 13 – Power windows – with power rear windows 2012 to 2017

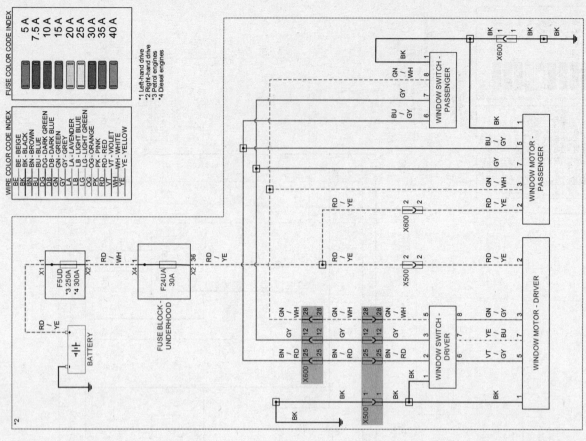

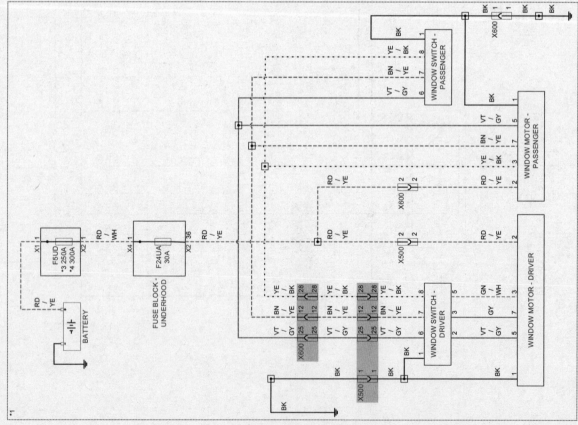

Diagram 14 – Power windows – without power rear windows 2009 to 2011

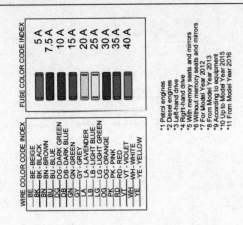

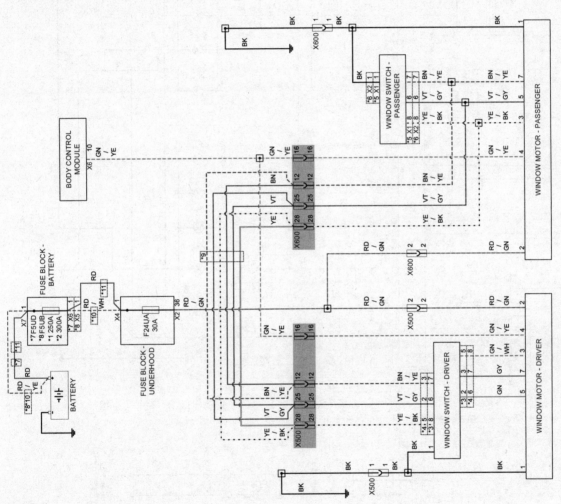

Diagram 15 – Power windows – without power rear windows 2012 to 2017

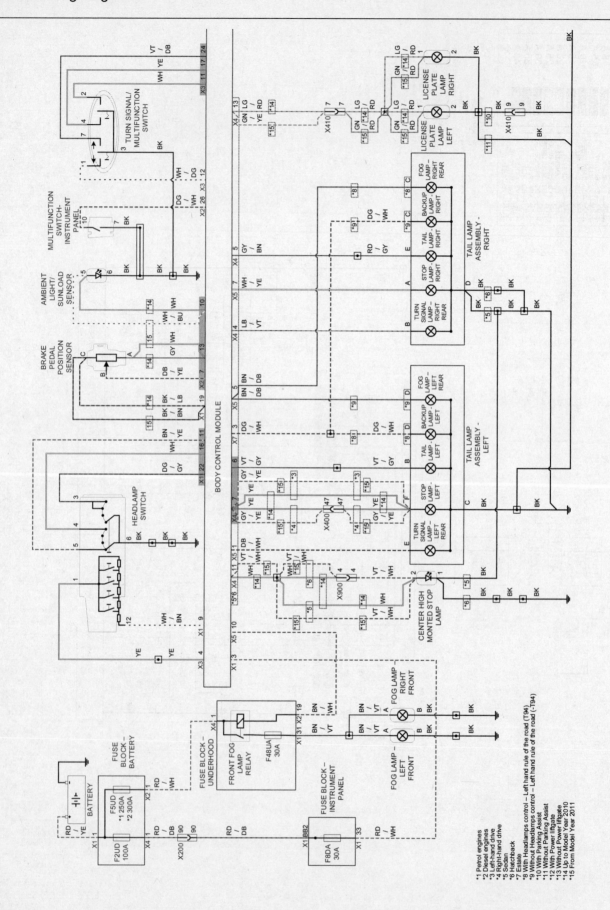

Diagram 16a – Fog lights, rear lights and light controls – 2009 to 2011 Part 1

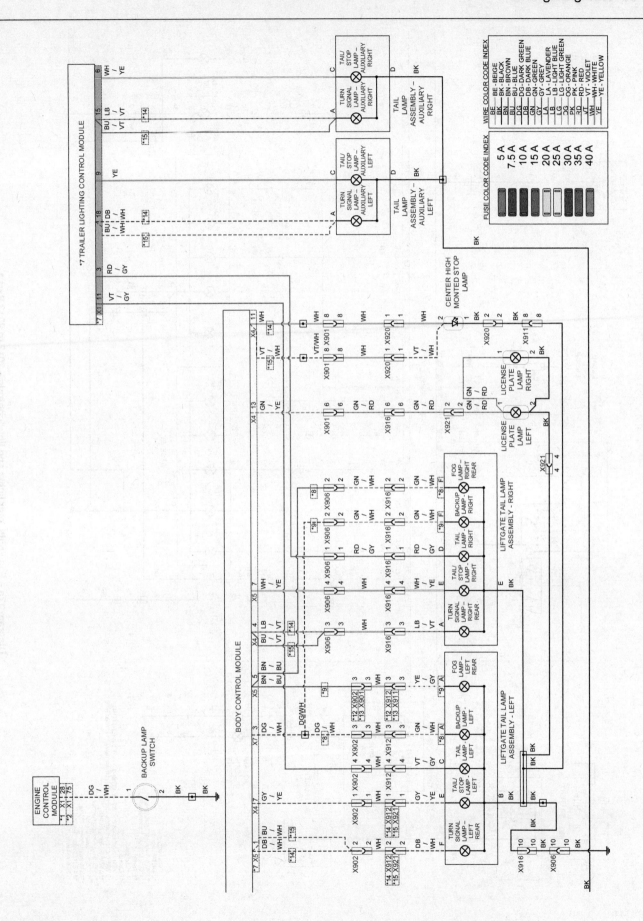

Diagram 16b – Fog lights, rear lights and light controls – 2009 to 2011 Part 2

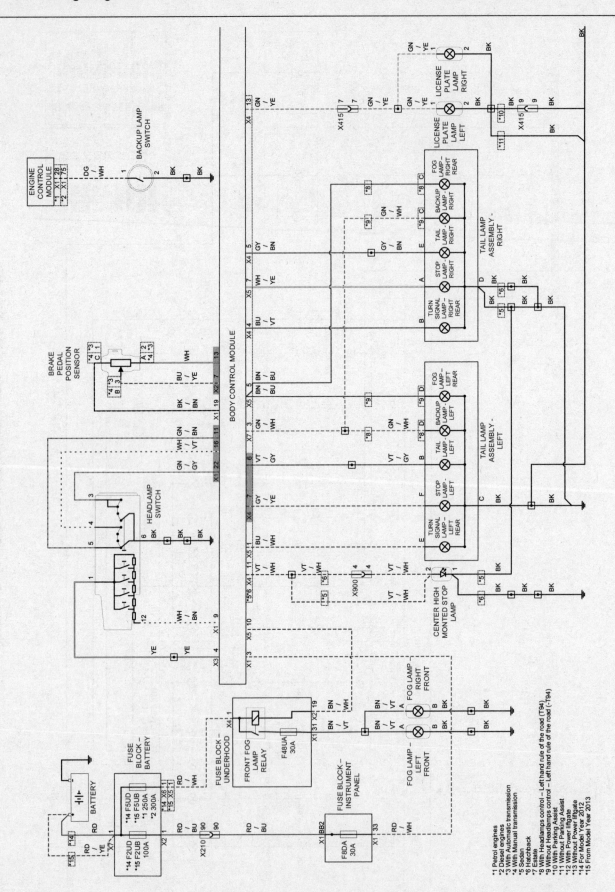

Diagram 17a – Fog lights, rear lights and light controls – 2012 to 2013 Part 1

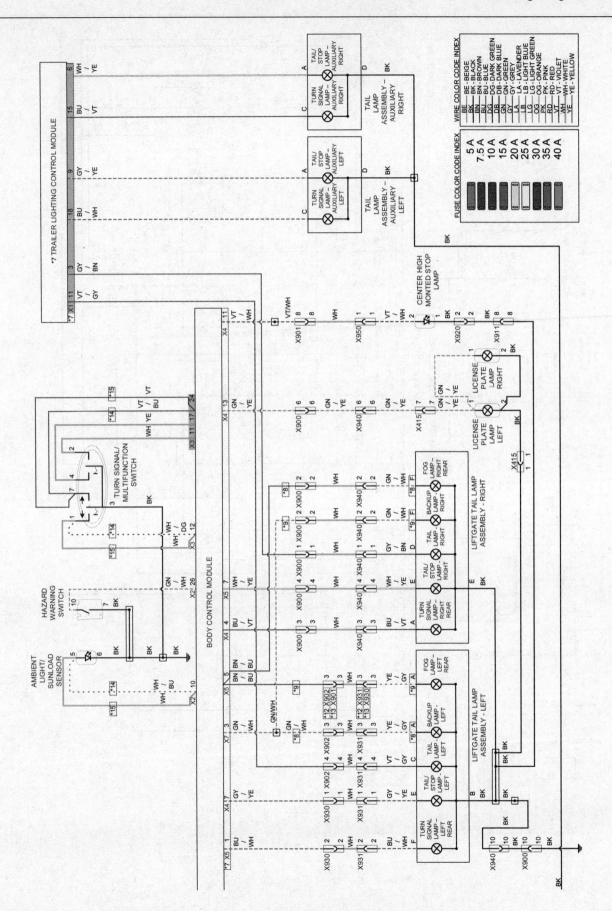

Diagram 17b – Fog lights, rear lights and light controls – 2012 to 2013 Part 2

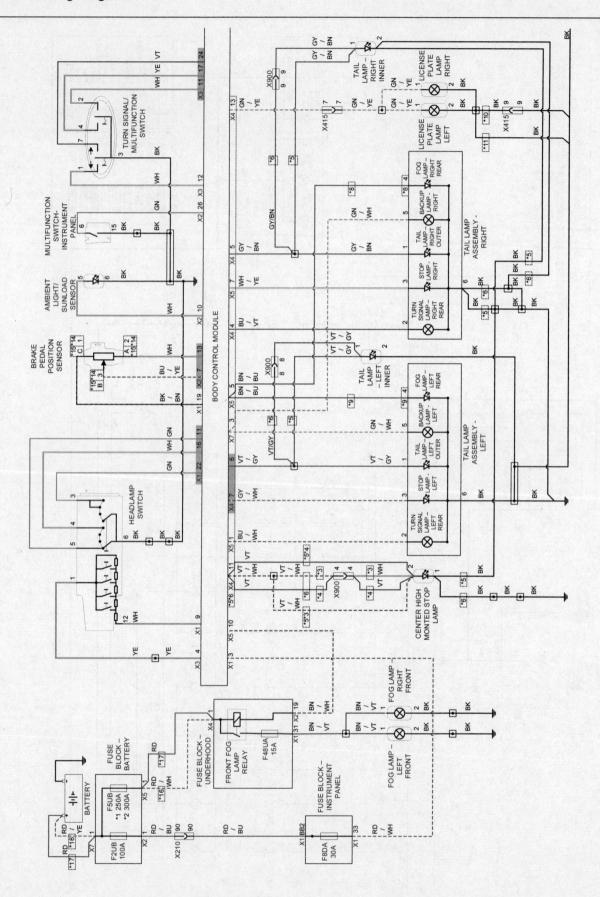

Diagram 18a – Fog lights, rear lights and light controls – 2014 to 2017 Part 1

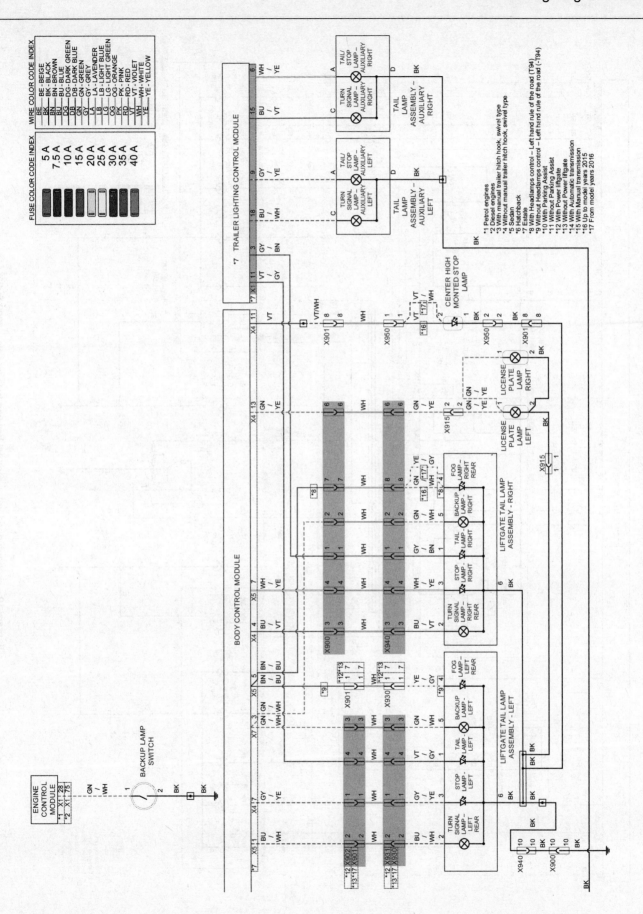

Diagram 18b – Fog lights, rear lights and light controls – 2014 to 2017 Part 2

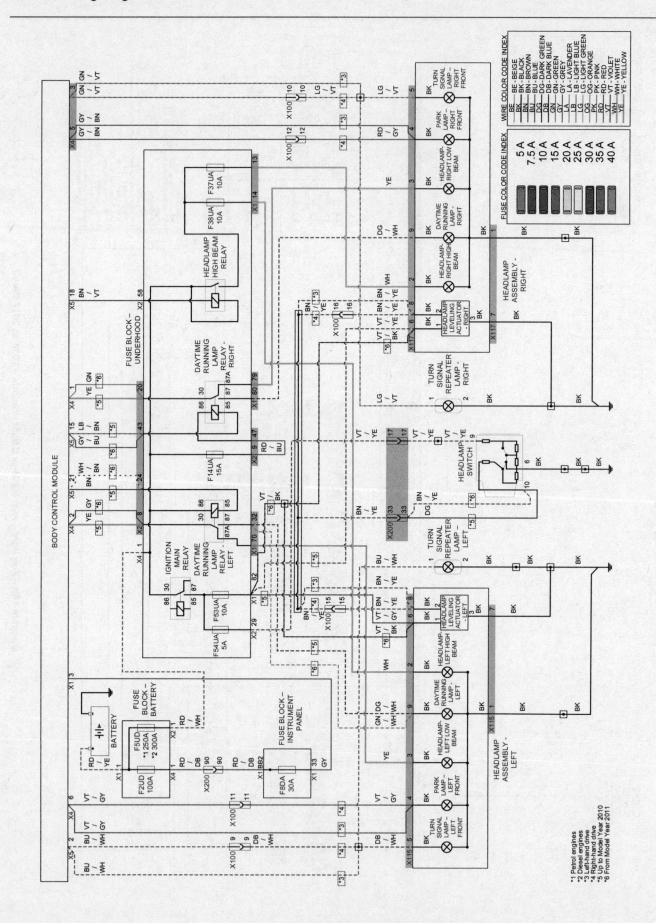

Diagram 19 – Halogen headlights, manual leveling turn signals – 2009 to 2011

*1 Petrol engines
*2 Diesel engines
*3 Left-hand drive
*4 Right-hand drive
*5 Up to Model Year 2010
*6 From Model Year 2011

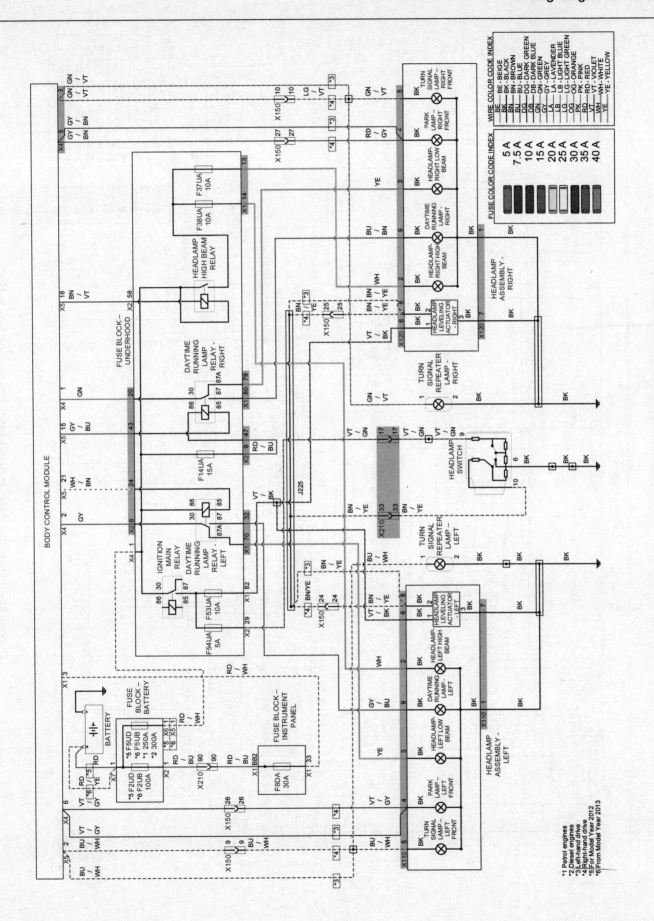

Diagram 20 – Halogen headlights, manual leveling turn signals – 2012 to 2013

*1 Petrol engines
*2 Diesel engines
*3 Left-hand drive
*4 Right-hand drive
*5 For Model Year 2012
*6 From Model Year 2013

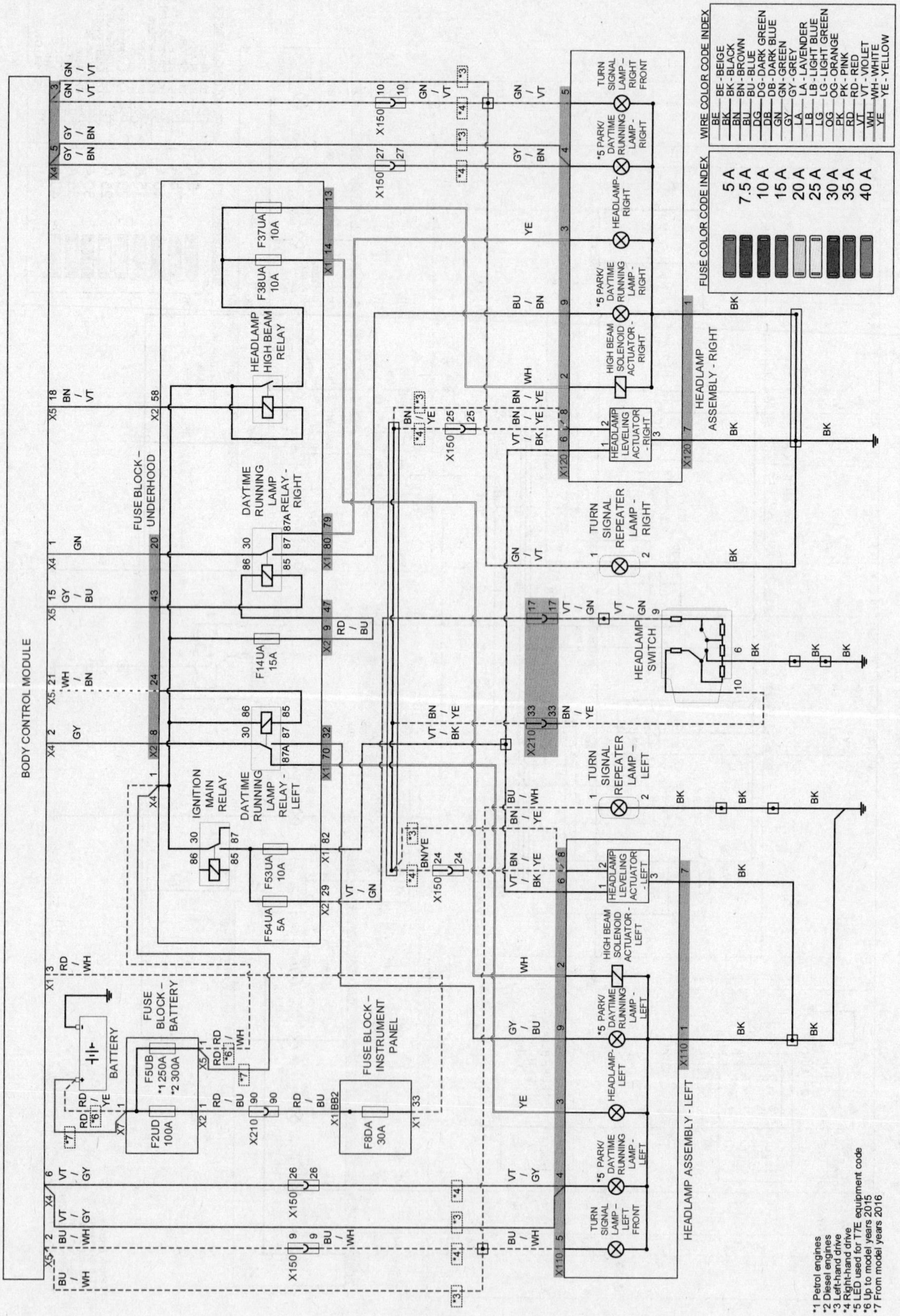

Diagram 21 – Halogen headlights, manual leveling turn signals – 2014 to 2017

*1 Petrol engines
*2 Diesel engines
*3 Left-hand drive
*4 Right-hand drive
*5 LED used for T7E equipment code
*6 Up to model years 2015
*7 From model years 2016

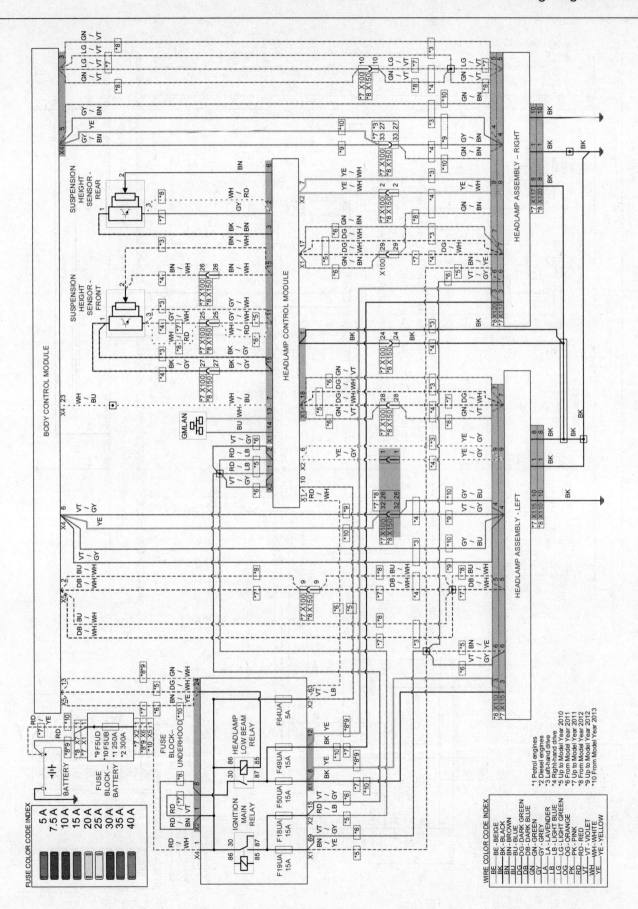

Diagram 22 – HID headlights, auto-leveling and adapting lighting – 2009 to 2013

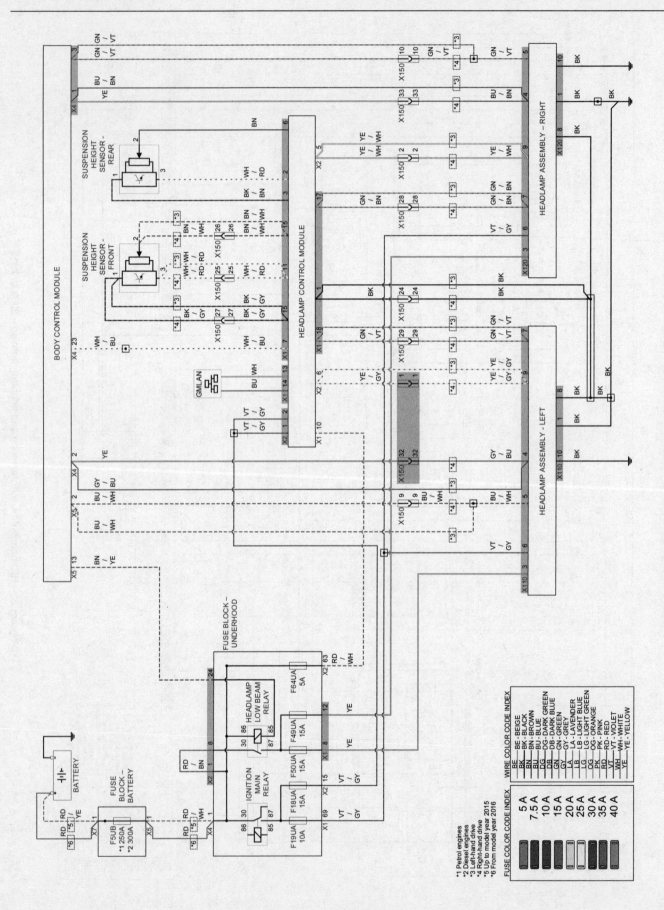

Diagram 23 – HID headlights, auto-leveling and adapting lighting – 2014 to 2017

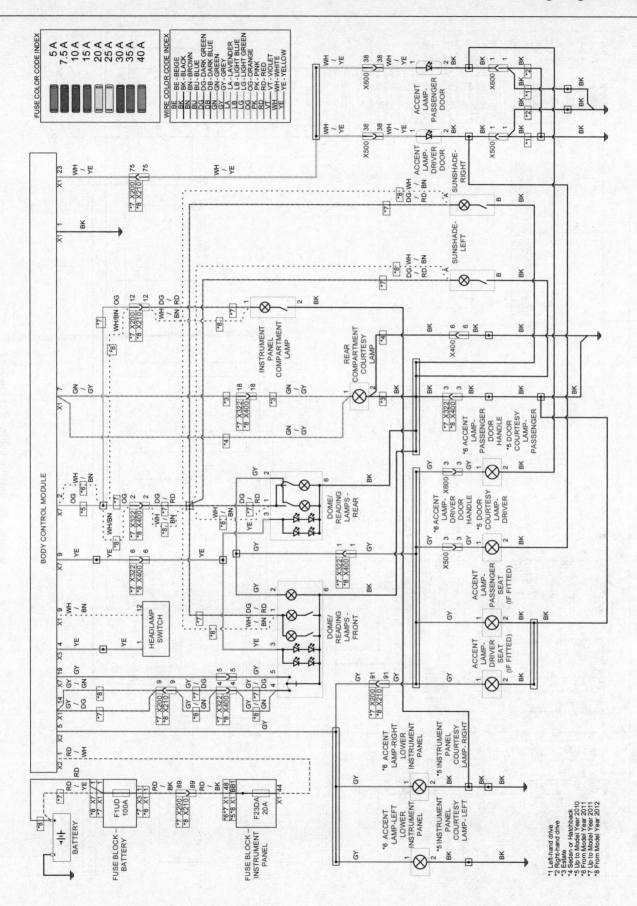

Diagram 24 – Interior lights – 2009 to 2012

*1 Left-hand drive
*2 Right-hand drive
*3 Estate
*4 Sedan or Hatchback
*5 Up to Model Year 2010
*6 From Model Year 2011
*7 Up to Model Year 2011
*8 From Model Year 2012

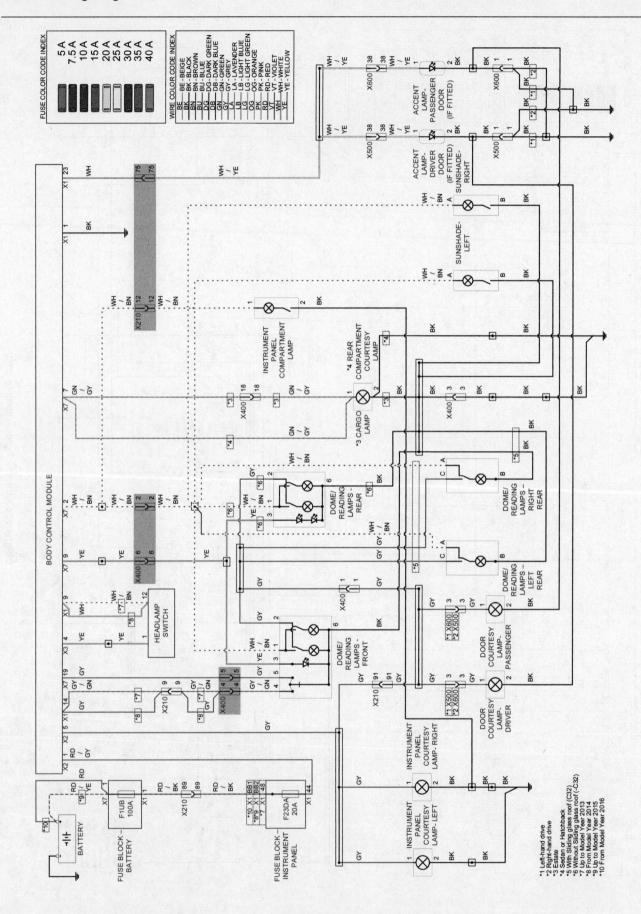

Diagram 25 – Interior lights – 2013 to 2017

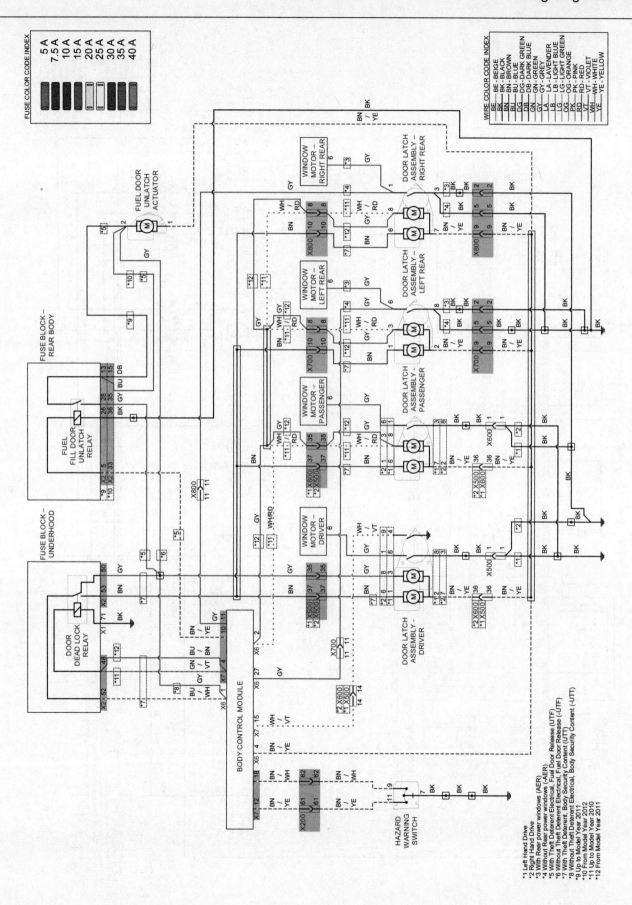

Diagram 26 – Door and fuel flap locks – 2009 to 2013

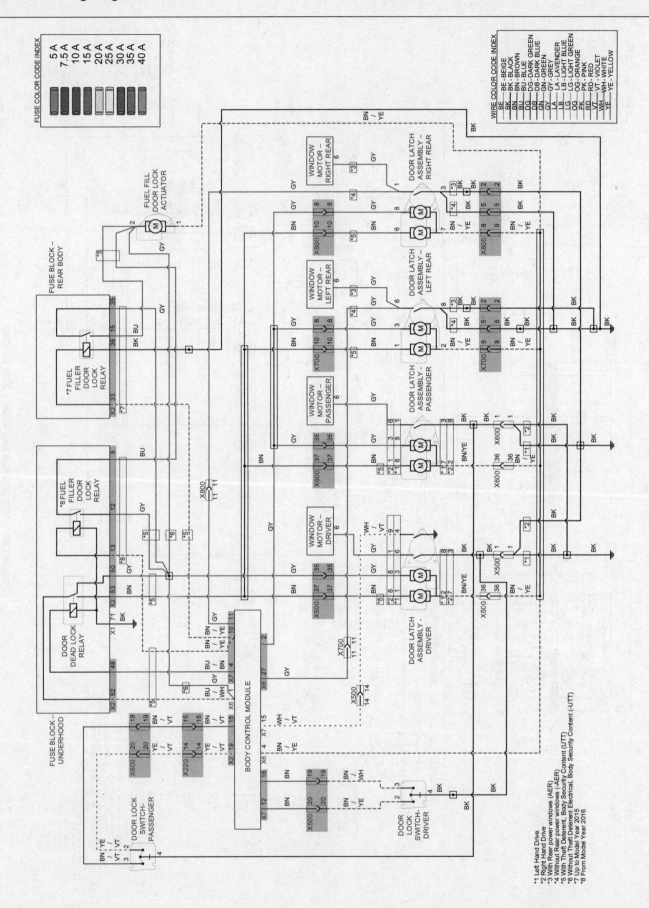

Diagram 27 – Door and fuel flap locks – 2014 to 2017

*1 Left Hand Drive
*2 Right Hand Drive
*3 With Rear power windows (AER)
*4 Without Rear power windows (-AER)
*5 With Theft Deterrent, Body Security Content (UTT)
*6 Without Theft Deterrent, Electrical, Body Security Content (-UTT)
*7 Up to Model Year 2015
*8 From Model Year 2016

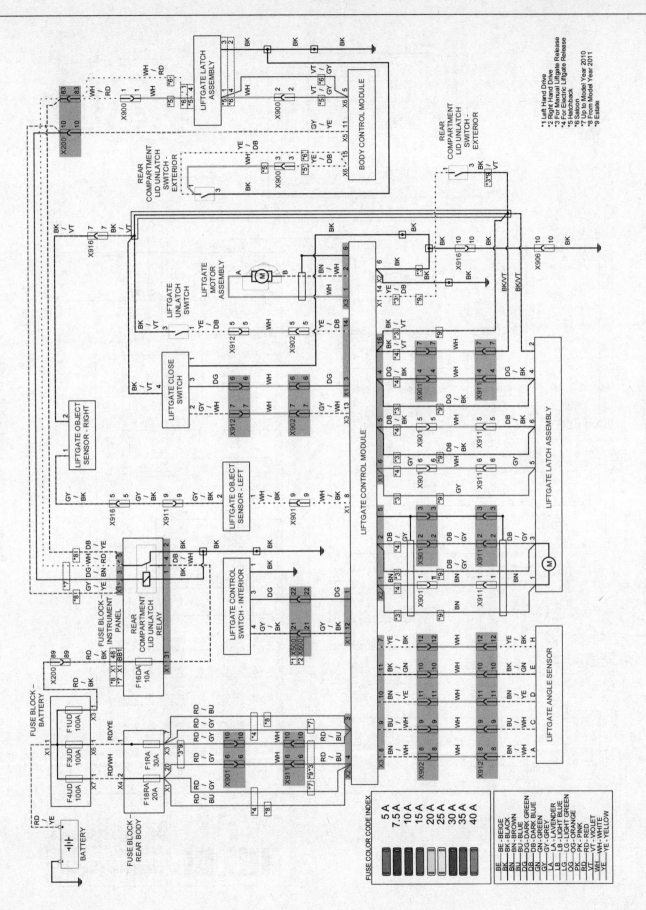

Diagram 28 – Liftgate lock – 2009 to 2011

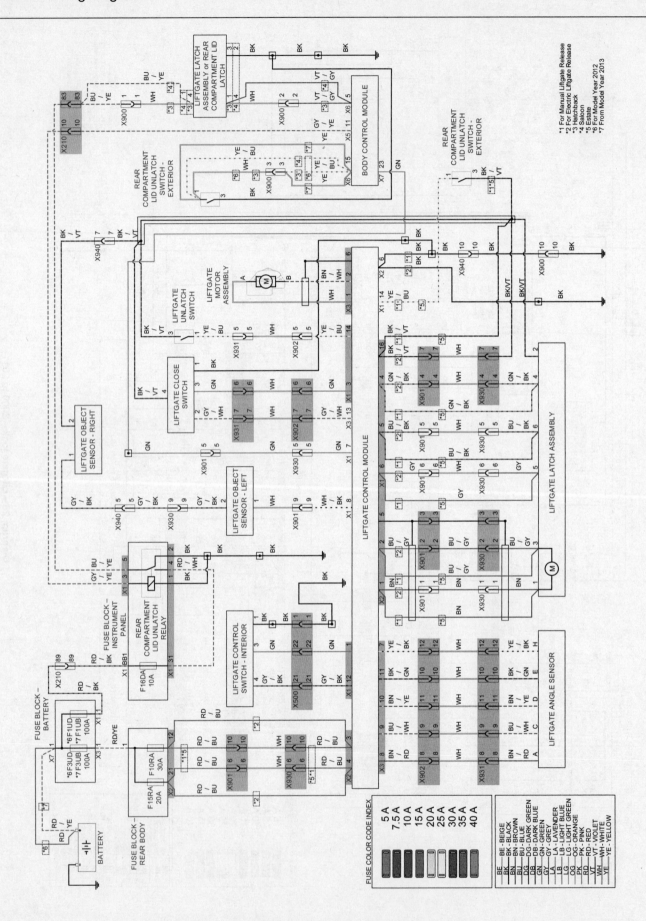

Diagram 29 – Liftgate lock – 2012 to 2013

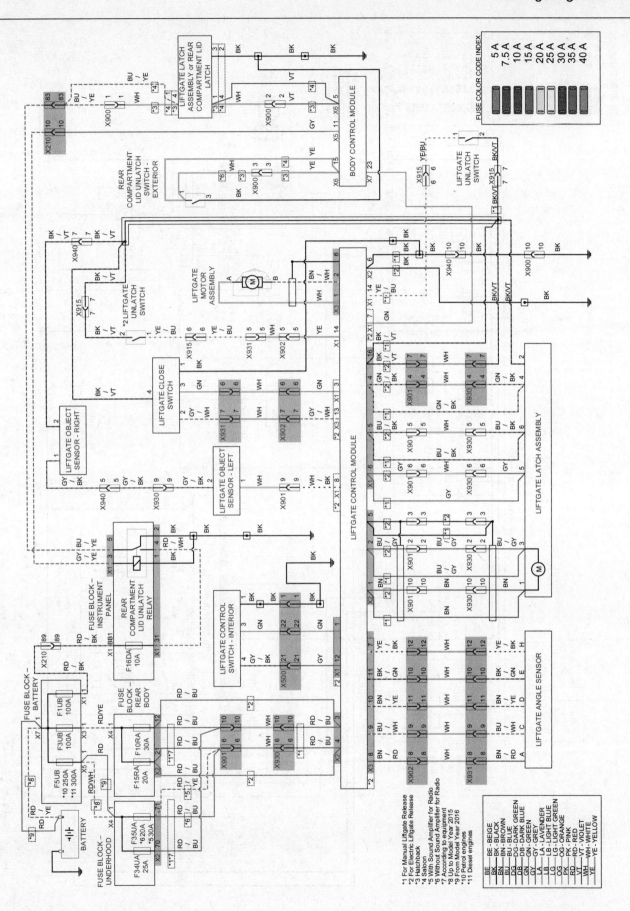

Diagram 30 – Liftgate lock – 2014 to 2017

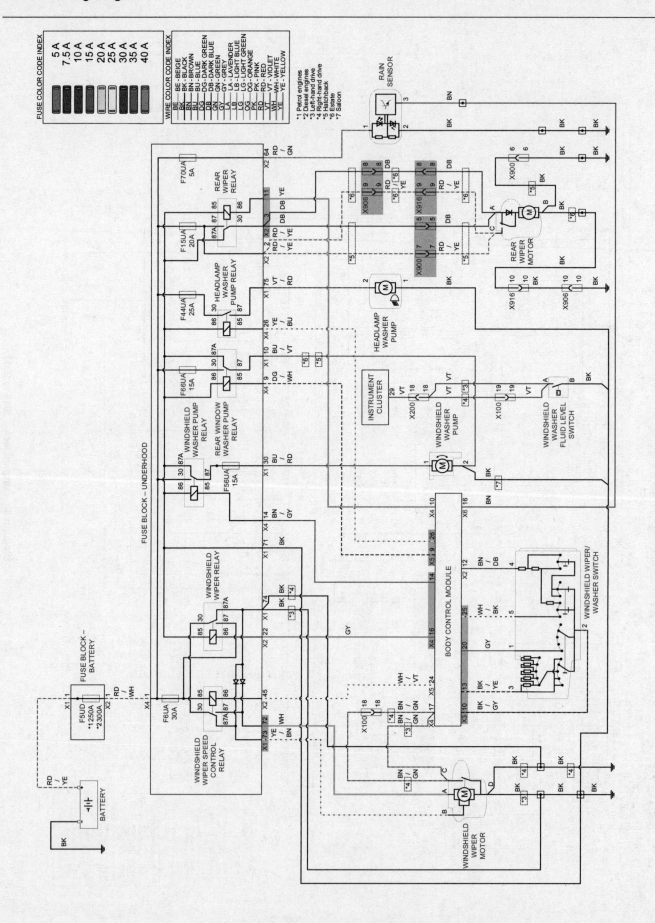

Diagram 31 – Wipers and washers – 2009 to 2011

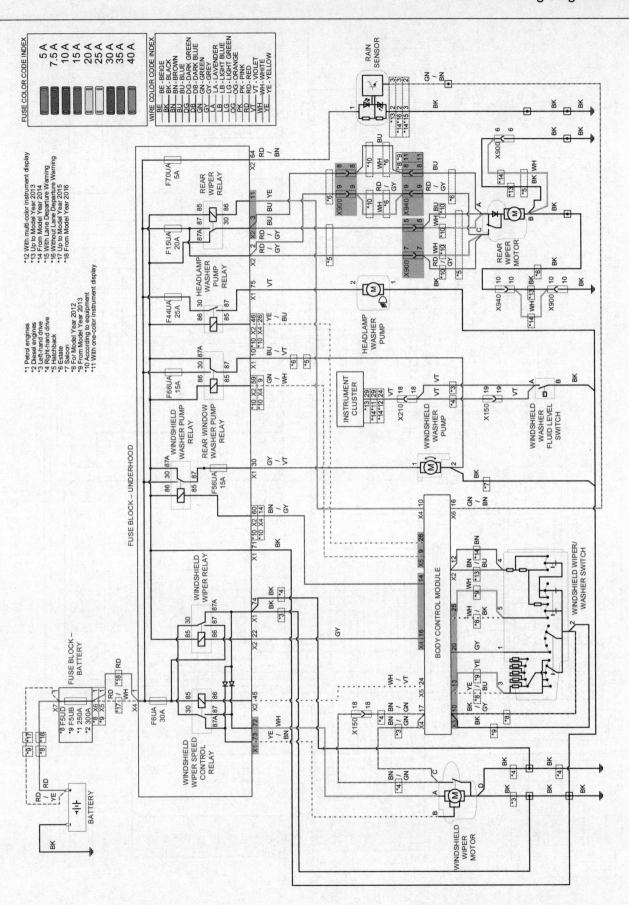

Diagram 32 – Wipers and washers – 2012 to 2017

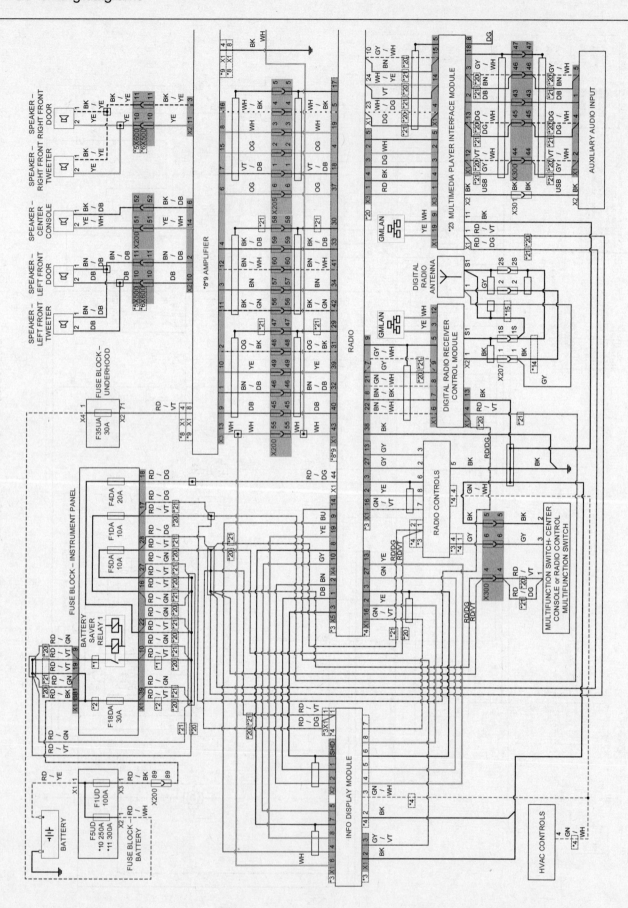

Diagram 33a – Radio, navigation and info display – 2009 to 2011 Part 1

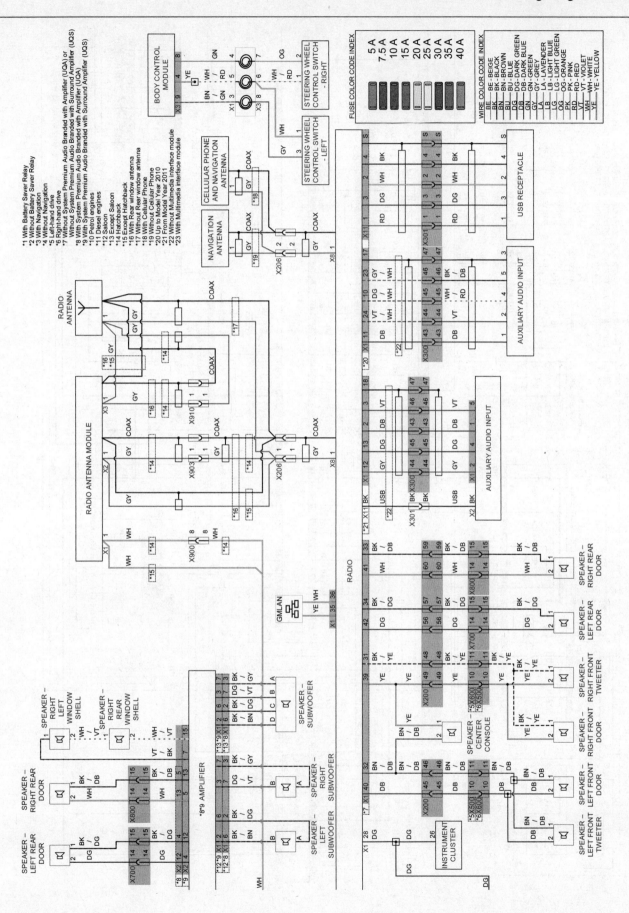

Diagram 33b – Radio, navigation and info display – 2009 to 2011 Part 2

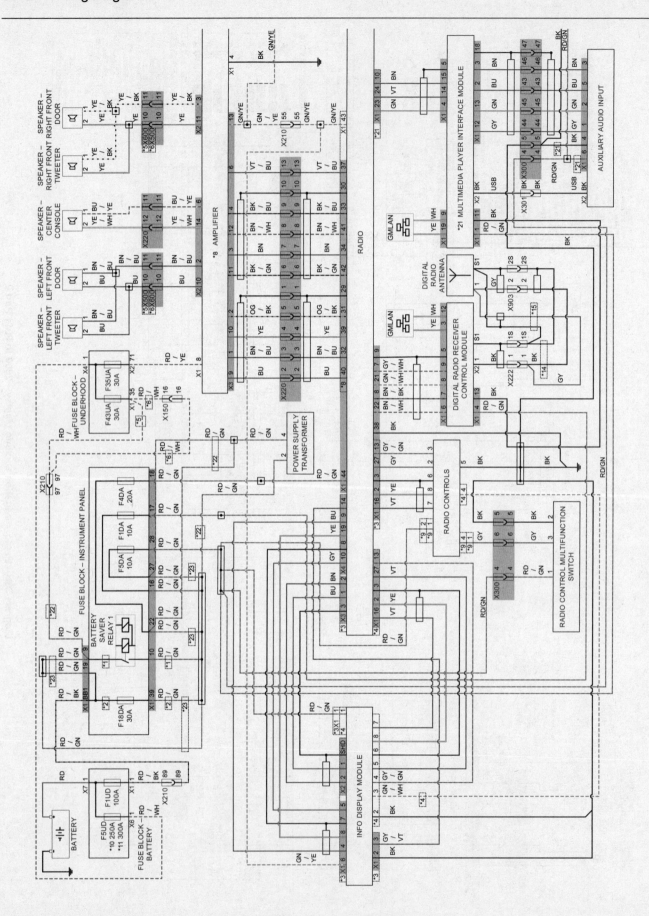

Diagram 34a – Radio, navigation and info display – 2012 Part 1

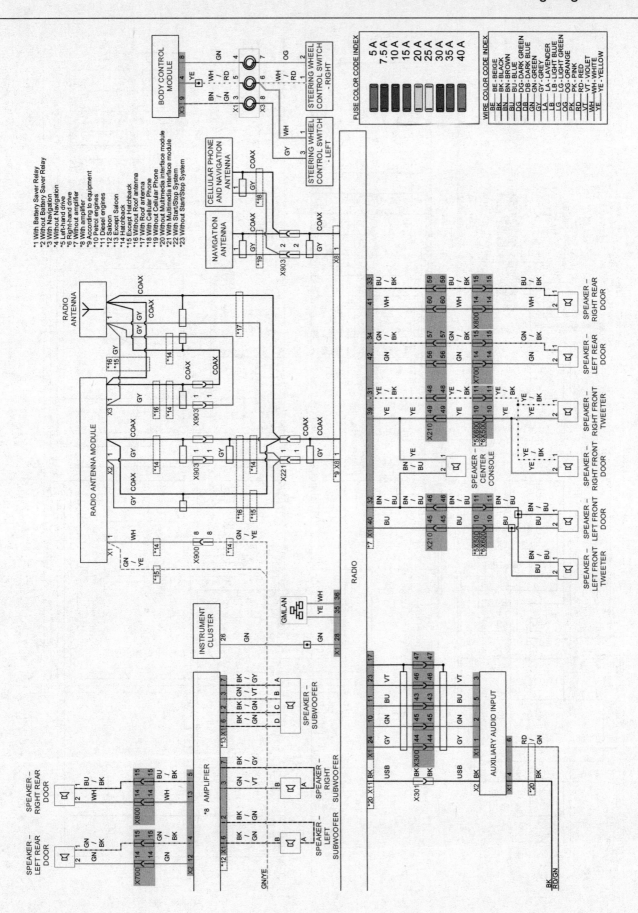

Diagram 34b – Radio, navigation and info display – 2012 Part 2

FUSE COLOR CODE INDEX

5 A
7.5 A
10 A
15 A
20 A
25 A
30 A
35 A
40 A

WIRE COLOR CODE INDEX
BE - BEIGE
BK - BLACK
BN - BROWN
BU - BLUE
DG - DARK GREEN
DB - DARK BLUE
GN - GREEN
GY - GREY
LA - LAVENDER
LB - LIGHT BLUE
LG - LIGHT GREEN
OG - ORANGE
PK - PINK
RD - RED
VT - VIOLET
WH - WHITE
YE - YELLOW

*1 With Battery Saver Relay
*2 Without Battery Saver Relay
*3 With Navigation
*4 Without Navigation
*5 Left-hand drive
*6 Right-hand drive
*7 Without amplifier
*8 With amplifier
*9 According to equipment
*10 Petrol engines
*11 Diesel engines
*12 Saloon
*13 Except Saloon
*14 Hatchback
*15 Except Hatchback
*16 Without Roof antenna
*17 With Roof antenna
*18 Without Cellular Phone
*19 With Cellular Phone
*20 Without Multimedia interface module
*21 With Multimedia interface module
*22 With Start/Stop System
*23 Without Start/Stop System

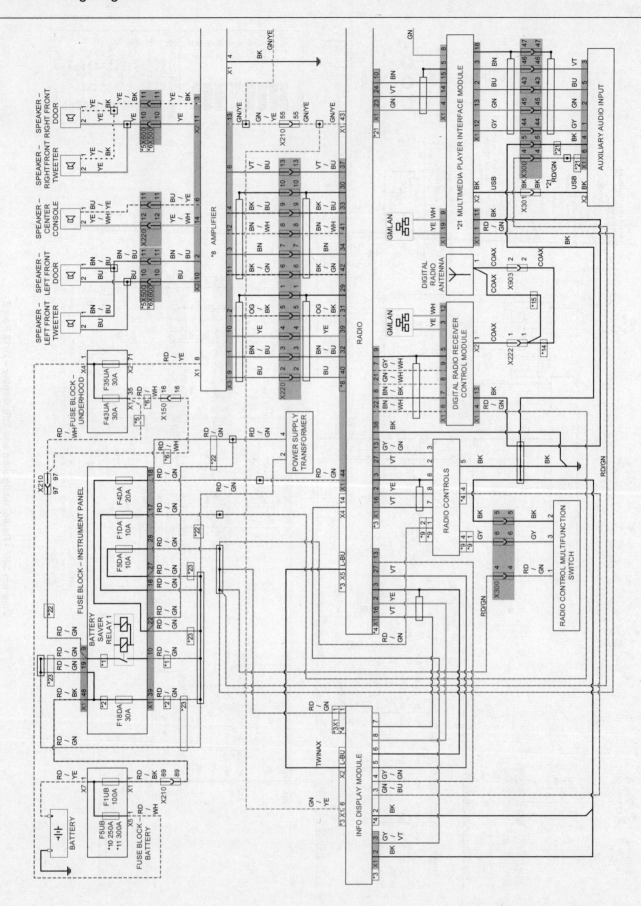

Diagram 35a – Radio, navigation and info display – 2013 Part 1

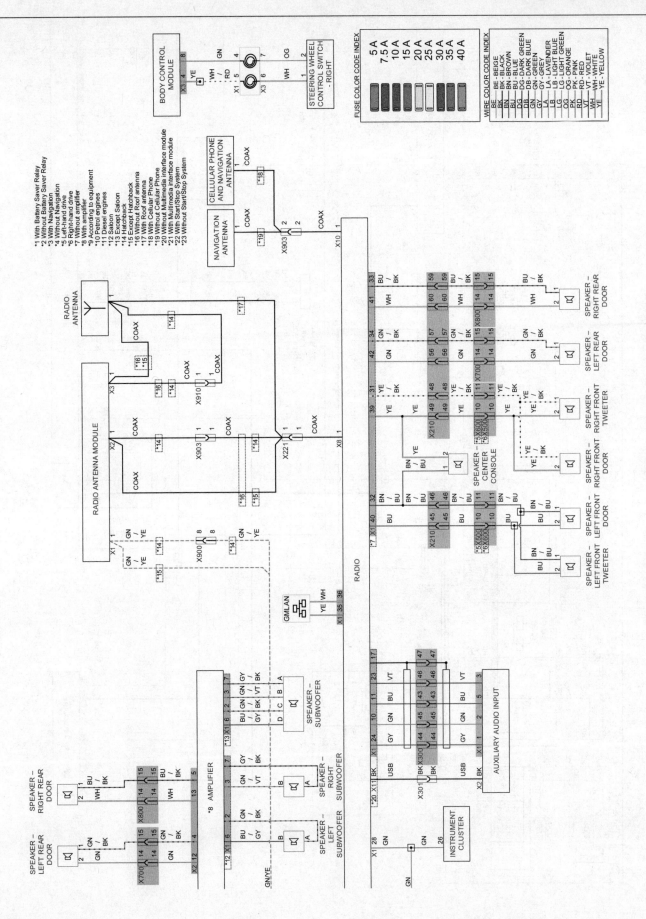

Diagram 35b – Radio, navigation and info display – 2013 Part 2

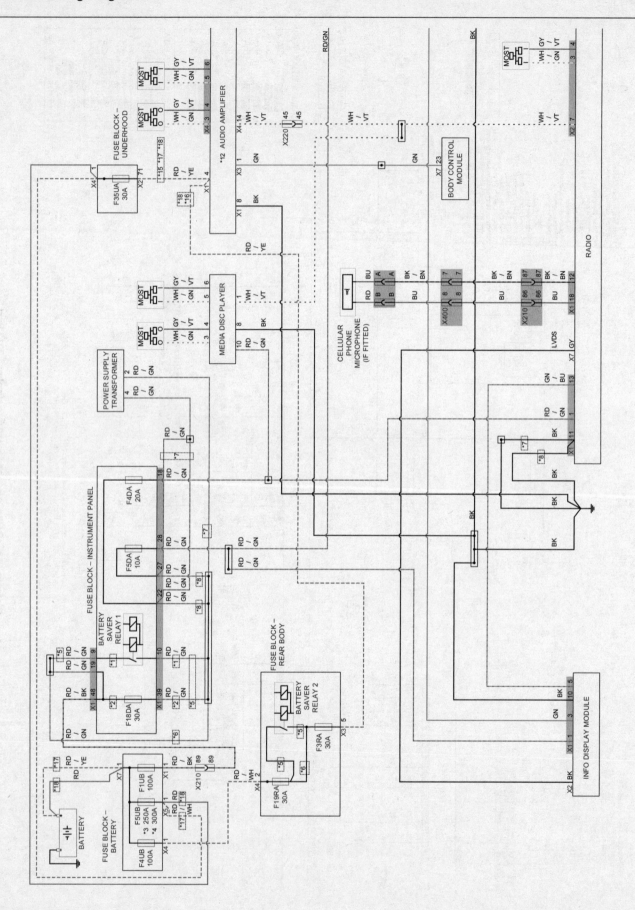

Diagram 36a – Information and sound system – 2014 to 2017 IO3 or IO7 Part 1

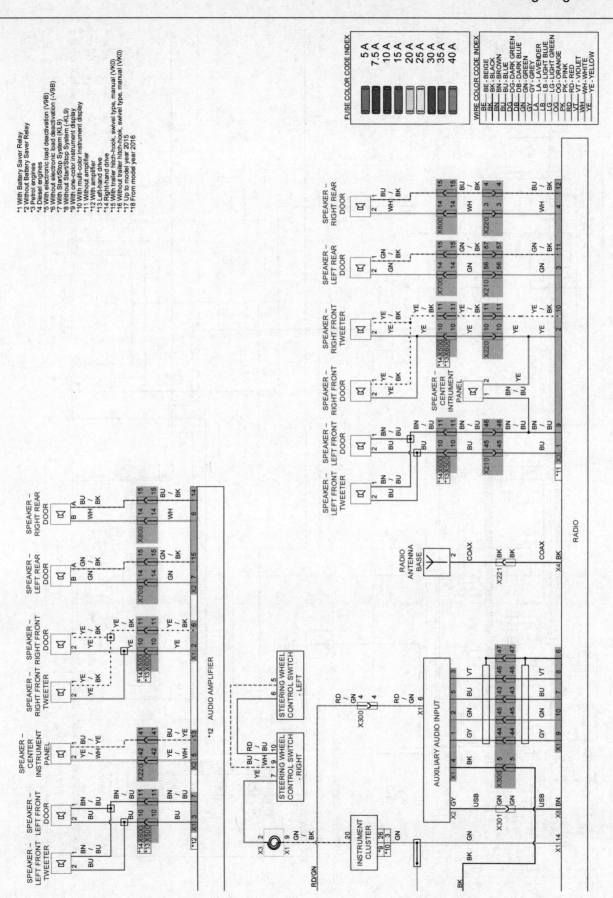

Diagram 36b – Information and sound system – 2014 to 2017 IO3 or IO7 Part 2

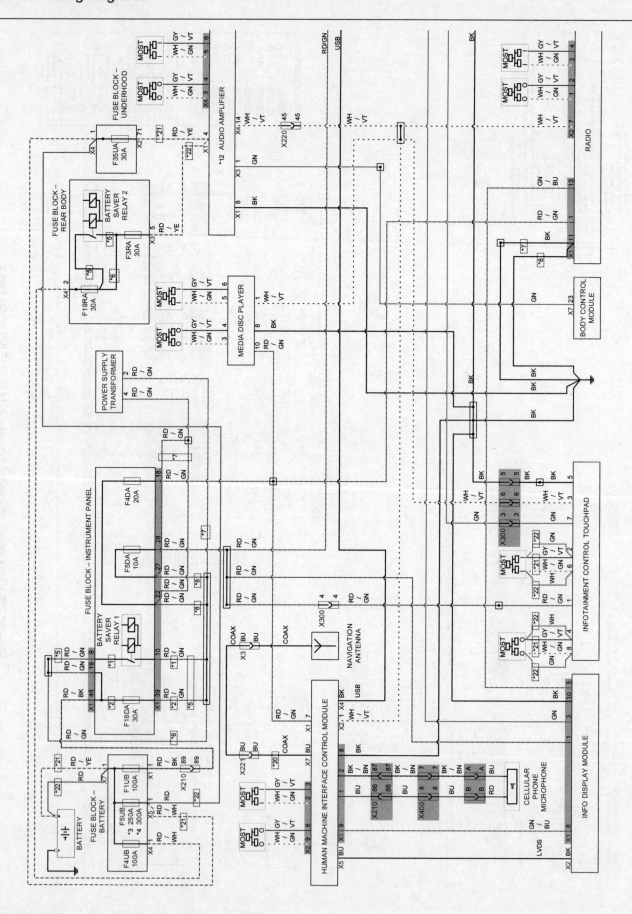

Diagram 37a – Information and sound system – 2014 to 2017 I05 or I06 Part 1

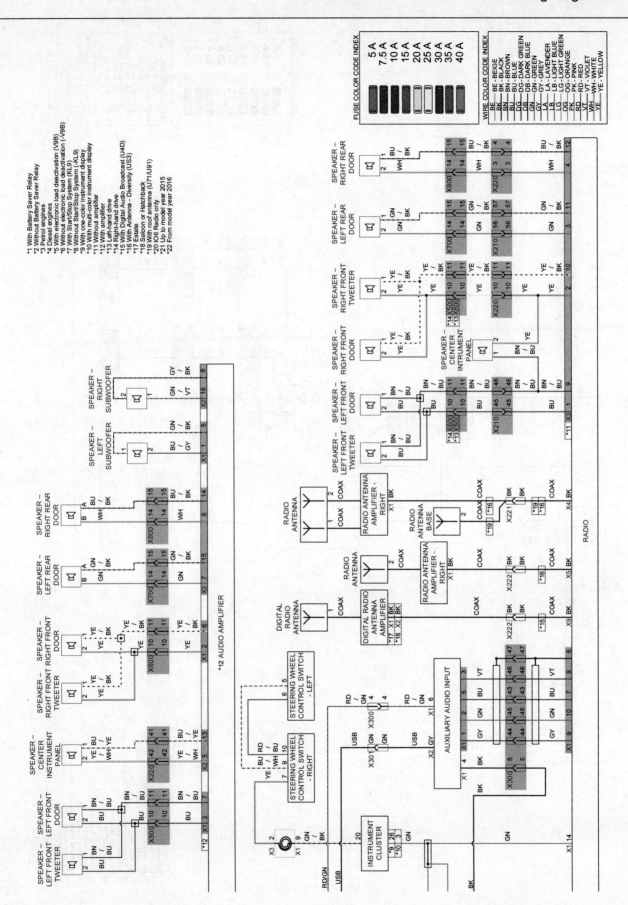

Diagram 37b – Information and sound system – 2014 to 2017 IO5 or IO6 Part 2

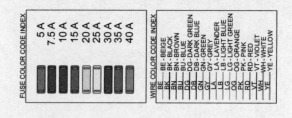

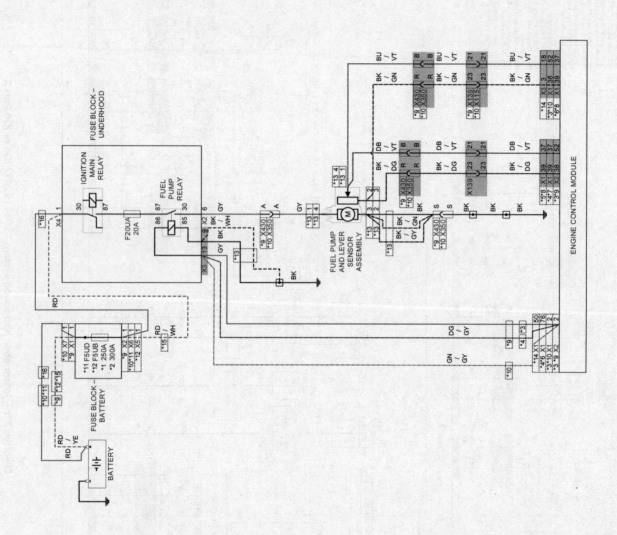

Diagram 38 – Fuel pump

Dimensions and Weights

Note: *All figures are approximate and may vary according to model. Refer to manufacturer's data for exact figures.*

Dimensions

Overall length:	
Saloon and Hatchback	4830 mm
Estate	4908 mm
Overall width (including door mirrors)	2084 mm
Overall height (unladen):	
Saloon and Hatchback	1498 mm
Estate	1520 mm
Wheelbase	2737 mm
Turning circle diameter (wall to wall)	11.40 metres
Front track	1536 mm
Rear track	1525 mm

Weights

Kerb weight:	
Petrol engine models:	
Saloon	1503 to 1692 kg
Hatchback	1503 to 1707 kg
Estate	1613 to 1799 kg
Diesel engine models:	
Saloon	1613 to 1806 kg
Hatchback	1613 to 1821 kg
Estate	1733 to 1918 kg
Gross vehicle weight	Refer to information contained on the vehicle identification plate
Maximum roof load (including weight of rack)	100 kg

Length (distance)

Inches (in)	x 25.4	= Millimetres (mm)	x 0.0394	= Inches (in)
Feet (ft)	x 0.305	= Metres (m)	x 3.281	= Feet (ft)
Miles	x 1.609	= Kilometres (km)	x 0.621	= Miles

Volume (capacity)

Cubic inches (cu in; in³)	x 16.387	= Cubic centimetres (cc; cm³)	x 0.061	= Cubic inches (cu in; in³)
Imperial pints (Imp pt)	x 0.568	= Litres (l)	x 1.76	= Imperial pints (Imp pt)
Imperial quarts (Imp qt)	x 1.137	= Litres (l)	x 0.88	= Imperial quarts (Imp qt)
Imperial quarts (Imp qt)	x 1.201	= US quarts (US qt)	x 0.833	= Imperial quarts (Imp qt)
US quarts (US qt)	x 0.946	= Litres (l)	x 1.057	= US quarts (US qt)
Imperial gallons (Imp gal)	x 4.546	= Litres (l)	x 0.22	= Imperial gallons (Imp gal)
Imperial gallons (Imp gal)	x 1.201	= US gallons (US gal)	x 0.833	= Imperial gallons (Imp gal)
US gallons (US gal)	x 3.785	= Litres (l)	x 0.264	= US gallons (US gal)

Mass (weight)

Ounces (oz)	x 28.35	= Grams (g)	x 0.035	= Ounces (oz)
Pounds (lb)	x 0.454	= Kilograms (kg)	x 2.205	= Pounds (lb)

Force

Ounces-force (ozf; oz)	x 0.278	= Newtons (N)	x 3.6	= Ounces-force (ozf; oz)
Pounds-force (lbf; lb)	x 4.448	= Newtons (N)	x 0.225	= Pounds-force (lbf; lb)
Newtons (N)	x 0.1	= Kilograms-force (kgf; kg)	x 9.81	= Newtons (N)

Pressure

Pounds-force per square inch (psi; lbf/in²; lb/in²)	x 0.070	= Kilograms-force per square centimetre (kgf/cm²; kg/cm²)	x 14.223	= Pounds-force per square inch (psi; lbf/in²; lb/in²)
Pounds-force per square inch (psi; lbf/in²; lb/in²)	x 0.068	= Atmospheres (atm)	x 14.696	= Pounds-force per square inch (psi; lbf/in²; lb/in²)
Pounds-force per square inch (psi; lbf/in²; lb/in²)	x 0.069	= Bars	x 14.5	= Pounds-force per square inch (psi; lbf/in²; lb/in²)
Pounds-force per square inch (psi; lbf/in²; lb/in²)	x 6.895	= Kilopascals (kPa)	x 0.145	= Pounds-force per square inch (psi; lbf/in²; lb/in²)
Kilopascals (kPa)	x 0.01	= Kilograms-force per square centimetre (kgf/cm²; kg/cm²)	x 98.1	= Kilopascals (kPa)
Millibar (mbar)	x 100	= Pascals (Pa)	x 0.01	= Millibar (mbar)
Millibar (mbar)	x 0.0145	= Pounds-force per square inch (psi; lbf/in²; lb/in²)	x 68.947	= Millibar (mbar)
Millibar (mbar)	x 0.75	= Millimetres of mercury (mmHg)	x 1.333	= Millibar (mbar)
Millibar (mbar)	x 0.401	= Inches of water (inH₂O)	x 2.491	= Millibar (mbar)
Millimetres of mercury (mmHg)	x 0.535	= Inches of water (inH₂O)	x 1.868	= Millimetres of mercury (mmHg)
Inches of water (inH₂O)	x 0.036	= Pounds-force per square inch (psi; lbf/in²; lb/in²)	x 27.68	= Inches of water (inH₂O)

Torque (moment of force)

Pounds-force inches (lbf in; lb in)	x 1.152	= Kilograms-force centimetre (kgf cm; kg cm)	x 0.868	= Pounds-force inches (lbf in; lb in)
Pounds-force inches (lbf in; lb in)	x 0.113	= Newton metres (Nm)	x 8.85	= Pounds-force inches (lbf in; lb in)
Pounds-force inches (lbf in; lb in)	x 0.083	= Pounds-force feet (lbf ft; lb ft)	x 12	= Pounds-force inches (lbf in; lb in)
Pounds-force feet (lbf ft; lb ft)	x 0.138	= Kilograms-force metres (kgf m; kg m)	x 7.233	= Pounds-force feet (lbf ft; lb ft)
Pounds-force feet (lbf ft; lb ft)	x 1.356	= Newton metres (Nm)	x 0.738	= Pounds-force feet (lbf ft; lb ft)
Newton metres (Nm)	x 0.102	= Kilograms-force metres (kgf m; kg m)	x 9.804	= Newton metres (Nm)

Power

Horsepower (hp)	x 745.7	= Watts (W)	x 0.0013	= Horsepower (hp)

Velocity (speed)

Miles per hour (miles/hr; mph)	x 1.609	= Kilometres per hour (km/hr; kph)	x 0.621	= Miles per hour (miles/hr; mph)

Fuel consumption*

Miles per gallon, Imperial (mpg)	x 0.354	= Kilometres per litre (km/l)	x 2.825	= Miles per gallon, Imperial (mpg)
Miles per gallon, US (mpg)	x 0.425	= Kilometres per litre (km/l)	x 2.352	= Miles per gallon, US (mpg)

Temperature

Degrees Fahrenheit = (°C x 1.8) + 32   Degrees Celsius (Degrees Centigrade; °C) = (°F - 32) x 0.56

It is common practice to convert from miles per gallon (mpg) to litres/100 kilometres (l/100km), where mpg x l/100 km = 282

Spare parts are available from many sources, including maker's appointed garages, accessory shops, and motor factors. To be sure of obtaining the correct parts, it will sometimes be necessary to quote the vehicle identification number. If possible, it can also be useful to take the old parts along for positive identification. Items such as starter motors and alternators may be available under a service exchange scheme – any parts returned should be clean.

Our advice regarding spare parts is as follows.

Officially appointed garages

This is the best source of parts which are peculiar to your car, and which are not otherwise generally available (eg, badges, interior trim, certain body panels, etc). It is also the only place at which you should buy parts if the car is still under warranty.

Accessory shops

These are very good places to buy materials and components needed for the maintenance of your car (oil, air and fuel filters, light bulbs, drivebelts, greases, brake pads, touch-up paint, etc). Components of this nature sold by a reputable shop are usually of the same standard as those used by the car manufacturer.

Besides components, these shops also sell tools and general accessories, usually have convenient opening hours, charge lower prices, and can often be found close to home. Some accessory shops have parts counters where components needed for almost any repair job can be purchased or ordered.

Motor factors

Good factors will stock all the more important components which wear out comparatively quickly, and can sometimes supply individual components needed for the overhaul of a larger assembly (eg, brake seals and hydraulic parts, bearing shells, pistons, valves). They may also handle work such as cylinder block reboring, crankshaft regrinding, etc.

Engine reconditioners

These specialise in engine overhaul and can also supply components. It is recommended that the establishment is a member of the Federation of Engine Re-Manufacturers, or a similar society.

Tyre and exhaust specialists

These outlets may be independent, or members of a local or national chain. They frequently offer competitive prices when compared with a main dealer or local garage, but it will pay to obtain several quotes before making a decision. When researching prices, also ask what extras may be added – for instance fitting a new valve, balancing the wheel and tyre disposal all both commonly charged on top of the price of a new tyre.

Other sources

Beware of parts or materials obtained from market stalls, car boot sales, on-line auctions or similar outlets. Such items are not invariably sub-standard, but there is little chance of compensation if they do prove unsatisfactory. In the case of safety-critical components such as brake pads, there is the risk not only of financial loss, but also of an accident causing injury or death.

Second-hand components or assemblies obtained from a car breaker can be a good buy in some circumstances, but this sort of purchase is best made by the experienced DIY mechanic.

Vehicle identification

Modifications are a continuing and unpublished process in vehicle manufacture, quite apart from major model changes. Spare parts manuals and lists are compiled upon a numerical basis, the individual vehicle numbers being essential to correct identification of the component required.

When ordering spare parts, always give as much information as possible. Quote the car model, year of manufacture and vehicle identification and/or engine numbers as appropriate.

The *vehicle identification label* is attached to the front left-hand side door pillar **(see illustration)** and includes the Vehicle Identification Number (VIN), vehicle weight information and paint and trim colour codes.

The *Vehicle Identification Number (VIN)* is given on the vehicle identification label and may also be viewed through the base of the windscreen on the passenger's side **(see illustration)**.

The VIN is also stamped into the front section of the plenum chamber (scuttle) panel **(see illustration)**. A check should always be made to ensure that all three VIN numbers are identical.

The engine number is stamped on a horizontal flat located on the front of the cylinder block, at the transmission end. The first part of the engine number gives the engine code – eg LBS/A20DTH. Engine codes are shown in the table below.

Vauxhall/Opel use a 'Car pass' scheme for vehicle identification. This is a card which is issued to the customer when the car is first purchased. It contains important information, eg, VIN number, key number and radio code. It also includes a special code for diagnostic equipment, therefore it must be kept in a secure place and not in the vehicle.

Engine codes are as follows:

1.6 litre (1598 cc) DOHC 16-valve diesel engine	B16DTH/LVL and B16DTJ/LVL
1.8 litre (1796 cc) DOHC 16-valve petrol engine	2HO/A18XER
2.0 litre (1956 cc) DOHC 16-valve diesel engine A20	LBS/A20DTH, LBX/A20DTJ, LBR/A20DT and LHV/A20DTE
2.0 litre (1956 cc) DOHC 16-valve diesel engine B20	LFS/B20DTH

Vehicle identification label (arrowed) attached to the front left-hand side door pillar

The VIN number viewed through the windscreen

The third VIN number locatio

Whenever servicing, repair or overhaul work is carried out on the car or its components, observe the following procedures and instructions. This will assist in carrying out the operation efficiently and to a professional standard of workmanship.

Joint mating faces and gaskets

When separating components at their mating faces, never insert screwdrivers or similar implements into the joint between the faces in order to prise them apart. This can cause severe damage which results in oil leaks, coolant leaks, etc upon reassembly. Separation is usually achieved by tapping along the joint with a soft-faced hammer in order to break the seal. However, note that this method may not be suitable where dowels are used for component location.

Where a gasket is used between the mating faces of two components, a new one must be fitted on reassembly; fit it dry unless otherwise stated in the repair procedure. Make sure that the mating faces are clean and dry, with all traces of old gasket removed. When cleaning a joint face, use a tool which is unlikely to score or damage the face, and remove any burrs or nicks with an oilstone or fine file.

Make sure that tapped holes are cleaned with a pipe cleaner, and keep them free of jointing compound, if this is being used, unless specifically instructed otherwise.

Ensure that all orifices, channels or pipes are clear, and blow through them, preferably using compressed air.

Oil seals

Oil seals can be removed by levering them out with a wide flat-bladed screwdriver or similar implement. Alternatively, a number of self-tapping screws may be screwed into the seal, and these used as a purchase for pliers or some similar device in order to pull the seal free.

Whenever an oil seal is removed from its working location, either individually or as part of an assembly, it should be renewed.

The very fine sealing lip of the seal is easily damaged, and will not seal if the surface it contacts is not completely clean and free from scratches, nicks or grooves. If the original sealing surface of the component cannot be restored, and the manufacturer has not made provision for slight relocation of the seal relative to the sealing surface, the component should be renewed.

Protect the lips of the seal from any surface which may damage them in the course of fitting. Use tape or a conical sleeve where possible. Where indicated, lubricate the seal lips with oil before fitting and, on dual-lipped seals, fill the space between the lips with grease.

Unless otherwise stated, oil seals must be fitted with their sealing lips toward the lubricant to be sealed.

Use a tubular drift or block of wood of the appropriate size to install the seal and, if the seal housing is shouldered, drive the seal down to the shoulder. If the seal housing is unshouldered, the seal should be fitted with its face flush with the housing top face (unless otherwise instructed).

Screw threads and fastenings

Seized nuts, bolts and screws are quite a common occurrence where corrosion has set in, and the use of penetrating oil or releasing fluid will often overcome this problem if the offending item is soaked for a while before attempting to release it. The use of an impact driver may also provide a means of releasing such stubborn fastening devices, when used in conjunction with the appropriate screwdriver bit or socket. If none of these methods works, it may be necessary to resort to the careful application of heat, or the use of a hacksaw or nut splitter device. Before resorting to extreme methods, check that you are not dealing with a left-hand thread!

Studs are usually removed by locking two nuts together on the threaded part, and then using a spanner on the lower nut to unscrew the stud. Studs or bolts which have broken off below the surface of the component in which they are mounted can sometimes be removed using a stud extractor.

Always ensure that a blind tapped hole is completely free from oil, grease, water or other fluid before installing the bolt or stud. Failure to do this could cause the housing to crack due to the hydraulic action of the bolt or stud as it is screwed in.

For some screw fastenings, notably cylinder head bolts or nuts, torque wrench settings are no longer specified for the latter stages of tightening, "angle-tightening" being called up instead. Typically, a fairly low torque wrench setting will be applied to the bolts/nuts in the correct sequence, followed by one or more stages of tightening through specified angles.

When checking or retightening a nut or bolt to a specified torque setting, slacken the nut or bolt by a quarter of a turn, and then retighten to the specified setting. However, this should not be attempted where angular tightening has been used.

Locknuts, locktabs and washers

Any fastening which will rotate against a component or housing during tightening should always have a washer between it and the relevant component or housing.

Spring or split washers should always be renewed when they are used to lock a critical component such as a big-end bearing retaining bolt or nut. Locktabs which are folded over to retain a nut or bolt should always be renewed.

Self-locking nuts can be re-used in non-critical areas, providing resistance can be felt when the locking portion passes over the bolt or stud thread. However, it should be noted that self-locking stiffnuts tend to lose their effectiveness after long periods of use, and should then be renewed as a matter of course.

Split pins must always be replaced with new ones of the correct size for the hole.

When thread-locking compound is found on the threads of a fastener which is to be re-used, it should be cleaned off with a wire brush and solvent, and fresh compound applied on reassembly.

Special tools

Some repair procedures in this manual entail the use of special tools such as a press, two or three-legged pullers, spring compressors, etc. Wherever possible, suitable readily-available alternatives to the manufacturer's special tools are described, and are shown in use. In some instances, where no alternative is possible, it has been necessary to resort to the use of a manufacturer's tool, and this has been done for reasons of safety as well as the efficient completion of the repair operation. Unless you are highly-skilled and have a thorough understanding of the procedures described, never attempt to bypass the use of any special tool when the procedure described specifies its use. Not only is there a very great risk of personal injury, but expensive damage could be caused to the components involved.

Environmental considerations

When disposing of used engine oil, brake fluid, antifreeze, etc, give due consideration to any detrimental environmental effects. Do not, for instance, pour any of the above liquids down drains into the general sewage system, or onto the ground to soak away, as this is likely to pollute your local environment. Many local council refuse tips provide a facility for waste oil disposal, as do some garages. You can find your nearest disposal point by calling the Environment Agency on 03708 506 506 or by visiting www.oilbankline.org.uk.

Note: It is illegal and anti-social to dump oil down the drain. To find the location of your local oil recycling bank, call 03708 506 506 or visit www.oilbankline.org.uk.

The jack supplied with the car's tool kit should only be used for changing the roadwheels – see Wheel changing at the front of this book. When carrying out any other kind of work, raise the car using a hydraulic (or 'trolley') jack, and always supplement the jack with axle stands positioned under the jacking/support points. If the roadwheels do not have to be removed, consider using wheel ramps – if wished, these can be placed under the wheels once the car has been raised using a hydraulic jack, and then lowered onto the ramps so that it is resting on its wheels.

Only ever jack the car up on a solid, level surface. If there is even a slight slope, take great care that the car cannot move as the wheels are lifted off the ground. Jacking up on an uneven or gravelled surface is not recommended, as the weight of the car will not be evenly distributed, and the jack may slip as the car is raised.

As far as possible, do not leave the car unattended once it has been raised, particularly if children are playing nearby.

Before jacking up the front of the car, ensure that the handbrake is firmly applied. When jacking up the rear of the car, place wooden chocks in front of the front wheels, and engage first gear (manual transmission) or PARK (automatic transmission).

To raise the front and/or rear of the car, use the main jacking/support points which are the reinforced areas of the underbody behind the front wheels and in front of the rear wheels. These reinforced area can be identified by the two holes in the reinforced section (front) or single hole (rear) (see illustration). The jacking points at the front and rear ends of the door sills, which are located at the places marked by a notch in the sill's lower flange can also be used for jacking or for location of an axle stand (see illustration). Position a block of wood with a groove cut in it on the jack head to prevent the car's weight resting on the sill edge; align the sill edge with the groove in the wood so that the car's weight is spread evenly over the surface of the block. Supplement the jack with axle stands (also with slotted blocks of wood) positioned as close as possible to the jacking points.

Do not jack the car under any other part of the sill, sump, floor pan, or directly under any of the steering or suspension components.

Never work under, around, or near a raised vehicle, unless it is adequately supported on stands. Do not rely on a jack alone, as even a hydraulic jack could fail under load.

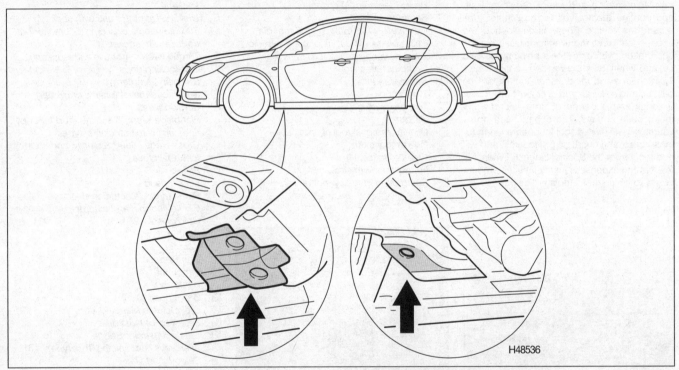

Front and rear reinforced jacking/support points

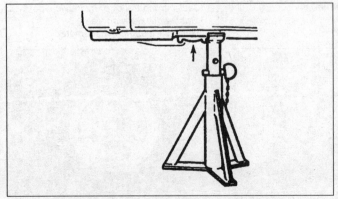

Axle stands should be placed under, or adjacent to the jacking point (arrowed)

A small section of card protects the sill

Introduction

A selection of good tools is a fundamental requirement for anyone contemplating the maintenance and repair of a motor vehicle. For the owner who does not possess any, their purchase will prove a considerable expense, offsetting some of the savings made by doing-it-yourself. However, provided that the tools purchased meet the relevant national safety standards and are of good quality, they will last for many years and prove an extremely worthwhile investment.

To help the average owner to decide which tools are needed to carry out the various tasks detailed in this manual, we have compiled three lists of tools under the following headings: *Maintenance and minor repair*, *Repair and overhaul*, and *Special*. Newcomers to practical mechanics should start off with the *Maintenance and minor repair* tool kit, and confine themselves to the simpler jobs around the vehicle. Then, as confidence and experience grow, more difficult tasks can be undertaken, with extra tools being purchased as, and when, they are needed. In this way, a *Maintenance and minor repair* tool kit can be built up into a *Repair and overhaul* tool kit over a considerable period of time, without any major cash outlays. The experienced do-it-yourselfer will have a tool kit good enough for most repair and overhaul procedures, and will add tools from the *Special* category when it is felt that the expense is justified by the amount of use to which these tools will be put.

Maintenance and minor repair tool kit

The tools given in this list should be considered as a minimum requirement if routine maintenance, servicing and minor repair operations are to be undertaken. We recommend the purchase of combination spanners (ring one end, open-ended the other); although more expensive than open-ended ones, they do give the advantages of both types of spanner.

☐ *Combination spanners:*
Metric - 8 to 19 mm inclusive
☐ *Adjustable spanner - 35 mm jaw (approx.)*
☐ *Spark plug spanner (with rubber insert) - petrol models*
☐ *Spark plug gap adjustment tool - petrol models*
☐ *Set of feeler gauges*
☐ *Brake bleed nipple spanner*
☐ *Screwdrivers:*
Flat blade - 100 mm long x 6 mm dia
Cross blade - 100 mm long x 6 mm dia
Torx - various sizes (not all vehicles)
☐ *Combination pliers*
☐ *Hacksaw (junior)*
☐ *Tyre pump*
☐ *Tyre pressure gauge*
☐ *Oil can*
☐ *Oil filter removal tool (if applicable)*
☐ *Fine emery cloth*
☐ *Wire brush (small)*
☐ *Funnel (medium size)*
☐ *Sump drain plug key (not all vehicles)*

Repair and overhaul tool kit

These tools are virtually essential for anyone undertaking any major repairs to a motor vehicle, and are additional to those given in the *Maintenance and minor repair* list. Included in this list is a comprehensive set of sockets. Although these are expensive, they will be found invaluable as they are so versatile - particularly if various drives are included in the set. We recommend the half-inch square-drive type, as this can be used with most proprietary torque wrenches.

The tools in this list will sometimes need to be supplemented by tools from the *Special* list:

☐ *Sockets to cover range in previous list (including Torx sockets)*
☐ *Reversible ratchet drive (for use with sockets)*
☐ *Extension piece, 250 mm (for use with sockets)*
☐ *Universal joint (for use with sockets)*
☐ *Flexible handle or sliding T "breaker bar" (for use with sockets)*
☐ *Torque wrench (for use with sockets)*
☐ *Self-locking grips*
☐ *Ball pein hammer*
☐ *Soft-faced mallet (plastic or rubber)*
☐ *Screwdrivers:*
Flat blade - long & sturdy, short (chubby), and narrow (electrician's) types
Cross blade - long & sturdy, and short (chubby) types
☐ *Pliers:*
Long-nosed
Side cutters (electrician's)
Circlip (internal and external)
☐ *Cold chisel - 25 mm*
☐ *Scriber*
☐ *Scraper*
☐ *Centre-punch*
☐ *Pin punch*
☐ *Hacksaw*
☐ *Brake hose clamp*
☐ *Brake/clutch bleeding kit*
☐ *Selection of twist drills*
☐ *Steel rule/straight-edge*
☐ *Allen keys (inc. splined/Torx type)*
☐ *Selection of files*
☐ *Wire brush*
☐ *Axle stands*
☐ *Jack (strong trolley or hydraulic type)*
☐ *Light with extension lead*
☐ *Universal electrical multi-meter*

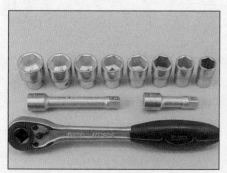

Sockets and reversible ratchet drive

Brake bleeding kit

Torx key, socket and bit

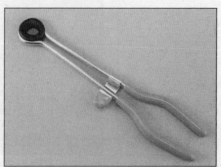

Hose clamp

Angular-tightening gauge

Special tools

The tools in this list are those which are not used regularly, are expensive to buy, or which need to be used in accordance with their manufacturers' instructions. Unless relatively difficult mechanical jobs are undertaken frequently, it will not be economic to buy many of these tools. Where this is the case, you could consider clubbing together with friends (or joining a motorists' club) to make a joint purchase, or borrowing the tools against a deposit from a local garage or tool hire specialist.

The following list contains only those tools and instruments freely available to the public, and not those special tools produced by the vehicle manufacturer specifically for its dealer network. You will find occasional references to these manufacturers' special tools in the text of this manual. Generally, an alternative method of doing the job without the vehicle manufacturers' special tool is given. However, sometimes there is no alternative to using them. Where this is the case and the relevant tool cannot be bought or borrowed, you will have to entrust the work to a dealer.

☐ Angular-tightening gauge
☐ Valve spring compressor
☐ Valve grinding tool
☐ Piston ring compressor
☐ Piston ring removal/installation tool
☐ Cylinder bore hone
☐ Balljoint separator
☐ Coil spring compressors (where applicable)
☐ Two/three-legged hub and bearing puller
☐ Impact screwdriver
☐ Micrometer and/or vernier calipers
☐ Dial gauge
☐ Tachometer
☐ Fault code reader
☐ Cylinder compression gauge
☐ Hand-operated vacuum pump and gauge
☐ Clutch plate alignment set
☐ Brake shoe steady spring cup removal tool
☐ Bush and bearing removal/installation set
☐ Stud extractors
☐ Tap and die set
☐ Lifting tackle

Buying tools

Reputable motor accessory shops and superstores often offer excellent quality tools at discount prices, so it pays to shop around.

Remember, you don't have to buy the most expensive items on the shelf, but it is always advisable to steer clear of the very cheap tools. Beware of 'bargains' offered on market stalls, on-line or at car boot sales. There are plenty of good tools around at reasonable prices, but always aim to purchase items which meet the relevant national safety standards. If in doubt, ask the proprietor or manager of the shop for advice before making a purchase.

Care and maintenance of tools

Having purchased a reasonable tool kit, it is necessary to keep the tools in a clean and serviceable condition. After use, always wipe off any dirt, grease and metal particles using a clean, dry cloth, before putting the tools away. Never leave them lying around after they have been used. A simple tool rack on the garage or workshop wall for items such as screwdrivers and pliers is a good idea. Store all normal spanners and sockets in a metal box. Any measuring instruments, gauges, meters, etc, must be carefully stored where they cannot be damaged or become rusty.

Take a little care when tools are used. Hammer heads inevitably become marked, and screwdrivers lose the keen edge on their blades from time to time. A little timely attention with emery cloth or a file will soon restore items like this to a good finish.

Working facilities

Not to be forgotten when discussing tools is the workshop itself. If anything more than routine maintenance is to be carried out, a suitable working area becomes essential.

It is appreciated that many an owner-mechanic is forced by circumstances to remove an engine or similar item without the benefit of a garage or workshop. Having done this, any repairs should always be done under the cover of a roof.

Wherever possible, any dismantling should be done on a clean, flat workbench or table at a suitable working height.

Any workbench needs a vice; one with a jaw opening of 100 mm is suitable for most jobs. As mentioned previously, some clean dry storage space is also required for tools, as well as for any lubricants, cleaning fluids, touch-up paints etc, which become necessary.

Another item which may be required, and which has a much more general usage, is an electric drill with a chuck capacity of at least 8 mm. This, together with a good range of twist drills, is virtually essential for fitting accessories.

Last, but not least, always keep a supply of old newspapers and clean, lint-free rags available, and try to keep any working area as clean as possible.

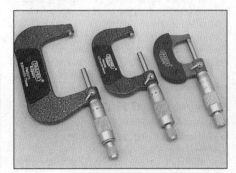
Micrometers

Dial test indicator ("dial gauge")

Oil filter removal tool (strap wrench type)

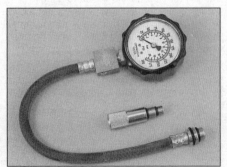
Compression tester

Bearing puller

This is a guide to getting your vehicle through the MOT test. Obviously it will not be possible to examine the vehicle to the same standard as the professional MOT tester. However, working through the following checks will enable you to identify any problem areas before submitting the vehicle for the test.

It has only been possible to summarise the test requirements here, based on the regulations in force at the time of printing. Test standards are becoming increasingly stringent, although there are some exemptions for older vehicles.

An assistant will be needed to help carry out some of these checks.

The checks have been sub-divided into four categories, as follows:

1 Checks carried out **FROM THE VEHICLE INTERIOR**

2 Checks carried out **WITH THE VEHICLE ON THE GROUND**

3 Checks carried out **WITH THE VEHICLE RAISED AND THE WHEELS FREE TO TURN**

4 Checks carried out on **YOUR VEHICLE'S EXHAUST EMISSION SYSTEM**

1 Checks carried out **FROM THE VEHICLE INTERIOR**

Handbrake (parking brake)

☐ Test the operation of the handbrake. Excessive travel (too many clicks) indicates incorrect brake or cable adjustment.
☐ Check that the handbrake cannot be released by tapping the lever sideways. Check the security of the lever mountings.

☐ If the parking brake is foot-operated, check that the pedal is secure and without excessive travel, and that the release mechanism operates correctly.
☐ Where applicable, test the operation of the electronic handbrake. The brake should engage and disengage without excessive delay. If the warning light does not extinguish, or a warning message is displayed when the brake is disengaged, this could indicate a fault which will need further investigation.

Footbrake

☐ Depress the brake pedal and check that it does not creep down to the floor, indicating a master cylinder fault. Release the pedal, wait a few seconds, then depress it again. If the pedal travels nearly to the floor before firm resistance is felt, brake adjustment or repair is necessary. If the pedal feels spongy, there is air in the hydraulic system which must be removed by bleeding.

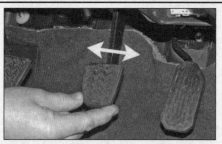

☐ Check that the brake pedal is secure and in good condition. Check also for signs of fluid leaks on the pedal, floor or carpets, which would indicate failed seals in the brake master cylinder.
☐ Check the servo unit (when applicable) by operating the brake pedal several times, then keeping the pedal depressed and starting the engine. As the engine starts, the pedal will move down. If not, the vacuum hose or the servo itself may be faulty.

Steering wheel and column

☐ Examine the steering wheel for fractures or looseness of the hub, spokes or rim.
☐ Move the steering wheel from side to side and then up and down. Check that the steering wheel is not loose on the column, indicating wear or a loose retaining nut. Continue moving the steering wheel as before, but also turn it slightly from left to right.
☐ Check that the steering wheel is not loose on the column, and that there is no abnormal movement of the steering wheel, indicating wear in the column support bearings or couplings.

☐ Check that the ignition lock (where fitted) engages and disengages correctly.
☐ Steering column adjustment mechanisms (where fitted) must be able to lock the column securely in place with no play evident.

Windscreen, mirrors and sunvisor

☐ The windscreen must be free of cracks or other significant damage within the 'swept area' of the windscreen. This is the area swept by the windscreen wipers. A second test area, known as 'Zone A', is the part of the swept area 290 mm wide, centred on the steering wheel centre line. Any damage in Zone A that cannot be contained in a 10 mm diameter circle, or any damage in the remainder of the swept area that cannot be contained in a 40 mm diameter circle, may cause the vehicle to fail the test.

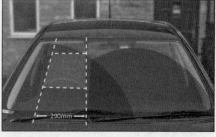

☐ Any items that may obscure the drivers view, such as stickers, sat-navs, anything hanging from the interior mirror, should be removed prior to the test.
☐ Vehicles registered after 1st August 1978 must have a drivers side mirror, and either an interior mirror, or a passenger's side mirror. Cameras (or indirect vision devices) may replace the mirrors, but they must function correctly.
☐ The driver's sunvisor must be capable of being stored in the "up" position.

Seat belts, seats and supplementary restraint systems (SRS)

Note: *The following checks are applicable to all seat belts, front and rear.*

☐ Examine the webbing of all the belts (including rear belts if fitted) for cuts, serious fraying or deterioration. Fasten and unfasten each belt to check the buckles. If applicable, check the retracting mechanism. Check the security of all seat belt mountings accessible from inside the vehicle, ensuring any height adjustable mountings lock securely in place.

☐ Where the seat belt is attached to a seat, the frame and mountings of the seat form part of the belt mountings, and are to be inspected as such.

☐ Any airbag, or SRS warning light must extinguish a few seconds after the ignition is switched on. Failure to do so indicates a fault which must be investigated.

☐ Seat belts with pre-tensioners, once activated, have a "flag" or similar showing on the seat belt stalk. This, in itself, is a reason for test failure.

☐ Check that the original airbag(s) is/are present, and not obviously defective.

☐ The seats themselves must be securely attached and the backrests must lock in the upright position. The driver's seat must also be able to slide forwards/rearwards, and lock in several positions.

Doors

☐ Both front doors must be able to be opened and closed from outside and inside, and must latch securely when closed.

☐ The rear doors must open from the outside.

☐ Examine all door hinges, catches and striker plates for missing, deteriorated, or insecure parts that could effect the opening and closing of the doors.

Speedometer

☐ The vehicle speedometer must be present, and appear operative. The figures on the speedometer must be legible, and illuminated when the lights are switched on.

2 Checks carried out WITH THE VEHICLE ON THE GROUND

Vehicle identification

☐ Number plates must be in good condition, secure and legible, with letters and numbers correctly spaced – spacing at (A) should be 33 mm and at (B) 11 mm. At the front, digits must be black on a white background and at the rear

black on a yellow background. Other background designs (such as honeycomb) are not permitted.

☐ The VIN plate and/or homologation plate must be permanently displayed and legible.

Electrical equipment

☐ Switch on the ignition and check the operation of the horn.

☐ Check the windscreen washers and wipers, examining the wiper blades; renew damaged or perished blades. The wiper blades must clear a large enough area of the windscreen to provide an 'adequate' view of the road, and be able to be parked in a position where they will not affect the drivers' view.

☐ On vehicles first used from 1st September 2009, the headlight washers (where fitted) must operate correctly.

☐ Check the operation of the stop-lights. This includes any lights that appear to be connected – Eg. high-level lights.

☐ Check the operation of the sidelights and number plate lights. The lenses and reflectors must be secure, clean and undamaged.

☐ Check the operation and alignment of the headlights. The headlight reflectors must not be tarnished and the lenses must be undamaged. Where plastic lenses are fitted, check they haven't deteriorated to the extent where they affect the light ouput or beam image. It's often possible to restore the plastic lens using a suitable polish or aftermarket treatment.

☐ Where HID or LED headlights are fitted, check the operation of the cleaning and self-levelling functions.

☐ The headlight main beam warning lamp must be functional.

☐ On vehicles first used from 1st March 2018, the daytime running lights (where fitted) must operate correctly.

☐ Switch on the ignition and check the operation of the direction indicators (including the instrument panel tell-tale) and the hazard warning lights. Operation of the sidelights and stop-lights must not affect the indicators – if it does, the cause is usually a bad earth at the rear light cluster. Indicators should flash at a rate of between 60 and 120 times per minute – faster or slower than this could indicate a fault with the flasher unit or a bad earth at one of the light units.

☐ The hazard warning lights must operate with the ignition on and off.

☐ Check the operation of the rear foglight(s), including the warning light on the instrument panel or in the switch. Note that the foglight

must be positioned in the centre or driver's side of the vehicle. If only the passenger's side illuminates, the test will fail.

☐ The warning lights must illuminate in accordance with the manufacturers' design (this includes any warning messages). For most vehicles, the ABS and other warning lights should illuminate when the ignition is switched on, and (if the system is operating properly) extinguish after a few seconds. Refer to the owner's handbook.

☐ On vehicles first used from 1st September 2009, the reversing lights must operate correctly when reverse gear is selected.

☐ Check the vehicle battery for security and leakage.

☐ Check the visible/accessible vehicle wiring is adequately supported, with no evidence of damage or deterioration that could result in a short-circuit.

Footbrake

☐ Examine the master cylinder, brake pipes and servo unit for leaks, loose mountings, corrosion or other damage. If ABS is fitted, this unit should also be examined for signs of leaks or corrosion.

☐ The fluid reservoir must be secure and the fluid level must be between the upper (A) and lower (B) markings.

☐ Check the fluid in the reservoir for signs of contamination.

☐ Inspect both front brake flexible hoses for cracks or deterioration of the rubber. Turn the steering from lock to lock, and ensure that the hoses do not contact the wheel, tyre, or any part of the steering or suspension mechanism. With the brake pedal firmly depressed, check the hoses for bulges or leaks under pressure.

Steering and suspension

☐ Have your assistant turn the steering wheel from side to side slightly, up to the point where the steering gear just begins to transmit this movement to the roadwheels. Check for excessive free play between the steering wheel and the steering gear, indicating wear or insecurity of the steering column joints, the column-to-steering gear coupling, or the steering gear itself. With a standard (380 mm diameter) steering wheel, there should be no more than 13 mm of free play for rack-and-pinion systems, and no more than 75 mm for non-rack-and-pinion designs.

☐ Have your assistant turn the steering

wheel more vigorously in each direction, so that the roadwheels just begin to turn. As this is done, examine all the steering joints, linkages, fittings and attachments. Renew any component that shows signs of wear or damage. On vehicles with hydraulic power steering, check the security and condition of the steering pump, drivebelt and hoses.

☐ Note that all movement checks on power steering systems are carried out with the engine running.

☐ Check that the vehicle is standing level, and at approximately the correct ride height.

Exhaust system

☐ Start the engine. With your assistant holding a rag over the tailpipe, check the entire system for leaks. Repair or renew leaking sections.

3 Checks carried out WITH THE VEHICLE RAISED AND THE WHEELS FREE TO TURN

Jack up the front and rear of the vehicle, and securely support it on axle stands. Position the stands clear of the suspension assemblies. Ensure that the wheels are clear of the ground and that the steering can be turned from lock to lock.

Steering mechanism

☐ Have your assistant turn the steering from lock to lock. Check that the steering turns smoothly, and that no part of the steering mechanism, including a wheel or tyre, fouls any brake hose or pipe or any part of the body structure.

☐ Examine the steering rack rubber gaiters for damage or insecurity of the retaining clips. If power steering is fitted, check for signs of damage or leakage of the fluid hoses, pipes or connections. Also check for excessive stiffness or binding of the steering, a missing split pin or locking device, or severe corrosion of the body structure within 30 cm of any steering component attachment point.

☐ Check the track rod end ball joint dust covers. Any covers that are missing, seriously damaged, deteriorated or insecure, may fail inspection.

Front and rear suspension and wheel bearings

☐ Starting at the front right-hand side, grasp the roadwheel at the 3 o'clock and 9 o'clock positions and rock gently but firmly. Check for free play or insecurity at the wheel bearings, suspension balljoints, or suspension mountings, pivots and attachments.

☐ Now grasp the wheel at the 12 o'clock and 6 o'clock positions and repeat the previous inspection. Spin the wheel, and check for roughness or tightness of the front wheel bearing.

☐ If excess free play is suspected at a component pivot point, this can be confirmed by using a large screwdriver or similar tool and levering between the mounting and the component attachment. This will confirm whether the wear is in the pivot bush, its retaining bolt, or in the mounting itself (the bolt holes can often become elongated).

☐ Carry out all the above checks at the other front wheel, and then at both rear wheels.

Springs and shock absorbers

☐ Examine the suspension struts (when applicable) for serious fluid leakage, corrosion, or damage to the casing. Also check the security of the mounting points.

☐ If coil springs are fitted, check that the spring ends locate in their seats, and that the spring is not corroded, cracked or broken.

☐ If leaf springs are fitted, check that all leaves are intact, that the axle is securely attached to each spring, and that there is no deterioration of the spring eye mountings, bushes, and shackles.

☐ The same general checks apply to vehicles fitted with other suspension types, such as torsion bars, hydraulic displacer units, etc. Ensure that all mountings and attachments are secure, that there are no signs of excessive wear, corrosion or damage, and (on hydraulic types) that there are no fluid leaks or damaged pipes.

☐ Check any suspension and anti-roll bar link ball joint dust covers. Any covers that are missing, seriously damaged, deteriorated or insecure, may fail inspection.

☐ Examine each shock absorber for signs of leakage, corrosion of the casing, missing, detached or worn pivots and/or rubber bushes.

Driveshafts (fwd vehicles only)

☐ Rotate each front wheel in turn and inspect the inner and outer joint gaiters for splits or damage. Also check that each driveshaft is straight and undamaged.

Braking system

☐ If possible without dismantling, check brake pad wear and disc condition. Ensure that the friction lining material has not worn excessively, (A) and that the discs are not fractured, pitted, scored or badly worn (B). As a general rule, if the friction material is less than 1.5 mm thick, the inspection will fail.

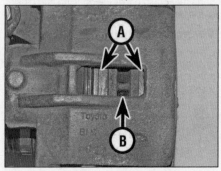

☐ Examine all the rigid brake pipes underneath the vehicle, and the flexible hose(s) at the rear. Look for corrosion, chafing or insecurity of the pipes, and for signs of bulging under pressure, chafing, splits or deterioration of the flexible hoses.

☐ Look for signs of fluid leaks at the brake calipers or on the brake backplates. Repair or renew leaking components.

☐ Slowly spin each wheel, while your assistant depresses and releases the footbrake. Ensure that each brake is operating and does not bind when the pedal is released.

☐ Examine the handbrake mechanism, checking for frayed or broken cables, excessive corrosion, or wear or insecurity of the linkage. Check that the mechanism works on each relevant wheel, and releases fully, without binding.

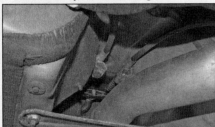

☐ Check the ABS sensors' wiring for signs of damage, deterioration or insecurity.

☐ It is not possible to test brake efficiency without special equipment, but a road test can be carried out later to check that the vehicle pulls up in a straight line.

Fuel and exhaust systems

☐ Inspect the fuel tank (including the filler cap), fuel pipes, hoses and unions. All components must be secure and free from leaks. Locking fuel caps must lock securely and the key must be provided for the MOT test.

☐ Examine the exhaust system over its entire length, checking for any damaged, broken or missing mountings, security of the retaining clamps and rust or corrosion.

☐ If the vehicle was originally equipped with a catalytic converter or particulate filter, one must be fitted.

Wheels and tyres

☐ Examine the sidewalls and tread area of each tyre in turn. Check for cuts, tears, lumps, bulges, separation of the tread, and exposure of the ply or cord due to wear or damage. Check that the tyre bead is correctly seated on the wheel rim, that the valve is sound and properly seated, and that the wheel is not distorted or damaged.

☐ Check that the tyres are of the correct size for the vehicle, that they are of the same size and type on each axle, and that the pressures are correct. The vehicle will fail the test if the tyres are obviously under-inflated.

☐ Check the tyre tread depth. The legal minimum at the time of writing is 1.6 mm over the central three-quarters of the tread width. Abnormal tread wear may indicate incorrect front wheel alignment or wear in steering or suspension components.

☐ Check that all wheel bolts/nuts are present.

☐ If the spare wheel is fitted externally or in a separate carrier beneath the vehicle, check that mountings are secure and free of excessive corrosion.

Body corrosion

☐ Check the condition of the entire vehicle structure for signs of corrosion in load-bearing areas. (These include chassis box sections, side sills, cross-members, pillars, and all suspension, steering, braking system and seat belt mountings and anchorages.) Any corrosion which has seriously reduced the thickness of a load-bearing area (or is within 30 cm of safety-related components such as steering or suspension) is likely to cause the vehicle to fail. In this case professional repairs are likely to be needed.

☐ Damage or corrosion which causes sharp or otherwise dangerous edges to be exposed will also cause the vehicle to fail.

Towbars

☐ Check the condition of mounting points (both beneath the vehicle and within boot/hatchback areas) for signs of corrosion, ensuring that all fixings are secure and not worn or damaged. There must be no excessive play in detachable tow ball arms or quick-release mechanisms.

☐ Examine the security and condition of the towbar electrics socket. If the later 13-pin socket is fitted, the MOT tester will check its' wiring functions/connections are correct.

General leaks

☐ The vehicle will fail the test if there is a fluid leak of any kind that poses an environmental risk.

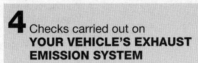

4 Checks carried out on **YOUR VEHICLE'S EXHAUST EMISSION SYSTEM**

Petrol models

☐ The engine should be warmed up, and running well (ignition system in good order, air filter element clean, etc).

☐ Before testing, run the engine at around 2500 rpm for 20 seconds. Let the engine drop to idle, and watch for smoke from the exhaust. If the idle speed is too high, or if dense blue or black smoke emerges for more than 5 seconds, the vehicle will fail. Typically, blue smoke signifies oil burning (engine wear); black smoke means unburnt fuel (dirty air cleaner element, or other fuel system fault).

☐ An exhaust gas analyser for measuring carbon monoxide (CO) and hydrocarbons (HC) is now needed. If one cannot be hired or borrowed, have a local garage perform the check.

CO emissions (mixture)

☐ The MOT tester has access to the CO limits for all vehicles from 1st August 1992. The CO level is measured at idle speed, and at 'fast idle' (2500 to 3000 rpm). The following limits are given as a general guide:

  At idle speed – Less than 0.3% CO
  At 'fast idle' – Less than 0.2% CO
  Lambda reading – 0.97 to 1.03

☐ If the CO level is too high, this may point to poor maintenance, a fuel injection system problem, faulty lambda (oxygen) sensor or catalytic converter. Try an injector cleaning treatment, and check the vehicle's ECU for fault codes.

HC emissions

☐ The MOT tester has access to HC limits for all vehicles. The HC level is measured at 'fast idle' (2500 to 3000 rpm). The following limits are given as a general guide:

  At 'fast idle' – Less than 200 ppm

☐ Excessive HC emissions are typically caused by oil being burnt (worn engine), or by a blocked crankcase ventilation system ('breather'). If the engine oil is old and thin, an oil change may help. If the engine is running badly, check the vehicle's ECU for fault codes.

Diesel models

☐ If the vehicle was fitted with a DPF (Diesel Particulate Filter) when it left the factory, it will fail the test if the MOT tester can see smoke of any colour emitting from the exhaust, or finds evidence that the filter has been tampered with.

☐ The only emission test for diesel engines is measuring exhaust smoke density, using a calibrated smoke meter.

☐ This test involves accelerating the engine to its maximum unloaded speed a minimum of once, and a maximum of 6 times. With the smoke meter connected, the engine is accelerated quickly to its maximum speed. If the smoke level is at or below the limit specified, the vehicle will pass. If the level is more than the specified limit then two further accelerations are carried out, and an average of the readings calculated. If the vehicle is still over the limit, a further three accelerations are carried out, with the average of the last three calculated after each check.

Note: On engines with a timing belt, it is VITAL that the belt is in good condition before the test is carried out.

Vehicles registered after 1st July 2008

  Smoke level must not exceed 1.5m-1 – Turbo-charged and non-Turbocharged engines

Vehicles registered before 1st July 2008

  Smoke level must not exceed 2.5m-1 – Non-turbo vehicles
  Smoke level must not exceed 3.0m-1 – Turbocharged vehicles:

☐ If excess smoke is produced, try fitting a new air cleaner element, or using an injector cleaning treatment. If the engine is running badly, where applicable, check the vehicle's ECU for fault codes. Also check the vehicle's EGR system, where applicable. At high mileages, the injectors may require professional attention.

Engine

- ☐ Engine fails to rotate when attempting to start
- ☐ Engine rotates, but will not start
- ☐ Engine difficult to start when cold
- ☐ Engine difficult to start when hot
- ☐ Starter motor noisy or excessively-rough in engagement
- ☐ Engine starts, but stops immediately
- ☐ Engine idles erratically
- ☐ Engine misfires at idle speed
- ☐ Engine misfires throughout the driving speed range
- ☐ Engine hesitates on acceleration
- ☐ Engine stalls
- ☐ Engine lacks power
- ☐ Engine backfires
- ☐ Oil pressure warning light illuminated with engine running
- ☐ Engine runs-on after switching off
- ☐ Engine noises

Cooling system

- ☐ Overheating
- ☐ Overcooling
- ☐ External coolant leakage
- ☐ Internal coolant leakage
- ☐ Corrosion

Fuel and exhaust systems

- ☐ Excessive fuel consumption
- ☐ Fuel leakage and/or fuel odour
- ☐ Excessive noise or fumes from exhaust system

Clutch

- ☐ Pedal travels to floor – no pressure or very little resistance
- ☐ Clutch fails to disengage (unable to select gears)
- ☐ Clutch slips (engine speed increases, with no increase in vehicle speed)
- ☐ Judder as clutch is engaged
- ☐ Noise when depressing or releasing clutch pedal

Manual transmission

- ☐ Noisy in neutral with engine running
- ☐ Noisy in one particular gear
- ☐ Difficulty engaging gears
- ☐ Jumps out of gear
- ☐ Vibration
- ☐ Lubricant leaks

Automatic transmission

- ☐ Fluid leakage
- ☐ Transmission fluid brown, or has burned smell
- ☐ General gear selection problems
- ☐ Transmission will not downshift (kickdown) with accelerator pedal fully depressed
- ☐ Engine will not start in any gear, or starts in gears other than Park or Neutral
- ☐ Transmission slips, shifts roughly, is noisy, or has no drive in forward or reverse gears

Driveshafts

- ☐ Vibration when accelerating or decelerating
- ☐ Clicking or knocking noise on turns (at slow speed on full-lock)

Braking system

- ☐ Vehicle pulls to one side under braking
- ☐ Noise (grinding or high-pitched squeal) when brakes applied
- ☐ Excessive brake pedal travel
- ☐ Brake pedal feels spongy when depressed
- ☐ Excessive brake pedal effort required to stop vehicle
- ☐ Judder felt through brake pedal or steering wheel when braking
- ☐ Brakes binding
- ☐ Rear wheels locking under normal braking

Suspension and steering

- ☐ Vehicle pulls to one side
- ☐ Wheel wobble and vibration
- ☐ Excessive pitching and/or rolling around corners, or during braking
- ☐ Wandering or general instability
- ☐ Excessively-stiff steering
- ☐ Excessive play in steering
- ☐ Lack of power assistance
- ☐ Tyre wear excessive

Electrical system

- ☐ Battery will not hold a charge for more than a few days
- ☐ Ignition/no-charge warning light remains illuminated with engine running
- ☐ Ignition/no-charge warning light fails to come on
- ☐ Lights inoperative
- ☐ Instrument readings inaccurate or erratic
- ☐ Horn inoperative, or unsatisfactory in operation
- ☐ Windscreen wipers inoperative, or unsatisfactory in operation
- ☐ Windscreen washers inoperative, or unsatisfactory in operation
- ☐ Electric windows inoperative, or unsatisfactory in operation
- ☐ Central locking system inoperative, or unsatisfactory in operation

Introduction

The vehicle owner who does his or her own maintenance according to the recommended service schedules should not have to use this section of the manual very often. Modern component reliability is such that, provided those items subject to wear or deterioration are inspected or renewed at the specified intervals, sudden failure is comparatively rare. Faults do not usually just happen as a result of sudden failure, but develop over a period of time. Major mechanical failures in particular are usually preceded by characteristic symptoms over hundreds or even thousands of miles. Those components which do occasionally fail without warning are often small and easily carried in the vehicle.

With any fault-finding, the first step is to decide where to begin investigations. Sometimes this is obvious, but on other occasions, a little detective work will be necessary. The owner who makes half a dozen haphazard adjustments or replacements may be successful in curing a fault (or its symptoms), but will be none the wiser if the fault recurs, and ultimately may have spent more time and money than was necessary. A calm and logical approach will be found to be more satisfactory in the long run. Always take into account any warning signs or abnormalities that may have been noticed in the period preceding the fault – power loss, high or low gauge readings, unusual smells,

etc – and remember that failure of components such as fuses or spark plugs may only be pointers to some underlying fault.

The pages which follow provide an easy-reference guide to the more common problems which may occur during the operation of the vehicle. These problems and their possible causes are grouped under headings denoting various components or systems, such as Engine, Cooling system, etc. The general Chapter which deals with the problem is also shown in brackets; refer to the relevant part of that Chapter for system-specific information. Whatever the fault, certain basic principles apply. These are as follows:

Verify the fault. This is simply a matter of

being sure that you know what the symptoms are before starting work. This is particularly important if you are investigating a fault for someone else, who may not have described it very accurately.

Don't overlook the obvious. For example, if the vehicle won't start, is there fuel in the tank? (Don't take anyone else's word on this particular point, and don't trust the fuel gauge either!) If an electrical fault is indicated, look for loose or broken wires before digging out the test gear.

Cure the disease, not the symptom. Substituting a flat battery with a fully-charged one will get you off the hard shoulder, but if the underlying cause is not attended to, the new battery will go the same way. Similarly, changing oil-fouled spark plugs for a new set will get you moving again, but remember that the reason for the fouling (if it wasn't simply an incorrect grade of plug) will have to be established and corrected.

Don't take anything for granted. Particularly, don't forget that a 'new' component may itself be defective (especially if it's been rattling around in the boot for months), and don't leave components out of a fault diagnosis sequence just because they are new or recently-fitted. When you do finally diagnose a difficult fault, you'll probably realise that all the evidence was there from the start.

Consider what work, if any, has recently been carried out. Many faults arise through careless or hurried work. For instance, if any work has been performed under the bonnet, could some of the wiring have been dislodged or incorrectly routed, or a hose trapped? Have all the fasteners been properly tightened? Were new, genuine parts and new gaskets used? There is often a certain amount of detective work to be done in this case, as an apparently-unrelated task can have far-reaching consequences.

Diesel fault diagnosis

The majority of starting problems on small diesel engines are electrical in origin. The mechanic who is familiar with petrol engines but less so with diesel may be inclined to view the diesel's injectors and pump in the same light as the spark plugs and distributor, but this is generally a mistake.

When investigating complaints of difficult starting for someone else, make sure that the correct starting procedure is understood and is being followed. Some drivers are unaware of the significance of the preheating warning light – many modern engines are sufficiently forgiving for this not to matter in mild weather, but with the onset of winter, problems begin. Glow plugs in particular are often neglected – just one faulty plug will make cold-weather starting very difficult.

As a rule of thumb, if the engine is difficult to start but runs well when it has finally got going, the problem is electrical (battery, starter motor or preheating system). If poor performance is combined with difficult starting, the problem is likely to be in the fuel system. The low-pressure (supply) side of the fuel system should be checked before suspecting the injectors and high-pressure pump. The most common fuel supply problem is air getting into the system, and any pipe from the fuel tank forwards must be scrutinised if air leakage is suspected.

Engine

Engine fails to rotate when attempting to start

- ☐ Battery terminal connections loose or corroded (see *Weekly checks*)
- ☐ Battery discharged or faulty (Chapter 5A)
- ☐ Broken, loose or disconnected wiring in the starting circuit (Chapter 12)
- ☐ Defective starter solenoid or ignition switch (Chapter 5A or 12)
- ☐ Defective starter motor (Chapter 5A)
- ☐ Starter pinion or flywheel ring gear teeth loose or broken (Chapter 2A, 2B, 2C, 2D or 5A)
- ☐ Engine earth strap broken or disconnected (Chapter 5A)
- ☐ Engine suffering 'hydraulic lock' (eg from water drawn into the engine after traversing flooded roads, or from a serious internal coolant leak) – consult a main dealer for advice
- ☐ If it's a model with manual transmission, make sure that the clutch and brake pedals are fully depressed
- ☐ On models with automatic transmission, make sure the selector is in P or N and the brake pedal is fully depressed

Engine rotates, but will not start

- ☐ Fuel tank empty
- ☐ Battery discharged (engine rotates slowly) (Chapter 5A)
- ☐ Battery terminal connections loose or corroded (see *Weekly checks*)
- ☐ Ignition components damp or damaged – petrol models (Chapter 1A or 5B)
- ☐ Immobiliser fault, or 'uncoded' ignition key being used (Chapter 12 or *Roadside repairs*)
- ☐ Broken, loose or disconnected wiring in the ignition circuit – petrol models (Chapter 1A or 5B)
- ☐ Worn, faulty or incorrectly-gapped spark plugs – petrol models (Chapter 1A)
- ☐ Preheating system faulty – diesel models (Chapter 5A)
- ☐ Fuel injection/engine management system fault (Chapter 4A or 4B)
- ☐ Air in fuel system – diesel models (Chapter 4B)
- ☐ Major mechanical failure (eg timing belt snapped) (Chapter 2A, 2B, 2C or 2D)

Engine difficult to start when cold

- ☐ Battery discharged (Chapter 5A)
- ☐ Battery terminal connections loose or corroded (see *Weekly checks*)
- ☐ Worn, faulty or incorrectly-gapped spark plugs – petrol models (Chapter 1A)
- ☐ Other ignition system fault – petrol models (Chapter 1A or 5B)
- ☐ Preheating system faulty – diesel models (Chapter 5A)
- ☐ Fuel injection/engine management system fault (Chapter 4A or 4B)
- ☐ Wrong grade of engine oil used (*Weekly checks*, Chapter 1A or 1B)
- ☐ Low cylinder compression (Chapter 2A, 2B, 2C or 2D)

Engine difficult to start when hot

- ☐ Air filter element dirty or clogged (Chapter 1A or 1B)
- ☐ Fuel injection/engine management system fault (Chapter 4A or 4B)
- ☐ Low cylinder compression (Chapter 2A, 2B, 2C or 2D)

Starter motor noisy or excessively-rough in engagement

- ☐ Starter pinion or flywheel ring gear teeth loose or broken (Chapter 2A, 2B, 2C, 2D or 5A)
- ☐ Starter motor mounting bolts loose or missing (Chapter 5A)
- ☐ Starter motor internal components worn or damaged (Chapter 5A)

Engine starts, but stops immediately

- ☐ Loose or faulty electrical connections in the ignition circuit – petrol models (Chapter 1A or 5B)
- ☐ Vacuum leak at the throttle housing or inlet manifold – petrol models (Chapter 4A)
- ☐ Blocked injectors/fuel injection system fault (Chapter 4A or 4B)

Engine idles erratically

- ☐ Air filter element clogged (Chapter 1A or 1B)
- ☐ Vacuum leak at the throttle housing, inlet manifold or associated hoses – petrol models (Chapter 4A)
- ☐ Worn, faulty or incorrectly-gapped spark plugs – petrol models (Chapter 1A)
- ☐ Low cylinder compression (Chapter 2A, 2B, 2C or 2D)
- ☐ Camshaft lobes worn (Chapter 2A, 2B, 2C or 2D)
- ☐ Blocked injectors/fuel injection system fault (Chapter 4A or 4B)

Engine (continued)

Engine misfires at idle speed

- ☐ Worn, faulty or incorrectly-gapped spark plugs – petrol models (Chapter 1A)
- ☐ Vacuum leak at the throttle housing, inlet manifold or associated hoses – petrol models (Chapter 4A)
- ☐ Blocked injectors/fuel injection system fault (Chapter 4A or 4B)
- ☐ Faulty injector(s) – diesel models (Chapter 4B)
- ☐ Uneven or low cylinder compression (Chapter 2A, 2B, 2C or 2D)
- ☐ Disconnected, leaking, or perished crankcase ventilation hoses (Chapter 4C)

Engine misfires throughout the driving speed range

- ☐ Fuel filter choked – diesel models (Chapter 1B)
- ☐ Fuel pump faulty, or delivery pressure low – petrol models (Chapter 4A)
- ☐ Fuel tank vent blocked, or fuel pipes restricted (Chapter 4A or 4B)
- ☐ Vacuum leak at the throttle housing, inlet manifold or associated hoses – petrol models (Chapter 4A)
- ☐ Worn, faulty or incorrectly-gapped spark plugs – petrol models (Chapter 1A)
- ☐ Faulty injector(s) – diesel models (Chapter 4B)
- ☐ Faulty ignition module – petrol models (Chapter 5B)
- ☐ Uneven or low cylinder compression (Chapter 2A, 2B, 2C or 2D)
- ☐ Blocked injector/fuel injection system fault (Chapter 4A or 4B)
- ☐ Blocked catalytic converter (Chapter 4A or 4B)
- ☐ Engine overheating (Chapter 3)

Engine hesitates on acceleration

- ☐ Worn, faulty or incorrectly-gapped spark plugs – petrol models (Chapter 1A)
- ☐ Vacuum leak at the throttle housing, inlet manifold or associated hoses – petrol models (Chapter 4A)
- ☐ Blocked injectors/fuel injection system fault (Chapter 4A or 4B)
- ☐ Faulty injector(s) – diesel models (Chapter 4B)

Engine stalls

- ☐ Vacuum leak at the throttle housing, inlet manifold or associated hoses – petrol models (Chapter 4A)
- ☐ Fuel filter choked – diesel models (Chapter 1B)
- ☐ Fuel pump faulty, or delivery pressure low – petrol models (Chapter 4A)
- ☐ Fuel tank vent blocked, or fuel pipes restricted (Chapter 4A or 4B)
- ☐ Blocked injectors/fuel injection system fault (Chapter 4A or 4B)
- ☐ Faulty injector(s) – diesel models (Chapter 4B)

Engine lacks power

- ☐ Air filter element blocked (Chapter 1A or 1B)
- ☐ Fuel filter choked – diesel models (Chapter 1B)
- ☐ Fuel pipes blocked or restricted (Chapter 1A or 1B)
- ☐ Worn, faulty or incorrectly-gapped spark plugs – petrol models (Chapter 1A)
- ☐ Engine overheating (Chapter 3)
- ☐ Accelerator pedal position sensor faulty (Chapter 4A or 4B)
- ☐ Vacuum leak at the throttle housing, inlet manifold or associated hoses – petrol models (Chapter 4A)
- ☐ Blocked injectors/fuel injection system fault (Chapter 4A or 4B)
- ☐ Faulty injector(s) – diesel models (Chapter 4B)
- ☐ Fuel pump faulty, or delivery pressure low – petrol models (Chapter 4A)
- ☐ Uneven or low cylinder compression (Chapter 2A, 2B, 2C or 2D)
- ☐ Blocked catalytic converter (Chapter 4A or 4B)
- ☐ Brakes binding (Chapter 1A, 1B or 9)
- ☐ Clutch slipping (Chapter 6)

Engine backfires

- ☐ Vacuum leak at the throttle housing, inlet manifold or associated hoses – petrol models (Chapter 4A)
- ☐ Blocked injectors/fuel injection system fault (Chapter 4A or 4B)
- ☐ Blocked catalytic converter (Chapter 4A or 4B)
- ☐ Faulty ignition module – petrol models (Chapter 5B)

Oil pressure warning light illuminated with engine running

- ☐ Low oil level, or incorrect oil grade (see *Weekly checks*)
- ☐ Faulty oil pressure sensor, or wiring damaged (Chapter 5A)
- ☐ Worn engine bearings and/or oil pump (Chapter 2A, 2B, 2C or 2D)
- ☐ High engine operating temperature (Chapter 3)
- ☐ Oil pump pressure relief valve defective (Chapter 2A, 2B, 2C or 2D)
- ☐ Oil pump pick-up strainer clogged (Chapter 2A, 2B, 2C or 2D)

Engine runs-on after switching off

- ☐ Excessive carbon build-up in engine (Chapter 2A, 2B, 2C or 2D)
- ☐ High engine operating temperature (Chapter 3)
- ☐ Fuel injection/engine management system fault (Chapter 4A or 4B)

Engine noises

Pre-ignition (pinking) or knocking during acceleration or under load

- ☐ Ignition system/engine management system fault – petrol models (Chapter 1A, 4A or 5B)
- ☐ Incorrect grade of spark plug – petrol models (Chapter 1A)
- ☐ Incorrect grade of fuel (Chapter 4A or 4B)
- ☐ Knock sensor faulty – petrol models (Chapter 4A or 5B)
- ☐ Vacuum leak at the throttle housing, inlet manifold or associated hoses – petrol models (Chapter 4A)
- ☐ Excessive carbon build-up in engine (Chapter 2A, 2B, 2C or 2D)
- ☐ Fuel injection/engine management system fault (Chapter 4A or 4B)
- ☐ Faulty injector(s) – diesel models (Chapter 4B)

Whistling or wheezing noises

- ☐ Leaking inlet manifold or throttle housing gasket – petrol models (Chapter 4A)
- ☐ Leaking exhaust manifold gasket or pipe-to-manifold joint (Chapter 4A or 4B)
- ☐ Leaking vacuum hose (Chapter 9)
- ☐ Blowing cylinder head gasket (Chapter 2A, 2B, 2C or 2D)
- ☐ Partially blocked or leaking crankcase ventilation system (Chapter 4C)

Tapping or rattling noises

- ☐ Worn valve gear or camshaft (Chapter 2A, 2B, 2C or 2D)
- ☐ Ancillary component fault (coolant pump, alternator, etc) (Chapter 3, 5A, etc)

Knocking or thumping noises

- ☐ Worn big-end bearings (regular heavy knocking, perhaps less under load) (Chapter 2E)
- ☐ Worn main bearings (rumbling and knocking, perhaps worsening under load) (Chapter 2E)
- ☐ Piston slap – most noticeable when cold, caused by piston/bore wear (Chapter 2E)
- ☐ Ancillary component fault (coolant pump, alternator, etc) (Chapter 3, 5A, etc)
- ☐ Engine mountings worn or defective (Chapter 2A, 2B, 2C or 2D)
- ☐ Front suspension or steering components worn (Chapter 10)

Cooling system

Overheating

- ☐ Insufficient coolant in system (see *Weekly checks*)
- ☐ Thermostat faulty (Chapter 3)
- ☐ Radiator core blocked, or grille restricted (Chapter 3)
- ☐ Cooling fan or cooling module faulty (Chapter 3)
- ☐ Inaccurate coolant temperature sensor (Chapter 3)
- ☐ Airlock in cooling system (Chapter 1A or 1B)
- ☐ Expansion tank pressure cap faulty (Chapter 3)
- ☐ Engine management system fault (Chapter 4A or 4B)

Overcooling

- ☐ Thermostat faulty (Chapter 3)
- ☐ Inaccurate coolant temperature sensor (Chapter 3)
- ☐ Cooling fan faulty (Chapter 3)
- ☐ Engine management system fault (Chapter 4A or 4B)

External coolant leakage

- ☐ Deteriorated or damaged hoses or hose clips (Chapter 1A or 1B)
- ☐ Radiator core or heater matrix leaking (Chapter 3)
- ☐ Expansion tank pressure cap faulty (Chapter 3)
- ☐ Coolant pump internal seal leaking (Chapter 3)
- ☐ Coolant pump gasket leaking (Chapter 3)
- ☐ Boiling due to overheating (Chapter 3)
- ☐ Cylinder block core plug leaking (Chapter 2E)

Internal coolant leakage

- ☐ Leaking cylinder head gasket (Chapter 2A, 2B, 2C or 2D)
- ☐ Cracked cylinder head or cylinder block (Chapter 2A, 2B, 2C or 2D)

Corrosion

- ☐ Infrequent draining and flushing (Chapter 1A or 1B)
- ☐ Incorrect coolant mixture or inappropriate coolant type (see *Weekly checks*)

Fuel and exhaust systems

Excessive fuel consumption

- ☐ Air filter element dirty or clogged (Chapter 1A or 1B)
- ☐ Fuel injection system fault (Chapter 4A or 4B)
- ☐ Engine management system fault (Chapter 4A or 4B)
- ☐ Crankcase ventilation system blocked (Chapter 4C)
- ☐ Tyres under-inflated (see *Weekly checks*)
- ☐ Brakes binding (Chapter 1A, 1B or 9)
- ☐ Fuel leak, causing apparent high consumption (Chapter 1A or 1B)

Fuel leakage and/or fuel odour

- ☐ Damaged or corroded fuel tank, pipes or connections (Chapter 4A or 4B)
- ☐ Evaporative emissions system fault – petrol models (Chapter 4C)

Excessive noise or fumes from exhaust system

- ☐ Leaking exhaust system or manifold joints (Chapter 1A, 1B, 4A or 4B)
- ☐ Leaking, corroded or damaged silencers or pipe (Chapter 1A, 1B, 4A or 4B)
- ☐ Broken mountings causing body or suspension contact (Chapter 1A, 1B, 4A or 4B)

Clutch

Pedal travels to floor – no pressure or very little resistance

- ☐ Air in hydraulic system/faulty master or release cylinder (Chapter 6)
- ☐ Faulty hydraulic release system (Chapter 6)
- ☐ Clutch pedal return spring detached or broken (Chapter 6)
- ☐ Faulty clutch release cylinder (Chapter 6)
- ☐ Broken diaphragm spring in clutch pressure plate (Chapter 6)

Clutch fails to disengage (unable to select gears)

- ☐ Air in hydraulic system/faulty master or release cylinder (Chapter 6)
- ☐ Faulty hydraulic release system (Chapter 6)
- ☐ Clutch disc sticking on transmission input shaft splines (Chapter 6)
- ☐ Clutch disc sticking to flywheel or pressure plate (Chapter 6)
- ☐ Faulty pressure plate assembly (Chapter 6)
- ☐ Clutch release mechanism worn or incorrectly assembled (Chapter 6)

Clutch slips (engine speed increases, with no increase in vehicle speed)

- ☐ Faulty hydraulic release system (Chapter 6)
- ☐ Clutch disc linings excessively worn (Chapter 6)
- ☐ Clutch disc linings contaminated with oil or grease (Chapter 6)
- ☐ Faulty pressure plate or weak diaphragm spring (Chapter 6)

Judder as clutch is engaged

- ☐ Clutch disc linings contaminated with oil or grease (Chapter 6)
- ☐ Clutch disc linings excessively worn (Chapter 6)
- ☐ Faulty or distorted pressure plate or diaphragm spring (Chapter 6).
- ☐ Worn or loose engine or transmission mountings (Chapter 2A, 2B, 2C or 2D)
- ☐ Clutch disc hub or transmission input shaft splines worn (Chapter 6)

Noise when depressing or releasing clutch pedal

- ☐ Faulty clutch release cylinder (Chapter 6)
- ☐ Worn or dry clutch pedal bushes (Chapter 6)
- ☐ Faulty pressure plate assembly (Chapter 6)
- ☐ Pressure plate diaphragm spring broken (Chapter 6)
- ☐ Broken clutch disc cushioning springs (Chapter 6)

Manual transmission

Noisy in neutral with engine running

☐ Lack of oil (Chapter 7A)
☐ Input shaft bearings worn (noise apparent with clutch pedal released, but not when depressed) (Chapter 7A)*
☐ Clutch release cylinder faulty (noise apparent with clutch pedal depressed, possibly less when released) (Chapter 6)

Noisy in one particular gear

☐ Worn, damaged or chipped gear teeth (Chapter 7A)*

Difficulty engaging gears

☐ Clutch fault (Chapter 6)
☐ Worn, damaged, or poorly-adjusted gearchange (Chapter 7A)
☐ Lack of oil (Chapter 7A)
☐ Worn synchroniser units (Chapter 7A)*

Jumps out of gear

☐ Worn, damaged, or poorly-adjusted gearchange (Chapter 7A)
☐ Worn synchroniser units (Chapter 7A)*
☐ Worn selector forks (Chapter 7A)*

Vibration

☐ Lack of oil (Chapter 7A)
☐ Worn bearings (Chapter 7A)*

Lubricant leaks

☐ Leaking driveshaft or selector shaft oil seal (Chapter 7A)
☐ Leaking housing joint (Chapter 7A)*
☐ Leaking input shaft oil seal (Chapter 7A)*

*Although the corrective action necessary to remedy the symptoms described is beyond the scope of the home mechanic, the above information should be helpful in isolating the cause of the condition, so that the owner can communicate clearly with a professional mechanic.

Automatic transmission

Note: Due to the complexity of the automatic transmission, it is difficult for the home mechanic to properly diagnose and service this unit. For problems other than the following, the vehicle should be taken to a dealer service department or automatic transmission specialist. Do not be too hasty in removing the transmission if a fault is suspected, as most of the testing is carried out with the unit still fitted. Remember that, besides the sensors specific to the transmission, many of the engine management system sensors described in the relevant Part of Chapter 4 are essential to the correct operation of the transmission.

Fluid leakage

☐ Automatic transmission fluid is usually dark red in colour. Fluid leaks should not be confused with engine oil, which can easily be blown onto the transmission by airflow.
☐ To determine the source of a leak, first remove all built-up dirt and grime from the transmission housing and surrounding areas using a degreasing agent, or by steam-cleaning. Drive the vehicle at low speed, so airflow will not blow the leak far from its source. Raise and support the vehicle, and determine where the leak is coming from. The following are common areas of leakage:
a) Fluid pan
b) Dipstick tube
c) Transmission-to-fluid cooler unions

Transmission fluid brown, or has burned smell

☐ Transmission fluid level low (Chapter 7B)

General gear selection problems

☐ Chapter 7B deals with checking the selector cable on automatic transmissions. The following are common problems which may be caused by a faulty cable or sensor:

a) Engine starting in gears other than Park or Neutral.
b) Indicator panel indicating a gear other than the one actually being used.
c) Vehicle moves when in Park or Neutral.
d) Poor gear shift quality or erratic gear changes.

Transmission will not downshift (kickdown) with accelerator pedal fully depressed

☐ Low transmission fluid level (Chapter 7B)
☐ Engine management system fault (Chapter 7B)
☐ Faulty transmission sensor or wiring (Chapter 7B)
☐ Incorrect selector cable adjustment (Chapter 7B)

Engine will not start in any gear, or starts in gears other than Park or Neutral

☐ Incorrect selector cable adjustment (Chapter 7B)
☐ Faulty transmission sensor or wiring (Chapter 7B)
☐ Engine management system fault (Chapter 7B)

Transmission slips, shifts roughly, is noisy, or has no drive in forward or reverse gears

☐ Transmission fluid level low (Chapter 7B)
☐ Faulty transmission sensor or wiring (Chapter 7B)
☐ Engine management system fault (Chapter 7B)

Note: There are many probable causes for the above problems, but diagnosing and correcting them is considered beyond the scope of this manual. Having checked the fluid level and all the wiring as far as possible, a dealer or transmission specialist should be consulted if the problem persists.

Driveshafts

Vibration when accelerating or decelerating

☐ Worn inner constant velocity joint (Chapter 8)
☐ Bent or distorted driveshaft (Chapter 8)
☐ Worn intermediate shaft bearing (Chapter 8)

Clicking or knocking noise on turns (at slow speed on full-lock)

☐ Worn outer constant velocity joint (Chapter 8)
☐ Lack of constant velocity joint lubricant, possibly due to damaged gaiter (Chapter 8)

Braking system

Note: *Before assuming that a brake problem exists, make sure that the tyres are in good condition and correctly inflated, that the front wheel alignment is correct, and that the vehicle is not loaded with weight in an unequal manner. Apart from checking the condition of all pipe and hose connections, any faults occurring on the anti-lock braking system should be referred to a Vauxhall/Opel dealer for diagnosis.*

Vehicle pulls to one side under braking

☐ Worn, defective, damaged or contaminated brake pads on one side (Chapter 1A, 1B or 9)
☐ Seized or partially-seized brake caliper piston (Chapter 1A, 1B or 9)
☐ A mixture of brake pad lining materials fitted between sides (Chapter 1A, 1B or 9)
☐ Brake caliper mounting bolts loose (Chapter 9)
☐ Worn or damaged steering or suspension components (Chapter 1A, 1B or 10)

Noise (grinding or high-pitched squeal) when brakes applied

☐ Brake pad wear sensor indicating worn brake pads (Chapter 1A, 1B or 9)
☐ Brake pad friction lining material worn down to metal backing (Chapter 1A, 1B or 9)
☐ Excessive corrosion of brake disc (may be apparent after the vehicle has been standing for some time (Chapter 1A, 1B or 9)
☐ Foreign object (stone chipping, etc) trapped between brake disc and shield (Chapter 1A, 1B or 9)

Excessive brake pedal travel

☐ Faulty master cylinder (Chapter 9)
☐ Air in hydraulic system (Chapter 1A, 1B or 9)
☐ Faulty vacuum servo unit (Chapter 9)

Brake pedal feels spongy when depressed

☐ Air in hydraulic system (Chapter 1A, 1B or 9)
☐ Deteriorated flexible rubber brake hoses (Chapter 1A, 1B or 9)
☐ Master cylinder mounting nuts loose (Chapter 9)
☐ Faulty master cylinder (Chapter 9)

Excessive brake pedal effort required to stop vehicle

☐ Faulty vacuum servo unit (Chapter 9)
☐ Faulty vacuum pump (Chapter 9)
☐ Disconnected, damaged or insecure brake servo vacuum hose (Chapter 9)
☐ Primary or secondary hydraulic circuit failure (Chapter 9)
☐ Seized brake caliper piston (Chapter 9)
☐ Brake pads incorrectly fitted (Chapter 9)
☐ Incorrect grade of brake pads fitted (Chapter 9)
☐ Brake pad linings contaminated (Chapter 9)

Judder felt through brake pedal or steering wheel when braking

Note: *Under heavy braking on vehicles equipped with ABS, vibration may be felt through the brake pedal. This is a normal feature of ABS operation, and does not constitute a fault.*
☐ Excessive run-out or distortion of discs (Chapter 9)
☐ Brake pad linings worn (Chapter 9)
☐ Brake caliper mounting bolts loose (Chapter 9)
☐ Wear in suspension or steering components or mountings (Chapter 1A, 1B or 10)
☐ Front wheels out of balance (see *Weekly checks*)

Brakes binding

☐ Seized brake caliper piston (Chapter 9)
☐ Faulty master cylinder (Chapter 9)

Rear wheels locking under normal braking

☐ Rear brake pad linings contaminated or damaged (Chapter 1A or 1B)
☐ Rear brake discs warped (Chapter 1A or 1B)

Suspension and steering

Note: *Before diagnosing suspension or steering faults, be sure that the trouble is not due to incorrect tyre pressures, mixtures of tyre types, or binding brakes.*

Vehicle pulls to one side

☐ Defective tyre (see *Weekly checks*)
☐ Excessive wear in suspension or steering components (Chapter 1A, 1B or 10)
☐ Incorrect front wheel alignment (Chapter 10)
☐ Accident damage to steering or suspension components (Chapter 1A or 1B)

Wheel wobble and vibration

☐ Front wheels out of balance (vibration felt mainly through the steering wheel) (see *Weekly checks*)
☐ Rear wheels out of balance (vibration felt throughout the vehicle) (see *Weekly checks*)
☐ Roadwheels damaged or distorted (see *Weekly checks*)
☐ Faulty or damaged tyre (see *Weekly checks*)
☐ Worn steering or suspension joints, bushes or components (Chapter 1A, 1B or 10)
☐ Wheel nuts loose (Chapter 1A or 1B)

Excessive pitching and/or rolling around corners, or during braking

☐ Defective shock absorbers (Chapter 1A, 1B or 10)
☐ Broken or weak spring and/or suspension component (Chapter 1A, 1B or 10)
☐ Worn or damaged anti-roll bar or mountings (Chapter 1A, 1B or 10)

Wandering or general instability

☐ Incorrect front wheel alignment (Chapter 10)
☐ Worn steering or suspension joints, bushes or components (Chapter 1A, 1B or 10)
☐ Roadwheels out of balance (see *Weekly checks*)
☐ Faulty or damaged tyre (see *Weekly checks*)
☐ Wheel nuts loose (Chapter 1A or 1B)
☐ Defective shock absorbers (Chapter 1A, 1B or 10)
☐ Power steering system fault (Chapter 10)

Excessively-stiff steering

☐ Seized steering linkage balljoint or suspension balljoint (Chapter 1A, 1B or 10)
☐ Incorrect front wheel alignment (Chapter 10)
☐ Steering rack damaged (Chapter 10)
☐ Power steering system fault (Chapter 10)

Excessive play in steering

☐ Worn steering column/intermediate shaft joints (Chapter 10)
☐ Worn track rod end balljoints (Chapter 1A, 1B or 10)
☐ Worn steering rack (Chapter 10)
☐ Worn steering or suspension joints, bushes or components (Chapter 1A, 1B or 10)

Lack of power assistance

☐ Power steering system fault (Chapter 10)
☐ Faulty steering rack (Chapter 10)

Tyre wear excessive

Tyres worn on inside or outside edges

☐ Tyres under-inflated (wear on both edges) (see *Weekly checks*)
☐ Incorrect camber or castor angles (wear on one edge only) (Chapter 10)
☐ Worn steering or suspension joints, bushes or components (Chapter 1A, 1B or 10)
☐ Excessively-hard cornering or braking
☐ Accident damage

Tyre treads exhibit feathered edges

☐ Incorrect toe-setting (Chapter 10)

Tyres worn in centre of tread

☐ Tyres over-inflated (see *Weekly checks*)

Tyres worn on inside and outside edges

☐ Tyres under-inflated (see *Weekly checks*)

Tyres worn unevenly

☐ Tyres/wheels out of balance (see *Weekly checks*)
☐ Excessive wheel or tyre run-out
☐ Worn shock absorbers (Chapter 1A, 1B or 10)
☐ Faulty tyre (see *Weekly checks*)

Electrical system

Note: *For problems associated with the starting system, refer to the faults listed under 'Engine' earlier in this Section.*
Note: *Some of the faults described below may be associated with the vehicle electronic control system modules. If the procedures described below fail to eliminate the problem, it will be necessary to have the control system modules interrogated, to identify the nature of the fault, using Vauxhall/Opel diagnostic test equipment.*

Battery will not hold a charge for more than a few days

☐ Battery defective internally (Chapter 5A)
☐ Battery terminal connections loose or corroded (see *Weekly checks*)
☐ Auxiliary drivebelt worn or faulty automatic adjuster (Chapter 1A or 1B)
☐ Alternator not charging at correct output (Chapter 5A)
☐ Alternator or voltage regulator faulty (Chapter 5A)
☐ Short-circuit causing continual battery drain (Chapter 5A or 12)

Ignition/no-charge warning light remains illuminated with engine running

☐ Auxiliary drivebelt broken, worn, or or faulty automatic adjuster (Chapter 1A or 1B)
☐ Internal fault in alternator or voltage regulator (Chapter 5A)
☐ Broken, disconnected, or loose wiring in charging circuit (Chapter 5A or 12)

Ignition/no-charge warning light fails to come on

☐ Broken, disconnected, or loose wiring in warning light circuit (Chapter 5A or 12)
☐ Alternator faulty (Chapter 5A)

Electrical system (continued)

Lights inoperative

- ☐ Bulb blown (Chapter 12)
- ☐ Corrosion of bulb or bulbholder contacts (Chapter 12)
- ☐ Blown fuse (Chapter 12)
- ☐ Faulty relay (Chapter 12)
- ☐ Broken, loose, or disconnected wiring (Chapter 12)
- ☐ Faulty switch (Chapter 12)

Horn inoperative, or unsatisfactory in operation

Horn operates all the time

- ☐ Horn push either earthed or stuck down (Chapter 12)
- ☐ Horn cable-to-horn push earthed (Chapter 12)

Horn fails to operate

- ☐ Blown fuse (Chapter 12)
- ☐ Cable or connections loose, broken or disconnected (Chapter 12)
- ☐ Faulty horn (Chapter 12)

Horn emits intermittent or unsatisfactory sound

- ☐ Cable connections loose (Chapter 12)
- ☐ Horn mountings loose (Chapter 12)
- ☐ Faulty horn (Chapter 12)

Windscreen wipers inoperative, or unsatisfactory in operation

Wipers fail to operate, or operate very slowly

- ☐ Wiper blades stuck to screen, or linkage seized or binding (Chapter 12)
- ☐ Blown fuse (Chapter 12)
- ☐ Battery discharged (Chapter 5A)
- ☐ Cable or connections loose, broken or disconnected (Chapter 12)
- ☐ Faulty relay (Chapter 12)
- ☐ Faulty wiper motor (Chapter 12)

Wiper blades sweep over too large or too small an area of the glass

- ☐ Wiper blades incorrectly fitted, or wrong size used (see *Weekly checks*)
- ☐ Wiper arms incorrectly positioned on spindles (Chapter 12)
- ☐ Excessive wear of wiper linkage (Chapter 12)
- ☐ Wiper motor or linkage mountings loose or insecure (Chapter 12)

Wiper blades fail to clean the glass effectively

- ☐ Wiper blade rubbers dirty, worn or perished (see *Weekly checks*)
- ☐ Wiper blades incorrectly fitted, or wrong size used (see *Weekly checks*)
- ☐ Wiper arm tension springs broken, or arm pivots seized (Chapter 12)
- ☐ Insufficient windscreen washer additive to adequately remove road film (see *Weekly checks*)

Windscreen washers inoperative, or unsatisfactory in operation

One or more washer jets inoperative

- ☐ Blocked washer jet
- ☐ Disconnected, kinked or restricted fluid hose (Chapter 12)
- ☐ Insufficient fluid in washer reservoir (see *Weekly checks*)

Washer pump fails to operate

- ☐ Broken or disconnected wiring or connections (Chapter 12)
- ☐ Blown fuse (Chapter 12)
- ☐ Faulty washer switch (Chapter 12)
- ☐ Faulty washer pump (Chapter 12)

Washer pump runs for some time before fluid is emitted from jets

- ☐ Faulty one-way valve in fluid supply hose (Chapter 12)

Electric windows inoperative, or unsatisfactory in operation

Window glass will only move in one direction

- ☐ Faulty switch (Chapter 12)

Window glass slow to move

- ☐ Battery discharged (Chapter 5A)
- ☐ Regulator seized or damaged, or in need of lubrication (Chapter 11)
- ☐ Door internal components or trim fouling regulator (Chapter 11)
- ☐ Faulty motor (Chapter 11)

Window glass fails to move

- ☐ Blown fuse (Chapter 12)
- ☐ Faulty relay (Chapter 12)
- ☐ Broken or disconnected wiring or connections (Chapter 12)
- ☐ Faulty motor (Chapter 11)

Central locking system inoperative, or unsatisfactory in operation

Complete system failure

- ☐ Remote handset battery discharged, where applicable (Chapter 1A or 1B)
- ☐ Blown fuse (Chapter 12)
- ☐ Faulty relay (Chapter 12)
- ☐ Broken or disconnected wiring or connections (Chapter 12)
- ☐ Faulty motor (Chapter 11)

Latch locks but will not unlock, or unlocks but will not lock

- ☐ Remote handset battery discharged, where applicable (Chapter 1A or 1B)
- ☐ Broken or disconnected latch operating rods or levers (Chapter 11)
- ☐ Faulty relay (Chapter 12)
- ☐ Faulty motor (Chapter 11)

One solenoid/motor fails to operate

- ☐ Broken or disconnected wiring or connections (Chapter 12)
- ☐ Faulty operating assembly (Chapter 11)
- ☐ Broken, binding or disconnected latch operating rods or levers (Chapter 11)
- ☐ Fault in door latch (Chapter 11)

Note: *References throughout this index are in the form* "**Chapter number**" • "**Page number**". *So, for example, 2C•15 refers to page 15 of Chapter 2C.*

Note: *References throughout this index are in the form "**Chapter number**" • "**Page number**". So, for example, 2C•15 refers to page 15 of Chapter 2C.*

Note: *References throughout this index are in the form* "**Chapter number**" • "**Page number**". *So, for example, 2C•15 refers to page 15 of Chapter 2C.*

Note: *References throughout this index are in the form* "**Chapter number**" • "**Page number**". *So, for example, 2C•15 refers to page 15 of Chapter 2C.*

Note: *References throughout this index are in the form* **"Chapter number"** • **"Page number"**. *So, for example, 2C•15 refers to page 15 of Chapter 2C.*